Cisco CCENT/ CCNA
ICND1 100-101
Official Cert Guide
Academic Edition

WENDELL ODOM, CCIE No. 1624

Cisco Press
800 East 96th Street
Indianapolis, IN 46240

Cisco CCENT/CCNA ICND1 100-101
Official Cert Guide, Academic Edition

Wendell Odom, CCIE No. 1624

Copyright © 2013 Pearson Education, Inc.

Published by:
Cisco Press
800 East 96th Street
Indianapolis, IN 46240 USA

Printed in the United States of America

Second Printing: November 2013

Library of Congress Control Number: 2013939886

ISBN-13: 978-1-58714-485-1

ISBN-10: 1-58714-485-9

Warning and Disclaimer

This book is designed to provide information about the Cisco 100-101 ICND1 and 200-120 CCNA exams. Every effort has been made to make this book as complete and as accurate as possible, but no warranty or fitness is implied.

The information is provided on an "as is" basis. The authors, Cisco Press, and Cisco Systems, Inc. shall have neither liability nor responsibility to any person or entity with respect to any loss or damages arising from the information contained in this book or from the use of the discs or programs that may accompany it.

The opinions expressed in this book belong to the author and are not necessarily those of Cisco Systems, Inc.

Trademark Acknowledgments

All terms mentioned in this book that are known to be trademarks or service marks have been appropriately capitalized. Cisco Press or Cisco Systems, Inc., cannot attest to the accuracy of this information. Use of a term in this book should not be regarded as affecting the validity of any trademark or service mark.

Images in Figures 2-7 (2960S-F48TS-L switch), 2-8, and 7-1 used with permission from Cisco Systems, Inc.

Corporate and Government Sales

The publisher offers excellent discounts on this book when ordered in quantity for bulk purchases or special sales, which may include electronic versions and/or custom covers and content particular to your business, training goals, marketing focus, and branding interests. For more information, please contact:
U.S. Corporate and Government Sales   1-800-382-3419   corpsales@pearsontechgroup.com

For sales outside the United States, please contact: **International Sales**   international@pearsoned.com

Feedback Information

At Cisco Press, our goal is to create in-depth technical books of the highest quality and value. Each book is crafted with care and precision, undergoing rigorous development that involves the unique expertise of members from the professional technical community.

Readers' feedback is a natural continuation of this process. If you have any comments regarding how we could improve the quality of this book, or otherwise alter it to better suit your needs, you can contact us through email at feedback@ciscopress.com. Please make sure to include the book title and ISBN in your message.

We greatly appreciate your assistance.

Publisher: Paul Boger

Associate Publisher: Dave Dusthimer

Business Operation Manager, Cisco Press: Jan Cornelssen

Executive Editor: Brett Bartow

Managing Editor: Sandra Schroeder

Development Editor: Andrew Cupp

Senior Project Editor: Tonya Simpson

Copy Editor: John Edwards

Technical Editor: Elan Beer

Editorial Assistant: Vanessa Evans

Book Designer: Mark Shirar

Illustrator: Michael Tanamachi

Composition: Studio Galou

Indexer: Tim Wright

Proofreader: Dan Knott

CISCO

Americas Headquarters
Cisco Systems, Inc.
San Jose, CA

Asia Pacific Headquarters
Cisco Systems (USA) Pte. Ltd.
Singapore

Europe Headquarters
Cisco Systems International BV
Amsterdam, The Netherlands

Cisco has more than 200 offices worldwide. Addresses, phone numbers, and fax numbers are listed on the Cisco Website at www.cisco.com/go/offices.

CCDE, CCENT, Cisco Eos, Cisco HealthPresence, the Cisco logo, Cisco Lumin, Cisco Nexus, Cisco StadiumVision, Cisco TelePresence, Cisco WebEx, DCE, and Welcome to the Human Network are trademarks; Changing the Way We Work, Live, Play, and Learn and Cisco Store are service marks; and Access Registrar, Aironet, AsyncOS, Bringing the Meeting To You, Catalyst, CCDA, CCDP, CCIE, CCIP, CCNA, CCNP, CCSP, CCVP, Cisco, the Cisco Certified Internetwork Expert logo, Cisco IOS, Cisco Press, Cisco Systems, Cisco Systems Capital, the Cisco Systems logo, Cisco Unity, Collaboration Without Limitation, EtherFast, EtherSwitch, Event Center, Fast Step, Follow Me Browsing, FormShare, GigaDrive, HomeLink, Internet Quotient, IOS, iPhone, iQuick Study, IronPort, the IronPort logo, LightStream, Linksys, MediaTone, MeetingPlace, MeetingPlace Chime Sound, MGX, Networkers, Networking Academy, Network Registrar, PCNow, PIX, PowerPanels, ProConnect, ScriptShare, SenderBase, SMARTnet, Spectrum Expert, StackWise, The Fastest Way to Increase Your Internet Quotient, TransPath, WebEx, and the WebEx logo are registered trademarks of Cisco Systems, Inc. and/or its affiliates in the United States and certain other countries.

All other trademarks mentioned in this document or website are the property of their respective owners. The use of the word partner does not imply a partnership relationship between Cisco and any other company. (0812R)

About the Author

Wendell Odom, CCIE No. 1624, has been in the networking industry since 1981. He has worked as a network engineer, consultant, systems engineer, instructor, and course developer; he currently works writing and creating certification tools. He is author of all the previous books in the Cisco Press CCNA Official Certification Guide series, as well as the *CCNP ROUTE 642-902 Official Certification Guide*, the *QoS 642-642 Exam Certification Guide*, coauthor of the *CCIE Routing and Switch Official Certification Guide*, and several other titles. He is also a consultant for the CCNA 640-802 Network Simulator from Pearson and for a forthcoming replacement version of that product. He maintains study tools, links to his blogs, and other resources at www.certskills.com.

About the Technical Reviewer

Elan Beer, CCIE No. 1837, is a senior consultant and Cisco instructor specializing in data center architecture and multiprotocol network design. For the past 25 years, Elan has designed networks and trained thousands of industry experts in data center architecture, routing, and switching. Elan has been instrumental in large-scale professional service efforts designing and troubleshooting internetworks, performing data center and network audits, and assisting clients with their short- and long-term design objectives. Elan has a global perspective of network architectures through his international clientele. Elan has used his expertise to design and troubleshoot data centers and internetworks in Malaysia, North America, Europe, Australia, Africa, China, and the Middle East. Most recently, Elan has been focused on data center design, configuration, and troubleshooting as well as service provider technologies. In 1993, Elan was among the first to obtain the Cisco Certified System Instructor (CCSI) certification, and in 1996, Elan was among the first to attain Cisco System's highest technical certification, the Cisco Certified Internetworking Expert. Since then, Elan has been involved in numerous large-scale data center and telecommunications networking projects worldwide.

Dedication

In memory of William E. York: Mom's dad, Paw Paw, wearing blue-jean overalls, always smiling, tagging along at the water works, fishing on Juliet Lake, the Catawba worm tree, and his big-belly laugh.

Acknowledgments

While this book is published as a first edition for various reasons, this book and the companion *Cisco CCNA Routing and Switching ICND2 200-101 Official Cert Guide* represent the seventh books in a long line of Cisco Press books focused on helping people pass the CCENT and CCNA Routing and Switching certifications. Given the long history, many people have worked on these books from their inception back in 1998. To those many people who have touched these books over these past 15 years—technical edits, development, copyedits, project editing, proofing, indexing, managing the production process, interior design, cover design, marketing, and all the other details that happen to get these books out the door—thanks so much for playing a role in this CCENT/CCNA franchise.

Many of the contributors to the previous editions returned to work on creating these new editions, including Development Editor Drew Cupp. Drew kept all the details straight, with my frequent changes to the outlines and titles, keeping the sequencing on track, while still doing his primary job: keeping the text and features clear and consistent throughout the book. Thanks, Drew, for walking me through the development.

As for the technical editor, Elan Beer did his normal job. That is, he did his usual amazing job of doing every part of the technical edit job well, from finding the tiny little cross-reference errors that sit pages apart, to anticipating how readers might misunderstand certain phrasing, to being all over the details of every technical feature. Fantastic job as usual—thanks, Elan.

Brett Bartow again served as Executive Editor on the book, as he has almost since the beginning of these titles. When my family has asked me over the years about Brett's role with these books, the best single word definition is "teammate." Brett might be employed at Pearson Education, but he is always working with me and for me, watching out for the business end of the books and finding ways to make the publisher/author relationship work seamlessly. Thanks for another great ride through these books, Brett!

Word docs go in and out come these beautiful finished products. Thanks to Sandra Schroeder, Tonya Simpson, and all the production team for working through the magic that takes those Word docs and makes the beautiful finished product. From fixing all my grammar, crummy word choices, and passive-voice sentences, and then pulling the design and layout together, they do it all—thanks for putting it all together and making it look easy. And Tonya, managing the details through several process steps for roughly 100 elements between the pair of CCNA books in a short time frame—thanks for the amazing juggling act! And thanks especially for the attention to detail.

The figures for these books go through a little different process than they do for other books. Together we invested a large amount of labor in updating the figures for these books, both for the design, the volume of figures, and for the color versions of the figures for the electronic versions of the books. A special thanks goes out to Laura Robbins for working with me on the color and design standards early in the process. Also, thanks to Mike Tanamachi for drawing all the figures so well—and then redrawing them every time I changed my mind about something.

Thanks to Chris Burns of Certskills for all the work on the mind maps, both those used in the final product and those used to build the book, as well as for being a bit of a test case for some of the chapters.

A special thanks you to you readers who write in with suggestions, possible errors, and especially those of you who post online at the Cisco Learning Network. Without question, the comments I receive directly and overhear by participating at CLN made this edition a better book.

Thanks to my wife, Kris. Book schedules have a bigger impact than I would like, but you always make it work. Thanks to my daughter, Hannah, for all the great study/work breaks on some of these busy school days. And thanks to Jesus Christ, for this opportunity to write.

Contents at a Glance

Contents

Icons Used in This Book

Printer	PC	Laptop	Server	Phone
IP Phone	Router	Switch	Frame Relay Switch	Cable Modem
Access Point	ASA	DSLAM	WAN Switch	CSU/DSU
Hub	PIX Firewall	Bridge	Layer 3 Switch	Network Cloud
Ethernet Connection	Serial Line	Virtual Circuit	Ethernet WAN	Wireless

Command Syntax Conventions

The conventions used to present command syntax in this book are the same conventions used in the IOS Command Reference. The Command Reference describes these conventions as follows:

- **Boldface** indicates commands and keywords that are entered literally as shown. In actual configuration examples and output (not general command syntax), boldface indicates commands that are manually input by the user (such as a **show** command).

- *Italic* indicates arguments for which you supply actual values.

- Vertical bars (|) separate alternative, mutually exclusive elements.

- Square brackets ([ ]) indicate an optional element.

- Braces ({ }) indicate a required choice.

- Braces within brackets ([{ }]) indicate a required choice within an optional element.

Introduction

About the Book and the Exams

This book serves first as a textbook in some college networking courses. At the same time, you might want a career in networking somewhere down the road, and this book helps you with a big step in that journey by helping you pass a Cisco certification exam.

If you want to succeed as a technical person in the networking industry, you need to know Cisco. Cisco has a ridiculously high market share in the router and switch marketplace, with more than an 80 percent share in some markets. In many geographies and markets around the world, networking equals Cisco. If you want to be taken seriously as a network engineer, Cisco certification makes perfect sense.

The Exams That Help You Achieve CCENT and CCNA

Cisco announced changes to the CCENT and CCNA Routing and Switching certifications, and the related 100-101 ICND1, 200-101 ICND2, and 200-120 CCNA exams, early in 2013. For those of you who understand the how the old Cisco ICND1, ICND2, and CCNA exams worked, the structure remains the same. For those of you new to Cisco certifications, this Introduction begins by discussing the basics.

Almost everyone new to Cisco certifications begins with either CCENT or CCNA Routing and Switching. CCENT certification requires knowledge and skills on about half as much material as does CCNA Routing and Switching, so CCENT is the easier first step.

The CCENT certification requires a single step: pass the ICND1 exam. Simple enough.

The CCNA Routing and Switching certification gives you two options, as show in Figure I-1: Pass both the ICND1 and ICND2 exams, or just pass the CCNA exam. (Note that there is no separate certification for passing the ICND2 exam.)

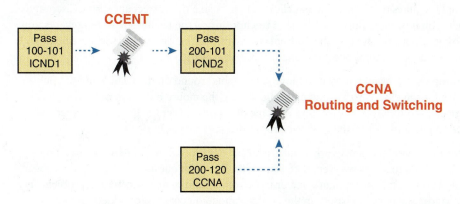

Figure I-1 *Cisco Entry-Level Certifications and Exams*

As you can see, although you can obtain the CCENT certification by taking the ICND1 exam, you do not have to be CCENT certified before you get your CCNA Routing and Switching certification. You can choose to take the CCNA exam and bypass the CCENT certification.

As for the topics themselves, the ICND1 and ICND2 exams cover different topics, but with some overlap required. For example, ICND1 covers the basics of the Open Shortest Path First (OSPF) routing protocol. ICND2 covers more detail about OSPF, but to discuss those additional details, ICND2 must rely on the parts of OSPF included in ICND1. Many topics in ICND2 build upon topics in ICND1, causing some overlap.

The CCNA exam covers all the topics in both ICND1 and ICND2—no more, no less.

Types of Questions on the Exams

The ICND1, ICND2, and CCNA exams all follow the same general format. At the testing center, you will sit in a quiet room with a PC. Before the exam timer begins, you will have a chance to do a few other tasks on the PC—for example, you can take a sample quiz just to get accustomed to the PC and the testing engine. Anyone who has user-level skills in getting around a PC should have no problems with the testing environment.

After the exam starts, the screen shows you question after question. The questions typically fall into one of the following categories:

- Multiple-choice (MC) single answer
- Multiple-choice (MC) multiple answer
- Testlet
- Drag-and-drop (DND)
- Simulated lab (Sim)
- Simlet

The first three items in the list are all actually multiple-choice questions. The multiple-choice format simply requires that you point and click a circle beside the correct answer(s). Cisco traditionally tells you how many answers you need to choose, and the testing software prevents you from choosing too many answers. The Testlet style gives you one larger scenario statement, with multiple different multichoice questions about that one scenario.

Drag-and-drop questions require you to move some items around on the GUI. You left-click and hold, move a button or icon to another area, and release the mouse button to place the object somewhere else—typically into a list. So, for some questions, to get the question correct, you might need to put a list of five things in the proper order.

The last two types both use a network simulator to ask questions. Interestingly, the two types actually allow Cisco to assess two very different skills. First, Sim questions generally describe a problem, and your task is to configure one or more routers and switches to fix the problem. The exam then grades the question based on the configuration you changed or added.

The Simlet questions might well be the most difficult style of question on the exams. Simlet questions also use a network simulator, but instead of answering the question by changing the configuration, the question includes one or more MC questions. The questions require that you use the simulator to examine the current behavior of a network, interpreting the output of any show commands that you can remember to answer the question. While Sim questions require you to troubleshoot problems related to a configuration, Simlets require you to both analyze both working and broken networks, correlating show command output with your knowledge of networking theory and configuration commands.

You can watch and even experiment with these command types using the Cisco Exam Tutorial. To find the Cisco Certification Exam Tutorial, go to www.cisco.com and search for "exam tutorial."

What's on the CCNA Exam(s)?

Ever since I was in grade school, whenever the teacher announced that we were having a test soon, someone would always ask, "What's on the test?" Even in college, people would try to get more information about what would be on the exams. At heart, the goal is to know what to study hard, what to study a little, and what to not study at all.

Cisco tells the world the topics on each of its exams. Cisco wants the public to know both the variety of topics, and an idea about the kinds of knowledge and skills required for each topic, for every Cisco certification exam. To that end, Cisco publishes a set of exam topics for each exam.

Many Cisco exam topics list both a networking topic and an important verb. The verb tells us to what degree the topic must be understood, and what skills are required. The topic also implies the kinds of skills required for that topic. For example, one topic might start with "Describe…," another with "Configure…," another with "Verify…," and another might begin with "Troubleshoot…." That last topic has the highest required skill level, because to trouble-shoot, you must understand the topic, be able to configure it (to see what's wrong with the configuration), and verify it (to find the root cause of the problem). By listing the topics and skill level, Cisco helps us all prepare for its exams.

Although the exam topics are helpful, keep in mind that Cisco adds a disclaimer that the posted exam topics for all of its certification exams are guidelines. Cisco makes the effort to keep the exam questions within the confines of the stated exam topics, and I know from talking to those involved that every question is analyzed for whether it fits within the stated exam topics.

ICND1 Exam Topics

Tables I-1 through I-7 lists the exam topics for the ICND1 exam. Following those tables, Tables I-8 through I-12 list the exam topics for ICND2. These tables note the book chapters in which each exam topic is covered.

The tables follow the Cisco organization of topics, by both grouping similar topics and listing subtopics. The subtopics simply give more specific terms and concepts to provide more detail about some exam topics. The tables show the main topics with bold, and the subtopics as indented text inside the tables.

Table I-1   ICND1 Exam Topics: Operation of IP Data Networks

Chapter	Operation of IP Data Networks
1–4, 6, 15	**Recognize the purpose and functions of various network devices such as Routers, Switches, Bridges and Hubs.**
1–4, 6, 15	**Select the components required to meet a given network specification.**
5	**Identify common applications and their impact on the network**
1	**Describe the purpose and basic operation of the protocols in the OSI and TCP/IP models.**
2–5, 6, 9, 16, 24, 25	**Predict the data flow between two hosts across a network.**
2, 6, 15	**Identify the appropriate media, cables, ports, and connectors to connect Cisco network devices to other network devices and hosts in a LAN**

Table I-2   ICND1 Exam Topics: LAN Switching Technologies

Chapter	LAN Switching Technologies
2, 6	**Determine the technology and media access control method for Ethernet networks**
6, 8, 9	**Identify basic switching concepts and the operation of Cisco switches**
6, 8	Collision Domains
6, 9	Broadcast Domains
6	Types of switching
6, 8, 9	CAM Table
7	**Configure and verify initial switch configuration including remote access management.**
7	Cisco IOS commands to perform basic switch setup
7, 18, 28	**Verify network status and switch operation using basic utilities such as ping, telnet and ssh.**
9	**Describe how VLANs create logically separate networks and the need for routing between them.**
9	**Explain network segmentation and basic traffic management concepts**
9	**Configure and verify VLANs**
9, 10	**Configure and verify trunking on Cisco switches**
9, 10	DTP
10	Auto negotiation

Table I-3   ICND1 Exam Topics: IP Addressing (IPv4 / IPv6)

Chapter	IP Addressing (IPv4/IPv6)
11	**Describe the operation and necessity of using private and public IP addresses for IPv4 addressing**
25, 26	**Identify the appropriate IPv6 addressing scheme to satisfy addressing requirements in a LAN/WAN environment.**
11, 19, 20, 21	**Identify the appropriate IPv4 addressing scheme using VLSM and summarization to satisfy addressing requirements in a LAN/WAN environment.**
27, 28, 29	**Describe the technological requirements for running IPv6 in conjunction with IPv4 such as dual stack**
25–28	**Describe IPv6 addresses**
25, 26	Global unicast
27	Multicast
27	Link local
26	Unique local
27	eui 64
28	autoconfiguration

Table I-4   ICND1 Exam Topics: IP Routing Technologies

Chapter	IP Routing Technologies
16	**Describe basic routing concepts**
16	CEF
16	Packet forwarding
16	Router lookup process
15–18, 27	**Configure and verify utilizing the CLI to set basic Router configuration**

Chapter	IP Routing Technologies
16–18, 27	Cisco IOS commands to perform basic router setup
16, 27	**Configure and verify operation status of an ethernet interface**
16–18, 27–29	**Verify router configuration and network connectivity**
16–18, 27, 29	Cisco IOS commands to review basic router information and network connectivity
16, 29	**Configure and verify routing configuration for a static or default route given specific routing requirements**
4, 16, 17, 25, 29	**Differentiate methods of routing and routing protocols**
4, 17, 29	Static vs. Dynamic
17	Link state v. Distance Vector
16, 25	next hop
16, 25	ip routing table
17, 29	Passive interfaces
17, 29	**Configure and verify OSPF (single area)**
17, 29	Benefit of single area
17	Configure OSPF v2
29	Configure OSPF v3
17, 29	Router ID
17, 29	Passive interface
16	**Configure and verify interVLAN routing (Router on a stick)**
16	sub interfaces
16	upstream routing
16	encapsulation
8, 16	**Configure SVI interfaces**

Table I-5   ICND1 Exam Topics: IP Services

Chapter	IP Services
18, 28	**Configure and verify DHCP (IOS Router)**
18, 28	configuring router interfaces to use DHCP
18	DHCP options
18	excluded addresses
18	lease time
22, 23	**Describe the types, features, and applications of ACLs**
22	Standard
23	Sequence numbers
23	Editing
23	Extended
23	Named
22, 23	Numbered
22	Log option
22, 23	**Configure and verify ACLs in a network environment**
23	Named
22, 23	Numbered
22	Log option
24	**Identify the basic operation of NAT**
24	Purpose
24	Pool

Chapter	IP Services
24	Static
24	1 to 1
24	Overloading
24	Source addressing
24	One way NAT
24	**Configure and verify NAT for given network requirements**
23	**Configure and verify NTP as a client**

Table I-6   ICND1 Exam Topics: Network Device Security

Chapter	Network Device Security
8, 15	**Configure and verify network device security features such as**
8, 15	Device password security
8, 15	Enable secret vs enable
23	Transport
23	Disable telnet
8	SSH
8	VTYs
23	Physical security
8	Service password
8	Describe external authentication methods
8, 10	**Configure and verify Switch Port Security features such as**
8	Sticky MAC
8	MAC address limitation
8, 10	Static / dynamic
8, 10	Violation modes
8, 10	Err disable
8, 10	Shutdown
8, 10	Protect restrict
8	Shutdown unused ports
8	Err disable recovery
8	Assign unused ports to an unused VLAN
23	Setting native VLAN to other than VLAN 1
22, 23	**Configure and verify ACLs to filter network traffic**
23	**Configure and verify an ACLs to limit telnet and SSH access to the router**

Table I-7   ICND1 Exam Topics: Troubleshooting

Chapter	Troubleshooting
12–15, 18–21, 25–28	**Troubleshoot and correct common problems associated with IP addressing and host configurations.**
9, 10	**Troubleshoot and Resolve VLAN problems**
9, 10	identify that VLANs are configured
9, 10	port membership correct
9, 10	IP address configured
9, 10	**Troubleshoot and Resolve trunking problems on Cisco switches**
9, 10	correct trunk states

Chapter	Troubleshooting
9, 10	correct encapsulation configured
9, 10	correct vlans allowed
22, 23	**Troubleshoot and Resolve ACL issues**
22, 23	Statistics
22, 23	Permitted networks
22, 23	Direction
22, 23	Interface
10	**Troubleshoot and Resolve Layer 1 problems**
10	Framing
10	CRC
10	Runts
10	Giants
10	Dropped packets
10	Late collision
10	Input / Output errors

ICND2 Exam Topics

Tables I-8 through I-12 list the exam topics for ICND2. These tables note the book chapters in which each exam topic is covered in the ICND2 book. Note that each table covers a main exam topic. Cisco released further information on each topic to several sublevels of hierarchy. In this table, those sublevels are indented to indicate the topic above them that they are related to.

Table I-8   ICND2 Exam Topics: LAN Switching Technologies

Chapters	LAN Switching Technologies
1	**Identify enhanced switching technologies**
1	RSTP
1	PVSTP
1	Etherchannels
1, 2	**Configure and verify PVSTP operation**
1, 2	describe root bridge election
2	spanning tree mode

Table I-9   ICND2 Exam Topics, IP Routing Technologies

Chapters	IP Routing Technologies
20	**Describe the boot process of Cisco IOS routers**
20	POST
20	Router bootup process
12	**Configure and verify operation status of a Serial interface.**
20, 21	**Manage Cisco IOS Files**
20	Boot preferences
20	Cisco IOS image(s)
21	Licensing
21	Show license
21	Change license

Chapters	IP Routing Technologies
8–11, 16–18	**Differentiate methods of routing and routing protocols**
8	Administrative distance
9	split horizon
8, 9, 17, 18	metric
8, 9, 17, 18	next hop
8, 17	**Configure and verify OSPF (single area)**
8, 11, 17	neighbor adjacencies
8, 11, 17	OSPF states
8, 17	Discuss Multi area
8	Configure OSPF v2
17	Configure OSPF v3
8, 17	Router ID
8, 17	LSA types
9, 10, 18	**Configure and verify EIGRP (single AS)**
9, 10, 18	Feasible Distance / Feasible Successors /Administrative distance
9, 18	Feasibility condition
9, 18	Metric composition
9, 10, 18	Router ID
9, 10	Auto summary
9, 10, 18	Path selection
9, 10, 18	Load balancing
9, 10, 18	Equal
9, 10, 18	Unequal
9, 10, 18	Passive interface

Table I-10   ICND2 Exam Topics, IP Services

Chapters	IP Services
6	**Recognize High availability (FHRP)**
6	VRRP
6	HSRP
6	GLBP
19	**Configure and verify Syslog**
19	Utilize Syslog Output
19	**Describe SNMP v2 & v3**

Table I-11   ICND2 Exam Topics, Troubleshooting

Chapters	Troubleshooting
3, 4, 5, 16	**Identify and correct common network problems**
19	**Utilize netflow data**
2	**Troubleshoot and Resolve Spanning Tree operation issues**
2	root switch
2	priority
2	mode is correct
2	port states
4, 5, 16	**Troubleshoot and Resolve routing issues**
4, 5, 16	routing is enabled

Chapters	Troubleshooting
4, 5, 16	routing table is correct
4, 5, 16	correct path selection
11, 17	**Troubleshoot and Resolve OSPF problems**
11, 17	neighbor adjacencies
11, 17	Hello and Dead timers
11, 17	OSPF area
11, 17	Interface MTU
11, 17	Network types
11, 17	Neighbor states
11, 17	OSPF topology database
11, 18	**Troubleshoot and Resolve EIGRP problems**
11, 18	neighbor adjacencies
11, 18	AS number
11, 18	Load balancing
11, 18	Split horizon
3, 5	**Troubleshoot and Resolve interVLAN routing problems**
5	Connectivity
5	Encapsulation
5	Subnet
3, 5	Native VLAN
3, 5	Port mode trunk status
12, 14	**Troubleshoot and Resolve WAN implementation issues**
12	Serial interfaces
12	PPP
14	Frame relay
19	**Monitor NetFlow statistics**
2	**Troubleshoot etherchannel problems**

Table I-12   ICND2 Exam Topics: WAN Technologies

Chapters	WAN Technologies
15, 13, 7	**Identify different WAN Technologies**
15	Metro Ethernet
15	VSAT
15	Cellular 3G / 4G
15	MPLS
12, 15	T1 / E1
15	ISDN
15	DSL
13	Frame relay
15	Cable
7	VPN
12	**Configure and verify a basic WAN serial connection**
12	**Configure and verify a PPP connection between Cisco routers**
14	**Configure and verify Frame Relay on Cisco routers**
15	**Implement and troubleshoot PPPoE**

200-120 CCNA Exam Topics

The 200-120 CCNA exam actually covers everything from both the ICND1 and ICND2 exams, at least based on the published exam topics. As of this writing, the CCNA exam topics include all topics in Tables I-1 through I-12. In short, CCNA = ICND1 + ICND2.

> **NOTE** Because it is possible that the exam topics can change over time, it might be worth the time to double-check the exam topics as listed on the Cisco website (www.cisco.com/go/ccent and www.cisco.com/go/ccna). If Cisco does happen to add exam topics at a later date, note that Appendix B, "ICND1 Exam Updates," describes how to go to www.ciscopress.com and download additional information about those newly added topics.

About This Book

This book discusses the content and skills needed to pass the 100-101 ICND1 exam. That content also serves as basically the first half of the CCNA content, with this book's companion title, *CCNA ICND2 200-101 Official Cert Guide*, Academic Edition, discussing the second half of the content.

Each of these books uses the same kinds of book features, so if you are reading both this book and the ICND2 book, there is no need to read the Introduction to the other book. Also, for those of you using both books to prepare for the 200-120 CCNA exam (rather than taking the two-exam option), the end of this Introduction lists a suggested reading plan.

Book Features

The most important and somewhat obvious objective of this book is to help you pass the ICND1 exam or the CCNA exam. In fact, if the primary objective of this book were different, the book's title would be misleading! However, the methods used in this book to help you pass the exams are also designed to make you much more knowledgeable about how to do your job.

This book uses several tools to help you discover your weak topic areas, to help you improve your knowledge and skills with those topics, and to prove that you have retained your knowledge of those topics. So, this book does not try to help you pass the exams only by memorization, but by truly learning and understanding the topics. The CCNA Routing and Switching certification is the foundation for many of the Cisco professional certifications, and it would be a disservice to you if this book did not help you truly learn the material. Therefore, this book helps you pass the CCNA exam by using the following methods:

- Helping you discover which exam topics you have not mastered
- Providing explanations and information to fill in your knowledge gaps
- Supplying exercises that enhance your ability to recall and deduce the answers to test questions
- Providing practice exercises on the topics and the testing process through test questions on the DVD

Chapter Features

To help you customize your study time using these books, the core chapters have several features that help you make the best use of your time:

- **Introduction and Exam Topics:** Each chapter begins with an introduction to the chapter's main topics and a listing of the official exam topics covered in that chapter.

- **Foundation Topics:** These are the core sections of each chapter. They explain the protocols, concepts, and configurations for the topics in that chapter.
- **Review Activities:** At the end of the "Foundation Topics" section of each chapter, the "Review Activities" section lists a series of study activities that should be done at the end of the chapter. Each chapter includes the activities that make the most sense for studying the topics in that chapter. The activities include the following:
  - **Chapter Summaries:** This is a thorough summary of the main chapter topics for you to review. Be sure you understand all these points in detail, and refer to the chapter if not.
  - **Review Questions:** These questions offer a chance for you to assess how well you retained particular facts from the Foundation Topics.
  - **Review Key Topics:** The Key Topic icon is shown next to the most important items in the "Foundation Topics" section of the chapter. The Key Topics Review activity lists the key topics from the chapter and their corresponding page numbers. Although the contents of the entire chapter could be on the exam, you should definitely know the information listed in each key topic.
  - **Complete Tables and Lists from Memory:** To help you exercise your memory and memorize some lists of facts, many of the more important lists and tables from the chapter are included in a document on the DVD. This document lists only partial information, allowing you to complete the table or list.
  - **Define Key Terms:** Although the exams are unlikely to ask a question like, "Define this term," the CCNA exams require that you learn and know a lot of networking terminology. This section lists the most important terms from the chapter, asking you to write a short definition and compare your answer to the Glossary at the end of this book.
  - **Command Reference Tables:** Some book chapters cover a large amount of configuration and EXEC commands. These tables list the commands introduced in the chapter, along with an explanation. For exam preparation, use it for reference, but also read the table once when performing the Review Activities to make sure that you remember what all the commands do.

Part Review

The Part Review tasks help you prepare to apply all the concepts in this part of the book. (Each book part contains a number of related chapters.) The part review includes sample test questions, which require you to apply the concepts from multiple chapters in that part, uncovering what you truly understood and what you did not quite yet understand. The part review also uses mind map exercises that help you mentally connect concepts, configuration, and verification, so that no matter what perspective a single exam question takes, you can analyze and answer the question.

The part reviews list tasks, along with checklists so that you can track your progress. The following list explains the most common tasks you will see in the Part Review sections; note that not all Part Review sections use every type of task:

- **Repeat Chapter Review Questions:** Although you have already seen the Chapter Review questions from the chapters in a part, reanswering those questions can be a useful way to review facts. The Part Review section suggests that you repeat the Chapter Review questions, but using the PCPT exam software that comes with the book, for extra practice in answering multichoice questions on a computer.
- **Answer Part Review Questions:** The PCPT exam software includes several exam databases. One exam database holds Part Review questions, written specifically for Part Review. These questions purposefully include multiple concepts in each question, sometimes from multiple chapters, to help build the skills needed for the more challenging analysis questions on the exams.

- **Review Key Topics:** Yes, again! They are indeed the most important topics in each chapter.

- **Create Configuration Mind Maps:** Mind maps are graphical organizing tools that many people find useful when learning and processing how concepts fit together. The process of creating mind maps helps you build mental connections between concepts and configuration commands, as well as develop your recall of the individual commands. For this task, you can create the mind map on paper or using any mind-mapping or graphic organizer software. (For more information on mind maps, refer to this book's Introduction, in the section "About Mind Maps.")

- **Create Verification Mind Maps:** These mind-mapping exercises focus on helping you connect router and switch show commands to either networking concepts or to configuration commands. Simply create the mind maps on paper or use any mind-mapping or graphic organizer software.

- **Repeat Chapter Review Tasks:** (Optional) Browse through all the Review Activities, and repeat any that you think might help you with review at this point.

Final Prep Tasks

Chapter 30, "Final Review," near the end of this book, lists a series of preparation tasks that you can best use for your final preparation before taking the exam.

Other Features

In addition to the features in each of the core chapters, this book, as a whole, has additional study resources, including

- **DVD-based practice exam:** The companion DVD contains the powerful Pearson IT Certification Practice Test exam engine. You can take simulated ICND1 exams, as well as simulated CCNA exams, with the DVD and activation code included in this book. (You can take simulated ICND2 and CCNA exams with the DVD in the *Cisco CCNA Routing and Switching ICND2 200-101 Official Cert Guide*, Academic Edition.)

- **CENT/CCNA ICND1 Simulator Lite:** This lite version of the best-selling CCNA Network Simulator from Pearson provides you with a means, right now, to experience the Cisco command-line interface (CLI). There's no need to go buy real gear or buy a full simulator to start learning the CLI. Just install it from the DVD in the back of this book.

- **eBook:** This Academic Edition comes complete with a free copy of the *Cisco CCENT/CCNA ICND1 100-101 Official Cert Guide Premium Edition eBook and Practice Test*. The Premium Edition eBook provides you with three different eBook files: PDF, EPUB, and Mobi (native Kindle format). In addition, the Premium Edition enables you to link all the questions from the practice test software to the PDF file of the book, so you can link directly to the book content from each question for further study. Instructions for accessing your Premium Edition can be found on the access code card in the DVD sleeve.

- **Subnetting videos:** The companion DVD contains a series of videos that show you how to calculate various facts about IP addressing and subnetting (in particular, using the shortcuts described in this book).

- **Subnetting practice:** The companion DVD contains five appendices (D through H), and each appendix contains a set of IPv4 subnetting practice problems, with the answers, and with explanations of how the answers were found. This is a great resource to get ready to do subnetting well and fast.

- **Other practice:** The companion DVD contains four other appendices (I through L) that each contain other practice problems related to a particular chapter from the book. Use these for more practice on the particulars with some of the math- and process-oriented activities in the chapters.

- **Mentoring videos:** The DVD included with this book includes four other instructional videos, about the following topics: Switch Basics, CLI Navigation, Router Configuration, and VLANs.

- **Companion website:** The website www.ciscopress.com/title/9781587144851 posts up-to-the-minute materials that further clarify complex exam topics. Check this site regularly for new and updated postings written by the author that provide further insight into the more troublesome topics on the exam.

- **PearsonITCertification.com:** The www.pearsonitcertification.com website is a great resource for all things IT-certification related. Check out the great CCNA Routing and Switching articles, videos, blogs, and other certification preparation tools from the industry's best authors and trainers.

- **CCNA Simulator:** If you are looking for more hands-on practice, you might want to consider purchasing the CCNA Network Simulator. You can purchase a copy of this software from Pearson at http://pearsonitcertification.com/networksimulator or from other retail outlets. To help you with your studies, I have created a mapping guide that maps each of the labs in the simulator to the specific sections in these CCNA Cert Guides. You can get this mapping guide for free on the "Extras" tab of the companion website.

- **Author's website and blogs:** The author maintains a website that hosts tools and links useful when studying for CCENT and CCNA Routing and Switching. The site lists information to help you build your own lab, study pages that correspond to each chapter of this book and the ICND2 book, and links to the author's CCENT Skills blog and CCNA Skills blog. Start at www.certskills.com; check the tabs for study and blogs in particular.

Book Organization, Chapters, and Appendices

This book contains 29 core chapters, Chapters 1 through 29, with Chapter 30 including some suggestions for how to approach the actual exams. Each core chapter covers a subset of the topics on the ICND1 exam. The core chapters are organized into sections. The core chapters cover the following topics:

Part I: Networking Fundamentals

- Chapter 1, "The TCP/IP and OSI Networking Models," introduces the terminology surrounding two different networking architectures, namely Transmission Control Protocol/Internet Protocol (TCP/IP) and Open Systems Interconnection (OSI).

- Chapter 2, "Fundamental of Ethernet LANs," covers the concepts and terms used for the most popular option for the data link layer for local-area networks (LAN), namely Ethernet.

- Chapter 3, "Fundamentals of WANs," covers the concepts and terms used for the most popular options for the data link layer for wide-area networks (WAN), including High-Level Data Link Control (HDLC).

- Chapter 4, "Fundamentals of IPv4 Addressing and Routing": The Internet Protocol (IP) is the main network layer protocol for TCP/IP. This chapter introduces the basics of IP version 4 (IPv4), including IPv4 addressing and routing.

- Chapter 5, "Fundamentals of TCP/IP Transport and Applications": The Transmission Control Protocol (TCP) and User Datagram Protocol (UDP) are the main transport layer protocols for TCP/IP. This chapter introduces the basics of TCP and UDP.

Part II: Ethernet LANs and Switches

- Chapter 6, "Building Ethernet LANs with Switches," deepens and expands the introduction to LANs from Chapter 2, discussing the roles and functions of LAN switches.

- **Chapter 7, "Installing and Operating Cisco LAN Switches,"** explains how to access, examine, and configure Cisco Catalyst LAN switches.

- **Chapter 8, "Configuring Ethernet Switching,"** shows how to configure a variety of switch features, including duplex and speed, port security, securing the CLI, and the switch IP address.

- **Chapter 9, "Implementing Ethernet Virtual LANs":** This chapter explains the concepts and configuration surrounding virtual LANs, including VLAN trunking and the VLAN Trunking Protocol.

- **Chapter 10, "Troubleshooting Ethernet LANs,"** focuses on how to tell whether the switch is doing what it is supposed to be doing, mainly through the use of show commands.

Part III: IP Version 4 Addressing and Subnetting

- **Chapter 11, "Perspectives on IPv4 Subnetting,"** walks you through the entire concept of subnetting, from starting with a Class A, B, or C network; analyzing requirements; making choices; calculating the resulting subnets; and assigning those on paper, all in preparation to deploy and use those subnets by configuring the devices.

- **Chapter 12, "Analyzing Classful IPv4 Networks":** IPv4 addresses originally fell into several classes, with unicast IP addresses being in Class A, B, and C. This chapter explores all things related to address classes and the IP network concept created by those classes.

- **Chapter 13, "Analyzing Subnet Masks":** In most jobs, someone else came before you and chose the subnet mask used in a network. What does that mean? What does that mask do for you? This chapter focuses on how to look at the mask (and IP network) to discover key facts, like the size of a subnet (number of hosts) and the number of subnets in the network.

- **Chapter 14, "Analyzing Existing Subnets":** Most troubleshooting of IP connectivity problems starts with an IP address and mask. This chapter takes that paired information and shows you how to find and analyze the subnet in which that IP address resides, including finding the subnet ID, range of addresses in the subnet, and subnet broadcast address.

Part IV: Implementing IP Version 4

- **Chapter 15, "Operating Cisco Routers,"** is like Chapter 8, but it focuses on routers instead of switches.

- **Chapter 16, "Configuring IPv4 Addresses and Routes,"** discusses how to add IPv4 address configuration to router interfaces, the routes that the router creates as a result, and how to configure static IPv4 routes.

- **Chapter 17, "Learning IPv4 Routes with OSPFv2,"** explains how routers work together to find all the best routes to each subnet using a routing protocol. This chapter also shows how to configure the OSPF routing protocol for use with IPv4.

- **Chapter 18, "Configuring and Verifying Host Connectivity,"** discusses several tools useful when working with IPv4 configuration on hosts. In particular, this chapter discusses DHCP, ping, and traceroute and how to configure IPv4 settings on a host.

Part V: Advanced IPv4 Addressing Concepts

- **Chapter 19, "Subnet Design,"** reverses the approach to IPv4 subnetting as compared to Part III of this book. Instead, this chapter consider questions about why a particular mask might be chosen, and if chosen, what subnet IDs exist.

- **Chapter 20, "Variable-Length Subnet Masks,"** takes IPv4 subnetting to another challenge level, in which different subnets in the same network can use a different subnet mask so that the subnets in the same network have different sizes.

■ **Chapter 21, "Route Summarization,"** looks at a process that can be configured for routing protocols so that the protocol advertises one route, for a larger set of addresses, rather than many routes, each for a smaller set of addresses.

Part VI: IPv4 Services

■ **Chapter 22, "Basic IPv4 Access Control Lists":** This chapter examines how standard IP ACLs can filter packets based on the source IP address so that a router will not forward the packet.

■ **Chapter 23, "Advanced IPv4 ACLs and Device Security":** This chapter examines both named and numbered ACLs, with emphasis on how extended IP ACLs can match packets based on both source and destination IP address, and by matching source and destination TCP and UDP port numbers.

■ **Chapter 24, "Network Address Translation":** This chapter closely examines the concepts behind the depletion of the IPv4 address space, and how NAT, in particular the Port Address Translation (PAT) option, helps solve the problem. The chapter also shows how to configure NAT on routers using the IOS CLI.

Part VII: IP Version 6

■ **Chapter 25, "Fundamentals of IP Version 6,"** discusses the most basic concepts of IP version 6, focusing on the rules for writing and interpreting IPv6 addresses.

■ **Chapter 26, "IPv6 Addressing and Subnetting,"** works through the two branches of unicast IPv6 addresses—global unicast addresses and unique local addresses—that act somewhat like IPv4 public and private addresses, respectively. This chapter also shows how IPv6 implements subnetting.

■ **Chapter 27, "Implementing IPv6 Addressing on Routers,"** shows how to configure IPv6 routing and addresses on routers. It also shows the link-local unicast address, plus other special addresses used by routers.

■ **Chapter 28, "Implementing IPv6 Addressing on Hosts,"** shows how to add IPv6 configuration on hosts, with emphasis on the two methods by which hosts can learn IPv6 settings: stateful DHCPv6 and Stateless Address Autoconfiguration (SLAAC).

■ **Chapter 29, "Implementing IPv6 Routing,"** shows how to adds routes to an IPv6 router's routing table, both through static configuration and with OSPF version 3 (OSPFv3).

Part VIII: Final Preparation

■ **Chapter 30, "Final Review,"** suggests a plan for final preparation after you have finished the core parts of the book, in particular explaining the many study options available in the book.

Part IX: Appendices (In Print)

■ **Appendix A, "Numeric Reference Tables,"** lists several tables of numeric information, including a binary-to-decimal conversion table and a list of powers of 2.

■ **Appendix B, "ICND1 Exam Updates,"** covers a variety of short topics that either clarify or expand upon topics covered earlier in the book. This appendix is updated from time to time, and posted at www.ciscopress.com/title/1587143852, with the most recent version available at the time of printing included here as Appendix B. (The first page of the appendix includes instructions on how to check to see whether a later version of Appendix B is available online.)

■ The **Glossary** contains definitions for all the terms listed in the "Definitions of Key Terms" sections at the conclusion of Chapters 1 through 29.

Appendixes (on the DVD)

The following appendices are available in digital format on the DVD that accompanies this book:

- **Appendix C, "Answers to the Review Questions,"** includes the explanations to all the questions from Chapters 1 through 29.

- **Appendix D, "Practice for Chapter 12: Analyzing Classful IPv4 Networks,"** lists practice problems associated with Chapter 12. In particular, the practice questions ask you to find the classful network number in which an address resides, and all other facts about that network.

- **Appendix E, "Practice for Chapter 13: Analyzing Subnet Masks,"** lists practice problems associated with Chapter 13. In particular, the practice questions ask you to convert masks between the three formats, and to examine an existing mask, determine the structure of the IP addresses, and calculate the number of hosts/subnet and number of subnets.

- **Appendix F, "Practice for Chapter 14: Analyzing Existing Subnets,"** lists practice problems associated with Chapter 14. In particular, the practice questions ask you to take an IP address and mask, and find the subnet ID, subnet broadcast address, and range of IP addresses in the subnet.

- **Appendix G, "Practice for Chapter 19: Subnet Design,"** lists practice problems associated with Chapter 19. In particular, the practice questions ask you to examine a set of requirements, determine which mask (if any) meets those requirements, and choose the best mask based on the requirements. It also asks you to find all the subnet IDs in a classful network when given a single mask used throughout the network.

- **Appendix H, "Practice for Chapter 20: Variable-Length Subnet Masks,"** lists practice problems associated with Chapter 20, including problems in which you look for a place to add a new VLSM subnet so that no VLSM overlap is created.

- **Appendix I, "Practice for Chapter 21: Route Summarization,"** lists practice problems associated with Chapter 21. In particular, the practice questions ask you to find the best summary route that includes all the subnets in a list.

- **Appendix J, "Practice for Chapter 22: Basic IPv4 Access Control Lists,"** lists practice problems associated with Chapter 22. In particular, the practice questions give you a chance to practice working with ACL wildcard masks.

- **Appendix K, "Practice for Chapter 25: Fundamentals of IP Version 6,"** lists practice problems associated with Chapter 25. In particular, it provides practice for abbreviating full IPv6 addresses and expanded abbreviated IPv6 addresses.

- **Appendix L, "Practice for Chapter 27: Implementing IPv6 on Routers,"** lists practice problems associated with Chapter 27. In particular, it provides practice in using the EUI-64 process to build an IPv6 address, and in how to find the solicited node multicast used based on a unicast address.

- **Appendix M, "Memory Tables,"** holds the key tables and lists from each chapter, with some of the content removed. You can print this appendix and, as a memory exercise, complete the tables and lists. The goal is to help you memorize facts that can be useful on the exams.

- **Appendix N, "Memory Tables Answer Key,"** contains the answer key for the exercises in Appendix M.

- **Appendix O, "Mind Map Solutions,"** shows an image of sample answers for all the part-ending mind map exercises.

- **Appendix P, "Study Planner,"** is a spreadsheet with major study milestones, where you can track your progress through your study.

Reference Information

This short section contains a few topics available for reference elsewhere in the book. You can read these when you first use the book, but you can also skip these topics and refer back to them later. In particular, make sure to note the final page of this Introduction, which lists several contact details, including how to get in touch with Cisco Press.

Install the Pearson IT Certification Practice Test Engine and Questions

The DVD in the book includes the Pearson IT Certification Practice Test (PCPT) engine—software that displays and grades a set of exam-realistic multiple-choice, drag and drop, fill-in-the-blank, and Testlet questions. Using the Pearson IT Certification Practice Test engine, you can either study by going through the questions in Study Mode, or take a simulated ICND1 or CCNA exam that mimics real exam conditions.

The installation process requires two major steps. The DVD in the back of this book has a recent copy of the Pearson IT Certification Practice Test engine. The practice exam—the database of ICND1 and CCNA exam questions—is not on the DVD. After you install the software, the PCPT software will download the latest versions of both the software and the question databases for this book using your Internet connection.

NOTE The cardboard DVD case in the back of this book includes both the DVD and a piece of thick paper. The paper lists the digital product voucher code and instructions for accessing the eBook files and for the practice exams associated with this book. *Do not lose the code.*

Redeem Your Digital Product Voucher to Access the eBook and Practice Test Code

To use the practice test software, you must first redeem your digital product voucher found on the card in the DVD sleeve. To do so, follow these steps:

Step 1. If you have a Cisco Press account, go to www.ciscopress.com/account and log in. If you do not have a Cisco Press account, go to www.ciscopress.com/join and create an account.

Step 2. On your Account page, find the "Digital Product Voucher" box at the top of the right column.

Step 3. Type in your digital product voucher code found on the DVD card, and click Submit.

NOTE Codes are one-time use and may not be shared.

Step 4. The products and download link will now be listed under Digital Purchases on your Account page. Click the "refresh" links to generate your eBook files for download. Use the access code to unlock and download the Premium Edition practice exams in the Pearson IT Certification Practice Test software, as described in the following sections.

Install the Software from the DVD

The software installation process is pretty routine as compared with other software installation processes. If you have already installed the Pearson IT Certification Practice Test software from another Pearson product, there is no need for you to reinstall the software. Simply launch the software on your desktop and proceed to activate the practice exam from this book by using the activation code included in the DVD sleeve. The following steps outline the installation process:

Step 1. Insert the DVD into your PC.

Step 2. The software that automatically runs is the Cisco Press software to access and use all DVD-based features, including the exam engine and the DVD-only appendices. From the main menu, click the Install the Exam Engine option.

Step 3. Respond to windows prompts as with any typical software installation process.

The installation process will give you the option to activate your exam with the activation code supplied on the paper in the DVD sleeve. This process requires that you establish a Pearson website login. You will need this login to activate the exam, so please do register when prompted. If you already have a Pearson website login, there is no need to register again. Just use your existing login.

Activate and Download the Practice Exam

When the exam engine is installed, you should then activate the exam associated with this book (if you did not do so during the installation process) as follows:

Step 1. Start the PCPT software from the Windows **Start** menu or from your desktop shortcut icon.

Step 2. To activate and download the exam associated with this book, from the **My Products** or **Tools** tab, click the **Activate** button.

Step 3. At the next screen, enter the activation key listed under the Premium Edition product on your account page on www.ciscopress.com. When it is entered, click the **Activate** button.

Step 4. The activation process will download the practice exam. Click **Next**, and then click **Finish**.

After the activation process is completed, the **My Products** tab should list your new exam. If you do not see the exam, make sure that you have selected the **My Products** tab on the menu. At this point, the software and practice exam are ready to use. Simply select the exam and click the **Open Exam** button.

To update a particular product's exams that you have already activated and downloaded, simply select the Tools tab and click the **Update Products** button. Updating your exams will ensure that you have the latest changes and updates to the exam data.

If you want to check for updates to the PCPT software, simply select the Tools tab and click the **Update Application** button. This will ensure that you are running the latest version of the software engine.

Activating Other Products

The exam software installation process and the registration process only have to happen once. Then for each new product, only a few steps are required. For example, if you buy another new Cisco Press Official Cert Guide or Pearson IT Certification Cert Guide, extract the activation code from the DVD sleeve in the back of that book—you don't even need the DVD at this point. From there, all you have to do is start PCPT (if not still up and running) and perform Steps 2 through 4 from the previous list.

PCPT Exam Databases with This Book

The practice test questions come in different exams or exam databases. When you install the PCPT software, and type in the activation code, the PCPT software downloads the latest version of all these exam databases. And with the ICND1 book alone, you get 10 different "exams," or 10 different sets of questions, as listed in Figure I-2.

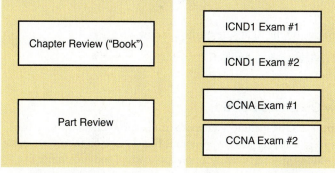

Use for Part Review   Use for Exam Review

Figure I-2 *PCPT Exams/Exam Databases and When to Use Them*

You can choose to use any of these exam databases at any time, both in study mode and practice exam mode. However, many people find it best to save some of the exams until exam review time, after you have finished reading the entire book. Figure I-2 begins to suggest a plan, spelled out here:

- During part review, use PCPT to review the Chapter Review questions (designated as "Book Questions" in the software) for that part, using study mode.
- During part review, use the questions built specifically for part review (the Part Review questions) for that part of the book, using study mode.
- Save the remaining exams to use with the Final Review chapter, using practice exam mode, as discussed in Chapter 30.

The two modes inside PCPT give you better options for study versus practicing a timed exam event. In study mode, you can see the answers immediately, so you can study the topics more easily. Also, you can choose a subset of the questions in an exam database—for example, you can view questions from only the chapters in one part of the book.

Practice exam mode creates an event somewhat like the actual exam. It gives you a preset number of questions, from all chapters, with a timed event. Practice exam mode also gives you a score for that timed event.

How to View Only Chapter Review Questions by Part

Each Part Review section asks you to repeat the Chapter Review questions from the chapters in that part. While you can simply scan the book pages to review these questions, it is slightly better to review these questions from inside the PCPT software, just to get a little more practice in how to read questions from the testing software. But, you can just read them in the book as well.

To view these Chapter Review (book) questions inside the PCPT software, you need to select "Book Questions" and the chapters in this part, using the PCPT menus. To do so, follow these steps:

Step 1.   Start the PCPT software.

Step 2.   From the main (home) menu, select the item for this product, with a name like **Cisco CCENT/CCNA ICND1 100-101 Official Cert Guide**, and click **Open Exam**.

Step 3. The top of the next window that appears should list some exams; select the check box beside **ICND1 Book Questions** and deselect the other check boxes. This selects the "book" questions, that is, the Chapter Review questions from the end of each chapter.

Step 4. In this same window, click at the bottom of the screen to deselect all objectives (chapters). Then select the box beside each chapter in the part of the book you are reviewing.

Step 5. Select any other options on the right side of the window.

Step 6. Click **Start** to start reviewing the questions.

How to View Only Part Review Questions by Part

The exam databases you get with this book include a database of questions created solely for study during the Part Review process. Chapter Review questions focus more on facts, with basic application. The Part Review questions instead focus more on application, and look more like real exam questions.

To view these questions, follow the same process as you did with Chapter Review/Book questions, but select the "Part Review" database instead of the "Book" database. Specifically:

Step 1. Start the PCPT software.

Step 2. From the main (home) menu, select the item for this product, with a name like **CCENT/CCNA ICND1 100-101 Official Cert Guide**, and click **Open Exam**.

Step 3. The top of the next window should list some exams; select the check box beside **Part Review Questions** and deselect the other check boxes. This selects the questions intended for part-ending review.

Step 4. In this same window, click at the bottom of the screen to deselect all objectives, and then select (check) the box beside the book part you want to review. This tells the PCPT software to give you Part Review questions from the selected part.

Step 5. Select any other options on the right side of the window.

Step 6. Click **Start** to start reviewing the questions.

About Mind Maps

Mind maps are a type of visual organization tool that can be used for many purposes. For example, mind maps can be used as an alternative way to take notes.

Mind maps can also be used to improve how your brain organizes concepts. Mind maps stress the connections and relationships between ideas. When you spend time thinking about an area of study, and organize your ideas into a mind map, you strengthen existing mental connections, create new connections, all into your own frame of reference.

In short, mind maps help you internalize what you learn.

Mind Map Mechanics

Each mind map begins with a blank piece of paper or blank window in an application. You then add a large central idea, with branches that move out in any direction. The branches contain smaller concepts, ideas, commands, pictures—whatever idea needs to be represented. Any concepts that can be grouped should be put near each other. As need be, you can create deeper and deeper branches, although for this book's purposes, most mind maps will not go beyond a couple of levels.

> **NOTE**   While many books have been written about mind maps, Tony Buzan often gets credit for formalizing and popularizing mind maps. You can learn more about mind maps at his website, www.thinkbuzan.com.

For example, Figure I-3 shows a sample mind map that begins to output some of the IPv6 content from Part VII of the book. The central concept of the mind map is IPv6 addressing, and the Part Review activity asks you to think of all facts you learned about IPv6 addressing and organize them with a mind map. The mind map allows a more visual representation of the concepts as compared with just written notes.

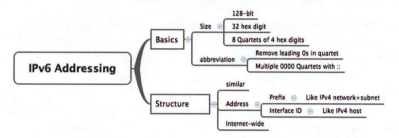

Figure I-3   *Sample Mind Map*

About Mind Maps Used During Part Review

This book suggests mind-mapping exercises during Part Review. This short topic lists some details about the Part Review mind-mapping exercises, listed in one place for reference.

The Part Review sections use two main types of mind mapping exercises:

Configuration exercises ask you to recall the related configuration commands and group them. For example, in a configuration exercise, related commands that happen to be interface subcommands should be grouped, but as shown as being inside interface configuration mode.

Verification exercises ask you to think about the output of show commands and link the output to either the configuration commands that cause that output or the concepts that explain the meaning of some of that output.

Create these configuration mind maps on paper, using any mind-mapping software, or even any drawing application. Many mind-mapping apps exist as well. Regardless of how you draw them, follow these rules:

- If you have only a little time for this exercise, spend your time making your own mind map, instead of looking at suggested answers. The learning happens when thinking through the problem of making your own mind map.

- Set aside the book and all your notes, and do not look at them when first creating these maps, and do as much as you can without looking at the book or your notes (or Google, or anything else).

- Try all the mind maps listed in a Part Review section before looking at your notes.

- Finally, look at your notes to complete all the mind maps.

- Make a note of where you put your final results so that you can find them later during final exam review.

Finally, when learning to use these tools, take two other important suggestions as well. First, use as few words as possible for each node in your mind map. The point is for you to remember the idea and its connections, rather than explain the concept to someone else. Just write enough to remind yourself of the concept. Second, if the mind map process just is not working for you, discard the tool. Instead, take freeform notes on a blank piece of paper. Try to do the important part of the exercise—the thinking about what concepts go together—without letting the tool get in the way.

About Building Hands-On Skills

You need skills in using Cisco routers and switches, specifically the Cisco command-line interface (CLI). The Cisco CLI is a text-based command-and-response user interface in which you type a command and the device (a router or switch) displays messages in response. To answer Sim and Simlet questions on the exams, you need to know a lot of commands, and you need to be able to navigate to the right place in the CLI to use those commands.

The best way to master these commands is to use them. Sometime during your initial reading of the first part of this book, you need to decide how you personally plan to build your CLI skills. This next topic discusses your options for getting the tools you need to build CLI skills.

Overview of Lab Options

To effectively build your hands-on CLI skills, you either need real routers and switches, or at least something that acts like routers and switches. People who are new to Cisco technology often choose from a few options to get those skills.

First, you can use real Cisco routers and switches. You can buy them, new or used, or borrow them at work. You can rent them for a fee. You can even rent virtual Cisco router and switch lab pods from Cisco, in an offering called Cisco Learning Labs.

Simulators provide another option. Router and switch Simulators are software products that mimic the behavior of the Cisco CLI, generally for the purpose of allowing people to learn. These products have an added advantage when learning: They usually have lab exercises as well.

Simulators come in many shapes and sizes, but the publisher sells Simulators that are designed to help you with CCENT and CCNA study—plus they match this book! The Pearson CCENT Network Simulator and the Pearson CCNA Network Simulator both provide an excellent environment to practice the commands, as well as hundreds of focused labs to help you learn what you need to know for the exams. Both products have the same software code base. The CCNA product simply has labs for both ICND1 and ICND2, while the CCENT product has only the ICND1 labs.

This book does not tell you what option you have to use, but you should plan on getting some hands-on practice somehow. The important thing to know is that most people need to practice using the Cisco CLI to be ready to pass these exams.

I (Wendell) have collected some information and opinions about this decision on my website, at certskills.com/labgear. Those pages link to sites for Dynamips and for the Pearson Simulator. Also, because the information never seemed to exist in any one place, this website includes many details about how to build a CCNA lab using used real Cisco routers and switches.

A Quick Start with Pearson Network Simulator Lite

The decision of how to get hands-on skills can be a little scary at first. The good news: You have a free and simple first step: Install the Pearson NetSim Lite that comes with this book.

This lite version of the best-selling CCNA Network Simulator from Pearson provides you with a means, right now, to experience the Cisco command-line interface (CLI). There's no need to go buy real gear or buy a full simulator to start learning the CLI. Just install it from the DVD in the back of this book.

Of course, one reason that NetSim Lite comes on the DVD is that the publisher hopes you will buy the full product. However, even if you do not use the full product, you can still learn from the labs that come with NetSim Lite while deciding about what options to pursue.

NOTE The ICND1 and ICND2 books each contain a different version of the Sim Lite product, each with labs related to the matching book. If you bought both books, make sure that you install both Sim Lite products.

For More Information

If you have any comments about the book, submit them through www.ciscopress.com. Just go to the website, select Contact Us, and type your message.

Cisco might make changes that affect the CCNA Routing and Switching certification from time to time. You should always check www.cisco.com/go/ccna and www.cisco.com/go/ccent for the latest details.

The *Cisco CCENT/CCNA ICND1 100-101 Official Cert Guide*, Academic Edition helps you attain both CCENT and CCNA Routing and Switching certifications. This is the CCENT/CCNA ICND1 certification book from the only Cisco-authorized publisher. We at Cisco Press believe that this book certainly can help you achieve CCNA Routing and Switching certification, but the real work is up to you! I trust that your time will be well spent.

Getting Started

This Getting Started section provides some valuable advice about how to use the study features in this book. Taking a few minutes to read through this short section before going on to Chapter 1 helps you get the most out of the book, regardless of whether you are using it with the end goal of preparing for the CCNA Routing and Switching certification exams or just learning basic networking concepts.

A Brief Perspective on Cisco Certification Exams

Cisco sets the bar pretty high for passing the ICND1, ICND2, and/or CCNA exams. Most anyone can study and pass these exams, but it takes more than just a quick read through the book and the cash to pay for the exam.

The challenge of these exams comes from many angles. Each of these exams covers a lot of concepts, as well as many commands specific to Cisco devices. Beyond knowledge, these Cisco exams also require deep skills. You must be able to analyze and predict what really happens in a network. You must be able to configure Cisco devices to work correctly in those networks. And you must be ready to troubleshoot problems when the network does not work correctly.

The more challenging questions on these exams work a lot like a jigsaw puzzle—but with four out of every five puzzle pieces not even in the room. To solve the puzzle, you have to mentally re-create the missing pieces. To do that, you must know each networking concept and remember how the concepts work together. You also have to match the concepts with what happens on the devices with the configuration commands that tell the devices what to do. You also have to connect the concepts, and the configuration, with the meaning of the output of various troubleshooting commands, to analyze how the network is working and why it is not working right now.

For example, you need to know IP subnetting well, and that topic includes some math. A simple question—one that might be too simple to be a real exam question—would tell you enough of the numbers so that all you have to do is the equivalent of a little addition or multiplication to find a number called a subnet ID.

A more exam-realistic question makes you connect concepts together to set up the math problem. For example, a question might give you a network diagram and ask you to list the subnet ID used in one part of the diagram. But the diagram has no numbers at all. Instead, you have the output of a command from a router, for example, the **show ip ospf database** command, which does list some numbers. But before you can use those numbers, you might need to predict how the devices are configured and what other troubleshooting commands would tell you. So you end up with a question like a puzzle, as shown in Figure 1. The question puts some pieces in the right place; you have to find other pieces using different commands and by applying your knowledge. And some pieces will just remain unknown for a given question.

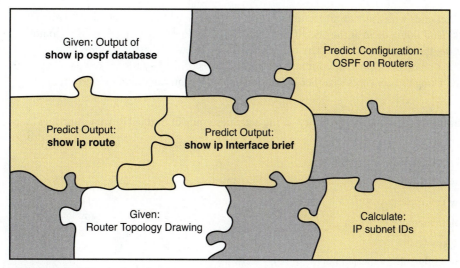

Figure 1 *Filling in Puzzle Pieces with Your Analysis Skills*

These skills require that you prepare by doing more than just reading and memorizing what you read. Of course, you will need to read many pages in this book to learn many individual facts and how these facts are related to each other. But a big part of this book lists exercises beyond reading, exercises that help you build the skills to solve these networking puzzles.

Suggestions for How to Approach Your Study with This Book

Whether you are using this book with the goal of learning introductory networking concepts or to prepare for the CCNA Routing and Switching exams, there are a few things you should consider about how to use it to achieve your goals. What do you need to do to be ready to pass the CCNA Routing and Switching exams or to be successful as a networking professional, beyond reading and remembering all the facts? You need to develop skills. You need to mentally link each idea with other related ideas. Doing that requires additional work. To help you along the way, the next few pages give you five key perspectives about how to use this book to build those skills and make those connections, before you dive into this exciting but challenging world of learning networking on Cisco gear.

Not One Book: 29 Short Read-and-Review Sessions

First, look at your study as a series of read-and-review tasks, each on a relatively small set of related topics.

Each of the core chapters of this book (1 through 29) have around 22 pages of content on average. If you glance around any of those chapters, you will find a heading called "Foundation Topics" on about the fifth page of each chapter. From there to the "Review Activities" section at the end of the chapter, the chapters average about 22 pages.

So, do not approach this book as one big book. Treat the task of your first read of a chapter as a separate task. Anyone can read 22 pages. Having a tough day? Each chapter has two or three major sections, so read just one of them. Or, do some related labs or review something you have already read. This book organizes the content into topics of a more manageable size to give you something more digestible to manage your study time throughout the book.

For Each Chapter, Do Not Neglect Practice

Next, plan to do the Review Activities at the end of each chapter.

Each chapter ends with practice and study tasks under a heading "Review Activities." Doing these tasks, and doing them at the end of the chapter, really does help you get ready. Do not put off using these tasks until later! The chapter-ending "Review Activities" section helps you with the first phase of deepening your knowledge and skills of the key topics, remembering terms and linking the concepts together in your brain so that you can remember how it all fits together.

The following list describes the majority of the activities you will find in "Review Activities" sections:

- Chapter summary
- Review questions
- Review key topics
- Complete memory tables
- Define key terms
- Review command summary tables
- Review feature configuration checklists
- Do subnetting exercises

Use Book Parts for Major Milestones

Third, view the book as having seven major milestones, one for each major topic.

Beyond the more obvious organization into chapters, this book also organizes the chapters into seven major topic areas called book parts. Completing each part means that you have completed a major area of study. At the end of each part, take a little extra time. Do the Part Review tasks at the end of each part. Ask yourself where you are weak and where you are strong. And give yourself some reward for making it to a major milestone. Figure 2 lists the seven parts in this book.

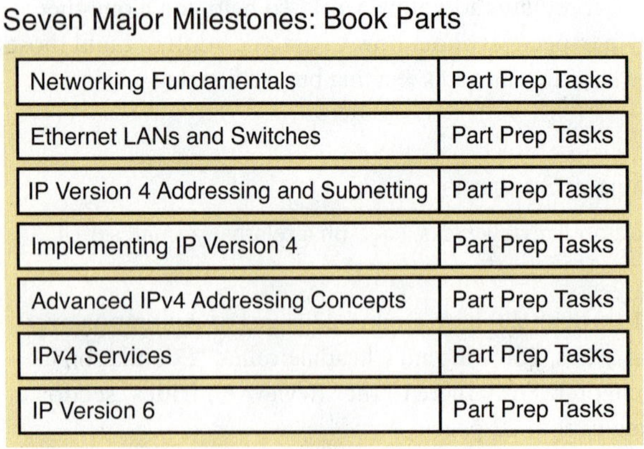

Seven Major Milestones: Book Parts

Networking Fundamentals	Part Prep Tasks
Ethernet LANs and Switches	Part Prep Tasks
IP Version 4 Addressing and Subnetting	Part Prep Tasks
Implementing IP Version 4	Part Prep Tasks
Advanced IPv4 Addressing Concepts	Part Prep Tasks
IPv4 Services	Part Prep Tasks
IP Version 6	Part Prep Tasks

Figure 2 *Parts as Major Milestones*

The tasks in the Part Review sections focus on helping you apply concepts (from that book part) to new scenarios for the exam. Some tasks use sample test questions so that you can think through and analyze a problem. This process helps you refine what you know and to realize what you did not quite yet understand. Some tasks use mind map exercises that help you mentally connect the theoretical concepts with the configuration and verification commands. These Part Review activities help build these skills.

Note that the part review directs you to use the Pearson Certification Practice Test (PCPT) software to access the practice questions. Each part review tells you to repeat the Chapter Review questions, but using the PCPT software. Each part review also directs you how to access a specific set of questions reserved for reviewing concepts at part review. Note that the PCPT software and exam databases with this book give you the rights to additional questions as well; Chapter 30, "Final Review," gives some recommendations on how to best use those questions for your final exam preparation.

Also, consider setting a goal date for finishing each part of the book, and a reward as well! Plan a break, some family time, some time out exercising, eating some good food—whatever helps you get refreshed and motivated for the next part.

Use the Final Review Chapter to Refine Skills

Fourth, do the tasks outlined in the final preparation chapter (Chapter 30) at the end of this book.

The Final Review chapter has two major goals. First, it helps you further develop the analysis skills you need to answer the more complicated questions on the exam. Many questions require that you connect ideas about concepts, configuration, verification, and troubleshooting. More reading on your part does not develop all these skills; this chapter's tasks give you activities to further develop these skills.

The tasks in the Final Review chapter also help you find your weak areas. This final element gives you repetition with high-challenge exam questions, uncovering any gaps in your knowledge. Many of the questions are purposefully designed to test your knowledge of the most common mistakes and misconceptions, helping you avoid some of the common pitfalls people experience with the actual exam.

Set Goals and Track Your Progress

Finally, before you start reading the book and doing the rest of these study tasks, take the time to make a plan, set some goals, and be ready to track your progress.

While making lists of tasks might or might not appeal to you, depending on your personality, goal setting can help everyone studying for these exams. And to do the goal setting, you need to know what tasks you plan to do.

As for the list of tasks to do when studying, you do not have to use a detailed task list. (You could list every single task in every chapter-ending "Review Activities" section, every task in the Part Review tasks section, and every task in the Final Preparation Tasks chapter.) However, listing the major tasks can be enough.

You should track at least two tasks for each typical chapter: reading the "Foundation Topics" section and doing the "Review Activities" section at the end of the chapter. And of course, do not forget to list tasks for Part Reviews and Final Review. Table 1 shows a sample for Part I of this book.

Table 1 Sample Excerpt from a Planning Table

Element	Task	Goal Date	First Date Completed	Second Date Completed (Optional)
Chapter 1	Read Foundation Topics			
Chapter 1	Do Review Activities			
Chapter 2	Read Foundation Topics			
Chapter 2	Do Review Activities			
Chapter 3	Read Foundation Topics			
Chapter 3	Do Review Activities			
Chapter 4	Read Foundation Topics			
Chapter 4	Do Review Activities			
Chapter 5	Read Foundation Topics			
Chapter 5	Do Review Activities			
Part I Review	Do Part Review Activities			

NOTE Appendix P, "Study Planner," on the DVD that comes with this book, contains a complete planning checklist like Table 1 for the tasks in this book. This spreadsheet allows you to update and save the file to note your goal dates and the tasks you have completed.

Use your goal dates as a way to manage your study, and not as a way to get discouraged if you miss a date. Pick reasonable dates that you can meet. When setting your goals, think about how fast you read and the length of each chapter's "Foundation Topics" section, as listed in the Table of Contents. Then, when you finish a task sooner than planned, move up the next few goal dates.

If you miss a few dates, do not start skipping the tasks listed at the ends of the chapters! Instead, think about what is impacting your schedule—real life, commitments, and so on—and either adjust your goals or work a little harder on your study.

Other Small Tasks Before Getting Started

You will need to do a few overhead tasks to install software, find some PDFs, and so on. You can do these tasks now, or do them in your spare moments when you need a study break during the first few chapters of the book. But do these early, so that if you do stumble upon an installation problem, you have time to work through it before you need a particular tool.

Register (for free) at the Cisco Learning Network (CLN, http://learningnetwork.cisco.com) and join the CCENT and CCNA study groups. These mailing lists allow you to lurk and participate in discussions about topics related to CCENT (ICND1) and CCNA (ICND1 + ICND2). Register, join the groups, and set up an email filter to redirect the messages to a separate folder. Even if you do not spend time reading all the posts yet, later, when you have time to read, you can browse through the posts to find interesting topics. Or just search the posts from the CLN website.

Find and print a copy of Appendix M, "Memory Tables." Many of the Chapter Review sections use this tool, in which you take the incomplete tables from the appendix and complete the table to help you remember some key facts.

If you bought an eBook version of this book, find and download the media files (videos and Sim Lite software) per the instructions supplied on the last page of the eBook file under the heading "Where Are the Companion Files?"

Install the PCPT exam software and activate the exams. For more details on how to load the software, refer to the Introduction, under the heading "Install the Pearson IT Certification Practice Test Engine and Questions."

Finally, install the Sim Lite software (unless you bought the full simulator product already). The Sim Lite that comes with this book contains a subset of the lab exercises in the full Pearson Network Simulator product.

Getting Started—Now

Now dive in to your first of many short, manageable tasks: reading Chapter 1, "The TCP/IP and OSI Networking Models." Enjoy!

This first part of the book introduces the most important topics in TCP/IP networking. Chapter 1 introduces the terms, concepts, and protocols for TCP/IP. Chapters 2 and 3 look at how networking devices send data to each other over a physical link, with Chapter 2 focusing on links between nearby devices (local-area networks) and Chapter 3 focusing on links between far-away devices (wide-area networks).

Chapter 4 focuses on the rules of IP routing, which pulls the LAN and WAN links together by forwarding data all the way from one user device to another. Finally, Chapter 5 looks at several other topics, mostly related to how applications make use of the TCP/IP network.

Part I

Networking Fundamentals

Chapter 1: The TCP/IP and OSI Networking Models

Chapter 2: Fundamentals of Ethernet LANs

Chapter 3: Fundamentals of WANs

Chapter 4: Fundamentals of IPv4 Addressing and Routing

Chapter 5: Fundamentals of TCP/IP Transport and Applications

Part I Review

Chapter 1

The TCP/IP and OSI Networking Models

Welcome to the first chapter in your study for CCENT and CCNA! This chapter begins Part I, which focuses on the basics of networking. Because networks require all the devices to follow the rules, this part starts with a discussion of networking models, which gives you a big-picture view of the networking rules.

You can think of a networking model as you think of a set of architectural plans for building a house. A lot of different people work on building your house, such as framers, electricians, bricklayers, painters, and so on. The blueprint helps ensure that all the different pieces of the house work together as a whole. Similarly, the people who make networking products, and the people who use those products to build their own computer networks, follow a particular networking model. That networking model defines rules about how each part of the network should work, as well as how the parts should work together, so that the entire network functions correctly.

The CCNA exams include detailed coverage of one networking model: Transmission Control Protocol/Internet Protocol (TCP/IP). TCP/IP is the most pervasively used networking model in the history of networking. You can find support for TCP/IP on practically every computer operating system (OS) in existence today, from mobile phones to mainframe computers. Every network built using Cisco products today supports TCP/IP. And not surprisingly, the CCNA exams focus heavily on TCP/IP.

The ICND1 exam, and the ICND2 exam to a small extent, also covers a second networking model, called the Open Systems Interconnection (OSI) reference model. Historically, OSI was the first large effort to create a vendor-neutral networking model. Because of that timing, many of the terms used in networking today come from the OSI model, so this chapter's section on OSI discusses OSI and the related terminology.

This chapter covers the following exam topics:

Operation of IP Data Networks

Recognize the purpose and functions of various network devices such as Routers, Switches, Bridges and Hubs.

Select the components required to meet a given network specification.

Describe the purpose and basic operation of the protocols in the OSI and TCP/IP models.

Foundation Topics

This chapter introduces some of the most basic ideas about computer networking, while also defining the structure of two networking models: TCP/IP and OSI. The chapter begins with a brief introduction of how most people view a network, which hopefully connects with where you are to start your CCNA journey. The middle of this chapter introduces networking by explaining some of the key features of TCP/IP. The chapter closes with some additional concepts and terminology related to the OSI model.

Perspectives on Networking

So, you are new to networking. Like many people, your perspective about networks might be that of a user of the network, as opposed to the network engineer who builds networks. For some, your view of networking might be based on how you use the Internet, from home, using a high-speed Internet connection like DSL or cable TV, as shown in Figure 1-1.

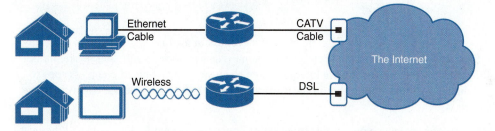

Figure 1-1 *End-User Perspective on High-Speed Internet Connections*

The top part of the figure shows a typical high-speed cable Internet user. The PC connects to a cable modem using an Ethernet cable. The cable modem then connects to a cable TV (CATV) outlet in the wall using a round coaxial cable—the same kind of cable used to connect your TV to the CATV wall outlet. Because cable Internet services provide service continuously, the user can just sit down at the PC and start sending e-mail, browsing websites, making Internet phone calls, and using other tools and applications as well.

The lower part of the figure uses two different technologies. First, the tablet computer uses wireless technology that goes by the name wireless local-area network (wireless LAN), or Wi-Fi, instead of using an Ethernet cable. In this example, the router uses a different technology, digital subscriber line (DSL), to communicate with the Internet.

The CCNA exams, and particularly the ICND1 (100-101) exam, include the technologies used to create networks at a home (as shown in Figure 1-1), but with even more focus on networking technology used inside a company. The Information Technology (IT) world refers to a network created by one corporation, or enterprise, for the purpose of allowing its employees to communicate, as an *enterprise network*. The smaller networks at home, when used for business purposes, often go by the name small office home office (SOHO) networks.

Users of enterprise networks have some idea about the enterprise network at their company or school. People realize that they use a network for many tasks. PC users might realize that their PC connects through an Ethernet cable to a matching wall outlet, as shown at the top of Figure 1-2. Those same users might use wireless LANs with their laptop when going to a meeting in the conference room as well. Figure 1-2 shows these two end-user perspectives on an enterprise network.

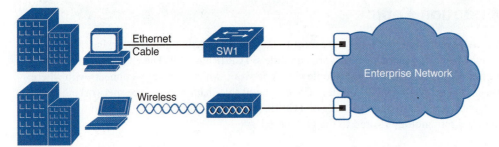

Figure 1-2 *Example Representation of an Enterprise Network*

> **NOTE**   In networking diagrams, a cloud represents a part of a network whose details are not important to the purpose of the diagram. In this case, Figure 1-2 ignores the details of how to create an Enterprise network.

Some users might not even have a concept of the network at all. Instead, these users just enjoy the functions of the network—the ability to post messages to social media sites, make phone calls, search for information on the Internet, listen to music, and download countless apps to their phones—without caring about how it works or how their favorite device connects to the network.

Regardless of how much you already know about how networks work, this book, and the related certifications, help you learn how networks do their job. That job is simply this: moving data from one device to another. The rest of this chapter, and the rest of this first part of the book, reveals the basics of how to build both SOHO and enterprise networks so that they can deliver data between two devices.

In the building business, much work happens before you nail the first boards together. The process starts with some planning, an understanding of how to build a house, and some architectural blueprints of how to build that specific house. Similarly, the journey toward building any computer network does not begin by installing devices and cables, but instead by looking at the architectural plans for those modern networks: the TCP/IP model.

TCP/IP Networking Model

A *networking model*, sometimes also called either a *networking architecture* or *networking blueprint*, refers to a comprehensive set of documents. Individually, each document describes one small function required for a network; collectively, these documents define everything that should happen for a computer network to work. Some documents define a *protocol*, which is a set of logical rules that devices must follow to communicate. Other documents define some physical requirements for networking. For example, a document could define the voltage and current levels used on a particular cable when transmitting data.

You can think of a networking model as you think of an architectural blueprint for building a house. Sure, you can build a house without the blueprint. However, the blueprint can ensure that the house has the right foundation and structure so that it will not fall down, and it has the correct hidden spaces to accommodate the plumbing, electrical, gas, and so on. Also, the many different people that build the house using the blueprint—such as framers, electricians, bricklayers, painters, and so on—know that if they follow the blueprint, their part of the work should not cause problems for the other workers.

Similarly, you could build your own network—write your own software, build your own networking cards, and so on—to create a network. However, it is much easier to simply buy and

1

use products that already conform to some well-known networking model or blueprint. Because the networking product vendors build their products with some networking model in mind, their products should work well together.

History Leading to TCP/IP

Today, the world of computer networking uses one networking model: TCP/IP (Transmission Control Protocol/Internet Protocol). However, the world has not always been so simple. Once upon a time, networking protocols didn't exist, including TCP/IP. Vendors created the first networking protocols; these protocols supported only that vendor's computers. For example, IBM published its Systems Network Architecture (SNA) networking model in 1974. Other vendors also created their own proprietary networking models. As a result, if your company bought computers from three vendors, network engineers often had to create three different networks based on the networking models created by each company, and then somehow connect those networks, making the combined networks much more complex. The left side of Figure 1-3 shows the general idea of what a company's enterprise network might have looked back in the 1980s, before TCP/IP became common in enterprise internetworks.

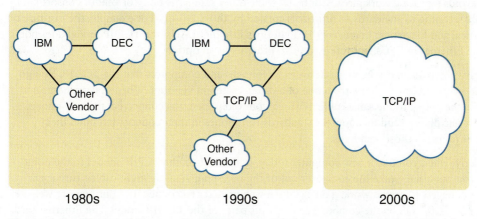

Figure 1-3 *Historical Progression: Proprietary Models to the Open TCP/IP Model*

Although vendor-defined proprietary networking models often worked well, having an open, vendor-neutral networking model would aid competition and reduce complexity. The International Organization for Standardization (ISO) took on the task to create such a model, starting as early as the late 1970s, beginning work on what would become known as the Open Systems Interconnection (OSI) networking model. ISO had a noble goal for the OSI model: to standardize data networking protocols to allow communication between all computers across the entire planet. ISO worked toward this ambitious and noble goal, with participants from most of the technologically developed nations on Earth participating in the process.

A second, less formal effort to create an open, vendor-neutral, public networking model sprouted forth from a U.S. Department of Defense (DoD) contract. Researchers at various universities volunteered to help further develop the protocols surrounding the original DoD work. These efforts resulted in a competing open networking model called TCP/IP.

During the 1990s, companies began adding OSI, TCP/IP, or both to their enterprise networks. However, by the end of the 1990s, TCP/IP had become the common choice, and OSI fell away. The center part of Figure 1-3 shows the general idea behind enterprise networks in that decade—still with networks built upon multiple networking models, but including TCP/IP.

Here in the twenty-first century, TCP/IP dominates. Proprietary networking models still exist, but they have mostly been discarded in favor of TCP/IP. The OSI model, whose development suffered in part because of a slower formal standardization process as compared with

TCP/IP, never succeeded in the marketplace. And TCP/IP, the networking model originally created almost entirely by a bunch of volunteers, has become the most prolific network model ever, as shown on the right side of Figure 1-3.

In this chapter, you will read about some of the basics of TCP/IP. Although you will learn some interesting facts about TCP/IP, the true goal of this chapter is to help you understand what a networking model or networking architecture really is and how it works.

Also in this chapter, you will learn about some of the jargon used with OSI. Will any of you ever work on a computer that is using the full OSI protocols instead of TCP/IP? Probably not. However, you will often use terms relating to OSI. Also, the ICND1 exam covers the basics of OSI, so this chapter also covers OSI to prepare you for questions about it on the exam.

Overview of the TCP/IP Networking Model

The TCP/IP model both defines and references a large collection of protocols that allow computers to communicate. To define a protocol, TCP/IP uses documents called Requests for Comments (RFC). (You can find these RFCs using any online search engine.) The TCP/IP model also avoids repeating work already done by some other standards body or vendor consortium by simply referring to standards or protocols created by those groups. For example, the Institute of Electrical and Electronic Engineers (IEEE) defines Ethernet LANs; the TCP/IP model does not define Ethernet in RFCs, but refers to IEEE Ethernet as an option.

An easy comparison can be made between telephones and computers that use TCP/IP. You go to the store and buy a phone from one of a dozen different vendors. When you get home and plug in the phone to the same cable in which your old phone was connected, the new phone works. The phone vendors know the standards for phones in their country and build their phones to match those standards.

Similarly, when you buy a new computer today, it implements the TCP/IP model to the point that you can usually take the computer out of the box, plug in all the right cables, turn it on, and it connects to the network. You can use a web browser to connect to your favorite website. How? Well, the OS on the computer implements parts of the TCP/IP model. The Ethernet card, or wireless LAN card, built into the computer implements some LAN standards referenced by the TCP/IP model. In short, the vendors that created the hardware and software implemented TCP/IP.

To help people understand a networking model, each model breaks the functions into a small number of categories called *layers*. Each layer includes protocols and standards that relate to that category of functions. TCP/IP actually has two alternative models, as shown in Figure 1-4.

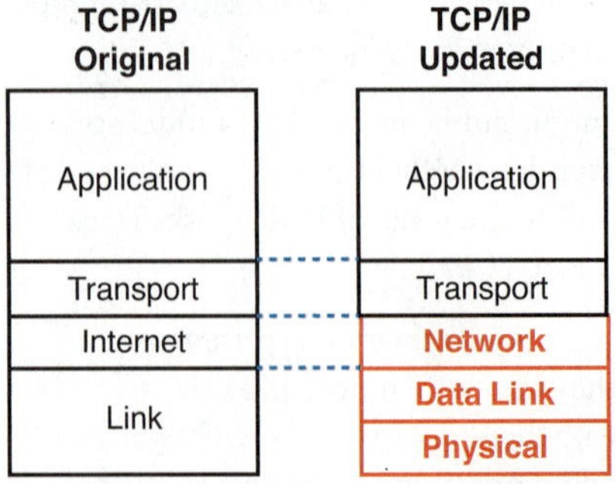

Figure 1-4 *Two TCP/IP Networking Models*

The model on the left shows the original TCP/IP model listed in RFC 1122, which breaks TCP/IP into four layers. The top two layers focus more on the applications that need to send and receive data. The bottom layer focuses on how to transmit bits over each individual link, with the internet layer focusing on delivering data over the entire path from the original sending computer to the final destination computer.

The TCP/IP model on the right is a common method used today to refer to the layers formed by expanding the original model's link layer on the left into two separate layers: data link and physical (similar to the lower two layers of the OSI model). Note that the model on the right is used more often today.

> **NOTE** The original TCP/IP model's link layer has also been referred to as the *network access* and *network interface* layer.

Many of you will have already heard of several TCP/IP protocols, like the examples listed in Table 1-1. Most of the protocols and standards in this table will be explained in more detail as you work through this book. Following the table, this section takes a closer look at the layers of the TCP/IP model.

Table 1-1   TCP/IP Architectural Model and Example Protocols

TCP/IP Architecture Layer	Example Protocols
Application	HTTP, POP3, SMTP
Transport	TCP, UDP
Internet	IP
Link	Ethernet, Point-to-Point Protocol (PPP), T1

TCP/IP Application Layer

TCP/IP application layer protocols provide services to the application software running on a computer. The application layer does not define the application itself, but it defines services that applications need. For example, application protocol HTTP defines how web browsers can pull the contents of a web page from a web server. In short, the application layer provides an interface between software running on a computer and the network itself.

Arguably, the most popular TCP/IP application today is the web browser. Many major software vendors either have already changed or are changing their application software to support access from a web browser. And thankfully, using a web browser is easy: You start a web browser on your computer and select a website by typing the name of the website, and the web page appears.

HTTP Overview

What really happens to allow that web page to appear on your web browser?

Imagine that Bob opens his browser. His browser has been configured to automatically ask for web server Larry's default web page, or *home page*. The general logic looks like Figure 1-5.

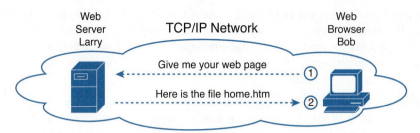

Figure 1-5   *Basic Application Logic to Get a Web Page*

So, what really happened? Bob's initial request actually asks Larry to send his home page back to Bob. Larry's web server software has been configured to know that the default web page is contained in a file called home.htm. Bob receives the file from Larry and displays the contents of the file in Bob's web-browser window.

HTTP Protocol Mechanisms

Taking a closer look, this example shows how applications on each endpoint computer—specifically, the web-browser application and web-server application—use a TCP/IP application layer protocol. To make the request for a web page and return the contents of the web page, the applications use the Hypertext Transfer Protocol (HTTP).

HTTP did not exist until Tim Berners-Lee created the first web browser and web server in the early 1990s. Berners-Lee gave HTTP functions to ask for the contents of web pages, specifically by giving the web browser the ability to request files from the server, and giving the server a way to return the content of those files. The overall logic matches what was shown in Figure 1-5; Figure 1-6 shows the same idea, but with details specific to HTTP.

> **NOTE**   The full version of most web addresses—also called Uniform Resource Locators (URL)—begins with the letters "http," which means that HTTP is used to transfer the web pages.

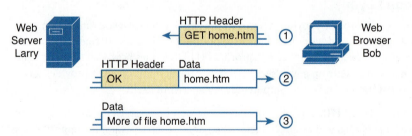
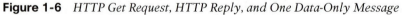

Figure 1-6   *HTTP Get Request, HTTP Reply, and One Data-Only Message*

To get the web page from Larry, at Step 1, Bob sends a message with an HTTP header. Generally, protocols use headers as a place to put information used by that protocol. This HTTP header includes the request to "get" a file. The request typically contains the name of the file (home.htm, in this case), or if no filename is mentioned, the web server assumes that Bob wants the default web page.

Step 2 in Figure 1-6 shows the response from web server Larry. The message begins with an HTTP header, with a return code (200), which means something as simple as "OK" returned in the header. HTTP also defines other return codes so that the server can tell the browser whether the request worked. (Here is another example: If you ever looked for a web page that was not found, and then received an HTTP 404 "not found" error, you received an HTTP return code of 404.) The second message also includes the first part of the requested file.

Step 3 in Figure 1-6 shows another message from web server Larry to web browser Bob, but this time without an HTTP header. HTTP transfers the data by sending multiple messages, each with a part of the file. Rather than wasting space by sending repeated HTTP headers that list the same information, these additional messages simply omit the header.

TCP/IP Transport Layer

Although many TCP/IP application layer protocols exist, the TCP/IP transport layer includes a smaller number of protocols. The two most commonly used transport layer protocols are the *Transmission Control Protocol (TCP)* and the *User Datagram Protocol (UDP)*.

Transport layer protocols provide services to the application layer protocols that reside one layer higher in the TCP/IP model. How does a transport layer protocol provide a service to a higher-layer protocol? This section introduces that general concept by focusing on a single service provided by TCP: error recovery. Later chapters examine the transport layer in more detail, and discuss more functions of the transport layer.

TCP Error Recovery Basics

To appreciate what the transport layer protocols do, you must think about the layer above the transport layer, the application layer. Why? Well, each layer provides a service to the layer above it, like the error-recovery service provided to application layer protocols by TCP.

For example, in Figure 1-5, Bob and Larry used HTTP to transfer the home page from web server Larry to Bob's web browser. But what would have happened if Bob's HTTP GET request had been lost in transit through the TCP/IP network? Or, what would have happened if Larry's response, which included the contents of the home page, had been lost? Well, as you might expect, in either case, the page would not have shown up in Bob's browser.

TCP/IP needs a mechanism to guarantee delivery of data across a network. Because many application layer protocols probably want a way to guarantee delivery of data across a network, the creators of TCP included an error-recovery feature. To recover from errors, TCP uses the concept of acknowledgments. Figure 1-7 outlines the basic idea behind how TCP notices lost data and asks the sender to try again.

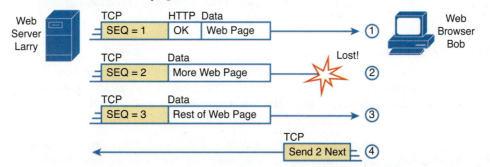

Figure 1-7 *TCP Error-Recovery Services as Provided to HTTP*

Figure 1-7 shows web server Larry sending a web page to web browser Bob, using three separate messages. Note that this figure shows the same HTTP headers as Figure 1-6, but it also shows a TCP header. The TCP header shows a sequence number (SEQ) with each message. In this example, the network has a problem, and the network fails to deliver the TCP message (called a segment) with sequence number 2. When Bob receives messages with sequence numbers 1 and 3, but does not receive a message with sequence number 2, Bob realizes that message 2 was lost. That realization by Bob's TCP logic causes Bob to send a TCP segment back to Larry, asking Larry to send message 2 again.

Same-Layer and Adjacent-Layer Interactions

The example in Figure 1-7 also demonstrates a function called *adjacent-layer interaction*, which refers to the concepts of how adjacent layers in a networking model, on the same computer, work together. In this example, the higher-layer protocol (HTTP) wants error recovery, and the higher layer uses the next lower-layer protocol (TCP) to perform the service of error recovery; the lower layer provides a service to the layer above it.

Figure 1-7 also shows an example of a similar function called *same-layer interaction.* When a particular layer on one computer wants to communicate with the same layer on another computer, the two computers use headers to hold the information that they want to communicate. For example, in Figure 1-7, Larry set the sequence numbers to 1, 2, and 3 so that Bob could notice when some of the data did not arrive. Larry's TCP process created that TCP header with the sequence number; Bob's TCP process received and reacted to the TCP segments. This process through which two computers set and interpret the information in the header used by that layer is called *same-layer interaction*, and it occurs between computers that are communicating over a network.

Table 1-2 summarizes the key points about how adjacent layers work together on a single computer and how one layer on one computer works with the same networking layer on another computer.

Table 1-2   Summary: Same-Layer and Adjacent-Layer Interactions

Concept	Description
Same-layer interaction on different computers	The two computers use a protocol (an agreed-to set of rules) to communicate with the same layer on another computer. The protocol defined by each layer uses a header that is transmitted between the computers to communicate what each computer wants to do. Header information added by a layer of the sending computer is processed by the same layer of the receiving computer.
Adjacent-layer interaction on the same computer	On a single computer, one layer provides a service to a higher layer. The software or hardware that implements the higher layer requests that the next lower layer perform the needed function.

TCP/IP Network Layer

The application layer includes many protocols. The transport layer includes fewer, most notably, TCP and UDP. The TCP/IP network layer includes a small number of protocols, but only one major protocol: the *Internet Protocol (IP)*. In fact, the name *TCP/IP* is simply the names of the two most common protocols (TCP and IP) separated by a /.

IP provides several features, most importantly, addressing and routing. This section begins by comparing IP's addressing and routing with another commonly known system that uses addressing and routing: the postal service. Following that, this section introduces IP addressing and routing. (More details follow in Chapter 4, "Fundamentals of IPv4 Addressing and Routing.")

Internet Protocol and the Postal Service

Imagine that you just wrote two letters: one to a friend on the other side of the country and one to a friend on the other side of town. You addressed the envelopes and put on the stamps, so both are ready to give to the postal service. Is there much difference in how you treat each letter? Not really. Typically, you would just put them in the same mailbox and expect the postal service to deliver both letters.

The postal service, however, must think about each letter separately, and then make a decision of where to send each letter so that it is delivered. For the letter sent across town, the people in the local post office probably just need to put the letter on another truck.

For the letter that needs to go across the country, the postal service sends the letter to another post office, then another, and so on, until the letter gets delivered across the country. At each post office, the postal service must process the letter and choose where to send it next.

To make it all work, the postal service has regular routes for small trucks, large trucks, planes, boats, and so on, to move letters between postal service sites. The service must be able to receive and forward the letters, and it must make good decisions about where to send each letter next, as shown in Figure 1-8.

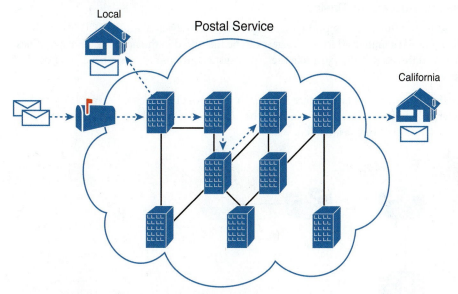

Figure 1-8   *Postal Service Forwarding (Routing) Letters*

Still thinking about the postal service, consider the difference between the person sending the letter and the work that the postal service does. The person sending the letters expects that the postal service will deliver the letter most of the time. However, the person sending the letter does not need to know the details of exactly what path the letters take. In contrast, the postal service does not create the letter, but they accept the letter from the customer. Then, the postal service must know the details about addresses and postal codes that group addresses into larger groups, and it must have the ability to deliver the letters.

The TCP/IP application and transport layers act like the person sending letters through the postal service. These upper layers work the same way regardless of whether the endpoint host computers are on the same LAN or are separated by the entire Internet. To send a message, these upper layers ask the layer below them, the network layer, to deliver the message.

The lower layers of the TCP/IP model act more like the postal service to deliver those messages to the correct destinations. To do so, these lower layers must understand the underlying physical network because they must choose how to best deliver the data from one host to another.

So, what does this all matter to networking? Well, the network layer of the TCP/IP networking model, primarily defined by the *Internet Protocol (IP)*, works much like the postal service. IP defines that each host computer should have a different IP address, just as the postal service defines addressing that allows unique addresses for each house, apartment, and business. Similarly, IP defines the process of routing so that devices called routers can work like the post office, forwarding packets of data so that they are delivered to the correct destinations. Just as the postal service created the necessary infrastructure to deliver letters—post offices, sorting machines, trucks, planes, and personnel—the network layer defines the details of how a network infrastructure should be created so that the network can deliver data to all computers in the network.

> **NOTE**   TCP/IP defines two versions of IP: IP Version 4 (IPv4) and IP Version 6 (IPv6). The world still mostly uses IPv4, so this introductory part of the book uses IPv4 for all references to IP. Later in this book, Part VII, "IP Version 6," discusses this newer version of the IP protocol.

Internet Protocol Addressing Basics

IP defines addresses for several important reasons. First, each device that uses TCP/IP—each TCP/IP *host*—needs a unique address so that it can be identified in the network. IP also defines how to group addresses together, just like the postal system groups addresses based on postal codes (like ZIP codes in the United States).

To understand the basics, examine Figure 1-9, which shows the familiar web server Larry and web browser Bob; but now, instead of ignoring the network between these two computers, part of the network infrastructure is included.

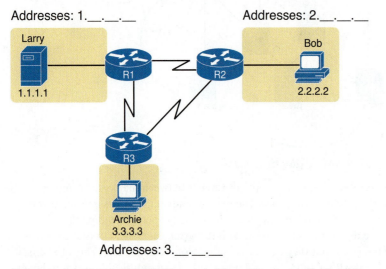

Figure 1-9   *Simple TCP/IP Network: Three Routers with IP Addresses Grouped*

First, note that Figure 1-9 shows some sample IP addresses. Each IP address has four numbers, separated by periods. In this case, Larry uses IP address 1.1.1.1, and Bob uses 2.2.2.2. This style of number is called a *dotted-decimal notation (DDN)*.

Figure 1-9 also shows three groups of address. In this example, all IP address that begin with 1 must be on the upper left, as shown in shorthand in the figure as 1.__.__. All addresses that begin with 2 must be on the right, as shown in shorthand as 2.__.__. Finally, all IP addresses that begin with 3 must be at the bottom of the figure.

Additionally, Figure 1-9 also introduces icons that represent IP routers. Routers are networking devices that connect the parts of the TCP/IP network together for the purpose of routing (forwarding) IP packets to the correct destination. Routers do the equivalent of the work done by each post office site: They receive IP packets on various physical interfaces, make decisions based on the IP address included with the packet, and then physically forward the packet out some other network interface.

IP Routing Basics

The TCP/IP network layer, using the IP protocol, provides a service of forwarding IP packets from one device to another. Any device with an IP address can connect to the TCP/IP network and send packets. This section shows a basic IP routing example for perspective.

> **NOTE** The term *IP host* refers to any device, regardless of size or power, that has an IP address and connects to any TCP/IP network.

Figure 1-10 repeats the familiar case in which web server Larry wants to send part of a web page to Bob, but now with details related to IP. On the lower left, note that server Larry has the familiar application data, HTTP header, and TCP header ready to send. Additionally, the message now also contains an IP header. The IP header includes a source IP address of Larry's IP address (1.1.1.1) and a destination IP address of Bob's IP address (2.2.2.2).

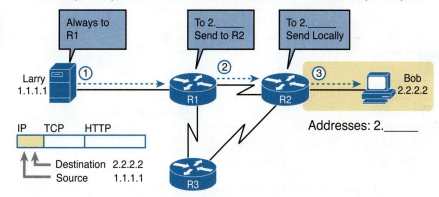

Figure 1-10 *Basic Routing Example*

Step 1, on the left of Figure 1-10, begins with Larry being ready to send an IP packet. Larry's IP process chooses to send the packet to some router—a nearby router on the same LAN—with the expectation that the router will know how to forward the packet. (This logic is much like you or me sending all our letters by putting them in a nearby post office box.) Larry doesn't need to know anything more about the topology or the other routers.

At Step 2, router R1 receives the IP packet, and R1's IP process makes a decision. R1 looks at the destination address (2.2.2.2), compares that address to its known IP routes, and chooses to forward the packet to router R2. This process of forwarding the IP packet is called *IP routing* (or simply *routing*).

At Step 3, router R2 repeats the same kind of logic used by router R1. R2's IP process will compare the packet's destination IP address (2.2.2.2) to R2's known IP routes and make a choice to forward the packet to the right, on to Bob.

All the CCNA exams cover IP fairly deeply. Practically half the chapters in this book discuss some feature that relates to addressing, IP routing, and how routers perform routing.

TCP/IP Link Layer (Data Link Plus Physical)

The TCP/IP model's original link layer defines the protocols and hardware required to deliver data across some physical network. The term *link* refers to the physical connections, or links, between two devices and the protocols used to control those links.

Just like every layer in any networking model, the TCP/IP link layer provides services to the layer above it in the model. When a host's or router's IP process chooses to send an IP packet to another router or host, that host or router then uses link-layer details to send that packet to the next host/router.

Because each layer provides a service to the layer above it, take a moment to think about the IP logic related to Figure 1-10. In that example, host Larry's IP logic chooses to send the IP packet to a nearby router (R1), with no mention of the underlying Ethernet. The Ethernet network, which implements link-layer protocols, must then be used to deliver that packet from host Larry over to router R1. Figure 1-11 shows four steps of what occurs at the link layer to allow Larry to send the IP packet to R1.

> **NOTE**   Figure 1-11 depicts the Ethernet as a series of lines. Networking diagrams often use this convention when drawing Ethernet LANs, in cases where the actual LAN cabling and LAN devices are not important to some discussion, as is the case here. The LAN would have cables and devices, like LAN switches, which are not shown in this figure.

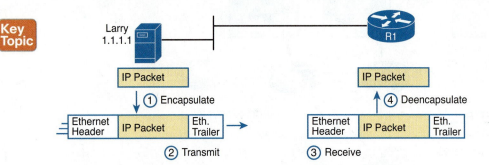

Figure 1-11   *Larry Using Ethernet to Forward an IP Packet to Router R1*

Figure 1-11 shows four steps. The first two occur on Larry, and the last two occur on router R1, as follows:

Step 1.   Larry encapsulates the IP packet between an Ethernet header and Ethernet trailer, creating an Ethernet *frame*.

Step 2.   Larry physically transmits the bits of this Ethernet frame, using electricity flowing over the Ethernet cabling.

Step 3.   Router R1 physically receives the electrical signal over a cable, and re-creates the same bits by interpreting the meaning of the electrical signals.

Step 4.   Router R1 deencapsulates the IP packet from the Ethernet frame by removing and discarding the Ethernet header and trailer.

By the end of this process, the link-layer processes on Larry and R1 have worked together to deliver the packet from Larry to router R1.

> **NOTE**   Protocols define both headers and trailers for the same general reason, but headers exist at the beginning of the message and trailers exist at the end.

The link layer includes a large number of protocols and standards. For example, the link layer includes all the variations of Ethernet protocols, along with several other LAN standards that were more popular in decades past. The link layer includes wide-area network (WAN) standards for different physical media, which differ significantly compared to LAN standards because of the longer distances involved in transmitting the data. This layer also includes the popular WAN standards that add headers and trailers as shown generally in Figure 1-11—protocols such as the Point-to-Point Protocol (PPP) and Frame Relay. Chapter 2, "Fundamentals of Ethernet LANs," and Chapter 3, "Fundamentals of WANs," further develop these topics for LANs and WANs, respectively.

In short, the TCP/IP link layer includes two distinct functions: functions related to the physical transmission of the data, plus the protocols and rules that control the use of the physical media. The five-layer TCP/IP model simply splits out the link layer into two layers (data link and physical) to match this logic.

TCP/IP Model and Terminology

Before completing this introduction to the TCP/IP model, this section examines a few remaining details of the model and some related terminology.

Comparing the Original and Modern TCP/IP Models

The original TCP/IP model defined a single layer—the link layer—below the internetwork layer. The functions defined in the original link layer can be broken into two major categories: functions related directly to the physical transmission of data and those only indirectly related to the physical transmission of data. For example, in the four steps shown in Figure 1-11, Steps 2 and 3 were specific to sending the data, but Steps 1 and 4—encapsulation and deencapsulation—were only indirectly related. This division will become clearer as you read about additional details of each protocol and standard.

Today, most documents use a more modern version of the TCP/IP model, as shown in Figure 1-12. Comparing the two, the upper layers are identical, except a name change from "internet" to "network." The lower layers differ in that the single link layer in the original model is split into two layers to match the division of physical transmission details from the other functions. Figure 1-12 shows the two versions of the TCP/IP model again, with emphasis on these distinctions.

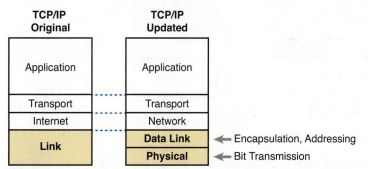

Figure 1-12   *Link Versus Data Link and Physical Layers*

Data Encapsulation Terminology

As you can see from the explanations of how HTTP, TCP, IP, and Ethernet do their jobs, each layer adds its own header (and for data-link protocols, also a trailer) to the data supplied by the higher layer. The term *encapsulation* refers to the process of putting headers (and sometimes trailers) around some data.

Many of the examples in this chapter show the encapsulation process. For example, web server Larry encapsulated the contents of the home page inside an HTTP header in Figure 1-6. The TCP layer encapsulated the HTTP headers and data inside a TCP header in Figure 1-7. IP encapsulated the TCP headers and the data inside an IP header in Figure 1-10. Finally, the Ethernet link layer encapsulated the IP packets inside both a header and a trailer in Figure 1-11.

The process by which a TCP/IP host sends data can be viewed as a five-step process. The first four steps relate to the encapsulation performed by the four TCP/IP layers, and the last step is the actual physical transmission of the data by the host. In fact, if you use the five-layer TCP/IP model, one step corresponds to the role of each layer. The steps are summarized in the following list:

Step 1.   **Create and encapsulate the application data with any required application layer headers.** For example, the HTTP OK message can be returned in an HTTP header, followed by part of the contents of a web page.

Step 2.   **Encapsulate the data supplied by the application layer inside a transport layer header.** For end-user applications, a TCP or UDP header is typically used.

Step 3.   **Encapsulate the data supplied by the transport layer inside a network layer (IP) header.** IP defines the IP addresses that uniquely identify each computer.

Step 4.   **Encapsulate the data supplied by the network layer inside a data link layer header and trailer.** This layer uses both a header and a trailer.

Step 5.   **Transmit the bits.** The physical layer encodes a signal onto the medium to transmit the frame.

The numbers in Figure 1-13 correspond to the five steps in this list, graphically showing the same concepts. Note that because the application layer often does not need to add a header, the figure does not show a specific application layer header.

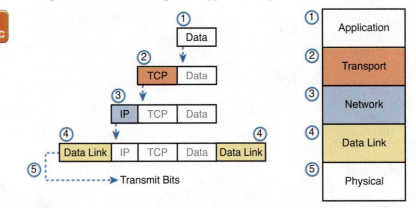

Figure 1-13   *Five Steps of Data Encapsulation: TCP/IP*

Names of TCP/IP Messages

Finally, take particular care to remember the terms *segment*, *packet*, and *frame* and the meaning of each. Each term refers to the headers (and possibly trailers) defined by a particular layer and the data encapsulated following that header. Each term, however, refers to a different layer: segment for the transport layer, packet for the network layer, and frame for the link layer. Figure 1-14 shows each layer along with the associated term.

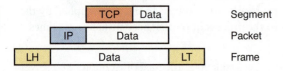
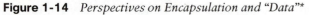

Figure 1-14   *Perspectives on Encapsulation and "Data"**

* The letters LH and LT stand for link header and link trailer, respectively, and refer to the data link layer header and trailer.

Figure 1-14 also shows the encapsulated data as simply "data." When focusing on the work done by a particular layer, the encapsulated data typically is unimportant. For example, an IP packet can indeed have a TCP header after the IP header, an HTTP header after the TCP header, and data for a web page after the HTTP header. However, when discussing IP, you probably just care about the IP header, so everything after the IP header is just called "data." So, when drawing IP packets, everything after the IP header is typically shown simply as "data."

OSI Networking Model

At one point in the history of the OSI model, many people thought that OSI would win the battle of the networking models discussed earlier. If that had occurred, instead of running TCP/IP on every computer in the world, those computers would be running with OSI.

However, OSI did not win that battle. In fact, OSI no longer exists as a networking model that could be used instead of TCP/IP, although some of the original protocols referenced by the OSI model still exist.

So, why is OSI even in this book? Terminology. During those years in which many people thought the OSI model would become commonplace in the world of networking (mostly in the late 1980s and early 1990s), many vendors and protocol documents started using terminology from the OSI model. That terminology remains today. So, while you will never need to work with a computer that uses OSI, to understand modern networking terminology, you need to understand something about OSI.

Comparing OSI and TCP/IP

The OSI model has many similarities to the TCP/IP model from a basic conceptual perspective. It has (seven) layers, and each layer defines a set of typical networking functions. As with TCP/IP, the OSI layers each refer to multiple protocols and standards that implement the functions specified by each layer. In other cases, just as for TCP/IP, the OSI committees did not create new protocols or standards, but instead referenced other protocols that were already defined. For example, the IEEE defines Ethernet standards, so the OSI committees did not waste time specifying a new type of Ethernet; it simply referred to the IEEE Ethernet standards.

Today, the OSI model can be used as a standard of comparison to other networking models. Figure 1-15 compares the seven-layer OSI model with both the four-layer and five-layer TCP/IP models.

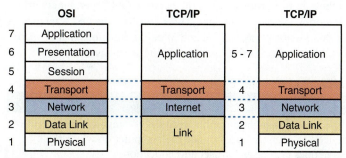

Figure 1-15 *OSI Model Compared to the Two TCP/IP Models*

Next, this section will examine two ways in which we still use OSI terminology today: to describe other protocols and to describe the encapsulation process. Along the way, the text will briefly examine each layer of the OSI model.

Describing Protocols by Referencing the OSI Layers

Even today, networking documents often describe TCP/IP protocols and standards by referencing OSI layers, both by layer number and layer name. For example, a common description of a LAN switch is "layer 2 switch," with "layer 2" referring to OSI layer 2. Because OSI did have a well-defined set of functions associated with each of its seven layers, if you know those functions, you can understand what people mean when they refer to a product or function by its OSI layer.

For another example, TCP/IP's original internet layer, as implemented mainly by IP, equates most directly to the OSI *network* layer. So, most people say that IP is a *network layer protocol*, or a *Layer 3 protocol*, using OSI terminology and numbers for the layer. Of course, if you numbered the TCP/IP model, starting at the bottom, IP would be either Layer 2 or 3, depending on what version of the TCP/IP model you care to use. However, even though IP is a TCP/IP protocol, everyone uses the OSI model layer names and numbers when describing IP or any other protocol for that matter.

The claim that a particular TCP/IP layer is similar to a particular OSI layer is a general comparison, but not a detailed comparison. The comparison is a little like comparing a car to a truck: Both can get you from point A to point B, but they have many specific differences, like the truck having a truck bed in which to carry cargo. Similarly, both the OSI and TCP/IP network layers define logical addressing and routing. However, the addresses have a different size, and the routing logic even works differently. So the comparison of OSI layers to other protocol models is a general comparison of major goals, and not a comparison of the specific methods.

OSI Layers and Their Functions

Cisco requires that CCENTs demonstrate a basic understanding of the functions defined by each OSI layer, as well as remember the names of the layers. It is also important that, for each device or protocol referenced throughout the book, you understand which layers of the OSI model most closely match the functions defined by that device or protocol.

Today, because most people happen to be much more familiar with TCP/IP functions than with OSI functions, one of the best ways to learn about the function of different OSI layers is to think about the functions in the TCP/IP model and to correlate those with the OSI model. If you use the five-layer TCP/IP model, the bottom four layers of OSI and TCP/IP map closely together. The only difference in these bottom four layers is the name of OSI Layer 3 (network) compared to the original TCP/IP model (internet). The upper three layers of the OSI reference model (application, presentation, and session—Layers 7, 6, and 5) define functions that all map to the TCP/IP application layer. Table 1-3 defines the functions of the seven layers.

Table 1-3   OSI Reference Model Layer Definitions

Layer	Functional Description
7	**Application layer.** This layer provides an interface between the communications software and any applications that need to communicate outside the computer on which the application resides. It also defines processes for user authentication.
6	**Presentation layer.** This layer's main purpose is to define and negotiate data formats, such as ASCII text, EBCDIC text, binary, BCD, and JPEG. Encryption is also defined by OSI as a presentation layer service.
5	**Session layer.** This layer defines how to start, control, and end conversations (called sessions). This includes the control and management of multiple bidirectional messages so that the application can be notified if only some of a series of messages are completed. This allows the presentation layer to have a seamless view of an incoming stream of data.

Layer	Functional Description
4	**Transport layer.** This layer's protocols provide a large number of services, as described in Chapter 5, "Fundamentals of TCP/IP Transport and Applications." Although OSI Layers 5 through 7 focus on issues related to the application, Layer 4 focuses on issues related to data delivery to another computer (for example, error recovery and flow control).
3	**Network layer.** This layer defines three main features: logical addressing, routing (forwarding), and path determination. Routing defines how devices (typically routers) forward packets to their final destination. Logical addressing defines how each device can have an address that can be used by the routing process. Path determination refers to the work done by routing protocols to learn all possible routes and choose the best route.
2	**Data link layer.** This layer defines the rules that determine when a device can send data over a particular medium. Data link protocols also define the format of a header and trailer that allows devices attached to the medium to successfully send and receive data.
1	**Physical layer.** This layer typically refers to standards from other organizations. These standards deal with the physical characteristics of the transmission medium, including connectors, pins, use of pins, electrical currents, encoding, light modulation, and the rules for how to activate and deactivate the use of the physical medium.

Table 1-4 lists a sampling of the devices and protocols covered in the CCNA exams and their comparable OSI layers. Note that many network devices must actually understand the protocols at multiple OSI layers, so the layer listed in Table 1-4 actually refers to the highest layer that the device normally thinks about when performing its core work. For example, routers need to think about Layer 3 concepts, but they must also support features at both Layers 1 and 2.

Table 1-4   OSI Reference Model—Example Devices and Protocols

Layer Name	Protocols and Specifications	Devices
Application, presentation, session (Layers 5–7)	Telnet, HTTP, FTP, SMTP, POP3, VoIP, SNMP	Hosts, firewalls
Transport (Layer 4)	TCP, UDP	Hosts, firewalls
Network (Layer 3)	IP	Router
Data link (Layer 2)	Ethernet (IEEE 802.3), HDLC	LAN switch, wireless access point, cable modem, DSL modem
Physical (Layer 1)	RJ-45, Ethernet (IEEE 802.3)	LAN hub, LAN repeater, cables

Besides remembering the basics of the features of each OSI layer (as in Table 1-3), and some example protocols and devices at each layer (as in Table 1-4), you should also memorize the names of the layers. You can simply memorize them, but some people like to use a mnemonic phrase to make memorization easier. In the following three phrases, the first letter of each word is the same as the first letter of an OSI layer name, in the order specified in parentheses:

- All People Seem To Need Data Processing (Layers 7 to 1)
- Please Do Not Take Sausage Pizzas Away (Layers 1 to 7)
- Pew! Dead Ninja Turtles Smell Particularly Awful (Layers 1 to 7)

OSI Layering Concepts and Benefits

While networking models use layers to help humans categorize and understand the many functions in a network, networking models use layers for many reasons. For example, consider another postal service analogy. A person writing a letter does not have to think about how the postal service will deliver a letter across the country. The postal worker in the middle of the country does not have to worry about the contents of the letter. Likewise, networking models that divide functions into different layers enable one software package or hardware device to implement functions from one layer, and assume that other software/hardware will perform the functions defined by the other layers.

The following list summarizes the benefits of layered protocol specifications:

- **Less complex:** Compared to not using a layered model, network models break the concepts into smaller parts.

- **Standard interfaces:** The standard interface definitions between each layer allow multiple vendors to create products that fill a particular role, with all the benefits of open competition.

- **Easier to learn:** Humans can more easily discuss and learn about the many details of a protocol specification.

- **Easier to develop:** Reduced complexity allows easier program changes and faster product development.

- **Multivendor interoperability:** Creating products to meet the same networking standards means that computers and networking gear from multiple vendors can work in the same network.

- **Modular engineering:** One vendor can write software that implements higher layers—for example, a web browser—and another vendor can write software that implements the lower layers—for example, Microsoft's built-in TCP/IP software in its OSs.

OSI Encapsulation Terminology

Like TCP/IP, each OSI layer asks for services from the next lower layer. To provide the services, each layer makes use of a header and possibly a trailer. The lower layer encapsulates the higher layer's data behind a header. The final topic of this chapter explains some of the terminology and concepts related to OSI encapsulation.

The TCP/IP model uses terms such as *segment*, *packet*, and *frame* to refer to various layers and their respective encapsulated data (refer to Figure 1-13). OSI uses a more generic term: *protocol data unit (PDU)*.

A PDU represents the bits that include the headers and trailers for that layer, as well as the encapsulated data. For example, an IP packet, as shown in Figure 1-14, using OSI terminology, is a PDU. In fact, an IP packet is a *Layer 3 PDU* (abbreviated L3PDU) because IP is a Layer 3 protocol. So, rather than use the terms *segment*, *packet*, or *frame*, OSI simply refers to the "Layer x PDU" (LxPDU), with "x" referring to the number of the layer being discussed.

Figure 1-16 represents the typical encapsulation process, with the top of the figure showing the application data and application layer header and the bottom of the figure showing the L2PDU that is transmitted onto the physical link.

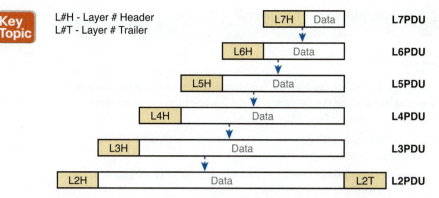

Figure 1-16   *OSI Encapsulation and Protocol Data Units*

Review Activities

Chapter Summary

- Network connectivity varies depending on how the network is used; for example, a home network most likely would use DSL or CATV connectivity, a work network most likely would use Ethernet or wireless connectivity.

- A *networking model*, sometimes also called either a *networking architecture* or *networking blueprint*, refers to a comprehensive set of documents.

- Today, the world of computer networking uses one networking model: Transmission Control Protocol/Internet Protocol (TCP/IP).

- The TCP/IP model both defines and references a large collection of protocols that enable computers to communicate.

- The original TCP/IP model had four layers: application, transport, Internet, and link. The current updated TCP/IP model has five layers: application, transport, and network, and the link layer is now broken into two layers, the data link and physical layers.

- TCP/IP application layer protocols provide services to the application software running on a computer. The application layer does not define the application itself, but it defines services that applications need.

- The two most commonly used transport layer protocols are the Transmission Control Protocol (TCP) and the User Datagram Protocol (UDP).

- Transport layer protocols provide services to the application layer protocols that reside one layer higher in the TCP/IP model.

- TCP/IP needs a mechanism to guarantee delivery of data across a network. Because many application layer protocols probably want a way to guarantee delivery of data across a network, the creators of TCP included an error recovery feature. To recover from errors, TCP uses the concept of acknowledgments.

- IP provides several features, most importantly, addressing and routing.

- The TCP/IP network layer, using the IP protocol, provides a service of forwarding IP packets from one device to another. Any device with an IP address can connect to the TCP/IP network and send packets.

- The TCP/IP model's original link layer defines the protocols and hardware required to deliver data across a physical network. The term *link* refers to the physical connections, or links, between two devices, and the protocols used to control those links.

- The process by which a TCP/IP host sends data can be viewed as a five-step process. The first four steps relate to the encapsulation performed by the four TCP/IP layers, and the last step is the actual physical transmission of the data by the host.

- The OSI model consists of seven layers: application, presentation, session, transport, network, data link, and physical.

- Cisco requires CCENTs to demonstrate a basic understanding of the functions defined by each OSI layer and remember the names of the layers. It is also important that, for each device or protocol referenced throughout the book, you understand which layers of the OSI model most closely match the functions defined by that device or protocol.

- Today, because most people are much more familiar with TCP/IP functions than with OSI functions, one of the best ways to learn about the function of different OSI layers is to think about the functions in the TCP/IP model, and correlate those with the OSI model.

- If you use the five-layer TCP/IP model, the bottom four layers of OSI and TCP/IP map closely together. The only difference in these bottom four layers is the name of OSI Layer 3 (network) compared to the original TCP/IP model (Internet).

- The upper three layers of the OSI reference model (application, presentation, and session Layers 7, 6, and 5) define functions that all map to the TCP/IP application layer.

Review Questions

Answer these review questions. You can find the answers at the bottom of the last page of the chapter. For thorough explanations, see DVD Appendix C, "Answers to Review Questions."

1. Which of the following protocols are examples of TCP/IP transport layer protocols? (Choose two answers.)

   A. Ethernet

   B. HTTP

   C. IP

   D. UDP

   E. SMTP

   F. TCP

2. Which of the following protocols are examples of TCP/IP data link layer protocols? (Choose two answers.)

   A. Ethernet

   B. HTTP

   C. IP

   D. UDP

   E. SMTP

   F. TCP

   G. PPP

3. The process of HTTP asking TCP to send some data and making sure that it is received correctly is an example of what?

   A. Same-layer interaction

   B. Adjacent-layer interaction

   C. OSI model

   D. All of these answers are correct.

4. The process of TCP on one computer marking a TCP segment as segment 1, and the receiving computer then acknowledging the receipt of TCP segment 1 is an example of what?

   A. Data encapsulation

   B. Same-layer interaction

   C. Adjacent-layer interaction

   D. OSI model

   E. All of these answers are correct.

5. The process of a web server adding a TCP header to the contents of a web page, followed by adding an IP header and then adding a data link header and trailer is an example of what?

    A. Data encapsulation

    B. Same-layer interaction

    C. OSI model

    D. All of these answers are correct.

6. Which of the following terms is used specifically to identify the entity created when encapsulating data inside data link layer headers and trailers?

    A. Data

    B. Chunk

    C. Segment

    D. Frame

    E. Packet

7. Which OSI layer defines the functions of logical network-wide addressing and routing?

    A. Layer 1

    B. Layer 2

    C. Layer 3

    D. Layer 4

    E. Layer 5, 6, or 7

8. Which OSI layer defines the standards for cabling and connectors?

    A. Layer 1

    B. Layer 2

    C. Layer 3

    D. Layer 4

    E. Layer 5, 6, or 7

9. Which of the following terms are not valid terms for the names of the seven OSI layers? (Choose two answers.)

    A. Application

    B. Data link

    C. Transmission

    D. Presentation

    E. Internet

    F. Session

Review All the Key Topics

Review the most important topics from this chapter, noted with the Key Topic icon. Table 1-5 lists these key topics and where each is discussed.

Table 1-5   Key Topics for Chapter 1

Key Topic Elements	Description	Page Number
Table 1-2	Provides definitions of same-layer and adjacent-layer interaction	18
Figure 1-10	Shows the general concept of IP routing	21
Figure 1-11	Depicts the data link services provided to IP for the purpose of delivering IP packets from host to host	22
Figure 1-13	Five steps to encapsulate data on the sending host	24
Figure 1-14	Shows the meaning of the terms *segment*, *packet*, and *frame*	24
Figure 1-15	Compares the OSI and TCP/IP network models	25
List	Lists the benefits of using a layered networking model	28
Figure 1-16	Terminology related to encapsulation	29

Definitions of Key Terms

After your first reading of the chapter, try to define these key terms, but do not be concerned about getting them all correct at that time. Chapter 30 directs you in how to use these terms for late-stage preparation for the exam.

adjacent-layer interaction, deencapsulation, encapsulation, frame, networking model, packet, protocol data unit (PDU), same-layer interaction, segment

---

Answers to Review Questions:

1 D and F **2** A and G **3** B **4** B **5** A **6** D **7** C **8** A **9** C and E

Chapter 2

Fundamentals of Ethernet LANs

Most every enterprise computer network can be separated into two general types of technology: local-area networks (LAN) and wide-area networks (WAN). LANs typically connect nearby devices: devices in the same room, in the same building, or in a campus of buildings. In contrast, WANs connect devices that are typically relatively far apart. Together, LANs and WANs create a complete enterprise computer network, working together to do the job of a computer network: delivering data from one device to another.

While many types of LANs have existed over the years, today's networks use two general types of LANs: Ethernet LANs and wireless LANs. Ethernet LANs happen to use cables for the links between nodes, and because many types of cables use copper wires, Ethernet LANs are often called *wired LANs*. In comparison, wireless LANs do not use wires or cables, instead using radio waves for the links between nodes.

This chapter introduces Ethernet LANs, with more detailed coverage in Part II (Chapters 6 through 10).

This chapter covers the following exam topics:

Operation of IP Data Networks

Recognize the purpose and functions of various network devices such as Routers, Switches, Bridges and Hubs.

Select the components required to meet a given network specification.

Predict the data flow between two hosts across a network.

Identify the appropriate media, cables, ports, and connectors to connect Cisco network devices to other network devices and hosts in a LAN

LAN Switching Technologies

Determine the technology and media access control method for Ethernet networks

Foundation Topics

An Overview of LANs

The term *Ethernet* refers to a family of LAN standards that together define the physical and data link layers of the world's most popular wired LAN technology. The standards, defined by the Institute of Electrical and Electronics Engineers (IEEE), defines the cabling, the connectors on the ends of the cables, the protocol rules, and everything else required to create an Ethernet LAN.

Typical SOHO LANs

To begin, first think about a Small Office / Home Office (SOHO) LAN today, specifically a LAN that uses only Ethernet LAN technology. First, the LAN needs a device called an Ethernet *LAN switch*, which provides many physical ports into which cables can be connected. An Ethernet uses *Ethernet cables*, which is a general reference to any cable that conforms to any of several Ethernet standards. The LAN uses Ethernet cables to connect different Ethernet devices or nodes to one of the switch's Ethernet ports.

Figure 2-1 shows a drawing of a SOHO Ethernet LAN. The figure shows a single LAN switch, five cables, and five other Ethernet nodes: three PCs, a printer, and one network device called a router. (The router connects the LAN to the WAN, in this case to the Internet.)

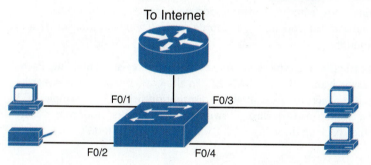

Figure 2-1 *Typical Small Ethernet-Only SOHO LAN*

Although Figure 2-1 shows a simple Ethernet LAN, many SOHO Ethernet LANs today combine the router and switch into a single device. Vendors sell consumer-grade integrated networking devices that work as a router and Ethernet switch, as well as doing other functions. These devices typically have "router" on the packaging, but many models also have four-port or eight-port Ethernet LAN switch ports built into the device.

Typical SOHO LANs today also support wireless LAN connections. Ethernet defines wired LAN technology only; in other words, Ethernet LANs use cables. However, you can build one LAN that uses both Ethernet LAN technology as well as wireless LAN technology, which is also defined by the IEEE. Wireless LANs, defined by the IEEE using standards that begin with 802.11, use radio waves to send the bits from one node to the next.

Most wireless LANs rely on yet another networking device: a wireless LAN *access point (AP)*. The AP acts somewhat like an Ethernet switch, in that all the wireless LAN nodes communicate with the Ethernet switch by sending and receiving data with the wireless AP. Of course, as a wireless device, the AP does not need Ethernet ports for cables, other than for a single Ethernet link to connect the AP to the Ethernet LAN, as shown in Figure 2-2.

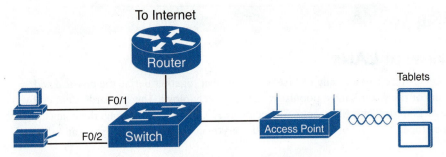

Figure 2-2   *Typical Small Wired and Wireless SOHO LAN*

Note that this drawing shows the router, Ethernet switch, and wireless LAN access point as three separate devices so that you can better understand the different roles. However, most SOHO networks today would use a single device, often labeled as a "wireless router" that does all these functions.

Typical Enterprise LANs

Enterprise networks have similar needs compared to a SOHO network, but on a much larger scale. For example, enterprise Ethernet LANs begin with LAN switches installed in a wiring closet behind a locked door on each floor of a building. The electricians install the Ethernet cabling from that wiring closet to cubicles and conference rooms where devices might need to connect to the LAN. At the same time, most enterprises also support wireless LANs in the same space, to allow people to roam around and still work and to support a growing number of devices that do not have an Ethernet LAN interface.

Figure 2-3 shows a conceptual view of a typical enterprise LAN in a three-story building. Each floor has an Ethernet LAN switch and a wireless LAN AP. To allow communication between floors, each per-floor switch connects to one centralized distribution switch. For example, PC3 can send data to PC2, but it would first flow through switch SW3 to the first floor to the distribution switch (SWD) and then back up through switch SW2 on the second floor.

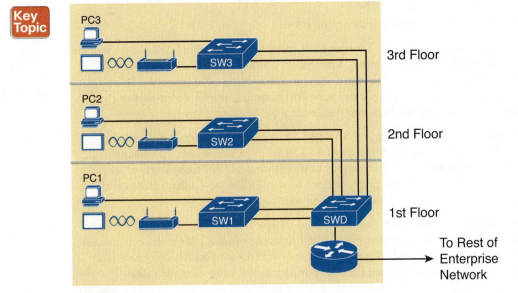

Figure 2-3   *Single-Building Enterprise Wired and Wireless LAN*

The figure also shows the typical way to connect a LAN to a WAN using a router. LAN switches and wireless access points work to create the LAN itself. Routers connect to both the LAN and the WAN. To connect to the LAN, the router simply uses an Ethernet LAN interface and an Ethernet cable, as shown on the lower right of Figure 2-3.

The rest of this chapter focuses on Ethernet in particular.

The Variety of Ethernet Physical Layer Standards

The term *Ethernet* refers to an entire family of standards. Some standards define the specifics of how to send data over a particular type of cabling, and at a particular speed. Other standards define protocols, or rules, that the Ethernet nodes must follow to be a part of an Ethernet LAN. All these Ethernet standards come from the IEEE and include the number 802.3 as the beginning part of the standard name.

Ethernet supports a large variety of options for physical Ethernet links given its long history over the last 40 or so years. Today, Ethernet includes many standards for different kinds of optical and copper cabling, and for speeds from 10 megabits per second (Mbps) up to 100 gigabits per second (100 Gbps). The standards also differ as far as the types of cabling and the allowed length of the cabling.

The most fundamental cabling choice has to do with the materials used inside the cable for the physical transmission of bits: either copper wires or glass fibers. The use of *unshielded twisted-pair (UTP)* cabling saves money compared to optical fibers, with Ethernet nodes using the wires inside the cable to send data over electrical circuits. Fiber-optic cabling, the more expensive alternative, allows Ethernet nodes to send light over glass fibers in the center of the cable. Although more expensive, optical cables typically allow longer cabling distances between nodes.

To be ready to choose the products to purchase for a new Ethernet LAN, a network engineer must know the names and features of the different Ethernet standards supported in Ethernet products. The IEEE defines Ethernet physical layer standards using a couple of naming conventions. The formal name begins with "802.3" followed by some suffix letters. The IEEE also uses more meaningful shortcut names that identify the speed, as well as a clue about whether the cabling is UTP (with a suffix that includes "T") or fiber (with a suffix that includes "X").

Table 2-1 lists a few Ethernet physical layer standards. First, the table lists enough names so that you get a sense of the IEEE naming conventions. It also lists the four most common standards that use UTP cabling, because this book's discussion of Ethernet focuses mainly on the UTP options.

Key Topic

Table 2-1   Examples of Types of Ethernet

Speed	Common Name	Informal IEEE Standard Name	Formal IEEE Standard Name	Cable Type, Maximum Length
10 Mbps	Ethernet	10BASE-T	802.3	Copper, 100 m
100 Mbps	Fast Ethernet	100BASE-T	802.3u	Copper, 100 m
1000 Mbps	Gigabit Ethernet	1000BASE-LX	802.3z	Fiber, 5000 m
1000 Mbps	Gigabit Ethernet	1000BASE-T	802.3ab	Copper, 100 m
10 Gbps	10 Gig Ethernet	10GBASE-T	802.3an	Copper, 100 m

NOTE   Fiber-optic cabling contains long thin strands of fiberglass. The attached Ethernet nodes send light over the glass fiber in the cable, encoding the bits as changes in the light.

Consistent Behavior over All Links Using the Ethernet Data Link Layer

Although Ethernet includes many physical layer standards, Ethernet acts like a single LAN technology because it uses the same data link layer standard over all types of Ethernet physical links. That standard defines a common Ethernet header and trailer. (As a reminder, the header and trailer are bytes of overhead data that Ethernet uses to do its job of sending data over a LAN.) No matter whether the data flows over a UTP cable, or any kind of fiber cable, and no matter the speed, the data link header and trailer use the same format.

While the physical layer standards focus on sending bits over a cable, the Ethernet data link protocols focus on sending an *Ethernet frame* from source to destination Ethernet node. From a data link perspective, nodes build and forward frames. As first defined in Chapter 1, "The TCP/IP and OSI Networking Models," the term *frame* specifically refers to the header and trailer of a data link protocol, plus the data encapsulated inside that header and trailer. The various Ethernet nodes simply forward the frame, over all the required links, to deliver the frame to the correct destination.

Figure 2-4 shows an example of the process. In this case, PC1 sends an Ethernet frame to PC3. The frame travels over a UTP link to Ethernet switch SW1, then over fiber links to Ethernet switches SW2 and SW3, and finally over another UTP link to PC3. Note that the bits actually travel at four different speeds in this example: 10 Mbps, 1 Gbps, 10 Gbps, and 100 Mbps, respectively.

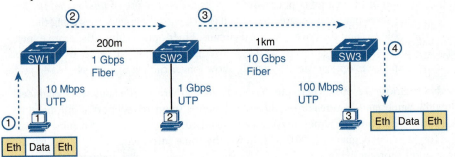

Figure 2-4   *Ethernet LAN Forwards a Data Link Frame over Many Types of Links*

So, what is an Ethernet LAN? It is a combination of user devices, LAN switches, and different kinds of cabling. Each link can use different types of cables, at different speeds. However, they all work together to deliver Ethernet frames from the one device on the LAN to some other device.

The rest of this chapter takes these concepts a little deeper, first looking at the details of building the physical Ethernet network, followed by some discussion of the rules for forwarding frames through an Ethernet LAN. *Ethernet frame* from source to destination Ethernet node.

Building Physical Ethernet Networks with UTP

For this second of three major sections of this chapter, focus on the individual physical links between any two Ethernet nodes. Before the Ethernet network as a whole can send Ethernet frames between user devices, each node must be ready and able to send data over an individual physical link. This section looks at some of the particulars of how Ethernet sends data over these links.

This section focuses on the three most commonly used Ethernet standards: 10BASE-T (Ethernet), 100BASE-T (Fast Ethernet, or FE), and 1000BASE-T (Gigabit Ethernet, or GE). Specifically, this section looks at the details of sending data in both directions over a UTP cable. It then examines the specific wiring of the UTP cables used for 10-Mbps, 100-Mbps, and 1000-Mbps Ethernet.

Transmitting Data Using Twisted Pairs

While it is true that Ethernet sends data over UTP cables, the physical means to send the data uses electricity that flows over the wires inside the UTP cable. To better understand how Ethernet sends data using electricity, break the idea down into two parts: how to create an electrical circuit and then how to make that electrical signal communicate 1s and 0s.

First, to create one electrical circuit, Ethernet defines how to use the two wires inside a single twisted pair of wires, as shown Figure 2-5. The figure does not show a UTP cable between two nodes, but instead shows two individual wires that are inside the UTP cable. An electrical circuit requires a complete loop, so the two nodes, using circuitry on their Ethernet ports, connect the wires in one pair to complete a loop, allowing electricity to flow.

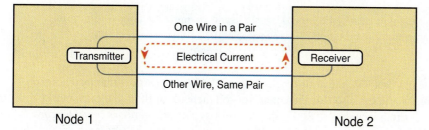
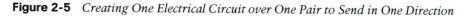

Figure 2-5 *Creating One Electrical Circuit over One Pair to Send in One Direction*

To send data, the two devices follow some rules called an *encoding scheme*. The idea works a lot like when two people talk, using the same language: The speaker says some words in a particular language, and the listener, because she speaks the same language, can understand the spoken words. With an encoding scheme, the transmitting node changes the electrical signal over time, while the other node, the receiver, using the same rules, interprets those changes as either 0s or 1s. (For example, 10BASE-T uses an encoding scheme that encodes a binary 0 as a transition from higher voltage to lower voltage during the middle of a 1/10,000,000th-of-a-second interval.)

Note that in an actual UTP cable, the wires will be twisted together and not parallel, as shown in Figure 2-5. The twisting helps solve some important physical transmission issues. When electrical current passes over any wire, it creates *electromagnetic interference (EMI)* that interferes with the electrical signals in nearby wires, including the wires in the same cable. (EMI between wire pairs in the same cable is called *crosstalk*.) Twisting the wire pairs together helps cancel out most of the EMI, so most networking physical links that use copper wires used twisted pairs.

Breaking Down a UTP Ethernet Link

The term *Ethernet link* refers to any physical cable between two Ethernet nodes. To learn about how a UTP Ethernet link works, it helps to break down the physical link into those basic pieces, as shown in Figure 2-6: the cable itself, the connectors on the ends of the cable, and the matching ports on the devices into which the connectors will be inserted.

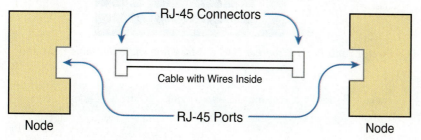

Figure 2-6 *Basic Components of an Ethernet Link*

First, think about the UTP cable itself. The cable holds some copper wires, grouped as twisted pairs. The 10BASE-T and 100BASE-T standards require two pairs of wires, while the 1000BASE-T standard requires four pairs. Each wire has a color-coded plastic coating, with the wires in a pair having a color scheme. For example, for the blue wire pair, one wire's coating is all blue, while the other wire's coating is blue-and-white striped.

Many Ethernet UTP cables use an RJ-45 connector on both ends. The RJ-45 connector has eight physical locations into which the eight wires in the cable can be inserted, called *pin positions*, or simply *pins*. These pins create a place where the ends of the copper wires can touch the electronics inside the nodes at the end of the physical link so that electricity can flow.

NOTE If available, find a nearby Ethernet UTP cable and examine the connectors closely. Look for the pin positions and the colors of the wires in the connector.

To complete the physical link, the nodes each need an RJ-45 *Ethernet port* that matches the RJ-45 connectors on the cable so that the connectors on the ends of the cable can connect to each node. PCs often include this RJ-45 Ethernet port as part of a *network interface card (NIC)*, which can be an expansion card on the PC or can be built into the system itself. Switches typically have many RJ-45 ports because switches give user devices a place to connect to the Ethernet LAN.

Figure 2-7 shows photos of the cables, connectors, and ports.

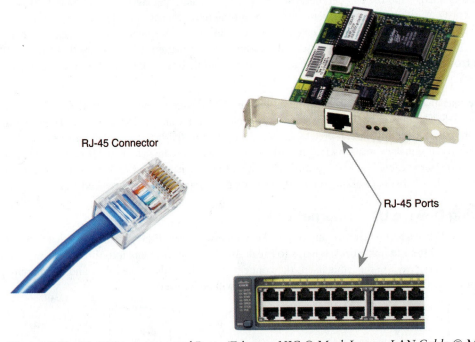

Figure 2-7   *RJ-45 Connectors and Ports (Ethernet NIC © Mark Jansen, LAN Cable © Mikko Pitkänen)*

NOTE The RJ-45 connector is slightly wider, but otherwise similar, to the RJ-11 connectors commonly used for telephone cables in homes in North America.

The figure shows a connector on the left and ports on the right. The left shows the eight pin positions in the end of the RJ-45 connector. The upper right shows an Ethernet NIC that is not yet installed in a computer. The lower-right part of the figure shows the side of a Cisco 2960 switch, with multiple RJ-45 ports, allowing multiple devices to easily connect to the Ethernet network.

Finally, while RJ-45 connectors with UTP cabling can be common, Cisco LAN switches often support other types of connectors as well. When you buy one of the many models of Cisco switches, you need to think about the mix and numbers of each type of physical ports you want on the switch.

To give its customers flexibility as to the type of Ethernet links, even after the customer has bought the switch, Cisco switches include some physical ports whose port hardware can be changed later, after you purchase the switch. One type of port is called a *gigabit interface converter (GBIC)*, which happened to first arrive on the market around the same time as Gigabit Ethernet, so it was given the same "gigabit" name. More recently, improved smaller types of removable interfaces, called *small form-factor pluggables (SFP),* provide the same function of giving users the ability to swap hardware and change the type of physical link. Figure 2-8 shows a photo of a Cisco switch, with an SFP sitting slightly outside the SFP slot.

Figure 2-8   *Gigabit Fiber SFP Sitting Just Outside a Switch SFP Port*

UTP Cabling Pinouts for 10BASE-T and 100BASE-T

So far in this section, you have learned about the equivalent of how to drive a truck on a 1000-acre ranch, but you do not know the equivalent of the local traffic rules. If you worked the ranch, you could drive the truck all over the ranch, any place you wanted to go, and the police would not mind. However, as soon as you get on the public roads, the police want you to behave and follow the rules. Similarly, so far this chapter has discussed the general principles of how to send data, but it has not yet detailed some important rules for Ethernet cabling: the rules of the road so that all the devices send data using the right wires inside the cable.

This next topic discusses conventions for 10BASE-T and 100BASE-T together, because they use UTP cabling in similar ways (including the use of only two wire pairs). A short comparison of the wiring for 1000BASE-T (Gigabit Ethernet), which uses four pairs, follows.

Straight-Through Cable Pinout

10BASE-T and 100BASE-T use two pair of wires in a UTP cable, one for each direction, as shown in Figure 2-9. The figure shows four wires, all of which sit inside a single UTP cable that connects a PC and a LAN switch. In this example, the PC on the left transmits using the top pair, and the switch on the right transmits using the bottom pair.

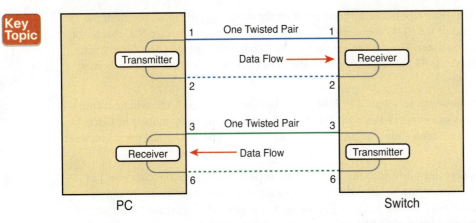

Figure 2-9 *Using One Pair for Each Transmission Direction with 10- and 100-Mbps Ethernet*

For correct transmission over the link, the wires in the UTP cable must be connected to the correct pin positions in the RJ-45 connectors. For example, in Figure 2-9, the transmitter on the PC on the left must know the pin positions of the two wires it should use to transmit. Those two wires must be connected to the correct pins in the RJ-45 connector on the switch, so that the switch's receiver logic can use the correct wires.

To understand the wiring of the cable—which wires need to be in which pin positions on both ends of the cable—you need to first understand how the NICs and switches work. As a rule, Ethernet NIC transmitters use the pair connected to pins 1 and 2; the NIC receivers use a pair of wires at pin positions 3 and 6. LAN switches, knowing those facts about what Ethernet NICs do, do the opposite: Their receivers use the wire pair at pins 1 and 2, and their transmitters use the wire pair at pins 3 and 6.

To allow a PC NIC to communicate with a switch, the UTP cable must also use a *straight-through cable pinout*. The term *pinout* refers to the wiring of which color wire is placed in each of the eight numbered pin positions in the RJ-45 connector. An Ethernet straight-through cable connects the wire at pin 1 on one end of the cable to pin 1 at the other end of the cable; the wire at pin 2 needs to connect to pin 2 on the other end of the cable; pin 3 on one end connects to pin 3 on the other, and so on. Also, it uses the wires in one wire pair at pins 1 and 2, and another pair at pins 3 and 6.

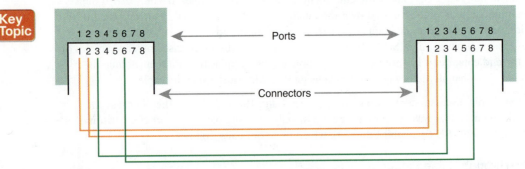

Figure 2-10 *10BASE-T and 100BASE-T Straight-Through Cable Pinout*

Figure 2-11 shows one final perspective on the straight-through cable pinout. In this case, PC Larry connects to a LAN switch. Note that the figure again does not show the UTP cable, but instead shows the wires that sit inside the cable, to emphasize the idea of wire pairs and pins.

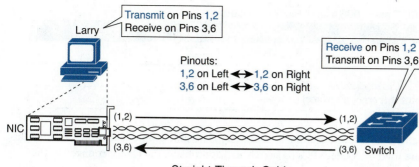

Figure 2-11 *Ethernet Straight-Through Cable Concept*

Crossover Cable Pinout

A straight-through cable works correctly when the nodes use opposite pairs for transmitting data. However, when two like devices connect to an Ethernet link, they both transmit on over the same pins. In that case, you then need another type of cabling pinout called a *crossover cable*. The crossover cable pinout crosses the pair at the transmit pins on each device to the receive pins on the opposite device.

While that previous sentence is true, this concept is much clearer with a figure such as Figure 2-12. The figure shows what happens on a link between two switches. The two switches both transmit on the pair at pins 3 and 6, and they both receive on the pair at pins 1 and 2. So, the cable must connect a pair at pins 3 and 6 on each side to pins 1 and 2 on the other side, connecting to the other node's receiver logic. The top of the figure shows the literal pinouts, and the bottom half shows a conceptual diagram.

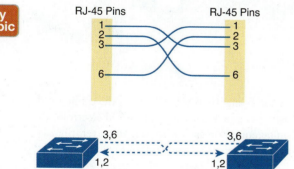

Figure 2-12 *Crossover Ethernet Cable*

Choosing the Right Cable Pinouts

For the exam, you should be well prepared to choose which type of cable (straight-through or crossover) is needed in each part of the network. The key is to know whether a device acts like a PC NIC, transmitting at pins 1 and 2, or like a switch, transmitting at pins 3 and 6. Then, just apply the following logic:

Crossover cable: If the endpoints transmit on the same pin pair

Straight-through cable: If the endpoints transmit on different pin pairs

Table 2-2 lists the devices mentioned in this book and the pin pairs they use, assuming that they use 10BASE-T and 100BASE-T.

Table 2-2   10BASE-T and 100BASE-T Pin Pairs Used

Transmits on Pins 1,2	Transmits on Pins 3,6
PC NICs	Hubs
Routers	Switches
Wireless access point (Ethernet interface)	—

For example, Figure 2-13 shows a campus LAN in a single building. In this case, several straight-through cables are used to connect PCs to switches. Additionally, the cables connecting the switches require crossover cables.

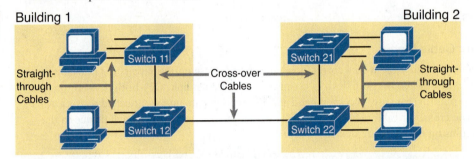

Figure 2-13   *Typical Uses for Straight-Through and Crossover Ethernet Cables*

> **NOTE**   If you have some experience with installing LANs, you might be thinking that you have used the wrong cable before (straight-through or crossover), but the cable worked. Cisco switches have a feature called *auto-mdix* that notices when the wrong cable is used and automatically changes its logic to make the link work. However, for the exams, be ready to identify whether the correct cable is shown in the figures.

UTP Cabling Pinouts for 1000BASE-T

1000BASE-T (Gigabit Ethernet) differs from 10BASE-T and 100BASE-T as far as the cabling and pinouts. First, 1000BASE-T requires four wire pairs. Second, it uses more advanced electronics that allow both ends to transmit and receive simultaneously on each wire pair. However, the wiring pinouts for 1000BASE-T work almost identically to the earlier standards, adding details for the additional two pairs.

The straight-through cable connects each pin with the same numbered pin on the other side, but it does so for all eight pins—pin 1 to pin 1, pin 2 to pin 2, up through pin 8. It keeps one pair at pins 1 and 2 and another at pins 3 and 6, just like in the earlier wiring. It adds a pair at pins 4 and 5 and the final pair at pins 7 and 8 (refer to Figure 2-12).

The Gigabit Ethernet crossover cable crosses the same two-wire pairs as the crossover cable for the other types of Ethernet (the pairs at pins 1,2 and 3,6). It also crosses the two new pairs as well (the pair at pins 4,5 with the pair at pins 7,8).

Sending Data in Ethernet Networks

Although physical layer standards vary quite a bit, other parts of the Ethernet standards work the same way, regardless of the type of physical Ethernet link. Next, this final major section of this chapter looks at several protocols and rules that Ethernet uses regardless of the type of link. In particular, this section examines the details of the Ethernet data link layer protocol, plus how Ethernet nodes, switches, and hubs forward Ethernet frames through an Ethernet LAN.

Ethernet Data Link Protocols

One of the most significant strengths of the Ethernet family of protocols is that these protocols use the same data link standard. In fact, the core parts of the data link standard date back to the original Ethernet standards.

The Ethernet data link protocol defines the Ethernet frame: an Ethernet header at the front, the encapsulated data in the middle, and an Ethernet trailer at the end. Ethernet actually defines a few alternate formats for the header, with the frame format shown in Figure 2-14 being commonly used today.

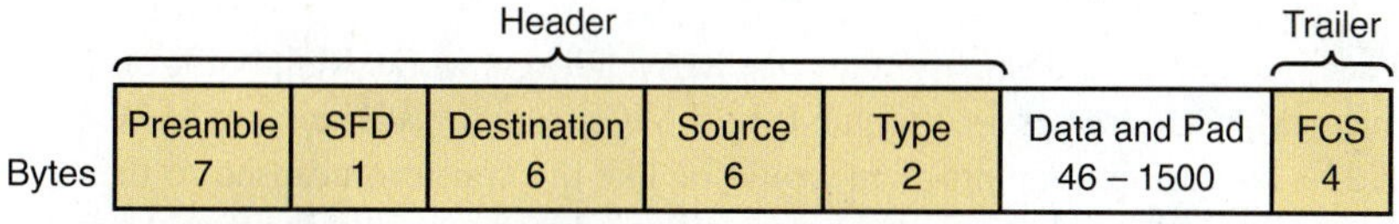

Figure 2-14 *Commonly Used Ethernet Frame Format*

While all the fields in the frame matter, some matter more to the topics discussed in this book. Table 2-3 lists the fields in the header and trailer, and a brief description for reference, with the upcoming pages including more detail about a few of these fields.

Table 2-3 IEEE 802.3 Ethernet Header and Trailer Fields

Field	Field Length in Bytes	Description
Preamble	7	Synchronization
Start Frame Delimiter (SFD)	1	Signifies that the next byte begins the Destination MAC Address field
Destination MAC Address	6	Identifies the intended recipient of this frame
Source MAC Address	6	Identifies the sender of this frame
Type	2	Defines the type of protocol listed inside the frame; today, most likely identifies IP version 4 (IPv4) or IP version 6 (IPv6)
Data and Pad*	46–1500	Holds data from a higher layer, typically an L3PDU (usually an IPv4 or IPv6 packet). The sender adds padding to meet the minimum length requirement for this field (46 bytes).
Frame Check Sequence (FCS)	4	Provides a method for the receiving NIC to determine whether the frame experienced transmission errors

* The IEEE 802.3 specification limits the data portion of the 802.3 frame to a minimum of 46 and a maximum of 1500 bytes. The term *maximum transmission unit (MTU)* defines the maximum Layer 3 packet that can be sent over a medium. Because the Layer 3 packet rests inside the data portion of an Ethernet frame, 1500 bytes is the largest IP MTU allowed over an Ethernet.

Ethernet Addressing

The source and destination Ethernet address fields play a big role in much of the Ethernet logic included in the CCENT and CCNA certifications. The general idea for each is relatively simple: The sending node puts its own address in the source address field and the intended Ethernet destination device's address in the destination address field. The sender transmits the frame, expecting that the Ethernet LAN, as a whole, will deliver the frame to that correct destination.

Ethernet addresses, also called *Media Access Control (MAC)* addresses, are 6-byte-long (48-bit-long) binary numbers. For convenience, most computers list MAC addresses as 12-digit hexadecimal numbers. Cisco devices typically add some periods to the number for easier readability as well; for example, a Cisco switch might list a MAC address as 0000.0C12.3456.

Most MAC addresses represent a single NIC or other Ethernet port, so these addresses are often called a *unicast* Ethernet address. The term *unicast* is simply a formal way to refer to the fact that the address represents one interface to the Ethernet LAN. (This term also contrasts with two other types of Ethernet addresses, *broadcast* and *multicast*, which will be defined later in this section.)

The entire idea of sending data to a destination unicast MAC address works well, but it only works if all the unicast MAC addresses are unique. If two NICs tried to use the same MAC address, there could be confusion. (The problem would be like the confusion caused to the postal service, if you and I both tried to use the same mailing address—would the postal service deliver mail to your house or mine?). If two PCs on the same Ethernet tried to use the same MAC address, to which PC should frames sent to that MAC address be delivered?

Ethernet solves this problem using an administrative process so that, at the time of manufacture, all Ethernet devices are assigned a universally unique MAC address. Before a manufacturer can build Ethernet products, it must ask the IEEE to assign the manufacturer a universally unique 3-byte code, called the *organizationally unique identifier (OUI)*. The manufacturer agrees to give all NICs (and other Ethernet products) a MAC address that begins with its assigned 3-byte OUI. The manufacturer also assigns a unique value for the last 3 bytes, a number that manufacturer has never used with that OUI. As a result, the MAC address of every device in the universe is unique.

NOTE   The IEEE also calls these universal MAC addresses global MAC addresses.

Figure 2-15 shows the structure of the unicast MAC address, with the OUI.

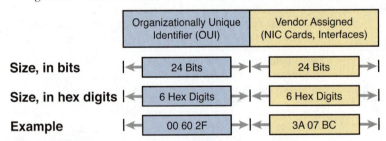

Figure 2-15   *Structure of Unicast Ethernet Addresses*

Ethernet addresses go by many names: LAN address, Ethernet address, hardware address, burned-in address, physical address, universal address, or MAC address. For example, the term *burned-in address (BIA)* refers to the idea that a permanent MAC address has been encoded (burned into) the ROM chip on the NIC. As another example, the IEEE uses the term *universal address* to emphasize the fact that the address assigned to a NIC by a manufacturer should be unique among all MAC addresses in the universe.

In addition to unicast addresses, Ethernet also uses group addresses. *Group addresses* identify more than one LAN interface card. A frame sent to a group address might be delivered to a small set of devices on the LAN, or even to all devices on the LAN. In fact, the IEEE defines two general categories of group addresses for Ethernet:

Broadcast address: Frames sent to this address should be delivered to all devices on the Ethernet LAN. It has a value of FFFF.FFFF.FFFF.

Multicast addresses: Frames sent to a multicast Ethernet address will be copied and forwarded to a subset of the devices on the LAN that volunteers to receive frames sent to a specific multicast address.

Table 2-4 summarizes most of the details about MAC addresses.

Table 2-4   LAN MAC Address Terminology and Features

LAN Addressing Term or Feature	Description
MAC	Media Access Control. 802.3 (Ethernet) defines the MAC sublayer of IEEE Ethernet.
Ethernet address, NIC address, LAN address	Other names often used instead of MAC address. These terms describe the 6-byte address of the LAN interface card.
Burned-in address	The 6-byte address assigned by the vendor making the card.
Unicast address	A term for a MAC address that represents a single LAN interface.
Broadcast address	An address that means "all devices that reside on this LAN right now."
Multicast address	On Ethernet, a multicast address implies some subset of all devices currently on the Ethernet LAN.

Identifying Network Layer Protocols with the Ethernet Type Field

While the Ethernet header's address fields play an important and more obvious role in Ethernet LANs, the Ethernet Type field plays a much less obvious role. The Ethernet Type field, or EtherType, sits in the Ethernet data link layer header, but its purpose is to directly help the network processing on routers and hosts. Basically, the Type field identifies the type of network layer (Layer 3) packet that sits inside the Ethernet frame.

First, think about what sits inside the data part of the Ethernet frame shown earlier in Figure 2-14. Typically, it holds the network layer packet created by the network layer protocol on some device in the network. Over the years, those protocols have included IBM Systems Network Architecture (SNA), Novell NetWare, Digital Equipment Corporation's DECnet, and Apple Computer's AppleTalk. Today, the most common network layer protocols are both from TCP/IP: IP version 4 (IPv4) and IP version 6 (IPv6).

The original host has a place to insert a value (a hexadecimal number) to identify the type of packet encapsulated inside the Ethernet frame. However, what number should the sender put in the header to identify an IPv4 packet as the type? Or an IPv6 packet? As it turns out, the IEEE manages a list of EtherType values, so that every network layer protocol that needs a unique EtherType value can have a number. The sender just has to know the list. (Anyone can view the list; just go to www.ieee.org and search for *EtherType*.)

For example, a host can send one Ethernet frame with an IPv4 packet and the next Ethernet frame with an IPv6 packet. Each frame would have a different Ethernet Type field value, using the values reserved by the IEEE, as shown in Figure 2-16.

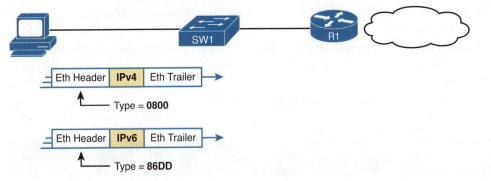

Figure 2-16   *Use of Ethernet Type Field*

Error Detection with FCS

Ethernet also defines a way for nodes to find out whether a frame's bits changed while crossing over an Ethernet link. (Usually, the bits could change because of some kind of electrical interference, or a bad NIC.) Ethernet, like most every other data link protocol covered on the CCNA exams, uses a field in the data link trailer for the purpose of error detection.

The Ethernet *Frame Check Sequence (FCS)* field in the Ethernet trailer—the only field in the Ethernet trailer—gives the receiving node a way to compare results with the sender, to discover whether errors occurred in the frame. The sender applies a complex math formula to the frame before sending it, storing the result of the formula in the FCS field. The receiver applies the same math formula to the received frame. The receiver then compares its own results with the sender's results. If the results are the same, the frame did not change; otherwise, an error occurred, and the receiver discards the frame.

Note that *error detection* does not also mean *error recovery*. Ethernet defines that the errored frame should be discarded, but Ethernet does not attempt to recover the lost frame. Other protocols, notably TCP, recover the lost data by noticing that it is lost and sending the data again.

Sending Ethernet Frames with Switches and Hubs

Ethernet LANs behave slightly differently depending on whether the LAN has mostly modern devices, in particular, LAN switches instead of some older LAN devices called LAN hubs. Basically, the use of more modern switches allows the use of full-duplex logic, which is much faster and simpler than half-duplex logic, which is required when using hubs. The final topic in this chapter looks at these basic differences.

Sending in Modern Ethernet LANs Using Full-Duplex

Modern Ethernet LANs use a variety of Ethernet physical standards, but with standard Ethernet frames that can flow over any of these types of physical links. Each individual link can run at a different speed, but each link allows the attached nodes to send the bits in the frame to the next node. They must work together to deliver the data from the sending Ethernet node to the destination node.

The process is relatively simple, on purpose; the simplicity lets each device send a large number of frames per second. Figure 2-17 shows an example, in which PC1 sends an Ethernet frame to PC2.

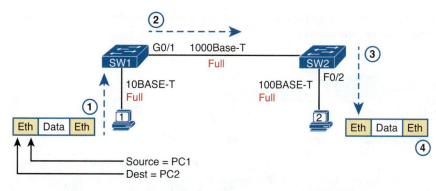

Figure 2-17 *Example of Sending Data in a Modern Ethernet LAN*

Following the steps in the figure:

1. PC1 builds and sends the original Ethernet frame, using its own MAC address as the source address and PC2's MAC address as the destination address.

2. Switch SW1 receives and forwards the Ethernet frame out its G0/1 interface (short for Gigabit interface 0/1) to SW2.

3. Switch SW2 receives and forwards the Ethernet frame out its F0/2 interface (short for Fast Ethernet interface 0/2) to PC2.

4. PC2 receives the frame, recognizes the destination MAC address as its own, and processes the frame.

The Ethernet network in Figure 2-17 uses full-duplex on each link, but the concept might be difficult to see. Full-duplex means that the NIC or switch port has no half-duplex restrictions. So, to understand full-duplex, you need to understand half-duplex, as follows:

> **Half-duplex:** Logic in which a port sends data only when it is not also receiving data; in other words, it cannot send and receive at the same time.
>
> **Full-duplex:** The absence of the half-duplex restriction.

So, with all PCs and LAN switches, and no LAN hubs, all the nodes can use full-duplex. All nodes can send and receive on their port at the same instant in time. For example, in Figure 2-17, PC1 and PC2 could send frames to each other simultaneously, in both directions, without any half-duplex restrictions.

Using Half-Duplex with LAN Hubs

To understand the need for half-duplex logic in some cases, you have to understand a little about an older type of networking device called a LAN hub. When the IEEE first introduced 10BASE-T in 1990, the Ethernet did not yet include LAN switches. Instead of switches, vendors created LAN hubs. The LAN hub provided a number of RJ-45 ports as a place to connect links to PCs, just like a LAN switch, but it used different rules for forwarding data.

LAN hubs forward data using physical layer standards, and are therefore considered to be Layer 1 devices. When an electrical signal comes in one hub port, the hub repeats that electrical signal out all other ports (except the incoming port). By doing so, the data reaches all the rest of the nodes connected to the hub, so the data hopefully reaches the correct destination. The hub has no concept of Ethernet frames, of addresses, and so on.

The downside of using LAN hubs is that if two or more devices transmitted a signal at the same instant, the electrical signal collides and becomes garbled. The hub repeats all received electrical signals, even if it receives multiple signals at the same time. For example, Figure 2-18 shows the idea, with PCs Archie and Bob sending an electrical signal at the same instant of time (at Steps 1A and 1B) and the hub repeating both electrical signals out toward Larry on the left (Step 2).

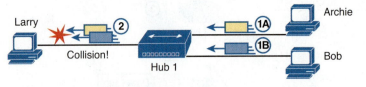

Figure 2-18   *Collision Occurring Because of LAN Hub Behavior*

NOTE   For completeness, note that the hub floods each frame out all other ports (except the incoming port). So, Archie's frame goes to both Larry and Bob; Bob's frame goes to Larry and Archie.

If you replace the hub in Figure 2-18 with a LAN switch, the switch prevents the collision on the left. The switch operates as a Layer 2 device, meaning that it looks at the data link header and trailer. A switch would look at the MAC addresses, and even if the switch needed to forward both frames to Larry on the left, the switch would send one frame and queue the other frame until the first frame was finished.

Now back to the issue created by the hub's logic: collisions. To prevent these collisions, the Ethernet nodes must use half-duplex logic instead of full-duplex logic. A problem only occurs when two or more devices send at the same time; half-duplex logic tells the nodes that if someone else is sending, wait before sending.

For example, back in Figure 2-18, imagine that Archie began sending his frame early enough so that Bob received the first bits of that frame before Bob tried to send his own frame. Bob, at Step 1B, would notice that he was receiving a frame from someone else, and using half-duplex logic, would simply wait to send the frame listed at Step 1B.

Nodes that use half-duplex logic actually use a relatively well-known algorithm called CSMA/CD (carrier sense multiple access with collision detection). The algorithm takes care of the obvious cases but also the cases caused by unfortunate timing. For example, two nodes could check for an incoming frame at the exact same instant, both realize that no other node is sending, and both send their frames at the exact same instant, causing a collision. CSMA/CD covers these cases as well, as follows:

Step 1.   A device with a frame to send listens until the Ethernet is not busy.

Step 2.   When the Ethernet is not busy, the sender begins sending the frame.

Step 3.   The sender listens while sending to discover whether a collision occurs; collisions might be caused by many reasons, including unfortunate timing. If a collision occurs, all currently sending nodes do the following:

   A. They send a jamming signal that tells all nodes that a collision happened.

   B. They independently choose a random time to wait before trying again, to avoid unfortunate timing

   C. The next attempt starts again at Step 1.

Although most modern LANs do not often use hubs, and therefore do not need to use half-duplex, enough old hubs still exist in enterprise networks so that you need to be ready to understand duplex issues. Each NIC and switch port has a duplex setting. For all links between PCs and switches, or between switches, use full-duplex. However, for any link connected to a LAN hub, the connected LAN switch and NIC port should use half-duplex. Note that the hub itself does not use half-duplex logic, instead just repeating incoming signals out every other port.

Figure 2-19 shows an example, with full-duplex links on the left and a single LAN hub on the right. The hub then requires SW2's F0/2 interface to use half-duplex logic, along with the PCs connected to the hub.

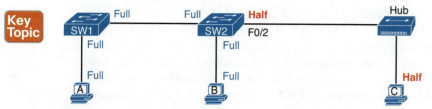

Figure 2-19 *Full- and Half-Duplex in an Ethernet LAN*

Review Activities

Chapter Summary

- LANs usually connect nearby devices: devices in the same room or the same building, or in a campus of buildings.

- Although many types of LANs have existed over the years, today's networks use two general types of LANs: Ethernet LANs and wireless LANs.

- Ethernet LANs use cables for the links between nodes, and because many types of cables use copper wires, Ethernet LANs are often called *wired LANs*. In comparison, wireless LANs do not use wires or cables; instead, they use radio waves for the links between nodes.

- The term *Ethernet* refers to a family of LAN standards that together define the physical and data link layers of the world's most popular wired LAN technology. The standards, defined by the Institute of Electrical and Electronics Engineers (IEEE), defines the cabling, the connectors on the ends of the cables, the protocol rules, and everything else required to create an Ethernet LAN.

- *Ethernet* defines wired LAN technology only; in other words, Ethernet LANs use cables.

- All Ethernet standards come from the IEEE and include the number 802.3 as the beginning part of the standard name.

- The most fundamental cabling choice has to do with the materials used inside the cable for the physical transmission of bits: either copper wires or glass fibers.

  - The use of unshielded twisted-pair (UTP) cabling saves money compared to optical fibers, with Ethernet nodes using the wires inside the cable to send data over electrical circuits.

  - Fiber optic cabling, the more expensive alternative, enables Ethernet nodes to send light over glass fibers in the center of the cable.

- Ethernet acts like a single LAN technology because it uses the same data link layer standard over all types of Ethernet physical links.

- The term *Ethernet link* refers to any physical cable between two Ethernet nodes.

- The UTP cable holds some copper wires, grouped as twisted pairs. The 10BASE-T and 100BASE-T standards require two pairs of wires, while the 1000BASE-T standard requires four pairs.

- Many Ethernet UTP cables use an RJ-45 connector on both ends. The RJ-45 connector has eight physical locations into which the eight wires in the cable can be inserted, called *pin positions* or simply *pins*. These pins create a place where the ends of the copper wires can touch the electronics inside the nodes at the end of the physical link, so that electricity can flow.

- The Ethernet data link protocol defines the Ethernet frame: an Ethernet header at the front, the encapsulated data in the middle, and an Ethernet trailer at the end.

- Ethernet addresses, also called Media Access Control (MAC) addresses, are 6-byte long (48-bit long) binary numbers.

- For convenience, most computers list MAC addresses as 12-digit hexadecimal numbers.

- At the time of manufacture, all Ethernet devices are assigned a universally unique MAC address.

  - The first part of the MAC address is a universally unique 3-byte code, called the *organizationally unique identifier (OUI)* that has been assigned to the manufacturer by the IEEE.

  - *The manufacturer then* assigns a unique value for the last 3 bytes, a number that manufacturer has never used with that OUI.

  - As a result, the MAC address of every device is unique in the universe.

- Ethernet addresses go by many names: LAN addresses, Ethernet addresses, hardware addresses, burned-in addresses, physical addresses, universal addresses, or MAC addresses.

- The Ethernet Frame Check Sequence (FCS) field in the Ethernet trailer is the only field in the Ethernet trailer that gives the receiving node a way to compare results with the sender, to discover whether errors occurred in the frame.

- The use of more modern switches enables the use of full-duplex logic, which is much faster and simpler than half-duplex logic, which is required when using hubs.

Review Questions

Answer these review questions. You can find the answers at the bottom of the last page of the chapter. For thorough explanations, see DVD Appendix C, "Answers to Review Questions."

1. In the LAN for a small office, some user devices connect to the LAN using a cable, while others connect using wireless technology (and no cable). Which of the following is true regarding the use of Ethernet in this LAN?

   A. Only the devices that use cables are using Ethernet.

   B. Only the devices that use wireless are using Ethernet.

   C. Both the devices using cables and those using wireless are using Ethernet.

   D. None of the devices are using Ethernet.

2. Which of the following Ethernet standards defines Gigabit Ethernet over UTP cabling?

   A. 10GBASE-T

   B. 100BASE-T

   C. 1000BASE-T

   D. None of the other answers is correct.

3. Which of the following is true about Ethernet crossover cables for Fast Ethernet?

   A. Pins 1 and 2 are reversed on the other end of the cable.

   B. Pins 1 and 2 on one end of the cable connect to pins 3 and 6 on the other end of the cable.

   C. Pins 1 and 2 on one end of the cable connect to pins 3 and 4 on the other end of the cable.

   D. The cable can be up to 1000 meters long to cross over between buildings.

   E. None of the other answers is correct.

4. Each answer lists two types of devices used in a 100BASE-T network. If these devices were connected with UTP Ethernet cables, which pairs of devices would require a straight-through cable? (Choose three answers.)

   A. PC and router

   B. PC and switch

   C. Hub and switch

   D. Router and hub

   E. Wireless access point (Ethernet port) and switch

5. Which of the following is true about the CSMA/CD algorithm?

    A. The algorithm never allows collisions to occur.

    B. Collisions can happen, but the algorithm defines how the computers should notice a collision and how to recover.

    C. The algorithm works with only two devices on the same Ethernet.

    D. None of the other answers is correct.

6. Which of the following is true about the Ethernet FCS field?

    A. Ethernet uses FCS for error recovery.

    B. It is 2 bytes long.

    C. It resides in the Ethernet trailer, not the Ethernet header.

    D. It is used for encryption.

7. Which of the following are true about the format of Ethernet addresses? (Choose three answers.)

    A. Each manufacturer puts a unique OUI code into the first 2 bytes of the address.

    B. Each manufacturer puts a unique OUI code into the first 3 bytes of the address.

    C. Each manufacturer puts a unique OUI code into the first half of the address.

    D. The part of the address that holds this manufacturer's code is called the MAC.

    E. The part of the address that holds this manufacturer's code is called the OUI.

    F. The part of the address that holds this manufacturer's code has no specific name.

8. Which of the following terms describe Ethernet addresses that can be used to send one frame that is delivered to multiple devices on the LAN? (Choose two answers.)

    A. Burned-in address

    B. Unicast address

    C. Broadcast address

    D. Multicast address

Review All the Key Topics

Review the most important topics from this chapter, noted with the Key Topic icon. Table 2-5 lists these key topics and where each is discussed.

Key Topic

Table 2-5   Key Topics for Chapter 2

Key Topic Element	Description	Page Number
Figure 2-3	Drawing of a typical wired and wireless enterprise LAN	36
Table 2-1	Several types of Ethernet LANs and some details about each	37
Figure 2-9	Conceptual drawing of transmitting in one direction each over two different electrical circuits between two Ethernet nodes	42
Figure 2-10	10- and 100-Mbps Ethernet straight-through cable pinouts	42
Figure 2-12	10- and 100-Mbps Ethernet crossover cable pinouts	43
Table 2-2	List of devices that transmit on wire pair 1,2 and pair 3,6	44
Figure 2-13	Typical Uses for Straight-Through and Crossover Ethernet Cables	44
Figure 2-15	Format of Ethernet MAC addresses	46
List	Definitions of half-duplex and full-duplex	49
Figure 2-19	Examples of which interfaces use full-duplex and which interfaces use half-duplex	51

Complete the Tables and Lists from Memory

Print a copy of DVD Appendix M, "Memory Tables," or at least the section for this chapter, and complete the tables and lists from memory. DVD Appendix N, "Memory Tables Answer Key," includes completed tables and lists for you to check your work.

Definitions of Key Terms

After your first reading of the chapter, try to define these key terms, but do not be concerned about getting them all correct at that time. Chapter 30 directs you in how to use these terms for late-stage preparation for the exam.

Ethernet, IEEE, wired LAN, wireless LAN, Ethernet frame, 10BASE-T, 100BASE-T, 1000BASE-T, Fast Ethernet, Gigabit Ethernet, Ethernet link, RJ-45, Ethernet port, network interface card (NIC), straight-through cable, crossover cable, Ethernet address, MAC address, unicast address, broadcast address, Frame Check Sequence

---

Answers to Review Questions:

1 A **2** C **3** B **4** B, D, and E **5** B **6** C **7** B, C, and E **8** C and D

Chapter 3

Fundamentals of WANs

Most Layer 1 and 2 networking technology falls into one of two primary categories: wide-area networks (WAN) and LANs. Because both WANs and LANs match OSI Layers 1 and 2, they have many similarities: Both define cabling details, transmission speeds, encoding, and how to send data over physical links, as well as data link frames and forwarding logic.

Of course, WANs and LANs have many differences as well, most notably the distances between nodes and the business model for paying for the network. First, in terms of the distance, the terms *local* and *wide* give us a small hint: LANs typically include nearby devices, while WANs connect devices that can be far apart, potentially hundreds or thousands of miles apart.

The other big difference between the two is this: You pay for and own LANs, but you lease WANs. With LANs, you buy the cables and LAN switches and install them in spaces you control. WANs physically pass through other people's property, and you do not have the right to put your cables and devices there. So, a few companies, like a telephone company or cable company, install and own their own devices and cables, creating their own networks, and lease the right to send data over their networks.

This chapter introduces WANs in three major sections. The first introduces leased line WANs, a type of WAN link that has been part of enterprise networks since the 1960s. The second part shows how Ethernet can be used to create WAN services by taking advantage of the longer cable length possibilities of modern fiber-optic Ethernet standards. The last part of the chapter takes a survey of common WAN technology used to access the Internet.

This chapter covers the following exam topics:

Operation of IP Data Networks

Recognize the purpose and functions of various network devices such as Routers, Switches, Bridges and Hubs.

Select the components required to meet a given network specification.

Predict the data flow between two hosts across a network.

Foundation Topics

Leased Line WANs

Imagine that you are the primary network engineer for an enterprise TCP/IP internetwork. Your company is building a new building at a site 100 miles away from your corporate headquarters. You will of course install a LAN throughout the new building, but you also need to connect that new remote LAN to the rest of the existing enterprise TCP/IP network.

To connect the new building's LAN to the rest of the existing corporate network, you need some kind of a WAN. At a minimum, that WAN needs to be able to send data from the remote LAN back to the rest of the existing network and vice versa. Leased line WANs do exactly that, forwarding data between two routers.

From a basic point of view, a leased line WAN works a lot like an Ethernet crossover cable connecting two routers, but with few distance limitations. Each router can send at any time (full-duplex) over the leased line, for tens, hundreds, or even thousands of miles.

This section begins by giving some perspective about where leased lines fit with LANs and routers, because one main goal for a WAN is to move data between LANs. The rest of this first section explains the physical details about leased lines, followed with information about data link protocols.

Positioning Leased Lines with LANs and Routers

The vast majority of end-user devices in an enterprise or SOHO network connect directly into a LAN. Many PCs use an Ethernet NIC that connects to a switch. More and more, devices use 802.11 wireless LANs, with some devices like phones and tablets supporting only wireless LAN connections.

Now think about a typical company that has many different locations. From a human resources perspective, it might have lots of employees that work at many locations. From a facilities perspective, the company might have a few large sites, with hundreds or even thousands of individual branch offices, stores, or other small locations. However, from a networking perspective, think of each site as being one or more LANs that need to communicate with each other, and to communicate, those LANs need to be connected to each other using a WAN.

To connect LANs together using a WAN, the internetwork uses a router connected to each LAN, with a WAN link between the routers. First, the enterprise's network engineer would order some kind of WAN link. A router at each site connects to both the WAN link and the LAN, as shown in Figure 3-1. Note that crooked line between the routers is the common way to represent a leased line when the drawing does not need to show any of the physical details of the line.

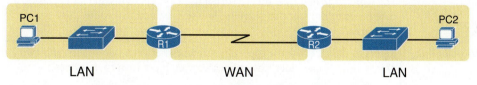

Figure 3-1 *Small Enterprise Network with One Leased Line*

The world of WAN technologies includes many different options in addition to the leased line shown in the figure. WAN technology includes a large number of options for physical links, as well as the data link protocols that control those links. By comparison, the wired LAN world basically has one major option today—Ethernet—because Ethernet won the wired LAN battle in the marketplace back in the 1980s and 1990s.

Physical Details of Leased Lines

The leased line service delivers bits in both directions, at a predetermined speed, using full-duplex logic. In fact, conceptually it acts as if you had a full-duplex crossover Ethernet link between two routers, as shown in Figure 3-2. The leased line uses two pair of wires, one pair for each direction of sending data, which allows full-duplex operation.

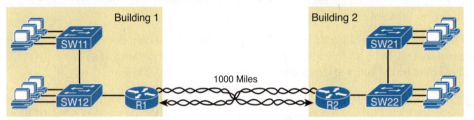

Figure 3-2   *Conceptual View of the Leased Line Service*

Of course, leased lines have many differences compared to an Ethernet crossover cable. To create such possibly long links, or circuits, a leased line does not actually exist as a single long cable between the two sites. Instead, the telco installs a large network of cables and specialized switching devices to create its own computer network. The telco network creates a service that acts like a crossover cable between two points, but the physical reality is hidden from the customer.

Leased lines come with their own set of terminology as well. First, the term *leased line* refers to the fact that the company using the leased line does not own the line, but instead pays a monthly lease fee to use it. However, many people today use the generic term *service provider* to refer to a company that provides any form of WAN connectivity, including Internet services.

Given its long history, leased lines have had many names. Table 3-1 lists some of those names, mainly so that in a networking job, you have a chance to translate from the terms each person uses with a basic description as to the meaning of the name.

Table 3-1   Different Names for a Leased Line

Name	Meaning or Reference
Leased circuit, Circuit	The words *line* and *circuit* are often used as synonyms in telco terminology; *circuit* makes reference to the electrical circuit between the two endpoints.
Serial link, Serial line	The words *link* and *line* are also often used as synonyms. *Serial* in this case refers to the fact that the bits flow serially, and that routers use serial interfaces.
Point-to-point link, Point-to-point line	Refers to the fact that the topology stretches between two points, and two points only. (Some older leased lines allowed more than two devices.)
T1	A specific type of leased line that transmits data at 1.544 megabits per second (1.544 Mbps).
WAN link, Link	Both these terms are very general, with no reference to any specific technology.
Private line	Refers to the fact that the data sent over the line cannot be copied by other telco customers, so the data is private.

Leased Line Cabling

To create a leased line, some physical path must exist between the two routers on the ends of the link. The physical cabling must leave the buildings where each router sits. However, the telco does not simply install one cable between the two buildings. Instead, it uses what is typically a large and complex network that creates the appearance of a cable between the two routers.

Figure 3-3 gives a little insight into the cabling that could exist inside the telco for a short leased line. Telcos put their equipment in buildings called central offices (CO). The telco installs cables from the CO to most every other building in the city, expecting to sell services to the people in those buildings one day. The telco would then configure its switches to use some of the capacity on each cable to send data in both directions, creating the equivalent of a crossover cable between the two routers.

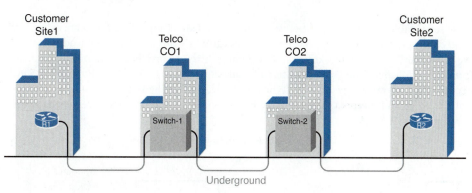

Figure 3-3   *Possible Cabling Inside a Telco for a Short Leased Line*

Although what happens inside the telco is completely hidden from the telco customer, enterprise engineers do need to know about the parts of the link that exist inside the customer's building at the router.

First, each site has *customer premises equipment (CPE)*, which includes the router, serial interface card, and CSU/DSU. Each router uses a serial interface card that acts somewhat like an Ethernet NIC, sending and receiving data over the physical link. The physical link requires a function called a channel service unit/data service unit (CSU/DSU). The CSU/DSU can either be integrated into the serial interface card in the router or sit outside the router as an external device. Figure 3-4 shows the CPE devices, along with the cabling.

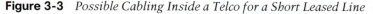
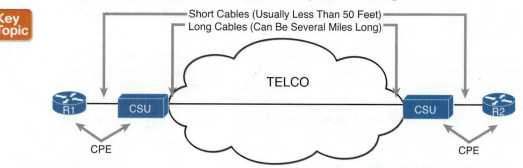

Figure 3-4   *Point-to-Point Leased Line: Components and Terminology*

The cabling includes a short serial cable (only if an external CSU/DSU is used) plus the cable installed by the telco for the leased line itself. The serial cable connects the router serial interface to the external CSU/DSU. (Many cable options exist; the cable just needs to match the connector of the serial interface on one end and the CSU/DSU on the other end.) The four-wire cable from the telco plugs into the CSU/DSU, typically using an RJ-48 connector that has the same size and shape as an RJ-45 connector (as seen in Chapter 2's Figure 2-7).

Telcos offer a wide variety of speeds for leased lines. However, you cannot pick the exact speed you want; instead, you must pick from a long list of predefined speeds. Slower-speed links run at multiples of 64 kbps (kilobits per second), while faster links run at multiples of about 1.5 Mbps (megabits per second).

Building a WAN Link in a Lab

On a practical note, to prepare for the CCENT and CCNA exams, you can choose to buy some used router and switch hardware for hands-on practice. If you do, you can create the equivalent of a leased line without a real leased line from a telco, and without CSU/DSUs, just using a cabling trick. This short topic tells you enough information to create a WAN link in your home lab.

First, the serial cables normally used between a router and an external CSU/DSU are called *data terminal equipment (DTE) cables*. To create a physical WAN link in a lab, you need two serial cables: one serial DTE cable, plus a similar but slightly different matching *data communications equipment (DCE) cable*. The DCE cable has a female connector, while the DTE cable has a male connector, which allows the two cables to be attached directly. The DCE cable also does the equivalent task of an Ethernet crossover cable by swapping the transmit and receive wire pairs, as shown in Figure 3-5.

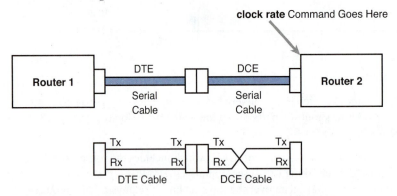

Figure 3-5 *Serial Cabling Uses a DTE Cable and a DCE Cable*

The figure shows the cable details at the top, with the wiring details inside the cable at the bottom. In particular, at the bottom of the figure, note that the DTE serial cable acts as a straight-through cable, and does not swap the transmit and receive pair, while the DCE cable does swap the pairs.

Finally, to make the link work, the router with the DCE cable installed must do one function normally done by the CSU/DSU. The CSU/DSU normally provides a function called *clocking*, in which it tells the router exactly when to send each bit through signaling over the serial cable. A router serial interface can provide clocking, but the router does not do so unless configured with the **clock rate** command. Chapter 15's section "Bandwidth and Clock Rate on Serial Interfaces" shows a sample configuration.

Data Link Details of Leased Lines

A leased line provides a Layer 1 service. In other words, it promises to deliver bits between the devices connected to the leased line. However, the leased line itself does not define a data link layer protocol to be used on the leased line.

Because leased lines define only the Layer 1 transmission service, many companies and standards organizations have created data link protocols to control and use leased lines. Today, the two most popular data link layer protocols used for leased lines between two routers are High-Level Data Link Control (HDLC) and Point-to-Point Protocol (PPP). This next topic takes a brief look at HDLC, just to show one example, plus a few comments about how routers use WAN data link protocols.

HDLC Basics

All data link protocols perform a similar role: to control the correct delivery of data over a physical link of a particular type. For example, the Ethernet data link protocol uses a destination address field to identify the correct device that should receive the data, and an FCS field that allows the receiving device to determine whether the data arrived correctly. HDLC provides similar functions.

HDLC has less work to do because of the simple point-to-point topology of a point-to-point leased line. When one router sends an HDLC frame, it can only go one place: to the other end of the link. So, while HDLC has an address field, the destination is implied. The idea is sort of like when I have lunch with my friend Gary, and only Gary. I do not need to start every sentence with "Hey Gary"—he knows I am talking to him.

> **NOTE**   In case you wonder why HDLC has an address field at all, in years past, the telcos offered multidrop circuits. These circuits included more than two devices, so there was more than one possible destination, requiring an address field to identify the correct destination.

HDLC has other fields and functions similar to Ethernet as well. Table 3-2 lists the HDLC fields, with the similar Ethernet header/trailer field, just for the sake of learning HDLC based on something you have already learned about (Ethernet).

Table 3-2   Comparing HDLC Header Fields to Ethernet

HDLC Header or Trailer Field	Ethernet Equivalent	Description
Flag	Preamble	Lists a recognizable bit pattern so that the receiving nodes realize that a new frame is arriving
Address	Destination Address	Identifies the destination device
Type	Type	Identifies the type of Layer 3 packet encapsulated inside the frame
FCS	FCS	A field used by the error detection process; it is the only trailer field in this table

HDLC exists today as a standard of the International Organization for Standardization (ISO), the same organization that brought us the OSI model. However, ISO standard HDLC does not have a Type field, and routers need to know the type of packet inside the frame. So, Cisco routers use a Cisco-proprietary variation of HDLC that adds a Type field, as shown in Figure 3-6.

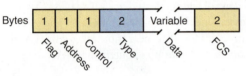

Figure 3-6 *HDLC Framing*

How Routers Use a WAN Data Link

Today, most leased lines connect to routers, and routers focus on delivering packets to a destination host. However, routers physically connect to both LANs and WANs, with those LANs and WANs requiring that data be sent inside data link frames. So, now that you know a little about HDLC, it helps to think about how routers use the HDLC protocol when sending data.

First, the TCP/IP network layer focuses on forwarding IP packets from the sending host to the destination host. The underlying LANs and WANs just act as a way to move the packets to the next router or end-user device. Figure 3-7 shows that network layer perspective.

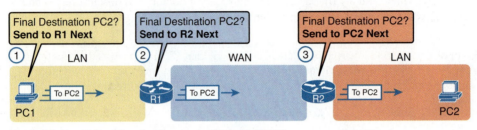

Figure 3-7 *IP Routing Logic over LANs and WANs*

Following the steps in the figure, for a packet sent by PC1 to PC2's IP address:

1. PC1's network layer (IP) logic tells it to send the packet to a nearby router (R1).

2. Router R1's network layer logic tells it to forward (route) the packet out the leased line to router R2 next.

3. Router R2's network layer logic tells it to forward (route) the packet out the LAN link to PC2 next.

While Figure 3-7 shows the network layer logic, the PCs and routers must rely on the LANs and WANs in the figure to actually move the bits in the packet. Figure 3-8 shows the same figure, with the same packet, but this time showing some of the data link layer logic used by the hosts and routers. Basically, three separate data link layer steps encapsulate the packet, inside a data link frame, over three hops through the internetwork: from PC1 to R1, from R1 to R2, and from R2 to PC2.

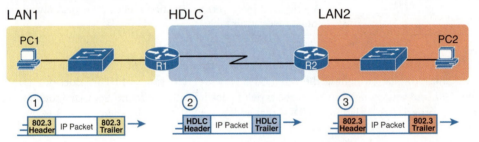

Figure 3-8 *General Concept of Routers Deencapsulating and Reencapsulating IP Packets*

Following the steps in the figure, again for a packet sent by PC1 to PC2's IP address:

1. To send the IP packet to router R1 next, PC1 encapsulates the IP packet in an Ethernet frame that has the destination MAC address of R1.

2. Router R1 deencapsulates (removes) the IP packet from the Ethernet frame, encapsulates the packet into an HDLC frame using an HDLC header and trailer, and forwards the HDLC frame to router R2 next.

3. Router R2 deencapsulates (removes) the IP packet from the HDLC frame, encapsulates the packet into an Ethernet frame that has the destination MAC address of PC2, and forwards the Ethernet frame to PC2.

In summary, a leased line with HDLC creates a WAN link between two routers so that they can forward packets for the devices on the attached LANs. The leased line itself provides the physical means to transmit the bits, in both directions. The HDLC frames provide the means to encapsulate the network layer packet correctly so that it crosses the link between routers.

Leased lines have many benefits that have led to their relatively long life in the WAN marketplace. These lines are simple for the customer, are widely available, are of high quality, and are private. However, they do have some negatives as well compared to newer WAN technologies, including a higher cost and typically longer lead times to get the service installed. The next section looks at an alternative WAN technology used in some examples in this book: Ethernet.

Ethernet as a WAN Technology

For the first several decades of the existence of Ethernet, Ethernet was only appropriate for LANs. The restrictions on cable lengths and devices might allow a LAN that stretched a kilometer or two, to support a campus LAN, but that was the limit.

As time passed, the IEEE improved Ethernet standards in ways that made Ethernet a reasonable WAN technology. For example, the 1000BASE-LX standard uses single-mode fiber cabling, with support for a 5-km cable length; the 1000BASE-ZX standard supports an even longer 70-km cable length. As time went by, and as the IEEE improved cabling distances for fiber Ethernet links, Ethernet became a reasonable WAN technology.

Today, in this second decade of the twenty-first century, many WAN service providers (SP) offer WAN services that take advantage of Ethernet. SPs offer a wide variety of these Ethernet WAN services, with many different names. But all of them use a similar model, with Ethernet used between the customer site and the SP's network, as shown in Figure 3-9.

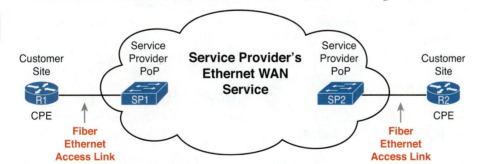

Figure 3-9 *Fiber Ethernet Link to Connect a CPE Router to a Service Provider's WAN*

The model shown in Figure 3-9 has many of the same ideas of how a telco creates a leased line, as seen earlier in Figure 3-3, but now with Ethernet links and devices. The customer connects to an Ethernet link using a router interface. The (fiber) Ethernet link leaves the customer building and connects to some nearby SP location called a point of presence (POP). Instead of a telco switch as seen in Figure 3-3, the SP uses an Ethernet switch. Inside the SP's network, the SP uses any technology that it wants to create the specific Ethernet WAN services.

Ethernet WANs that Create a Layer 2 Service

The WAN services implied by Figure 3-9 include a broad number of services, with a lot of complex networking concepts needed to understand those services. Yet, we sit here at the third chapter of what is probably your first Cisco certification book, so clearly, getting into depth on these WAN services makes little sense. So, for the purposes of the CCENT certification, this book focuses on one specific Ethernet WAN service that can be easily understood if you understand how Ethernet LANs work.

> **NOTE**   For perspective about the broad world of the service provider network shown in Figure 3-9, consider the Cisco certification paths for a moment. Cisco has CCNA, CCNP, and CCIE certifications in many areas: routing and switching, voice, security, and so on. Two paths— Service Provider and Service Provider Operations—focus on technologies and tasks in the service provider arena. See www.cisco.com/go/certifications for more details.

The one Ethernet WAN service used for CCENT and CCNA Routing and Switching examples goes by two names: Ethernet emulation and Ethernet over MPLS (EoMPLS). Ethernet emulation is a general term, meaning that the service acts like one Ethernet link. EoMPLS refers to Multiprotocol Label Switching (MPLS), which is one technology that can be used inside the SP's cloud. This book will refer to this specific service either as Ethernet emulation or EoMPLS.

The type of EoMPLS service discussed in this book gives the customer an Ethernet link between two sites. In other words, the EoMPLS service provides

- A point-to-point connection between two customer devices
- Behavior as if a fiber Ethernet link existed between the two devices

So, if you can imagine two routers, with a single Ethernet link between the two routers, you understand what this particular EoMPLS service does.

Figure 3-10 shows the idea. In this case, the two routers, R1 and R2, connect with an EoMPLS service instead of a serial link. The routers use Ethernet interfaces, and they can send data in both directions at the same time. Physically, each router actually connects to some SP PoP, as shown earlier in Figure 3-9, but logically, the two routers can send Ethernet frames to each other over the link.

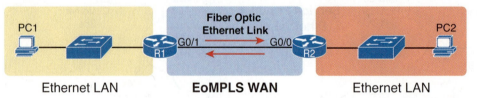

Figure 3-10   *EoMPLS Acting Like a Simple Ethernet Link Between Two Routers*

How Routers Route IP Packets Using Ethernet Emulation

WANs, by their very nature, give IP routers a way to forward IP packets from a LAN at one site, over the WAN, and to another LAN at another site. Routing over an EoMPLS WAN link still uses the WAN like a WAN, as a way to forward IP packets from one site to another. However, the WAN link happens to use the same Ethernet protocols as the Ethernet LAN links at each site.

The EoMPLS link uses Ethernet for both Layer 1 and Layer 2 functions. That means the link uses the same familiar Ethernet header and trailer, as seen in the middle of Figure 3-11.

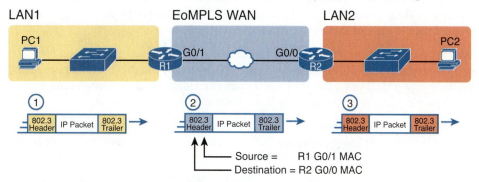

Figure 3-11   *Routing over an EoMPLS Link*

> **NOTE**   This book shows EoMPLS connections as a familiar single black line, like other Ethernet links, but with a small cloud overlaid to note that this particular Ethernet link is through an Ethernet WAN service.

The figure shows the same three routing steps as shown with the serial link in the earlier Figure 3-8. In this case, all three routing steps use the same Ethernet (802.3) protocol. However, note that each frame's data link header and trailer are different. Each router discards the old data link header/trailer and adds a new set, as described in these steps. Focus mainly on Step 2, because compared to the similar example shown in Figure 3-8, Steps 1 and 3 are unchanged:

1. To send the IP packet to router R1 next, PC1 encapsulates the IP packet in an Ethernet frame that has the destination MAC address of R1.

2. Router R1 deencapsulates (removes) the IP packet from the Ethernet frame and encapsulates the packet into a new Ethernet frame, with a new Ethernet header and trailer. The destination MAC address is R2's G0/0 MAC address, and the source MAC address is R1's G0/1 MAC address. R1 forwards this frame over the EoMPLS service to R2 next.

3. Router R2 deencapsulates (removes) the IP packet from the Ethernet frame, encapsulates the packet into an Ethernet frame that has the destination MAC address of PC2, and forwards the Ethernet frame to PC2.

Accessing the Internet

Many people begin their CCENT and CCNA study never having heard of leased lines, but many people have heard of two other WAN technologies used to gain access to the Internet: digital subscriber line (DSL) and cable. These two WAN technologies do not replace leased lines in all cases, but they do play an important role in the specific case of creating a WAN connection between a home or office and the Internet.

This last major section of the chapter begins by introducing the basic networking concepts behind the Internet, followed with some specifics of how DSL and cable provide a way to send data to/from the Internet.

The Internet as a Large WAN

The Internet is an amazing cultural phenomenon. Most of us use it every day. We post messages on social media sites, we search for information using a search engine like Google, and we send emails. We use apps on our phones to pull down information, like weather reports, maps, and movie reviews. We use the Internet to purchase physical products and to buy and download digital products like music and videos. The Internet has created completely new things to do and changed the old ways of living life compared to a generation ago.

However, if you instead focus on the networking technology that creates the Internet, the Internet is simply one huge TCP/IP network. In fact, the name "Internet" comes from the core network layer protocol: Internet Protocol. The Internet includes many LANs, and because the Internet spans the globe, it of course needs WAN links to connect different sites.

As a network of networks, the Internet is actually owned by countless companies and people. The Internet includes most every enterprise TCP/IP network and a huge number of home-based networks, as well as a huge number of individuals from their phones and other wireless devices, as shown in Figure 3-12.

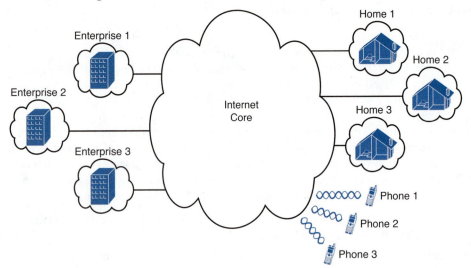

Figure 3-12   *Internet with Enterprise, Home, and Phone Subscribers*

The middle of the Internet, called the *Internet core*, exists as LANs and WANs owned and operated by Internet service providers (ISP). (Figure 3-12 shows the Internet core as a cloud, because network diagrams show a cloud when hiding the details of a part of the network.) ISPs cooperate to create a mesh of links between each other in the Internet core, so that no matter through which ISP a particular company or person connects, some path exists to every device.

Figure 3-13 shows a slightly different version of Figure 3-12, in this case showing the concept of the Internet core: ISP networks that connect to both their customers, as well as each other, so that IP packets can flow from every customer of every ISP to every other customer of every other ISP.

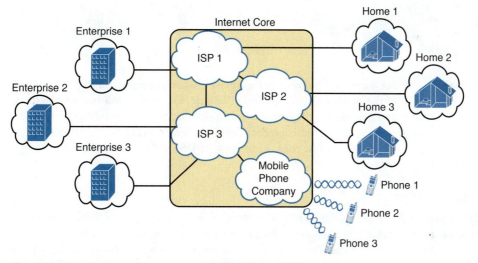

Figure 3-13 *Internet Core with Multiple ISPs and Telcos*

Internet Access (WAN) Links

The Internet also happens to use a huge number of WAN links. All of those lines connecting an enterprise or home to one of the ISPs in Figure 3-13 represent some kind of WAN link that uses a cable, while the phones create their WAN link using wireless technology. These links usually go by the name *Internet access link*.

Historically, businesses tend to use one set of WAN technologies as Internet access links, while home-based consumers use others. Businesses often use leased lines, connecting a router at the business to a router at the ISP. The top of Figure 3-14 shows just such an example.

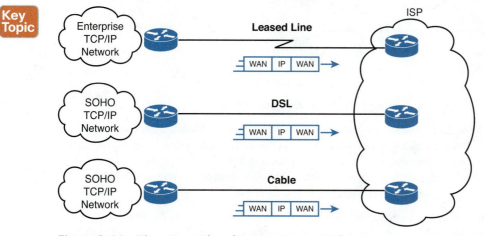

Figure 3-14 *Three Examples of Internet Access Links*

Consumers often use technologies like DSL and cable for Internet access links. These technologies use cabling that is already installed in most homes, making these services somewhat inexpensive for home users. DSL uses the analog phone lines that are already installed in homes, while cable Internet uses the cable TV (CATV) cable.

> **NOTE**   While mostly home-based consumers use DSL and cable, there is no restriction against businesses using them as well.

All three of the Internet access technologies in Figure 3-14 happen to use a pair of routers: one at the customer side of the WAN link and one at the ISP side. The routers will continue to think about network layer logic, of sending IP packets to their destination by forwarding the packets to the next router. However, the physical and data link layer details on the WAN link differ as compared to leased lines. The next few pages examine both DSL and cable Internet to show some of those differences.

Digital Subscriber Line

Digital subscriber line (DSL) creates a relatively short (miles long, not tens of miles) high-speed link WAN between a telco customer and an ISP. To do so, it uses the same single-pair telephone line used for a typical home phone line. DSL, as a technology, does not try to replace leased lines, which run between any two sites, for potentially very long distances. DSL instead just provides a short physical link from a home to the telco's network, allowing access to the Internet.

First, to get an idea about the cabling, think about typical home telephone service in the United States, before adding DSL service. Each home has one phone line that runs from a nearby telco CO to the home. As shown on the left side of Figure 3-15, the telephone wiring splits out and terminates at several wall plates, often with RJ-11 ports that are a slightly skinnier cousin of the RJ-45 connector.

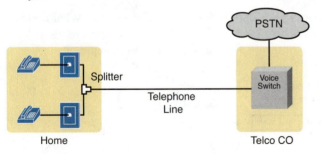

Figure 3-15   *Typical Voice Cabling Concepts in the United States*

Next, think about the telephone line and the equipment at the CO. Sometime in the past, the telco installed all the telephone lines from its local CO to each neighborhood, apartment, and so on. At the CO, each line connects to a port on a telco switch. This switch supports the ability to set up voice calls, take them down, and forward the voice through the worldwide voice network, called the public switched telephone network, or PSTN.

To add DSL service at the home in Figure 3-15, two changes need to be made. First, you need to add DSL-capable devices at the home. Second, the telco has to add DSL equipment at the CO. Together, the DSL equipment at each side of the local telephone line can send data while still supporting the same voice traffic.

The left side of Figure 3-16 shows the changes. A new *DSL modem* now connects to a spare phone outlet. The DSL modem follows the DSL physical and data link layer standards to send data to/from the telco. The home now has a small LAN, implemented with a consumer-grade router, which often includes an Ethernet switch and possibly a wireless LAN access point.

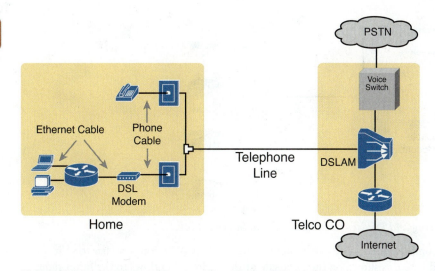

Figure 3-16   *Wiring and Devices for a Home DSL Link*

The home-based router on the left needs to be able to send data to/from the Internet. To make that happen, the telco CO uses a product called a DSL Access Multiplexer (DSLAM). The DSLAM splits out the data over to the router on the lower right, which completes the connection to the Internet. The DSLAM also splits out the voice signals over to the voice switch on the upper right.

DSL gives telcos a useful high-speed Internet service to offer their customers. Telcos have had other offerings that happen to use the same telephone line for data, but these options ran much slower than DSL. DSL supports asymmetric speeds, meaning that the transmission speed from the ISP toward the home (downstream) is much faster than the transmissions toward the ISP (upstream). Asymmetric speeds work better for consumer Internet access from the home, because clicking a web page sends only a few hundred bytes upstream into the Internet, but can trigger many megabytes of data to be delivered downstream to the home.

Cable Internet

Cable Internet creates an Internet access service which, when viewed generally rather than specifically, has many similarities to DSL. Like DSL, cable Internet takes full advantage of existing cabling, using the existing cable TV (CATV) cable to send data. Like DSL, cable Internet uses asymmetric speeds, sending data faster downstream than upstream, which works better than symmetric speeds for most consumer locations. And like DSL, cable Internet does not attempt to replace long leased lines between any two sites, instead focusing on the short WAN links from a customer to an ISP.

Cable Internet also uses the same basic in-home cabling concepts as does DSL. Figure 3-17 shows a figure based on the earlier DSL Figure 3-16, but with the DSL details replaced with cable Internet details. The telephone line has been replaced with coaxial cable from the CATV company, and the DSL modem has been replaced by a cable modem. Otherwise, the details in the home follow the same overall plan.

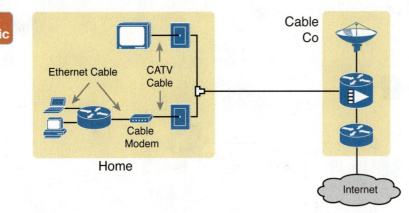

Figure 3-17   *Wiring and Devices for a Home Cable Internet Link*

On the CATV company side of the cable Internet service, the CATV company has to split out the data and video, as shown on the right side of the figure. Data flows to the lower right, through a router, while video comes in from video dishes for distribution out to the TVs in people's homes.

Cable Internet service and DSL directly compete for consumer and small-business Internet access. Generally speaking, while both offer high speeds, cable Internet typically runs at faster speeds than DSL, with DSL providers keeping their prices a little lower to compete. Both support asymmetric speeds, and both provide an "always on" service, in that you can communicate with the Internet without the need to first take some action to start the Internet connection.

Review Activities

Chapter Summary

- Because both WANs and LANs match OSI Layers 1 and 2, they have many similarities: Both define cabling details, transmission speeds, encoding, how to send data over physical links, and data link frames and forwarding logic.

- WANs connect devices that can be far apart, potentially hundreds or thousands of miles apart.

- To connect LANs using a WAN, the internetwork uses a router connected to each LAN, with a WAN link between the routers.

- The term leased line refers to the fact that the company using the leased line does not own the line, but instead pays a monthly lease fee to use it. However, many people today use the generic term *service provider* to refer to a company that provides any form of WAN connectivity, including Internet services.

- Each site has customer premise equipment (CPE), which includes the router, serial interface card, and CSU/DSU.

  - Each router uses a serial interface card that basically acts like an Ethernet NIC, sending and receiving data over the physical link.

  - The physical link requires a function called a channel service unit/data service unit (CSU/DSU).

  - The cabling includes a short serial cable (only if an external CSU/DSU is used), plus the cable installed by the telco for the leased line itself.

- The CSU/DSU normally provides a function called clocking, in which it tells the router exactly when to send each bit by signaling over the serial cable. A router serial interface can provide clocking, but the router does not do so unless configured with the **clock rate** command.

- A leased line with HDLC protocol creates a WAN link between two routers so that they can forward packets for the devices on the attached LANs. The leased line itself provides the physical means to transmit the bits, in both directions. The HDLC frames provide the means to encapsulate the network layer packet correctly so it crosses the link between routers.

- The one Ethernet WAN service used for CCNA examples goes by two names: Ethernet emulation and Ethernet over MPLS (EoMPLS). Ethernet emulation is a general term, meaning that the service acts like one Ethernet link. EoMPLS refers to Multiprotocol Label Switching (MPLS), which is one technology that can be used inside the service provider's cloud.

- By their very nature, WANs give IP routers a way to forward IP packets from a LAN at one site, over the WAN, and to another LAN at another site.

- Consumers often use technologies such as DSL and cable. These technologies use cabling that is already installed in most homes, making these services somewhat inexpensive for home users. DSL uses the analog phone lines that are already installed in homes, while cable Internet uses the cable TV (CATV) cable.

  - Digital Subscriber Line (DSL) creates a relatively short (miles long, not tens of miles) high-speed link between a telco customer and an ISP. To do so, it uses the same single-pair telephone line used for a typical home phone line.

  - Cable Internet takes full advantage of existing cabling, using the existing cable TV (CATV) cable to send data.

Review Questions

Answer these review questions. You can find the answers at the bottom of the last page of the chapter. For thorough explanations, see DVD Appendix C, "Answers to Review Questions."

1. Which of the following best describes the main function of OSI Layer 1 as used in WANs?

    A. Framing

    B. Delivery of bits from one device to another

    C. Addressing

    D. Error detection

2. In the cabling for a leased line, which of the following typically connects to a four-wire line provided by a telco?

    A. Router serial interface without internal CSU/DSU

    B. CSU/DSU

    C. Router serial interface with internal transceiver

    D. Switch serial interface

3. Which of the following is an accurate speed at which a leased line can operate in the United States?

    A. 100 Mbps

    B. 100 Kbps

    C. 256 Kbps

    D. 6.4 Mbps

4. Which of the following fields in the HDLC header used by Cisco routers does Cisco add, beyond the ISO standard HDLC?

    A. Flag

    B. Type

    C. Address

    D. FCS

5. Two routers, R1 and R2, connect using an Ethernet over MPLS service. The service provides point-to-point service between these two routers only, as a Layer 2 Ethernet service. Which of the following are the most likely to be true about this WAN? (Choose two answers.)

    A. R1 will connect to a physical Ethernet link, with the other end of the cable connected to R2.

    B. R1 will connect to a physical Ethernet link, with the other end of the cable connected to a device at the WAN service provider point of presence.

    C. R1 will forward data link frames to R2 using an HDLC header/trailer.

    D. R1 will forward data link frames to R2 using an Ethernet header/trailer.

6. Which of the following Internet access technologies, used to connect a site to an ISP, offers asymmetric speeds? (Choose two answers.)

   A. Leased lines

   B. DSL

   C. Cable Internet

   D. BGP

7. Fred has just added DSL service at his home, with a separate DSL modem and consumer-grade router with four Ethernet ports. Fred wants to use the same old phone he was using before the installation of DSL. Which is most likely true about the phone cabling and phone used with his new DSL installation?

   A. He uses the old phone, cabled to one of the router/switch device's Ethernet ports.

   B. He uses the old phone, cabled to the DSL modem's ports.

   C. He uses the old phone, cabled to an existing telephone port, and not to any new device.

   D. The old phone must be replaced with a digital phone.

Review All the Key Topics

Review the most important topics from this chapter, noted with the Key Topic icon. Table 3-3 lists these key topics and where each is discussed.

Key Topic

Table 3-3   Key Topics for Chapter 3

Key Topic Element	Description	Page Number
Figure 3-4	Typical cabling diagram of CPE for a leased line	59
Figure 3-9	Ethernet over MPLS—physical connections	63
Figure 3-14	Common Internet access links	67
Figure 3-16	Typical DSL cabling at home	69
Figure 3-17	Typical cable Internet cabling at home	70

Complete the Tables and Lists from Memory

Print a copy of DVD Appendix M, "Memory Tables," or at least the section for this chapter, and complete the tables and lists from memory. DVD Appendix N, "Memory Tables Answer Key," includes completed tables and lists to check your work.

Definitions of Key Terms

After your first reading of the chapter, try to define these key terms, but do not be concerned about getting them all correct at that time. Chapter 30 directs you in how to use these terms for late-stage preparation for the exam.

leased line, wide-area network (WAN), telco, serial interface, HDLC, DSL, cable Internet, DSL modem, Ethernet over MPLS

Answers to Review Questions:

1 B **2** B **3** C **4** B **5** B and D **6** B and C **7** C

Chapter 4

Fundamentals of IPv4 Addressing and Routing

The TCP/IP network layer (Layer 3) defines how to deliver IP packets over the entire trip, from the original device that creates the packet to the device that needs to receive the packet. That process requires cooperation between several different jobs and concepts on a number of devices. This chapter begins with an overview of all these cooperating functions, and then it dives into more detail about each area, as follows:

IP routing: The process of hosts and routers forwarding IP packets (Layer 3 PDUs), while relying on the underlying LANs and WANs to forward the bits.

IP addressing: Addresses used to identify a packet's source and destination host computer. Addressing rules also organize addresses into groups, which greatly assists the routing process.

IP routing protocol: A protocol that aids routers by dynamically learning about the IP address groups so that a router knows where to route IP packets so that they go to the right destination host.

Other utilities: The network layer also relies on other utilities. For TCP/IP, these utilities include Domain Name System (DNS), Address Resolution Protocol (ARP), and ping.

Note that all these functions have variations both for the well-established IP version 4 (IPv4) and for the emerging newer IP version 6 (IPv6). This chapter focuses on IPv4 and the related protocols. Part VII of this book looks at the same kinds of functions for IPv6.

This chapter covers the following exam topics:

Operation of IP Data Networks

Recognize the purpose and functions of various network devices such as Routers, Switches, Bridges and Hubs.

Select the components required to meet a given network specification.

Predict the data flow between two hosts across a network.

IP Routing Technologies

Differentiate methods of routing and routing protocols

Static vs. Dynamic

Foundation Topics

Overview of Network Layer Functions

While many protocol models have existed over the years, today the TCP/IP model dominates. And at the network layer of TCP/IP, two options exist for the main protocol around which all other network layer functions revolve: IP version 4 (IPv4) and IP version 6 (IPv6). Both IPv4 and IPv6 define the same kinds of network layer functions, but with different details. This chapter introduces these network layer functions for IPv4, leaving the IPv6 details until Part VII of this book.

> **NOTE** All references to IP in this chapter refer to the older and more established IPv4.

IP focuses on the job of routing data, in the form of IP packets, from the source host to the destination host. IP does not concern itself with the physical transmission of data, instead relying on the lower TCP/IP layers to do the physical transmission of the data. Instead, IP concerns itself with the logical details, instead of physical details, of delivering data. In particular, the network layer specifies how packets travel end to end over a TCP/IP network, even when the packet crosses many different types of LAN and WAN links.

This first section of the chapter begins a broad discussion of the TCP/IP network layer by looking at IP routing and addressing. The two topics work together, because IP routing relies on the structure and meaning of IP addresses, and IP addressing was designed with IP routing in mind. Following that, this overview section looks at routing protocols, which let routers learn the information they need to know to do routing correctly.

Network Layer Routing (Forwarding) Logic

Routers and end-user computers (called *hosts* in a TCP/IP network) work together to perform IP routing. The host operating system (OS) has TCP/IP software, including the software that implements the network layer. Hosts use that software to choose where to send IP packets, oftentimes to a nearby router. Those routers make choices of where to send the IP packet next. Together, the hosts and routers deliver the IP packet to the correct destination, as seen in the example in Figure 4-1.

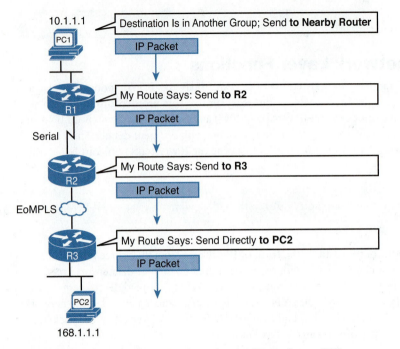

Figure 4-1   *Routing Logic: PC1 Sending an IP Packet to PC2*

The IP packet, created by PC1, goes from the top of the figure all the way to PC2 at the bottom of the figure. The next few pages discuss the network layer routing logic used by each device along the path.

NOTE   The term *path selection* is sometimes used to refer to the routing process shown in Figure 4-1. At other times, it refers to routing protocols, specifically how routing protocols select the best route among the competing routes to the same destination.

Host Forwarding Logic: Send the Packet to the Default Router

In this example, PC1 does some basic analysis, and then chooses to send the IP packet to the router so that the router will forward the packet. PC1 analyzes the destination address and realizes that PC2's address (168.1.1.1) is not on the same LAN as PC1. So PC1's logic tells it to send the packet to a device whose job it is to know where to route data: a nearby router, on the same LAN, called PC1's default router.

To send the IP packet to the default router, the sender sends a data link frame across the medium to the nearby router; this frame includes the packet in the data portion of the frame. That frame uses data link layer (Layer 2) addressing in the data link header to ensure that the nearby router receives the frame.

> **NOTE**   The *default router* is also referred to as the *default gateway*.

R1 and R2's Logic: Routing Data Across the Network

All routers use the same general process to route the packet. Each router keeps an *IP routing table*. This table lists IP address *groupings*, called *IP networks* and *IP subnets*. When a router receives a packet, it compares the packet's destination IP address to the entries in the routing table and makes a match. This matching entry also lists directions that tell the router where to forward the packet next.

In Figure 4-1, R1 would have matched the destination address (168.1.1.1) to a routing table entry, which in turn told R1 to send the packet to R2 next. Similarly, R2 would have matched a routing table entry that told R2 to send the packet, over an Ethernet over MPLS (EoMPLS) link, to R3 next.

The routing concept works a little like driving down the freeway when approaching a big interchange. You look up and see signs for nearby towns, telling you which exits to take to go to each town. Similarly, the router looks at the IP routing table (the equivalent of the road signs) and directs each packet over the correct next LAN or WAN link (the equivalent of a road).

R3's Logic: Delivering Data to the End Destination

The final router in the path, R3, uses almost the same logic as R1 and R2, but with one minor difference. R3 needs to forward the packet directly to PC2, not to some other router. On the surface, that difference seems insignificant. In the next section, when you read about how the network layer uses LANs and WANs, the significance of the difference will become obvious.

How Network Layer Routing Uses LANs and WANs

While the network layer routing logic ignores the physical transmission details, the bits still have to be transmitted. To do that work, the network layer logic in a host or router must hand off the packet to the data link layer protocols, which, in turn, ask the physical layer to actually send the data. And as was described in Chapter 2, "Fundamentals of Ethernet LANs," the data link layer adds the appropriate header and trailer to the packet, creating a frame, before sending the frames over each physical network.

The routing process forwards the network layer packet from end to end through the network, while each data link frame only takes a smaller part of the trip. Each successive data link layer frame moves the packet to the next device that thinks about network layer logic. In short, the network layer thinks about the bigger view of the goal, like "Send this packet to the specified next device...," while the data link layer thinks about the specifics, like "Encapsulate the packet in a data link frame and transmit it." Figure 4-2 points out the key encapsulation logic on each device, using the same examples as shown in Figure 4-1.

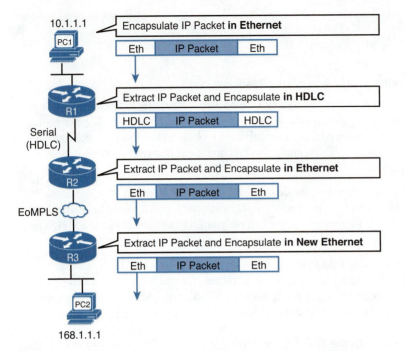

Figure 4-2 *Network Layer and Data Link Layer Encapsulation*

Because the routers build new data link headers and trailers, and because the new headers contain data link addresses, the PCs and routers must have some way to decide what data link addresses to use. An example of how the router determines which data link address to use is the IP Address Resolution Protocol (ARP). *ARP dynamically learns the data link address of an IP host connected to a LAN.* For example, at the last step, at the bottom of Figure 4-2, router R3 would use ARP once to learn PC2's MAC address before sending any packets to PC2.

Routing as covered so far has two main concepts:

■ The process of routing forwards Layer 3 packets, also called *Layer 3 protocol data units (L3 PDU)*, based on the destination Layer 3 address in the packet.

■ The routing process uses the data link layer to encapsulate the Layer 3 packets into Layer 2 frames for transmission across each successive data link.

IP Addressing and How Addressing Helps IP Routing

IP defines network layer addresses that identify any host or router interface that connects to a TCP/IP network. The idea basically works like a postal address: Any interface that expects to receive IP packets needs an IP address, just like you need a postal address before receiving mail from the postal service.

TCP/IP groups IP addresses together so that IP addresses used on the same physical network are part of the same group. IP calls these address groups an *IP network* or an *IP subnet*. Using that same postal service analogy, each IP network and IP subnet works like a postal code (or in the United States, a ZIP code). All nearby postal addresses are in the same postal code (ZIP code), while all nearby IP addresses must be in the same IP network or IP subnet.

> **NOTE**   IP defines the word *network* to mean a very specific concept. To avoid confusion when writing about IP addressing, this book (and others) often avoid using the term *network* for other uses. In particular, this book uses the term *internetwork* to refer more generally to a network made up of routers, switches, cables, and other equipment.

IP defines specific rules about which IP address should be in the same IP network or IP subnet. Numerically, the addresses in the same group have the same value in the first part of the addresses. For example, Figures 4-1 and 4-2 could have used the following conventions:

- Hosts on the top Ethernet: Addresses start with 10
- Hosts on the R1-R2 serial link: Addresses start with 168.10
- Hosts on the R2-R3 EoMPLS link: Addresses start with 168.11
- Hosts on the bottom Ethernet: Addresses start with 168.1

It's similar to the USPS ZIP code system and how it requires local governments to assign addresses to new buildings. It would be ridiculous to have two houses, next door to each other, whose addresses had different ZIP codes. Similarly, it would be silly to have people who live on opposite sides of the country to have addresses with the same ZIP code.

Similarly, to make routing more efficient, network layer protocols group addresses, both by their location and by the actual address values. A router can list one routing table entry for each IP network or subnet, instead of one entry for every single IP address.

The routing process also makes use of the IPv4 header, as shown in Figure 4-3. The header lists a 32-bit source IP address, as well as a 32-bit destination IP address. The header of course has other fields, a few of which matter for other discussions in this book. The book will refer back to this figure as needed, but otherwise, be aware of the 20-byte IP header and the existence of the source and destination IP address fields.

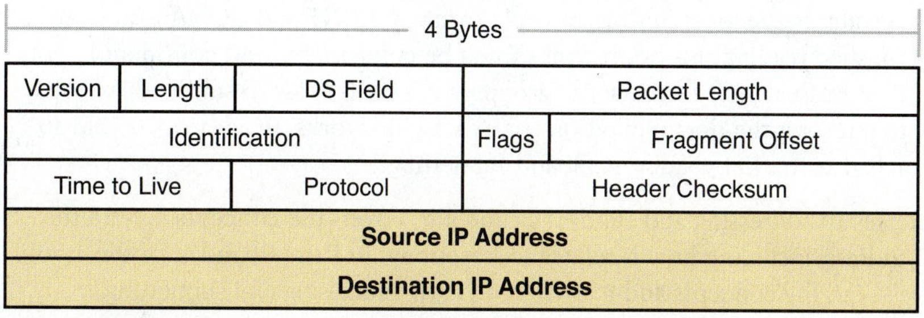

4 Bytes				
Version	Length	DS Field	Packet Length	
Identification			Flags	Fragment Offset
Time to Live		Protocol	Header Checksum	
Source IP Address				
Destination IP Address				

Figure 4-3   *IPv4 Header, Organized as Four Bytes Wide for a Total of 20 Bytes*

Routing Protocols

For routing logic to work on both hosts and routers, each needs to know something about the TCP/IP internetwork. Hosts need to know the IP address of their default router so that hosts can send packets to remote destinations. Routers, however, need to know routes so that routers know how to forward packets to each and every IP network and IP subnet.

Although a network engineer could configure (type) all the required routes, on every router, most network engineers instead simply enable a routing protocol on all routers. If you enable the same routing protocol on all the routers in a TCP/IP internetwork, with the correct settings, the routers will send routing protocol messages to each other. As a result, all the routers will learn routes for all the IP networks and subnets in the TCP/IP internetwork.

Figure 4-4 shows an example, using the same diagram as in Figures 4-1 and 4-2. In this case, IP network 168.1.0.0, which consists of all addresses that begin with 168.1, sits on the Ethernet at the bottom of the figure. R3, knowing this fact, sends a routing protocol message to R2 (Step 1). R2 learns a route for network 168.1.0.0 as a result, as shown on the left. At Step 2, R2 turns around and sends a routing protocol message to R1 so that R1 now has a route for that same IP network (168.1.0.0).

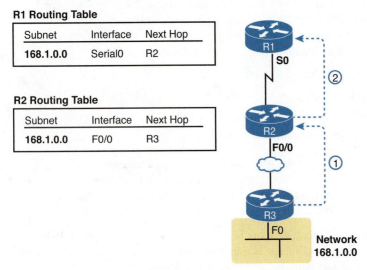

R1 Routing Table

Subnet	Interface	Next Hop
168.1.0.0	Serial0	R2

R2 Routing Table

Subnet	Interface	Next Hop
168.1.0.0	F0/0	R3

Figure 4-4   *Example of How Routing Protocols Advertise About Networks and Subnets*

This concludes the overview of how the TCP/IP network layer works. The rest of this chapter reexamines the key components in more depth.

IPv4 Addressing

IPv4 addressing is absolutely the most important topic for the CCENT and CCNA exams. By the time you have finished reading this book, you should be comfortable and confident in your understanding of IP addresses, their formats, the grouping concepts, how to subdivide groups into subnets, how to interpret the documentation for existing networks' IP addressing, and so on. Simply put, you had better know addressing and subnetting!

This section introduces IP addressing and subnetting and also covers the concepts behind the structure of an IP address, including how it relates to IP routing. In Parts III and V of this book, you will read more about the concepts and math behind IPv4 addressing and subnetting.

Rules for IP Addresses

If a device wants to communicate using TCP/IP, it needs an IP address. When the device has an IP address and the appropriate software and hardware, it can send and receive IP packets. Any device that has at least one interface with an IP address can send and receive IP packets and is called an *IP host*.

IP addresses consist of a 32-bit number, usually written in *dotted-decimal notation (DDN)*. The "decimal" part of the term comes from the fact that each byte (8 bits) of the 32-bit IP address is shown as its decimal equivalent. The four resulting decimal numbers are written in sequence, with "dots," or decimal points, separating the numbers—hence the name *dotted-decimal*. For example, 168.1.1.1 is an IP address written in dotted-decimal form; the actual binary version is 10101000 00000001 00000001 00000001. (You almost never need to write down the binary version, but you can use the conversion chart in Appendix A to easily convert from DDN to binary or vice versa.)

Each DDN has four decimal *octets*, separated by periods. The term *octet* is just a vendor-neutral term for *byte*. Because each octet represents an 8-bit binary number, the range of decimal numbers in each octet is between 0 and 255, inclusive. For example, the IP address of 168.1.1.1 has a first octet of 168, the second octet of 1, and so on.

Finally, note that each network interface uses a unique IP address. Most people tend to think that their computer has an IP address, but actually their computer's network card has an IP address. For example, if your laptop has both an Ethernet network interface card (NIC) and a wireless NIC, with both working at the same time, both will have an IP address. Similarly, routers, which typically have many network interfaces that forward IP packets, have an IP address for each interface.

Rules for Grouping IP Addresses

The original specifications for TCP/IP grouped IP addresses into sets of consecutive addresses called *IP networks*. The addresses in a single IP network have the same numeric value in the first part of all addresses in the network. Figure 4-5 shows a simple internetwork that has three separate IP networks.

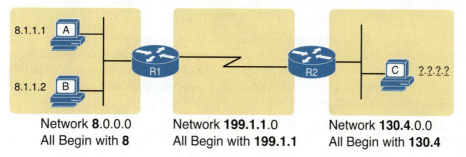

Figure 4-5   *Sample TCP/IP Internetwork Using IPv4 Network Numbers*

The figure lists a network identifier (network ID) for each network, as well as a text description of the DDN values in each network. For example, the hosts in the Ethernet LAN on the far left use IP addresses that begin with a first octet of 8; the network ID happens to be 8.0.0.0. As another example, the serial link between R1 and R2 consists of only two interfaces—a serial interface on each router—and uses an IP address that begins with the three octets 199.1.1.

Figure 4-5 also provides a good figure with which to discuss two important facts about how IPv4 groups IP addresses:

Key Topic

- All IP addresses in the same group must not be separated from each other by a router.
- IP addresses separated from each other by a router must be in different groups.

Take the first of the two rules, and look at hosts A and B on the left. Hosts A and B are in the same IP network and have IP addresses that begin with 8. Per the first rule, hosts A and B cannot be separated from each other by a router (and they are indeed not separated from each other by a router).

Next, take the second of the two rules and add host C to the discussion. Host C is separated from host A by at least one router, so host C cannot be in the same IP network as host A. Host C's address cannot begin with 8.

NOTE   This example assumes the use of IP networks only, and no subnets, simply because the discussion has not yet dealt with the details of subnetting.

As mentioned earlier in this chapter, IP address grouping behaves similarly to ZIP codes. Everyone in my ZIP code lives in a little town in Ohio. If some addresses in my ZIP code were in California, some mail might be delivered to the wrong local post office, because the postal service delivers the letters based on the postal (ZIP) codes. The post system relies on all address-es in one postal code being near to each other.

Likewise, IP routing relies on all addresses in one IP network or IP subnet to be in the same location, specifically on a single instance of a LAN or WAN data link. Otherwise, the routers might deliver IP packets to the wrong locations.

For any TCP/IP internetwork, each LAN and WAN link will use either an IP network or an IP subnet. Next, this chapter looks more closely at the concepts behind IP networks, followed by IP subnets.

Class A, B, and C IP Networks

The IPv4 address space includes all possible combinations of numbers for a 32-bit IPv4 address. Literally 2^{32} different values exist with a 32-bit number, for more than 4 billion different num-bers. With DDN values, these numbers include all combinations of the values 0 through 255 in all four octets: 0.0.0.0, 0.0.0.1, 0.0.0.2, and all the way up to 255.255.255.255.

IP standards first subdivide the entire address space into classes, as identified by the value of the first octet. Class A gets roughly half of the IPv4 address space, with all DDN numbers that begin with 1–126, as shown in Figure 4-6. Class B gets one-fourth of the address space, with all DDN numbers that begin with 128–191 inclusive, while Class C gets one-eighth of the address space, with all numbers that begin with 192–223.

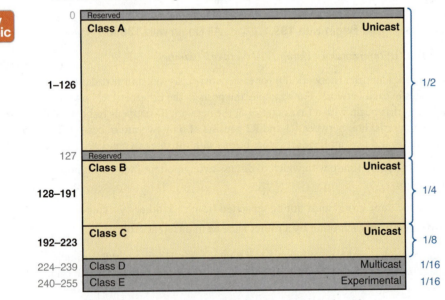

Figure 4-6 *Division of the Entire IPv4 Address Space by Class*

Figure 4-6 also notes the purpose for the five address classes. Classes A, B, and C define unicast IP addresses, meaning that the address identifies a single host interface. Class D defines multi-cast addresses, used to send one packet to multiple hosts, while Class E defines experimental addresses.

IPv4 standards also subdivide the Class A, B, and C unicast classes into predefined IP networks. Each IP network makes up a subset of the DDN values inside the class.

IPv4 uses three classes of unicast addresses so that the IP networks in each class can be different sizes, and therefore meet different needs. Class A networks each support a very large number of IP addresses (over 16 million host addresses per IP network). However, because each Class A network is so large, Class A holds only 126 Class A networks. Class B defines IP networks that have 65,534 addresses per network, but with space for over 16,000 such networks. Class C defines much smaller IP networks, with 254 addresses each, as shown in Figure 4-7.

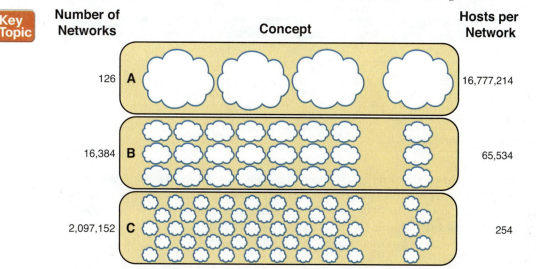

Figure 4-7   *Size of Network and Host Parts of Class A, B, and C Addresses*

Figure 4-7 shows a visual perspective, as well as the literal numbers, for all the Class A, B, and C IPv4 networks in the entire world. The figure shows clouds for IP networks. It of course does not show one cloud for every possible network, but shows the general idea, with a small number of large clouds for Class A and a large number of small clouds for Class C.

The Actual Class A, B, and C IP Networks

Figure 4-7 shows the number of Class A, B, and C IP networks in the entire world. Eventually, you need to actually pick and use some of these IP networks to build a working TCP/IP inter-network, so you need to be able to answer the question: What are the specific IP networks?

First, you must be able to identify each network briefly using a *network identifier* (network ID). The network ID is just one reserved DDN value per network that identifies the IP network. (The network ID cannot be used by a host as an IP address.) For example, Table 4-1 shows the network IDs that match the earlier Figure 4-5.

Table 4-1   Network IDs Used in Figure 4-5

Concept	Class	Network ID
All addresses that begin with 8	A	8.0.0.0
All addresses that begin with 130.4	B	130.4.0.0
All addresses that begin with 199.1.1	C	199.1.1.0

NOTE   Many people use the term *network ID*, but others use the terms *network number* and *network address*. Be ready to use all three terms.

So, what are the actual Class A, B, and C IP networks, and what are their network IDs? First, consider the Class A networks. Per Figure 4-7, only 126 Class A networks exist. As it turns out, they consist of all addresses that begin with 1, all addresses that begin with 2, all addresses that begin with 3, and so on, up through the 126th such network of "all addresses that begin with 126." Table 4-2 lists a few of these networks.

Table 4-2   Sampling of IPv4 Class A Networks

Concept	Class	Network ID
All addresses that begin with 8	A	8.0.0.0
All addresses that begin with 13	A	13.0.0.0
All addresses that begin with 24	A	24.0.0.0
All addresses that begin with 125	A	125.0.0.0
All addresses that begin with 126	A	126.0.0.0

Class B networks have a first octet value between 128 and 191, inclusive, but in a single Class B network, the addresses have the same value in the first two octets. For example, Figure 4-5 uses Class B network 130.4.0.0. The DDN value 130.4.0.0 must be in Class B, because the first octet is between 128 and 191, inclusive. However, the first two octets define the addresses in a single Class B network. Table 4-3 lists some sample IPv4 Class B networks.

Table 4-3   Sampling of IPv4 Class B Networks

Concept	Class	Network ID
All addresses that begin with 128.1	B	128.1.0.0
All addresses that begin with 172.20	B	172.20.0.0
All addresses that begin with 191.191	B	191.191.0.0
All addresses that begin with 150.1	B	150.1.0.0

Class C networks can also be easily identified, with a first octet value between 192 and 223, inclusive. With Class C networks and addresses, the first three octets define the group, with addresses in one Class C network having the same value in the first three octets. Table 4-4 shows some samples.

Table 4-4   Sampling of IPv4 Class C Networks

Concept	Class	Network ID
All addresses that begin with 199.1.1	C	199.1.1.0
All addresses that begin with 200.1.200	C	200.1.200.0
All addresses that begin with 223.1.10	C	223.1.10.0
All addresses that begin with 209.209.1	C	209.209.1.0

Listing all the Class A, B, and C networks would of course take too much space. For study review, Table 4-5 summarizes the first octet values that identify the class and summarizes the range of Class A, B, and C network numbers available in the entire IPv4 address space.

Key Topic

Table 4-5 All Possible Valid Network Numbers

Class	First Octet Range	Valid Network Numbers
A	1 to 126	1.0.0.0 to 126.0.0.0
B	128 to 191	128.0.0.0 to 191.255.0.0
C	192 to 223	192.0.0.0 to 223.255.255.0

> **NOTE** The term *classful IP network* refers to any Class A, B, or C network, because it is defined by Class A, B, and C rules.

IP Subnetting

Subnetting is one of the most important topics on the exams related to the CCENT and CCNA certifications. You need to know how subnetting works and how to "do the math" to figure out issues when subnetting is in use, both in real life and on the exam. Parts III and V of this book cover the details of subnetting concepts, motivation, and math, but you should have a basic understanding of the concepts before covering the topics between here and Part III.

Subnetting defines methods of further subdividing the IPv4 address space into groups that are smaller than a single IP network. IP subnetting defines a flexible way for anyone to take a single Class A, B, or C IP network and further subdivide it into even smaller groups of consecutive IP addresses. In fact, the name *subnet* is just shorthand for *subdivided network*. Then, in each location where you used to use an entire Class A, B, or C network, you can use a smaller subnet, wasting fewer IP addresses.

To make it clear how an internetwork can use both classful IPv4 networks as well as subnets of classful IPv4 networks, the next two figures show the same internetwork, one with classful networks only and one with subnets only. Figure 4-8 shows the first such example, which uses five Class B networks, with no subnetting.

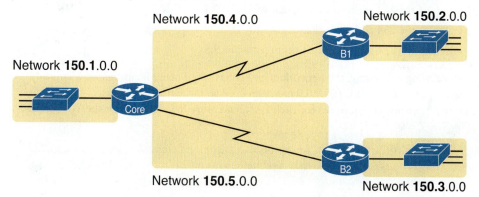

Figure 4-8 *Example That Uses Five Class B Networks*

The design in Figure 4-8 requires five groups of IP addresses, each of which is a Class B network in this example. Specifically, the three LANs each use a single Class B network, and the two serial links each use a Class B network.

Figure 4-8 wastes many IP addresses, because each Class B network has $2^{16} - 2$ host addresses—far more than you will ever need for each LAN and WAN link. For example, the Ethernet on the left uses an entire Class B network, which supports 65,534 IP addresses that begin with 150.1. However, a single LAN seldom grows past a few hundred devices, so many of the IP addresses in Class B network 150.1.0.0 would be wasted. Even more waste occurs on the point-to-point serial links, which only need two IP addresses.

Figure 4-9 illustrates a more common design today, one that uses basic subnetting. As in the previous figure, this figure needs five groups of addresses. However, in this case, the figure uses five subnets of Class B network 150.9.0.0.

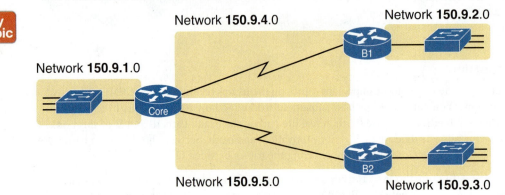

Figure 4-9 *Using Subnets for the Same Design as the Previous Figure*

Subnetting allows the network engineer for the TCP/IP internetwork to choose to use a longer part of the addresses that must have the same value. Subnetting allows quite a bit of flexibility, but Figure 4-9 shows one of the simplest forms of subnetting. In this case, each subnet includes the addresses that begin with the same value in the first three octets, as follows:

- One group of the 254 addresses that begin with 150.9.1
- One group of the 254 addresses that begin with 150.9.2
- One group of the 254 addresses that begin with 150.9.3
- One group of the 254 addresses that begin with 150.9.4
- One group of the 254 addresses that begin with 150.9.5

As a result of using subnetting, the network engineer has saved many IP addresses. First, only a small part of Class B network 150.9.0.0 has been used so far. Each subnet has 254 addresses, which should be plenty of addresses for each LAN, and more than enough for the WAN links.

> **NOTE**   All chapters of Parts III and V of this book explain the details of IP addressing, including the methods to choose an IP network and subnet it into smaller subnets.

In summary, you now know some of the details of IP addressing, with a focus on how it relates to routing. Each host and router interface will have an IP address. However, the IP addresses will not be randomly chosen, but will instead be grouped together to aid the routing process. The groups of addresses can be an entire Class A, B, or C network number or it can be a subnet.

IPv4 Routing

In the first section of this chapter ("Overview of Network Layer Functions"), you read about the basics of IPv4 routing using a network with three routers and two PCs. Armed with more knowledge of IP addressing, you now can take a closer look at the process of routing IP. This section begins with the simple two-part routing logic on the originating host, and then moves on to discuss how routers choose where to route or forward packets to the final destination.

IPv4 Host Routing

Hosts actually use some simple routing logic when choosing where to send a packet. If you assume that the design uses subnets (which is typical), this two-step logic is as follows:

Key Topic

Step 1. If the destination IP address is in the same IP subnet as I am, send the packet directly to that destination host.

Step 2. Otherwise, send the packet to my *default gateway*, also known as a *default router*. (This router has an interface on the same subnet as the host.)

For example, consider Figure 4-10 and focus on the Ethernet LAN on the left. When PC1 sends an IP packet to PC11 (150.9.1.11), PC1 first considers some match related to subnetting. PC1 concludes that PC11's IP address is in the same subnet as PC1, so PC1 ignores its default router (Core, 150.9.1.1), sending the packet directly to PC11, as shown in Step 1 of the figure.

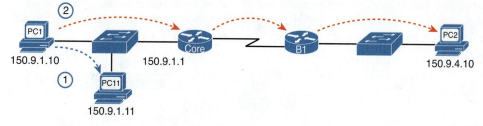

Figure 4-10 *Host Routing: Forwarding to a Host on the Same Subnet*

Alternatively, when PC1 sends a packet to PC2 (150.9.4.10), PC1 does the same kind of subnetting math, and realizes that PC2 is not on the same subnet as PC1. So, PC1 forwards the packet (Step 2) to its default gateway, 150.9.1.1, which then routes the packet to PC2.

Router Forwarding Decisions and the IP Routing Table

Earlier in this chapter, Figure 4-1 shows the network layer concepts of routing, while Figure 4-2 shows the data link encapsulation logic related to routing. This next topic dives a little deeper into that same process, using an example with three routers forwarding (routing) one packet. But before looking at the example, the text first summarizes how a router thinks about forwarding a packet.

A Summary of Router Forwarding Logic

First, when a router receives a data link frame addressed to that router's data link address, the router needs to think about processing the contents of the frame. When such a frame arrives, the router uses the following logic on the data link frame:

Key Topic

Step 1. Use the data link Frame Check Sequence (FCS) field to ensure that the frame had no errors; if errors occurred, discard the frame.

Step 2. Assuming that the frame was not discarded at Step 1, discard the old data link header and trailer, leaving the IP packet.

Step 3.   Compare the IP packet's destination IP address to the routing table, and find the route that best matches the destination address. This route identifies the outgoing interface of the router, and possibly the next-hop router IP address.

Step 4.   Encapsulate the IP packet inside a new data link header and trailer, appropriate for the outgoing interface, and forward the frame.

With these steps, each router forwards the packet to the next location, inside a data link frame. With each router repeating this process, the packet reaches its final destination.

While the router does all the steps in the list, Step 3 is the main routing or forwarding step. The packet has a destination IP address in the header, whereas the routing table lists slightly different numbers, typically a list of networks and subnets. To match a routing table entry, the router thinks like this:

> Network numbers and subnet numbers represent a group of addresses that begin with the same prefix. Think about those numbers as groups of addresses. In which of the groups does this packet's destination address reside?

The next example shows specific examples of matching the routing table.

A Detailed Routing Example

The routing example uses Figure 4-11. In this example, all routers happen to use the Open Shortest Path First (OSPF) routing protocol, and all routers know routes for all subnets. In particular, PC2, at the bottom, sits in subnet 150.150.4.0, which consists of all addresses that begin with 150.150.4. In the example, PC1 sends an IP packet to 150.150.4.10, PC2's IP address.

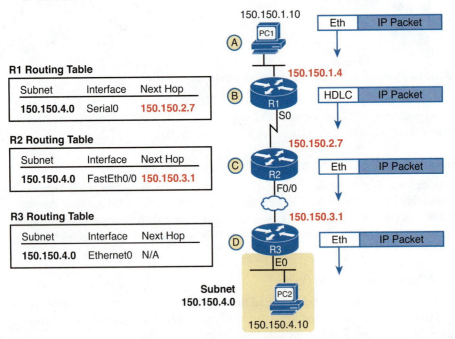

Figure 4-11   *Simple Routing Example, with IP Subnets*

> **NOTE**   Note that the routers all know in this case that "subnet 150.150.4.0" means "all addresses that begin with 150.150.4."

The following list explains the forwarding logic at each step in the figure. (Note that the text refers to Steps 1, 2, 3, and 4 of the routing logic shown in the previous section.)

Step A.   **PC1 sends the packet to its default router.** PC1 first builds the IP packet, with a destination address of PC2's IP address (150.150.4.10). PC1 needs to send the packet to R1 (PC1's default router) because the destination address is on a different subnet. PC1 places the IP packet into an Ethernet frame, with a destination Ethernet address of R1's Ethernet address. PC1 sends the frame onto the Ethernet. (Note that the figure omits the data link trailers.)

Step B.   **R1 processes the incoming frame and forwards the packet to R2.** Because the incoming Ethernet frame has a destination MAC of R1's Ethernet MAC, R1 copies the frame off the Ethernet for processing. R1 checks the frame's FCS, and no errors have occurred (Step 1). R1 then discards the Ethernet header and trailer (Step 2). Next, R1 compares the packet's destination address (150.150.4.10) to the routing table and finds the entry for subnet 150.150.4.0—which includes addresses 150.150.4.0 through 150.150.4.255 (Step 3). Because the destination address is in this group, R1 forwards the packet out interface Serial0 to next-hop router R2 (150.150.2.7) after encapsulating the packet in a High-Level Data Link Control (HDLC) frame (Step 4).

Step C.   **R2 processes the incoming frame and forwards the packet to R3.** R2 repeats the same general process as R1 when R2 receives the HDLC frame. R2 checks the FCS field and finds that no errors occurred (Step 1). R2 then discards the HDLC header and trailer (Step 2). Next, R2 finds its route for subnet 150.150.4.0—which includes the address range 150.150.4.0–150.150.4.255—and realizes that the packet's destination address 150.150.4.10 matches that route (Step 3). Finally, R2 sends the packet out interface Fast Ethernet 0/0 to next-hop router 150.150.3.1 (R3) after encapsulating the packet in an Ethernet header (Step 4).

Step D.   **R3 processes the incoming frame and forwards the packet to PC2.** Like R1 and R2, R3 checks the FCS, discards the old data link header and trailer, and matches its own route for subnet 150.150.4.0. R3's routing table entry for 150.150.4.0 shows that the outgoing interface is R3's Ethernet interface, but there is no next-hop router, because R3 is connected directly to subnet 150.150.4.0. All R3 has to do is encapsulate the packet inside a new Ethernet header and trailer, with a destination Ethernet address of PC2's MAC address, and forward the frame.

Next, this chapter briefly introduces the concepts behind IP routing protocols.

IPv4 Routing Protocols

The routing (forwarding) process depends heavily on having an accurate and up-to-date IP routing table on each router. This section takes another look at routing protocols, considering the goals of a routing protocol, the methods routing protocols use to teach and learn routes, and an example based on the same internetwork shown in the routing example around Figure 4-10.

First, consider the goals of a routing protocol, regardless of how the routing protocol works:

- To dynamically learn and fill the routing table with a route to each subnet in the internetwork.
- If more than one route to a subnet is available, to place the best route in the routing table.
- To notice when routes in the table are no longer valid, and to remove them from the routing table.

- If a route is removed from the routing table and another route through another neighboring router is available, to add the route to the routing table. (Many people view this goal and the preceding one as a single goal.)
- To work quickly when adding new routes or replacing lost routes. (The time between losing the route and finding a working replacement route is called *convergence* time.)
- To prevent routing loops.

Routing protocols all use some similar ideas to allow routers to learn routing information from each other. Of course, each routing protocol works differently; otherwise, you would not need more than one routing protocol. However, many routing protocols use the same general steps for learning routes:

Step 1. Each router, independent of the routing protocol, adds a route to its routing table for each subnet directly connected to the router.

Step 2. Each router's routing protocol tells its neighbors about the routes in its routing table, including the directly connected routes, and routes learned from other routers.

Step 3. After learning a new route from a neighbor, the router's routing protocol adds a route to its IP routing table, with the next-hop router of that route typically being the neighbor from which the route was learned.

For example, Figure 4-12 shows the same sample network as in Figure 4-11, but now with a focus on how the three routers each learned about subnet 150.150.4.0. Note that routing protocols do more work than is implied in the figure; this figure just focuses on how the routers learn about subnet 150.150.4.0.

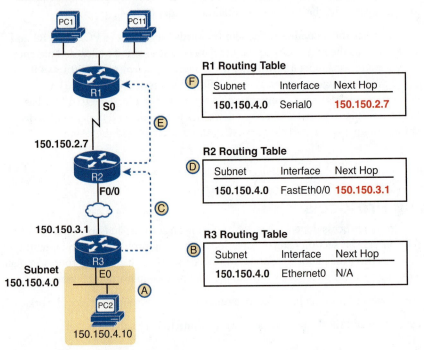

Figure 4-12 *Router R1 Learning About Subnet 150.150.4.0*

Follow items A through F shown in the figure to see how each router learns its route to 150.150.4.0. All references to Steps 1, 2, and 3 refer to the list just before Figure 4-12.

Step A.   Subnet 150.150.4.0 exists as a subnet at the bottom of the figure, connected to router R3.

Step B.   R3 adds a connected route for 150.150.4.0 to its IP routing table (Step 1); this happens without help from the routing protocol.

Step C.   R3 sends a routing protocol message, called a *routing update*, to R2, causing R2 to learn about subnet 150.150.4.0 (Step 2).

Step D.   R2 adds a route for subnet 150.150.4.0 to its routing table (Step 3).

Step E.   R2 sends a similar routing update to R1, causing R1 to learn about subnet 150.150.4.0 (Step 2).

Step F.   R1 adds a route for subnet 150.150.4.0 to its routing table (Step 3). The route lists R1's own Serial0 as the outgoing interface and R2 as the next-hop router IP address (150.150.2.7).

Chapter 17, "Learning IPv4 Routes with OSPFv2," covers routing protocols in more detail. Next, the final major section of this chapter introduces several additional functions related to how the network layer forwards packets from source to destination through an internetwork.

Other Network Layer Features

The TCP/IP network layer defines many functions beyond the function defined by the IPv4 protocol. Sure, IPv4 plays a huge role in networking today, defining IP addressing and IP routing. However, other protocols and standards, defined in other RFCs, play an important role for network layer functions as well. For example, routing protocols like OSPF exist as separate protocols, defined in separate RFCs.

This last short section of the chapter introduces three other network layer features that should be helpful to you when reading through the rest of this book. These last three topics just help fill in a few holes, helping to give you some perspective, and helping you make sense of later discussions as well. The three topics are

- Domain Name System (DNS)
- Address Resolution Protocol (ARP)
- Ping

Using Names and the Domain Name System

Can you imagine a world in which every time you used an application, you had to think about the other computer and refer to it by IP address? Instead of using easy names like google.com or facebook.com, you would have to remember and type IP addresses, like 74.125.225.5. Certainly, that would not be user friendly and could drive some people away from using computers at all.

Thankfully, TCP/IP defines a way to use *host names* to identify other computers. The user either never thinks about the other computer or refers to the other computer by name. Then, protocols dynamically discover all the necessary information to allow communications based on that name.

For example, when you open a web browser and type in the host name **www.google.com**, your computer does not send an IP packet with destination IP address www.google.com; it sends an IP packet to an IP address used by the web server for Google. TCP/IP needs a way to let a computer find the IP address used by the listed host name, and that method uses the *Domain Name System (DNS)*.

Enterprises use the DNS process to resolve names into the matching IP address, as shown in the example in Figure 4-13. In this case, PC11, on the left, needs to connect to a server named Server1. At some point, the user either types in the name Server1 or some application on PC11 refers to that server by name. At Step 1, PC11 sends a DNS message—a DNS query—to the DNS server. At Step 2, the DNS server sends back a DNS reply that lists Server1's IP address. At Step 3, PC11 can now send an IP packet to destination address 10.1.2.3, the address used by Server1.

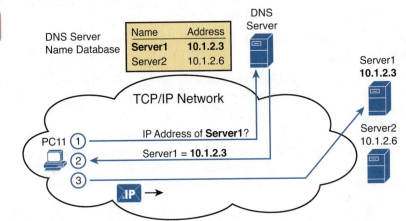

Figure 4-13   *Basic DNS Name Resolution Request*

Note that the example in Figure 4-13 shows a cloud for the TCP/IP network because the details of the network, including routers, do not matter to the name resolution process. Routers treat the DNS messages just like any other IP packet, routing them based on the destination IP address. For example, at Step 1 in the figure, the DNS query will list the DNS server's IP address as the destination address, which any routers will use to forward the packet.

Finally, DNS defines much more than just a few messages. DNS defines protocols, as well as standards for the text names used throughout the world, and a worldwide set of distributed DNS servers. The domain names that people use every day when web browsing, which look like www.example.com, follow the DNS naming standards. Also, no single DNS server knows all the names and matching IP addresses, but the information is distributed across many DNS servers. So, the DNS servers of the world work together, forwarding queries to each other, until the server that knows the answer supplies the desired IP address information.

The Address Resolution Protocol

IP routing logic requires that hosts and routers encapsulate IP packets inside data link layer frames. In fact, Figure 4-11 shows how every router deencapsulates each IP packet and encapsulates the IP packet inside a new data link frame.

On Ethernet LANs, whenever a host or router needs to encapsulate an IP packet in a new Ethernet frame, the host or router knows all the important facts to build that header—except for the destination MAC address. The host knows the IP address of the next device, either another host IP address or the default router IP address. A router knows the IP route used for forwarding the IP packet, which lists the next router's IP address. However, the hosts and routers do not know those neighboring devices' MAC addresses beforehand.

TCP/IP defines the *Address Resolution Protocol (ARP)* as the method by which any host or router on a LAN can dynamically learn the MAC address of another IP host or router on the same LAN. ARP defines a protocol that includes the *ARP Request*, which is a message that asks the simple request "if this is your IP address, please reply with your MAC address." ARP also defines the *ARP Reply* message, which indeed lists both the original IP address and the matching MAC address.

Figure 4-14 shows an example that uses the same router and host from the bottom part of the earlier Figure 4-11. The figure shows the ARP Request on the left as a LAN broadcast, so all hosts receive the frame. On the right, at Step 2, host PC2 sends back an ARP Reply, identifying PC2's MAC address. The text beside each message shows the contents inside the ARP message itself, which lets PC2 learn R3's IP address and matching MAC address, and R3 learn PC2's IP address and matching MAC address.

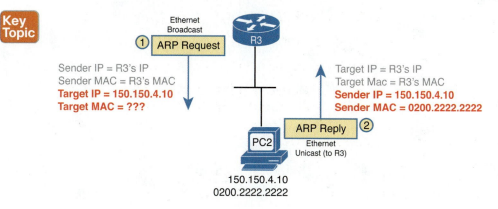

Figure 4-14   *Sample ARP Process*

Note that hosts remember the ARP results, keeping the information in their *ARP cache* or *ARP table*. A host or router only needs to use ARP occasionally, to build the ARP cache the first time. Each time a host or router needs to send a packet encapsulated in an Ethernet frame, it first checks its ARP cache for the correct IP address and matching MAC address. Hosts and routers will let ARP cache entries time out to clean up the table, so occasional ARP Requests can be seen.

NOTE   You can see the contents of the ARP cache on most PC operating systems by using the **arp -a** command from a command prompt.

ICMP Echo and the ping Command

After you have implemented a TCP/IP internetwork, you need a way to test basic IP connectivity without relying on any applications to be working. The primary tool for testing basic network connectivity is the **ping** command.

Ping (Packet Internet Groper) uses the *Internet Control Message Protocol (ICMP)*, sending a message called an *ICMP echo request* to another IP address. The computer with that IP address should reply with an *ICMP echo reply*. If that works, you successfully have tested the IP network. In other words, you know that the network can deliver a packet from one host to the other and back. ICMP does not rely on any application, so it really just tests basic IP connectivity—Layers 1, 2, and 3 of the OSI model. Figure 4-15 outlines the basic process.

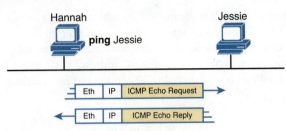

Figure 4-15   *Sample Network,* **ping** *Command*

Note that while the **ping** command uses ICMP, ICMP does much more. ICMP defines many messages that devices can use to help manage and control the IP network. Chapter 18, "Configuring and Verifying Host Connectivity," gives you more information about and examples of ping and ICMP.

Review Activities

Chapter Summary

- The TCP/IP network layer (Layer 3) defines how to deliver IP packets over the entire trip from the original device that creates the packet, to the device that needs to receive the packet.

- IP concerns itself with the logical details, instead of physical details, of delivering data.

- Routers and end-user computers (called *hosts* in a TCP/IP network) work together to perform IP routing.

- The host operating system (OS) has TCP/IP software, including the software that implements the network layer.

- Hosts use that software to choose where to send IP packets, often to a nearby router. Those routers make choices of where to send the IP packet next.

- The term *path selection* is sometimes used to refer to the routing process.

- Each router keeps an IP routing table. This table lists IP address groupings, called IP networks and IP subnets.

- Address Resolution Protocol (ARP) dynamically learns the data-link address of an IP host connected to a LAN.

- If a device wants to communicate using TCP/IP, it needs an IP address. When the device has an IP address and the appropriate software and hardware, it can send and receive IP packets. Any device that has at least one interface with an IP address can send and receive IP packets and is called an *IP host*.

- IP addresses consist of a 32-bit number, usually written in dotted-decimal notation. The decimal part of the term comes from the fact that each byte (8 bits) of the 32-bit IP address is shown as its decimal equivalent. The four resulting decimal numbers are written in sequence, with "dots," or decimal points, separating the numbers, hence the name *dotted decimal*.

- IP standards first subdivide the entire address space into classes, as identified by the value of the first octet.

  - Class A gets roughly half of the IPv4 address space, with all DDN numbers that begin with 1–126.

  - Class B gets one-fourth of the address space, with all DDN numbers that begin with 128–191.

  - Class C gets one-eighth of the address space, with all numbers that begin with 192–223.

  - Class D defines multicast addresses, used to send one packet to multiple hosts, with numbers that begin with 224–239.

  - Class E defines experimental addresses, with numbers that begin with 240–255.

- Subnetting defines a method of further subdividing the IPv4 address space into groups that are smaller than a single IP network. IP subnetting defines a flexible way for anyone to take a single class A, B, or C IP network and further subdivide it into even smaller groups of consecutive IP addresses.

- Hosts use some simple routing logic when choosing where to send a packet. If you assume the design uses subnets (which is typical), this two-step logic is as follows:

  - If the destination IP address is in the same IP subnet as I am, send the packet directly to that destination host.

  - Otherwise, send the packet to my *default gateway*, also known as a *default router*. (This router has an interface on the same subnet as the host.)

- When a router receives a data link frame addressed to that router's data link address, the router needs to think about processing the contents of the frame. When such a frame arrives, the router uses the following logic on the data link frame:

    Step 1. Use the data link FCS field to ensure that the frame had no errors; if errors occurred, discard the frame.

    Step 2. Assuming the frame was not discarded at Step 1, discard the old data link header and trailer, leaving the IP packet.

    Step 3. Compare the IP packet's destination IP address to the routing table, and find the route that best matches the destination address. This route identifies the outgoing interface of the router, and possibly the next-hop router IP address.

    Step 4. Encapsulate the IP packet inside a new data link header and trailer, appropriate for the outgoing interface, and forward the frame.

- TCP/IP needs a way to let a computer find the IP address used by the listed hostname, and that method uses the Domain Name System (DNS).

- TCP/IP defines the Address Resolution Protocol (ARP) as the method by which any host or router on a LAN can dynamically learn the MAC address of another IP host or router on the same LAN.

- The primary tool for testing basic network connectivity is the **ping** command. **ping** (Packet Internet Groper) uses the Internet Control Message Protocol (ICMP), sending a message called an *ICMP echo request* to another IP address. The computer with that IP address should reply with an ICMP echo reply.

Review Questions

Answer these review questions. You can find the answers at the bottom of the last page of the chapter. For thorough explanations, see DVD Appendix C, "Answers to Review Questions."

1. Which of the following are functions of OSI Layer 3 protocols? (Choose two answers.)

    A. Logical addressing

    B. Physical addressing

    C. Path selection

    D. Arbitration

    E. Error recovery

2. Imagine that PC1 needs to send some data to PC2, and PC1 and PC2 are separated by several routers. Both PC1 and PC2 sit on different Ethernet LANs. What are the largest entities (in size) that make it from PC1 to PC2? (Choose two answers.)

    A. Frame

    B. Segment

    C. Packet

    D. L5 PDU

    E. L3 PDU

    F. L1 PDU

3. Which of the following is a valid Class C IP address that can be assigned to a host?

   A. 1.1.1.1

   B. 200.1.1.1

   C. 128.128.128.128

   D. 224.1.1.1

4. What is the assignable range of values for the first octet for Class A IP networks?

   A. 0 to 127

   B. 0 to 126

   C. 1 to 127

   D. 1 to 126

   E. 128 to 191

   F. 128 to 192

5. PC1 and PC2 are on two different Ethernet LANs that are separated by an IP router. PC1's IP address is 10.1.1.1, and no subnetting is used. Which of the following addresses could be used for PC2? (Choose two answers.)

   A. 10.1.1.2

   B. 10.2.2.2

   C. 10.200.200.1

   D. 9.1.1.1

   E. 225.1.1.1

   F. 1.1.1.1

6. Imagine a network with two routers that are connected with a point-to-point HDLC serial link. Each router has an Ethernet, with PC1 sharing the Ethernet with Router1 and PC2 sharing the Ethernet with Router2. When PC1 sends data to PC2, which of the following is true?

   A. Router1 strips the Ethernet header and trailer off the frame received from PC1, never to be used again.

   B. Router1 encapsulates the Ethernet frame inside an HDLC header and sends the frame to Router2, which extracts the Ethernet frame for forwarding to PC2.

   C. Router1 strips the Ethernet header and trailer off the frame received from PC1, which is exactly re-created by Router2 before forwarding data to PC2.

   D. Router1 removes the Ethernet, IP, and TCP headers and rebuilds the appropriate headers before forwarding the packet to Router2.

7. Which of the following does a router normally use when making a decision about routing TCP/IP packets?

   A. Destination MAC address

   B. Source MAC address

   C. Destination IP address

   D. Source IP address

   E. Destination MAC and IP address

8. Which of the following are true about a LAN-connected TCP/IP host and its IP routing (forwarding) choices? (Choose two answers.)

   A. The host always sends packets to its default gateway.

   B. The host sends packets to its default gateway if the destination IP address is in a different class of IP network than the host.

   C. The host sends packets to its default gateway if the destination IP address is in a different subnet than the host.

   D. The host sends packets to its default gateway if the destination IP address is in the same subnet as the host.

9. Which of the following are functions of a routing protocol? (Choose two answers.)

   A. Advertising known routes to neighboring routers

   B. Learning routes for subnets directly connected to the router

   C. Learning routes, and putting those routes into the routing table, for routes advertised to the router by its neighboring routers

   D. Forwarding IP packets based on a packet's destination IP address

10. A company implements a TCP/IP network, with PC1 sitting on an Ethernet LAN. Which of the following protocols and features requires PC1 to learn information from some other server device?

   A. ARP

   B. ping

   C. DNS

   D. None of the other answers are correct

Review All the Key Topics

Review the most important topics from this chapter, noted with the Key Topic icon. Table 4-6 lists these key topics and where each is discussed.

Table 4-6   Key Topics for Chapter 4

Key Topic Element	Description	Page Number
List	Two statements about how IP expects IP addresses to be grouped into networks or subnets	81
Figure 4-6	Breakdown of IPv4 address space	82
Figure 4-7	Sizes of Class A, B, and C Networks	83
Table 4-5	List of the three types of unicast IP networks and the size of the network and host parts of each type of network	85
Figure 4-9	Conceptual view of how subnetting works	86
List	Two-step process of how hosts route (forward) packets	87
List	Four-step process of how routers route (forward) packets	87
List	Goals of IP routing protocols	89
Figure 4-13	Example that shows the purpose and process of DNS name resolution	92
Figure 4-14	Example of the purpose and process of ARP	93

Complete the Tables and Lists from Memory

Print a copy of DVD Appendix M, "Memory Tables," or at least the section for this chapter, and complete the tables and lists from memory. DVD Appendix N, "Memory Tables Answer Key," includes completed tables and lists for you to check your work.

Definitions of Key Terms

After your first reading of the chapter, try to define these key terms, but do not be concerned about getting them all correct at that time. Chapter 30 directs you in how to use these terms for late-stage preparation for the exam.

default router (default gateway), routing table, IP network, IP subnet, IP packet, routing protocol, dotted-decimal notation (DDN), IPv4 address, unicast IP address, subnetting, host name, DNS, ARP, ping

---

Answers to Review Questions:

1 A and C **2** C and E **3** B **4** D **5** D and F **6** A **7** C **8** B and C **9** A and C **10** C

Chapter 5

Fundamentals of TCP/IP Transport and Applications

The CCENT and CCNA exams focus mostly on functions at the lower layers of TCP/IP, which define how IP networks can send IP packets from host to host using LANs and WANs. This chapter explains the basics of a few topics that receive less attention on the exams: the TCP/IP transport layer and the TCP/IP application layer. The functions of these higher layers play a big role in real TCP/IP networks, so it helps to have some basic understanding before moving into the rest of the book, where you go deeper into LANs and IP routing.

This chapter begins by examining the functions of two transport layer protocols: Transmission Control Protocol (TCP) and User Datagram Protocol (UDP). The second major section of the chapter examines the TCP/IP application layer, including some discussion of how Domain Name System (DNS) name resolution works.

This chapter covers the following exam topics:

Operation of IP Data Networks

Identify common applications and their impact on the network

Predict the data flow between two hosts across a network.

TCP/IP Layer 4 Protocols: TCP and UDP

The OSI transport layer (Layer 4) defines several functions, the most important of which are error recovery and flow control. Likewise, the TCP/IP transport layer protocols also implement these same types of features. Note that both the OSI model and the TCP/IP model call this layer the transport layer. But as usual, when referring to the TCP/IP model, the layer name and number are based on OSI, so any TCP/IP transport layer protocols are considered Layer 4 protocols.

The key difference between TCP and UDP is that TCP provides a wide variety of services to applications, whereas UDP does not. For example, routers discard packets for many reasons, including bit errors, congestion, and instances in which no correct routes are known. As you have read already, most data link protocols notice errors (a process called *error detection*) but then discard frames that have errors. TCP provides retransmission (error recovery) and helps to avoid congestion (flow control), whereas UDP does not. As a result, many application protocols choose to use TCP.

However, do not let UDP's lack of services make you think that UDP is worse than TCP. By providing fewer services, UDP needs fewer bytes in its header compared to TCP, resulting in fewer bytes of overhead in the network. UDP software does not slow down data transfer in cases where TCP can purposefully slow down. Also, some applications, notably today Voice over IP (VoIP) and video over IP, do not need error recovery, so they use UDP. So, UDP also has an important place in TCP/IP networks today.

Table 5-1 lists the main features supported by TCP and/or UDP. Note that only the first item listed in the table is supported by UDP, whereas all items in the table are supported by TCP.

Key Topic

Table 5-1 TCP/IP Transport Layer Features

Function	Description
Multiplexing using ports	Function that allows receiving hosts to choose the correct application for which the data is destined, based on the port number.
Error recovery (reliability)	Process of numbering and acknowledging data with Sequence and Acknowledgment header fields.
Flow control using windowing	Process that uses window sizes to protect buffer space and routing devices from being overloaded with traffic.
Connection establishment and termination	Process used to initialize port numbers and Sequence and Acknowledgment fields.
Ordered data transfer and data segmentation	Continuous stream of bytes from an upper-layer process that is "segmented" for transmission and delivered to upper-layer processes at the receiving device, with the bytes in the same order.

Next, this section describes the features of TCP, followed by a brief comparison to UDP.

Transmission Control Protocol

Each TCP/IP application typically chooses to use either TCP or UDP based on the application's requirements. For example, TCP provides error recovery, but to do so, it consumes more bandwidth and uses more processing cycles. UDP does not perform error recovery, but it takes less bandwidth and uses fewer processing cycles. Regardless of which of these two TCP/IP transport layer protocols the application chooses to use, you should understand the basics of how each of these transport layer protocols works.

TCP, as defined in RFC 793, accomplishes the functions listed in Table 5-1 through mechanisms at the endpoint computers. TCP relies on IP for end-to-end delivery of the data, including routing issues. In other words, TCP performs only part of the functions necessary to deliver the data between applications. Also, the role that it plays is directed toward providing services for the applications that sit at the endpoint computers. Regardless of whether two computers are on the same Ethernet, or are separated by the entire Internet, TCP performs its functions the same way.

Figure 5-1 shows the fields in the TCP header. Although you don't need to memorize the names of the fields or their locations, the rest of this section refers to several of the fields, so the entire header is included here for reference.

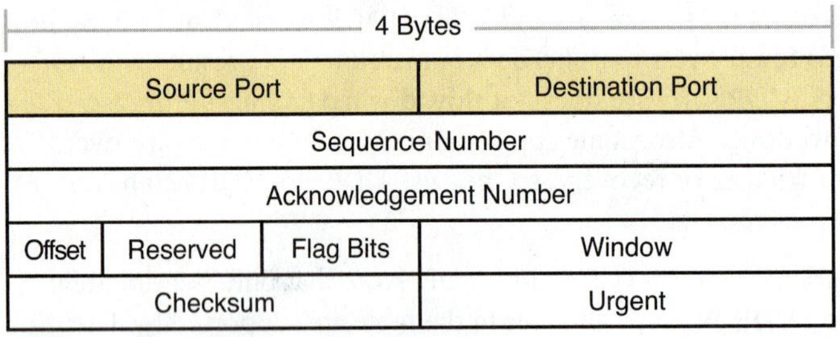

4 Bytes				
Source Port			Destination Port	
Sequence Number				
Acknowledgement Number				
Offset	Reserved	Flag Bits	Window	
Checksum			Urgent	

Figure 5-1 *TCP Header Fields*

The message created by TCP that begins with the TCP header, followed by any application data, is called a *TCP segment*. Alternately, the more generic term *Layer 4 PDU*, or *L4PDU*, can also be used.

Multiplexing Using TCP Port Numbers

TCP and UDP both use a concept called *multiplexing*. Therefore, this section begins with an explanation of multiplexing with TCP and UDP. Afterward, the unique features of TCP are explored.

Multiplexing by TCP and UDP involves the process of how a computer thinks when receiving data. The computer might be running many applications, such as a web browser, an email package, or an Internet VoIP application (for example, Skype). TCP and UDP multiplexing tells the receiving computer to which application to give the received data.

Some examples will help make the need for multiplexing obvious. The sample network consists of two PCs, labeled Hannah and Jessie. Hannah uses an application that she wrote to send advertisements that appear on Jessie's screen. The application sends a new ad to Jessie every 10 seconds. Hannah uses a second application, a wire-transfer application, to send Jessie some money. Finally, Hannah uses a web browser to access the web server that runs on Jessie's PC. The ad application and wire-transfer application are imaginary, just for this example. The web application works just like it would in real life.

Figure 5-2 shows the sample network, with Jessie running three applications:

■ A UDP-based ad application

■ A TCP-based wire-transfer application

■ A TCP web server application

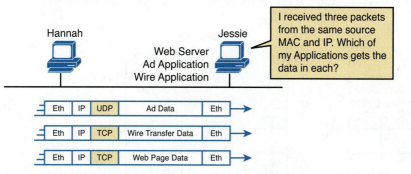

Figure 5-2   *Hannah Sending Packets to Jessie, with Three Applications*

Jessie needs to know which application to give the data to, but *all three packets are from the same Ethernet and IP address.* You might think that Jessie could look at whether the packet contains a UDP or TCP header, but as you see in the figure, two applications (wire transfer and web) are using TCP.

TCP and UDP solve this problem by using a port number field in the TCP or UDP header, respectively. Each of Hannah's TCP and UDP segments uses a different *destination port number* so that Jessie knows which application to give the data to. Figure 5-3 shows an example.

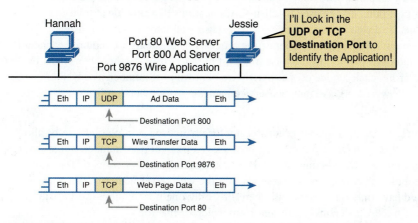

Figure 5-3   *Hannah Sending Packets to Jessie, with Three Applications Using Port Numbers to Multiplex*

Multiplexing relies on a concept called a *socket*. A socket consists of three things:

■ An IP address

■ A transport protocol

■ A port number

So, for a web server application on Jessie, the socket would be (10.1.1.2, TCP, port 80) because, by default, web servers use the well-known port 80. When Hannah's web browser connects to the web server, Hannah uses a socket as well—possibly one like this: (10.1.1.1, TCP, 1030). Why 1030? Well, Hannah just needs a port number that is unique on Hannah, so Hannah sees that port 1030 is available and uses it. In fact, hosts typically allocate *dynamic port numbers* starting at 1024 because the ports below 1024 are reserved for well-known applications.

In Figure 5-3, Hannah and Jessie use three applications at the same time—hence, three socket connections are open. Because a socket on a single computer should be unique, a connection between two sockets should identify a unique connection between two computers. This unique-ness means that you can use multiple applications at the same time, talking to applications running on the same or different computers. Multiplexing, based on sockets, ensures that the data is delivered to the correct applications. Figure 5-4 shows the three socket connections between Hannah and Jessie.

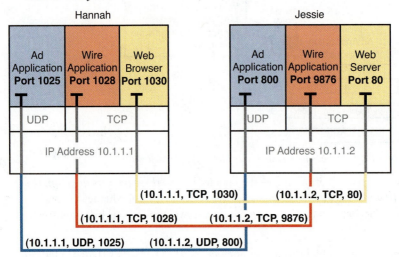

Figure 5-4   *Connections Between Sockets*

Port numbers are a vital part of the socket concept. Well-known port numbers are used by servers; other port numbers are used by clients. Applications that provide a service, such as FTP, Telnet, and web servers, open a socket using a well-known port and listen for connection requests. Because these connection requests from clients are required to include both the source and destination port numbers, the port numbers used by the servers must be well-known. Therefore, each service uses a specific well-known port number. The well-known ports are listed at www.iana.org/assignments/service-names-port-numbers/service-names-port-numbers.txt.

On client machines, where the requests originate, any locally unused port number can be allo-cated. The result is that each client on the same host uses a different port number, but a server uses the same port number for all connections. For example, 100 web browsers on the same host computer could each connect to a web server, but the web server with 100 clients con-nected to it would have only one socket and, therefore, only one port number (port 80, in this case). The server can tell which packets are sent from which of the 100 clients by looking at the source port of received TCP segments. The server can send data to the correct web client (browser) by sending data to that same port number listed as a destination port. The combination of source and destination sockets allows all participating hosts to dis-tinguish between the data's source and destination. Although the example explains the concept using 100 TCP connections, the same port-numbering concept applies to UDP sessions in the same way.

NOTE   You can find all RFCs online at www.rfc-editor.org/rfc/rfc*xxxx*.txt, where *xxxx* is the number of the RFC. If you do not know the number of the RFC, you can try searching by topic at www.rfc-editor.org.

Popular TCP/IP Applications

Throughout your preparation for the CCNA exams, you will come across a variety of TCP/IP applications. You should at least be aware of some of the applications that can be used to help manage and control a network.

The World Wide Web (WWW) application exists through web browsers accessing the content available on web servers. Although it is often thought of as an end-user application, you can actually use WWW to manage a router or switch. You enable a web server function in the router or switch and use a browser to access the router or switch.

The Domain Name System (DNS) allows users to use names to refer to computers, with DNS being used to find the corresponding IP addresses. DNS also uses a client/server model, with DNS servers being controlled by networking personnel and DNS client functions being part of most any device that uses TCP/IP today. The client simply asks the DNS server to supply the IP address that corresponds to a given name.

Simple Network Management Protocol (SNMP) is an application layer protocol used specifically for network device management. For example, Cisco supplies a large variety of network management products, many of them in the Cisco Prime network management software product family. They can be used to query, compile, store, and display information about a network's operation. To query the network devices, Cisco Prime software mainly uses SNMP protocols.

Traditionally, to move files to and from a router or switch, Cisco used Trivial File Transfer Protocol (TFTP). TFTP defines a protocol for basic file transfer—hence the word *trivial*. Alternatively, routers and switches can use File Transfer Protocol (FTP), which is a much more functional protocol, to transfer files. Both work well for moving files into and out of Cisco devices. FTP allows many more features, making it a good choice for the general end-user population. TFTP client and server applications are very simple, making them good tools as embedded parts of networking devices.

Some of these applications use TCP, and some use UDP. For example, Simple Mail Transfer Protocol (SMTP) and Post Office Protocol version 3 (POP3), both used for transferring mail, require guaranteed delivery, so they use TCP. Regardless of which transport layer protocol is used, applications use a well-known port number so that clients know which port to attempt to connect to. Table 5-2 lists several popular applications and their well-known port numbers.

Table 5-2   Popular Applications and Their Well-Known Port Numbers

Port Number	Protocol	Application
20	TCP	FTP data
21	TCP	FTP control
22	TCP	SSH
23	TCP	Telnet
25	TCP	SMTP
53	UDP, TCP	DNS
67, 68	UDP	DHCP
69	UDP	TFTP
80	TCP	HTTP (WWW)
110	TCP	POP3
161	UDP	SNMP
443	TCP	SSL

Connection Establishment and Termination

TCP connection establishment occurs before any of the other TCP features can begin their work. Connection establishment refers to the process of initializing sequence and acknowledgment fields and agreeing on the port numbers used. Figure 5-5 shows an example of connection establishment flow.

Figure 5-5 *TCP Connection Establishment*

This three-way connection establishment flow (also called a three-way handshake) must complete before data transfer can begin. The connection exists between the two sockets, although the TCP header has no single socket field. Of the three parts of a socket, the IP addresses are implied based on the source and destination IP addresses in the IP header. TCP is implied because a TCP header is in use, as specified by the protocol field value in the IP header. Therefore, the only parts of the socket that need to be encoded in the TCP header are the port numbers.

TCP signals connection establishment using 2 bits inside the flag fields of the TCP header. Called the SYN and ACK flags, these bits have a particularly interesting meaning. SYN means "synchronize the sequence numbers," which is one necessary component in initialization for TCP.

Figure 5-6 shows TCP connection termination. This four-way termination sequence is straightforward and uses an additional flag, called the *FIN bit*. (FIN is short for "finished," as you might guess.) One interesting note: Before the device on the right sends the third TCP segment in the sequence, it notifies the application that the connection is coming down. It then waits on an acknowledgment from the application before sending the third segment in the figure. Just in case the application takes some time to reply, the PC on the right sends the second flow in the figure, acknowledging that the other PC wants to take down the connection. Otherwise, the PC on the left might resend the first segment repeatedly.

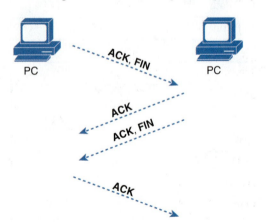

Figure 5-6 *TCP Connection Termination*

TCP establishes and terminates connections between the endpoints, whereas UDP does not. Many protocols operate under these same concepts, so the terms *connection-oriented* and *connectionless* are used to refer to the general idea of each. More formally, these terms can be defined as follows:

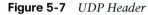

- **Connection-oriented protocol:** A protocol that requires an exchange of messages before data transfer begins, or that has a required preestablished correlation between two endpoints.

- **Connectionless protocol:** A protocol that does not require an exchange of messages and that does not require a preestablished correlation between two endpoints.

User Datagram Protocol

UDP provides a service for applications to exchange messages. Unlike TCP, UDP is connectionless and provides no reliability, no windowing, no reordering of the received data, and no segmentation of large chunks of data into the right size for transmission. However, UDP provides some functions of TCP, such as data transfer and multiplexing using port numbers, and it does so with fewer bytes of overhead and less processing required than TCP.

UDP data transfer differs from TCP data transfer in that no reordering or recovery is accomplished. Applications that use UDP are tolerant of the lost data, or they have some application mechanism to recover lost data. For example, VoIP uses UDP because if a voice packet is lost, by the time the loss could be noticed and the packet retransmitted, too much delay would have occurred, and the voice would be unintelligible. Also, DNS requests use UDP because the user will retry an operation if the DNS resolution fails. As another example, the Network File System (NFS), a remote file system application, performs recovery with application layer code, so UDP features are acceptable to NFS.

Figure 5-7 shows the UDP header format. Most importantly, note that the header includes source and destination port fields, for the same purpose as TCP. However, the UDP has only 8 bytes, in comparison to the 20-byte TCP header shown in Figure 5-1. UDP needs a shorter header than TCP simply because UDP has less work to do.

4 Bytes	
Source Port	Destination Port
Length	Checksum

Figure 5-7   *UDP Header*

TCP/IP Applications

The whole goal of building an enterprise network, or connecting a small home or office network to the Internet, is to use applications—applications such as web browsing, text messaging, email, file downloads, voice, and video. This section examines a few issues related to network design in light of the applications expected in an internetwork. This is followed by a much deeper look at one particular application—web browsing using Hypertext Transfer Protocol (HTTP).

QoS Needs and the Impact of TCP/IP Applications

Applications need to send data over a TCP/IP internetwork. However, they need more than the ability to move the data from one application on one device to another application on another device. That communication has different characteristics, or qualities, and the networking world refers to these qualities as quality of service (QoS).

5

QoS in general defines the quality of the data transfer between two applications and in the network as a whole. QoS often breaks down these qualities into four competing characteristics:

Bandwidth: The volume of bits per second needed for the application to work well; it can be biased with more volume in one direction, or balanced.

Delay: The amount of time it takes one IP packet to flow from sender to receiver.

Jitter: The variation in delay.

Loss: The percentage of packets discarded by the network before they reach the destination, which when using TCP, requires a retransmission.

Today's TCP/IP internetworks support many types of applications, and each type has different QoS requirements. The next few pages look at the QoS requirements for three general categories of applications: batch, interactive, and real-time.

Defining Interactive and Batch Applications

TCP/IP networks began in the 1970s and 1980s with data applications only, with no widely used voice and video applications. Data applications send bits, and the bits represent data: text to be displayed for a user, graphical images to be displayed for a user, customer information, and so on.

Data applications have different QoS requirements depending on whether they are interactive or batch. Interactive data applications usually have a human user at one end of a flow, and the IP packets must flow in both directions for meaningful work to happen. For example, the user takes some action, sending a packet to a server; before the user sees more data on the screen, the server must send a packet back. So, the delay and jitter have a big impact on the user experience.

Batch applications focus more on the bandwidth between two software processes. Batch applications often do not even have a human in the picture. For example, you can have an application on your device that backs up your device data overnight, copying it to some server in the network. You personally might not care how long it takes, but the IT department cares how much bandwidth (how many bits/second) is needed. Why? The IT department might need to support thousands of devices that need to do their backups between 2 a.m. and 5 a.m. each day, so it has to build a network with enough bandwidth to meet that need.

Real-Time Voice and Video Applications

Most modern enterprise TCP/IP internetworks support voice applications as well. Most commonly, the network includes IP phones, which are telephones that connect to the TCP/IP network using an Ethernet or wireless LAN connection. The phone sends the voice as bits inside IP packets, as shown in Figure 5-8.

VoIP Packet

| IP | UDP | RTP | Digital Voice Bits |

Figure 5-8   *IP Packet Sent by a Voice Call*

NOTE   Sending voice traffic as bits inside an IP packet is generally called *Voice over IP (VoIP)*, while the use of telephones that connect to LANs as shown in Figure 5-8 is called *IP telephony*.

While a phone call between two IP phones has similar kinds of QoS requirements as an interactive data application, because the QoS requirements are much higher, voice is considered to be a real-time application instead of an interactive application. For example, a one-way network delay of 1 second works well for most web-browsing experiences. However, for a quality voice call, that same one-way delay needs to be less than 0.2 seconds. Also, interactive applications do not suffer much when packets are lost in transit, but a real-time voice call does suffer, with less voice quality.

The QoS requirements for video are similar to those for voice. Like voice, two-way video applications, like videoconferencing, require low delay, low jitter, and low loss.

Table 5-3 compares the QoS requirements of three example applications: interactive web browsing, real-time voice, and real-time video. Use the table to review the comparisons between data applications versus voice and video, as opposed to using it as a set of random facts to memorize.

Table 5-3   *Comparing Interactive and Real-Time Application Requirements*

Category of Application	Delay	Jitter	Loss
Web browsing (interactive)	Medium	Medium	Medium
VoIP phone call	Low	Low	Low
Videoconferencing	Low	Low	Low

To support the QoS requirements of the various applications, routers and switches can be configured with a wide variety of QoS tools. They are beyond the scope of the CCNA exams (but are covered on several of the Cisco professional-level certifications). However, the QoS tools must be used for a modern network to be able to support high-quality VoIP and video over IP.

Next, we examine the most popular application layer protocol for interactive data applications today—HTTP and the World Wide Web (WWW). The goal is to show one example of how application layer protocols work.

The World Wide Web, HTTP, and SSL

The *World Wide Web (WWW)* consists of all the Internet-connected web servers in the world, plus all Internet-connected hosts with web browsers. *Web servers*, which consist of web server software running on a computer, store information (in the form of *web pages*) that might be useful to different people. *Web browsers*, which is software installed on an end user's computer, provide the means to connect to a web server and display the web pages stored on the web server.

NOTE   Although most people use the term *web browser*, or simply *browser*, web browsers are also called *web clients*, because they obtain a service from a web server.

For this process to work, several specific application layer functions must occur. The user must somehow identify the server, the specific web page, and the protocol used to get the data from the server. The client must find the server's IP address, based on the server's name, typically using DNS. The client must request the web page, which actually consists of multiple separate files, and the server must send the files to the web browser. Finally, for electronic commerce (e-commerce) applications, the transfer of data, particularly sensitive financial data, needs to be secure. The following sections address each of these functions.

Uniform Resource Locators

For a browser to display a web page, the browser must identify the server that has the web page, plus other information that identifies the particular web page. Most web servers have many web pages. For example, if you use a web browser to browse www.cisco.com and you click around that web page, you'll see another web page. Click again, and you'll see another web page. In each case, the clicking action identifies the server's IP address and the specific web page, with the details mostly hidden from you. (These clickable items on a web page, which in turn bring you to another web page, are called *links*.)

The browser user can identify a web page when you click something on a web page or when you enter a *Uniform Resource Locator (URL)* (often called a *web address* and sometimes a universal resource locator) in the browser's address area. Both options—clicking a link and entering a URL—refer to a URL, because when you click a link on a web page, that link actually refers to a URL.

NOTE   Most browsers support some way to view the hidden URL referenced by a link. In several browsers, hover the mouse pointer over a link, right-click, and select **Properties**. The pop-up window should display the URL to which the browser would be directed if you clicked that link.

Each URL defines the protocol used to transfer data, the name of the server, and the particular web page on that server. The URL can be broken into three parts:

- The protocol is listed before the //.
- The host name is listed between the // and the /.
- The name of the web page is listed after the /.

For example, consider the following:

  http://www.certskills.com/ICND1

In this case, the protocol is *Hypertext Transfer Protocol (HTTP)*, the host name is www.certskills.com, and the name of the web page is ICND1.

Finding the Web Server Using DNS

As mentioned in Chapter 4, "Fundamentals of IPv4 Addressing and Routing," a host can use DNS to discover the IP address that corresponds to a particular host name. Although URLs can include the IP address of the web server instead of the name of the web server, URLs typically list the host name. So, before the browser can send a packet to the web server, the browser typically needs to resolve the name in the URL to that name's corresponding IP address.

To pull together several concepts, Figure 5-9 shows the DNS process as initiated by a web browser, as well as some other related information. From a basic perspective, the user enters the URL (http://www.cisco.com/go/learningnetwork), resolves the www.cisco.com name into the correct IP address, and starts sending packets to the web server.

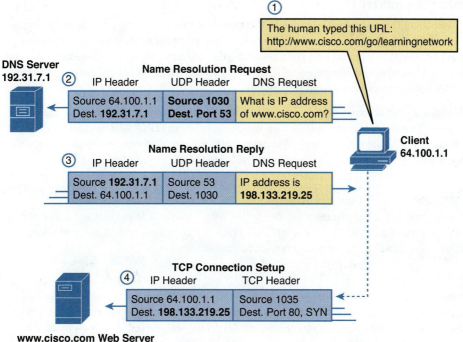

Figure 5-9 *DNS Resolution and Requesting a Web Page*

The steps shown in the figure are as follows:

1.   The user enters the URL, http://www.cisco.com/go/learningnetwork, into the browser's address area.

2.   The client sends a DNS request to the DNS server. Typically, the client learns the DNS server's IP address through DHCP. Note that the DNS request uses a UDP header, with a destination port of the DNS well-known port of 53. (See Table 5-2, earlier in this chapter, for a list of popular well-known ports.)

3.   The DNS server sends a reply, listing IP address 198.133.219.25 as www.cisco.com's IP address. Note also that the reply shows a destination IP address of 64.100.1.1, the client's IP address. It also shows a UDP header, with source port 53; the source port is 53 because the data is sourced, or sent by, the DNS server.

4.   The client begins the process of establishing a new TCP connection to the web server. Note that the destination IP address is the just-learned IP address of the web server. The packet includes a TCP header, because HTTP uses TCP. Also note that the destination TCP port is 80, the well-known port for HTTP. Finally, the SYN bit is shown, as a reminder that the TCP connection establishment process begins with a TCP segment with the SYN bit turned on (binary 1).

At this point in the process, the web browser is almost finished setting up a TCP connection to the web server. The next section picks up the story at that point, examining how the web browser then gets the files that comprise the desired web page.

Transferring Files with HTTP

After a web client (browser) has created a TCP connection to a web server, the client can begin requesting the web page from the server. Most often, the protocol used to transfer the web page is HTTP. The HTTP application layer protocol, defined in RFC 2616, defines how files can be transferred between two computers. HTTP was specifically created for the purpose of transferring files between web servers and web clients.

HTTP defines several commands and responses, with the most frequently used being the HTTP GET request. To get a file from a web server, the client sends an HTTP GET request to the server, listing the filename. If the server decides to send the file, the server sends an HTTP GET response, with a return code of 200 (meaning "OK"), along with the file's contents.

> **NOTE**   Many return codes exist for HTTP requests. For example, when the server does not have the requested file, it issues a return code of 404, which means "file not found." Most web browsers do not show the specific numeric HTTP return codes, instead displaying a response such as "page not found" in reaction to receiving a return code of 404.

Web pages typically consist of multiple files, called *objects*. Most web pages contain text as well as several graphical images, animated advertisements, and possibly voice or video. Each of these components is stored as a different object (file) on the web server. To get them all, the web browser gets the first file. This file can (and typically does) include references to other URLs, so the browser then also requests the other objects. Figure 5-10 shows the general idea, with the browser getting the first file and then two others.

In this case, after the web browser gets the first file—the one called "/go/ccna" in the URL—the browser reads and interprets that file. Besides containing parts of the web page, the file refers to two other files, so the browser issues two additional HTTP get requests. Note that, even though it isn't shown in the figure, all these commands flow over one (or possibly more) TCP connections between the client and the server. This means that TCP would provide error recovery, ensuring that the data was delivered.

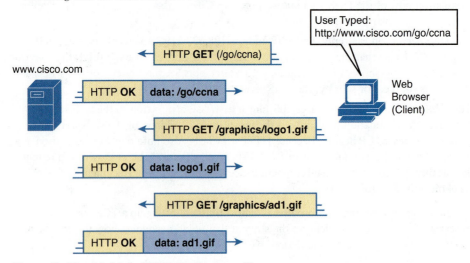

Figure 5-10   *Multiple HTTP Get Requests/Responses*

Review Activities

Chapter Summary

- The OSI transport layer (Layer 4) defines several functions, the most important of which are error recovery and flow control. Likewise, the TCP/IP transport layer protocols implement these same types of features.

- The key difference between TCP and UDP is that TCP provides a wide variety of services to applications, whereas UDP does not.

  - For example, TCP provides error recovery, but to do so, it consumes more bandwidth and uses more processing cycles.

  - UDP does not perform error recovery, but it takes less bandwidth and uses fewer processing cycles.

- Multiplexing by TCP and UDP involves the process of how a computer thinks when receiving data. The computer might be running many applications, such as a web browser, an e-mail package, or an Internet VoIP application (for example, Skype). TCP and UDP multiplexing enables the receiving computer to know which application to give the data.

- Multiplexing relies on a concept called a *socket*. A socket consists of three things:

  - An IP address

  - A transport protocol

  - A port number

- Port numbers are a vital part of the socket concept. Well-known port numbers are used by servers; other port numbers are used by clients. Applications that provide a service, such as FTP, Telnet, and web servers, open a socket using a well-known port and listen for connection requests.

- TCP connection establishment occurs before any of the other TCP features can begin their work. Connection establishment refers to the process of initializing sequence and acknowledgment fields and agreeing on the port numbers used.

- TCP establishes and terminates connections between the endpoints, whereas UDP does not. Many protocols operate under these same concepts, so the terms *connection-oriented* and *connectionless* are used to refer to the general idea of each.

  - **Connection-oriented protocol:** A protocol that requires an exchange of messages before data transfer begins or that has a required pre-established correlation between two endpoints.

  - **Connectionless protocol:** A protocol that does not require an exchange of messages and that does not require a pre-established correlation between two endpoints.

- UDP provides a service for applications to exchange messages. Unlike TCP, UDP is connectionless and provides no reliability, no windowing, no reordering of the received data, and no segmentation of large chunks of data into the right size for transmission.

- Today's TCP/IP internetworks support many types of applications, and each type has different Quality of Service (QoS) requirements.

- QoS in general defines the quality of the data transfer between two applications and in the network as a whole. QoS often breaks down these qualities into four competing characteristics:

  - **Bandwidth:** The volume of bits per second needed for the application to work well; it may be biased with more volume in one direction, or balanced.

  - **Delay:** The amount of time it takes one IP packet to flow from sender to receiver.

5

- **Jitter:** The variation in delay.
- **Loss:** The percentage of packets discarded by the network before they reach the destination, which when using TCP, requires a retransmission.

- Today's TCP/IP internetworks support many types of applications, and each type has different QoS requirements. Three general categories of applications are batch, interactive, and real time.

  - Batch applications focus more on the bandwidth between two software processes. Batch applications often do not even have a human in the picture.

  - Interactive data applications usually have a human user at one end of a flow, and the IP packets must flow in both directions for meaningful work to happen. For example, the user takes some action, sending a packet to a server; before the user sees more data on the screen, the server must send a packet back. So, the delay and jitter have a big impact on the user experience.

  - Real-time applications, such as voice and video, require low delay, low jitter, and low loss.

- The World Wide Web (WWW) consists of all the Internet-connected web servers in the world, plus all Internet-connected hosts with web browsers.

  - *Web servers*, which consist of web server software running on a computer, store information (in the form of *web pages*) that might be useful to different people.

  - *Web browsers*, which is software installed on an end user's computer, provide the means to connect to a web server and display the web pages stored on the web server.

- The browser user can identify a web page when you click something on a web page or when you enter a Uniform Resource Locator (URL)—often called a *web address* and sometimes a *universal resource locator*—in the browser's address area.

- After a web client (browser) has created a TCP connection to a web server, the client can begin requesting the web page from the server. Usually, the protocol used to transfer the web page is HTTP.

Review Questions

Answer these review questions. You can find the answers at the bottom of the last page of the chapter. For thorough explanations, see DVD Appendix C, "Answers to Review Questions."

1. Which of the following is not a feature of a protocol that is considered to match OSI Layer 4?

   A. Error recovery

   B. Flow control

   C. Segmenting of application data

   D. Conversion from binary to ASCII

2. Which of the following header fields identify which TCP/IP application gets data received by the computer? (Choose two answers.)

   A. Ethernet Type

   B. SNAP Protocol Type

   C. IP Protocol

   D. TCP Port Number

   E. UDP Port Number

3. Which of the following are typical functions of TCP? (Choose four answers.)

   A. Flow Control (windowing)

   B. Error recovery

   C. Multiplexing using port numbers

   D. Routing

   E. Encryption

   F. Ordered data transfer

4. Which of the following functions is performed by both TCP and UDP?

   A. Windowing

   B. Error recovery

   C. Multiplexing using port numbers

   D. Routing

   E. Encryption

   F. Ordered data transfer

5. What do you call data that includes the Layer 4 protocol header, and data given to Layer 4 by the upper layers, not including any headers and trailers from Layers 1 to 3? (Choose two answers.)

   A. L3PDU

   B. Chunk

   C. Segment

   D. Packet

   E. Frame

   F. L4PDU

6. In the URL http://www.certskills.com/ICND1, which part identifies the web server?

   A. http

   B. www.certskills.com

   C. certskills.com

   D. http://www.certskills.com

   E. The file name.html includes the host name.

7. When comparing VoIP with an HTTP-based mission-critical business application, which of the following statements are accurate about the quality of service needed from the network? (Choose two answers.)

   A. VoIP needs better (lower) packet loss.

   B. HTTP needs less bandwidth.

   C. HTTP needs better (lower) jitter.

   D. VoIP needs better (lower) delay.

Review All the Key Topics

Review the most important topics from this chapter, noted with the Key Topic icon. Table 5-4 lists these key topics and where each is discussed.

Table 5-4   Key Topics for Chapter 5

Key Topic Element	Description	Page Number
Table 5-1	Functions of TCP and UDP	101
Table 5-2	Well-known TCP and UDP port numbers	105
Figure 5-5	Example of TCP connection establishment	106
List	Definitions of connection-oriented and connectionless	107

Complete the Tables and Lists from Memory

Print a copy of DVD Appendix M, "Memory Tables," or at least the section for this chapter, and complete the tables and lists from memory. DVD Appendix N, "Memory Tables Answer Key," includes completed tables and lists for you to check your work.

Definitions of Key Terms

After your first reading of the chapter, try to define these key terms, but do not be concerned about getting them all correct at that time. Chapter 30 directs you in how to use these terms for late-stage preparation for the exam.

connection establishment, error detection, error recovery, flow control, forward acknowledgment, HTTP, ordered data transfer, port, segment, sliding windows, URL, VoIP, web server

---

Answers to Review Questions:

1 D **2** D and E **3** A, B, C, and F **4** C **5** C and F **6** B **7** A and D

Part I Review

Keep track of your part review progress with the checklist shown in Table P1-1. Details on each task follow the table.

Table P1-1 Part I Review Checklist

Activity	First Date Completed	Second Date Completed
Repeat all Chapter Review Questions		
Answer Part Review Questions		
Review Key Topics		
Create Terminology Mind Map		

Repeat All Chapter Review Questions

For this task, answer the chapter review questions again for the chapters in this part of the book, using the PCPT software. Refer to the Introduction to this book, heading "How to View Only Chapter Review Questions by Part," for help with how to make the PCPT software show you chapter review questions for this part only.

Answer Part Review Questions

For this task, answer the Part Review questions for this part of the book, using the PCPT software. Refer to the Introduction to this book, heading "How to View Only Part Review Questions by Part," for help with how to make the PCPT software show you Part Review questions for this part only.

Review Key Topics

Key Topic

Browse back through the chapters, and look for the Key Topic icons. If you do not remember some details, take the time to reread those topics.

Create Terminology Mind Maps

The first part of this book introduces a large amount of terminology. The sheer number of terms can be overwhelming. But more and more, while you work through each new chapter, you will become more comfortable with the terms. And the better you can remember the core meaning of a term, the easier your reading will be going forward.

For your first mind map exercise in this book, without looking back at the chapters or your notes, you will create six mind maps. The mind maps will each list a number in the center, 1 through 6, to match the numbers shown in Figure P1-1. Your job is as follows:

- Think of every term that you can remember from Part I of the book.
- Think of each of the six mind maps as being about the item next to the number in Figure P1-1. For example, number 1 is about the user PC, number 2 is about an Ethernet cable that connects PC1 to a switch, and so on.
- Add each term that you can recall to all mind maps to which it applies. For example, "leased line" would apply to mind map number 5.
- If a term seems to apply to multiple places, add it to all those mind maps.
- After you have written every term you can remember into one of the mind maps, review the Key Topics lists at the end of Chapters 1 through 5. Add any terms you forgot to your mind maps.

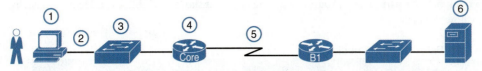

Figure P1-1   *Sample Network to Use with Mind Map Exercise*

The goal of these minds maps is to help you recall the terms with enough meaning to associate the terms with the right part of a simple network design. On your first review of Part I, do not be concerned if you cannot fully explain each term, because you will learn many of these terms more fully just by reading the rest of the book.

> **NOTE**   For more information on mind mapping, refer to the Introduction, in the section "About Mind Maps."

Create the mind maps in Table P1-2 on paper, using any mind-mapping software, or even any drawing application. If you use an application, note the filename and location where you saved the file, for later reference. Sample answers are listed in DVD Appendix O, "Mind Map Solutions."

Table P1-2   Configuration Mind Maps for Part I Review

Map	Description	Where You Saved It
1	Client PC	
2	Ethernet Link	
3	LAN Switch	
4	Router	
5	Leased Line	
6	Server	

Part II discusses how to build a small- to medium-sized Ethernet LAN today. Chapter 6 completes the discussion of Ethernet LAN concepts, building on the introduction to LANs found in Chapter 2. Chapters 7 and 8 unravel how Cisco switches work, first looking at administrative settings, and then discussing settings that impact how the switch forwards Ethernet frames. Chapter 9 moves on to discuss virtual LANs (VLAN), a widely used tool to use one set of switches to create many different LANs. Finally, Chapter 10 discusses how to troubleshoot Ethernet LANs.

Part II

Ethernet LANs and Switches

Chapter 6

Building Ethernet LANs with Switches

While Ethernet defines what happens on each Ethernet link, the more interesting and more detailed work happens on the devices connected to those links: the NICs inside devices and the LAN switches. This chapter takes the Ethernet LAN basics introduced in Chapter 2, "Fundamentals of Ethernet LANs," and dives deeply into many aspects of a modern Ethernet LAN, while focusing on the primary device used to create these LANs: LAN switches.

This chapter breaks down the discussion of Ethernet and LAN switching into two sections. The first major section looks at the logic used by LAN switches when forwarding Ethernet frames, along with the related terminology. The second section considers design and implementation issues, as if you were building a new Ethernet LAN in a building or campus. This second section considers design issues, including using switches for different purposes, when to choose different types of Ethernet links, and how to take advantage of Ethernet autonegotiation.

This chapter covers the following exam topics:

Operation of IP Data Networks

Recognize the purpose and functions of various network devices such as Routers, Switches, Bridges and Hubs.

Select the components required to meet a given network specification.

Predict the data flow between two hosts across a network.

Identify the appropriate media, cables, ports, and connectors to connect Cisco network devices to other network devices and hosts in a LAN

LAN Switching Technologies

Determine the technology and media access control method for Ethernet networks

Identify basic switching concepts and the operation of Cisco switches.

Collision Domains

Broadcast Domains

Types of switching

CAM Table

LAN Switching Concepts

Ethernet switches receive Ethernet frames in one port and then forward (switch) the frames out one (or more) other port. This first major section focuses on how switches make these switching decisions. Along the way, this section discusses several related concepts that you need to know to have a more complete understanding of how switches forward Ethernet frames.

In particular, this section first discusses some older Ethernet LANs, using hubs, so that some current terminology makes more sense. The bulk of this section focuses on the core switch forwarding logic and ends with a short discussion of some options for how switches from Cisco Systems process Ethernet frames internally.

Historical Progression: Hubs, Bridges, and Switches

First, think back to the first UTP-based Ethernet standard, 10BASE-T, introduced in 1990. 10BASE-T used a centralized cabling model similar to today's Ethernet LANs, with each device connecting to the LAN using a UTP cable. However, instead of a LAN switch, the early 10BASE-T networks used hubs, because LAN switches had not yet been created. Figure 6-1 depicts the typical topology for 10BASE-T with a hub.

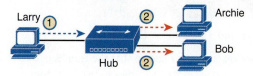

Figure 6-1 *10BASE-T (with a Hub)*

Although using 10BASE-T with a hub improved Ethernet as compared to the older standards, several drawbacks continued to exist, even with 10BASE-T using hubs:

- When hubs receive an electrical signal in one port (step 1 in Figure 6-1), the hub repeats the signal out all other ports (step 2 in the figure).

- When two or more devices send at the same time, an electrical collision occurs, making both signals corrupt.

- As a result, devices must take turns by using carrier sense multiple access with collision detection (CSMA/CD) logic, so the devices share the (10-Mbps) bandwidth.

- Broadcasts sent by one device are heard by, and processed by, all other devices on the LAN.

- Unicast frames are heard by all other devices on the LAN.

Over time, the performance of many Ethernet networks based on hubs started to degrade. People developed applications to take advantage of the LAN bandwidth. More devices were added to each Ethernet. However, the devices on the same Ethernet could not send (collectively) more than 10 Mbps of traffic because they all shared the 10 Mbps of bandwidth. In addition, the increase in traffic volumes resulted in an increased number of collisions, requiring more retransmissions and wasting more LAN capacity.

Ethernet transparent bridges, or simply bridges, helped solve this performance problem with 10BASE-T. After they were added to a 10BASE-T LAN, the following improvements were made:

■ Bridges separated devices into groups called *collision domains*.

■ Bridges reduced the number of collisions that occurred in the network, because frames inside one collision domain did not collide with frames in another collision domain.

■ Bridges increased bandwidth by giving each collision domain its own separate bandwidth, with one sender at a time per collision domain.

Figure 6-2 shows the effect of migrating from using a 10BASE-T hub without a bridge (as in Figure 6-1) to a network that uses a bridge. The bridge in this case separates the network into two separate collision domains (CD).

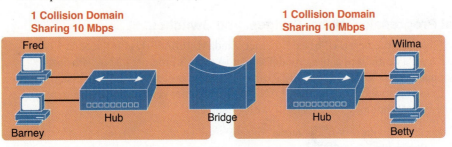

Figure 6-2   *Bridge Creates Two Collision Domains and Two Shared Ethernets*

The bridge, a predecessor to today's Ethernet LAN switch, uses logic so that the frames in one CD do not collide with frames in the other CD. The bridge forwards frames between its two interfaces, and unlike a hub, a bridge will buffer or queue the frame until the outgoing interface can send the frame. For example, Fred and Betty can both send a frame to Barney at the same time, and the bridge will queue the frame sent by Betty, waiting to forward it to the CD on the left, until the CD on the left is not busy.

Adding the bridge in Figure 6-2 really creates two separate 10BASE-T networks—one on the left and one on the right. The 10BASE-T network on the left has its own 10 Mbps to share, as does the network on the right. So, in this example, the total network bandwidth is doubled to 20 Mbps as compared with the 10BASE-T network in Figure 6-1, because devices on each side of the network can send at 10 Mbps at the same time.

LAN switches perform the same basic core functions as bridges, but at much faster speeds and with many enhanced features. Like bridges, switches segment a LAN into separate collision domains, each with its own capacity. And if the network does not have a hub, each single link is considered its own CD, even if no collisions can actually occur in that case.

For example, Figure 6-3 shows a simple LAN with a switch and four PCs. The switch creates four CDs, with the ability to send at 100 Mbps in this case on each of the four links. And with no hubs, each link can run at full-duplex, doubling the capacity of each link.

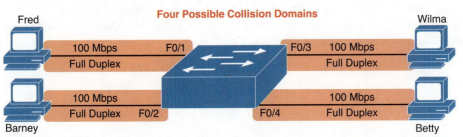

Figure 6-3   *Switch Creates Four Collision Domains and Four Ethernet Segments*

Switching Logic

Ultimately, the role of a LAN switch is to forward Ethernet frames. To achieve that goal, switches use logic—logic based on the source and destination MAC address in each frame's Ethernet header.

This book discusses how switches forward unicast frames and broadcast frames, ignoring multicast Ethernet frames. Unicast frames have a unicast address as a destination; these addresses represent a single device. A broadcast frame has a destination MAC address of FFFF.FFFF.FFFF; this frame should be delivered to all devices on the LAN.

LAN switches receive Ethernet frames and then make a switching decision: either forward the frame out some other port(s) or ignore the frame. To accomplish this primary mission, transparent bridges perform three actions:

1. Deciding when to forward a frame or when to filter (not forward) a frame, based on the destination MAC address.

2. Learning MAC addresses by examining the source MAC address of each frame received by the switch.

3. Creating a (Layer 2) loop-free environment with other switches by using Spanning Tree Protocol (STP).

The first action is the switch's primary job, whereas the other two items are overhead functions. The next sections examine each of these steps in order.

> **NOTE** Throughout this book's discussion of LAN switches, the terms *switch port* and *switch interface* are synonymous.

The Forward-Versus-Filter Decision

To decide whether to forward a frame, a switch uses a dynamically built table that lists MAC addresses and outgoing interfaces. Switches compare the frame's destination MAC address to this table to decide whether the switch should forward a frame or simply ignore it. For example, consider the simple network shown in Figure 6-4, with Fred sending a frame to Barney.

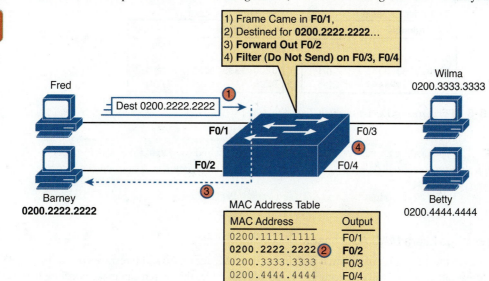

Figure 6-4 *Sample Switch Forwarding and Filtering Decision*

In this figure, Fred sends a frame with destination address 0200.2222.2222 (Barney's MAC address). The switch compares the destination MAC address (0200.2222.2222) to the MAC address table, matching the bold table entry. That matched table entry tells the switch to forward the frame out port F0/2, and only port F0/2.

> **NOTE**   A switch's MAC address table is also called the *switching table*, or *bridging table*, or even the *Content Addressable Memory (CAM)* table, in reference to the type of physical memory used to store the table.

A switch's MAC address table lists the location of each MAC relative to that one switch. In LANs with multiple switches, each switch makes an independent forwarding decision based on its own MAC address table. Together, they forward the frame so that it eventually arrives at the destination.

For example, Figure 6-5 shows the same four PCs as in Figure 6-4, but now with two LAN switches. In this case, Fred sends a frame to Wilma, with destination MAC 0200.3333.3333. Switch SW1 sends the frame out its G0/1 port, per SW1's MAC address table. Then at Step 2, switch SW2 forwards the frame out its F0/3 port, based on SW2's MAC address table.

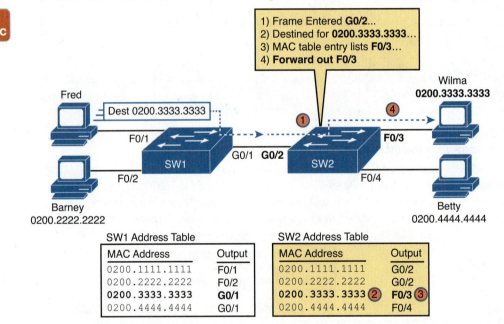

Figure 6-5   *Forwarding Decision with Two Switches*

> **NOTE**   The forwarding choice by a switch was formerly called a *forward-versus-filter* decision, because the switch also chooses to not forward (to filter) frames, not sending the frame out some ports.

How Switches Learn MAC Addresses

The second main function of a switch is to learn the MAC addresses and interfaces to put into its address table. With a full and accurate MAC address table, the switch can make accurate forwarding and filtering decisions.

Switches build the address table by listening to incoming frames and examining the *source MAC address* in the frame. If a frame enters the switch and the source MAC address is not in the MAC address table, the switch creates an entry in the table. That table entry lists the interface from which the frame arrived. Switch learning logic is that simple.

Figure 6-6 depicts the same network as Figure 6-4, but before the switch has built any address table entries. The figure shows the first two frames sent in this network—first a frame from Fred, addressed to Barney, and then Barney's response, addressed to Fred.

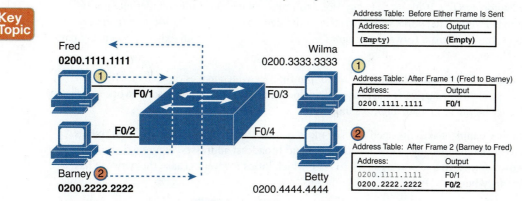

Figure 6-6   *Switch Learning: Empty Table and Adding Two Entries*

As shown in the figure, after Fred sends his first frame (labeled "1") to Barney, the switch adds an entry for 0200.1111.1111, Fred's MAC address, associated with interface F0/1. When Barney replies in Step 2, the switch adds a second entry, this one for 0200.2222.2222, Barney's MAC address, along with interface F0/2, which is the interface in which the switch received the frame. Learning always occurs by looking at the source MAC address in the frame.

Switches keep a timer for each entry in the MAC address table, called an *inactivity timer*. The switch sets the timer to 0 for new entries. Each time the switch receives another frame with that same source MAC address, the timer is reset to 0. The timer counts upward, so the switch can tell which entries have gone the longest time since receiving a frame from that device. The switch then removes entries from the table when they become old. Or, if the switch ever runs out of space for entries in the MAC address table, the switch can then remove table entries with the oldest (largest) inactivity timers.

Flooding Frames

Now again turn your attention to the forwarding process, using Figure 6-6. What do you suppose the switch does with Fred's first frame in Figure 6-6, the one that occurred when there were no entries in the MAC address table? As it turns out, when there is no matching entry in the table, switches forward the frame out all interfaces (except the incoming interface) using a process called *flooding*.

Switches flood *unknown unicast frames* (frames whose destination MAC addresses are not yet in the address table). Flooding means that the switch forwards copies of the frame out all ports, except the port on which the frame was received. If the unknown device receives the frame and sends a reply, the reply frame's source MAC address will allow the switch to build a correct MAC table entry for that device.

Switches also forward LAN broadcast frames, because this process helps deliver a copy of the frame to all devices in the LAN.

For example, Figure 6-6 shows the first frame, sent to Barney's MAC address, just going to Barney. However, in reality, the switch floods this frame out F0/2, F0/3, and F0/4, even though 0200.2222.2222 (Barney) is only off F0/2. The switch does not forward the frame back out F0/1, because a switch never forwards a frame out the same interface on which it arrived.

Avoiding Loops Using Spanning Tree Protocol

The third primary feature of LAN switches is loop prevention, as implemented by *Spanning Tree Protocol (STP)*. Without STP, any flooded frames would loop for an indefinite period of time in Ethernet networks with physically redundant links. To prevent looping frames, STP blocks some ports from forwarding frames so that only one active path exists between any pair of LAN segments.

The result of STP is good: Frames do not loop infinitely, which makes the LAN usable. However, STP has negative features as well, including the fact that it takes some work to balance traffic across the redundant alternate links.

A simple example makes the need for STP more obvious. Remember, switches flood frames sent to both unknown unicast MAC addresses and broadcast addresses. Figure 6-7 shows an unknown unicast frame, sent by Larry to Bob, which loops forever because the network has redundancy but no STP.

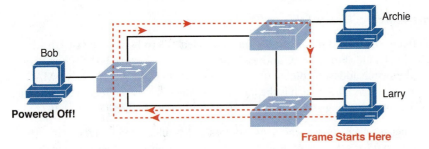

Figure 6-7 *Network with Redundant Links but Without STP: The Frame Loops Forever*

Because none of the switches list Bob's MAC address in their address tables, each switch floods the frame. A physical loop exists through the three switches. The switches keep forwarding the frame out all ports, and copies of the frame go around and around.

To avoid Layer 2 loops, all switches need to use STP. STP causes each interface on a switch to settle into either a blocking state or a forwarding state. *Blocking* means that the interface cannot forward or receive data frames, while *forwarding* means that the interface can send and receive data frames. If a correct subset of the interfaces is blocked, only a single currently active logical path exists between each pair of LANs.

> **NOTE**   STP behaves identically for a transparent bridge and a switch. Therefore, the terms *bridge*, *switch*, and *bridging device* all are used interchangeably when discussing STP.

Chapters 1 and 2 in the *Cisco CCNA Routing and Switching ICND2 200-101 Official Cert Guide*, Academic Edition cover the details of how STP prevents loops.

Internal Processing on Cisco Switches

This chapter has already explained how switches decide whether to forward or filter a frame. As soon as a Cisco switch decides to forward a frame, the switch can use a couple of different types of internal processing variations. Almost all of the more recently released switches use store-and-forward processing, but all three types of these internal processing methods are supported in at least one type of Cisco switch.

Some switches, and transparent bridges in general, use *store-and-forward processing*. With store-and-forward, the switch must receive the entire frame before forwarding the first bit of the frame. However, Cisco also offers two other internal processing methods for switches: *cut-through* and *fragment-free*. Because the destination MAC address occurs very early in the Ethernet header, a switch can make a forwarding decision long before the switch has received all the bits in the frame. The cut-through and fragment-free processing methods allow the switch to start forwarding the frame before the entire frame has been received, reducing time required to send the frame (the latency, or delay).

With *cut-through* processing, the switch starts sending the frame out the output port as soon as possible. Although this might reduce latency, it also propagates errors. Because the Frame Check Sequence (FCS) is in the Ethernet trailer, the switch cannot determine whether the frame had any errors before starting to forward the frame. So, the switch reduces the frame's latency, but with the price of having forwarded some frames that contain errors.

Fragment-free processing works similarly to cut-through, but it tries to reduce the number of errored frames that it forwards. One interesting fact about Ethernet CSMA/CD logic is that collisions should be detected within the first 64 bytes of a frame. Fragment-free processing works like cut-through logic, but it waits to receive the first 64 bytes before forwarding a frame. The frames experience less latency than with store-and-forward logic and slightly more latency than with cut-through, but frames that have errors as a result of collisions are not forwarded.

With many links to the desktop running at 100 Mbps, uplinks at 1 Gbps, and faster application-specific integrated circuits (ASIC), today's switches typically use store-and-forward processing, because the improved latency of the other two switching methods is negligible at these speeds.

The internal processing algorithms used by switches vary among models and vendors; regardless, the internal processing can be categorized as one of the methods listed in Table 6-1.

Table 6-1   Switch Internal Processing

Switching Method	Description
Store-and-forward	The switch fully receives all bits in the frame (store) before forwarding the frame (forward). This allows the switch to check the FCS before forwarding the frame.
Cut-through	The switch forwards the frame as soon as it can. This reduces latency but does not allow the switch to discard frames that fail the FCS check.
Fragment-free	The switch forwards the frame after receiving the first 64 bytes of the frame, thereby avoiding forwarding frames that were errored because of a collision.

LAN Switching Summary

Switches provide many additional features not offered by older LAN devices such as hubs and bridges. In particular, LAN switches provide the following benefits:

- Switch ports connected to a single device microsegment the LAN, providing dedicated bandwidth to that single device.
- Switches allow multiple simultaneous conversations between devices on different ports.

- Switch ports connected to a single device support full-duplex, in effect doubling the amount of bandwidth available to the device.

- Switches support rate adaptation, which means that devices that use different Ethernet speeds can communicate through the switch (hubs cannot).

Switches use Layer 2 logic, examining the Ethernet data link header to choose how to process frames. In particular, switches make decisions to forward and filter frames, learn MAC address-es, and use STP to avoid loops, as follows:

Step 1. Switches forward frames based on the destination address:

    A. If the destination address is a broadcast, multicast, or unknown destination uni-cast (a unicast not listed in the MAC table), the switch floods the frame.

    B. If the destination address is a known unicast address (a unicast address found in the MAC table):

        i. If the outgoing interface listed in the MAC address table is different from the interface in which the frame was received, the switch forwards the frame out the outgoing interface.

        ii. If the outgoing interface is the same as the interface in which the frame was received, the switch filters the frame, meaning that the switch simply ignores the frame and does not forward it.

Step 2. Switches use the following logic to learn MAC address table entries:

    A. For each received frame, examine the source MAC address and note the inter-face from which the frame was received.

    B. If it is not already in the table, add the MAC address and interface it was learned on, setting the inactivity timer to 0.

    C. If it is already in the table, reset the inactivity timer for the entry to 0.

Step 3. Switches use STP to prevent loops by causing some interfaces to block, meaning that they do not send or receive frames.

Design Choices in Ethernet LANs

The first of the two major sections of this chapter explained the details of how LAN switches work. The second major section now examines a variety of topics related to LAN design.

This section moves around between many different topics. The first topic explains the concept of collision domains as compared to broadcast domains, both of which impact LAN perfor-mance. These two topics give you enough background to then understand the most commonly used tool mentioned in this section: virtual LANs (VLAN). Then this section examines some Ethernet LAN design issues, and closes with how to more easily migrate Ethernet LANs over time to use the latest standards by using autonegotiation.

Collision Domains, Broadcast Domains, and VLANs

When creating any Ethernet LAN today, you use LAN switches and routers. You also have to think about older legacy devices like hubs and bridges, just in case some still exist. The differ-ent parts of an Ethernet LAN can behave differently, in terms of function and performance, depending on which types of devices are used. These differences then affect a network engi-neer's decision when choosing how to design a LAN.

The terms *collision domain* and *broadcast domain* define two important effects of the process of segmenting LANs using various devices. This section defines these terms to explain how hubs, switches, and routers impact collision domains and broadcast domains.

Collision Domains

Originally, the term *collision domain* referred to an Ethernet concept of all ports whose transmitted frames would cause a collision with frames sent by other devices in the collision domain. To review the core concept, Figure 6-8 illustrates collision domains.

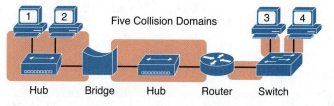

Figure 6-8   *Collision Domains*

> **NOTE**   The LAN design in Figure 6-8 is not a typical design today. Instead, it simply provides enough information to help you compare hubs, switches, and routers.

First, pay attention to the devices in the figure. Of the four types of networking devices in the figure, only the hub allows a CD to spread from one side of the device to the other. The rest of the networking devices (routers, switches, bridges) all separate the LAN into separate ports.

Today, modern networks might not allow a collision to physically occur, but we still describe links as being in separate CDs. For example, consider the link from the switch to PC3. Physically, no collision could possibly occur. However, if PC3 and the LAN switch both enabled half-duplex, which uses CSMA/CD, they would consider their frames to collide if they were sent and received at the same time. So even today, we still talk about collision domains.

Broadcast Domains

Take any Ethernet LAN, and pick any device. Then think of that device sending an Ethernet broadcast. An Ethernet *broadcast domain* is the set of devices to which that broadcast is delivered.

Of all the network devices shown in Figure 6-8, only routers separate the LAN into multiple broadcast domains. LAN switches flood Ethernet broadcast frames, extending the scope of the broadcast domain. Routers do not forward Ethernet broadcast frames, either ignoring the frames, or processing and then discarding some broadcast from some overhead protocols used by routers. (Of the older Ethernet devices, bridges act like switches with broadcasts, and hubs repeat the signal, again not stopping the broadcasts.)

For perspective, Figure 6-9 provides the broadcast domains for the same network depicted in Figure 6-8.

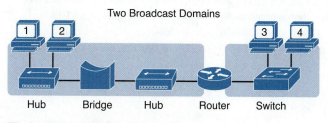
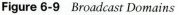

Figure 6-9   *Broadcast Domains*

By definition, broadcasts sent by a device in one broadcast domain are not forwarded to devices in another broadcast domain. In this example, there are two broadcast domains. For example, the router does not forward a LAN broadcast sent by a PC on the left to the network segment on the right.

General definitions for a collision domain and a broadcast domain are as follows:

Key Topic

■ A *collision domain* is a set of network interface cards (NIC) for which a frame sent by one NIC could result in a collision with a frame sent by any other NIC in the same collision domain.

■ A *broadcast domain* is a set of NICs for which a broadcast frame sent by one NIC is received by all other NICs in the same broadcast domain.

The Impact of Collision and Broadcast Domains on LAN Design

When designing a LAN, you need to keep in mind the trade-offs when choosing the number of devices in each collision domain and broadcast domain. First, consider the devices in a single collision domain for a moment. For a single collision domain:

■ The devices share the available bandwidth.

■ The devices might inefficiently use that bandwidth because of the effects of collisions, particularly under higher utilization.

For perspective on the impact of collision domains, it helps to compare an old design using LAN hubs to a newer design that uses the same speeds for each link, but instead uses a LAN switch. Consider a design with ten PCs, with each link using 100BASE-T. With a hub, only one PC can send at a time, for a theoretical maximum capacity of 100 Mbps for the entire LAN. Replace the hub with a switch, and you get

■ 100 Mbps per link, for a total of 1000 Mbps (1 Gbps)

■ The ability to use full-duplex on each link, effectively doubling the capacity to 2000 Mbps (2 Gbps)

The example of using hubs versus switches is admittedly a little old, but it shows one reason why no one chooses to use hubs, and why vendors now sell switches instead of hubs.

Now consider the issue of broadcasts. When a host receives a broadcast, the host must process the received frame. This means that the NIC must interrupt the computer's CPU, and the CPU must spend time thinking about the received broadcast frame. All hosts need to send some broadcasts to function properly. (For example, IP ARP messages are LAN broadcasts, as mentioned in Chapter 4, "Fundamentals of IPv4 Addressing and Routing.") So, broadcasts happen, which is good, but broadcasts do require all the hosts to spend time processing each broadcast frame.

Next, consider a large LAN, with multiple switches with all ports assigned to the same virtual LAN (by default), with 500 PCs total. The switches create a single broadcast domain, so a broadcast sent by any of the 500 hosts should be sent to, and then processed by, all 499 other hosts. Depending on the number of broadcasts, the broadcasts could start to impact performance of the end-user PCs. However, a design that separated the 500 PCs into five groups of 100, separated from each other by a router, would create five broadcast domains. Now, a broadcast by one host would interrupt only 99 other hosts, and not the other 400 hosts, resulting in generally better performance on the PCs.

> **NOTE**   Using smaller broadcast domains can also improve security, because of limiting broadcasts and because of robust security features in routers.

The choice about when to use a hub versus a switch was straightforward, but the choice of when to use a router to break up a large broadcast domain is more difficult. A meaningful discussion of the trade-offs and options is beyond the scope of this book. However, you should understand the concepts behind broadcast domains—specifically, that a router breaks LANs into multiple broadcast domains, but switches and hubs do not.

More importantly for the CCNA exams, you should be ready to react to questions in terms of the benefits of LAN segmentation instead of just asking for the facts related to collision domains and broadcast domains. Table 6-2 lists some of the key benefits. The features in the table should be interpreted within the following context: "Which of the following benefits are gained by using a hub/switch/router between Ethernet devices?" The table assumes all switch ports are in the same VLAN.

Table 6-2   Benefits of Segmenting Ethernet Devices Using Hubs, Switches, and Routers

Feature	Hub	Switch	Router
Greater cabling distances are allowed	Yes	Yes	Yes
Creates multiple collision domains	No	Yes	Yes
Increases bandwidth	No	Yes	Yes
Creates multiple broadcast domains	No	No	Yes

Virtual LANs (VLAN)

Most every enterprise network today uses the concept of virtual LANs (VLAN). Before understanding VLANs, you must have a very specific understanding of the definition of a LAN. Although you can think about and define the term "LAN" from many perspectives, one perspective in particular will help you understand VLANs:

   A LAN consists of all devices in the same broadcast domain.

Without VLANs, a switch considers all interfaces on the switch, and the devices connected to those links, to be in the same broadcast domain. In other words, all connected devices are in the same LAN. (Cisco switches accomplish this by putting all interfaces in VLAN 1 by default.)

With VLANs, a switch groups interfaces into different VLANs (broadcast domains) based on configuration, with each interface in a specific VLAN. Essentially, the switch creates multiple broadcast domains by putting some interfaces into one VLAN and other interfaces into other VLANs. So, instead of all ports on a switch forming a single broadcast domain, the switch separates them into many, based on configuration. It's really that simple.

The next two figures compare two LANs for the purpose of explaining a little more about VLANs. First, before VLANs existed, if a design specified two separate broadcast domains, two switches would be used—one for each broadcast domain, as shown in Figure 6-10.

Figure 6-10 *Sample Network with Two Broadcast Domains and No VLANs*

Alternately, you can create multiple broadcast domains using a single switch. Figure 6-11 shows the same two broadcast domains as in Figure 6-10, now implemented as two different VLANs on a single switch.

Key Topic

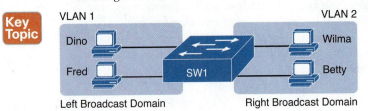

Figure 6-11 *Sample Network with Two VLANs Using One Switch*

This section briefly introduces the concept of VLANs, but Chapter 9, "Implementing Ethernet Virtual LANs," discusses VLANs in more depth, including the details of how to configure VLANs in campus LANs.

Choosing Ethernet Technology for a Campus LAN

The term *campus LAN* refers to the LAN created to support larger buildings, or multiple buildings in somewhat close proximity to one another. For example, a company might lease office space in several buildings in the same office park. The network engineers can then build a campus LAN that includes switches in each building, plus Ethernet links between the switches in the buildings, to create a larger campus LAN.

When planning and designing a campus LAN, the engineers must consider the types of Ethernet available and the cabling lengths supported by each type. The engineers also need to choose the speeds required for each Ethernet segment. Additionally, some thought needs to be given to the idea that some switches should be used to connect directly to end-user devices, whereas other switches might need to simply connect to a large number of these end-user switches. Finally, most projects require that the engineer consider the type of equipment that is already installed and whether an increase in speed on some segments is worth the cost of buying new equipment.

This section discusses campus LAN design. It begins with some terminology Cisco uses for campus LAN design. Then, the text looks at the choice of what Ethernet standards to use for each link in the campus LAN, and why you might choose one versus another. This section ends with a popular tool to allow easy migration from older to newer (faster) Ethernet links using an Ethernet feature called autonegotiation.

Campus Design Terminology

To sift through all the requirements for a campus LAN, and then have a reasonable conversation about it with peers, most Cisco-oriented LAN designs use some common terminology to refer to the design. For this book's purposes, you should be aware of some of the key campus LAN design terminology.

Figure 6-12 shows a typical design of a large campus LAN, with the terminology included in the figure. This LAN has around 1000 PCs connected to switches that support around 25 ports each. Explanations of the terminology follow the figure.

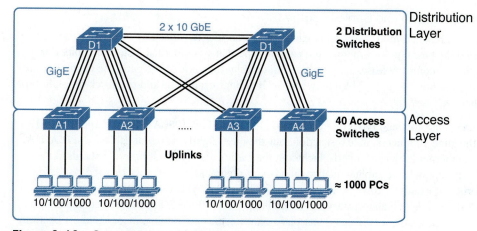

Figure 6-12 *Campus LAN with Design Terminology Listed*

Cisco uses three terms to describe the role of each switch in a campus design: *access*, *distribution*, and *core*. The roles differ based on whether the switch forwards traffic from user devices and the rest of the LAN (access), or whether the switch forwards traffic between other LAN switches (distribution and core).

Access switches connect directly to end users, providing user device access to the LAN. Access switches normally send traffic to and from the end-user devices to which they are connected and sit at the edge of the LAN.

In larger campus LANs, *distribution switches* provide a path through which the access switches can forward traffic to each other. By design, each of the access switches connects to at least one distribution switch, relying on distribution switches to forward traffic to other parts of the LAN. Note that most designs use at least two uplinks to two different distribution switches (as shown in Figure 6-12) for redundancy.

Using designs that connect a larger number of access switches to a small number of distribution switches reduces cabling needs while still allowing all devices to send data to all other devices in the LAN. For example, in Figure 6-12, the design could use a pair of links from each access switch to each of the two distribution switches, providing a great deal of redundancy. With four links for each of 40 access switches, the design uses 160 uplinks. If the design instead did not use distribution switches, to connect a single link between each pair of access switches would require 780 links.

The largest campus LANs often use *core switches* to forward traffic between distribution switches. For example, imagine a campus in which you had a LAN like Figure 6-12 in 12 buildings in the same office park. You could add two additional core switches, that serve a similar role as the distribution switches, connecting every distribution switch to the core. However, medium to smaller campus LANs often forego the concept of core switches.

The following list summarizes the terms that describe the roles of campus switches:

■ **Access:** Provides a connection point (access) for end-user devices. Does not forward frames between two other access switches under normal circumstances.

■ **Distribution:** Provides an aggregation point for access switches, forwarding frames between switches, but not connecting directly to end-user devices.

■ **Core:** Aggregates distribution switches in very large campus LANs, providing very high forwarding rates.

Ethernet LAN Media and Cable Lengths

When designing a campus LAN, an engineer must consider the length of each cable run and then find the best type of Ethernet and cabling type that supports that length of cable. For example, if a company leases space in five buildings in the same office park, the engineer needs to figure out how long the cables between the buildings need to be and then pick the right type of Ethernet.

The three most common types of Ethernet today (10BASE-T, 100BASE-T, and 1000BASE-T) have the same 100-meter cable restriction, but they use slightly different cables. The EIA/TIA defines Ethernet cabling standards, including the cable's quality. Each Ethernet standard that uses UTP cabling lists a cabling quality category as the minimum category that the standard supports. For example, 10BASE-T allows for Category 3 (CAT3) cabling or better, whereas 100BASE-T calls for higher-quality CAT5 cabling, and 1000BASE-T requires even higher-quality CAT5e or CAT6 cabling. If an engineer plans on using existing cabling, he or she must be aware of the types of UTP cables and the speed restrictions implied by the type of Ethernet the cabling supports.

Several types of Ethernet define the use of fiber-optic cables. UTP cables include copper wires over which electrical currents can flow, whereas optical cables include ultrathin strands of glass through which light can pass. To send bits, the switches can alternate between sending brighter and dimmer light to encode 0s and 1s on the cable.

Optical cables support a variety of much longer distances than the 100 meters supported by Ethernet on UTP cables. Optical cables experience much less interference from outside sources as compared to copper cables. Additionally, switches can use lasers to generate the light, as well as light-emitting diodes (LED). Lasers allow for even longer cabling distances, in the thousands of meters, at higher cost, whereas less-expensive LEDs might well support plenty of distance for campus LANs in most office parks.

Finally, the type of optical cabling can also impact the maximum distances per cable. Of the two types, multimode fiber supports shorter distances, but it is generally cheaper cabling and it works fine with less-expensive LEDs. The other optical cabling type, single-mode fiber, supports the longest distances but is more expensive. Also note that LED-based hardware, often used with multimode fiber, is much less expensive than laser-based hardware, often used with single-mode fiber.

Table 6-3 lists the more common types of Ethernet and their cable types and length limitations.

Table 6-3 Ethernet Types, Media, and Segment Lengths (Per IEEE)

Ethernet Type	Media	Maximum Segment Length
10BASE-T	TIA CAT3 or better, two pair	100 m (328 feet)
100BASE-T	TIA CAT5 UTP or better, two pair	100 m (328 feet)
1000BASE-T	TIA CAT5e UTP or better, four pair	100 m (328 feet)
1000BASE-SX	Multimode fiber	550 m (1804.5 feet) for 50-micron fiber
1000BASE-LX	Multimode fiber	550 m (1804.5 feet) for 50- and 62.5-micron fiber
1000BASE-LX	9-micron single-mode fiber	5 km (3.1 miles)

Most engineers simply remember the general distance limitations and then use a reference chart (such as Table 6-4) to remember each specific detail. An engineer must also consider the physical paths that the cables will use to run through a campus or building and the impact on the required cable length. For example, a cable might have to run from one end of the building to the other, then through a conduit that connects the floors of the building, and then horizontally to a wiring closet on another floor. Often those paths are not the shortest way to get from one place to the other. So, the chart's details are important to the LAN planning process and the resulting choice of LAN media.

Autonegotiation

Ethernet devices on the ends of a link must use the same standard or they cannot correctly send data. For example, a NIC cannot use 100BASE-T, which uses a two-pair UTP cable with a 100-Mbps speed, while the switch port on the other end of the link uses 1000BASE-T. Even if you used a cable that works with Gigabit Ethernet, the link would not work with one end trying to send at 100 Mbps while the other tried to receive the data at 1000 Mbps.

Upgrading to new and faster Ethernet standards becomes a problem because both ends have to use the same standard. For example, if you replace an old PC with a new one, the old one might have been using 100BASE-T while the new one uses 1000BASE-T. The switch port on the other end of the link needs to now use 1000BASE-T, so you upgrade the switch. If that switch had ports that would only use 1000BASE-T, you would need to upgrade all the other PCs connected to the switch.

The IEEE gives us a nice solution to this migration problem: IEEE autonegotiation. IEEE autonegotiation (IEEE standard 802.3u) defines a protocol that lets the two UTP-based Ethernet nodes on a link negotiate so that they each choose to use the same speed and duplex settings. The protocol messages flow outside the normal Ethernet electrical frequencies as out-of-band signals over the UTP cable. Basically, each node states what it can do, and then each node picks the best options that both nodes support: the fastest speed and the best duplex setting, with full-duplex being better than half-duplex.

> **NOTE** Autonegotiation relies on the fact that the IEEE uses the same wiring pinouts for 10BASE-T and 100BASE-T, and that 1000BASE-T simply adds to those pinouts, adding two pair.

Many networks use autonegotiation every day, particularly between user devices and the access layer LAN switches, as shown in Figure 6-13. The company installed four-pair cabling to be ready to support Gigabit Ethernet, so the wiring works for the 10-Mbps, 100-Mbps, and 1000-Mbps Ethernet options. Both nodes on each link send autonegotiation messages to each other. The switch in this case has all 10/100/1000 ports, while the PC NICs support different options.

6

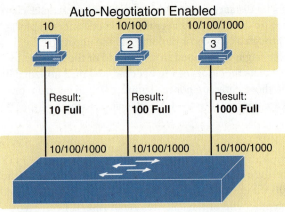

Figure 6-13   *IEEE Autonegotiation Results with Both Nodes Working Correctly*

The following list breaks down the logic, one PC at a time:

PC1: The switch port claims it can go as fast as 1000 Mbps, but PC1's NIC claims a top speed of 10 Mbps. Both the PC and switch choose the best speed both support (10 Mbps) and the best duplex (full).

PC2: PC2 claims a best speed of 100 Mbps, which means it can use 10BASE-T or 100BASE-T. The switch port and NIC negotiate to use the best speed of 100 Mbps and full-duplex.

PC3: It uses a 10/100/1000 NIC, supporting all three speeds and standards, so both the NIC and switch port choose 1000 Mbps and full-duplex.

Autonegotiation Results When Only One Node Uses Autonegotiation

Figure 6-13 shows the IEEE autonegotiation results when both nodes use the process. However, most Ethernet devices can disable autonegotiation, so it is just as important to know what happens when a node tries to use autonegotiation but the node gets no response.

Disabling autonegotiation is not always a bad idea, but generally you should either use it on both ends of the link or disable it on both ends of the link. For example, many network engineers disable autonegotiation on links between switches and simply configure the desired speed and duplex on both switches. If enabled on both ends of the link, the nodes should pick the best speed and duplex. However, when enabled on only one end, many issues can arise: The link might not work at all, or it might just work poorly.

IEEE autonegotiation defines some rules (defaults) that nodes should use when autonegotiation fails, as follows:

■ **Speed:** Use your slowest supported speed (often 10 Mbps).

■ **Duplex:** If your speed = 10 or 100, use half-duplex; otherwise, use full-duplex.

Cisco switches also add to the base IEEE logic, because Cisco switches can actually sense the speed used by other node, even without IEEE autonegotiation. As a result, Cisco switches use this slightly different logic when autonegotiation fails:

Key Topic

■ **Speed:** Sense the speed (without using autonegotiation), or if that fails, use the IEEE default (slowest supported speed, often 10 Mbps).

■ **Duplex:** Use the IEEE defaults: If speed = 10 or 100, use half-duplex; otherwise, use full-duplex.

Figure 6-14 shows three examples in which three users change their NIC settings and disable autonegotiation. The switch has all 10/100/1000 ports, with autonegotiation enabled. The top of the figure shows the configured settings on each PC NIC, with the choices made by the switch listed next to each switch port.

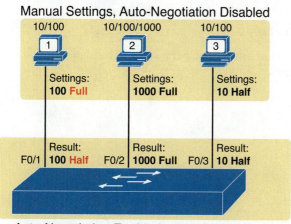

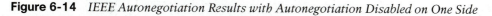

Figure 6-14 *IEEE Autonegotiation Results with Autonegotiation Disabled on One Side*

Reviewing each link, left to right:

- **PC1:** The switch receives no autonegotiation messages, so it senses the electrical signal to learn that PC1 is sending data at 100 Mbps. The switch uses the IEEE default duplex based on the 100 Mbps speed (half-duplex).

- **PC2:** The switch uses the same steps and logic as with the link to PC1, except that the switch chooses to use full-duplex, because the speed is 1000 Mbps.

- **PC3:** The user picks poorly, choosing the slower speed (10 Mbps) and the worse duplex setting (half). However, the Cisco switch senses the speed without using IEEE autonegotiation and then uses the IEEE duplex default for 10-Mbps links (half-duplex).

PC1 shows a classic and unfortunately common end result: a *duplex mismatch*. The two nodes (PC1 and SW1's port F0/1) both use 100 Mbps, so they can send data. However, PC1, using full-duplex, does not attempt to use CSMA/CD logic and sends frames at any time. Switch port F0/1, with half-duplex, does use CSMA/CD. As a result, switch port F0/1 will believe collisions occur on the link, even if none physically occur. The switch port will stop transmitting, back off, resend frames, and so on. As a result, the link is up, but it performs poorly.

Autonegotiation and LAN Hubs

LAN hubs also impact how autonegotiation works. Basically, hubs do not react to autonegotiation messages, and they do not forward the messages. As a result, devices connected to a hub must use the IEEE rules for choosing default settings, which often results in the devices using 10 Mbps and half-duplex.

Figure 6-15 shows an example of a small Ethernet LAN that uses a 20-year-old 10BASE-T hub. In this LAN, all devices and switch ports are 10/100/1000 ports. The hub supports only 10BASE-T.

Figure 6-15 *IEEE Autonegotiation with a LAN Hub*

Note that the devices on the right need to use half-duplex, because the hub requires the use of the CSMA/CD algorithm to avoid collisions.

Review Activities

Chapter Summary

- Ethernet switches receive Ethernet frames in one port, and then forward (switch) the frames out one (or more) other port.

- LAN switches receive Ethernet frames and then make a switching decision: either forward the frame out some other ports or ignore the frame. To accomplish this primary mission, transparent bridges perform three actions:

  - Deciding when to forward a frame or when to filter (not forward) a frame, based on the destination MAC address

  - Learning MAC addresses by examining the source MAC address of each frame received by the bridge

  - Creating a (Layer 2) loop-free environment with other bridges by using Spanning Tree Protocol (STP)

- To decide whether to forward a frame, a switch uses a dynamically built table that lists MAC addresses and outgoing interfaces. Switches compare the frame's destination MAC address to this table to decide whether the switch should forward a frame to a single port or flood it out all ports except the port on which it received it.

- Switches build the address table by listening to incoming frames and examining the source MAC address in the frame. If a frame enters the switch and the source MAC address is not in the MAC address table, the switch creates an entry in the table. That table entry lists the interface from which the frame arrived. Switch learning logic is that simple.

- When there is no matching entry in the table, switches forward the frame out all interfaces (except the incoming interface) using a process called *flooding*.

- The third primary feature of LAN switches is loop prevention, as implemented by Spanning Tree Protocol (STP). Without STP, any flooded frames would loop for an indefinite period of time in Ethernet networks with physically redundant links. To prevent looping frames, STP blocks some ports from forwarding frames so that only one active path exists between any pair of LAN segments.

- With *store-and-forward* processing, the switch must receive the entire frame before forwarding the first bit of the frame.

- With *cut-through* processing, the switch starts sending the frame out the output port as soon as possible. Although this might reduce latency, it also propagates errors. Because the frame check sequence (FCS) is in the Ethernet trailer, the switch cannot determine whether the frame had any errors before starting to forward the frame. So, the switch reduces the frame's latency, but with the price of having forwarded some frames that contain errors.

- *Fragment-free* processing works similarly to cut-through, but it tries to reduce the number of errored frames that it forwards. One interesting fact about Ethernet carrier sense multiple access with collision detection (CSMA/CD) logic is that collisions should be detected within the first 64 bytes of a frame. Fragment-free processing works like cut-through logic, but it waits to receive the first 64 bytes before forwarding a frame. The frames experience less latency than with store-and-forward logic and slightly more latency than with cut-through, but frames that have errors as a result of collisions are not forwarded.

- The term *collision domain* refers to an Ethernet concept of all ports whose transmitted frames would cause a collision with frames sent by other devices in the collision domain.

- An Ethernet *broadcast domain* is the set of devices to which that broadcast is delivered.

- By definition, broadcasts sent by a device in one broadcast domain are not forwarded to devices in another broadcast domain.

- Most Enterprise networks today use the concept of virtual LANs (VLAN). With VLANs, a switch groups interfaces into different VLANs (broadcast domains) based on configuration, with each interface in a different VLAN. Essentially, the switch creates multiple broadcast domains by putting some interfaces into one VLAN and other interfaces into other VLANs. So, instead of all ports on a switch forming a single broadcast domain, the switch separates them into many, based on configuration.

- The term *campus LAN* refers to the LAN created to support larger buildings or multiple buildings in somewhat close proximity to one another.

- Cisco uses three terms to describe the role of each switch in a campus design: *access*, *distribution*, and *core*.

  - *Access switches* connect directly to end users, providing user device access to the LAN. Access switches normally send traffic to and from the end-user devices to which they are connected, and sit at the edge of the LAN.

  - *Distribution switches* provide a path through which the access switches can forward traffic to each other. By design, each access switch connects to at least one distribution switch, relying on distribution switches to forward traffic to other parts of the LAN.

  - *Core switches* are used to forward traffic between distribution switches.

- IEEE autonegotiation (IEEE standard 802.3u) defines a protocol that lets the two UTP-based Ethernet nodes on a link negotiate so that they each choose to use the same speed and duplex settings.

Review Questions

Answer these review questions. You can find the answers at the bottom of the last page of the chapter. For thorough explanations, see DVD Appendix C, "Answers to Review Questions."

1. Which of the following statements describes part of the process of how a switch decides to forward a frame destined for a known unicast MAC address?

   A. It compares the unicast destination address to the bridging, or MAC address, table.

   B. It compares the unicast source address to the bridging, or MAC address, table.

   C. It forwards the frame out all interfaces in the same VLAN except for the incoming interface.

   D. It compares the destination IP address to the destination MAC address.

   E. It compares the frame's incoming interface to the source MAC entry in the MAC address table.

2. Which of the following statements describes part of the process of how a LAN switch decides to forward a frame destined for a broadcast MAC address?

   A. It compares the unicast destination address to the bridging, or MAC address, table.

   B. It compares the unicast source address to the bridging, or MAC address, table.

   C. It forwards the frame out all interfaces in the same VLAN except for the incoming interface.

   D. It compares the destination IP address to the destination MAC address.

   E. It compares the frame's incoming interface to the source MAC entry in the MAC address table.

3. Which of the following statements best describes what a switch does with a frame destined for an unknown unicast address?

   A. It forwards out all interfaces in the same VLAN except for the incoming interface.

   B. It forwards the frame out the one interface identified by the matching entry in the MAC address table.

   C. It compares the destination IP address to the destination MAC address.

   D. It compares the frame's incoming interface to the source MAC entry in the MAC address table.

4. Which of the following comparisons does a switch make when deciding whether a new MAC address should be added to its MAC address table?

   A. It compares the unicast destination address to the bridging, or MAC address, table.

   B. It compares the unicast source address to the bridging, or MAC address, table.

   C. It compares the VLAN ID to the bridging, or MAC address, table.

   D. It compares the destination IP address's ARP cache entry to the bridging, or MAC address, table.

5. PC1, with MAC address 1111.1111.1111, is connected to Switch SW1's Fa0/1 interface. PC2, with MAC address 2222.2222.2222, is connected to SW1's Fa0/2 interface. PC3, with MAC address 3333.3333.3333, connects to SW1's Fa0/3 interface. The switch begins with no dynamically learned MAC addresses, followed by PC1 sending a frame with a destination address of 2222.2222.2222. If the next frame to reach the switch is a frame sent by PC3, destined for PC2's MAC address of 2222.2222.2222, which of the following are true? (Choose two answers.)

   A. The switch forwards the frame out interface Fa0/1.

   B. The switch forwards the frame out interface Fa0/2.

   C. The switch forwards the frame out interface Fa0/3.

   D. The switch discards (filters) the frame.

6. Which of the following devices would be in the same collision domain as PC1?

   A. PC2, which is separated from PC1 by an Ethernet hub

   B. PC3, which is separated from PC1 by a transparent bridge

   C. PC4, which is separated from PC1 by an Ethernet switch

   D. PC5, which is separated from PC1 by a router

7. Which of the following devices would be in the same broadcast domain as PC1? (Choose three answers.)

   A. PC2, which is separated from PC1 by an Ethernet hub

   B. PC3, which is separated from PC1 by a transparent bridge

   C. PC4, which is separated from PC1 by an Ethernet switch

   D. PC5, which is separated from PC1 by a router

8. Which of the following Ethernet standards support a maximum cable length of longer than 100 meters? (Choose two answers.)

   A. 100BASE-T

   B. 1000BASE-LX

   C. 1000BASE-T

   D. 100BASE-FX

9. A Cisco LAN switch connects to three PCs (PC1, PC2, and PC3), each directly using a cable that supports Ethernet UTP speeds up through 1000 Mbps (1 Gbps). PC1 uses a NIC that supports only 10BASE-T, while PC2 has a 10/100 NIC, and PC3 has a 10/100/1000 NIC. Assuming that the PCs and switch use IEEE autonegotiation, which PCs will use half-duplex?

   A. PC1

   B. PC2

   C. PC3

   D. None of the PCs will use half-duplex.

Review All the Key Topics

Review the most important topics from this chapter, noted with the Key Topic icon. Table 6-4 lists these key topics and where each is discussed.

Table 6-4   Key Topics for Chapter 6

Key Topic Element	Description	Page Number
List	LAN switch actions	127
Figure 6-4	Example of switch forwarding logic	127
Figure 6-5	Example of switch filtering logic	128
Figure 6-6	Example of how a switch learns MAC addresses	129
Table 6-1	Summary of three switch internal forwarding options	131
List	Some of the benefits of switching	131
List	Summary of logic used to forward and filter frames and to learn MAC addresses	132
List	Definitions of collision domain and broadcast domain	134
Table 6-2	Four LAN design feature comparisons with hubs, switches, and routers	135
Figure 6-11	Illustration of the concept of a VLAN	136
List	Default autonegotiation actions with added Cisco switch logic to sense the speed	140

Complete the Tables and Lists from Memory

Print a copy of Appendix M, "Memory Tables" (found on the DVD), or at least the section for this chapter, and complete the tables and lists from memory. Appendix N, "Memory Tables Answer Key," also on the DVD, includes completed tables and lists for you to check your work.

Definitions of Key Terms

After your first reading of the chapter, try to define these key terms, but do not be concerned about getting them all correct at that time. Chapter 30 directs you in how to use these terms for late-stage preparation for the exam.

autonegotiation, broadcast domain, broadcast frame, collision domain, cut-through switching, flooding, fragment-free switching, Spanning Tree Protocol (STP), store-and-forward switching, unknown unicast frame, virtual LAN

Answers to Review Questions:

1 B **2** C **3** A **4** B **5** A and B **6** A **7** A, B, and C **8** B and D **9** D

6

Chapter 7

Installing and Operating Cisco LAN Switches

When you buy a Cisco Catalyst switch, you can take it out of the box, power on the switch by connecting the power cable to the switch and a power outlet, and connect hosts to the switch using the correct UTP cables, and the switch works. You do not have to do anything else, and you certainly do not have to tell the switch to start forwarding Ethernet frames. The switch uses default settings so that all interfaces will work, assuming that the right cables and devices connect to the switch, and the switch forwards frames in and out of each interface.

However, most enterprises will want to be able to check on the switch's status, look at information about what the switch is doing, and possibly configure specific features of the switch. Engineers will also want to enable security features that allow them to securely access the switches without being vulnerable to malicious people breaking into the switches. To perform these tasks, a network engineer needs to connect to the switch's user interface.

This chapter explains the details of how to access a Cisco switch's user interface, how to use commands to find out how the switch is currently working, and how to configure the switch to tell it what to do. This chapter focuses on the processes, introducing several commands while introducing the process. The remaining chapters in Part II of the book focus on commands to do particular tasks.

This chapter covers the following exam topics:

LAN Switching Technologies

Configure and verify initial switch configuration including remote access management.

Cisco IOS commands to perform basic switch setup

Verify network status and switch operation using basic utilities such as ping, telnet and ssh.

Accessing the Cisco Catalyst 2960 Switch CLI

Cisco uses the concept of a *command-line interface (CLI)* with its router products and most of its Catalyst LAN switch products. The CLI is a text-based interface in which the user, typically a network engineer, enters a text command and presses Enter. Pressing Enter sends the command to the switch, which tells the device to do something. The switch does what the command says, and in some cases, the switch replies with some messages stating the results of the command.

Cisco Catalyst switches also support other methods to both monitor and configure a switch. For example, a switch can provide a web interface, so that an engineer can open a web browser to connect to a web server running in the switch. Switches also can be controlled and operated using network management software, as discussed briefly in the ICND2 book.

This book discusses only Cisco Catalyst enterprise-class switches, and in particular, how to use the Cisco CLI to monitor and control these switches. This first major section of the chapter first examines these Catalyst switches in more detail, and then explains how a network engineer can get access to the CLI to issue commands.

Cisco Catalyst Switches and the 2960 Switch

Within the Cisco Catalyst brand of LAN switches, Cisco produces a wide variety of switch series or families. Each switch series includes several specific models of switches that have similar features, similar price-versus-performance trade-offs, and similar internal components.

Cisco positions the 2960 series (family) of switches as full-featured, low-cost wiring closet switches for enterprises. That means that you would expect to use 2960 switches as access switches, as shown in Figure 6-12 in Chapter 6, "Building Ethernet LANs with Switches."

Figure 7-1 shows a photo of the 2960 switch series from Cisco. Each switch is a different specific model of switch inside the 2960 series. For example, three of the five switches have 48 RJ-45 UTP 10/100 ports, meaning that these ports can autonegotiate the use of 10BASE-T or 100BASE-T Ethernet. These switches also have a few 10/100/1000 interfaces on the right, intended to connect to the core of an enterprise campus LAN.

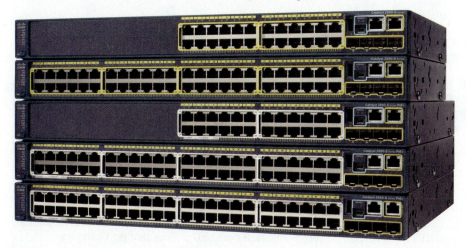

Figure 7-1 *Cisco 2960 Catalyst Switch Series*

Cisco refers to a switch's physical connectors as either *interfaces* or *ports*. Each interface has a number in the style x/y, where x and y are two different numbers. On a 2960, the numbering of 10/100 interfaces starts at 0/1, the second is 0/2, and so on. The interfaces also have names; for example, "interface FastEthernet 0/1" is the first of the 10/100 interfaces. Any Gigabit-capable interfaces would be called "GigabitEthernet" interfaces. For example, the first 10/100/1000 interface on a 2960 would be "interface GigabitEthernet 1/1."

Switch Status from LEDs

When an engineer needs to examine how a switch is working to verify its current status and to troubleshoot any problems, the vast majority of the time is spent using commands from the Cisco IOS CLI. However, the switch hardware does include several LEDs that provide some status and troubleshooting information, both during the time right after the switch has been powered on and during ongoing operations. Before moving on to discuss the CLI, this brief section examines the switch LEDs and their meanings.

Most Cisco Catalyst switches have some LEDs, including an LED for each physical Ethernet interface. For example, Figure 7-2 shows the front of a 2960 series switch, with five LEDs on the left, one LED over each port, and a mode button.

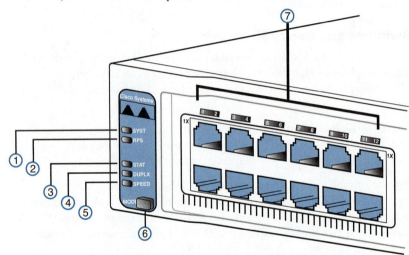

Figure 7-2 *2960 LEDs and a Mode Button*

The figure points out the various LEDs, with various meanings. Table 7-1 summarizes the LEDs, and additional explanations follow the table.

Table 7-1 LEDs and One Button in Figure 7-2

Number in Figure 7-2	Name	Description
1	SYST (system)	Implies the overall system status.
2	RPS (Redundant Power Supply)	Suggests the status of the extra (redundant) power supply.
3	STAT (Status)	If on (green), implies that each port LED implies that port's status.
4	DUPLX (duplex)	If on (green), each port LED implies that port's duplex (on/green is full; off means half).

Number in Figure 7-2	Name	Description
5	SPEED	If on (green), each port LED implies the speed of that port, as follows: off means 10 Mbps, solid green means 100 Mbps, and flashing green means 1 Gbps.
6	MODE	A button that cycles the meaning of the LEDs through three states (STAT, DUPLX, SPEED).
7	Port	LED that has different meanings, depending on the port mode as toggled using the mode button.

A few specific examples can help make sense of the LEDs. For example, consider the SYST LED for a moment. This LED provides a quick overall status of the switch, with three simple states on most 2960 switch models:

- **Off:** The switch is not powered on.
- **On (green):** The switch is powered on and operational (Cisco IOS has been loaded).
- **On (amber):** The system has power, but is not functioning properly.

So, a quick look at the SYST LED on the switch tells you whether the switch is working and, if it isn't, whether this is because of a loss of power (the SYST LED is off) or some kind of problem loading IOS (LED amber). In this last case, the typical response is to power the switch off and back on again. If the same failure occurs, a call to the Cisco Technical Assistance Center (TAC) is typically the next step.

Besides the straightforward SYST LED, the port LEDs—the LEDs sitting above or below each Ethernet port—mean something different depending on which of three port LED modes is currently used on the switch. The switches have a mode button (labeled with the number 6 in Figure 7-2) that, when pressed, cycles the port LEDs through three modes: STAT, DUPLX, and SPEED. The current port LED mode is signified by a solid green STAT, DUPLX, or SPEED LED (the lower three LEDs on the left part of Figure 7-2, labeled 3, 4, and 5). To move to another port LED mode, the engineer simply presses the mode button another time or two.

For example, in STAT (status) mode, each port LED implies the state of the matching port, as follows:

- **Off:** The link is currently not working (including if shut down).
- **Solid green:** The link is working, but there's no current traffic.
- **Flashing green:** The link is working, and traffic is currently passing over the interface.
- **Flashing amber:** The port is blocked by spanning tree.

In contrast, in SPEED port LED mode, the port LEDs imply the operating speed of the interface, with an unlit LED meaning 10 Mbps, a solid green light meaning 100 Mbps, and flashing green meaning 1000 Mbps (1 Gbps).

The particular details of how each LED works differ between different Cisco switch families and with different models inside the same switch family. So, memorizing the specific meaning of particular LED combinations is probably not required, and this chapter does not attempt to cover all combinations for even a single switch. However, it is important to remember the general ideas, the concept of a mode button that changes the meaning of the port LEDs, and the three meanings of the SYST LED mentioned earlier in this section.

The vast majority of the time, switches power up just fine and load Cisco IOS, and then the engineer simply accesses the CLI to operate and examine the switch. Next, the chapter focuses on the details of how to access the CLI.

7

Accessing the Cisco IOS CLI

Like any other piece of computer hardware, Cisco switches need some kind of operating system software. Cisco calls this OS the *Internetwork Operating System (IOS)*.

Cisco IOS Software for Catalyst switches implements and controls logic and functions performed by a Cisco switch. Besides controlling the switch's performance and behavior, Cisco IOS also defines an interface for humans called the CLI. The Cisco IOS CLI allows the user to use a terminal emulation program, which accepts text entered by the user. When the user presses Enter, the terminal emulator sends that text to the switch. The switch processes the text as if it is a command, does what the command says, and sends text back to the terminal emulator.

The switch CLI can be accessed through three popular methods—the console, Telnet, and Secure Shell (SSH). Two of these methods (Telnet and SSH) use the IP network in which the switch resides to reach the switch. The console is a physical port built specifically to allow access to the CLI. Figure 7-3 depicts the options.

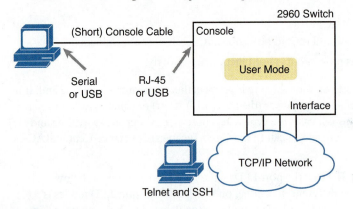

Figure 7-3 *CLI Access*

Console access requires both a physical connection between a PC (or other user device) and the switch's console port, as well as some software on the PC. Telnet and SSH require software on the user's device, but they rely on the existing TCP/IP network to transmit data. The next few pages detail how to connect the console and set up the software for each method to access the CLI.

Cabling the Console Connection

The physical console connection, both old and new, uses three main components: the physical console port on the switch, a physical serial port on the PC, and a cable that works with the console and serial ports. However, the physical cabling details have changed slowly over time, mainly because of advances and changes with PC hardware.

Older console connections use a PC serial port, a console cable, and an RJ-45 connector on the switch. The PC serial port typically has a D-shell connector (roughly rectangular) with nine pins (often called a DB-9). Older switches, as well as some current models, use an RJ-45 connector for the console port. Figure 7-4 shows the cabling on the left.

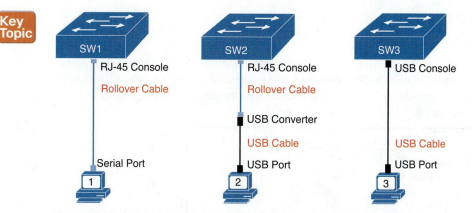

Figure 7-4 *Console Connection to a Switch*

You can use either a purpose-built console cable (which ships with new Cisco switches and routers) or make your own console cable using UTP cables and a standard RJ-45–to–DB-9 converter plug. You can buy the converter plug at most computer stores. Then, for the UTP cabling, the cable uses rollover cable pinouts, rather than any of the standard Ethernet cabling pinouts. Instead, it uses eight wires, rolling the wire at pin 1 to pin 8, pin 2 to pin 7, pin 3 to pin 6, and so on.

PCs have migrated away from using serial ports to instead use Universal Serial Bus (USB) ports for serial communications. Cisco has also begun building newer routers and switches with USB ports for console access as well. In the simplest form, you can use any USB port on the PC, with a USB cable, connected to the USB console port on the switch or router, as shown on the far right side of Figure 7-4.

The middle part of the figure shows yet another common option. Many PCs no longer have serial ports, but many existing Cisco routers and switches have only an RJ-45 console port and no USB console port. To connect such a PC to a router or switch console, you need some kind of converter that converts from the older console cable to a USB connector, as shown in the middle of Figure 7-4.

> **NOTE** When using the USB options, you typically also need to install a software driver so that your PC's OS knows that the device on the other end of the USB connection is the console of a Cisco device.

Configuring the Terminal Emulator for the Console

After the PC is physically connected to the console port, a terminal emulator software package must be installed and configured on the PC. The terminal emulator software treats all data as text. It accepts the text typed by the user and sends it over the console connection to the switch. Similarly, any bits coming into the PC over the console connection are displayed as text for the user to read.

The emulator must be configured to use the PC's serial port to match the settings on the switch's console port settings. The default console port settings on a switch are as follows. Note that the last three parameters are referred to collectively as "8N1":

- 9600 bits/second
- No hardware flow control
- 8-bit ASCII

- No parity bits
- 1 stop bit

Figure 7-5 shows one such terminal emulator, Zterm Pro. The image shows the window created by the emulator software in the background, with some output of a **show** command. The foreground, in the upper left, shows a settings window that lists the default console settings as listed just before this paragraph.

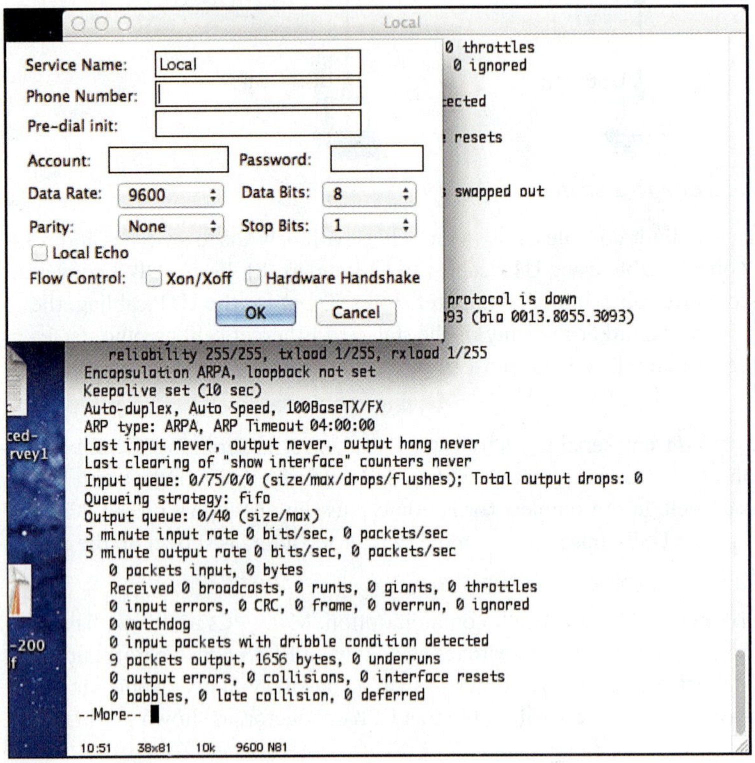

Figure 7-5   *Terminal Settings for Console Access*

Accessing the CLI with Telnet and SSH

The TCP/IP Telnet application allows a terminal emulator to communicate with another willing device. The process works much like what happens with an emulator on a PC connected to the console, except that the data flows over a TCP/IP network, instead of over a console cable. However, Telnet uses an IP network to send and receive the data, rather than a specialized cable and physical port on the device. The Telnet application protocols call the terminal emulator a *Telnet client* and the device that listens for commands and replies to them a *Telnet server*. Telnet is a TCP-based application layer protocol that uses well-known port 23.

To use Telnet, the user must install a Telnet client software package on his or her PC. (As mentioned earlier, most terminal emulator software packages today include both Telnet and SSH client functions.) The switch runs Telnet server software by default, but the switch does need to have an IP address configured so that it can send and receive IP packets. (Chapter 8, "Configuring Ethernet Switching," covers switch IP address configuration in greater detail.) Additionally, the network between the PC and switch needs to be up and working so that the PC and switch can exchange IP packets.

Many network engineers habitually use a Telnet client to monitor switches. The engineer can sit at his or her desk without having to walk to another part of the building—or go to another state or country—and still get into the CLI of that device.

While Telnet works well, many network engineers instead use *Secure Shell (SSH)* to over-come a serious security problem with Telnet. Telnet sends all data (including any username and password for login to the switch) as clear-text data. SSH encrypts the contents of all messages, including the passwords, avoiding the possibility of someone capturing packets in the network and stealing the password to network devices.

Secure Shell (SSH) does the same basic things as Telnet, but with added security. The user uses a terminal emulator that supports SSH. Like Telnet, SSH uses TCP, using well-known port 22 instead of Telnet's 23. As with Telnet, the SSH server (on the switch) receives the text from each SSH client, processes the text as a command, and sends messages back to the client.

Password Security for CLI Access

A Cisco switch, with default settings, remains relatively secure when locked inside a wiring clos-et, because by default, a switch allows console access only. However, when you enable Telnet and/or SSH access, you need to enable password security so that only authorized people have access to the CLI. Also, just to be safe, you should password-protect the console as well.

To add basic password checking for the console and for Telnet, the engineer needs to configure a couple of basic commands. The configuration process is covered a little later in this chapter, but you can get a general idea of the commands by looking in the last column of Table 7-2. The table lists the two commands that configure the console and vty passwords (used by Telnet users). After it is configured, the switch supplies a simple password prompt (as a result of the **login** command), and the switch expects the user to enter the password listed in the **password** command.

Table 7-2   CLI Password Configuration: Console and Telnet

Access From	Password Type	Sample Configuration

Console	Console password	line console 0
		  login
		  password faith

Telnet	vty password	line vty 0 15
		  login
		  password love

Cisco switches refer to the console as a console line—specifically, console line 0. Similarly, switches support 16 concurrent Telnet sessions, referenced as virtual terminal (vty) lines 0 through 15. (The term *vty* refers to an old name for terminal emulators.) The **line vty 0 15** configuration command tells the switch that the commands that follow apply to all 16 possible concurrent virtual terminal connections to the switch (0 through 15), which includes Telnet as well as SSH access.

After adding the configuration shown in Table 7-2, a user connecting to the console would be prompted for a password, and he or she would have to supply the word **faith** in this case. New Telnet users would also be prompted for a password, with **love** being the required password. Also, with this configuration, no username is required—just a simple password.

Configuring SSH requires a little more effort than the console and Telnet password configura-tion examples shown in Table 7-3. SSH uses public key cryptography to exchange a shared session key, which in turn is used for encryption. Additionally, SSH requires slightly better login security, requiring at least a password and a username. The section "Configuring Usernames and Secure Shell (SSH)" in Chapter 8 shows the configuration steps and a sample configuration to support SSH.

User and Enable (Privileged) Modes

All three CLI access methods covered so far (console, Telnet, and SSH) place the user in an area of the CLI called *user EXEC mode*. User EXEC mode, sometimes also called *user mode*, allows the user to look around but not break anything. The "EXEC mode" part of the name refers to the fact that in this mode, when you enter a command, the switch executes the command and then displays messages that describe the command's results.

Cisco IOS supports a more powerful EXEC mode called *enable* mode (also known as *privileged* mode or *privileged EXEC* mode). Enable mode gets its name from the **enable** command, which moves the user from user mode to enable mode, as shown in Figure 7-6. The other name for this mode, privileged mode, refers to the fact that powerful (or privileged) commands can be executed there. For example, you can use the **reload** command, which tells the switch to reinitialize or reboot Cisco IOS, only from enable mode.

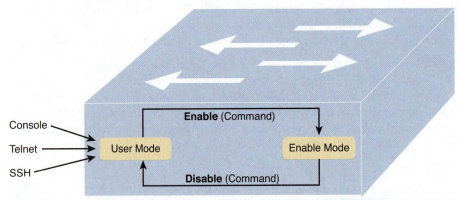

Figure 7-6   *User and Privileged Modes*

> **NOTE**   If the command prompt lists the host name followed by a >, the user is in user mode; if it is the host name followed by the #, the user is in enable mode.

Example 7-1 shows the output that you could see in a Telnet window. In this case, the user connects with Telnet and tries the **reload** command. The **reload** command tells the switch to reinitialize or reboot Cisco IOS. IOS allows this powerful command to be used only from enable mode, so in the example, IOS rejects the **reload** command when used in user mode and accepts the command when the user is in enable mode.

Example 7-1   *Navigating Between Different EXEC Modes on Switch Certskills1*

```
Press RETURN to get started.


User Access Verification


Password:
Certskills1>
Certskills1> reload
Translating "reload"
% Unknown command or computer name, or unable to find computer address
Certskills1> enable
Password:
Certskills1#
Certskills1# reload
```

```
Proceed with reload? [confirm] y
00:08:42: %SYS-5-RELOAD: Reload requested by console. Reload Reason: Reload Command.
```

> **NOTE** The commands that can be used in either user (EXEC) mode or enable (EXEC) mode are called EXEC commands.

This example is the first instance of this book showing you the output from the CLI, so it is worth noting a few conventions. The bold text represents what the user typed, while the non-bold text is what the switch sent back to the terminal emulator. Also, the typed passwords do not show up on the screen for security purposes. Finally, note that this switch has been preconfigured with a host name of "Certskills1," so the command prompt on the left shows that host name on each line.

So far, this chapter has pointed out some of the first things you should know when unpacking and installing a switch. The switch will work without any configuration—just plug in the power and Ethernet cables, and it works. However, you should at least connect to the switch console port and configure passwords for the console, Telnet, SSH, and the enable secret password. Next, this chapter examines some of the CLI features that exist regardless of how you access the CLI.

CLI Help Features

If you printed the Cisco IOS Command Reference documents, you would end up with a stack of paper several feet tall. No one should expect to memorize all the commands—and no one does. You can use several very easy, convenient tools to help remember commands and save time typing. As you progress through your Cisco certifications, the exams will cover progressively more commands. However, you should know the methods of getting command help.

Table 7-3 summarizes command-recall help options available at the CLI. Note that, in the first column, *command* represents any command. Likewise, *parm* represents a command's parameter. For example, the third row lists *command* **?**, which means that commands such as **show ?** and **copy ?** would list help for the **show** and **copy** commands, respectively.

Table 7-3 Cisco IOS Software Command Help

What You Enter	What Help You Get
?	Help for all commands available in this mode.
help	Text describing how to get help. No actual command help is given.
Command ?	Text help describing all the first parameter options for the command.
com?	A list of commands that start with **com**.
command parm?	This style of help lists all parameters beginning with the **parameter typed so far.** (Notice that there is no space between *parm* and the **?**.)
command parm<Tab>	If you press the Tab key midword, the CLI either spells the rest of this parameter at the command line or does nothing. If the CLI does nothing, it means that this string of characters represents more than one possible next parameter, so the CLI does not know which one to spell out.
command parm1 ?	If a space is inserted before the question mark, the CLI lists all the next parameters and gives a brief explanation of each.

When you enter the **?**, the Cisco IOS CLI reacts immediately; that is, you don't need to press the Enter key or any other keys. The device running Cisco IOS also redisplays what you entered before the **?** to save you some keystrokes. If you press Enter immediately after the **?**, Cisco IOS tries to execute the command with only the parameters you have entered so far.

The information supplied by using help depends on the CLI mode. For example, when **?** is entered in user mode, the commands allowed in user mode are displayed, but commands available only in enable mode (not in user mode) are not displayed. Also, help is available in configuration mode, which is the mode used to configure the switch. In fact, configuration mode has many different subconfiguration modes, as explained in the section "Configuration Submodes and Contexts," later in this chapter. So, you can get help for the commands available in each configuration submode as well. (Note that this might be a good time to use the free NetSim Lite product on the DVD—open any lab, use the question mark, and try some commands.)

Cisco IOS stores the commands that you enter in a history buffer, storing ten commands by default. The CLI allows you to move backward and forward in the historical list of commands and then edit the command before reissuing it. These key sequences can help you use the CLI more quickly on the exams. Table 7-4 lists the commands used to manipulate previously entered commands.

Table 7-4 Key Sequences for Command Edit and Recall

Keyboard Command	What Happens
Up arrow or Ctrl-P	This displays the most recently used command. If you press it again, the next most recent command appears, until the history buffer is exhausted. (The P stands for previous.)
Down arrow or Ctrl-N	If you have gone too far back into the history buffer, these keys take you forward to the more recently entered commands. (The N stands for next.)
Left arrow or Ctrl-B	This moves the cursor backward in the currently displayed command without deleting characters. (The B stands for back.)
Right arrow or Ctrl-F	This moves the cursor forward in the currently displayed command without deleting characters. (The F stands for forward.)
Backspace	This moves the cursor backward in the currently displayed command, deleting characters.
Ctrl-A	This moves the cursor directly to the first character of the currently displayed command.
Ctrl-E	This moves the cursor directly to the end of the currently displayed command.
Ctrl-R	This redisplays the command line with all characters. It's useful when messages clutter the screen.
Ctrl-D	This deletes a single character.
Ctrl-Shift-6	Interrupts the current command.

The debug and show Commands

By far, the single most popular Cisco IOS command is the **show** command. The **show** command has a large variety of options, and with those options, you can find the status of almost every feature of Cisco IOS. Essentially, the **show** command lists the currently known facts about the switch's operational status. The only work the switch does in react-ion to **show** commands is to find the current status and list the information in messages sent to the user.

The **debug** command has a similar role as compared with the **show** command. Like the **show** command, **debug** has many options. However, instead of just listing messages about the current status, the **debug** command asks the switch to continue monitoring different processes in the switch. The switch then sends ongoing messages to the user when different events occur.

The effects of the **show** and **debug** commands can be compared to a photograph (**show** command) and a movie (**debug** command). A **show** command shows what's true at a single point in time, and it takes less effort. A **debug** command shows what's true over time, but it requires more effort. As a result, the **debug** command requires more CPU cycles, but it lets you watch what is happening in a switch while it is happening.

Cisco IOS handles the messages from the **show** and **debug** commands very differently. IOS sends the output of **show** commands to the user that issued the **show** command, and to no other users. However, IOS reacts to **debug** commands by creating log messages related to that **debug** command's options. Any user logged in can choose to view the log messages, just by using the **terminal monitor** command from enable mode.

IOS also treats the **show** command as a very short-lived event and the **debug** command as an ongoing task. The options enabled by a single **debug** command are not disabled until the user takes action or until the switch is reloaded. A **reload** of the switch disables all currently enabled debug options. To disable a single debug option, repeat the same **debug** command with those options, prefaced by the word **no**. For example, if the **debug spanning-tree** command had been issued earlier, issue the **no debug spanning-tree** command to disable that same debug. Also, the **no debug all** and **undebug all** commands disable all currently enabled debugs.

Be aware that some **debug** options create so many messages that Cisco IOS cannot process them all, possibly resulting in a crash of Cisco IOS. You might want to check the current switch CPU utilization with the **show process** command before issuing any **debug** command. To be more careful, before enabling an unfamiliar **debug** command option, issue a **no debug all** command and then issue the **debug** that you want to use. Then quickly retrieve the **no debug all** command using the up arrow or Ctrl-P key sequence twice. If the debug quickly degrades switch performance, the switch might be too busy to listen to what you are typing. The process described in this paragraph saves a bit of typing and can be the difference between preventing the switch from failing or not.

Configuring Cisco IOS Software

You must understand how to configure a Cisco switch to succeed on the exam and in real networking jobs. This section covers the basic configuration processes, including the concept of a configuration file and the locations in which the configuration files can be stored. Although this section focuses on the configuration process, and not on the configuration commands themselves, you should know all the commands covered in this chapter for the exams, in addition to the configuration processes.

Configuration mode is another mode for the Cisco CLI, similar to user mode and privileged mode. User mode lets you issue nondisruptive commands and displays some information. Privileged mode supports a superset of commands compared to user mode, including commands that might harm the switch. However, none of the commands in user or privileged mode changes the switch's configuration. Configuration mode accepts *configuration commands*—commands that tell the switch the details of what to do and how to do it. Figure 7-7 illustrates the relationships among configuration mode, user EXEC mode, and privileged EXEC mode.

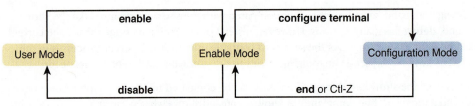

Figure 7-7   *CLI Configuration Mode Versus EXEC Modes*

Commands entered in configuration mode update the active configuration file. *These changes to the configuration occur immediately each time you press the Enter key at the end of a command.* Be careful when you enter a configuration command!

Configuration Submodes and Contexts

Configuration mode itself contains a multitude of subcommand modes. *Context-setting commands* move you from one configuration subcommand mode, or context, to another. These context-setting commands tell the switch the topic about which you will enter the next few configuration commands. More importantly, the context tells the switch the topic you care about right now, so when you use the **?** to get help, the switch gives you help about that topic only.

> **NOTE**   *Context-setting* is not a Cisco term—it's just a term used here to help make sense of configuration mode.

The **interface** command is one of the most commonly used context-setting configuration commands. For example, the CLI user could enter interface configuration mode by entering the **interface FastEthernet 0/1** configuration command. Asking for help in interface configuration mode displays only commands that are useful when configuring Ethernet interfaces. Commands used in this context are called *subcommands*—or, in this specific case, *interface subcommands*. When you begin practicing with the CLI with real equipment, the navigation between modes can become natural. For now, consider Example 7-2, which shows the following:

- Movement from enable mode to global configuration mode by using the **configure terminal** EXEC command
- Using a **hostname Fred** global configuration command to configure the switch's name
- Movement from global configuration mode to console line configuration mode (using the **line console 0** command)
- Setting the console's simple password to **hope** (using the **password hope** line subcommand)
- Movement from console configuration mode to interface configuration mode (using the **interface** command)
- Setting the speed to 100 Mbps for interface Fa0/1 (using the **speed 100** interface subcommand)
- Movement from interface configuration mode back to global configuration mode (using the **exit** command)

Example 7-2 *Navigating Between Different Configuration Modes*

```
Switch# configure terminal
Switch(config)# hostname Fred
Fred(config)# line console 0
Fred(config-line)# password hope
Fred(config-line)# interface FastEthernet 0/1
Fred(config-if)# speed 100
Fred(config-if)# exit
Fred(config)#
```

The text inside parentheses in the command prompt identifies the configuration mode. For example, the first command prompt after you enter configuration mode lists (config), meaning global configuration mode. After the **line console 0** command, the text expands to (config-line), meaning line configuration mode. Table 7-5 shows the most common command prompts in configuration mode, the names of those modes, and the context-setting commands used to reach those modes.

Key Topic

Table 7-5 Common Switch Configuration Modes

Prompt	Name of Mode	Context-Setting Command(s) to Reach This Mode
hostname(config)#	Global	None—first mode after **configure terminal**
hostname(config-line)#	Line	**line console 0** **line vty 0 15**
hostname(config-if)#	Interface	**interface** *type number*
hostname(vlan)#	VLAN	**vlan** *number*

You should practice until you become comfortable moving between the different configuration modes, back to enable mode, and then back into the configuration modes. However, you can learn these skills just doing labs about the topics in later chapters of the book. For now, Figure 7-8 shows most of the navigation between global configuration mode and the four configuration submodes listed in Table 7-5.

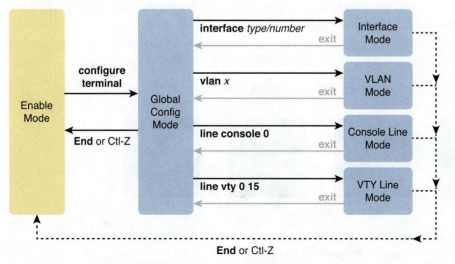

Figure 7-8 *Navigation In and Out of Switch Configuration Modes*

NOTE   You can also move directly from one configuration submode to another, without first using the **exit** command to move back to global configuration mode. Just use the commands listed in bold in the center of the figure.

No set rules exist for what commands are global commands or subcommands. Generally, however, when multiple instances of a parameter can be set in a single switch, the command used to set the parameter is likely a configuration subcommand. Items that are set once for the entire switch are likely global commands. For example, the **hostname** command is a global command because there is only one host name per switch. Conversely, the **duplex** command is an interface subcommand to allow the switch to use a different setting on the different interfaces.

Storing Switch Configuration Files

When you configure a switch, it needs to use the configuration. It also needs to be able to retain the configuration in case the switch loses power. Cisco switches contain random-access memory (RAM) to store data while Cisco IOS is using it, but RAM loses its contents when the switch loses power. To store information that must be retained when the switch loses power, Cisco switches use several types of more permanent memory, none of which has any moving parts. By avoiding components with moving parts (such as traditional disk drives), switches can maintain better uptime and availability.

The following list details the four main types of memory found in Cisco switches, as well as the most common use of each type:

- **RAM:** Sometimes called DRAM, for dynamic random-access memory, RAM is used by the switch just as it is used by any other computer: for working storage. The running (active) configuration file is stored here.

- **ROM:** Read-only memory (ROM) stores a bootstrap (or boothelper) program that is loaded when the switch first powers on. This bootstrap program then finds the full Cisco IOS image and manages the process of loading Cisco IOS into RAM, at which point Cisco IOS takes over operation of the switch.

- **Flash memory:** Either a chip inside the switch or a removable memory card, flash memory stores fully functional Cisco IOS images and is the default location where the switch gets its Cisco IOS at boot time. Flash memory also can be used to store any other files, including backup copies of configuration files.

- **NVRAM:** Nonvolatile RAM (NVRAM) stores the initial or startup configuration file that is used when the switch is first powered on and when the switch is reloaded.

Figure 7-9 summarizes this same information in a briefer and more convenient form for memorization and study.

Figure 7-9   *Cisco Switch Memory Types*

Cisco IOS stores the collection of configuration commands in a *configuration file*. In fact, switches use multiple configuration files—one file for the initial configuration used when powering on, and another configuration file for the active, currently used running configuration as stored in RAM. Table 7-6 lists the names of these two files, their purpose, and their storage location.

Key Topic

Table 7-6 Names and Purposes of the Two Main Cisco IOS Configuration Files

Configuration Filename	Purpose	Where It Is Stored
Startup config	Stores the initial configuration used anytime the switch reloads Cisco IOS.	NVRAM
Running config	Stores the currently used configuration commands. This file changes dynamically when someone enters commands in configuration mode.	RAM

Essentially, when you use configuration mode, you change only the running config file. This means that the configuration example earlier in this chapter (Example 7-2) updates only the running config file. However, if the switch lost power right after that example, all that configuration would be lost. If you want to keep that configuration, you have to copy the running config file into NVRAM, overwriting the old startup config file.

Example 7-3 demonstrates that commands used in configuration mode change only the running configuration in RAM. The example shows the following concepts and steps:

Step 1. The original **hostname** command on the switch, with the startup config file matching the running config file.

Step 2. The **hostname** command changes the host name, but only in the running config file.

Step 3. The **show running-config** and **show startup-config** commands are shown, with only the **hostname** commands displayed for brevity, to make the point that the two configuration files are now different.

Example 7-3 *How Configuration Mode Commands Change the Running Config File, Not the Startup Config File*

```
! Step 1 next (two commands)
!
hannah# show running-config
! (lines omitted)
hostname hannah
! (rest of lines omitted)

hannah# show startup-config
! (lines omitted)
hostname hannah
! (rest of lines omitted)
! Step 2 next. Notice that the command prompt changes immediately after
! the hostname command.
hannah# configure terminal
hannah(config)# hostname jessie
jessie(config)# exit
! Step 3 next (two commands)
!
jessie# show running-config
! (lines omitted)
hostname jessie
! (rest of lines omitted - notice that the running configuration reflects the
```

```
!  changed hostname)
jessie# show startup-config
! (lines omitted)
hostname hannah
! (rest of lines omitted - notice that the changed configuration is not
! shown in the startup config)
```

NOTE   Cisco uses the term *reload* to refer to what most PC operating systems call rebooting or restarting. In each case, it is a reinitialization of the software. The **reload** EXEC command causes a switch to reload.

Copying and Erasing Configuration Files

If you want to keep the new configuration commands you add in configuration mode (so that the changes are present the next time the system is rebooted), like the **hostname jessie** command in Example 7-3, you need to use the command **copy running-config startup-config**. This command overwrites the current startup config file with what is currently in the running configuration file.

The **copy** command can be used to copy files in a switch, most typically a configuration file or a new version of Cisco IOS Software. The most basic method for moving configuration files in and out of a switch is to use the **copy** command to copy files between RAM or NVRAM on a switch and a TFTP server. The files can be copied between any pair, as shown in Figure 7-10.

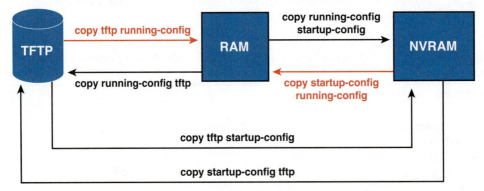

Figure 7-10   *Locations for Copying and Results from Copy Operations*

The commands for copying Cisco IOS configurations can be summarized as follows:

```
copy {tftp | running-config | startup-config} {tftp | running-config | startup-config}
```

The first set of parameters enclosed in braces ({ }) is the "from" location; the next set of parameters is the "to" location.

The **copy** command always replaces the existing file when the file is copied into NVRAM or into a TFTP server. In other words, it acts as if the destination file was erased and the new file completely replaced the old one. However, when the **copy** command copies a configuration file into the running config file in RAM, the configuration file in RAM is not replaced, but is merged instead. Effectively, any **copy** into RAM works just as if you entered the commands in the "from" configuration file in the order listed in the config file.

Who cares? Well, we do. If you change the running config and then decide that you want to revert to what's in the startup config file, the result of the **copy startup-config running-config** command might not cause the two files to actually match. One way to guarantee that the two configuration files match is to issue the **reload** command, which reloads, or reboots, the switch, which erases RAM and then copies the startup config into RAM as part of the reload process.

You can use three different commands to erase the contents of NVRAM. The **write erase** and **erase startup-config** commands are older, whereas the **erase nvram:** command is the more recent, and recommended, command. All three commands simply erase the contents of the NVRAM configuration file. Of course, if the switch is reloaded at this point, there is no initial configuration. Note that Cisco IOS does not have a command that erases the contents of the running config file. To clear out the running config file, simply erase the startup config file and then **reload** the switch.

> **NOTE**   Making a copy of all current switch and router configurations should be part of any network's overall security strategy, mainly so that you can replace a device's configuration if an attack changes the configuration.

7

Initial Configuration (Setup Mode)

Cisco IOS Software supports two primary methods of giving a switch an initial basic configuration—configuration mode, which has already been covered in this chapter, and setup mode. *Setup mode* leads a switch administrator by asking questions that prompt the administrator for basic configuration parameters. After the administrator answers the questions, IOS builds a configuration file, saves it as the startup config, and also loads it as the running config to start using the new configuration.

When a Cisco switch or router initializes, but the startup config file is empty, the switch or router asks the console user if he wants to use setup. Figure 7-11 shows the branches in the process. The left side of the figure, moving down, brings the user to the point at which IOS asks the user questions about what should be added to the configuration.

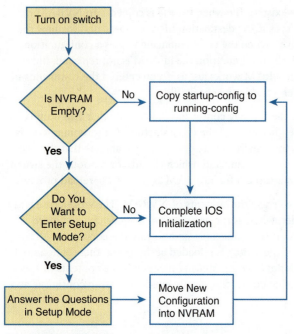

Figure 7-11 *Getting into Setup Mode*

Frankly, most network engineers never use setup mode, mainly because setup supports only a small percentage of modern switch configuration settings. However, you will still see some evidence of setup, because when you reload a switch or router that has no configuration, IOS will ask you whether you want to enter the "initial configuration dialogue" (the official term for setup mode). Just answer "no," as shown in Example 7-4, and use configuration mode to configure the device.

Example 7-4 *Initial Configuration Dialog (Setup)—Rejected*

```
--- System Configuration Dialog ---

Would you like to enter the initial configuration dialog? [yes/no]: no

Switch>
```

IOS Version and Other Reload Facts

To finish this first chapter about how Cisco IOS works, with the IOS CLI, this last topic looks at the switch **show version** command.

When a switch loads the IOS, it must do many tasks. The IOS software itself must be loaded into RAM. The IOS must become aware of the hardware available, for example, all the different LAN interfaces on the switch. After the software is loaded, the IOS keeps track of some statistics related to the current operation of the switch, like the amount of time since the IOS was last loaded and the reason why the IOS was most recently loaded.

The **show version** command lists these facts, plus many others. As you might guess from the command itself, the **show version** command does list information about the IOS, including the version of IOS software. However, as highlighted in Example 7-5, it lists many other interesting facts as well.

Example 7-5 *Example of a* **show version** *Command on a Cisco Switch*

```
SW1# show version
Cisco IOS Software, C2960 Software (C2960-LANBASEK9-M), Version 15.0(1)SE3, RELEASE
SOFTWARE (fc1)
Technical Support: http://www.cisco.com/techsupport
Copyright (c) 1986-2012 by Cisco Systems, Inc.
Compiled Wed 30-May-12 14:26 by prod_rel_team

ROM: Bootstrap program is C2960 boot loader
BOOTLDR: C2960 Boot Loader (C2960-HBOOT-M) Version 12.2(44)SE5, RELEASE SOFTWARE (fc1)

SW1 uptime is 2 days, 22 hours, 2 minutes
System returned to ROM by power-on
System image file is "flash:c2960-lanbasek9-mz.150-1.SE3.bin"


This product contains cryptographic features and is subject to United
States and local country laws governing import, export, transfer and
use…
! Lines omitted for brevity


cisco WS-C2960-24TT-L (PowerPC405) processor (revision P0) with 65536K bytes of memory.
Processor board ID FCQ1621X6QC
Last reset from power-on
1 Virtual Ethernet interface
24 FastEthernet interfaces
2 Gigabit Ethernet interfaces
The password-recovery mechanism is enabled.

64K bytes of flash-simulated non-volatile configuration memory.
Base ethernet MAC Address       : 18:33:9D:7B:13:80
Motherboard assembly number     : 73-11473-11
Power supply part number        : 341-0097-03
Motherboard serial number       : FCQ162103ZL
Power supply serial number      : ALD1619B37W
Model revision number           : P0
Motherboard revision number     : A0
Model number                    : WS-C2960-24TT-L
System serial number            : FCQ1621X6QC
Top Assembly Part Number        : 800-29859-06
Top Assembly Revision Number    : C0
Version ID                      : V10
CLEI Code Number                : COMCX00ARB
Hardware Board Revision Number  : 0x01


Switch Ports Model              SW Version          SW Image
------ ----- -----              ----------          ----------
*    1 26    WS-C2960-24TT-L    15.0(1)SE3          C2960-LANBASEK9-M


Configuration register is 0xF
```

Working through the highlighted parts of the example, top to bottom, this command lists

- The IOS version
- Time since last load of the IOS
- Reason for last load of the IOS
- Number of Fast Ethernet interfaces (24)
- Number of Gigabit Ethernet interfaces (2)
- Switch model number

Review Activities

Chapter Summary

- Cisco uses the concept of a command-line interface (CLI) with its router products and most of its Catalyst LAN switch products. The CLI is a text-based interface in which the user, typically a network engineer, enters a text command and presses Enter.

- Like any other piece of computer hardware, Cisco switches need some kind of operating system software. Cisco calls this OS the Internetwork Operating System (IOS).

- The switch CLI can be accessed through four popular methods: the console, Telnet, Secure Shell (SSH), and the AUX port. Two of these methods (Telnet and SSH) use the IP network in which the switch resides to reach the switch. The console is a physical port built specifically to allow access to the CLI. The AUX port is designed to be connected to a modem.

- The physical console connection, both old and new, uses three main components: the physical console port on the switch, a physical serial port on the PC, and a cable that works with the console and serial ports.

- When the PC is physically connected to the console port, a terminal emulator software package must be installed and configured on the PC. The terminal emulator software treats all data as text. It accepts the text typed by the user and sends it over the console connection to the switch. Similarly, any bits coming into the PC over the console connection is displayed as text for the user to read.

- The emulator must be configured to use the PC's serial port to match the settings on the switch's console port settings. The default console port settings on a switch are as follows; note that the last three parameters are referred to collectively as "8N1.":

  - 9600 bits per second
  - No hardware flow control
  - 8-bit ASCII
  - No parity bits
  - 1 stop bit

- A Cisco switch, with default settings, remains relatively secure when locked inside a wiring closet because, by default, a switch allows console access only. However, when you enable Telnet and/or SSH access, you must enable password security so that only authorized people have access to the CLI.

- User EXEC mode, sometimes also called *user mode*, enables the user to look around but not break anything. The "EXEC mode" part of the name refers to the fact that in this mode, when you enter a command, the switch executes the command and then displays messages that describe the command's results.

- Cisco IOS supports a more powerful EXEC mode called *enable* mode (also known as *privileged* mode or *privileged EXEC* mode). Enable mode gets its name from the **enable** command, which moves the user from user mode to enable mode.

- The information supplied by using help depends on the CLI mode. For example, when ? is entered in user mode, the commands allowed in user mode are displayed, but commands available only in enable mode (not in user mode) are not displayed. Also, help is available in configuration mode, which is the mode used to configure the switch. In fact, configuration mode has many different subconfiguration modes.

- Cisco IOS stores the commands that you enter in a history buffer, storing 10 commands by default. The CLI enables you to move backward and forward in the historical list of commands and then edit the command before reissuing it.

7

- The **show** command has a large variety of options, and with those options, you can find the status of almost every feature of Cisco IOS.

- The **debug** command has a similar role as the **show** command. Like the **show** command, **debug** has many options; however, instead of just listing messages about the current status, the **debug** command asks the switch to continue monitoring different processes in the switch. The switch then sends ongoing messages to the user when different events occur.

- *Configuration mode* is another mode for the Cisco CLI, similar to user mode and privileged mode. User mode lets you issue nondisruptive commands and displays some information. Privileged mode supports a superset of commands compared to user mode, including commands that might harm the switch. However, none of the commands in user or privileged mode changes the switch's configuration. Configuration mode accepts configuration commands that tell the switch the details of what to do and how to do it.

- Configuration mode itself contains a multitude of subcommand modes. *Context-setting commands* move you from one configuration subcommand mode, or context, to another.

- The **interface** command is one of the most commonly used context-setting configuration commands. For example, the CLI user could enter interface configuration mode by entering the **interface FastEthernet 0/1** configuration command.

- The startup-config file stores the initial configuration used any time the switch reloads Cisco IOS. It is stored in nonvolatile RAM (NVRAM).

- The running-config file stores the currently used configuration commands. This file changes dynamically when someone enters commands in the configuration mode. It is stored in RAM.

- If you want to keep the new configuration commands you add in configuration mode (so that the changes are present the next time the system is rebooted), you must use the command **copy running-config startup-config.**

- *Setup mode* leads a switch administrator by asking questions that prompt the administrator for basic configuration parameters. After the administrator answers the questions, IOS builds a configuration file, saves it as the startup-config, and loads it as the running-config to start using the new configuration.

- The show version command lists the following about the IOS:
  - The IOS version
  - Time since last load of the IOS
  - Reason for last load of the IOS
  - Number of FastEthernet interfaces
  - Number of GigabitEthernet interfaces
  - Switch model number

Review Questions

Answer these review questions. You can find the answers at the bottom of the last page of the chapter. For thorough explanations, see DVD Appendix C, "Answers to Review Questions."

1. In what modes can you execute the command **show mac address-table**? (Choose two answers.)

    A. User mode

    B. Enable mode

    C. Global configuration mode

    D. Interface configuration mode

2. In which of the following modes of the CLI could you issue the command **reload** to reboot the switch?

   A. User mode

   B. Enable mode

   C. Global configuration mode

   D. Interface configuration mode

3. Which of the following is a difference between Telnet and SSH as supported by a Cisco switch?

   A. SSH encrypts the passwords used at login, but not other traffic; Telnet encrypts nothing.

   B. SSH encrypts all data exchange, including login passwords; Telnet encrypts nothing.

   C. Telnet is used from Microsoft operating systems, and SSH is used from UNIX and Linux operating systems.

   D. Telnet encrypts only password exchanges; SSH encrypts all data exchanges.

4. What type of switch memory is used to store the configuration used by the switch when it is up and working?

   A. RAM

   B. ROM

   C. Flash

   D. NVRAM

   E. Bubble

5. What command copies the configuration from RAM into NVRAM?

   A. copy running-config tftp

   B. copy tftp running-config

   C. copy running-config start-up-config

   D. copy start-up-config running-config

   E. copy startup-config running-config

   F. copy running-config startup-config

6. A switch user is currently in console line configuration mode. Which of the following would place the user in enable mode? (Choose two answers.)

   A. Using the **exit** command once

   B. Using the **end** command once

   C. Pressing the Ctrl-Z key sequence once

   D. Using the **quit** command

Review All the Key Topics

Review the most important topics from this chapter, noted with the Key Topic icon. Table 7-7 lists these key topics and where each is discussed.

Key Topic

Table 7-7   Key Topics for Chapter 7

Key Topic Element	Description	Page Number
Figure 7-4	Cabling options for a console connection	153
List	A Cisco switch's default console port settings	153
Table 7-5	A list of configuration mode prompts, the name of the configuration mode, and the command used to reach each mode	161
Figure 7-9	Types of memory in a switch	162
Table 7-6	The names and purposes of the two configuration files in a switch or router	163

Complete the Tables and Lists from Memory

Print a copy of DVD Appendix M, "Memory Tables," or at least the section for this chapter, and complete the tables and lists from memory. DVD Appendix N, "Memory Tables Answer Key," includes completed tables and lists for you to check your work.

Definitions of Key Terms

After your first reading of the chapter, try to define these key terms, but do not be concerned about getting them all correct at that time. Chapter 30 directs you in how to use these terms for late-stage preparation for the exam.

command-line interface (CLI), Telnet, Secure Shell (SSH), enable mode, user mode, configuration mode, startup config file, running config file

Command References

Table 7-8 lists and briefly describes the configuration commands used in this chapter.

Table 7-8   Chapter 7 Configuration Commands

Command	Mode and Purpose
line console 0	Global command that changes the context to console configuration mode.
line vty *1st-vty last-vty*	Global command that changes the context to vty configuration mode for the range of vty lines listed in the command.
login	Line (console and vty) configuration mode. Tells IOS to prompt for a password (no username).
password *pass-value*	Line (console and vty) configuration mode. Lists the password required if the **login** command (with no other parameters) is configured.
interface *type port-number*	Global command that changes the context to interface mode—for example, **interface FastEthernet 0/1**.
hostname *name*	Global command that sets this switch's host name, which is also used as the first part of the switch's command prompt.
exit	Moves back to the next higher mode in configuration mode.

Command	Mode and Purpose
end	Exits configuration mode and goes back to enable mode from any of the configuration submodes.
Ctrl-Z	This is not a command, but rather a two-key combination (pressing the Ctrl key and the letter Z) that together do the same thing as the **end** command.

Table 7-9 lists and briefly describes the EXEC commands used in this chapter.

Table 7-9   Chapter 7 EXEC Command Reference

Command	Purpose
no debug all **undebug all**	Enable mode EXEC command to disable all currently enabled debugs.
terminal monitor	EXEC command that tells Cisco IOS to send a copy of all syslog messages, including debug messages, to the Telnet or SSH user who issues this command.
reload	Enable mode EXEC command that reboots the switch or router.
copy *from-location to-location*	Enable mode EXEC command that copies files from one file location to another. Locations include the startup config and running config in RAM, files TFTP and RCP servers, and flash memory.
copy running-config startup-config	Enable mode EXEC command that saves the active config, replacing the startup config file used when the switch initializes.
copy startup-config running-config	Enable mode EXEC command that merges the startup config file with the currently active config file in RAM.
show running-config	Lists the contents of the running config file.
write erase **erase startup-config**	These enable mode EXEC commands to erase the startup config file.
quit	EXEC command that disconnects the user from the CLI session.
show startup-config	Lists the contents of the startup config (initial config) file.
enable	Moves the user from user mode to enable (privileged) mode and prompts for a password if one is configured.
disable	Moves the user from enable mode to user mode.
configure terminal	Enable mode command that moves the user into configuration mode.

Answers to Review Questions:

1 A and B **2** B **3** B **4** A **5** F **6** B and C

Chapter 8

Configuring Ethernet Switching

Cisco LAN switches perform their core function—forwarding Ethernet frames—without any configuration. You can buy a Cisco switch, plug in the right cables to connect various devices to the switch, plug in the power cable, and the switch works. However, in most networks, the network engineer wants to configure and use various switch features.

This chapter explains a large variety of switch features, broken into two halves of the chapter. The first half of the chapter explains many switch administrative features that happen to work the same way on routers and switches; this chapter keeps these common features together so that you can easily refer to them later when working with routers. The second half of the chapter shows how to configure some switch-specific features, many of which impact how a switch forwards frames.

This chapter covers the following exam topics:

IP Routing Technologies

Configure SVI interfaces

Network Device Security

Configure and verify network device security features such as

Device password security

Enable secret vs enable

SSH

VTYs

Service password

Describe external authentication methods

Configure and verify Switch Port Security features such as

Sticky MAC

MAC address limitation

Static / dynamic

Violation modes

Err disable

Shutdown

Protect restrict

Shutdown unused ports

Err disable recovery

Assign unused ports to an unused VLAN

Configuration of Features in Common with Routers

This first of the two major sections of this chapter examines the configuration of several features that are configured the exact same way on both switches and routers. In particular, this section examines how to secure access to the CLI, plus various settings for the console. Note that this section will refer to only switches, and not routers, but the commands apply to both.

Securing the Switch CLI

The first step to securing a switch is to secure access to the CLI. Securing the CLI includes protecting access to enable mode, because from enable mode, an attacker could reload the switch or change the configuration. At the same time, protecting user mode is also important, because attackers can see the status of the switch, learn about the network, and find new ways to attack the network.

For example, consider a user who accesses a switch from the console. The default console configuration settings allow a console user to reach both user mode and enable mode without supplying a password. These defaults make some sense, because when you use the console, you are typically sitting near or next to the switch. If you can touch the switch, even if the console had all the available password protections, you could still perform the switch password recovery/ reset procedure in five minutes anyway and get into the switch. So, by default, console access is open. However, most network engineers add login security to the console as well.

> **NOTE** To see the password recovery/reset procedures, go to Cisco.com and search for the phrase "password recovery." The first listed item probably will be a web page with password recovery details for most every product made by Cisco.

On the other hand, the default configuration settings do not allow a vty (Telnet or SSH) session into a switch, either to user mode or to enable mode. To allow these users to reach user mode, the switch first needs a working IP configuration, as well as login security on the vty lines. To allow access to enable mode, the switch must be configured with enable mode security as well.

This section examines many of the configuration details related to accessing user and enable mode on a switch or router. Switch IP configuration is covered later in this chapter in the section "Enabling IP for Remote Access." In particular, this section covers the following topics:

- Simple password security to user mode from (a) the console and (b) Telnet
- Secure Shell (SSH)
- Password encryption
- Enable mode passwords

Securing Access with Simple Passwords

Cisco switches can protect user mode with a simple password—with no username—for console and Telnet users. Console users must supply the *console password*, as configured in console line configuration mode. Telnet users must supply the *Telnet password*, also called the vty password, so called because the configuration sits in vty line configuration mode.

Cisco switches protect enable mode for any user with the *enable password*. The user, in user mode, types the **enable** EXEC command and is prompted for this enable password; if the user types the correct password, IOS moves the user to enable mode. Figure 8-1 shows the names of these passwords and the associated configuration modes.

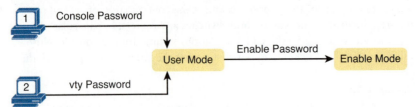

Figure 8-1 *Simple Password Security Concepts*

The configuration for these passwords does not require a lot of work. First, the console and vty password configuration uses the same two subcommands in console and vty line configuration modes, respectively. The **login** command tells IOS to use simple password security, and the **password** *password-value* command defines the password. IOS protects enable mode using the enable secret password, configured using the global command **enable secret** *password-value*.

> **NOTE** The later section "Hiding the Enable Password" explains two options for configuring the password required by the **enable** command, as configured with the **enable secret** and **enable password** commands, and describes why the **enable secret** command is preferred.

Example 8-1 shows a sample configuration process that sets the console password, the vty (Telnet) password, the enable secret password, and a host name for the switch. The example shows the entire process, including command prompts, that provides some reminders of the different configuration modes explained in Chapter 7, "Installing and Operating Cisco LAN Switches."

Key Topic

Example 8-1 *Configuring Basic Passwords and a Host Name*

```
Switch> enable
Switch# configure terminal
Switch(config)# enable secret cisco
Switch(config)# hostname Emma
Emma(config)# line console 0
Emma(config-line)# password hope
Emma(config-line)# login
Emma(config-line)# exit
Emma(config)# line vty 0 15
Emma(config-line)# password love
Emma(config-line)# login
Emma(config-line)# end
Emma#
```

Because you have probably not done many configurations yourself yet, the next few paragraphs walk you through Example 8-1 a few lines at a time, to use this example as an exercise in how the CLI works. First, focus on the first four lines, with the command prompts that begin with "Switch." By the publisher's conventions, this book lists all text output displayed by the switch in nonbold text and all text typed by the user in bold text. For example, the first line shows a command prompt supplied by the switch of "Switch>" (the default prompt, by the way), with the user typing **enable**. The ">" at the end of the prompt tells us that the user is in user mode.

Those first few lines show the user beginning in user mode, and then moving to enable mode (using the **enable** EXEC command). Then the user moves to global configuration mode (by using the **configure terminal** EXEC command). As soon as the user is in global configuration mode, he enters two global configuration commands (**enable secret** and **hostname**) that add configuration that applies to the entire switch.

The first line of output in Example 8-1 that begins with "Emma" shows the beginning of the configuration of the console password. First, the user needs to enter console line configuration mode using the **line console 0** command. (With only one console per switch, it is always numbered as console 0.) Next, the **password** command lists the simple text password (faith), and the **login** command tells the switch to ask for the simple text password as defined by the password command.

Continuing through the example, the next few lines repeat the same process, but for all 16 vty lines (vty lines 0 through 15). The 16 vty lines means that the switch can accept 16 concurrent Telnet connections into the switch. As for the password, the configuration uses a different vty line password of "love." Finally, the **end** command moves the user back to enable mode.

Moving on from the configuration, now focus on what the users will see because of the configuration in Example 8-1. A console user will now be prompted for a password (but no username), and he must type **hope**. Similarly, Telnet users will be prompted for a password, but no username, and they must type **love**. Both console and Telnet users must use the **enable** command, and use password "cisco," to reach enable mode. And SSH users cannot yet log in to this switch, because more configuration is needed to support SSH.

Example 8-2 shows the resulting configuration in the switch named Emma. The gray lines highlight the new configuration. Note that some lines have been omitted from the full output from a switch just to reduce the volume of unrelated lines on the page.

Example 8-2   *Resulting Running Config File on Switch Emma*

```
Emma# show running-config
!
Building configuration...

Current configuration : 1333 bytes
!
version 12.2
!
hostname Emma
!
enable secret 5 $1$YXRN$11zOe1Lb0Lv/nHyTquobd.
!
spanning-tree mode pvst
spanning-tree extend system-id
!
interface FastEthernet0/1
!
interface FastEthernet0/2
!
! Several lines have been omitted here - in particular, lines for FastEthernet
! interfaces 0/3 through 0/23.
!
interface FastEthernet0/24
!
```

8

```
interface GigabitEthernet0/1
!
interface GigabitEthernet0/2
!
interface Vlan1
 no ip address
 no ip route-cache
!
!
line con 0
 password faith
 login
!
line vty 0 4
 password love
 login
!
line vty 5 15
 password love
 login
```

NOTE   The output of the **show running-config** command, in the last six lines of Example 8-2, separates the first five vty lines (0 through 4) from the rest (5 through 15) for historical reasons.

Securing Access with Local Usernames and Passwords

A login method that uses simple text passwords (without usernames) works, but it requires that everyone know the same passwords. For example, all must know the same vty password to get access to the switch using Telnet.

Cisco switches support other login authentication methods that use a username and password so that each user has unique login details that do not have to be shared. One method configures the username/password pairs locally on the switch, and the other relies on an external server called an authentication, authorization, and accounting (AAA) server. (The server could be the same server used for logins for other servers in the network.) This book covers the configuration using locally configured usernames/passwords.

The migration from using the password-only login method to using locally configured user-names and passwords requires only some small configuration changes. The switch needs one or more **username** *name* **password** *password* global configuration commands to define the user-names and passwords. Then the vty and/or console line needs to be told to make use of a locally configured username and password (per the **login local** line subcommand). For example, Figure 8-2 shows the concept and configuration to migrate to using local usernames for Telnet users.

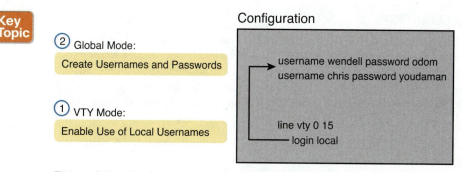

Figure 8-2   *Configuring Switches to Use Local Username Login Authentication*

When a Telnet user connects to the switch configured as shown in Figure 8-2, the user will be prompted first for a username and then for a password. The username/password pair must be from the list of local usernames, or the login is rejected.

> **NOTE**   Figure 8-2 lists the configuration commands in the same order as seen in the IOS **show running-config** command.

Securing Access with External Authentication Servers

Using a local list of usernames and passwords on a switch or router works well in small networks. However, using locally configured username/password pairs means that every switch and router needs the configuration for all users who might need to log in to the devices. Then, when any changes need to happen, like an occasional change to the passwords, the configuration of all devices must be changed.

Cisco switches and routers support an alternative way to keep track of valid usernames and passwords by using an external AAA server. When using a AAA server for authentication, the switch (or router) simply sends a message to the AAA server asking whether the username and password are allowed, and the AAA server replies. Figure 8-3 shows an example, with the user first supplying his username/password, the switch asking the AAA server, and the server replying to the switch stating that the username/password is valid.

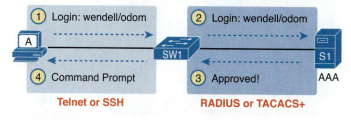
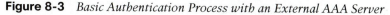

Figure 8-3   *Basic Authentication Process with an External AAA Server*

While the figure shows the general idea, note that the information flows with a couple of different protocols. On the left, the connection between the user and the switch or router uses Telnet or SSH. On the right, the switch and AAA server typically use either the RADIUS or TACACS+ protocol, both of which encrypt the passwords as they traverse the network.

Configuring Secure Shell (SSH)

To support SSH, Cisco switches require the base configuration used to support Telnet login with usernames, plus additional configuration. First, the switch already runs an SSH server by default, accepting incoming SSH connections from SSH clients. In addition, the switch needs a cryptography key, used to encrypt the data. The following list details the steps for a Cisco switch to support SSH using local usernames, with Step 3 listing the new commands specific to SSH support:

Step 1. Configure the vty lines to use usernames, with either locally configured usernames (using the **login local** command) or a AAA server.

Step 2. If using locally defined usernames, add one or more **username** global configuration commands to configure username/password pairs.

Step 3. Configure the switch to generate a matched public and private key pair to use for encryption, using two commands:

A. As a prerequisite for the next command, configure a DNS domain name with the **ip domain-name** *name* global configuration command.

B. Create the encryption keys using the **crypto key generate rsa** global configuration command.

Step 4. (Optional) Enable SSH Version 2 using the **ip ssh version 2** global command for enhanced security.

Figure 8-4 shows the three steps, with examples of the required configuration commands. Note that this figure adds to the configuration shown in Figure 8-2, with only two more commands added to support SSH.

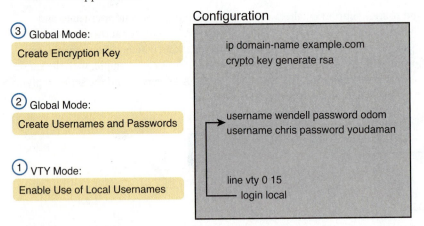

Figure 8-4   *Configuring a Switch to Support Inbound SSH Login*

NOTE   If you wonder why the figure shows the order from bottom to top, it is because the output of the **show running-config** command will list these configuration commands in the order shown in the figure.

Seeing the configuration happen in configuration mode, step by step, can be particularly helpful with SSH. Note in particular that the **crypto key** command actually prompts the user for more information and generates some messages while the key is being generated. Example 8-3 shows the commands in Figure 8-4 being configured, with the encryption key as the final step.

Example 8-3 *SSH Configuration Process*

```
Emma# configure terminal
Enter configuration commands, one per line.  End with CNTL/Z.
Emma(config)# line vty 0 15
! Step 1's key command happens next
Emma(config-line)# login local
Emma(config-line)# exit
!
! Step 2's command happens next
Emma(config)# username wendell password odom
Emma(config)# username chris password youdaman
!
! Step 3's two commands happen next
Emma(config)# ip domain-name example.com
Emma(config)# crypto key generate rsa
The name for the keys will be: Emma.example.com
Choose the size of the key modulus in the range of 360 to 2048 for your
  General Purpose Keys. Choosing a key modulus greater than 512 may take
  a few minutes.

How many bits in the modulus [512]: 1024
% Generating 1024 bit RSA keys, keys will be non-exportable...
[OK] (elapsed time was 4 seconds)

Emma(config)# ip ssh version 2
Emma(config)# ^Z
Emma#
```

Two key commands give some information about the status of SSH on the switch. First, the **show ip ssh** command lists status information about the SSH server itself. The **show ssh** command then lists information about each SSH client currently connected into the switch. Example 8-4 shows samples of each, with user Wendell currently connected to the switch.

Example 8-4 *Displaying SSH Status*

```
Emma# show ip ssh
SSH Enabled - version 2.0
Authentication timeout: 120 secs; Authentication retries: 3
Minimum expected Diffie Hellman key size : 1024 bits
IOS Keys in SECSH format(ssh-rsa, base64 encoded):
ssh-rsa AAAAB3NzaC1yc2EAAAADAQABAAAAgQC+/mp2iaeaGwjqkIgLNH+lN/04LTc2u6qHVHHv3hoq
/DDBd9vABNnJGsq8z0Hm9HcrSudC20N/cCuEb4x5+T9rvNkUeAqwEEoJALpdiWVOpBliomhPysvJi+m4
wI16AH31KI+GFCZv1AIjZSYHQEbvdCEqsYezAeKnPhvzTrUqaQ==

Emma# show ssh
Connection Version Mode Encryption  Hmac       State             Username
0          2.0     IN   aes128-cbc  hmac-sha1  Session started   wendell
0          2.0     OUT  aes128-cbc  hmac-sha1  Session started   wendell
%No SSHv1 server connections running.
```

Note that this example does use SSH Version 2 rather than Version 1. SSH v2 improves the underlying security algorithms over SSH v1 and adds some other small advantages, like banner support.

Finally, the switch supports both Telnet and SSH on the vty lines, but you can disable either or both for even tighter security. For example, your company might require that you avoid Telnet because of the security risk, so you need to disable Telnet support on the switch. Switches can control their support of Telnet and/or SSH on the vty lines using the **transport input {all | none | telnet | ssh}** vty subcommand, with the following options:

transport input all or **transport input telnet ssh:** Support both

transport input none: Support neither

transport input telnet: Support only Telnet

transport input ssh: Support only SSH

Encrypting and Hiding Passwords

Several of the configuration commands discussed so far in this chapter list passwords in clear text in the running config file (at least by default). In fact, of the commands discussed in this chapter so far, only the **enable secret** command automatically hides the password value. The other commands—the console and vty lines with the **password** command, plus the password in the **username password** command—store the password in clear text by default.

The next few sections discuss several options for hiding password values. Some tools use encryption, and some use a one-way hash algorithm. Regardless of the detail, the result is that the passwords cannot be seen by anyone who happens to see the output of the **show running-config** command.

Encrypting Passwords with the **service password** Command

To prevent password vulnerability in a printed version of the configuration file, or in a backup copy of the configuration file stored on a server, you can encrypt some passwords using the **service password-encryption** global configuration command. This command affects how IOS stores passwords for the **password** command, in both console and vty modes, and the **username password** global command. The rules for the **service password-encryption** command are as follows:

■ At the moment that the **service password-encryption** command is configured, IOS immediately encrypts all existing **password** commands (in console and vty modes) and **username password** (global command) passwords.

■ While the **service password-encryption** command remains in the configuration, IOS encrypts these same passwords if their values are changed.

■ At the moment the **no service password-encryption** command is used, disabling password encryption, IOS does nothing to the existing passwords, leaving them all as encrypted.

■ From that point forward, while the **service password-encryption** command is no longer in the configuration, IOS stores any changed password values for these commands as clear text.

Example 8-5 shows an example of these details.

Example 8-5 *Encryption and the* service password-encryption *Command*

```
Switch3# show running-config | begin line vty
line vty 0 4
 password cisco
 login
line vty 5 15
 password cisco
 login


Switch3# configure terminal
Enter configuration commands, one per line.  End with CNTL/Z.
Switch3(config)# service password-encryption
Switch3(config)# ^Z


Switch3# show running-config | begin line vty
line vty 0 4
 password 7 070C285F4D06
 login
line vty 5 15
 password 7 070C285F4D06
 login
end
Switch3# configure terminal
Enter configuration commands, one per line.  End with CNTL/Z.
Switch3(config)# no service password-encryption
Switch3(config)# ^Z
Switch3# show running-config | section vty
line vty 0 4
 password 7 070C285F4D06
 login
line vty 5 15
 password 7 070C285F4D06
 login
end


Switch3# configure terminal
Enter configuration commands, one per line.  End with CNTL/Z.
Switch3(config)# line vty 0 4
Switch3(config-line)# password cisco
Switch3(config-line)# ^Z


Switch3# show running-config | begin line vty
line vty 0 4
 password cisco
 login
line vty 5 15
 password 7 070C285F4D06
 login
end
```

8

> **NOTE**   The encryption type used by the **service password-encryption** command, as noted with the "7" in the **password** commands, is weak. You can search the Internet and find sites with tools to decrypt these passwords. In fact, you can take the encrypted password from this example, plug it into one of these sites, and it decrypts to "cisco." So, the **service password-encryption** command will slow down the curious, but it will not stop a knowledgeable attacker.

Example 8-5 also shows several examples of the pipe function (|), available at the end of CLI **show** commands. The | at the end of a **show** command sends (pipes) the output of the command to another function, like the **begin** and **section** functions shown in Example 8-5. The **begin** function, as shown in the **show running-config | begin line vty** command in the example, takes the output from the command and starts listing the text beginning when the first occurrence of the listed text ("vty" in this case) shows up. The | **section vty** parameters, also seen in Example 8-5, display only the section of output about the vty lines.

Hiding the Enable Password

Switches can protect enable mode by requiring that the user supply an enable password after using the **enable** EXEC command. However, the configuration can be based on two different commands: the older **enable password** *password* global command and the newer (and preferred) **enable secret** *password* global command.

IOS allows you to configure neither, one or the other, or even both of these commands. Then the switch chooses what password to require of a user based on the following rules:

- **Both commands configured:** Use the **enable secret** *password* command.
- **Only one command configured:** Use the password in that one command.
- **Neither command configured (default):** Console users are allowed into enable mode without a password prompt, while others are rejected.

The newer **enable secret** command provides much better security compared to the older **enable password** command. The older **enable password** command stores the password as clear text, and the only option to encrypt it is the weak **service password-encryption** command. The newer **enable secret** command automatically encodes the password, using a different process than the **service password-encryption** command. This newer command applies a mathematical function to the password, called a Message Digest 5 (MD5) hash, storing the results of the formula in the **enable secret** command in the configuration file.

Example 8-6 shows the creation of the **enable secret** command, and describes how it hides the password text. The example first lists the **enable secret fred** command, as typed by the user. Later, the **show running-configuration** command shows that IOS changed the **enable secret** command, now listing encryption type 5 (meaning it is an MD5 hash). The gobbledygook long text string is the MD5 hash, preventing others from reading the password.

Example 8-6   *Encryption and the* **enable secret** *Command*

```
Switch3(config)# enable secret ?
  0      Specifies an UNENCRYPTED password will follow
  5      Specifies an ENCRYPTED secret will follow
  LINE   The UNENCRYPTED (cleartext) 'enable' secret
  level  Set exec level password
```

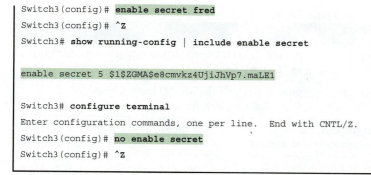

```
Switch3(config)# enable secret fred
Switch3(config)# ^Z
Switch3# show running-config | include enable secret

enable secret 5 $1$ZGMA$e8cmvkz4UjiJhVp7.maLE1

Switch3# configure terminal
Enter configuration commands, one per line.  End with CNTL/Z.
Switch3(config)# no enable secret
Switch3(config)# ^Z
```

The end of the example also shows an important point about deleting the enable secret pass-word: After you are in enable mode, you can delete the enable secret password using the **no enable secret** command, without even having to enter the password value. You can also over-write the old password by just repeating the command.

> **NOTE** Example 8-6 shows another shortcut with working through long **show** command out-put, using the pipe to the **include** command. The **show running-config | include enable secret** command lists the output from **show running-config**, but only lines that include the case-sensitive text "enable secret."

Finally, note that Cisco has added another hash algorithm to the **enable secret** command for routers: SHA-256. This algorithm is stronger than MD5, with IOS listing this algorithm as encryption type 4. Over time, Cisco will likely add SHA-256 support to switches as well. Regardless, the effect of using SHA-256 or MD5 is the same: The user configures a command like **enable secret fred**, typing the clear-text password, and IOS stores the hash value as either MD5 (older IOS versions) or SHA-256 (newer IOS versions).

Hiding the Passwords for Local Usernames

Cisco added the **enable secret** command, and its better password protection, back in the 1990s. More recently, Cisco has added the **username** *user* **secret** *password* global command as an alternative to the **username** *user* **password** *password* command. Note that this command uses an SHA-256 (type 4) hash.

Today, the **username secret** command is preferred over the **username password** command, much like the **enable secret** command is preferred over the **enable password** command. However, note that a username can be configured with either the **username secret** command or the **username password** command, but not both.

Console and vty Settings

This section covers a few small configuration settings that affect the behavior of the CLI con-nection from the console and/or vty (Telnet and SSH).

Banners

Cisco switches can display a variety of banners depending on what a router or switch administra-tor is doing. A banner is simply some text that appears on the screen for the user. You can con-figure a router or switch to display multiple banners, some before login and some after. Table 8-1 lists the three most popular banners and their typical use with Telnet.

8

Table 8-1   Banners and Their Use with Telnet

Banner	Typical Use
Message of the Day (MOTD)	Shown before the login prompt. Used for temporary messages that can change from time to time, such as "Router1 down for maintenance at midnight."
Login	Shown before the login prompt but after the MOTD banner. Used for permanent messages such as "Unauthorized Access Prohibited."
Exec	Shown after the login prompt. Used to supply information that should be hidden from unauthorized users.

The **banner** global configuration command can be used to configure all three types of these banners. In each case, the type of banner is listed as the first parameter, with MOTD being the default option. The first nonblank character after the banner type is called a beginning delimiter character. The banner text can span several lines, with the CLI user pressing Enter at the end of each line. The CLI knows that the banner has been configured as soon as the user enters the same delimiter character again.

Example 8-7 shows the configuration process for all three types of banners from Table 8-1, followed by a sample user login session that shows the banners in use. The first banner in the example, the MOTD banner, omits the banner type in the **banner** command as a reminder that **motd** is the default banner type. The first two **banner** commands use a # as the delimiter character. The third **banner** command uses a Z as the delimiter, just to show that any character can be used. Also, the last **banner** command shows multiple lines of banner text.

Example 8-7   *Banner Configuration*

```
! Below, the three banners are created in configuration mode. Note that any
! delimiter can be used, as long as the character is not part of the message
! text.


SW1(config)# banner #
Enter TEXT message.  End with the character '#'.
(MOTD) Switch down for maintenance at 11PM Today #
SW1(config)# banner login #
Enter TEXT message.  End with the character '#'.
(Login) Unauthorized Access Prohibited!!!!
#
SW1(config)# banner exec Z
Enter TEXT message.  End with the character 'Z'.
(Exec) Company picnic at the park on Saturday
 Don't tell outsiders!
Z
SW1(config)# end


! Below, the user of this router quits the console connection, and logs back in,
! seeing the motd and login banners, then the password prompt, and then the
! exec banner.
SW1#quit


SW1 con0 is now available


Press RETURN to get started.
```

```
(MOTD) Switch down for maintenance at 11PM Today
(Login) Unauthorized Access Prohibited!!!!

User Access Verification

Username: fred
Password:
(Exec) Company picnic at the park on Saturday
don't tell outsiders!
SW1>
```

History Buffer Commands

When you enter commands from the CLI, the last several commands are saved in the history buffer. As mentioned in Chapter 7, you can use the up-arrow key, or press Ctrl+P, to move back in the history buffer stack to retrieve a command you entered a few commands ago. This feature makes it very easy and fast to use a set of commands repeatedly. Table 8-2 lists some of the key commands related to the history buffer.

Table 8-2   Commands Related to the History Buffer

Command	Description
show history	Lists the commands currently held in the history buffer.
history size *x*	From console or vty line configuration mode, sets the default number of commands saved in the history buffer for the user(s) of the console or vty lines, respectively.
terminal history size *x*	From EXEC mode, this command allows a single user to set, just for this one login session, the size of his or her history buffer.

The **logging synchronous** and **exec-timeout** Commands

The next short section looks at a couple of ways to make using the console a little more user friendly, by asking the switch to not interrupt with log messages, and to control how long you can be connected to the console before getting forced out.

The console automatically receives copies of all unsolicited syslog messages on a switch. The idea is that if the switch needs to tell the network administrator some important and possibly urgent information, the administrator might be at the console and might notice the message.

The display of these messages at the console can be disabled and enabled with the **no logging console** and **logging console** global commands. For example, when working from the console, if you want to temporarily not be bothered by log messages, you can disable the display of these messages with the **no logging console** global configuration command, and then when finished, enable them again.

Unfortunately, IOS (by default) displays these syslog messages on the console's screen at any time—including right in the middle of a command you are entering, or in the middle of the output of a **show** command. Having a bunch of text show up unexpectedly can be a bit annoying.

IOS supplies a solution to this problem by telling the switch to display syslog messages only at more convenient times, such as at the end of output from a **show** command. To do so, just configure the **logging synchronous** console line subcommand.

Another way to improve the user experience at the console is to control timeouts from the console. By default, the switch automatically disconnects console and vty (Telnet and SSH) users after 5 minutes of inactivity. The **exec-timeout** *minutes seconds* line subcommand lets you set the length of that inactivity timer, with the special value of 0 minutes and 0 seconds meaning "never time out."

Example 8-8 shows the syntax for these two commands, both on the console line. Note that both can be applied to the vty lines as well, for the same reasons.

Example 8-8 *Defining Console Inactivity Timeouts and When to Display Log Messages*

```
line console 0
 login
 password cisco
 exec-timeout 0 0
 logging synchronous
```

NOTE This concludes the first half of this chapter. If you have not yet tried any commands on a router or switch, now would be a good time to pause from your reading and try some. If you have real gear, or the Pearson Simulator, do some labs about navigating the CLI, setting passwords, and other basic administration. If not, watch the videos from the DVD on CLI navigation and route configuration. Also, try a few labs from the ICND1 Simulator Lite on the DVD. Even if you do a lab on something you have not seen yet, you can get a little better idea about how to move around with the command-line interface.

LAN Switch Configuration and Operation

Cisco switches work very well when received from the factory, without any configuration added. Cisco switches leave the factory with default settings, with all interfaces enabled (a default configuration of **no shutdown**) and with autonegotiation enabled for ports that can use it (a default configuration of **duplex auto** and **speed auto**). All interfaces default to be part of VLAN 1 (**switchport access vlan 1**). All you have to do with a new Cisco switch is make all the physical connections—Ethernet cables and power cord—and the switch starts working.

In most enterprise networks, you will want the switch to operate with some different settings as compared with the factory defaults. The second half of this chapter discusses some of those settings, with Chapter 9 ("Implementing Ethernet Virtual LANs") discussing more. (Also note that the details in this section differ from the configuration on a router.) In particular, this section covers the following:

- IP for remote access
- Interface configuration (including speed and duplex)
- Port security
- Securing unused switch interfaces

Enabling IP for Remote Access

To allow Telnet or SSH access to the switch, and to allow other IP-based management protocols (for example, Simple Network Management Protocol) to function as intended, the switch needs an IP address. The IP address has nothing to do with how switches forward Ethernet frames; it simply exists to support overhead management traffic.

A switch's IP configuration works like a PC with a single Ethernet interface. For perspective, a PC has a CPU, with the operating system running on the CPU. It has an Ethernet network interface card (NIC). The OS configuration includes an IP address associated with the NIC, either configured or learned dynamically with DHCP. To support IP, the switch has the equivalent settings.

A switch uses concepts similar to a host, except that the switch can use a virtual NIC. Like a PC, a switch has a real CPU, running an OS (called IOS). The switch then uses a NIC-like concept called a *switched virtual interface (SVI)*, or more commonly, a *VLAN interface*, that acts like the switch's own NIC for connecting into a LAN to send IP packets. Like a host, the switch configuration assigns IP settings, like an IP address, to this VLAN interface, as seen in Figure 8-5.

Key Topic

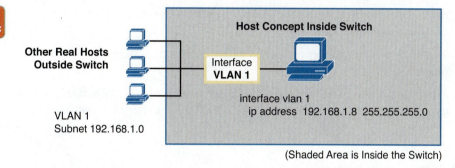

Figure 8-5 *Switch Virtual Interface (SVI) Concept Inside a Switch*

A typical Layer 2 Cisco LAN switch can use only one VLAN interface at a time, but the network engineer can choose which VLAN interface, putting the switch's management traffic into a particular VLAN. For example, Figure 8-6 shows a switch with some physical ports in two different VLANs (1 and 2). The network engineer needs to choose whether the switch IP address, used to access and manage the switch, should have an IP address in subnet 192.168.1.0 (in VLAN 1), or in subnet 192.168.2.0 (in VLAN 2).

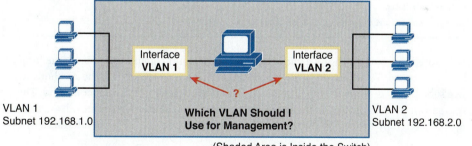

Figure 8-6 *Choosing One VLAN on Which to Configure a Switch IP Address*

> **NOTE** Some Cisco switches, called *Layer 2 switches*, forward Ethernet frames as discussed in depth in Chapter 6, "Building Ethernet LANs with Switches." Other Cisco switches, called *multilayer switches* or *Layer 3 switches*, can also route IP packets using the Layer 3 logic normally used by routers. Layer 3 switches configure IP addresses on more than one VLAN interface at a time. This chapter assumes all switches are Layer 2 switches. Chapter 9 further defines the differences between these types of LAN switches.

Configuring IPv4 on a Switch

A switch configures its IPv4 address and mask on this special NIC-like *VLAN interface*. The following steps list the commands used to configure IPv4 on a switch, assuming that the IP address is configured to be in VLAN 1, with Example 8-9 that follows showing an example configuration.

Step 1. Enter VLAN 1 configuration mode using the **interface vlan 1** global configuration command.

Step 2. Assign an IP address and mask using the **ip address** *ip-address mask* interface subcommand.

Step 3. If not already enabled, enable the VLAN 1 interface using the **no shutdown** interface subcommand.

Step 4. Add the **ip default-gateway** *ip-address* global command to configure the default gateway.

Step 5. (Optional) Add the **ip name-server** *ip-address1 ip-address2 . . .* global command to configure the switch to use DNS to resolve names into their matching IP address.

Example 8-9   *Switch Static IP Address Configuration*

```
Emma# configure terminal
Emma(config)# interface vlan 1
Emma(config-if)# ip address 192.168.1.200 255.255.255.0
Emma(config-if)# no shutdown
00:25:07: %LINK-3-UPDOWN: Interface Vlan1, changed state to up
00:25:08: %LINEPROTO-5-UPDOWN: Line protocol on Interface Vlan1, changed
  state to up
Emma(config-if)# exit
Emma(config)# ip default-gateway 192.168.1.1
```

On a side note, this example shows a particularly important and common command: the **[no] shutdown** command. To administratively enable an interface on a switch, use the **no shutdown** interface subcommand; to disable an interface, use the **shutdown** interface subcommand. The messages shown in Example 8-9, immediately following the **no shutdown** command, are syslog messages generated by the switch stating that the switch did indeed enable the interface.

The switch can also use DHCP to dynamically learn its IPv4 settings. Basically, all you have to do is tell the switch to use DHCP on the interface, and enable the interface. Assuming that DHCP works in this network, the switch will learn all its settings. The following list details the steps, again assuming the use of interface VLAN 1, with Example 8-10 that follows showing an example.

Step 1. Enter VLAN 1 configuration mode using the **interface vlan 1** global configuration command, and enable the interface using the **no shutdown** command as necessary.

Step 2. Assign an IP address and mask using the **ip address dhcp** interface subcommand.

Example 8-10 *Switch Dynamic IP Address Configuration with DHCP*

```
Emma# configure terminal
Enter configuration commands, one per line.  End with CNTL/Z.
Emma(config)# interface vlan 1
Emma(config-if)# ip address dhcp
Emma(config-if)# no shutdown
Emma(config-if)# ^Z
Emma#
00:38:20: %LINK-3-UPDOWN: Interface Vlan1, changed state to up
00:38:21: %LINEPROTO-5-UPDOWN: Line protocol on Interface Vlan1, changed state to up
```

Verifying IPv4 on a Switch

The switch IPv4 configuration can be checked in several places. First, you can always look at the current configuration using the **show running-config** command. Second, you can look at the IP address and mask information using the **show interface vlan** *x* command, which shows detailed status information about the VLAN interface in VLAN *x*. Finally, if using DHCP, use the **show dhcp lease** command to see the (temporarily) leased IP address and other parameters. (Note that the switch does not store the DHCP-learned IP configuration in the running-config file.) Example 8-11 shows sample output from these commands to match the configuration in Example 8-10.

Example 8-11 *Verifying DHCP-learned Information on a Switch*

```
Emma# show dhcp lease
Temp IP addr: 192.168.1.101  for peer on Interface: Vlan1
Temp  sub net mask: 255.255.255.0
   DHCP Lease server: 192.168.1.1, state: 3 Bound
   DHCP transaction id: 1966
   Lease: 86400 secs,  Renewal: 43200 secs,  Rebind: 75600 secs
Temp default-gateway addr: 192.168.1.1
   Next timer fires after: 11:59:45
   Retry count: 0   Client-ID: cisco-0019.e86a.6fc0-Vl1
   Hostname: Emma
Emma# show interfaces vlan 1
Vlan1 is up, line protocol is up
  Hardware is EtherSVI, address is 0019.e86a.6fc0 (bia 0019.e86a.6fc0)
  Internet address is 192.168.1.101/24
  MTU 1500 bytes, BW 1000000 Kbit, DLY 10 usec,
     reliability 255/255, txload 1/255, rxload 1/255
! lines omitted for brevity
Emma# show ip default-gateway
192.168.1.1
```

The output of the **show interfaces vlan 1** command lists two very important details related to switch IP addressing. First, this **show** command lists the interface status of the VLAN 1 interface—in this case, "up and up." If the VLAN 1 interface is not up, the switch cannot use its IP address to send and receive traffic. Notably, if you forget to issue the **no shutdown** command, the VLAN 1 interface remains in its default shutdown state and is listed as "administratively down" in the **show** command output.

8

Second, note that the output lists the interface's IP address on the third line. If you statically configure the IP address, as in Example 8-9, the IP address will always be listed. However, if you use DHCP, and DHCP fails, the **show interfaces vlan** *x* command will not list an IP address here. When DHCP works, you can see the IP address with this command, but it does not remind you whether the address is either statically configured or DHCP leased.

Configuring Switch Interfaces

IOS uses the term *interface* to refer to physical ports used to forward data to and from other devices. Each interface can be configured with several settings, each of which might differ from interface to interface.

IOS uses interface subcommands to configure these settings. For example, interfaces can be configured to use the **duplex** and **speed** interface subcommands to configure those settings statically, or an interface can use autonegotiation (the default). Example 8-12 shows how to configure duplex and speed, as well as the **description** command, which is simply a text description that can be configured by the administrator.

Example 8-12 *Interface Configuration Basics*

```
Emma# configure terminal
Enter configuration commands, one per line.  End with CNTL/Z.
Emma(config)# interface FastEthernet 0/1
Emma(config-if)# duplex full
Emma(config-if)# speed 100
Emma(config-if)# description Server1 connects here
Emma(config-if)# exit
Emma(config)# interface range FastEthernet 0/11 - 20
Emma(config-if-range)# description end-users connect_here
Emma(config-if-range)# ^Z
Emma#
Emma# show interfaces status

Port       Name              Status        Vlan      Duplex  Speed Type
Fa0/1      Server1 connects h notconnect   1         full    100   10/100BaseTX
Fa0/2                        notconnect    1         auto    auto  10/100BaseTX
Fa0/3                        notconnect    1         auto    auto  10/100BaseTX
Fa0/4                        connected     1         a-full  a-100 10/100BaseTX
Fa0/5                        notconnect    1         auto    auto  10/100BaseTX
Fa0/6                        connected     1         a-full  a-100 10/100BaseTX
Fa0/7                        notconnect    1         auto    auto  10/100BaseTX
Fa0/8                        notconnect    1         auto    auto  10/100BaseTX
Fa0/9                        notconnect    1         auto    auto  10/100BaseTX
Fa0/10                       notconnect    1         auto    auto  10/100BaseTX
Fa0/11     end-users connect notconnect    1         auto    auto  10/100BaseTX
Fa0/12     end-users connect notconnect    1         auto    auto  10/100BaseTX
Fa0/13     end-users connect notconnect    1         auto    auto  10/100BaseTX
Fa0/14     end-users connect notconnect    1         auto    auto  10/100BaseTX
Fa0/15     end-users connect notconnect    1         auto    auto  10/100BaseTX
Fa0/16     end-users connect notconnect    1         auto    auto  10/100BaseTX
Fa0/17     end-users connect notconnect    1         auto    auto  10/100BaseTX
```

Fa0/18	end-users connect	notconnect	1	auto	auto 10/100BaseTX
Fa0/19	end-users connect	notconnect	1	auto	auto 10/100BaseTX
Fa0/20	end-users connect	notconnect	1	auto	auto 10/100BaseTX
Fa0/21		notconnect	1	auto	auto 10/100BaseTX
Fa0/22		notconnect	1	auto	auto 10/100BaseTX
Fa0/23		notconnect	1	auto	auto 10/100BaseTX
Fa0/24		notconnect	1	auto	auto 10/100BaseTX
Gi0/1		notconnect	1	auto	auto 10/100/1000BaseTX
Gi0/2		notconnect	1	auto	auto 10/100/1000BaseTX

You can see some of the details of interface configuration with both the **show running-config** command (not shown in the example) and the handy **show interfaces status** command. This command lists a single line for each interface, the first part of the interface description, and the speed and duplex settings. Several of the early entries in the output purposefully show some differences, as follows:

FastEthernet 0/1 (Fa0/1): This output lists the configured speed of 100 and duplex full; however, it lists a status of notconnect. The notconnect status means that the physical link is not currently working, including reasons like no cable being connected, the other device being powered off, or the other device putting the port in a shutdown state. In this case, no cable had been installed when the output was gathered.

FastEthernet 0/2 (Fa0/2): This port also has no cable installed yet, but it uses all default configuration. So, the highlighted output shows this interface with the default setting of auto (meaning autonegotiate).

FastEthernet 0/4 (Fa0/4): Like Fa0/2, this port has all default configuration, but was cabled to another device that is up, causing the status to be listed as "connect." This device also completed the autonegotiation process, so the output lists the resulting speed and duplex (**a-full** and **a-100**), in which the **a-** refers to the fact that these values were autonegotiated.

Also, note that for the sake of efficiency, you can configure a command on a range of interfaces at the same time using the **interface range** command. In the example, the **interface range FastEthernet 0/11 - 20** command tells IOS that the next subcommand(s) apply to interfaces Fa0/11 through Fa0/20.

NOTE Configuring both the speed and duplex on a Cisco switch interface disables autonegotiation.

Port Security

If the network engineer knows what devices should be cabled and connected to particular interfaces on a switch, the engineer can use *port security* to restrict that interface so that only the expected devices can use it. This reduces exposure to attacks in which the attacker connects a laptop to some unused switch port. When that inappropriate device attempts to send frames to the switch interface, the switch can take different actions, ranging from simply issuing informational messages to effectively shutting down the interface.

Port security identifies devices based on the source MAC address of Ethernet frames the devices send. For example, in Figure 8-7, PC1 sends a frame, with PC1's MAC address as the source address. SW1's F0/1 interface can be configured with port security, and if so, SW1 would think about PC1's MAC address and whether PC1 was allowed to send frames into port F0/1.

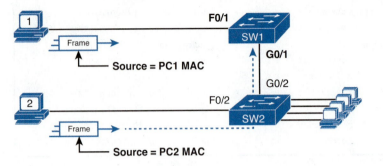

Figure 8-7 *Source MAC Addresses in Frames as They Enter a Switch*

Port security also has no restrictions on whether the frame came from a local device or it was forwarded through other switches. For example, switch SW1 could use port security on its G0/1 interface, checking the source MAC address of the frame from PC2, when forwarded up to SW1 from SW2.

Port security has several flexible options, but all operate with the same core concepts. First, switches enable port security per port, with different settings available per port. Each port has a maximum number of allowed MAC addresses, meaning that for all frames entering that port, only that number of *different* source MAC addresses can be used in different incoming frames before port security thinks a violation has occurred. When a frame with a new source MAC address arrives, pushing the number of MAC addresses past the allowed maximum, a port security violation occurs. At that point, the switch takes action—by default, discarding all future incoming traffic on that port.

The following list summarizes these ideas common to all variations of port security:

Key Topic

- Define a maximum number of source MAC addresses allowed for all frames coming in the interface.

- Watch all incoming frames, and keep a list of all source MAC addresses, plus a counter of the number of different source MAC addresses.

- When adding a new source MAC address to the list, if the number of MAC addresses pushes past the configured maximum, a port security violation has occurred. The switch takes action (the default action is to shutdown the interface).

While those rules define the basics, port security allows other options as well, including letting you configure the specific MAC address(es) allowed to send frames in an interface. For example, in Figure 8-7, switch SW1 connects through interface F0/1 to PC1, so the port security configuration could list PC1's MAC address as the specific allowed MAC address. But predefining MAC addresses for port security is optional: You can predefine all MAC addresses, none, or a subset of the MAC addresses.

You might like the idea of predefining the MAC addresses for port security, but finding the MAC address of each device can be a bother. Port security provides an easy way to discover the MAC addresses used off each port using a feature called *sticky secure MAC addresses*. With this feature, port security learns the MAC addresses off each port and stores those in the port security configuration (in the running-config file). This feature helps reduce the big effort of finding out the MAC address of each device.

As you can see, port security has a lot of detailed options. The next few sections walk you through these options to pull the ideas together.

Configuring Port Security

Port security configuration involves several steps. First, you need to disable the negotiation of a feature that is not discussed until Chapter 9: whether the port is an access or trunk port. For now, accept that port security requires a port to be configured to either be an access port or a trunking port. The rest of the commands enable port security, set the maximum allowed MAC addresses per port, and configure the actual MAC addresses, as detailed in this list:

Step 1. Make the switch interface either a static access or trunk interface, using the **switchport mode access** or the **switchport mode trunk** interface subcommands, respectively.

Step 2. Enable port security using the **switchport port-security** interface subcommand.

Step 3. (Optional) Override the default maximum number of allowed MAC addresses associated with the interface (1) by using the **switchport port-security maximum** *number* interface subcommand.

Step 4. (Optional) Override the default action to take upon a security violation (shutdown) using the **switchport port-security violation {protect | restrict | shutdown}** interface subcommand.

Step 5. (Optional) Predefine any allowed source MAC address(es) for this interface, using the **switchport port-security mac-address** *mac-address* command. Use the command multiple times to define more than one MAC address.

Step 6. (Optional) Tell the switch to "sticky learn" dynamically learned MAC addresses with the **switchport port-security mac-address sticky** interface subcommand.

Figure 8-8 and Example 8-13 show four examples of port security, each with different details just to show the different options.

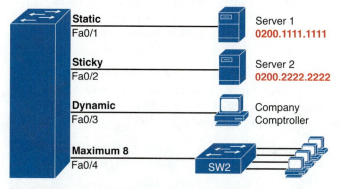

Figure 8-8 *Port Security Configuration Example*

Example 8-13 *Variations on Port Security Configuration*

```
SW1# show running-config
(Lines omitted for brevity)

interface FastEthernet0/1
 switchport mode access
 switchport port-security
 switchport port-security mac-address 0200.1111.1111
!
```

```
interface FastEthernet0/2
 switchport mode access
 switchport port-security
 switchport port-security mac-address sticky
!
interface FastEthernet0/3
 switchport mode access
 switchport port-security
!
interface FastEthernet0/4
 switchport mode access
 switchport port-security
 switchport port-security maximum 8
```

First, scan the configuration for all four interfaces in Example 8-13, focusing on the first two interface subcommands. Note that all four interfaces in the example use the same first two interface subcommands, matching the first two configuration steps noted before Figure 8-8. The **switchport port-security** command enables port security, with all defaults, with the **switchport mode access** command meeting the requirement to configure the port as either an access or trunk port.

Next, scan all four interfaces again, and note that the configuration differs on each interface after those first two interface subcommands. Each interface simply shows a different example for perspective.

The first interface, FastEthernet 0/1, adds one optional port security subcommand: **switchport port-security mac-address 0200.1111.1111**, which defines a specific source MAC address. With the default maximum source address setting of 1, only frames with source MAC 0200.1111.1111 will be allowed in this port. When a frame with a source other than 0200.1111.1111 enters F0/1, the switch will take the default violation action and disable the interface.

As a second example, FastEthernet 0/2 uses the same logic as FastEthernet 0/1, except that it uses the sticky learning feature instead of predefining a MAC address with the **switchport port-security mac-address sticky** command. The end of upcoming Example 8-14 shows the running config file that lists the sticky-learned MAC address in this case.

NOTE   Port security does not save the configuration of the sticky addresses, so use the **copy running-config startup-config** command if desired.

The other two interfaces do not predefine MAC addresses, nor do they sticky-learn the MAC addresses. The only difference between these two interfaces' port security configuration is that FastEthernet 0/4 supports eight MAC addresses, because it connects to another switch and should receive frames with multiple source MAC addresses. Interface F0/3 uses the default maximum of one MAC address.

Verifying Port Security

Example 8-14 lists the output of two examples of the **show port-security interface** command. This command lists the configuration settings for port security on an interface, plus it lists several important facts about the current operation of port security, including information about any security violations. The two commands in the example show interfaces F0/1 and F0/2, based on Example 8-13's configuration.

Example 8-14   *Using Port Security to Define Correct MAC Addresses of Particular Interfaces*

```
SW1# show port-security interface fastEthernet 0/1
Port Security               : Enabled
Port Status                 : Secure-shutdown
Violation Mode              : Shutdown
Aging Time                  : 0 mins
Aging Type                  : Absolute
SecureStatic Address Aging  : Disabled
Maximum MAC Addresses       : 1
Total MAC Addresses         : 1
Configured MAC Addresses    : 1
Sticky MAC Addresses        : 0
Last Source Address:Vlan    : 0013.197b.5004:1
Security Violation Count    : 1


SW1# show port-security interface fastEthernet 0/2
Port Security               : Enabled
Port Status                 : Secure-up
Violation Mode              : Shutdown
Aging Time                  : 0 mins
Aging Type                  : Absolute
SecureStatic Address Aging  : Disabled
Maximum MAC Addresses       : 1
Total MAC Addresses         : 1
Configured MAC Addresses    : 1
Sticky MAC Addresses        : 1
Last Source Address:Vlan    : 0200.2222.2222:1
Security Violation Count    : 0


SW1# show running-config
(Lines omitted for brevity)
interface FastEthernet0/2
 switchport mode access
 switchport port-security
 switchport port-security mac-address sticky
 switchport port-security mac-address sticky 0200.2222.2222
```

The first two commands in Example 8-14 confirm that a security violation has occurred on FastEthernet 0/1, but no violations have occurred on FastEthernet 0/2. The **show port-security interface fastethernet 0/1** command shows that the interface is in a *secure-shutdown* state, which means that the interface has been disabled because of port security. In this case, another device connected to port F0/1, sending a frame with a source MAC address other than 0200.1111.1111, is causing a violation. However, port Fa0/2, which used sticky learning, simply learned the MAC address used by Server 2.

The bottom of Example 8-14, as compared to the configuration in Example 8-13, shows the changes in the running-config because of sticky learning, with the **switchport port-security mac-address sticky 0200.2222.2222** interface subcommand.

Port Security Actions

Finally, the switch can be configured to use one of three actions when a violation occurs. All three options cause the switch to discard the offending frame, but some of the options make the switch take additional actions. The actions include the sending of syslog messages to the console, sending SNMP trap messages to the network management station, and disabling the interface. Table 8-3 lists the options of the **switchport port-security violation {protect | restrict | shutdown}** command and their meanings.

Table 8-3   Actions When Port Security Violation Occurs

Option on the switchport port-security violation Command	Protect	Restrict	Shutdown*
Discards offending traffic	Yes	Yes	Yes
Sends log and SNMP messages	No	Yes	Yes
Disables the interface, discarding all traffic	No	No	Yes

*__shutdown__ is the default setting.

Note that the shutdown option does not actually add the **shutdown** subcommand to the interface configuration. Instead, IOS puts the interface in an *error disabled* (err-disabled) state, which makes the switch stop all inbound and outbound frames. To recover from this state, someone must manually disable the interface with the **shutdown** interface command and then enable the interface with the **no shutdown** command.

Securing Unused Switch Interfaces

The default settings on Cisco switches work great if you want to buy a switch, unbox it, plug it in, and have it immediately work without any other effort. Those same defaults have an unfortunate side effect for worse security. With all default configuration, unused interfaces might be used by an attacker to gain access to the LAN. So, Cisco makes some general recommendations to override the default interface settings to make the unused ports more secure, as follows:

- Administratively disable the interface using the **shutdown** interface subcommand.
- Prevent VLAN trunking by making the port a nontrunking interface using the **switchport mode access** interface subcommand.
- Assign the port to an unused VLAN using the **switchport access vlan** *number* interface subcommand.
- Set the native VLAN to not be VLAN 1, but to instead be an unused VLAN, using the **switchport trunk native vlan** *vlan-id* interface subcommand. (The native VLAN is discussed in Chapter 9.)

Frankly, if you just shutdown the interface, the security exposure goes away, but the other tasks prevent any immediate problems if someone else comes around and enables the interface by configuring a **no shutdown** command.

Review Activities

Chapter Summary

- The first step in securing a switch is to secure access to the CLI. Securing the CLI includes protecting access to enable mode, because from enable mode an attacker could reload the switch or change the configuration.

- Cisco switches protect enable mode for any user with the *enable password*. The user, in user mode, types the **enable** EXEC command and is prompted for this enable password. If the user types the correct password, IOS moves the user to enable mode.

- The console and vty password configuration uses the same two subcommands in console and vty line configuration modes, respectively. The **login** command tells IOS to use simple password security, and the **password** *password_value* command defines the password. IOS protects enable mode using the enable secret password, configured using the global command **enable secret** *password_value*.

- The migration from using the password-only login method to using locally configured usernames and passwords requires only some small configuration changes. The switch needs one or more **username** *name* **password** *password* global configuration commands to define the usernames and passwords.

- Cisco switches and routers support an alternative way to keep track of valid usernames and passwords by using an external AAA server. When using a AAA server for authentication, the switch (or router) simply sends a message to the AAA server asking whether the username and password are allowed, and the AAA server replies.

- To support SSH, Cisco switches require the base configuration used to support Telnet login with usernames, plus additional configuration. First, the switch already runs an SSH server by default, accepting incoming SSH connections from both SSH version 1 and version 2 clients. In addition, the switch needs a cryptography key, used to encrypt the data.

- To prevent password vulnerability in a printed version of the configuration file, or in a back-up copy of the configuration file stored on a server, you can encrypt some passwords using the **service password-encryption** global configuration command.

- The **banner** global configuration command can be used to configure all three types of banners:

  - **The message of the day (MOTD):** Shown before the login prompt. For temporary messages that might change from time to time, such as "Router1 down for maintenance at midnight."

  - **The login banner:** Shown before the login prompt but after the MOTD banner. For permanent messages, such as "Unauthorized Access Prohibited."

  - **The Exec banner:** Shown after the login prompt. Used to supply information that should be hidden from unauthorized users.

- A switch configures its IPv4 address and mask on this special NIC-like *VLAN interface*. The following steps list the commands used to configure IPv4 on a switch, assuming the IP address is configured to be in VLAN 1:

  Step 1.   Enter VLAN 1 configuration mode using the **interface vlan 1** global configuration command.

  Step 2.   Assign an IP address and mask using the **ip address** *ip-address mask* interface subcommand.

  Step 3.   If not already enabled, enable the VLAN 1 interface using the **no shutdown** interface subcommand.

Step 4.   Add the **ip default-gateway** *ip-address* global command to configure the default gateway.

Step 5.   (Optional) Add the **ip name-server** *ip-address1 ip-address2...* global command to configure the switch to use DNS to resolve names into their matching IP addresses.

■ To administratively enable an interface on a switch, use the **no shutdown** interface subcommand. To disable an interface, use the **shutdown** interface subcommand.

■ If the network engineer knows what devices should be cabled and connected to particular interfaces on a switch, the engineer can use *port security* to restrict that interface so that only the expected devices can use it. This reduces exposure to attacks in which the attacker connects a laptop to some unused switch port. When that inappropriate device attempts to send frames to the switch interface, the switch can take different actions, ranging from simply issuing informational messages to effectively shutting down the interface.

Review Questions

Answer these review questions. You can find the answers at the bottom of the last page of the chapter. For thorough explanations, see DVD Appendix C, "Answers to Review Questions."

1. Imagine that you have configured the **enable secret** command, followed by the **enable password** command, from the console. You log out of the switch and log back in at the console. Which command defines the password that you had to enter to access privileged mode?

    A. enable password

    B. enable secret

    C. Neither

    D. The **password** command, if it's configured

2. An engineer had formerly configured a Cisco 2960 switch to allow Telnet access so that the switch expected a password of **mypassword** from the Telnet user. The engineer then changed the configuration to support Secure Shell. Which of the following commands could have been part of the new configuration? (Choose two answers.)

    A. A **username** *name* **password** *password* vty mode subcommand

    B. A **username** *name* **password** *password* global configuration command

    C. A **login local** vty mode subcommand

    D. A **transport input ssh** global configuration command

3. The following command was copied and pasted into configuration mode when a user was telnetted into a Cisco switch:

    ```
    banner login this is the login banner
    ```

    Which of the following is true about what occurs the next time a user logs in from the console?

    A. No banner text is displayed.

    B. The banner text "his is" is displayed.

    C. The banner text "this is the login banner" is displayed.

    D. The banner text "Login banner configured, no text defined" is displayed.

4. Which of the following is required when configuring port security with sticky learning?

   A. Setting the maximum number of allowed MAC addresses on the interface with the **switchport port-security maximum** interface subcommand

   B. Enabling port security with the **switchport port-security** interface subcommand

   C. Defining the specific allowed MAC addresses using the **switchport port-security mac-address** interface subcommand

   D. All the other answers list required commands

5. An engineer's desktop PC connects to a switch at the main site. A router at the main site connects to each branch office through a serial link, with one small router and switch at each branch. Which of the following commands must be configured on the branch office switches, in the listed configuration mode, to allow the engineer to telnet to the branch office switches? (Choose three answers.)

   A. The **ip address** command in interface configuration mode

   B. The **ip address** command in global configuration mode

   C. The **ip default-gateway** command in VLAN configuration mode

   D. The **ip default-gateway** command in global configuration mode

   E. The **password** command in console line configuration mode

   F. The **password** command in vty line configuration mode

6. Which of the following describes a way to disable IEEE standard autonegotiation on a 10/100 port on a Cisco switch?

   A. Configure the **negotiate disable** interface subcommand

   B. Configure the **no negotiate** interface subcommand

   C. Configure the **speed 100** interface subcommand

   D. Configure the **duplex half** interface subcommand

   E. Configure the **duplex full** interface subcommand

   F. Configure the **speed 100** and **duplex full** interface subcommands

7. In which of the following modes of the CLI could you configure the duplex setting for interface Fast Ethernet 0/5?

   A. User mode

   B. Enable mode

   C. Global configuration mode

   D. VLAN mode

   E. Interface configuration mode

8

Review All the Key Topics

Review the most important topics from this chapter, noted with the Key Topic icon. Table 8-4 lists these key topics and shows where each is discussed.

> **NOTE**   There is no need to memorize any configuration step list referenced as a key topic; these lists are just study aids.

Key Topic

Table 8-4   Key Topics for Chapter 8

Key Topic Element	Description	Page Number
Example 8-1	Example showing basic password configuration	176
Figure 8-2	Configuration steps to use local usernames	179
List	Configuration steps for SSH support on a switch	180
List	Key points about **enable secret** and **enable password**	184
Table 8-2	List of commands related to the command history buffer	187
Figure 8-5	Conceptual diagram of a switch VLAN interface	189
List	Configuration checklist for a switch's IP address and default gateway configuration	190
List	Configuration checklist for a switch to learn IP settings as a DHCP client	190
List	Key features of all variations of port security	194
List	Port security configuration checklist	195
Table 8-3	Port security actions and the results of each action	198
List	Suggested security actions for unused switch ports	198

Complete the Tables and Lists from Memory

Print a copy of DVD Appendix M, "Memory Tables," or at least the section for this chapter, and complete the tables and lists from memory. DVD Appendix N, "Memory Tables Answer Key," includes completed tables and lists for you to check your work.

Definitions of Key Terms

After your first reading of the chapter, try to define these key terms, but do not be concerned about getting them all correct at that time. Chapter 30 directs you in how to use these terms for late-stage preparation for the exam.

Telnet, SSH, local username, VLAN interface, port security

Command References

Tables 8-5 though 8-9 list the configuration commands used in this chapter, by general topic. Table 8-10, at the very end of the chapter, lists the EXEC commands from this chapter.

Table 8-5   Console, Telnet, and SSH Login Commands

Command	Mode/Purpose/Description
line console 0	Changes the context to console configuration mode.
line vty *1st-vty last-vty*	Changes the context to vty configuration mode for the range of vty lines listed in the command.
login	Console and vty configuration mode. Tells IOS to prompt for a password.
password *pass-value*	Console and vty configuration mode. Lists the password required if the **login** command (with no other parameters) is configured.
login local	Console and vty configuration mode. Tells IOS to prompt for a username and password, to be checked against locally configured **username** global configuration commands on this switch or router.
username *name* secret *pass-value*	Global command. Defines one of possibly multiple usernames and associated passwords, used for user authentication. Used when the **login local** line configuration command has been used.
crypto key generate rsa	Global command. Creates and stores (in a hidden location in flash memory) the keys required by SSH.
transport input {telnet | ssh | all | none}	vty line configuration mode. Defines whether Telnet and/or SSH access is allowed into this switch. Both values can be configured on one command to allow both Telnet and SSH access (the default).
service password-encryption	Global command that (weakly) encrypts passwords defined by the **username password**, **enable password**, and **login** commands.

Table 8-6   Switch IPv4 Configuration

Command	Mode/Purpose/Description
interface vlan *number*	Changes the context to VLAN interface mode. For VLAN 1, allows the configuration of the switch's IP address.
ip address *ip-address subnet-mask*	VLAN interface mode. Statically configures the switch's IP address and mask.
ip address dhcp	VLAN interface mode. Configures the switch as a DHCP client to discover its IP address, mask, and default gateway.

8

Command	Mode/Purpose/Description
ip default-gateway *address*	Global command. Configures the switch's default gateway IP address. Not required if the switch uses DHCP.
ip name-server *server-ip-1 server-ip-2 ...*	Global command. Configures the IP address(es) of DNS servers, so any commands when logged into the switch will use the DNS for name resolution.

Table 8-7 Switch Interface Configuration

Command	Mode/Purpose/Description
interface *type port-number*	Changes context to interface mode. The type is typically FastEthernet or GigabitEthernet. The possible port numbers vary depending on the model of switch—for example, Fa0/1, Fa0/2, and so on.
interface range *type port-range*	Changes the context to interface mode for a range of consecutively numbered interfaces. The subcommands that follow then apply to all interfaces in the range.
shutdown no shutdown	Interface mode. Disables or enables the interface, respectively.
speed {10 | 100 | 1000 | auto}	Interface mode. Manually sets the speed to the listed speed or, with the **auto** setting, automatically negotiates the speed.
duplex {auto | full | half}	Interface mode. Manually sets the duplex to half or full, or to autonegotiate the duplex setting.
description *text*	Interface mode. Lists any information text that the engineer wants to track for the interface, such as the expected device on the other end of the cable.

Table 8-8 Port Security

Command	Mode/Purpose/Description
switchport mode {access | trunk | negotiate}	Interface configuration mode command that tells the switch to always be an access port, or always be a trunk port, or to negotiate which to be.
switchport port-security mac-address *mac-address*	Interface configuration mode command that statically adds a specific MAC address as an allowed MAC address on the interface.
switchport port-security mac-address sticky	Interface subcommand that tells the switch to learn MAC addresses on the interface and add them to the configuration for the interface as secure MAC addresses.
switchport port-security maximum *value*	Interface subcommand that sets the maximum number of static secure MAC addresses that can be assigned to a single interface.
switchport port-security violation {protect | restrict | shutdown}	Interface subcommand that tells the switch what to do if an inappropriate MAC address tries to access the network through a secure switch port.

Table 8-9   Other Switch Configuration

Command	Mode/Purpose/Description
hostname *name*	Global command. Sets this switch's host name, which is also used as the first part of the switch's command prompt.
enable secret *pass-value*	Global command. Sets this switch's password that is required for any user to reach enable mode.
history size *length*	Line config mode. Defines the number of commands held in the history buffer, for later recall, for users of those lines.
logging synchronous	Console or vty mode. Tells IOS to send log messages to the user at natural break points between commands, rather than in the middle of a line of output.
[no] logging console	Global command that disables or enables the display of log messages to the console.
exec-timeout *minutes [seconds]*	Console or vty mode. Sets the inactivity timeout, so that after the defined period of no action, IOS closes the current user login session.
switchport access vlan *vlan-number*	Interface subcommand that defines the VLAN in which the interface resides.
banner [motd | exec | login] *delimiter banner-text delimiter*	Global command that defines a banner that is displayed at different times when users log in to the switch or router.

Table 8-10   Chapter 8 EXEC Command Reference

Command	Purpose
show running-config	Lists the currently used configuration.
show running-config | begin line vty	Pipes (sends) the command output to the **begin** command, which only lists output beginning with the first line that contains the text "line vty."
show mac address-table dynamic	Lists the dynamically learned entries in the switch's address (forwarding) table.
show dhcp lease	Lists any information the switch acquires as a DHCP client. This includes IP address, subnet mask, and default gateway information.
show crypto key mypubkey rsa	Lists the public and shared key created for use with SSH using the **crypto key generate rsa** global configuration command.
show ip ssh	Lists status information for the SSH server, including the SSH version.
show ssh	Lists status information for current SSH connections into and out of the local switch.
show interfaces status	Lists one output line per interface, noting the description, operating state, and settings for duplex and speed on each interface.
show interfaces vlan 1	Lists the interface status, the switch's IP address and mask, and much more.

8

Command	Purpose
show ip default-gateway	Lists the switch's setting for its IP default gateway.
show port-security interface *type number*	Lists an interface's port security configuration settings and security operational status.
terminal history size *x*	Changes the length of the history buffer for the current user only, only for the current login to the switch.
show history	Lists the commands in the current history buffer.

Answers to Review Questions:

1 B **2** B and C **3** B **4** B **5** A, D, and F **6** F **7** E

Chapter 9

Implementing Ethernet Virtual LANs

At their heart, Ethernet switches receive Ethernet frames, make decisions, and then forward (switch) those Ethernet frames. That core logic revolves around MAC addresses, the interface in which the frame arrives, and the interface(s) out which the switch forwards the frame. Several switch features have some impact on an individual switch's decisions about where to forward frames, but of all the topics in this book, virtual LANs (VLAN) easily have the biggest impact on those choices.

This chapter examines the concepts and configuration of VLANs. The first major section of the chapter explains the core concepts. These concepts include how VLANs work on a single switch, how to use VLAN trunking to create VLANs that span across multiple switches, and how to forward traffic between VLANs using a router. The second major section shows how to configure VLANs and VLAN trunks: how to statically assign interfaces to a VLAN.

This chapter covers the following exam topics:

Operation of IP Data Networks

Predict the data flow between two hosts across a network.

LAN Switching Technologies

Identify basic switching concepts and the operation of Cisco switches.

Broadcast Domains

CAM Table

Describe how VLANs create logically separate networks and the need for routing between them.

Explain network segmentation and basic traffic management concepts

Configure and verify VLANs

Configure and verify trunking on Cisco switches

DTP

Troubleshooting

Troubleshoot and Resolve VLAN problems

Identify that VLANs are configured

Port membership correct

IP address configured

Troubleshoot and Resolve trunking problems on Cisco switches

Correct trunk states

Correct encapsulation configured

Correct vlans allowed

Foundation Topics

Virtual LAN Concepts

Before understanding VLANs, you must first have a specific understanding of the definition of a LAN. For example, from one perspective, a LAN includes all the user devices, servers, switches, routers, cables, and wireless access points in one location. However, an alternative narrower definition of a LAN can help in understanding the concept of a virtual LAN:

A LAN includes all devices in the same broadcast domain.

A broadcast domain includes the set of all LAN-connected devices, so that when any of the devices sends a broadcast frame, all the other devices get a copy of the frame. So, from one perspective, you can think of a LAN and a broadcast domain as being basically the same thing.

Without VLANs, a switch considers all its interfaces to be in the same broadcast domain. That is, for one switch, when a broadcast frame entered one switch port, the switch forwarded that broadcast frame out all other ports. With that logic, to create two different LAN broadcast domains, you had to buy two different Ethernet LAN switches, as shown in Figure 9-1.

Figure 9-1   *Creating Two Broadcast Domains with Two Physical Switches and No VLANs*

With support for VLANs, a single switch can accomplish the same goals of the design in Figure 9-1—to create two broadcast domains—with a single switch. With VLANs, a switch can configure some interfaces into one broadcast domain and some into another, creating multiple broadcast domains. These individual broadcast domains created by the switch are called *virtual LANs (VLAN)*.

For example, in Figure 9-2, the single switch creates two VLANs, treating the ports in each VLAN as being completely separate. The switch would never forward a frame sent by Dino (in VLAN 1) over to either Wilma or Betty (in VLAN 2).

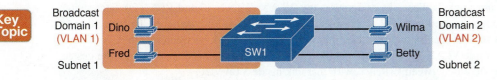

Figure 9-2   *Creating Two Broadcast Domains Using One Switch and VLANs*

Designing campus LANs to use more VLANs, each with a smaller number of devices, often helps improve the LAN in many ways. For example, a broadcast sent by one host in a VLAN will be received and processed by all the other hosts in the VLAN—but not by hosts in a different VLAN. Limiting the number of hosts that receive a single broadcast frame reduces the number of hosts that waste effort processing unneeded broadcasts. It also reduces security risks, because fewer hosts see frames sent by any one host. These are just a few reasons for separating hosts into different VLANs. The following list summarizes the most common reasons for choosing to create smaller broadcast domains (VLANs):

- To reduce CPU overhead on each device by reducing the number of devices that receive each broadcast frame

- To reduce security risks by reducing the number of hosts that receive copies of frames that the switches flood (broadcasts, multicasts, and unknown unicasts)

- To improve security for hosts that send sensitive data by keeping those hosts on a separate VLAN

- To create more flexible designs that group users by department, or by groups that work together, instead of by physical location

- To solve problems more quickly, because the failure domain for many problems is the same set of devices as those in the same broadcast domain

- To reduce the workload for the Spanning Tree Protocol (STP) by limiting a VLAN to a single access switch

This chapter does not examine all the reasons for VLANs in more depth. However, know that most enterprise networks use VLANs quite a bit. The rest of this chapter looks closely at the mechanics of how VLANs work across multiple Cisco switches, including the required configuration. To that end, the next section examines VLAN trunking, a feature required when installing a VLAN that exists on more than one LAN switch.

Creating Multiswitch VLANs Using Trunking

Configuring VLANs on a single switch requires only a little effort: You simply configure each port to tell it the VLAN number to which the port belongs. With multiple switches, you have to consider additional concepts about how to forward traffic between the switches.

When using VLANs in networks that have multiple interconnected switches, the switches need to use *VLAN trunking* on the links between the switches. VLAN trunking causes the switches to use a process called *VLAN tagging*, by which the sending switch adds another header to the frame before sending it over the trunk. This extra trunking header includes a *VLAN identifier* (VLAN ID) field so that the sending switch can associate the frame with a particular VLAN ID, and the receiving switch can then know in what VLAN each frame belongs.

Figure 9-3 shows an example that demonstrates VLANs that exist on multiple switches, but it does not use trunking. First, the design uses two VLANs: VLAN 10 and VLAN 20. Each switch has two ports assigned to each VLAN, so each VLAN exists in both switches. To forward traffic in VLAN 10 between the two switches, the design includes a link between switches, with that link fully inside VLAN 10. Likewise, to support VLAN 20 traffic between switches, the design uses a second link between switches, with that link inside VLAN 20.

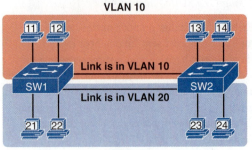

Figure 9-3 *Multiswitch VLAN Without VLAN Trunking*

The design in Figure 9-3 functions perfectly. For example, PC11 (in VLAN 10) can send a frame to PC14. The frame flows into SW1, over the top link (the one that is in VLAN 10) and over to SW2.

The design shown in Figure 9-3 works, but it simply does not scale very well. It requires one physical link between switches to support every VLAN. If a design needed 10 or 20 VLANs, you would need 10 or 20 links between switches, and you would use 10 or 20 switch ports (on each switch) for those links.

VLAN Tagging Concepts

VLAN trunking creates one link between switches that supports as many VLANs as you need. As a VLAN trunk, the switches treat the link as if it were a part of all the VLANs. At the same time, the trunk keeps the VLAN traffic separate, so frames in VLAN 10 would not go to devices in VLAN 20, and vice versa, because each frame is identified by VLAN number as it crosses the trunk. Figure 9-4 shows the idea, with a single physical link between the two switches.

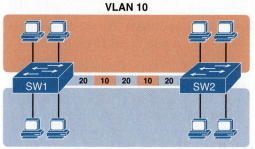

Figure 9-4   *Multiswitch VLAN with Trunking*

The use of trunking allows switches to pass frames from multiple VLANs over a single physical connection by adding a small header to the Ethernet frame. For example, Figure 9-5 shows PC11 sending a broadcast frame on interface Fa0/1 at Step 1. To flood the frame, switch SW1 needs to forward the broadcast frame to switch SW2. However, SW1 needs to let SW2 know that the frame is part of VLAN 10, so that after the frame is received, SW2 will flood the frame only into VLAN 10, and not into VLAN 20. So, as shown at Step 2, before sending the frame, SW1 adds a VLAN header to the original Ethernet frame, with the VLAN header listing a VLAN ID of 10 in this case.

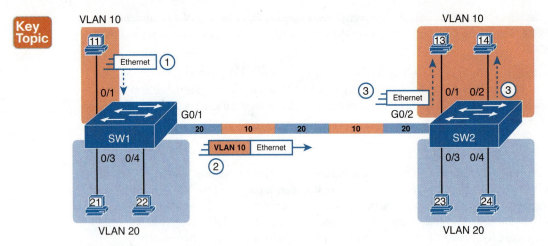

Figure 9-5   *VLAN Trunking Between Two Switches*

When SW2 receives the frame, it understands that the frame is in VLAN 10. SW2 then removes the VLAN header, forwarding the original frame out its interfaces in VLAN 10 (Step 3).

For another example, consider the case when PC21 (in VLAN 20) sends a broadcast. SW1 sends the broadcast out port Fa0/4 (because that port is in VLAN 20) and out Gi0/1 (because it is a trunk, meaning that it supports multiple different VLANs). SW1 adds a trunking header to the frame, listing a VLAN ID of 20. SW2 strips off the trunking header after noticing that the frame is part of VLAN 20, so SW2 knows to forward the frame out only ports Fa0/3 and Fa0/4, because they are in VLAN 20, and not out ports Fa0/1 and Fa0/2, because they are in VLAN 10.

The 802.1Q and ISL VLAN Trunking Protocols

Cisco has supported two different trunking protocols over the years: Inter-Switch Link (ISL) and IEEE 802.1Q. Cisco created the ISL long before 802.1Q, in part because the IEEE had not yet defined a VLAN trunking standard. Years later, the IEEE completed work on the 802.1Q standard, which defines a different way to do trunking. Today, 802.1Q has become the more popular trunking protocol, with Cisco not even supporting ISL in some of its newer models of LAN switches, including the 2960 switches used in the examples in this book.

While both ISL and 802.1Q tag each frame with the VLAN ID, the details differ. 802.1Q inserts an extra 4-byte 802.1Q VLAN header into the original frame's Ethernet header, as shown at the top of Figure 9-6. As for the fields in the 802.1Q header, only the 12-bit VLAN ID field inside the 802.1Q header matters for topics discussed in this book. This 12-bit field supports a theoretical maximum of 2^{12} (4096) VLANs, while in practice, it supports a maximum of 4094. (Both 802.1Q and ISL use 12 bits to tag the VLAN ID, with two reserved values [0 and 4095].)

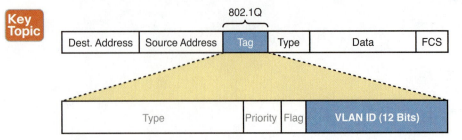

Figure 9-6   *802.1Q Trunking*

Cisco switches break the range of VLAN IDs (1–4094) into two ranges: the normal range and the extended range. All switches can use normal-range VLANs with values from 1 to 1005. Only some switches can use extended-range VLANs with VLAN IDs from 1006 to 4094. The rules for which switches can use extended-range VLANs depend on the configuration of the VLAN Trunking Protocol (VTP), which is discussed briefly in the section "VLAN Trunking Configuration," later in this chapter.

802.1Q also defines one special VLAN ID on each trunk as the *native VLAN* (defaulting to use VLAN 1). By definition, 802.1Q simply does not add an 802.1Q header to frames in the native VLAN. When the switch on the other side of the trunk receives a frame that does not have an 802.1Q header, the receiving switch knows that the frame is part of the native VLAN. Note that because of this behavior, both switches must agree on which VLAN is the native VLAN.

The 802.1Q native VLAN provides some interesting functions, mainly to support connections to devices that do not understand trunking. For example, a Cisco switch could be cabled to a switch that does not understand 802.1Q trunking. The Cisco switch could send frames in the native VLAN—meaning that the frame has no trunking header—so that the other switch would understand the frame. The native VLAN concept gives switches the capability of at least passing traffic in one VLAN (the native VLAN), which can allow some basic functions, like reachability to telnet into a switch.

Forwarding Data Between VLANs

If you create a campus LAN that contains many VLANs, you typically still need all devices to be able to send data to all other devices. This next topic discusses some concepts about how to route data between those VLANs.

First, it helps to know a few terms about some categories of LAN switches. All the Ethernet switch functions described in this book so far use the details and logic defined by OSI Layer 2 protocols. For example, Chapter 6, "Building Ethernet LANs with Switches," discussed how LAN switches receive Ethernet frames (a Layer 2 concept), look at the destination Ethernet MAC address (a Layer 2 address), and forward the Ethernet frame out some other interface. This chapter has already discussed the concept of VLANs as broadcast domains, which is yet another Layer 2 concept.

While some LAN switches work just as described so far in this book, some LAN switches have even more functions. LAN switches that forward data based on Layer 2 logic, as discussed so far in this book, often go by the name *Layer 2 switch*. However, some other switches can do some functions like a router, using additional logic defined by Layer 3 protocols. These switches go by the name *multilayer switch*, or *Layer 3 switch*. This section first discusses how to forward data between VLANs when using Layer 2 switches and ends with a brief discussion of how to use Layer 3 switches.

Routing Packets Between VLANs with a Router

When including VLANs in a campus LAN design, the devices in a VLAN need to be in the same subnet. Following the same design logic, devices in different VLANs need to be in different subnets. For example, in Figure 9-7, the two PCs on the left sit in VLAN 10, in subnet 10. The two PCs on the right sit in a different VLAN (20), with a different subnet (20).

Figure 9-7 *Layer 2 Switch Does Not Route Between the VLANs*

NOTE The figure refers to subnets somewhat generally, like "subnet 10," just so the subnet numbers do not distract. Also, note that the subnet numbers do not have to be the same number as the VLAN numbers.

Layer 2 switches will not forward data between two VLANs. In fact, one goal of VLANs is to separate traffic in one VLAN from another, preventing frames in one VLAN from leaking over to other VLANs. For example, when Dino (in VLAN 10) sends any Ethernet frame, if SW1 is a Layer 2 switch, that switch will not forward the frame to the PCs on the right in VLAN 20.

The network as a whole needs to support traffic flowing into and out of each VLAN, even though the Layer 2 switch does not forward frames outside a VLAN. The job of forwarding data into and out of a VLAN falls to routers. Instead of switching Layer 2 Ethernet frames between the two VLANs, the network must route Layer 3 packets between the two subnets.

That previous paragraph has some very specific wording related to Layers 2 and 3, so take a moment to reread and reconsider it for a moment. The Layer 2 logic does not let the Layer 2 switch forward the Layer 2 PDU (L2PDU), the Ethernet frame, between VLANs. However, routers can route Layer 3 PDUs (L3PDU) (packets) between subnets as their normal job in life.

For example, Figure 9-8 shows a router that can route packets between subnets 10 and 20. The figure shows the same Layer 2 switch as shown in Figure 9-7, with the same PCs and with the same VLANs and subnets. Now Router R1 has one LAN physical interface connected to the switch and assigned to VLAN 10, and a second physical interface connected to the switch and assigned to VLAN 20. With an interface connected to each subnet, the Layer 2 switch can keep doing its job—forwarding frames inside a VLAN, while the router can do its job—routing IP packets between the subnets.

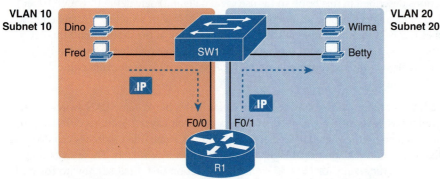
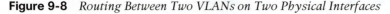

Figure 9-8 *Routing Between Two VLANs on Two Physical Interfaces*

The figure shows an IP packet being routed from Fred, which sits in one VLAN/subnet, to Betty, which sits in the other. The Layer 2 switch forwards two different Layer 2 Ethernet frames: one in VLAN 10, from Fred to R1's F0/0 interface, and the other in VLAN 20, from R1's F0/1 interface to Betty. From a Layer 3 perspective, Fred sends the IP packet to its default router (R1), and R1 routes the packet out another interface (F0/1) into another subnet where Betty resides.

While the design shown in Figure 9-8 works, it uses too many physical interfaces, one per VLAN. A much less expensive (and much preferred) option uses a VLAN trunk between the switch and router, requiring only one physical link between the router and switch, while supporting all VLANs. Trunking can work between any two devices that choose to support it: between two switches, between a router and a switch, or even between server hardware and a switch.

Figure 9-9 shows the same design idea as Figure 9-8, with the same packet being sent from Fred to Betty, except now R1 uses VLAN trunking instead of a separate link for each VLAN.

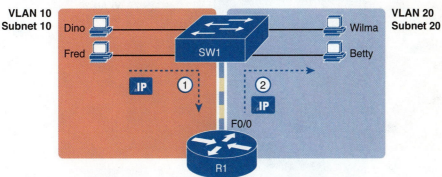

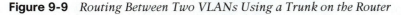

Figure 9-9 *Routing Between Two VLANs Using a Trunk on the Router*

NOTE Because the router has a single physical link connected to the LAN switch, this design is sometimes called a router-on-a-stick.

As a brief aside about terminology, many people describe the concept in Figures 9-8 and 9-9 as "routing packets between VLANs." You can use that phrase, and people know what you mean. However, for exam preparation purposes, note that this phrase is not literally true, because it refers to routing packets (a Layer 3 concept) and VLANs (a Layer 2 concept). It just takes fewer words to say something like "routing between VLANs" rather than the literally true but long "routing Layer 3 packets between Layer 3 subnets, with those subnets each mapping to a different Layer 2 VLAN."

Routing Packets with a Layer 3 Switch

Routing packets using a physical router, even with the VLAN trunk in the router-on-a-stick model shown in Figure 9-9, still has one significant problem: performance. The physical link puts an upper limit on how many bits can be routed, and less expensive routers tend to be less powerful, and might not be able to route a large enough number of packets per second (pps) to keep up with the traffic volumes.

The ultimate solution moves the routing functions inside the LAN switch hardware. Vendors long ago started combining the hardware and software features of their Layer 2 LAN switches, plus their Layer 3 routers, creating products called *Layer 3 switches* (also known as *multilayer switches*). Layer 3 switches can be configured to act only as a Layer 2 switch, or they can be configured to do both Layer 2 switching as well as Layer 3 routing.

Today, many medium- to large-sized enterprise campus LANs use Layer 3 switches to route packets between subnets (VLANs) in a campus.

In concept, a Layer 3 switch works a lot like the original two devices on which the Layer 3 switch is based: a Layer 2 LAN switch and a Layer 3 router. In fact, if you take the concepts and packet flow shown in Figure 9-8, with a separate Layer 2 switch and Layer 3 router, and then image all those features happening inside one device, you have the general idea of what a Layer 3 switch does. Figure 9-10 shows that exact concept, repeating many details of Figure 9-8, but with an overlay that shows the one Layer 3 switch doing the Layer 2 switch functions and the separate Layer 3 routing function.

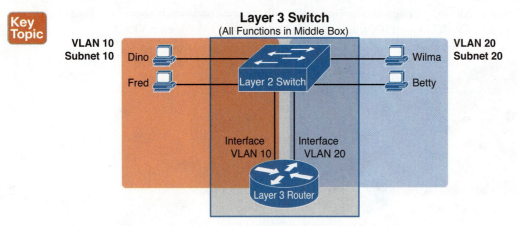

Figure 9-10   *Multilayer Switch: Layer 2 Switching with Layer 3 Routing in One Device*

This chapter introduces the core concepts of routing IP packets between VLANs (or more accurately, between the subnets on the VLANs). Chapter 16, "Configuring IPv4 Addresses and Routes," shows how to configure designs that use an external router with router-on-a-stick. This chapter now turns its attention to configuration and verification tasks for VLANs and VLAN trunks.

VLAN and VLAN Trunking Configuration and Verification

Cisco switches do not require any configuration to work. You can purchase Cisco switches, install devices with the correct cabling, turn on the switches, and they work. You would never need to configure the switch, and it would work fine, even if you interconnected switches, until you needed more than one VLAN. But if you want to use VLANs—and most every enterprise network does—you need to add some configuration.

This chapter separates the VLAN configuration details into two major sections. The first looks at how to configure access interfaces, which switch interfaces that do not use VLAN trunking. The second part shows how to configure interfaces that do use VLAN trunking.

Creating VLANs and Assigning Access VLANs to an Interface

This section shows how to create a VLAN, give the VLAN a name, and assign interfaces to a VLAN. To focus on these basic details, this section shows examples using a single switch, so VLAN trunking is not needed.

For a Cisco switch to forward frames in a particular VLAN, the switch must be configured to believe that the VLAN exists. Additionally, the switch must have nontrunking interfaces (called *access interfaces*) assigned to the VLAN, and/or trunks that support the VLAN. The configuration steps for access interfaces are as follows, with the trunk configuration shown later in the section "VLAN Trunking Configuration":

Step 1.   To configure a new VLAN, follow these steps:

  A.   From configuration mode, use the **vlan** *vlan-id* global configuration command to create the VLAN and to move the user into VLAN configuration mode.

  B.   (Optional) Use the **name** *name* VLAN subcommand to list a name for the VLAN. If not configured, the VLAN name is VLAN*ZZZZ*, where *ZZZZ* is the 4-digit decimal VLAN ID.

Step 2. For each access interface (each interface that does not trunk, but instead belongs to a single VLAN), follow these steps:

A. Use the **interface** command to move into interface configuration mode for each desired interface.

B. Use the **switchport access vlan** *id-number* interface subcommand to specify the VLAN number associated with that interface.

C. (Optional) To disable trunking on that same interface, so that the interface does not negotiate to become a trunk, use the **switchport mode access** interface subcommand.

While the list might look a little daunting, the process on a single switch is actually pretty simple. For example, if you want to put the switch's ports in three VLANs—11, 12, and 13—you just add three **vlan** commands: **vlan 11**, **vlan 12**, and **vlan 13**. Then, for each interface, add a **switchport access vlan 11** (or **12** or **13**) command to assign that interface to the proper VLAN.

VLAN Configuration Example 1: Full VLAN Configuration

Example 9-1 shows the configuration process of adding a new VLAN and assigning access interfaces to that VLAN. Figure 9-11 shows the network used in the example, with one LAN switch (SW1) and two hosts in each of three VLANs (1, 2, and 3). The example shows the details of the two-step process for VLAN 2 and the interfaces in VLAN 2, with the configuration of VLAN 3 deferred until the next example.

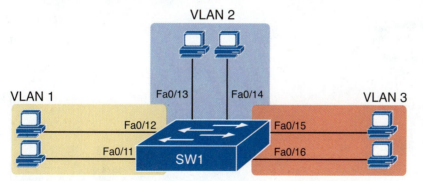

Figure 9-11 *Network with One Switch and Three VLANs*

Example 9-1 *Configuring VLANs and Assigning VLANs to Interfaces*

```
SW1# show vlan brief

VLAN Name                             Status    Ports
---- -------------------------------- --------- -------------------------------
1    default                          active    Fa0/1, Fa0/2, Fa0/3, Fa0/4
                                                Fa0/5, Fa0/6, Fa0/7, Fa0/8
                                                Fa0/9, Fa0/10, Fa0/11, Fa0/12
                                                Fa0/13, Fa0/14, Fa0/15, Fa0/16
                                                Fa0/17, Fa0/18, Fa0/19, Fa0/20
                                                Fa0/21, Fa0/22, Fa0/23, Fa0/24
                                                Gi0/1, Gi0/2
1002 fddi-default                     act/unsup
1003 token-ring-default               act/unsup
1004 fddinet-default                  act/unsup
1005 trnet-default                    act/unsup
! Above, VLANs 2 and 3 do not yet exist. Below, VLAN 2 is added, with name Freds-vlan,
! with two interfaces assigned to VLAN 2.
```

```
SW1# configure terminal
Enter configuration commands, one per line.  End with CNTL/Z.
SW1(config)# vlan 2
SW1(config-vlan)# name Freds-vlan
SW1(config-vlan)# exit
SW1(config)# interface range fastethernet 0/13 - 14
SW1(config-if)# switchport access vlan 2
SW1(config-if)# end

! Below, the show running-config command lists the interface subcommands on
! interfaces Fa0/13 and Fa0/14.
SW1# show running-config
! Many lines omitted for brevity
! Early in the output:
vlan 2
 name Freds-vlan
!
! more lines omitted for brevity
interface FastEthernet0/13
 switchport access vlan 2
 switchport mode access
!
interface FastEthernet0/14
 switchport access vlan 2
 switchport mode access
!

SW1# show vlan brief

VLAN Name                             Status    Ports
---- -------------------------------- --------- -------------------------------
1    default                          active    Fa0/1, Fa0/2, Fa0/3, Fa0/4
                                                Fa0/5, Fa0/6, Fa0/7, Fa0/8
                                                Fa0/9, Fa0/10, Fa0/11, Fa0/12
                                                Fa0/15, Fa0/16, Fa0/17, Fa0/18
                                                Fa0/19, Fa0/20, Fa0/21, Fa0/22
                                                Fa0/23, Fa0/24, Gi0/1, Gi0/2
2    Freds-vlan                       active    Fa0/13, Fa0/14
1002 fddi-default                     act/unsup
1003 token-ring-default               act/unsup
1004 fddinet-default                  act/unsup
1005 trnet-default                    act/unsup

SW1# show vlan id 2
VLAN Name                             Status    Ports
---- -------------------------------- --------- -------------------------------
2    Freds-vlan                       active    Fa0/13, Fa0/14

VLAN Type  SAID       MTU   Parent RingNo BridgeNo Stp  BrdgMode Trans1 Trans2
---- ----- ---------- ----- ------ ------ -------- ---- -------- ------ ------
2    enet  100010     1500  -      -      -        -    -        0      0
```

```
Remote SPAN VLAN

----------------

Disabled


Primary Secondary Type             Ports
------- --------- ----------------- -------------------------------------------
```

The example begins with the **show vlan brief** command, confirming the default settings of five nondeletable VLANs, with all interfaces assigned to VLAN 1. (VLAN 1 cannot be deleted, but can be used. VLANs 1002–1005 cannot be deleted and cannot be used as access VLANs today.) In particular, note that this 2960 switch has 24 Fast Ethernet ports (Fa0/1–Fa0/24) and two Gigabit Ethernet ports (Gi0/1 and Gi0/2), all of which are listed as being in VLAN 1 per that first command's output.

Next, the example shows the process of creating VLAN 2 and assigning interfaces Fa0/13 and Fa0/14 to VLAN 2. Note in particular that the example uses the **interface range** command, which causes the **switchport access vlan 2** interface subcommand to be applied to both interfaces in the range, as confirmed in the **show running-config** command output at the end of the example.

After the configuration has been added, to list the new VLAN, the example repeats the **show vlan brief** command. Note that this command lists VLAN 2, name Freds-vlan, and the interfaces assigned to that VLAN (Fa0/13 and Fa0/14).

The example surrounding Figure 9-11 uses six switch ports, all of which need to operate as access ports. That is, each port should not use trunking, but instead should be assigned to a single VLAN, as assigned by the **switchport access vlan** *vlan-id* command. However, as configured in Example 9-1, these interfaces could negotiate to later become trunk ports, because the switch defaults to allow the port to negotiate trunking and decide whether to act as an access interface or as a trunk interface.

For ports that should always act as access ports, add the optional interface subcommand **switchport mode access**. This command tells the switch to only allow the interface to be an access interface. The upcoming section "VLAN Trunking Configuration" discusses more details about the commands that allow a port to negotiate whether it should use trunking.

VLAN Configuration Example 2: Shorter VLAN Configuration

Example 9-1 shows several of the optional configuration commands, with a side effect of being a bit longer than is required. Example 9-2 shows a much briefer alternative configuration, picking up the story where Example 9-1 ended and showing the addition of VLAN 3 (as seen in Figure 9-11). Note that SW1 does not know about VLAN 3 at the beginning of this example.

Example 9-2 *Shorter VLAN Configuration Example (VLAN 3)*

```
SW1# configure terminal
Enter configuration commands, one per line.  End with CNTL/Z.
SW1(config)# interface range Fastethernet 0/15 - 16
SW1(config-if-range)# switchport access vlan 3
% Access VLAN does not exist. Creating vlan 3
SW1(config-if-range)# ^Z

SW1# show vlan brief
```

```
VLAN Name                             Status    Ports
---- -------------------------------- --------- ------------------------------
1    default                          active    Fa0/1, Fa0/2, Fa0/3, Fa0/4
                                                Fa0/5, Fa0/6, Fa0/7, Fa0/8
                                                Fa0/9, Fa0/10, Fa0/11, Fa0/12
                                                Fa0/17, Fa0/18, Fa0/19, Fa0/20
                                                Fa0/21, Fa0/22, Fa0/23, Fa0/24
                                                Gi0/1, Gi0/2
2    Freds-vlan                       active    Fa0/13, Fa0/14
3    VLAN0003                         active    Fa0/15, Fa0/16
1002 fddi-default                     act/unsup
1003 token-ring-default               act/unsup
1004 fddinet-default                  act/unsup
1005 trnet-default                    act/unsup
```

Example 9-2 shows how a switch can dynamically create a VLAN—the equivalent of the **vlan** *vlan-id* global config command—when the **switchport access vlan** interface subcommand refers to a currently unconfigured VLAN. This example begins with SW1 not knowing about VLAN 3. When the **switchport access vlan 3** interface subcommand was used, the switch realized that VLAN 3 did not exist, and as noted in the shaded message in the example, the switch created VLAN 3, using a default name (VLAN0003). No other steps are required to create the VLAN. At the end of the process, VLAN 3 exists in the switch, and interfaces Fa0/15 and Fa0/16 are in VLAN 3, as noted in the shaded part of the **show vlan brief** command output.

VLAN Trunking Protocol (VTP)

Before showing more configuration examples, you also need to know something about an older Cisco protocol and tool called the VLAN Trunking Protocol (VTP). VTP is a Cisco-proprietary tool on Cisco switches that advertises each VLAN configured in one switch (with the **vlan** *number* command) so that all the other switches in the campus learn about that VLAN. However, for various reasons, many enterprises choose not to use VTP.

This book does not discuss VTP as an end to itself. However, VTP has some small impact on how every Cisco Catalyst switch works, even if you do not try and use VTP. This brief section introduces enough details of VTP so that you can see these small differences in VTP that cannot be avoided.

Each switch can use one of three VTP modes: server, client, or transparent. Switches use either VTP server or client mode when the switch wants to use VTP for its intended purpose of dynamically advertising VLAN configuration information. However, with many Cisco switches and IOS versions, VTP cannot be completely disabled on a Cisco switch; instead, the switch disables VTP by using VTP transparent mode.

This book attempts to ignore VTP as much as is possible. To that end, all examples in this book use switches that have either been set to use VTP transparent mode (with the **vtp mode transparent** global command) or to disable it (with the **vtp mode off** global command). Both options allow the administrator to configure both standard- and extended-range VLANs, and the switch lists the **vlan** commands in the running config file.

Finally, on a practical note, if you happen to do lab exercises with real switches or with simulators, and you see unusual results with VLANs, check the VTP status with the **show vtp status** command. If your switch uses VTP server or client mode, you will find

- The server switches can configure VLANs in the standard range only (1–1005).
- The client switches cannot configure VLANs.
- The **show running-config** command does not list any **vlan** commands.

If possible, switch to VTP transparent mode and ignore VTP for your switch configuration practice for the CCENT and CCNA exam.

> **NOTE** If you experiment with VTP settings on a real lab switch, be very careful. If that switch connects to other switches, which in turn connect to switches used in the production LAN, it is possible to cause problems by overwriting the VLAN configuration in other switches. Be careful and never experiment with VTP settings on a switch unless it, and the other switches connected to it, have absolutely no physical links connected to the production LAN.

VLAN Trunking Configuration

Trunking configuration between two Cisco switches can be very simple if you just statically configure trunking. For example, if two Cisco 2960 switches connect to each other, they support only 802.1Q and not ISL. You could literally add one interface subcommand for the switch interface on each side of the link (**switchport mode trunk**), and you would create a VLAN trunk that supported all the VLANs known to each switch.

However, trunking configuration on Cisco switches includes many more options, including several options for dynamically negotiating various trunking settings. The configuration can either predefine different settings or tell the switch to negotiate the settings, as follows:

- The type of trunking: IEEE 802.1Q, ISL, or negotiate which one to use
- The *administrative mode*: Whether to always trunk, always not trunk, or negotiate

First, consider the type of trunking. Cisco switches that support ISL and 802.1Q can negotiate which type to use, using the Dynamic Trunking Protocol (DTP). If both switches support both protocols, they use ISL; otherwise, they use the protocol that both support. Today, many Cisco switches do not support the older ISL trunking protocol. Switches that support both types of trunking use the **switchport trunk encapsulation {dot1q | isl | negotiate}** interface subcommand to either configure the type or allow DTP to negotiate the type.

DTP can also negotiate whether the two devices on the link agree to trunk at all, as guided by the local switch port's administrative mode. The administrative mode refers to the configuration setting for whether trunking should be used. Each interface also has an *operational* mode, which refers to what is currently happening on the interface, and might have been chosen by DTP's negotiation with the other device. Cisco switches use the **switchport mode** interface subcommand to define the administrative trunking mode, as listed in Table 9-1.

Key Topic

Table 9-1 Trunking Administrative Mode Options with the **switchport mode** Command

Command Option	Description
access	Always act as an access (nontrunk) port
trunk	Always act as a trunk port
dynamic desirable	Initiates negotiation messages and responds to negotiation messages to dynamically choose whether to start using trunking
dynamic auto	Passively waits to receive trunk negotiation messages, at which point the switch will respond and negotiate whether to use trunking

For example, consider the two switches shown in Figure 9-12. This figure shows an expansion of the network of Figure 9-11, with a trunk to a new switch (SW2) and with parts of VLANs 1 and 3 on portsattached to SW2. The two switches use a Gigabit Ethernet link for the trunk. In this case, the trunk does not dynamically form by default, because both (2960) switches default to an administrative mode of *dynamic auto*, meaning that neither switch initiates the trunk negotiation process. By changing one switch to use *dynamic desirable* mode, which does initiate the negotiation, the switches negotiate to use trunking, specifically 802.1Q because the 2960s support only 802.1Q.

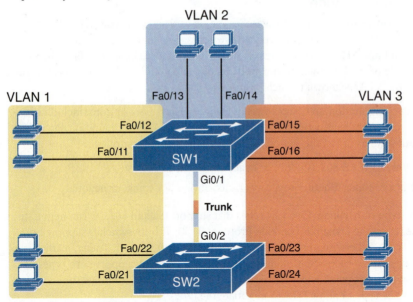

Figure 9-12 *Network with Two Switches and Three VLANs*

Example 9-3 begins by showing the two switches in Figure 9-12 with the default configuration so that the two switches do not trunk.

Example 9-3 *Initial (Default) State: Not Trunking Between SW1 and SW2*

```
SW1# show interfaces gigabit 0/1 switchport
Name: Gi0/1
Switchport: Enabled
Administrative Mode: dynamic auto
Operational Mode: static access
Administrative Trunking Encapsulation: dot1q
Operational Trunking Encapsulation: native
Negotiation of Trunking: On
```

```
Access Mode VLAN: 1 (default)
Trunking Native Mode VLAN: 1 (default)
Administrative Native VLAN tagging: enabled
Voice VLAN: none
Access Mode VLAN: 1 (default)
Trunking Native Mode VLAN: 1 (default)
Administrative Native VLAN tagging: enabled
Voice VLAN: none
Administrative private-vlan host-association: none
Administrative private-vlan mapping: none
Administrative private-vlan trunk native VLAN: none
Administrative private-vlan trunk Native VLAN tagging: enabled
Administrative private-vlan trunk encapsulation: dot1q
Administrative private-vlan trunk normal VLANs: none
Administrative private-vlan trunk private VLANs: none
Operational private-vlan: none
Trunking VLANs Enabled: ALL
Pruning VLANs Enabled: 2-1001
Capture Mode Disabled
Capture VLANs Allowed: ALL

Protected: false
Unknown unicast blocked: disabled
Unknown multicast blocked: disabled
Appliance trust: none

! Note that the next command results in a single empty line of output.
SW1# show interfaces trunk
SW1#
```

First, focus on the highlighted items from the output of the **show interfaces switchport** command at the beginning of Example 9-3. The output lists the default administrative mode setting of dynamic auto. Because SW2 also defaults to dynamic auto, the command lists SW1's operational status as access, meaning that it is not trunking. ("Dynamic auto" tells both switches to sit there and wait on the other switch to start the negotiations.) The third shaded line points out the only supported type of trunking (802.1Q) on this 2960 switch. (On a switch that supports both ISL and 802.1Q, this value would by default list "negotiate," to mean that the type of encapsulation is negotiated.) Finally, the operational trunking type is listed as "native," which is a reference to the 802.1Q native VLAN.

The end of the example shows the output of the **show interfaces trunk** command, but with no output. This command lists information about all interfaces that currently operationally trunk; that is, it list interfaces that currently use VLAN trunking. With no interfaces listed, this command also confirms that the link between switches is not trunking.

Next, consider Example 9-4, which shows the new configuration that enables trunking. In this case, SW1 is configured with the **switchport mode dynamic desirable** command, which asks the switch to both negotiate as well as to begin the negotiation process, rather than waiting on the other device. As soon as the command is issued, log messages appear showing that the interface goes down and then back up again, which happens when the interface transitions from access mode to trunk mode.

Example 9-4   *SW1 Changes from Dynamic Auto to Dynamic Desirable*

```
SW1# configure terminal
Enter configuration commands, one per line.  End with CNTL/Z.
SW1(config)# interface gigabit 0/1
SW1(config-if)# switchport mode dynamic desirable
SW1(config-if)# ^Z
SW1#
01:43:46: %LINEPROTO-5-UPDOWN: Line protocol on Interface GigabitEthernet0/1, changed
state to down
01:43:49: %LINEPROTO-5-UPDOWN: Line protocol on Interface GigabitEthernet0/1, changed
state to up
SW1# show interfaces gigabit 0/1 switchport
Name: Gi0/1
Switchport: Enabled
Administrative Mode: dynamic desirable
Operational Mode: trunk
Administrative Trunking Encapsulation: dot1q
Operational Trunking Encapsulation: dot1q
Negotiation of Trunking: On
Access Mode VLAN: 1 (default)
Trunking Native Mode VLAN: 1 (default)
! lines omitted for brevity


! The next command formerly listed a single empty line of output; now it lists
! information about the 1 operational trunk.
SW1# show interfaces trunk


Port        Mode          Encapsulation  Status        Native vlan
Gi0/1       desirable     802.1q         trunking      1


Port        Vlans allowed on trunk
Gi0/1       1-4094


Port        Vlans allowed and active in management domain
Gi0/1       1-3


Port        Vlans in spanning tree forwarding state and not pruned
Gi0/1       1-3


SW1# show vlan id 2
VLAN Name                             Status    Ports
---- -------------------------------- --------- -------------------------------
2    Freds-vlan                       active    Fa0/13, Fa0/14, G0/1


VLAN Type  SAID       MTU   Parent RingNo BridgeNo Stp  BrdgMode Trans1 Trans2
---- ----- ---------- ----- ------ ------ -------- ---- -------- ------ ------
2    enet  100010     1500  -      -      -        -    -        0      0


Remote SPAN VLAN
----------------
Disabled
```

```
Primary Secondary Type             Ports
------- --------- ----------------- -----------------------------------------
```

To verify that trunking is working now, the middle of Example 9-4 lists the **show interfaces switchport** command. Note that the command still lists the administrative settings, which denote the configured values along with the operational settings, which list what the switch is currently doing. In this case, SW1 now claims to be in an operational mode of *trunk*, with an operational trunking encapsulation of dot1Q.

The end of the example shows the output of the **show interfaces trunk** command, which now lists G0/1, confirming that G0/1 is now operationally trunking. The next section discusses the meaning of the output of this command.

For the exams, you should be ready to interpret the output of the **show interfaces switchport** command, realize the administrative mode implied by the output, and know whether the link should operationally trunk based on those settings. Table 9-2 lists the combinations of the trunking administrative modes and the expected operational mode (trunk or access) resulting from the configured settings. The table lists the administrative mode used on one end of the link on the left, and the administrative mode on the switch on the other end of the link across the top of the table.

Table 9-2 Expected Trunking Operational Mode Based on the Configured Administrative Modes

Administrative Mode	Access	Dynamic Auto	Trunk	Dynamic Desirable
access	Access	Access	Do Not Use[1]	Access
dynamic auto	Access	Access	Trunk	Trunk
trunk	Do Not Use[1]	Trunk	Trunk	Trunk
dynamic desirable	Access	Trunk	Trunk	Trunk

[1] When two switches configure a mode of "access" on one end and "trunk" on the other, problems occur. Avoid this combination.

Finally, before leaving the discussion of configuring trunks, Cisco recommends disabling trunk negotiation on most ports for better security. The majority of switch ports on most switches will be used to connect to users. As a matter of habit, you can disable DTP negotiations altogether using the **switchport nonegotiate** interface subcommand.

Controlling Which VLANs Can Be Supported on a Trunk

The *allowed VLAN list* feature provides a mechanism for engineers to administratively disable a VLAN from a trunk. By default, switches include all possible VLANs (1–4094) in each trunk's allowed VLAN list. However, the engineer can then limit the VLANs allowed on the trunk by using the following interface subcommand:

```
switchport trunk allowed vlan {add | all | except | remove} vlan-list
```

This command provides a way to easily add and remove VLANs from the list. For example, the **add** option permits the switch to add VLANs to the existing allowed VLAN list, and the **remove** option permits the switch to remove VLANs from the existing list. The **all** option means all VLANs, so you can use it to reset the switch to its original default setting (permitting VLANs 1–4094 on the trunk). The **except** option is rather tricky: It adds all VLANs to the list that are not part of the command. For example, the **switchport trunk allowed vlan except 100-200** interface subcommand adds VLANs 1 through 99 and 201 through 4094 to the existing allowed VLAN list on that trunk.

In addition to the allowed VLAN list, a switch has other reasons to prevent a particular VLAN's traffic from crossing a trunk. All five reasons are summarized in the following list:

Key Topic

- A VLAN has been removed from the trunk's *allowed VLAN* list.
- A VLAN does not exist in the switch's configuration (as seen with the **show vlan** command).
- A VLAN does exist, but has been administratively disabled (**shutdown**).
- A VLAN has been automatically pruned by VTP.
- A VLAN's STP instance has placed the trunk interface into a blocking state.

NOTE   The last two reasons in the list are outside the scope of this book, but are mentioned here for completeness.

While this section has already discussed the first reason—the allowed VLAN list—next consider the next two reasons in the list. If a switch does not know that a VLAN exists—for example, if the switch does not have a **vlan** *vlan-id* command configured, as confirmed by the output of the **show vlan** command—the switch will not forward frames in that VLAN over any interface. Additionally, a VLAN can exist in a switch's configuration, but also be administratively shut down either by using the **shutdown vlan** *vlan-id* global configuration command, or using the **shutdown** command in VLAN configuration mode. When disabled, a switch will no longer forward frames in that VLAN, even over trunks. So, switches do not forward frames in nonexistent VLANs or a shutdown VLAN over any of the switch's trunks.

This book has a motive for listing the reasons for limiting VLANs on a trunk: The **show interfaces trunk** command lists VLAN ID ranges as well, based on these same reasons. This command includes a progression of three lists of the VLANs supported over a trunk. These three lists are as follows:

- VLANs allowed on the trunk, 1–4094 by default
- VLANs from the first group that are also configured and active (not shut down)
- VLANs from the second group that are not VTP pruned and not STP blocked

To get an idea of these three lists inside the output of the **show interfaces trunk** command, Example 9-5 shows how VLANs might be disallowed on a trunk for various reasons. The command output is taken from SW1 in Figure 9-12, after the completion of the configuration as shown in all the earlier examples in this chapter. In other words, VLANs 1 through 3 exist in SW1's configuration, and are not shut down. Trunking is operational between SW1 and SW2. Then, during the example, the following items are configured on SW1:

Step 1.   VLAN 4 is configured.

Step 2.   VLAN 2 is shut down.

Step 3.   VLAN 3 is removed from the trunk's allowed VLAN list.

Example 9-5 *Allowed VLAN List and the List of Active VLANs*

```
! The three lists of VLANs in the next command list allowed VLANs (1-4094),
! Allowed and active VLANs (1-3), and allowed/active/not pruned/STP forwarding
! VLANs (1-3)
SW1# show interfaces trunk

Port        Mode         Encapsulation Status        Native vlan
Gi0/1       desirable    802.1q        trunking      1


Port        Vlans allowed on trunk
Gi0/1       1-4094


Port        Vlans allowed and active in management domain
Gi0/1       1-3


Port        Vlans in spanning tree forwarding state and not pruned
Gi0/1       1-3


! Next, the switch is configured with new VLAN 4; VLAN 2 is shutdown;
! and VLAN 3 is removed from the allowed VLAN list on the trunk.
SW1# configure terminal
Enter configuration commands, one per line.  End with CNTL/Z.
SW1(config)# vlan 4
SW1(config-vlan)# vlan 2
SW1(config-vlan)# shutdown
SW1(config-vlan)# interface gi0/1
SW1(config-if)# switchport trunk allowed vlan remove 3
SW1(config-if)# ^Z


! The three lists of VLANs in the next command list allowed VLANs (1-2, 4-4094),
! allowed and active VLANs (1,4), and allowed/active/not pruned/STP forwarding
! VLANs (1,4)
SW1# show interfaces trunk

Port        Mode         Encapsulation Status        Native vlan
Gi0/1       desirable    802.1q        trunking      1

! VLAN 3 is omitted next, because it was removed from the allowed VLAN list.
Port        Vlans allowed on trunk
Gi0/1       1-2,4-4094

! VLAN 2 is omitted below because it is shutdown. VLANs 5-4094 are omitted below
! because SW1 does not have them configured.
Port        Vlans allowed and active in management domain
Gi0/1       1,4


Port        Vlans in spanning tree forwarding state and not pruned
Gi0/1       1,4
```

Review Activities

Chapter Summary

- A LAN includes all devices in the same broadcast domain.

- Without VLANs, a switch considers all its interfaces to be in the same broadcast domain.

- With VLANs, a switch can configure some interfaces into one broadcast domain and some into another, creating multiple broadcast domains. These individual broadcast domains created by the switch are called virtual LANs (VLANs).

- The following list summarizes the most common reasons for choosing to create smaller broadcast domains (VLANs):

  - To reduce CPU overhead on each device by reducing the number of devices that receive each broadcast frame

  - To reduce security risks by reducing the number of hosts that receive copies of frames that the switches flood (broadcasts, multicasts, and unknown unicasts)

  - To improve security for hosts that send sensitive data, by keeping those hosts on a separate VLAN

  - To create more flexible designs that group users by department or by groups that work together, instead of by physical location

  - To solve problems more quickly, because the failure domain for many problems is the same set of devices as those in the same broadcast domain

- Configuring VLANs on a single switch requires only a little effort: You simply configure each port to tell it the VLAN number to which the port belongs.

- When using VLANs in networks that have multiple interconnected switches, the switches must use *VLAN trunking* on the links between the switches.

- VLAN trunking causes the switches to use a process called *VLAN tagging*, by which the sending switch adds another header to the frame before sending it over the trunk. This extra trunking header includes a *VLAN identifier* (VLAN ID) field so that the sending switch can associate the frame with a particular VLAN ID, and the receiving switch can then know in what VLAN each frame belongs.

- Cisco has supported two different trunking protocols over the years: Inter-Switch Link (ISL) and IEEE 802.1Q.

- 802.1Q also defines one special VLAN ID on each trunk as the *native VLAN* (defaulting to use VLAN 1). By definition, 802.1Q simply does not add an 802.1Q header to frames in the native VLAN.

- If you create a campus LAN that contains many VLANs, you typically still need all devices to be capable of sending data to all other devices. Layer 2 switches will not forward data between two VLANs. Traditionally, a router is used to route packets between VLANs.

- The ultimate solution moves the routing functions inside the LAN switch hardware. Vendors long ago started combining the hardware and software features of their Layer 2 LAN switches plus their Layer 3 routers, creating products called *Layer 3 switches* (also known as *multilayer switches*). Layer 3 switches can be configured to act only as a Layer 2 switch or to do both Layer 2 switching and Layer 3 routing.

- The configuration steps for access interfaces are as follows:

  Step 1. To configure a new VLAN, follow these steps:

  1. From configuration mode, use the **vlan** *vlan-id* global configuration command to create the VLAN and to move the user into VLAN configuration mode.

    2. (Optional) Use the **name** *name* VLAN subcommand to list a name for the VLAN. If not configured, the VLAN name is VLANZZZZ, where *ZZZZ* is the 4-digit decimal VLAN ID.

Step 2. For each access interface (each interface that does not trunk, but instead belongs to a single VLAN), follow these steps:

    1. Use the **interface** command to move into interface configuration mode for each desired interface.

    2. Use the **switchport access vlan** *id-number* interface subcommand to specify the VLAN number associated with that interface.

    3. (Optional) To disable trunking on that same interface, ensuring that the interface is an access interface, use the **switchport mode access** interface subcommand.

- VLAN Trunking Protocol (VTP) is a Cisco-proprietary tool on Cisco switches that advertises each VLAN configured in one switch (with the **vlan** *number* command) so that all the other switches in the campus learn about that VLAN.

Review Questions

Answer these review questions. You can find the answers at the bottom of the last page of the chapter. For thorough explanations, see DVD Appendix C, "Answers to Review Questions."

1. In a LAN, which of the following terms best equates to the term *VLAN*?

    A. Collision domain

    B. Broadcast domain

    C. Subnet

    D. Single switch

    E. Trunk

2. Imagine a switch with three configured VLANs. How many IP subnets are required, assuming that all hosts in all VLANs want to use TCP/IP?

    A. 0

    B. 1

    C. 2

    D. 3

    E. You can't tell from the information provided.

3. Switch SW1 sends a frame to switch SW2 using 802.1Q trunking. Which of the answers describes how SW1 changes or adds to the Ethernet frame before forwarding the frame to SW2?

    A. Inserts a 4-byte header and does change the MAC addresses

    B. Inserts a 4-byte header and does not change the MAC addresses

    C. Encapsulates the original frame behind an entirely-new Ethernet header

    D. None of the other answers are correct

4. For an 802.1Q trunk between two Ethernet switches, which answer most accurately defines which frames do not include an 802.1Q header?

   A. Frames in the native VLAN (only one)

   B. Frames in extended VLANs

   C. Frames in VLAN 1 (not configurable)

   D. Frames in all native VLANs (multiple allowed)

5. Imagine that you are told that switch 1 is configured with the **dynamic auto** parameter for trunking on its Fa0/5 interface, which is connected to switch 2. You have to configure switch 2. Which of the following settings for trunking could allow trunking to work? (Choose two answers.)

   A. Trunking turned **on**

   B. dynamic auto

   C. dynamic desirable

   D. access

   E. None of the other answers are correct.

6. A switch has just arrived from Cisco. The switch has never been configured with any VLANs, but VTP has been disabled. An engineer gets into configuration mode and issues the **vlan 22** command, followed by the **name Hannahs-VLAN** command. Which of the following are true? (Choose two answers.)

   A. VLAN 22 is listed in the output of the **show vlan brief** command.

   B. VLAN 22 is listed in the output of the **show running-config** command.

   C. VLAN 22 is not created by this process.

   D. VLAN 22 does not exist in that switch until at least one interface is assigned to that VLAN.

7. Which of the following commands identify switch interfaces as being trunking interfaces: interfaces that currently operate as VLAN trunks? (Choose two answers.)

   A. show interfaces

   B. show interfaces switchport

   C. show interfaces trunk

   D. show trunks

Review All the Key Topics

Review the most important topics from this chapter, noted with the Key Topic icon. Table 9-3 lists these key topics and where each is discussed.

Table 9-3 Key Topics for Chapter 9

Key Topic Element	Description	Page Number
Figure 9-2	Basic VLAN concept	209
List	Reasons for using VLANs	210
Figure 9-5	Diagram of VLAN trunking	212
Figure 9-6	802.1Q header	212
Figure 9-9	Routing between VLANs with router-on-a-stick	215
Figure 9-10	Routing between VLANs with Layer 3 switch	216
List	Configuration checklist for configuring VLANs and assigning to interfaces	216
Table 9-1	Options of the **switchport mode** command	222
Table 9-2	Expected trunking results based on the configuration of the **switchport mode** command	225
List	Reasons why a trunk does not pass traffic for a VLAN	226

Complete the Tables and Lists from Memory

Print a copy of Appendix M, "Memory Tables," (found on the DVD) or at least the section for this chapter, and complete the tables and lists from memory. Appendix N, "Memory Tables Answer Key," also on the DVD, includes completed tables and lists to check your work.

Definitions of Key Terms

After your first reading of the chapter, try to define these key terms, but do not be concerned about getting them all correct at that time. Chapter 30 directs you in how to use these terms for late-stage preparation for the exam.

802.1Q, trunk, trunking administrative mode, trunking operational mode, VLAN, VTP, VTP transparent mode, Layer 3 switch, access interface, trunk interface

Command Reference to Check Your Memory

While you should not necessarily memorize the information in the tables in this section, this section does include a reference for the configuration and EXEC commands covered in this chapter. Practically speaking, you should memorize the commands as a side effect of reading the chapter and doing all the activities in this exam preparation section. To check and see how well you have memorized the commands as a side effect of your other studies, cover the left side of the table with a piece of paper, read the descriptions in the right side, and see whether you remember the command.

Table 9-4   Chapter 9 Configuration Command Reference

Command	Description
vlan *vlan-id*	Global config command that both creates the VLAN and puts the CLI into VLAN configuration mode
name *vlan-name*	VLAN subcommand that names the VLAN
[no] shutdown	VLAN mode subcommand that enables (**no shutdown**) or disables (**shutdown**) the VLAN
[no] shutdown vlan *vlan-id*	Global config command that has the same effect as the [no] shutdown VLAN mode subcommands
vtp mode {server | client | transparent | off}	Global config command that defines the VTP mode
switchport mode {access | dynamic {auto | desirable} | trunk}	Interface subcommand that configures the trunking administrative mode on the interface
switchport trunk allowed vlan {add | all | except | remove} *vlan-list*	Interface subcommand that defines the list of allowed VLANs
switchport access vlan *vlan-id*	Interface subcommand that statically configures the interface into that one VLAN
switchport trunk encapsulation {dot1q | isl | negotiate}	Interface subcommand that defines which type of trunking to use, assuming that trunking is configured or negotiated
switchport trunk native vlan *vlan-id*	Interface subcommand that defines the native VLAN for a trunk port
switchport nonegotiate	Interface subcommand that disables the negotiation of VLAN trunking

Table 9-5   Chapter 9 EXEC Command Reference

Command	Description
show interfaces *interface-id* switchport	Lists information about any interface regarding administrative settings and operational state
show interfaces *interface-id* trunk	Lists information about all operational trunks (but no other interfaces), including the list of VLANs that can be forwarded over the trunk
show vlan [brief | id *vlan-id* | name *vlan-name* | summary]	Lists information about the VLAN
show vlan [*vlan*]	Displays VLAN information
show vtp status	Lists VTP configuration and status information

Answers to Review Questions::

1 B **2** D **3** B **4** A **5** A and C **6** A and B **7** B and C

Chapter 10

Troubleshooting Ethernet LANs

This chapter focuses on the processes of verification and troubleshooting. *Verification* refers to the process of confirming whether a network is working as designed. *Troubleshooting* refers to the follow-on process that occurs when the network is not working as designed, by trying to determine the real reason why the network is not working correctly, so that it can be fixed.

Over the years, the CCENT and CCNA exams have been asking more and more verification and troubleshooting questions. Each of these questions requires you to apply networking knowledge to unique problems, rather than just being ready to answer questions about lists of facts that you've memorized.

To help you prepare to answer troubleshooting questions, this book, as well as the ICND2 book, devotes different book elements (both full chapters and sections of chapters) to troubleshooting. These book elements do not just list the configuration, and they do not just list example output from different **show** commands. Instead, these elements discuss how to use different commands to verify what should be happening, and if not, how to find the root cause of the problem.

This chapter discusses a wide number of topics, many of which have already been discussed in Chapters 6, 7, 8, and 9. First, this chapter begins with some perspectives on troubleshooting networking problems, because it is the first book element that focuses on troubleshooting. At that point, this chapter looks at four key technical topics that matter to verifying and troubleshooting Ethernet LANs, as follows:

- Analyzing LAN Topology Using CDP
- Analyzing Switch Interface Status
- Predicting Where Switches Will Forward Frames
- Analyzing VLANs and VLAN Trunks

LAN Switching Technologies

Configure and verify trunking on Cisco switches

DTP

Autonegotiation

Network Device Security

Configure and verify Switch Port Security features such as

Static / dynamic

Violation modes

Err disable

Shutdown

Protect restrict

Troubleshooting

Troubleshoot and Resolve VLAN problems

identify that VLANs are configured

port membership correct

IP address configured

Troubleshoot and Resolve trunking problems on Cisco switches

correct trunk states

correct encapsulation configured

correct VLANs allowed

Troubleshoot and Resolve Layer 1 problems

Framing

CRC

Runts

Giants

Dropped packets

Late collision

Input / Output errors

Foundation Topics

Perspectives on Network Verification and Troubleshooting

> **NOTE**   The information in this section is a means to help you learn troubleshooting skills. However, the specific processes and comments in this section, up to the next major heading ("Analyzing LAN Topology Using Cisco Discovery Protocol"), do not cover any specific exam objective for any of the CCENT or CCNA exams.

You need several skills to be ready to answer the more challenging questions on today's CCENT and CCNA exams. However, the required skills differ when comparing the different types of questions. This section starts with some perspectives on the various question types, followed by some general comments on troubleshooting.

First, as a reminder, the Introduction to this book briefly describes a couple of different types of exam questions mentioned in this chapter: Sim, Simlet, and multiple choice (MC).

Sim and Simlet questions use a simulator, where you can use the CLI of simulated routers and switches. Sim questions require you to find a configuration problem and solve the problem by fixing or completing the configuration. Simlet questions require you to verify the current operation of the network and then answer MC questions about the current operation. MC questions simply ask a question, with multiple answers (choices) for the correct answer.

> **NOTE**   Refer to www.cisco.com/web/learning/wwtraining/certprog/training/cert_exam_tutorial.html for a tutorial about the various types of CCENT and CCNA exam questions.

Preparing to Use an Organized Troubleshooting Process

On exam day, you have one goal: answer enough questions correctly to pass the exam. However, before the exam, you should use a thorough and organized thought process. You can learn a lot by thinking through the troubleshooting process as you prepare for the exam so that you can be better prepared to attack problems quickly on exam day.

To that end, this book includes many suggested troubleshooting processes. The troubleshooting processes are not ends unto themselves, so you do not need to memorize them for the exams. They are learning tools, with the ultimate goal being to help you correctly and quickly find the answers to the more challenging questions on the exams.

This section gives an overview of a general troubleshooting process. As you progress through this book, the process will be mentioned occasionally as it relates to other technology areas, such as IP routing. The three major steps in this book's organized troubleshooting process are as follows:

Step 1.   **Analyzing/predicting normal operation:** Predict the details of what should happen if the network is working correctly, based on documentation, configuration, and **show** and **debug** command output.

Step 2.   **Problem isolation:** Determine how far along the expected path the frame/packet goes before it cannot be forwarded any farther, again based on documentation, configuration, and **show** and **debug** command output.

Step 3.   **Root cause analysis:** Identify the underlying causes of the problems identified in the preceding step—specifically, the causes that have a specific action with which the problem can be fixed.

Following this process requires a wide variety of learned skills. You need to remember the theory of how networks should work, as well as how to interpret the **show** command output that confirms how the devices are currently behaving. This process requires the use of testing tools, such as **ping** and **traceroute**, to isolate the problem. Finally, this approach requires the ability to think broadly about everything that could affect a single component.

For example, consider the following problem based on the network in Figure 10-1. PC1 and PC2 supposedly sit in the same VLAN (10). At one time, the **ping 10.1.1.2** command on PC1 worked; now it does not.

VLAN10

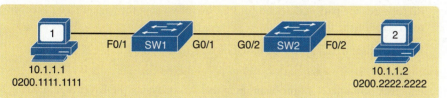

Figure 10-1   *Example Network with a ping Problem*

So, how do you attack this problem? If you doubt whether the figure is even correct, you could look at **show** command output to confirm the network topology. After it is confirmed, you could predict its normal working behavior based on your knowledge of LAN switching. As a result, you could predict where a frame sent by PC1 to PC2 should flow. To isolate the problem, you could look in the switch MAC tables to confirm the interfaces out which the frame should be forwarded, possibly then finding that the interface connected to PC2 has failed.

If you did conclude that an interface had failed, you still do not know the root cause: What caused the interface to fail? What could you do to fix that underlying problem? In that particular case, you would then need to broaden your thinking to any and all reasons why an interface might fail—from an unplugged cable, to electrical interference, to port security disabling the interface. **show** commands can either confirm that a specific root cause is the problem or at least give some hints as to the root cause.

The first example problem uses a simple LAN, with one subnet and no need for IP routing. However, many exam questions will include multiple IP subnets, with routers that must route IP packets between the hosts. In these cases, the troubleshooting process often begins with some analysis of how the Layer 3 routing process works when forwarding IP packets.

For example, the user of PC1 in Figure 10-2 can usually connect to the web server on the right by entering www.example.com in PC1's web browser. However, that web-browsing attempt fails right now. The user calls the help desk, and the problem is assigned to a network engineer to solve.

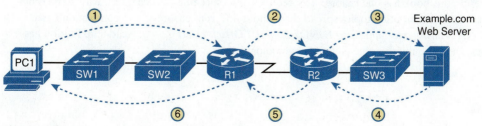

Figure 10-2   *Layer 3 Problem Isolation*

To begin the analysis, the network engineer can begin with the first tasks that would have to happen for a successful web-browsing session to occur. For example, the engineer would try to confirm that PC1 can resolve the host name (www.example.com) to the correct IP address used by the server on the right. At that point, the Layer 3 IP problem isolation process can proceed, to determine which of the six routing steps shown in the figure has failed. The routing steps shown in Figure 10-2 are as follows:

Step 1.   PC1 sends the packet to its default gateway (R1) because the destination IP address (of the web server) is in a different subnet.

Step 2.   R1 forwards the packet to R2 based on R1's routing table.

Step 3.   R2 forwards the packet to the web server based on R2's routing table.

Step 4.   The web server sends a packet back toward PC1 based on the web server's default gateway setting (R2).

Step 5.   R2 forwards the packet destined for PC1 by forwarding the packet to R1 according to R2's routing table.

Step 6.   R1 forwards the packet to PC1 based on R1's routing table.

Many engineers break down network problems as in this list, analyzing the Layer 3 path through the network, hop by hop, in both directions. This process helps you take the first attempt at problem isolation. When the analysis shows which hop in the layer path fails, you can then look further at those details. And if in this case the Layer 3 problem isolation process discovers that Step 1, 3, 4, or 6 fails, the root cause might be related to Ethernet.

For example, imagine that the Layer 3 analysis determined that PC1 cannot even send a packet to its default gateway (R1), meaning that Step 1 in Figure 10-2 fails. To further isolate the problem and find the root causes, the engineer would need to determine the following:

■ The MAC address of PC1 and of R1's LAN interface

■ The switch interfaces used on SW1 and SW2

■ The interface status of each switch interface

■ The VLANs that should be used

■ The expected forwarding behavior of a frame sent by PC1 to R1 as the destination MAC address

By gathering and analyzing these facts, the engineer can most likely isolate the problem's root cause and fix it.

Troubleshooting as Covered in This Book

In the current version of the ICND1 and ICND2 exams, Cisco spreads troubleshooting topics across both exams. However, in the current versions of the exams (100-101 ICND1 and 200-101 ICND2), more of the troubleshooting sits in the ICND2 exam, with less in the ICND1 exam. As a result, this book has one chapter devoted to troubleshooting (this chapter), with some other smaller troubleshooting topics spread throughout different chapters. The companion *Cisco CCNA Routing and Switching ICND2 200-101 Official Cert Guide*, Academic Edition has many more troubleshooting elements by comparison.

The rest of this chapter examines troubleshooting related to Ethernet LANs, with four major topics. Of these, only the first topic, about the Cisco Discovery Protocol (CDP), presents completely new material. The other three topics discuss familiar topics, but with a troubleshooting approach. The topics include the following:

- **Cisco Discovery Protocol (CDP):** Used to confirm the documentation, and learn about the network topology, to predict normal operation of the network.
- **Examining interface status:** Interfaces must be in a working state before a switch will forward frames on the interface. You must determine whether an interface is working, as well as determine the potential root causes for a failed switch interface.
- **Analyzing where frames will be forwarded:** You must know how to analyze a switch's MAC address table and how to then predict how a switch will forward a particular frame.
- **Analyzing VLANs and VLAN trunking:** Keeping a Layer 2 switch focus, this last section looks at what can go wrong with VLANs and VLAN trunks.

Analyzing LAN Topology Using Cisco Discovery Protocol

The proprietary Cisco Discovery Protocol (CDP) discovers basic information about neighboring routers and switches without needing to know the passwords for the neighboring devices. To discover information, routers and switches send CDP messages out each of their interfaces. The messages essentially announce information about the device that sent the CDP message. Devices that support CDP learn information about others by listening for the advertisements sent by other devices.

As is so often the case, Cisco created CDP as a proprietary solution to meet a need for Cisco customers. Since that time, the IEEE has standardized the Link Layer Discovery Protocol (LLDP), which serves the same role. However, most enterprises that use Cisco routers and switches use CDP, with LLDP as an option, so this chapter focuses solely on CDP instead of LLDP.

From a troubleshooting perspective, CDP can be used to either confirm or fix the documentation shown in a network diagram, or even discover the devices and interfaces used in a network. Confirming that the network is actually cabled to match the network diagram is a good step to take before trying to predict the normal flow of data in a network.

On media that support multicasts at the data link layer (like Ethernet), CDP uses multicast frames; on other media, CDP sends a copy of the CDP update to any known data link addresses. So, any CDP-supporting device that shares a physical medium with another CDP-supporting device can learn about the other device.

CDP discovers several useful details from the neighboring Cisco devices:

- **Device identifier:** Typically the host name
- **Address list:** Network and data link addresses
- **Port identifier:** The interface on the remote router or switch on the other end of the link that sent the CDP advertisement
- **Capabilities list:** Information on what type of device it is (for example, a router or a switch)
- **Platform:** The model and OS level running on the device

Examining Information Learned by CDP

CDP has **show** commands that list information about neighbors, **show** commands that list information about how CDP is working, and configuration commands to disable and enable CDP. Table 10-1 lists the three **show** commands that list the most important CDP information.

10

Key Topic

Table 10-1 **show cdp** Commands That List Information About Neighbors

Command	Description
show cdp neighbors [*type number*]	Lists one summary line of information about each neighbor, or just the neighbor found on a specific interface if an interface was listed.
show cdp neighbors detail	Lists one large set (approximately 15 lines) of information, one set for every neighbor.
show cdp entry *name*	Lists the same information as the **show cdp neighbors detail** command, but only for the named neighbor (case sensitive).

NOTE Cisco routers and switches support the same CDP commands, with the same parameters and same types of output.

The next example shows the power of the information in CDP commands. The example uses the network shown in Figure 10-3, with Example 10-1 that follows listing the output of several **show cdp** commands.

Cisco 2960 Switches (WS-2960-24TT-L)

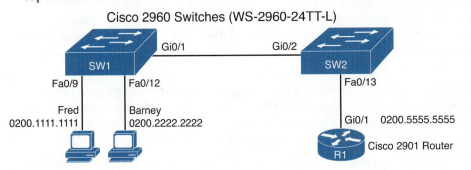

Figure 10-3 *Small Network Used in CDP Examples*

Example 10-1 **show cdp** *Command Examples: SW2*

```
! The show cdp neighbors command lists SW2's local interface, and both R1's
! and SW1's interfaces  (in the "port" column), along with other details.
!
SW2# show cdp neighbors
Capability Codes: R - Router, T - Trans Bridge, B - Source Route Bridge
                  S - Switch, H - Host, I - IGMP, r - Repeater, P - Phone,
                  D - Remote, C - CVTA, M - Two-port Mac Relay


Device ID      Local Intrfce    Holdtme    Capability  Platform  Port ID
SW1            Gig 0/2          170              S I    WS-C2960- Gig 0/1
R1             Fas 0/13         136            R S I    CISCO2901 Gig 0/1


SW2# show cdp neighbors detail
-------------------------
Device ID: SW1
Entry address(es):
  IP address: 172.16.1.1
Platform: cisco WS-C2960-24TT-L,  Capabilities: Switch IGMP
Interface: GigabitEthernet0/2,  Port ID (outgoing port): GigabitEthernet0/1
Holdtime : 161 sec
```

```
Version :
Cisco IOS Software, C2960 Software (C2960-LANBASEK9-M), Version 15.0(1)SE3, RELEASE
SOFTWARE (fc1)
Technical Support: http://www.cisco.com/techsupport
Copyright (c) 1986-2012 by Cisco Systems, Inc.
Compiled Wed 30-May-12 14:26 by prod_rel_team

advertisement version: 2
Protocol Hello:  OUI=0x00000C, Protocol ID=0x0112; payload len=27,
value=00000000FFFFFFFF010221FF00000000000018339D7B0E80FF0000
VTP Management Domain: ''
Native VLAN: 1
Duplex: full
Management address(es):
  IP address: 172.16.1.1

! This is a comment from the author: next lines are about R1.
-------------------------
Device ID: R1
Entry address(es):
  IP address: 10.1.1.9
Platform: Cisco CISCO2901/K9,  Capabilities: Router Switch IGMP
Interface: FastEthernet0/13,  Port ID (outgoing port): GigabitEthernet0/1
Holdtime : 127 sec

Version :
Cisco IOS Software, C2900 Software (C2900-UNIVERSALK9-M), Version 15.2(4)M1, RELEASE
SOFTWARE (fc1)
Technical Support: http://www.cisco.com/techsupport
Copyright (c) 1986-2012 by Cisco Systems, Inc.
Compiled Thu 26-Jul-12 20:54 by prod_rel_team

advertisement version: 2
VTP Management Domain: ''
Duplex: full
Management address(es):
```

10

The example begins with the **show cdp neighbors** command, which lists one line per neighbor. Each line lists the most important topology information: the neighbor's hostname (Device ID), the local device's interface, and the neighboring device's interface (under the Port heading). For example, SW2's **show cdp neighbors** command lists an entry for SW1, with SW2's local interface of Gi0/2 and SW1's interface of Gi0/1 (see Figure 10-3 for reference). This command also lists the platform, identifying the specific model of the neighboring router or switch. So, even using this basic information, you could either construct a figure like Figure 10-3 or confirm that the details in the figure are correct.

The **show cdp neighbors detail** command lists additional details, such as the full name of the model of switch (WS-2960-24TT-L) and the IP address configured on the neighboring device.

> **NOTE** The **show cdp entry** *name* command lists the exact same details shown in the output of the **show cdp neighbors detail** command, but for only the one neighbor listed in the command.

As you can see, you can sit on one device and discover a lot of information about a neighboring device—a fact that actually creates a security exposure. Cisco recommends that CDP be disabled on any interface that might not have a need for CDP. For switches, any switch port connected to another switch, a router, or to an IP phone should use CDP.

CDP can be disabled globally and per-interface. Per-interface, the **no cdp enable** and **cdp enable** interface subcommands toggle CDP off and on, respectively. Alternatively, the **no cdp run** and **cdp run** global commands toggle CDP off and on (respectively) for the entire switch.

Examining the Status of the CDP Protocols

CDP defines protocol messages that flow between devices. Cisco switches include a few commands that list statistics and other status information about how the CDP protocols are working, as summarized in Table 10-2 for easy reference.

Table 10-2   Commands Used to Verify CDP Operations

Command	Description
show cdp	States whether CDP is enabled globally, and lists the default update and holdtime timers.
show cdp interface [*type number*]	States whether CDP is enabled on each interface, or a single interface if the interface is listed, and states update and holdtime timers on those interfaces.
show cdp traffic	Lists global statistics for the number of CDP advertisements sent and received.

Example 10-2 lists sample output from each of the commands in Table 10-2, based on switch SW2 in Figure 10-3.

Example 10-2   show cdp *Commands That Show CDP Status*

```
SW2# show cdp
Global CDP information:
    Sending CDP packets every 60 seconds
    Sending a holdtime value of 180 seconds
    Sending CDPv2 advertisements is enabled


SW2# show cdp interface FastEthernet0/13
FastEthernet0/13 is up, line protocol is up
  Encapsulation ARPA
  Sending CDP packets every 60 seconds
  Holdtime is 180 seconds
SW2# show cdp traffic
CDP counters :
    Total packets output: 304, Input: 305
    Hdr syntax: 0, Chksum error: 0, Encaps failed: 0
    No memory: 0, Invalid packet: 0,
    CDP version 1 advertisements output: 0, Input: 0
    CDP version 2 advertisements output: 304, Input: 305
```

Analyzing Switch Interface Status

This section begins the third of five major sections in this chapter by looking at switch interfaces. That process begins with finding out whether each switch interface works. Unsurprisingly,

Cisco switches do not use interfaces at all unless the interface is first considered to be in a functional or working state. Additionally, the switch interface might be in a working state, but intermittent problems might still be occurring.

This section begins by looking at the Cisco switch interface status codes and what they mean so that you can know whether an interface is working. The rest of this section then looks at those more unusual cases in which the interface is working, but not working well.

Interface Status Codes and Reasons for Nonworking States

Cisco switches actually use two different sets of interface status codes—one set of two codes (words) that use the same conventions as do router interface status codes, and another set with a single code (word). Both sets of status codes can determine whether an interface is working.

The switch **show interfaces** and **show interfaces description** commands list the two-code status just like routers. The two codes are named the *line status* and *protocol status*. They *generally* refer to whether Layer 1 is working (line status) and whether Layer 2 is working (protocol status), respectively. LAN switch interfaces typically show an interface with both codes with the same value, either "up" or "down."

> **NOTE**   This book refers to these two status codes in shorthand by just listing the two codes with a slash between them, such as "up/up."

The **show interfaces status** command lists a different single interface status code. This single interface status code corresponds to different combinations of the traditional two-code interface status codes and can be easily correlated to those codes. For example, the **show interfaces status** command lists a "connected" state for working interfaces. It corresponds to the up/up state seen with the **show interfaces** and **show interfaces description** commands.

Any interface state other than *connected* or *up/up* means that the switch will not forward or receive frames on the interface. Each nonworking interface state has a small set of root causes. Also, note that the exams could easily ask a question that showed only one or the other type of status code, so be prepared to see both types of status codes on the exams, and know the meanings of both. Table 10-3 lists the code combinations and some root causes that could have caused a particular interface status.

Key Topic

Table 10-3   LAN Switch Interface Status Codes

Line Status	Protocol Status	Interface Status	Typical Root Cause
Administratively Down	Down	disabled	The interface is configured with the **shutdown** command.
Down	Down	notconnect	No cable; bad cable; wrong cable pinouts; the speeds are mismatched on the two connected devices; the device on the other end of the cable is (a) powered off, (b) **shutdown**, or (c) error disabled.
Up	Down	notconnect	An interface up/down state is not expected on LAN switch physical interfaces.
Down	Down (err-disabled)	err-disabled	Port security has disabled the interface.
Up	Up	connected	The interface is working.

10

Most of the reasons for the notconnect state were covered earlier in this book. For example, using incorrect cabling pinouts, instead of the correct pinouts explained in Chapter 2, "Fundamentals of Ethernet LANs," causes a problem. However, one topic can be particularly difficult to troubleshoot—the possibility for both speed and duplex mismatches, as explained in the next section.

As you can see in the table, having a bad cable is just one of many reasons for the down/down state (or notconnect, per the **show interfaces status** command). Interestingly, the Cisco CCENT and CCNA exams do not focus much on cabling itself. However, for some examples of the root causes of cabling problems:

- The installation of any equipment that uses electricity, even non-IT equipment, can interfere with the transmission on the cabling, and make the link fail.

- The cable could be damaged, for example, if it lies under carpet. If the user's chair keeps squashing the cable, eventually the electrical signal can degrade.

- While optical cables do not suffer from EMI, someone can try to be helpful and move a fiber-optic cable out of the way—bending it too much. A bend into too tight a shape can prevent the cable from transmitting bits (called *macrobending*).

For the other interface states listed in Table 10-3, only the up/up (connected) state needs more discussion. An interface can be in a working state, and it might really be working—or it might be working in a degraded state. The next few topics discuss how to examine an up/up interface to find out whether it is working well or having problems.

Interface Speed and Duplex Issues

Many UTP-based Ethernet interfaces support multiple speeds, either full- or half-duplex, and support IEEE standard autonegotiation (as discussed in Chapter 6's section "Autonegotiation"). These same interfaces can also be configured to use a specific speed using the **speed {10 | 100 | 1000}** interface subcommand, and a specific duplex using the **duplex {half | full}** interface sub-command. With both configured, a switch or router disables the IEEE-standard autonegotiation process on that interface.

The **show interfaces** and **show interfaces status** commands list both the actual speed and duplex settings on an interface, as demonstrated in Example 10-3.

Key Topic

Example 10-3 *Displaying Speed and Duplex Settings on Switch Interfaces*

```
SW1# show interfaces status


Port      Name            Status        Vlan      Duplex  Speed Type
Fa0/1                     notconnect    1           auto   auto 10/100BaseTX
Fa0/2                     notconnect    1           auto   auto 10/100BaseTX
Fa0/3                     notconnect    1           auto   auto 10/100BaseTX
Fa0/4                     connected     1         a-full  a-100 10/100BaseTX
Fa0/5                     connected     1         a-full  a-100 10/100BaseTX
Fa0/6                     notconnect    1           auto   auto 10/100BaseTX
Fa0/7                     notconnect    1           auto   auto 10/100BaseTX
Fa0/8                     notconnect    1           auto   auto 10/100BaseTX
Fa0/9                     notconnect    1           auto   auto 10/100BaseTX
Fa0/10                    notconnect    1           auto   auto 10/100BaseTX
Fa0/11                    connected     1         a-full     10 10/100BaseTX
Fa0/12                    connected     1           half    100 10/100BaseTX
Fa0/13                    connected     1         a-full  a-100 10/100BaseTX
Fa0/14                    disabled      1           auto   auto 10/100BaseTX
```

```
Fa0/15                        notconnect   3              auto   auto 10/100BaseTX
Fa0/16                        notconnect   3              auto   auto 10/100BaseTX
Fa0/17                        connected    1              a-full a-100 10/100BaseTX
Fa0/18                        notconnect   1              auto   auto 10/100BaseTX
Fa0/19                        notconnect   1              auto   auto 10/100BaseTX
Fa0/20                        notconnect   1              auto   auto 10/100BaseTX
Fa0/21                        notconnect   1              auto   auto 10/100BaseTX
Fa0/22                        notconnect   1              auto   auto 10/100BaseTX
Fa0/23                        notconnect   1              auto   auto 10/100BaseTX
Fa0/24                        notconnect   1              auto   auto 10/100BaseTX
Gi0/1                         connected    trunk          full   1000 10/100/1000BaseTX
Gi0/2                         notconnect   1              auto   auto 10/100/1000BaseTX


SW1# show interfaces fa0/13
FastEthernet0/13 is up, line protocol is up (connected)
  Hardware is Fast Ethernet, address is 0019.e86a.6f8d (bia 0019.e86a.6f8d)
  MTU 1500 bytes, BW 100000 Kbit, DLY 100 usec,
     reliability 255/255, txload 1/255, rxload 1/255
  Encapsulation ARPA, loopback not set
  Keepalive set (10 sec)
  Full-duplex, 100Mbps, media type is 10/100BaseTX
  input flow-control is off, output flow-control is unsupported
  ARP type: ARPA, ARP Timeout 04:00:00
  Last input 00:00:05, output 00:00:00, output hang never
  Last clearing of "show interface" counters never
  Input queue: 0/75/0/0 (size/max/drops/flushes); Total output drops: 0
  Queueing strategy: fifo
  Output queue: 0/40 (size/max)
  5 minute input rate 0 bits/sec, 0 packets/sec
  5 minute output rate 0 bits/sec, 0 packets/sec
     85022 packets input, 10008976 bytes, 0 no buffer
     Received 284 broadcasts (0 multicast)
     0 runts, 0 giants, 0 throttles
     0 input errors, 0 CRC, 0 frame, 0 overrun, 0 ignored
     0 watchdog, 281 multicast, 0 pause input
     0 input packets with dribble condition detected
     95226 packets output, 10849674 bytes, 0 underruns
     0 output errors, 0 collisions, 1 interface resets
     0 unknown protocol drops
     0 babbles, 0 late collision, 0 deferred
     0 lost carrier, 0 no carrier, 0 PAUSE output
     0 output buffer failures, 0 output buffers swapped out
```

Although both commands in the example can be useful, only the **show interfaces status** command implies how the switch determined the speed and duplex settings. The command output lists autonegotiated settings with a prefix of **a-**. For example, **a-full** means full-duplex as autonegotiated, whereas **full** means full-duplex but as manually configured. The example shades the command output that implies that the switch's Fa0/12 interface's speed and duplex were not found through autonegotiation, but Fa0/13 did use autonegotiation. Note that the **show interfaces fa0/13** command (without the **status** option) simply lists the speed and duplex for interface Fast Ethernet 0/13, with nothing implying that the values were learned through autonegotiation.

When the IEEE autonegotiation process works on both devices, both devices agree to the fastest speed supported by both devices. Additionally, the devices use full-duplex if it is supported by both devices, or half-duplex if it is not. However, when one device has disabled autonegotiation, and the other device uses autonegotiation, the device using autonegotiation chooses the default duplex setting based on the current speed. The defaults are as follows:

Key Topic

- If the speed is not known through any means, use 10 Mbps, half-duplex.
- If the switch successfully senses the speed without IEEE autonegotiation, by just looking at the signal on the cable:
  - If the speed is 10 or 100 Mbps, default to use half-duplex.
  - If the speed is 1,000 Mbps, default to use full-duplex.

NOTE Ethernet interfaces using speeds faster than 1 Gbps always use full-duplex.

While autonegotiation works well, these defaults allow for the possibility of a difficult-to-troubleshoot problem called a *duplex mismatch*. Chapter 6's section "Autonegotiation" explains how both devices could use the same speed, so the devices would consider the link to be up, but one side would use half-duplex, and the other side would use full-duplex.

The next example shows a specific case that causes a duplex mismatch. In Figure 10-4, imagine that SW2's Gi0/2 interface was configured with the **speed 100** and **duplex full** commands (these settings are not recommended on a Gigabit-capable interface, by the way). On Cisco switches, configuring both the **speed** and **duplex** commands disables IEEE autonegotiation on that port. If SW1's Gi0/1 interface tries to use autonegotiation, SW1 would also use a speed of 100 Mbps, but default to use half-duplex. Example 10-4 shows the results of this specific case on SW1.

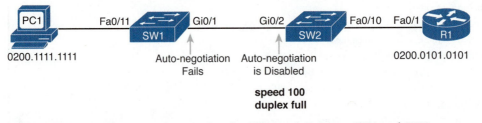

Figure 10-4 *Conditions to Create a Duplex Mismatch Between SW1 and SW2*

Example 10-4 *Confirming Duplex Mismatch on Switch SW1*

```
SW1# show interfaces gi0/1 status

Port      Name              Status       Vlan     Duplex  Speed Type
Gi0/1                       connected    trunk    a-half  a-100 10/100/1000BaseTX
```

First, focusing on the command output, the command confirms SW1's speed and duplex. It also lists a prefix of **a-** in the output, implying autonegotiation. Even with SW1 using autonegotiation defaults, the command still notes the values as being learned through autonegotiation.

Finding a duplex mismatch can be much more difficult than finding a speed mismatch, because *if the duplex settings do not match on the ends of an Ethernet segment, the switch interface will still be in a connected (up/up) state.* In this case, the interface works, but it might work poorly, with poor performance, and with symptoms of intermittent problems. The reason is that the device using half-duplex uses carrier sense multiple access collision detect (CSMA/CD) logic, waiting to send when receiving a frame, believing collisions occur when they physically do not—and actually stopping sending a frame because the switch thinks a collision occurred. With enough traffic load, the interface could be in a connect state, but it's extremely inefficient for passing traffic.

To identify duplex mismatch problems, check the duplex setting on each end of the link and watch for incrementing collision and late collision counters, as explained in the next section.

Common Layer 1 Problems on Working Interfaces

When the interface reaches the connect (up/up) state, the switch considers the interface to be working. The switch, of course, tries to use the interface, and at the same time, the switch keeps various interface counters. These interface counters can help identify problems that can occur even though the interface is in a connect state. This section explains some of the related concepts and a few of the most common problems.

Whenever the physical transmission has problems, the receiving device might receive a frame whose bits have changed values. These frames do not pass the error detection logic as implemented in the FCS field in the Ethernet trailer, as covered in Chapter 2. The receiving device discards the frame and counts it as some kind of *input error*. Cisco switches list this error as a CRC error, as highlighted in Example 10-5. (Cyclic redundancy check [CRC] is a term related to how the FCS math detects an error.)

Example 10-5 *Interface Counters for Layer 1 Problems*

```
SW1# show interfaces fa0/13
! lines omitted for brevity
    Received 284 broadcasts (0 multicast)
    0 runts, 0 giants, 0 throttles
    0 input errors, 0 CRC, 0 frame, 0 overrun, 0 ignored
    0 watchdog, 281 multicast, 0 pause input
    0 input packets with dribble condition detected
    95226 packets output, 10849674 bytes, 0 underruns
    0 output errors, 0 collisions, 1 interface resets
    0 unknown protocol drops
    0 babbles, 0 late collision, 0 deferred
    0 lost carrier, 0 no carrier, 0 PAUSE output
    0 output buffer failures, 0 output buffers swapped out
```

The number of input errors, and the number of CRC errors, are just a few of the counters in the output of the **show interfaces** command. The challenge is to decide which counters you need to think about, which ones show that a problem is happening, and which ones are normal and of no concern.

The example highlights several of the counters as examples so that you can start to understand which ones point to problems and which ones are just counting normal events that are not problems. The following list shows a short description of each highlighted counter, in the order shown in the example:

Runts: Frames that did not meet the minimum frame size requirement (64 bytes, including the 18-byte destination MAC, source MAC, Type, and FCS). Can be caused by collisions.

Giants: Frames that exceed the maximum frame size requirement (1518 bytes, including the 18-byte destination MAC, source MAC, Type, and FCS).

Input Errors: A total of many counters, including runts, giants, no buffer, CRC, frame, overrun, and ignored counts.

CRC: Received frames that did not pass the FCS math; can be caused by collisions.

Frame: Received frames that have an illegal format, for example, ending with a partial byte; can be caused by collisions.

Packets Output: Total number of packets (frames) forwarded out the interface.

Output Errors: Total number of packets (frames) that the switch port tried to transmit, but for which some problem occurred.

Collisions: Counter of all collisions that occur when the interface is transmitting a frame.

Late Collisions: The subset of all collisions that happen after the 64th byte of the frame has been transmitted. (In a properly working Ethernet LAN, collisions should occur within the first 64 bytes; late collisions today often point to a duplex mismatch.)

Note that many of these counters occur as part of the CSMA/CD process used when half-duplex is enabled. Collisions occur as a normal part of the half-duplex logic imposed by CSMA/CD, so a switch interface with an increasing collisions counter might not even have a problem. However, one problem, called late collisions, points to the classic duplex mismatch problem.

If a LAN design follows cabling guidelines, all collisions should occur by the end of the 64th byte of any frame. When a switch has already sent 64 bytes of a frame, and the switch receives a frame on that same interface, the switch senses a collision. In this case, the collision is a late collision, and the switch increments the late collision counter in addition to the usual CSMA/CD actions to send a jam signal, wait a random time, and try again.

With a duplex mismatch, like the mismatch between SW1 and SW2 in Figure 10-4, the half-duplex interface will likely see the late collisions counter increment. Why? The half-duplex interface sends a frame (SW1), but the full-duplex neighbor (SW2) sends at any time, even after the 64th byte of the frame sent by the half-duplex switch. So, just keep repeating the **show interfaces** command, and if you see the late collisions counter incrementing on a half-duplex interface, you might have a duplex mismatch problem.

A working interface (in an up/up state) can still suffer from issues related to the physical cabling as well. The cabling problems might not be bad enough to cause a complete failure, but the transmission failures result in some frames failing to pass successfully over the cable. For example, excessive interference on the cable can cause the various input error counters to keep growing larger, especially the CRC counter. In particular, if the CRC errors grow, but the collisions counters do not, the problem might simply be interference on the cable. (The switch counts each collided frame as one form of input error as well.)

Predicting Where Switches Will Forward Frames

This section begins the fourth of five major sections in this chapter. This section looks at a key part of the troubleshooting process for Ethernet LANs: predicting where frames should go in the LAN so that you can compare what should happen versus what is actually happening in a LAN.

Predicting the Contents of the MAC Address Table

As explained in Chapter 6, "Building Ethernet LANs with Switches," switches learn MAC addresses and then use the entries in the MAC address table to make a forwarding/filtering decision for each frame. To know exactly how a particular switch will forward an Ethernet frame, you need to examine the MAC address table on a Cisco switch.

The **show mac address-table** EXEC command displays the contents of a switch's MAC address table. This command lists all MAC addresses currently known by the switch. The output includes some static overhead MAC addresses used by the switch and any statically configured MAC addresses, such as those configured with the port security feature. The command also lists all dynamically learned MAC addresses. If you want to see only the dynamically learned MAC address table entries, simply use the **show mac address-table dynamic** EXEC command.

> **NOTE**   Some older switch IOS versions only support the older version of this command: **show mac-address-table**.

The more formal troubleshooting process begins with a mental process where you predict where frames should flow in the LAN. As an exercise, go back and review Figure 10-3 and try to create a MAC address table on paper for each switch. Include the MAC addresses for both PCs, as well as the Gi0/1 MAC address for R1. (Assume that all three are assigned to VLAN 10.) Then predict which interfaces would be used to forward a frame sent by Fred, Barney, and R1 to every other device.

The MAC table entries you predict in this case define where you think frames will flow. Even though this sample network in Figure 10-3 shows only one physical path through the Ethernet LAN, the exercise should be worthwhile, because it forces you to correlate what you'd expect to see in the MAC address table with how the switches forward frames. Figure 10-5 shows the resulting MAC table entries for PCs Fred and Barney, as well as for Router R1.

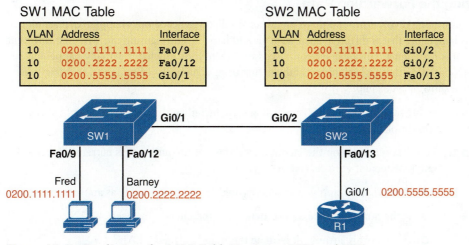

Figure 10-5   *Predictions for MAC Table Entries on SW1 and SW2*

While Figure 10-5 shows the concepts, Example 10-6 lists the same facts but in the form of the **show mac address-table dynamic** command on the switches. This command lists all dynamically learned MAC table entries on a switch, for all VLANs.

Example 10-6   *Examining SW1 and SW2 Dynamic MAC Address Table Entries*

```
SW1# show mac address-table dynamic
          Mac Address Table
-------------------------------------------

Vlan    Mac Address       Type       Ports
----    -----------       --------   -----
  10    0200.1111.1111    DYNAMIC    Fa0/9
  10    0200.2222.2222    DYNAMIC    Fa0/12
  10    0200.5555.5555    DYNAMIC    Gi0/1

SW2# show mac address-table dynamic
          Mac Address Table
```

```
--------------------------------------------------

Vlan    Mac Address      Type      Ports
----    -----------      --------  -----
  10    0200.1111.1111   DYNAMIC   Gi0/2
  10    0200.2222.2222   DYNAMIC   Gi0/2
  10    0200.5555.5555   DYNAMIC   Fa0/13
```

When predicting the MAC address table entries, you need to imagine a frame sent by a device to another device on the other side of the LAN and then determine *which switch ports the frame would enter* as it passes through the LAN. For example, if Barney sends a frame to Router R1, the frame would enter SW1's Fa0/12 interface, so SW1 has a MAC table entry that lists Barney's 0200.2222.2222 MAC address with Fa0/12. SW1 would forward Barney's frame to SW2, arriving on SW2's Gi0/2 interface, so SW2's MAC table lists Barney's MAC address (0200.2222.2222) with interface Gi0/2.

After you predict the expected contents of the MAC address tables, you can then examine what is actually happening on the switches, as described in the next section.

Analyzing the Forwarding Path

Troubleshooting revolves around three big ideas: predicting what should happen, determining what is happening that is different than what should happen, and figuring out why that different behavior is happening. This next section discusses how to look at what is actually happening in a VLAN based on those MAC address tables, first using a summary of switch forwarding logic and then showing an example.

The following list summarizes switch forwarding logic including the LAN switching features discussed in this book:

Step 1. Process functions on the incoming interface, if the interface is currently in an up/ up (connected) state, as follows:

   A. If configured, apply port security logic to filter the frame as appropriate.

   B. If the port is an access port, determine the interface's access VLAN.

   C. If the port is a trunk, determine the frame's tagged VLAN.

Step 2. Make a forwarding decision. Look for the frame's destination MAC address in the MAC address table, but only for entries in the VLAN identified in Step 1. If the destination MAC is...

   A. Found (unicast), forward the frame out the only interface listed in the matched address table entry.

   B. Not found (unicast), flood the frame out all other access ports (except the incoming port) in that same VLAN, plus out trunks that have not restricted the VLAN from that trunk (as discussed in Chapter 9, "Implementing Ethernet Virtual LANs," as related to the **show interfaces trunk** command).

   C. Broadcast, flood the frame, with the same rules as the previous step.

For an example of this process, consider a frame sent by Barney to its default gateway, R1 (0200.5555.5555). Using the steps just listed, the following occurs:

Step 1.   Input interface processing:

    A. The port does not happen to have port security enabled.

    B. SW1 receives the frame on its Fa0/12 interface, an access port in VLAN 10.

Step 2.   Make a forwarding decision: SW1 looks in its MAC address table for entries in VLAN 10:

    A. SW1 finds an entry (known unicast) for 0200.5555.5555, associated with VLAN 10, outgoing interface Gi0/1, so SW1 forwards the frame only out interface Gi0/1. (This link is a VLAN trunk, so SW1 adds a VLAN 10 tag to the 802.1Q trunking header.)

At this point, the frame with source 0200.2222.2222 (Barney) and destination 0200.5555.5555 (R1) is on its way to SW2. You can then apply the same logic for SW2, as follows:

Step 1.   Input interface processing:

    A. The port does not happen to have port security enabled.

    B. SW2 receives the frame on its Gi0/2 interface, a trunk; the frame lists a tag of VLAN 10. (SW2 will remove the 802.1Q header as well.)

Step 2.   Make a forwarding decision: SW2 looks for its MAC table for entries in VLAN 10:

    A. SW2 finds an entry (known unicast) for 0200.5555.5555, associated with VLAN 10, outgoing interface Fa0/13, so SW2 forwards the frame only out interface Fa0/13.

At this point, the frame should be on its way, over the Ethernet cable between SW2 and R1.

Port Security and Filtering

When tracing the path a frame takes through LAN switches, different kinds of filters can discard frames, even when all the interfaces are up. For example, LAN switches can use filters called access control lists (ACL) that filter based on the source and destination MAC address, discarding some frames. Additionally, routers can filter IP packets using IP ACLs. (This book does not discuss ACLs for LAN switches, but it does discuss IP ACLs for routers in Chapter 22, "Basic IPv4 Access Control Lists," and Chapter 23, "Advanced IPv4 ACLs and Device Security.")

Additionally, port security, as discussed in Chapter 8, "Configuring Ethernet Switching," also filters frames. In some cases, you can easily tell that port security has taken action, because port security shuts down the interface. However, in other cases, port security leaves the interface up, but simply discards the offending traffic. From a troubleshooting perspective, a port security configuration that leaves the interface up, but still discards frames, requires the network engineer to look closely at port security status, rather than just looking at interfaces and the MAC address table.

As a reminder, port security allows three violation modes (**shutdown**, **protect**, and **restrict**), but only the default setting of **shutdown** causes the switch to err-disable the interface.

For example, consider a case in which someone takes a working network and adds port security to filter frames sent by Barney. Use Figure 10-3 or 10-5, both of which show the same topology. Barney sends frames into SW1's Fa0/12 port, which is now configured with port security. The port security configuration considers frames with Barney's source MAC address as a violation, and it uses a violation mode set to **protect**.

10

What happens? SW1 now discards all frames sourced by Barney's MAC address. But SW1 does not disable any interfaces. The **show interfaces** or **show interfaces status** command on SW1 shows no changes to the interface status, and no evidence of what happened. You would need to look further at port security (**show port-security interface**) to find evidence that port security was discarding the frames sent by Barney.

The MAC address table gives some hints that port security might be enabled. Because port security manages the MAC addresses, any MAC addresses associated with a port on which port security is enabled show up as static MAC addresses. As a result, the **show mac address-table dynamic** command does not list MAC addresses off these interfaces on which port security is enabled. However, the **show mac address-table** and **show mac address-table static** commands do list these static MAC addresses.

Analyzing VLANs and VLAN Trunks

A switch's forwarding process, as discussed earlier in the section "Analyzing the Forwarding Path," depends in part on VLANs and VLAN trunking. Before a switch can forward frames in a particular VLAN, the switch must know about a VLAN and the VLAN must be active. And before a switch can forward a frame over a VLAN trunk, the trunk must currently allow that VLAN to pass over the trunk.

This final of the five major sections in this chapter focuses on VLAN and VLAN trunking issues, and specifically issues that impact the frame switching process. The four potential issues are as follows:

Step 1. Identify all access interfaces and their assigned access VLANs and reassign into the correct VLANs as needed.

Step 2. Determine whether the VLANs both exist (configured or learned with VTP) and are active on each switch. If not, configure and activate the VLANs to resolve problems as needed.

Step 3. Check the allowed VLAN lists, on the switches on both ends of the trunk, and ensure that the lists of allowed VLANs are the same.

Step 4. Ensure that for any links that should use trunking, one switch does not think it is trunking, while the other switch does not think it is trunking because of an unfortunate choice of configuration settings.

Ensuring That the Right Access Interfaces Are in the Right VLANs

To ensure that each access interface has been assigned to the correct VLAN, engineers simply need to determine which switch interfaces are access interfaces instead of trunk interfaces, determine the assigned access VLANs on each interface, and compare the information to the documentation. The **show** commands listed in Table 10-4 can be particularly helpful in this process.

Table 10-4   Commands That Can Find Access Ports and VLANs

EXEC Command	Description
show vlan brief show vlan	Lists each VLAN and all interfaces assigned to that VLAN (but does not include operational trunks)
show vlan id *num*	Lists both access and trunk ports in the VLAN

Key Topic

EXEC Command	Description
show interfaces *type number* **switchport**	Identifies the interface's access VLAN and voice VLAN, plus the configured and operational mode (access or trunk)
show mac address-table	Lists MAC table entries, including the associated VLAN

If possible, start this step with the **show vlan** and **show vlan brief** commands, because they list all the known VLANs and the access interfaces assigned to each VLAN. Be aware, however, that these two commands do not list operational trunks. The output does list all other interfaces (those not currently trunking), no matter whether the interface is in a working or nonworking state.

If the **show vlan** and **show interface switchport** commands are not available in a particular exam question, the **show mac address-table** command can also help identify the access VLAN. This command lists the MAC address table, with each entry including a MAC address, interface, and VLAN ID. If the exam question implies that a switch interface connects to a single device PC, you should only see one MAC table entry that lists that particular access interface; the VLAN ID listed for that same entry identifies the access VLAN. (You cannot make such assumptions for trunking interfaces.)

After you determine the access interfaces and associated VLANs, if the interface is assigned to the wrong VLAN, use the **switchport access vlan** *vlan-id* interface subcommand to assign the correct VLAN ID.

Access VLANs Not Being Defined

Switches do not forward frames for VLANs that are (a) not configured or (b) configured but disabled (shutdown). This section summarizes the best ways to confirm that a switch knows that a particular VLAN exists, and if it exists, determines the state of the VLAN.

First, on the issue of whether a VLAN is defined, a VLAN can be defined to a switch in two ways: using the **vlan** *number* global configuration command, or it can be learned from another switch using VTP. This book purposefully ignores VTP as much as possible, so for this discussion, consider that the only way for a switch to know about a VLAN is to have a **vlan** command configured on the local switch.

Next, the **show vlan** command always lists all VLANs known to the switch, but the **show running-config** command does not. Switches configured as VTP servers and clients do not list the **vlan** commands in the running-config nor the startup-config file; on these switches, you must use the **show vlan** command. Switches configured to use VTP transparent mode, or that disable VTP, list the **vlan** configuration commands in the configuration files. (Use the **show vtp status** command to learn the current VTP mode of a switch.)

After you determine that a VLAN does not exist, the problem might be that the VLAN simply needs to be defined. If so, follow the VLAN configuration process as covered in detail in Chapter 9.

Access VLANs Being Disabled

For any existing VLANs, also verify that the VLAN is active. The **show vlan** command should list one of two VLAN state values, depending on the current state: either *active* or *act/lshut*. The second of these states means that the VLAN is shutdown. Shutting down a VLAN disables the VLAN on that switch only, so that *the switch will not forward frames in that VLAN*.

10

Switch IOS gives you two similar configuration methods with which to disable (**shutdown**) and enable (**no shutdown**) a VLAN. Example 10-7 shows how, first by using the global command **[no] shutdown vlan** *number* and then using the VLAN mode subcommand **[no] shutdown**. The example shows the global commands enabling and disabling VLANs 10 and 20, respectively, and using VLAN subcommands to enable and disable VLANs 30 and 40 (respectively).

Example 10-7 *Enabling and Disabling VLANs on a Switch*

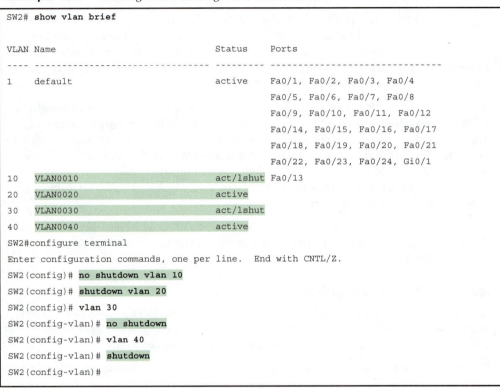

```
SW2# show vlan brief

VLAN Name                             Status    Ports
---- -------------------------------- --------- -------------------------------
1    default                          active    Fa0/1, Fa0/2, Fa0/3, Fa0/4
                                                Fa0/5, Fa0/6, Fa0/7, Fa0/8
                                                Fa0/9, Fa0/10, Fa0/11, Fa0/12
                                                Fa0/14, Fa0/15, Fa0/16, Fa0/17
                                                Fa0/18, Fa0/19, Fa0/20, Fa0/21
                                                Fa0/22, Fa0/23, Fa0/24, Gi0/1
10   VLAN0010                         act/lshut Fa0/13
20   VLAN0020                         active
30   VLAN0030                         act/lshut
40   VLAN0040                         active
SW2#configure terminal
Enter configuration commands, one per line.  End with CNTL/Z.
SW2(config)# no shutdown vlan 10
SW2(config)# shutdown vlan 20
SW2(config)# vlan 30
SW2(config-vlan)# no shutdown
SW2(config-vlan)# vlan 40
SW2(config-vlan)# shutdown
SW2(config-vlan)#
```

Check the Allowed VLAN List on Both Ends of a Trunk

The next item, and the one that follows, both occur when an engineer makes some poor configuration choices on a VLAN trunk. In real life, you should instead just configure the trunk correctly, as outlined in Chapter 9's section "VLAN Trunking Configuration" and the section that follows it, "Controlling Which VLANs Can Be Supported on a Trunk." But for the exams, you should be ready to notice a couple of oddities that happen with some unfortunate configuration choices on trunks.

First, it is possible to configure a different allowed VLAN list on the opposite ends of a VLAN trunk. When mismatched, the trunk cannot pass traffic for that VLAN.

Figure 10-6 shows an example. Both switches have defined VLANs 1 through 10, so both by default include VLANs 1 through 10 in their allowed VLAN list. However, SW2 has been configured with a **switchport trunk allowed vlan remove 10** command, removing VLAN 10 from SW2's G0/2 allowed list. In this case, SW1, which still allows VLAN 10, acts as normal, tagging and forwarding frames in VLAN 10 (Step 1 in the figure). SW2 simply discards any VLAN 10 frames received on that trunk (Step 2), because SW2 does not allow VLAN 10 traffic on that trunk.

Figure 10-6 *Mismatched VLAN-Allowed Lists on a Trunk*

And to emphasize the point, you cannot see this problem from just one side of the trunk or the other. The **show interfaces trunk** command output on both sides looks completely normal. You can only notice the problem by comparing the allowed lists on both ends of the trunk.

To compare the lists, you need to look at the second of three lists of VLANs listed by the **show interfaces trunk** command, as highlighted in the example output in Example 10-8. The highlighted text shows the second section, which lists VLANs that meet these criteria: the VLANs that exist on the switch, that are not shutdown, and that are not removed from the allowed list.

Example 10-8 *Second Set of VLANs: Existing, Not Shut Down, and Allowed*

```
SW2# show interfaces trunk

Port        Mode          Encapsulation  Status         Native vlan
Gi0/2       desirable     802.1q         trunking       1

Port        Vlans allowed on trunk
Gi0/2       1-4094

Port        Vlans allowed and active in management domain
Gi0/2       1-9

Port        Vlans in spanning tree forwarding state and not pruned
Gi0/2       1-9
```

Mismatched Trunking Operational States

Trunking can be configured correctly so that both switches forward frames for the same set of VLANs. However, trunks can also be misconfigured, with a couple of different results. In some cases, both switches conclude that their interfaces do not trunk. In other cases, one switch believes that its interface is correctly trunking, while the other switch does not.

The most common incorrect configuration—which results in both switches not trunking—is a configuration that uses the **switchport mode dynamic auto** command on both switches on the link. The word "auto" just makes us all want to think that the link would trunk automatically, but this command is both automatic and passive. As a result, both switches passively wait on the other device on the link to begin negotiations.

With this particular incorrect configuration, the **show interfaces switchport** command on both switches confirms both the administrative state (auto), as well as the fact that both switches operate as "static access" ports. Example 10-9 highlights those parts of the output from this command.

10

Example 10-9 *Operational Trunking State*

```
SW2# show interfaces gigabit0/2 switchport
Name: Gi0/2
Switchport: Enabled
Administrative Mode: dynamic auto
Operational Mode: static access
Administrative Trunking Encapsulation: dot1q
Operational Trunking Encapsulation: native
! lines omitted for brevity
```

A different incorrect trunking configuration results in one switch with an operational state of "trunk," while the other switch has an operational state of "static access." When this combination of events happens, the interface works a little. The status on each end will be up/up or connected. Traffic in the native VLAN will actually cross the link successfully. However, traffic in all the rest of the VLANs will not cross the link.

Figure 10-7 shows the incorrect configuration along with which side trunks and which does not. The side that trunks (SW1 in this case) enables trunking always, using the command **switchport mode trunk**. However, this command does not disable DTP negotiations. To cause this particular problem, SW1 also disables DTP negotiation using the **switchport nonegotiate** command. SW2's configuration also helps create the problem, by using a trunking option that relies on DTP. Because SW1 has disabled DTP, SW2's DTP negotiations fail, and SW2 does not trunk.

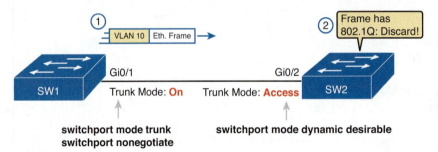

Figure 10-7 *Mismatched Trunking Operational States*

In this case, SW1 treats its G0/1 interface as a trunk, and SW2 treats its G0/2 interface as an access port (not a trunk). As shown in the figure at Step 1, SW1 could (for example) forward a frame in VLAN 10 (Step 1). However, SW2 would view any frame that arrives with an 802.1Q header as illegal, because SW2 treats its G0/2 port as an access port. So, SW2 discards any 802.1Q frames received on that port.

First, to deal with the possibility of this problem, always check the trunk's operational state on both sides of the trunk. The best commands to check trunking-related facts are **show interfaces trunk** and **show interfaces switchport**.

NOTE   Frankly, in real life, just avoid this kind of configuration. However, the switches do not prevent you from making these types of mistakes, so you need to be ready.

Review Activities

Chapter Summary

- The proprietary Cisco Discovery Protocol (CDP) discovers basic information about neighboring routers and switches without needing to know the passwords for the neighboring devices.

- To discover information, routers and switches send CDP messages out each of their interfaces. The messages essentially announce information about the device that sent the CDP message. Devices that support CDP learn information about others by listening for the advertisements sent by other devices.

- From a troubleshooting perspective, CDP can be used to either confirm or fix the documentation shown in a network diagram, or even discover the devices and interfaces used in a network.

- CDP discovers several useful details from the neighboring Cisco devices:

  - **Device identifier:** Typically the hostname

  - **Address list:** Network and data-link addresses

  - **Port identifier:** The interface on the remote router or switch on the other end of the link that sent the CDP advertisement

  - **Capabilities list:** Information about what type of device it is (for example, a router or a switch)

  - **Platform:** The model and OS level running in the device

- The switch **show interfaces** and **show interfaces description** commands list the two-code status just like routers. The two codes are named the *line status* and *protocol status*.

- The **show interfaces status** command lists a different single interface status code. This single interface status code corresponds to different combinations of the traditional two-code interface status codes and can be easily correlated to those codes.

- Any interface state other than *connected* or *up/up* means that the switch will not forward or receive frames on the interface.

- The following list shows a short description of each counter displayed in the output of a **show interfaces** command.

  - **Runts:** Frames that did not meet the minimum frame size requirement (64 bytes, including the 18-byte destination MAC, source MAC, Type, and FCS). May be caused by collisions.

  - **Giants:** Frames that exceed the maximum frame size requirement (1518 bytes, including the 18-byte destination MAC, source MAC, Type, and FCS).

  - **Input Errors:** A total of many counters, including runts, giants, no buffer, CRC, frame, overrun, and ignored counts.

  - **CRC:** Received frames that did not pass the FCS math; may be caused by collisions.

  - **Frame:** Received frames that have an illegal format (for example, ending with a partial byte); may be caused by collisions.

  - **Output Errors:** The total number of packets (frames) that the switch port tried to transmit but for which some problem occurred.

  - **Packets Output:** The total number of packets (frames) forwarded out the interface.

  - **Collisions:** The counter of all collisions that occur when the interface is transmitting a frame.

  - **Late Collisions:** The subset of all collisions that happen after the 64th byte of the frame has been transmitted. (In a properly working Ethernet LAN, collisions should occur within the first 64 bytes; late collisions today often point to a duplex mismatch.)

10

Review Questions

Answer these review questions. You can find the answers at the bottom of the last page of the chapter. For thorough explanations, see DVD Appendix C, "Answers to Review Questions."

1. Imagine that a switch connects through an Ethernet cable to a router, and the router's host name is Hannah. Which of the following commands could tell you information about the IOS version on Hannah without establishing a Telnet connection to Hannah? (Choose two answers.)

   A. show neighbors Hannah

   B. show cdp

   C. show cdp neighbors

   D. show cdp neighbors Hannah

   E. show cdp entry Hannah

   F. show cdp neighbors detail

2. A switch is cabled to a router whose host name is Hannah. Which of the following CDP commands could identify Hannah's model of hardware? (Choose two answers.)

   A. show neighbors

   B. show neighbors Hannah

   C. show cdp

   D. show cdp interface

   E. show cdp neighbors

   F. show cdp entry Hannah

3. The output of the **show interfaces status** command on a 2960 switch shows interface Fa0/1 in a "disabled" state. Which of the following is true about interface Fa0/1? (Choose three answers.)

   A. The interface is configured with the **shutdown** command.

   B. The **show interfaces fa0/1** command will list the interface with two status codes of administratively down and line protocol down.

   C. The **show interfaces fa0/1** command will list the interface with two status codes of up and down.

   D. The interface cannot currently be used to forward frames.

   E. The interface can currently be used to forward frames.

4. Switch SW1 uses its Gigabit 0/1 interface to connect to switch SW2's Gigabit 0/2 interface. SW2's Gi0/2 interface is configured with the **speed 1000** and **duplex full** commands. SW1 uses all defaults for interface configuration commands on its Gi0/1 interface. Which of the following are true about the link after it comes up? (Choose two answers.)

   A. The link works at 1000 Mbps (1 Gbps).

   B. SW1 attempts to run at 10 Mbps because SW2 has effectively disabled IEEE standard autonegotiation.

   C. The link runs at 1 Gbps, but SW1 uses half-duplex and SW2 uses full-duplex.

   D. Both switches use full-duplex.

5. The following line of output was taken from a **show interfaces fa0/1** command:

```
Full-duplex, 100Mbps, media type is 10/100BaseTX
```

Which of the following are true about the interface? (Choose two answers.)

   A. The speed was definitely configured with the **speed 100** interface subcommand.

   B. The speed might have been configured with the **speed 100** interface subcommand.

   C. The duplex was definitely configured with the **duplex full** interface subcommand.

   D. The duplex might have been configured with the **duplex full** interface subcommand.

6. Which of the following commands list the MAC address table entries for MAC addresses configured by port security? (Choose two answers.)

   A. show mac address-table dynamic

   B. show mac address-table

   C. show mac address-table static

   D. show mac address-table port-security

7. On a Cisco Catalyst switch, you issue a **show mac address-table** command. Which of the following answers list information you would likely see in most lines of output? (Choose two answers.)

   A. A MAC address

   B. An IP address

   C. A VLAN ID

   D. Type (broadcast, multicast, or unicast)

8. Layer 2 switches SW1 and SW2 connect through a link, with port G0/1 on SW1 and port G0/2 on SW2. The network engineer wants to use 802.1Q trunking on this link. The **show interfaces g0/1 switchport** command on SW1 shows the output listed here:

```
SW1# show interfaces gigabit0/1 switchport
Name: Gi0/1
Switchport: Enabled
Administrative Mode: trunk
Operational Mode: trunk
```

Which of the following must be true on switch SW2's G0/2 port?

   A. The operational state per the **show interfaces switchport** command must be "trunk."

   B. The administrative state per the **show interfaces switchport** command must be "trunk."

   C. SW2 must use the **switchport mode trunk** configuration command on G0/2, or the link will not use trunking.

   D. SW2 can use the **switchport mode dynamic auto** configuration command as one option to make the link use trunking.

10

Review All the Key Topics

Review the most important topics from this chapter, noted with the Key Topic icon. Table 10-5 lists these key topics and where each is discussed.

Table 10-5   Key Topics for Chapter 10

Key Topic Element	Description	Page Number
List	Information gathered by CDP	239
Table 10-1	Three CDP **show** commands that list information about neighbors	240
Table 10-3	Two types of interface state terms and their meanings	243
Example 10-3	Example that shows how to find the speed and duplex settings, as well as whether they were learned through autonegotiation	244
List	Defaults for IEEE autonegotiation	246
List	Summary of switch forwarding steps	250
Table 10-4	Commands that identify access VLANs assigned to ports	252

Complete the Tables and Lists from Memory

Print a copy of DVD Appendix M, "Memory Tables," or at least the section for this chapter, and complete the tables and lists from memory. DVD Appendix N, "Memory Tables Answer Key," includes completed tables and lists for you to check your work.

Definitions of Key Terms

After your first reading of the chapter, try to define these key terms, but do not be concerned about getting them all correct at that time. Chapter 30 directs you in how to use these terms for late-stage preparation for the exam.

CDP neighbor, up and up, connected, error disabled, problem isolation, root cause, duplex mismatch

Command References

Tables 10-6 and 10-7 list only commands specifically mentioned in this chapter, but the command references at the end of Chapters 8 and 9 also cover some related commands. Table 10-6 lists and briefly describes the configuration commands used in this chapter.

Table 10-6   Commands for Catalyst 2960 Switch Configuration

Command	Description
shutdown no shutdown	Interface subcommands that administratively disable and enable an interface, respectively.
switchport port-security violation {protect | restrict | shutdown}	Interface subcommand that tells the switch what to do if an inappropriate MAC address tries to access the network through a secure switch port.
cdp run no cdp run	Global commands that enable and disable, respectively, CDP for the entire switch or router.

Command	Description
cdp enable no cdp enable	Interface subcommands that enable and disable, respectively, CDP for a particular interface.
speed {auto | 10 | 100 | 1000}	Interface subcommand that manually sets the interface speed.
duplex {auto | full | half}	Interface subcommand that manually sets the interface duplex.

Table 10-7 lists and briefly describes the EXEC commands used in this chapter.

Table 10-7   Chapter 10 EXEC Command Reference

Command	Description
show mac address-table [dynamic | static] [address *hw-addr*] [interface *interface-id*] [vlan *vlan-id*]	Displays the MAC address table. The security option displays information about the restricted or static settings.
show port-security [interface *interface-id*] [address]	Displays information about security options configured on an interface.
show cdp neighbors [*type number*]	Lists one summary line of information about each neighbor, or just the neighbor found on a specific interface if an interface was listed.
show cdp neighbors detail	Lists one large set of information (approximately 15 lines) for every neighbor.
show cdp entry *name*	Displays the same information as the **show cdp neighbors detail** command, but only for the named neighbor.
show cdp	States whether CDP is enabled globally, and lists the default update and holdtime timers.
show cdp interface [*type number*]	States whether CDP is enabled on each interface, or a single interface if the interface is listed, and states update and holdtime timers on those interfaces.
show cdp traffic	Displays global statistics for the number of CDP advertisements sent and received.
show interfaces [*type number*]	Displays detailed information about interface status, settings, and counters.
show interfaces description	Displays one line of information per interface, with a two-item status (similar to the **show interfaces** command status), and includes any description that is configured on the interfaces.
show interfaces [*type number*] status	Displays summary information about interface status and settings, including actual speed and duplex, a single-item status code, and whether the interface was autonegotiated.
show interfaces [*type number*] switchport	Displays a large variety of configuration settings and current operational status, including VLAN trunking details, access and voice VLAN, and native VLAN.

10

Command	Description
show interfaces [*type number*] trunk	Lists information about the currently operational trunks (or just for the trunk listed in the command) and the VLANs supported on those trunks.
show vlan brief, show vlan	Lists each VLAN and all interfaces assigned to that VLAN but does not include trunks.
show vlan id *num*	Lists both access and trunk ports in the VLAN.
show vtp status	Lists the current VTP status, including the current mode.

Answers to Review Questions:

1 E and F 2 E and F 3 A, B, and D 4 A and D 5 B and D 6 B and C 7 A and C 8 D

Part II Review

Keep track of your part review progress with the checklist shown in Table P2-1. Details on each task follow the table.

Table P2-1 Part II Part Review Checklist

Activity	First Date Completed	Second Date Completed
Repeat all Chapter Review Questions		
Answer Part Review Questions		
Review Key Topics		
Create Command Mind Map by Category		

Repeat All Chapter Review Questions

For this task, answer the chapter review questions again for the chapters in this part of the book, using the PCPT software. Refer to the Introduction to this book, heading "How to View Only Chapter Review Questions by Part," for help with how to make the PCPT software show you chapter review questions for this part only.

Answer Part Review Questions

For this task, answer the Part Review questions for this part of the book, using the PCPT software. Refer to the Introduction to this book, heading "How to View Only Part Review Questions by Part," for help with how to make the PCPT software show you Part Review questions for this part only.

Review Key Topics

Key Topic

Browse back through the chapters, and look for the Key Topic icons. If you do not remember some details, take the time to reread those topics.

Create Command Mind Map by Category

Part II of this book both introduces the Cisco command-line interface (CLI) and introduces a large number of both configuration and EXEC commands. The sheer number of commands can be a bit overwhelming.

For the exam, you do not necessarily have to memorize every command and every parameter. However, you should be able to remember all the categories of topics that can be configured in LAN switches, and at least remember the first word or two of most of the commands. This mind map exercise is designed to help you work on organizing these commands in your mind.

Create a mind map with the following categories of commands from this part of the book:

> console and VTY, SSH, switch IPv4 support, port security, VLANs, VLAN trunks, CDP, other switch admin, other interface subcommands

For each category, think of all configuration commands and all EXEC commands (mostly **show** commands). For each category, group the configuration commands separately from the EXEC commands. Figure P2-1 shows a sample for the CDP branch of the commands.

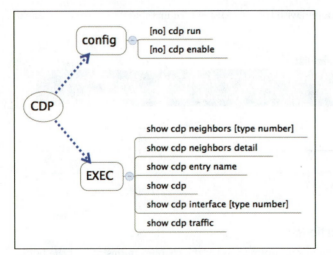

Figure P2-1 *Sample Mind Map from the CDP Branch*

> **NOTE** For more information on mind mapping, refer to the Introduction, in the section "About Mind Maps."

Finally, keep the following important points in mind when working on this project:

- Most of the learning with this exercise happens when you do it. Reading some other mind map, or just rereading command tables, does not work as well for helping you remember for yourself.

- Do this activity without notes and without looking at the book.

- After you finish, review it versus the command summary tables at the ends of the chapters, and note which commands you had originally forgotten.

- Do not worry about every last parameter or the exact syntax; just write down the first few words of the command.

- For later study, make a note about which commands you feel you truly understand and which ones about which you feel less confident.

- Repeat this exercise when you have ten spare minutes, as a way to see what you remember (again without your notes).

Appendix O, "Mind Map Solutions," lists a sample mind map answer, but as usual, your mind map can and will look different.

Parts III, IV, V, and VI all discuss features that make heavy use of IP version 4 (IPv4). This part focuses on the fundamentals of IPv4 addressing and subnetting. Chapter 11 takes a grand tour of IPv4 addressing as implemented inside a typical enterprise network. Chapters 12, 13, and 14 look at some of the specific questions people must ask themselves when operating an IPv4 network. Note that Part V also discusses other details related to IPv4 addressing.

Part III

IP Version 4 Addressing and Subnetting

Chapter 11

Perspectives on IPv4 Subnetting

Most entry-level networking jobs require you to operate and troubleshoot a network using a preexisting IP addressing and subnetting plan. The CCENT and CCNA exams assess your readiness to use preexisting IP addressing and subnetting information to perform typical operations tasks, like monitoring the network, reacting to possible problems, and troubleshooting those problems.

However, some exam questions, as well as many real-life issues at work, require that you understand the design of the network so that you can better operate the network. The process of monitoring any network requires that you continually answer the question, "Is the network working as *designed*?" If a problem exists, you must consider questions such as, "What happens when the network works normally, and what is different right now?" Both questions require you to understand the intended design of the network, including details of the IP addressing and subnetting design.

This chapter provides some perspectives and answers for the bigger issues in IPv4 addressing. What addresses can be used so that they work properly? What addresses should be used? When told to use certain numbers, what does that tell you about the choices made by some other network engineer? How do these choices impact the practical job of configuring switches, routers, hosts, and operating the network on a daily basis? This chapter hopes to answer these questions while revealing details of how IPv4 addresses work.

This chapter covers the following exam topics:

IP addressing (IPv4/IPv6)

Describe the operation and necessity of using private and public IP addresses for IPv4 addressing

Identify the appropriate IPv4 addressing scheme using VLSM and summarization to satisfy addressing requirements in a LAN/WAN environment.

Introduction to Subnetting

Say you just happened to be at the sandwich shop when they were selling the world's longest sandwich. You're pretty hungry, so you go for it. Now you have one sandwich, but at over 2 kilometers long, you realize it's a bit more than you need for lunch all by yourself. To make the sandwich more useful (and more portable), you chop the sandwich into meal-size pieces, and give the pieces to other folks around you, who are also ready for lunch.

Huh? Well, subnetting, at least the main concept, is similar to this sandwich story. You start with one network, but it is just one large network. As a single large entity, it might not be useful, and it is probably far too large. To make it useful, you chop it into smaller pieces, called subnets, and assign those subnets to be used in different parts of the enterprise internetwork.

This short section introduces IP subnetting. First, it shows the general ideas behind a completed subnet design that indeed chops (or subnets) one network into subnets. The rest of this section describes the many design steps that you would take to create just such a subnet design. By the end of this section, you should have the right context to then read through the subnetting design steps introduced throughout the rest of this chapter.

> **NOTE** This chapter, and in fact the rest of the chapters in this book up until Chapter 25, "Fundamentals of IP Version 6," focuses on IPv4 rather than IPv6. All references to "IP" refer to IPv4 unless otherwise stated.

Subnetting Defined Through a Simple Example

An IP network—in other words, a Class A, B, or C network—is simply a set of consecutively numbered IP addresses that follows some preset rules. These Class A, B, and C rules, first introduced back in Chapter 4's section, "Class A, B, and C IP Networks," define that for a given network, all the addresses in the network have the same value in some of the octets of the addresses. For example, Class B network 172.16.0.0 consists of all IP addresses that begin with 172.16: 172.16.0.0, 172.16.0.1, 172.16.0.2, and so on, through 172.16.255.255. Another example: Class A network 10.0.0.0 includes all addresses that begin with 10.

An IP subnet is simply a subset of a Class A, B, or C network. If fact, the word *subnet* is a shortened version of the phrase *subdivided network*. For example, one subnet of Class B network 172.16.0.0 could be the set of all IP addresses that begin with 172.16.1 would include 172.16.1.0, 172.16.1.1, 172.16.1.2, and so on, up through 172.16.1.255. Another subnet of that same Class B network could be all addresses that begin 172.16.2.

To give you a general idea, Figure 11-1 shows some basic documentation from a completed subnet design that could be used when an engineer subnets Class B network 172.16.0.0.

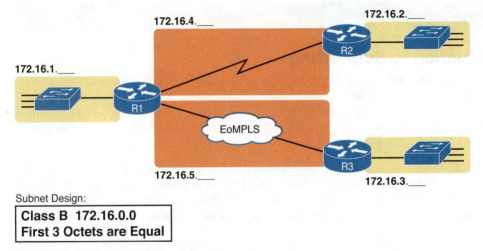

Figure 11-1   *Example Subnet Plan Document*

The design shows five subnets: one for each of the three LANs and one each for the two WAN links. The small text note shows the rationale used by the engineer for the subnets: Each subnet includes addresses that have the same value in the first three octets. For example, for the LAN on the left, the number shows 172.16.1.__, meaning "all addresses that begin with 172.16.1." Also, note that the design, as shown, does not use all the addresses in Class B network 172.16.0.0, so the engineer has left plenty of room for growth.

Operational View Versus Design View of Subnetting

Most IT jobs require you work with subnetting from an operational view. That is, someone else, before you got the job, designed how IP addressing and subnetting would work for that particular enterprise network. You need to interpret what someone else has already chosen.

To fully understand IP addressing and subnetting, you need to think about subnetting from both a design and operational perspective. For example, Figure 11-1 simply states that in all these subnets, the first three octets must be equal. Why was that convention chosen? What alternatives exist? Would those alternatives be better for your internetwork today? All these questions relate more to subnetting design rather than to operation.

To help you see both perspectives, some chapters in this part of the book focus more on design issues, while others focus more on operations by interpreting some existing design. This current chapter happens to move through the entire design process for the purpose of introducing the bigger picture of IP subnetting. Following this chapter, the rest of the chapters in this part of the book each take one topic from this chapter and examine it more closely, either from an operational or design perspective.

The remaining three main sections of this chapter examine each of the steps listed in Figure 11-2, in sequence.

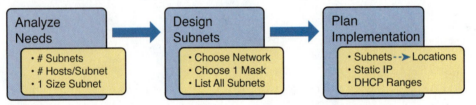

Figure 11-2   *Subnet Planning, Design, and Implementation Tasks*

> **NOTE**   This chapter shows a subset of the functions included in the Cisco formal design process, called PPDIOO: Prepare, Plan, Design, Implement, Operate, and Optimize.

Analyze Subnetting and Addressing Needs

This section discusses the meaning of four basic questions that can be used to analyze the addressing and subnetting needs for any new or changing enterprise network:

1. Which hosts should be grouped together into a subnet?
2. How many subnets does this network require?
3. How many host IP addresses does each subnet require?
4. Will we use a single subnet size for simplicity, or not?

Rules About Which Hosts Are in Which Subnet

Every device that connects to an IP internetwork needs to have an IP address. These devices include computers used by end users, servers, mobile phones, laptops, IP phones, tablets, and networking devices like routers, switches, and firewalls. In short, any device that uses IP to send and receive packets needs an IP address.

> **NOTE**   When discussing IP addressing, the term *network* has specific meaning: a Class A, B, or C IP network. To avoid confusion with that use of the term *network*, this book uses the terms *internetwork* and *enterprise network* when referring to a collection of hosts, routers, switches, and so on.

The IP addresses must be assigned according to some basic rules, and for good reasons. To make routing work efficiently, IP addressing rules group addresses into groups called subnets. The rules are as follows:

Key Topic

- Addresses in the same subnet are not separated by a router.
- Addresses in different subnets are separated by at least one router.

Figure 11-3 shows the general concept, with hosts A and B in one subnet and host C in another. In particular, note that hosts A and B are not separated from each other by any routers. However, host C, separated from A and B by at least one router, must be in a different subnet.

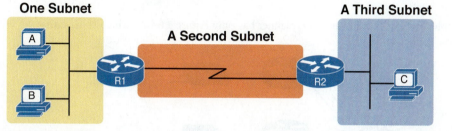

Figure 11-3   *PC A and B in One Subnet, and PC C in a Different Subnet*

The idea that hosts on the same link must be in the same subnet is much like the postal code concept. All mailing addresses in the same town use the same postal code (ZIP Codes in the United States). Addresses in another town, whether relatively nearby or on the other side of the country, have a different postal code. The postal code gives the postal service a better ability to automatically sort the mail to deliver it to the right location. For the same general reasons, hosts on the same LAN are in the same subnet, and hosts in different LANs are in different subnets.

Note that the point-to-point WAN link in the figure also needs a subnet. Figure 11-3 shows router R1 connected to the LAN subnet on the left and to a WAN subnet on the right. Router R2 connects to that same WAN subnet. To do so, both R1 and R2 will have IP addresses on their WAN interfaces, and the addresses will be in the same subnet. (An Ethernet over MPLS [EoMPLS] WAN link has the same IP addressing needs, with each of the two routers having an IP address in the same subnet.)

The Ethernet LANs in Figure 11-3 also show a slightly different style of drawing, using simple lines with no Ethernet switch. When drawing Ethernet LANs when the details of the LAN switches do not matter, drawings simply show each device connected to the same line, as seen in Figure 11-3. (This kind of drawing mimics the original Ethernet cabling before switches and hubs existed.)

Finally, because the routers' main job is to forward packets from one subnet to another, routers typically connect to multiple subnets. For example, in this case, router R1 connects to one LAN subnet on the left and one WAN subnet on the right. To do so, R1 will be configured with two different IP addresses, one per interface. These addresses will be in different subnets, because the interfaces connect the router to different subnets.

Determining the Number of Subnets

To determine the number of subnets required, the engineer must think about the internetwork as documented and apply the following rules. To do so, the engineer requires access to network diagrams, VLAN configuration details, and if you use Frame Relay WANs, details about the permanent virtual circuits (PVC). Based on this info, you should use these rules and plan for one subnet for every:

- VLAN
- Point-to-point serial link
- Ethernet emulation WAN link (EoMPLS)
- Frame Relay PVC

> **NOTE** WAN technologies like MPLS and Frame Relay allow subnetting options other than one subnet per pair of routers on the WAN, but this book only uses WAN technologies that have one subnet for each point-to-point WAN connection between two routers.

For example, imagine that the network planner has only Figure 11-4 on which to base the subnet design.

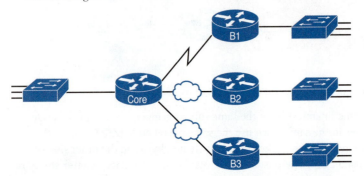

Figure 11-4 *Four-Site Internetwork with Small Central Site*

The number of subnets required cannot be fully predicted with only this figure. Certainly, three subnets will be needed for the WAN links, one per link. However, each LAN switch can be configured with a single VLAN, or with multiple VLANs. You can be certain that you need at least one subnet for the LAN at each site, but you might need more.

Next, consider the more detailed version of the same figure shown in Figure 11-5. In this case, the figure shows VLAN counts in addition to the same Layer 3 topology (the routers and the links connected to the routers). It also shows that the central site has many more switches, but the key fact on the left, regardless of how many switches exist, is that the central site has a total of 12 VLANs. Similarly, the figure lists each branch as having two VLANs. Along with the same three WAN subnets, this internetwork requires 21 subnets.

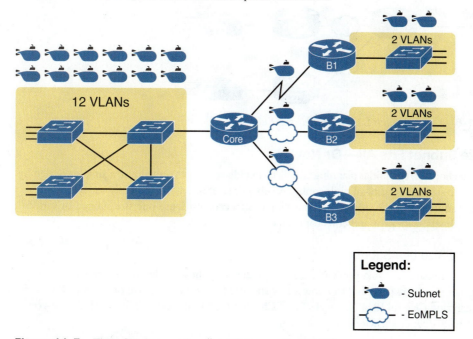

Figure 11-5 *Four-Site Internetwork with Larger Central Site*

Finally, in a real job, you would consider the needs today as well as how much growth you expect in the internetwork over time. Any subnetting plan should include a reasonable estimate of the number of subnets you need to meet future needs.

Determining the Number of Hosts per Subnet

Determining the number of hosts per subnet requires knowing a few simple concepts and then doing a lot of research and questioning. Every device that connects to a subnet needs an IP address. For a totally new network, you can look at business plans—numbers of people at the site, devices on order, and so on—to get some idea of the possible devices. When expanding an existing network to add new sites, you can use existing sites as a point of comparison, and then find out which sites will get bigger or smaller. And don't forget to count the router interface IP address in each subnet and the switch IP address used to remotely manage the switch.

Instead of gathering data for each and every site, planners often just use a few typical sites for planning purposes. For example, maybe you have some large sales offices and some small sales offices. You might dig in and learn a lot about only one large sales office and only one small sales office. Add that analysis to the fact that point-to-point links need a subnet with just two addresses, plus any analysis of more one-of-a-kind subnets, and you have enough information to plan the addressing and subnetting design.

For example, in Figure 11-6, the engineer has built a diagram that shows the number of hosts per LAN subnet in the largest branch, B1. For the two other branches, the engineer did not bother to dig to find out the number of required hosts. As long as the number of required IP addresses at sites B2 and B3 stays below the estimate of 50, based on larger site B1, the engineer can plan for 50 hosts in each branch LAN subnet and have plenty of addresses per subnet.

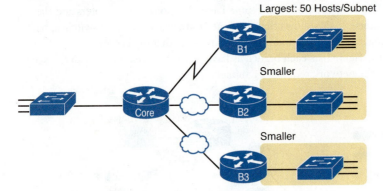

Figure 11-6   *Large Branch B1 with 50 Hosts/Subnet*

One Size Subnet Fits All—Or Not

The final choice in the initial planning step is to decide whether you will use a simpler design by using a one-size-subnet-fits-all philosophy. A subnet's size, or length, is simply the number of usable IP addresses in the subnet. A subnetting design can either use one size subnet, or varied sizes of subnets, with pros and cons for each choice.

Defining the Size of a Subnet

Before you finish this book, you will learn all the details of how to determine the size of the subnet. For now, you just need to know a few specific facts about the size of subnets. Chapter 12, "Analyzing Classful IPv4 Networks," and Chapter 13, "Analyzing Subnet Masks," give you a progressively deeper knowledge of the details.

The engineer assigns each subnet a *subnet mask*, and that mask, among other things, defines the size of that subnet. The mask sets aside a number of *host bits* whose purpose is to number different host IP addresses in that subnet. Because you can number 2^x things with x bits, if the mask defines H host bits, the subnet contains 2^H unique numeric values.

However, the subnet's size is not 2^H. It's $2^H - 2$, because two numbers in each subnet are reserved for other purposes. Each subnet reserves the numerically lowest value for the *subnet number* and the numerically highest value as the *subnet broadcast address*. As a result, the number of usable IP addresses per subnet is $2^H - 2$.

> **NOTE**   The terms *subnet number*, *subnet ID*, and *subnet address* all refer to the number that represents or identifies a subnet.

Figure 11-7 shows the general concept behind the three-part structure of an IP address, focusing on the host part and the resulting subnet size.

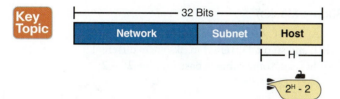

Figure 11-7 *Subnet Size Concepts*

One Size Subnet Fits All

To choose to use a single-size subnet in an enterprise network, you must use the same mask for all subnets, because the mask defines the size of the subnet. But which mask?

One requirement to consider when choosing that one mask is this: That one mask must provide enough host IP addresses to support the largest subnet. To do so, the number of host bits (H) defined by the mask must be large enough so that $2^H - 2$ is larger than (or equal to) the number of host IP addresses required in the largest subnet.

For example, consider Figure 11-8. It shows the required number of hosts per LAN subnet. (The figure ignores the subnets on the WAN links, which require only two IP addresses each.) The branch LAN subnets require only 50 host addresses, but the main site LAN subnet requires 200 host addresses. To accommodate the largest subnet, you need at least 8 host bits. Seven host bits would not be enough, because $2^7 - 2 = 126$. Eight host bits would be enough, because $2^8 - 2 = 254$, which is more than enough to support 200 hosts in a subnet.

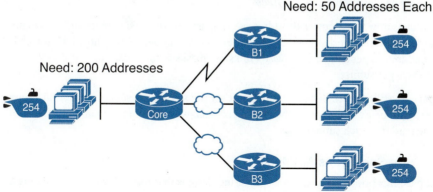

Figure 11-8 *Network Using One Subnet Size*

What's the big advantage when using a single-size subnet? Operational simplicity. In other words, keeping it simple. Everyone on the IT staff who has to work with networking can get used to working with one mask—and one mask only. They will be able to answer all subnetting questions more easily, because everyone gets used to doing subnetting math with that one mask.

The big disadvantage for using a single-size subnet is that it wastes IP addresses. For example, in Figure 11-8, all the branch LAN subnets support 254 addresses, while the largest branch subnet needs only 50 addresses. The WAN subnets only need two IP addresses, but each supports 254 addresses, again wasting more IP addresses.

The wasted IP addresses do not actually cause a problem in most cases, however. Most organizations use private IP networks in their enterprise internetworks, and a single Class A or Class B private network can supply plenty of IP addresses, even with the waste.

11

Multiple Subnet Sizes (Variable-Length Subnet Masks)

To create multiple sizes of subnets in one Class A, B, or C network, the engineer must create some subnets using one mask, some with another, and so on. Different masks mean different numbers of host bits, and a different number of hosts in some subnets based on the $2^H - 2$ formula.

For example, consider the requirements listed earlier in Figure 11-8. It showed one LAN subnet on the left that needs 200 host addresses, three branch subnets that need 50 addresses, and three WAN links that need two addresses. To meet those needs, but waste fewer IP addresses, three subnet masks could be used, creating subnets of three different sizes, as shown in Figure 11-9.

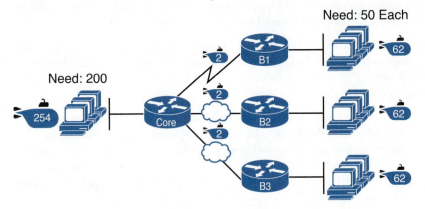

Figure 11-9   *Three Masks, Three Subnet Sizes*

The smaller subnets now waste fewer IP addresses compared to the design seen earlier in Figure 11-8. The subnets on the right that need 50 IP addresses have subnets with 6 host bits, for $2^6 - 2$ = 62 available addresses per subnet. The WAN links use masks with 2 host bits, for $2^2 - 2 = 2$ available addresses per subnet.

However, some are still wasted, because you cannot set the size of the subnet as some arbitrary size. All subnets will be a size based on the $2^H - 2$ formula, with H being the number of host bits defined by the mask for each subnet.

This Book: One Size Subnet Fits All (Mostly)

For the most part, this book explains subnetting using designs that use a single mask, creating a single subnet size for all subnets. Why? First, it makes the process of learning subnetting easier. Second, some types of analysis that you can do about a network—specifically, calculating the number of subnets in the classful network—only make sense when a single mask is used.

However, you still need to be ready to work with *variable-length subnet masks (VLSM)*, which is the practice of using different masks for different subnets in the same classful IP network. All of Chapter 20 focuses on VLSM, with Chapter 21, "Route Summarization," also using some math principles from VLSM. However, all the examples and discussion up until those chapters purposefully avoid VLSM just to keep the discussion simpler, for the sake of learning to walk before you run.

Make Design Choices

Now that you know how to analyze the IP addressing and subnetting needs, the next major step examines how to apply the rules of IP addressing and subnetting to those needs and mask some choices. In other words, now that you know how many subnets you need and how many host addresses you need in the largest subnet, how do you create a useful subnetting design that meets those requirements? The short answer is that you need to do the three tasks shown on the right side of Figure 11-10.

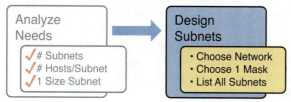

Figure 11-10   *Input to the Design Phase, and Design Questions to Answer*

Choose a Classful Network

In the original design for what we know of today as the Internet, companies used registered *public classful IP networks* when implementing TCP/IP inside the company. By the mid 1990s, an alternative became more popular: *private IP networks*. This section discusses the background behind these two choices, because it impacts the choice of what IP network a company will then subnet and implement in its enterprise internetwork.

Public IP Networks

The original design of the Internet required that any company that connected to the Internet had to use a *registered public IP network*. To do so, the company would complete some paperwork, describing the enterprise's internetwork and the number of hosts existing, plus plans for growth. After submitting the paperwork, the company would receive an assignment of either a Class A, B, or C network.

Public IP networks, and the administrative processes surrounding them, ensure that all the companies that connect to the Internet all use unique IP addresses. In particular, after a public IP network is assigned to a company, only that company should use the addresses in that network. That guarantee of uniqueness means that Internet routing can work well, because there are no duplicate public IP addresses.

For example, consider the example shown in Figure 11-11. Company 1 has been assigned public Class A network 1.0.0.0, and company 2 has been assigned public Class A network 2.0.0.0. Per the original intent for public addressing in the Internet, after these public network assignments have been made, no other companies can use addresses in Class A networks 1.0.0.0 or 2.0.0.0.

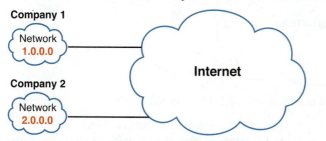

Figure 11-11   *Two Companies with Unique Public IP Networks*

This original address assignment process ensured unique IP addresses across the entire planet. The idea is much like the fact that your telephone number should be unique in the universe, your postal mailing address should also be unique, and your email address should also be unique. If someone calls you, your phone rings, but no one else's phone rings. Similarly, if company 1 is assigned Class A network 1.0.0.0, and it assigns address 1.1.1.1 to a particular PC, that address should be unique in the universe. A packet sent through the Internet, to destination 1.1.1.1, should only arrive at this one PC inside company 1, instead of being delivered to some other host.

Growth Exhausts the Public IP Address Space

By the early 1990s, the world was running out of public IP networks that could be assigned. During most of the 1990s, the number of hosts newly connected to the Internet was growing at a double-digit pace, *per month*. Companies kept following the rules, asking for public IP networks, and it was clear that the current address-assignment scheme could not continue without some changes. Simply put, the number of Class A, B, and C networks supported by the 32-bit address in IP version 4 (IPv4) was not enough to support one public classful network per organization, while also providing enough IP addresses in each company.

> **NOTE**   From one perspective, the universe ran out of public IPv4 addresses in early 2011. IANA, which assigns public IPv4 address blocks to the five Internet registries around the globe, assigned the last of the IPv4 address space in early 2011.

The Internet community worked hard during the 1990s to solve this problem, coming up with several solutions, including the following:

Key Topic

- A new version of IP (IPv6), with much larger addresses (128 bit)
- Assigning a subset of a public IP network to each company, instead of an entire public IP network, to reduce waste
- Network Address Translation (NAT), which allows the use of private IP networks

These three solutions matter to real networks today. However, to stay focused on the topic of subnet design, this chapter focuses on the third option, and in particular, the private IP networks that can be used by an enterprise when also using NAT.

NAT, which is detailed in Chapter 24, "Network Address Translation," allows multiple companies to use the exact same *private IP network*, using the same IP addresses as other companies, while still connecting to the Internet. For example, Figure 11-12 shows the same two companies connecting to the Internet as in Figure 11-11, but now with both using the same private Class A network 10.0.0.0.

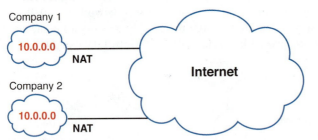

Figure 11-12   *Reusing the Same Private Network 10.0.0.0, with NAT*

Both companies use the same classful IP network (10.0.0.0). Both companies can implement their subnet design internal to their respective enterprise internetworks, without discussing their plans. The two companies can even using the exact same IP addresses inside network 10.0.0.0. And amazingly, at the same time, both companies can even communicate with each other through the Internet.

The technology called Network Address Translation (NAT) makes it possible for companies to reuse the same IP networks, as shown in Figure 11-12. NAT does this by translating the IP addresses inside the packets as they go from the enterprise to the Internet, using a small number of public IP addresses to support tens of thousands of private IP addresses. That one bit of information is not enough to understand how NAT works; however, to keep the focus on subnetting, the book defers the discussion of how NAT works until Chapter 24. For now, accept that most companies use NAT, and therefore, they can use private IP networks for their internetworks.

Private IP Networks

RFC 1918 defines the set of private IP networks, as listed in Table 11-1. By definition, these private IP networks

- Will never be assigned to an organization as a public IP network
- Can be used by organizations that will use NAT when sending packets into the Internet
- Can also be used by organizations that never need to send packets into the Internet

So, when using NAT—and almost every organization that connects to the Internet uses NAT—the company can simply pick one or more of the private IP networks from the list of reserved private IP network numbers. RFC 1918 defines the list, which is summarized in Table 11-1.

Table 11-1 RFC 1918 Private Address Space

Class of Networks	Private IP Networks	Number of Networks
A	10.0.0.0	1
B	172.16.0.0 through 172.31.0.0	16
C	192.168.0.0 through 192.168.255.0	256

NOTE According to an informal survey I ran in my blog back in late 2010, about half of the respondents said that their networks use private Class A network 10.0.0.0, as opposed to other private networks or public networks.

Choosing an IP Network During the Design Phase

Today, some organizations use private IP networks along with NAT, and some use public IP networks. Most new enterprise internetworks use private IP addresses throughout the network, along with NAT, as part of the connection to the Internet. Those organizations that already have a registered public IP networks—often obtained before the addresses started running short in the early 1990s—can continue to use those public addresses throughout their enterprise networks.

After the choice to use a private IP network has been made, just pick one that has enough IP addresses. You can have a small internetwork and still choose to use private Class A network 10.0.0.0. It might seem wasteful to choose a Class A network that has over 16 million IP addresses, especially if you only need a few hundred. However, there's no penalty or problem with using a private network that is too large for your current or future needs.

For the purposes of this book, most examples use private IP network numbers. For the design step to choose a network number, just choose a private Class A, B, or C network from the list of RFC 1918 private networks.

Regardless, from a math and concept perspective, the methods to subnet a public IP network versus a private IP network are the same.

11

Choose the Mask

If a design engineer followed the topics in this chapter so far, in order, he would know the following:

■ The number of subnets required

■ The number of hosts/subnet required

■ That a choice was made to use only one mask for all subnets, so that all subnets are the same size (same number of hosts/subnet)

■ The classful IP network number that will be subnetted

This section completes the design process, at least the parts described in this chapter, by discussing how to choose that one mask to use for all subnets. First, this section examines default masks, used when a network is not subnetted, as a point of comparison. Next, the concept of borrowing host bits to create subnet bits is explored. Finally, this section ends with an example of how to create a subnet mask based on the analysis of the requirements.

Classful IP Networks Before Subnetting

Before an engineer subnets a classful network, the network is a single group of addresses. In other words, the engineer has not yet subdivided the network into many smaller subsets called *subnets*.

When thinking about an unsubnetted classful network, the addresses in a network have only two parts: the network part and host part. Comparing any two addresses in the classful network:

■ The addresses have the same value in the network part.

■ The addresses have different values in the host part.

The actual sizes of the network and host part of the addresses in a network can be easily predicted, as shown in Figure 11-13.

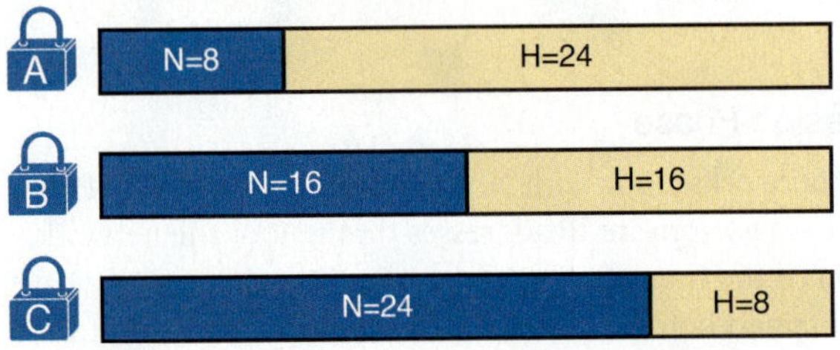

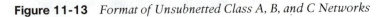

Figure 11-13   *Format of Unsubnetted Class A, B, and C Networks*

In Figure 11-13, N and H represent the number of network and host bits, respectively. Class rules define the number of network octets (1, 2, or 3) for Classes A, B, and C, respectively; the figure shows these values as a number of bits. The number of host octets is 3, 2, or 1, respectively.

Continuing the analysis of classful network before subnetting, the number of addresses in one classful IP network can be calculated with the same $2^H - 2$ formula previously discussed. In particular, the size of an unsubnetted Class A, B, or C network is as follows:

■ Class A: $2^{24} - 2 = 16,777,214$

■ Class B: $2^{16} - 2 = 65,534$

■ Class C: $2^8 - 2 = 254$

Borrowing Host Bits to Create Subnet Bits

To subnet a network, the designer thinks about the network and host parts, as shown in Figure 11-13, and then the engineer adds a third part in the middle: the subnet part. However, the designer cannot change the size of the network part or the size of the entire address (32 bits). To create a subnet part of the address structure, the engineer borrows bits from the host part. Figure 11-14 shows the general idea.

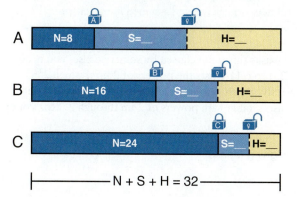

Figure 11-14   *Concept of Borrowing Host Bits*

Figure 11-14 shows a rectangle that represents the subnet mask. N, representing the number of network bits, remains locked at 8, 16, or 24, depending on the class. Conceptually, the designer moves a (dashed) dividing line into the host field, with subnet bits (S) between the network and host parts, and the remaining host bits (H) on the right. The three parts must add up to 32, because IPv4 addresses consist of 32 bits.

Choosing Enough Subnet and Host Bits

The design process requires a choice of where to place the dashed line shown in Figure 11-14. But what is the right choice? How many subnet and host bits should the designer choose? The answers hinge on the requirements gathered in the early stages of the planning process:

- Number of subnets required
- Number of hosts/subnet

The bits in the subnet part create a way to uniquely number the different subnets that the design engineer wants to create. With 1 subnet bit, you can number 2^1 or 2 subnets. With 2 bits, 2^2 or 4 subnets, with 3 bits, 2^3 or 8 subnets, and so on. The number of subnet bits must be large enough to uniquely number all the subnets, as determined during the planning process.

At the same time, the remaining number of host bits must also be large enough to number the host IP addresses in the largest subnet. Remember, in this chapter, we assume the use of a single mask for all subnets. This single mask must support both the required number of subnets and the required number of hosts in the largest subnet. Figure 11-15 shows the concept.

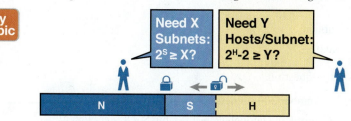

Figure 11-15   *Borrowing Enough Subnet and Host Bits*

Figure 11-15 shows the idea of the designer choosing a number of subnet (S) and host (H) bits and then checking the math. 2^S must be more than the number of required subnets, or the mask will not supply enough subnets in this IP network. Also, $2^H - 2$ must be more than the required number of hosts/subnet.

> **NOTE**   The idea of calculating the number of subnets as 2^S applies only in cases where a single mask is used for all subnets of a single classful network, as is being assumed in this chapter.

To effectively design masks, or to interpret masks that were chosen by someone else, you need a good working memory of the powers of 2. Table 11-2 lists the powers of 2 up through 2^{12}, along with a column with $2^H - 2$, for perspective when calculating the number of hosts/subnet. Appendix A, "Numeric Reference Tables," lists a table with powers of 2 up through 2^{24} for your reference.

Table 11-2   Powers of 2 Reference for Designing Masks

Number of Bits	2^X	$2^X - 2$
1	2	0
2	4	2
3	8	6
4	16	14
5	32	30
6	64	62
7	128	126
8	256	254
9	512	510
10	1024	1022
11	2048	2046
12	4096	4094

Example Design: 172.16.0.0, 200 Subnets, 200 Hosts

To help make sense of the theoretical discussion so far, consider an example that focuses on the design choice for the subnet mask. In this case, the planning and design choices so far tell us the following:

- Use a single mask for all subnets.
- Plan for 200 subnets.
- Plan for 200 host IP addresses per subnet.
- Use private Class B network 172.16.0.0.

To choose the mask, the designer asks this question:

How many subnet (S) bits do I need to number 200 subnets?

From Table 11-2, you can see that S = 7 is not large enough ($2^7 = 128$), but S = 8 is enough ($2^8 = 256$). So, you need *at least* 8 subnet bits.

Next, the designer asks a similar question, based on the number of hosts per subnet:

How many host (H) bits do I need to number 200 hosts per subnet?

The math is basically the same, but the formula subtracts 2 when counting the number of hosts/subnet. From Table 11-3, you can see that H = 7 is not large enough ($2^7 - 2 = 126$), but H = 8 is enough ($2^8 - 2 = 254$).

Only one possible mask meets all the requirements in this case. First, the number of network bits (N) must be 16, because the design uses a Class B network. The requirements tell us that the mask needs at least 8 subnet bits, and at least 8 host bits. The mask only has 32 bits in it; Figure 11-16 shows the resulting mask.

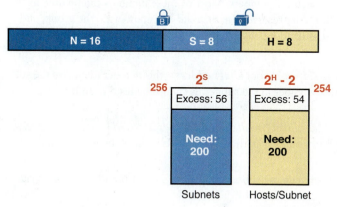

Figure 11-16   *Example Mask Choice, N = 16, S = 8, H = 8*

Masks and Mask Formats

Although engineers think about IP addresses in three parts when making design choices (network, subnet, and host), the subnet mask gives the engineer a way to communicate those design choices to all the devices in the subnet.

The subnet mask is a 32-bit binary number with a number of binary 1s on the left and with binary 0s on the right. By definition, the number of binary 0s equals the number of host bits—in fact, that is exactly how the mask communicates the idea of the size of the host part of the addresses in a subnet. The beginning bits in the mask equal binary 1, with those bit positions representing the combined network and subnet parts of the addresses in the subnet.

Because the network part always comes first, then the subnet part, and then the host part, the subnet mask, in binary form, cannot have interleaved 1s and 0s. Each subnet mask has one unbroken string of binary 1s on the left, with the rest of the bits as binary 0s.

After the engineer chooses the classful network and the number of subnet and host bits in a subnet, creating the binary subnet mask is easy. Just write down N 1s, S 1s, and then H 0s (assuming that N, S, and H represent the number of network, subnet, and host bits). Figure 11-17 shows the mask based on the previous example, which subnets a Class B network by creating 8 subnet bits, leaving 8 host bits.

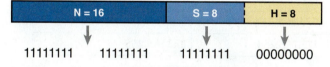

Figure 11-17   *Creating the Subnet Mask—Binary—Class B Network*

In addition to the binary mask shown in Figure 11-17, masks can also be written in two other formats: the familiar *dotted-decimal notation (DDN)* seen in IP addresses and an even briefer *prefix* notation. Chapter 13, "Analyzing Subnet Masks," discusses these formats and how to convert between the different formats.

Build a List of All Subnets

This final task of the subnet design step determines the actual subnets that can be used, based on all the earlier choices. The earlier design work determined the Class A, B, or C network to use, and the (one) subnet mask to use that supplies enough subnets and enough host IP addresses per subnet. But what are those subnets? How do you identify or describe a subnet? This section answers these questions.

A subnet consists of a group of consecutive numbers. Most of these numbers can be used as IP addresses by hosts. However, each subnet reserves the first and last numbers in the group, and these two numbers cannot be used as IP addresses. In particular, each subnet contains the following:

- **Subnet number:** Also called the *subnet ID* or *subnet address*, this number identifies the subnet. It is the numerically smallest number in the subnet. It cannot be used as an IP address by a host.

- **Subnet broadcast:** Also called the *subnet broadcast address* or *directed broadcast address*, this is the last (numerically highest) number in the subnet. It also cannot be used as an IP address by a host.

- **IP addresses:** All the numbers between the subnet ID and the subnet broadcast address can be used as a host IP address.

For example, consider the earlier case in which the design results were as follows:

Network   172.16.0.0 (Class B)

Mask   255.255.255.0 (for all subnets)

With some math, the facts about each subnet that exists in this Class B network can be calculated. In this case, Table 11-3 shows the first ten such subnets. It then skips many subnets and shows the last two (numerically largest) subnets.

Table 11-3   First Ten Subnets, Plus the Last Few, from 172.16.0.0, 255.255.255.0

Subnet Number	IP Addresses	Broadcast Address
172.16.0.0	172.16.0.1 – 172.16.0.254	172.16.0.255
172.16.1.0	172.16.1.1 – 172.16.1.254	172.16.1.255
172.16.2.0	172.16.2.1 – 172.16.2.254	172.16.2.255
172.16.3.0	172.16.3.1 – 172.16.3.254	172.16.3.255
172.16.4.0	172.16.4.1 – 172.16.4.254	172.16.4.255
172.16.5.0	172.16.5.1 – 172.16.5.254	172.16.5.255
172.16.6.0	172.16.6.1 – 172.16.6.254	172.16.6.255
172.16.7.0	172.16.7.1 – 172.16.7.254	172.16.7.255
172.16.8.0	172.16.8.1 – 172.16.8.254	172.16.8.255
172.16.9.0	172.16.9.1 – 172.16.9.254	172.16.9.255
Skipping many...		
172.16.254.0	172.16.254.1 – 172.16.254.254	172.16.254.255
172.16.255.0	172.16.255.1 – 172.16.255.254	172.16.255.255

After you have the network number and the mask, calculating the subnet IDs and other details for all subnets requires some math. In real life, most people use subnet calculators or subnet-planning tools. For the CCENT and CCNA exams, you need to be ready to find this kind of information; in this book, Chapter 19, "Subnet Design," shows you how to find all the subnets of a given network.

Plan the Implementation

The next step, planning the implementation, is the last step before actually configuring the devices to create a subnet. The engineer first needs to choose where to use each subnet. For example, at a branch office in a particular city, which subnet from the subnet planning chart (Table 11-3) should be used for each VLAN at that site? Also, for any interfaces that require static IP addresses, which addresses should be used in each case? Finally, what range of IP addresses from inside each subnet should be configured in the DHCP server, to be dynamically leased to hosts for use as their IP address? Figure 11-18 summarizes the list of implementation planning tasks.

Figure 11-18   *Facts Supplied to the Plan Implementation Step*

Assigning Subnets to Different Locations

The job is simple: Look at your network diagram, identify each location that needs a subnet, and pick one from the table you made of all the possible subnets. Then, track it so that you know which ones you use where, using a spreadsheet or some other purpose-built subnet-planning tool. That's it! Figure 11-19 shows a sample of a completed design using Table 11-3, which happens to match the initial design sample shown way back in Figure 11-1.

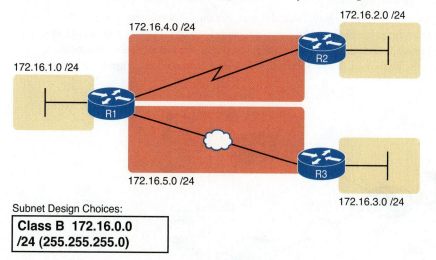

Figure 11-19   *Example of Subnets Assigned to Different Locations*

Although this design could have used any five subnets from Table 11-3, in real networks, engineers usually give more thought to some strategy for assigning subnets. For example, you might assign all LAN subnets lower numbers and WAN subnets higher numbers. Or you might slice off large ranges of subnets for different divisions of the company. Or you might follow that same strategy, but ignore organizational divisions in the company, paying more attention to geographies.

For example, for a U.S.-based company with a smaller presence in both Europe and Asia, you might plan to reserve ranges of subnets based on continent. This kind of choice is particularly useful when later trying to use a feature called route summarization, as discussed in Chapter 21, "Route Summarization." Figure 11-20 shows the general idea using the same subnets from Table 11-3 again.

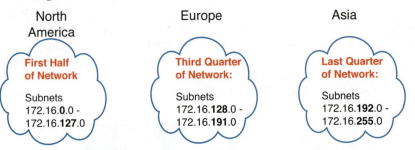

Figure 11-20 *Reserving 50% of Subnets for the U.S. and 25% Each for Europe and Asia*

Choose Static and Dynamic Ranges per Subnet

Devices receive their IP address and mask assignment in one of two ways: dynamically by using DHCP or statically through configuration. For DHCP to work, the network engineer must tell the DHCP server the subnets for which it must assign IP addresses. Additionally, that configuration limits the DHCP server to only a subset of the addresses in the subnet. For static addresses, you simply configure the device to tell it what IP address and mask to use.

To keep things as simple as possible, most shops use a strategy to separate the static IP addresses on one end of each subnet, and the DHCP-assigned dynamic addresses on the other. It does not really matter whether the static addresses sit on the low end of the range of addresses or the high end.

For example, imagine that the engineer decides that, for the LAN subnets in Figure 11-19, the DHCP pool comes from the high end of the range, namely, addresses that end in .101 through .254. (The address that ends in .255 is, of course, reserved.) The engineer also assigns static addresses from the lower end, with addresses ending in .1 through .100. Figure 11-21 shows the idea.

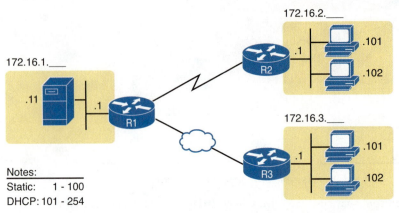

Figure 11-21 *Static from the Low End and DHCP from the High End*

Figure 11-21 shows all three routers with statically assigned IP addresses that end in .1. The only other static IP address in the figure is assigned to the server on the left, with address 172.16.1.11 (abbreviated simply as .11 in the figure).

On the right, each LAN has two PCs that use DHCP to dynamically lease their IP addresses. DHCP servers often begin by leasing the addresses at the bottom of the range of addresses, so in each LAN, the hosts have leased addresses that end in .101 and .102, which are at the low end of the range chosen by design.

11

Review Activities

Chapter Summary

- An IP subnet is a subset of a Class A, B, or C network. The word subnet is a shortened version of the phrase *subdivided network*.

- Every device that connects to an IP internetwork must have an IP address. These devices include computers used by end users; servers; mobile phones; laptops; IP phones; tablets; and networking devices such as routers, switches, and firewalls. In short, any device that uses IP to send and receive packets needs an IP address.

- IP addressing rules group addresses into groups called subnets. The rules are as follows:

  - Addresses in the same subnet are not separated by a router.

  - Addresses in different subnets are separated by at least one router.

- A subnet's size, or length, is the number of usable IP addresses in the subnet. A subnetting design can use either one sized subnet or varied sizes of subnets, with pros and cons for each choice.

- In particular, the size of an unsubnetted Class A, B, or C network is as follows:

  - **Class A:** $2^{24} - 2 = 16,777,214$

  - **Class B:** $2^{16} - 2 = 65,534$

  - **Class C:** $2^8 - 2 = 254$

- The decision of how to subnet a network lies with the answer to the following:

  - The number of subnets required (how many networks do I need?)

  - The number of hosts needed in each subnet

- Devices receive their IP address and mask assignments in one of two ways: dynamically, by using DHCP, or statically, through configuration. For DHCP to work, the network engineer must tell the DHCP server the subnets for which it must assign IP addresses. Additionally, that configuration limits the DHCP server to only a subset of the addresses in the subnet. For static addresses, you simply configure the device to tell it what IP address and mask to use.

Review Questions

Answer these review questions. You can find the answers at the bottom of the last page of the chapter. For thorough explanations, see DVD Appendix C, "Answers to Review Questions."

1. Host A is a PC, connected to switch SW1 and assigned to VLAN 1. Which of the following are typically assigned an IP address in the same subnet as host A? (Select two answers)

   A. The local router's WAN interface

   B. The local router's LAN interface

   C. All other hosts attached to the same switch

   D. Other hosts attached to the same switch and also in VLAN 1

2. Why does the formula for the number of hosts per subnet ($2^H - 2$) require the subtraction of two hosts?

   A. To reserve two addresses for redundant default gateways (routers)

   B. To reserve the two addresses required for DHCP operation

   C. To reserve addresses for the subnet ID and default gateway (router)

   D. To reserve addresses for the subnet broadcast address and subnet ID

3. A Class B network needs to be subnetted such that it supports 100 subnets and 100 hosts/ subnet. Which of the following answers list a workable combination for the number of network, subnet, and host bits? (Select two answers.)

   A. Network = 16, subnet = 7, host = 7

   B. Network = 16, subnet = 8, host = 8

   C. Network = 16, subnet = 9, host = 7

   D. Network = 8, subnet = 7, host = 17

4. Which of the following are private IP networks? (Select two answers.)

   A. 172.31.0.0

   B. 172.32.0.0

   C. 192.168.255.0

   D. 192.1.168.0

   E. 11.0.0.0

5. Which of the following are public IP networks? (Select three answers.)

   A. 9.0.0.0

   B. 172.30.0.0

   C. 192.168.255.0

   D. 192.1.168.0

   E. 1.0.0.0

6. Before Class B network 172.16.0.0 is subnetted by a network engineer, what parts of the structure of the IP addresses in this network already exist, with a specific size? (Select two answers.)

   A. Network

   B. Subnet

   C. Host

   D. Broadcast

7. A network engineer spends time thinking about the entire Class B network 172.16.0.0, and how to subnet that network. He then chooses how to subnet this Class B network and creates an addressing and subnetting plan, on paper, showing his choices. If you compare his thoughts about this network before subnetting the network, to his thoughts about this network after mentally subnetting the network, which of the following occurred to the parts of the structure of addresses in this network?

   A. The subnet part got smaller.

   B. The host part got smaller.

   C. The network part got smaller.

   D. The host part was removed.

   E. The network part was removed.

8. Which of the following terms are *not* used to reference the one number in each subnet used to uniquely identify the subnet? (Select two answers.)

   A. Subnet ID

   B. Subnet number

   C. Subnet broadcast

   D. Subnet name

   E. Subnet address

Review All the Key Topics

Review the most important topics from this chapter, noted with the Key Topic icon. Table 11-4 lists these key topics and where each is discussed.

Table 11-4   Key Topics for Chapter 11

Key Topic Element	Description	Page Number
List	Key facts about subnets	273
List	Rules about what places in a network topology need a subnet	274
Figure 11-7	Locations of the network, subnet, and host parts of an IPv4 address	277
List	Features that extended the life of IPv4	280
Figure 11-13	Formats of Class A, B, and C addresses when not subnetted	282
Figure 11-14	Formats of Class A, B, and C addresses when subnetted	283
Figure 11-15	General logic when choosing the size of the subnet and host parts of addresses in a subnet	283
List	Items that together define a subnet	286

Complete the Tables and Lists from Memory

Print a copy of DVD Appendix M, "Memory Tables," or at least the section for this chapter, and complete the tables and lists from memory. DVD Appendix N, "Memory Tables Answer Key," includes completed tables and lists for you to check your work.

Definitions of Key Terms

After your first reading of the chapter, try to define these key terms, but do not be concerned about getting them all correct at that time. Chapter 30 directs you in how to use these terms for late-stage preparation for the exam.

subnet, network, classful network, variable-length subnet masks (VLSM), network part, subnet part, host part, public IP network, private IP network, subnet mask

---

Answers to Review Questions:

1 B and D **2** D **3** B and C **4** A and C **5** A, D, and E **6** A and C **7** B **8** C and D

Chapter 12

Analyzing Classful IPv4 Networks

When operating a network, you often start investigating a problem based on an IP address and mask. Based on the IP address alone, you should be able to determine several facts about the Class A, B, or C network in which the IP address resides. These facts can be useful when troubleshooting some networking problems.

This chapter lists the key facts about classful IP networks and explains how to discover these facts. Following that, this chapter lists some practice problems. Before moving to the next chapter, you should practice until you can consistently determine all these facts, quickly and confidently, based on an IP address.

This chapter covers the following exam topics:

Troubleshooting

Troubleshoot and correct common problems associated with IP addressing and host configurations.

Foundation Topics

Classful Network Concepts

Imagine that you have a job interview for your first IT job. As part of the interview, you're given an IPv4 address and mask: 10.4.5.99, 255.255.255.0. What can you tell the interviewer about the classful network (in this case, the Class A network) in which the IP address resides?

This section, the first of two major sections in this chapter, reviews the concepts of *classful IP networks* (in other words, Class A, B, and C networks). In particular, this chapter examines how to begin with a single IP address and then determine the following facts:

- Class (A, B, or C)
- Default mask
- Number of network octets/bits
- Number of host octets/bits
- Number of host addresses in the network
- Network ID
- Network broadcast address
- First and last usable address in the network

IPv4 Network Classes and Related Facts

IP version 4 (IPv4) defines five address classes. Three of the classes, Classes A, B, and C, consist of unicast IP addresses. Unicast addresses identify a single host or interface so that the address uniquely identifies the device. Class D addresses serve as multicast addresses, so that one packet sent to a Class D multicast IPv4 address can actually be delivered to multiple hosts. Finally, Class E addresses are experimental.

The class can be identified based on the value of the first octet of the address, as shown in Table 12-1.

Key Topic

Table 12-1 IPv4 Address Classes Based on First Octet Values

Class	First Octet Values	Purpose
A	1–126	Unicast (large networks)
B	128–191	Unicast (medium-sized networks)
C	192–223	Unicast (small networks)
D	224–239	Multicast
E	240–255	Experimental

CCENT and CCNA focus mostly on the unicast classes (A, B, and C) rather than Classes D and E. After you identify the class as either A, B, or C, many other related facts can be derived just through memorization. Table 12-2 lists that information for reference and later study; each of these concepts is described in this chapter.

Key Topic

Table 12-2 Key Facts for Classes A, B, and C

	Class A	Class B	Class C
First octet range	1 – 126	128 – 191	192 – 223
Valid network numbers	1.0.0.0 – 126.0.0.0	128.0.0.0 – 191.255.0.0	192.0.0.0 – 223.255.255.0
Total networks	$2^7 - 2 = 126$	$2^{14} = 16{,}384$	$2^{21} = 2{,}097{,}152$
Hosts per network	$2^{24} - 2$	$2^{16} - 2$	$2^8 - 2$
Octets (bits) in network part	1 (8)	2 (16)	3 (24)
Octets (bits) in host part	3 (24)	2 (16)	1 (8)
Default mask	255.0.0.0	255.255.0.0	255.255.255.0

Actual Class A, B, and C Networks

Table 12-2 lists the range of Class A, B, and C network numbers. However, some key points can be lost just referencing a table of information. This section examines the Class A, B, and C network numbers, focusing on the more important points and the exceptions and unusual cases.

First, the number of networks from each class significantly differs. Only 126 Class A networks exist: network 1.0.0.0, 2.0.0.0, 3.0.0.0, and so on, up through network 126.0.0.0. However, 16,384 Class B networks exist, with over 2 million Class C networks.

Next, note that the size of networks from each class also significantly differs. Each Class A network is relatively large—over 16 million host IP addresses per network—so they were originally intended to be used by the largest companies and organizations. Class B networks are smaller, with over 65,000 hosts per network. Finally, Class C networks, intended for small organizations, have 254 hosts in each network. Figure 12-1 summarizes those facts.

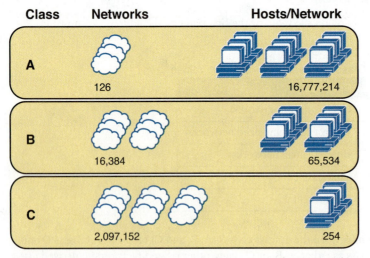

Figure 12-1 *Numbers and Sizes of Class A, B, and C Networks*

Address Formats

In some cases, an engineer might need to think about a Class A, B, or C network as if the network has not been subdivided through the subnetting process. In such a case, the addresses in the classful network have a structure with two parts: the *network part* (sometimes called the *prefix*) and the *host part*. Then, comparing any two IP addresses in one network, the following observations can be made:

Key Topic

The addresses in the same network have the same values in the network part.

The addresses in the same network have different values in the host part.

For example, in Class A network 10.0.0.0, by definition, the network part consists of the first octet. As a result, all addresses have an equal value in the network part, namely a 10 in the first octet. If you then compare any two addresses in the network, the addresses have a different value in the last three octets (the host octets). For example, IP addresses 10.1.1.1 and 10.1.1.2 have the same value (10) in the network part, but different values in the host part.

Figure 12-2 shows the format and sizes (in number of bits) of the network and host parts of IP addresses in Class A, B, and C networks, before any subnetting has been applied.

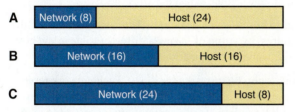

Figure 12-2 *Sizes (Bits) of the Network and Host Parts of Unsubnetted Classful Networks*

Default Masks

Although we humans can easily understand the concepts behind Figure 12-2, computers prefer numbers. To communicate those same ideas to computers, each network class has an associated *default mask* that defines the size of the network and host parts of an unsubnetted Class A, B, and C network. To do so, the mask lists binary 1s for the bits considered to be in the network part and binary 0s for the bits considered to be in the host part.

For example, Class A network 10.0.0.0 has a network part of the first single octet (8 bits) and a host part of last three octets (24 bits). As a result, the Class A default mask is 255.0.0.0, which in binary is

    11111111 00000000 00000000 00000000

Figure 12-3 shows default masks for each network class, both in binary and dotted-decimal format.

Key Topic

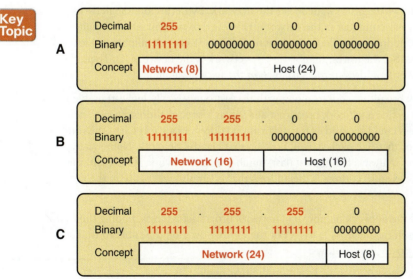

12

Figure 12-3 *Default Masks for Classes A, B, and C*

> **NOTE**   Decimal 255 converts to the binary value 11111111. Decimal 0, converted to 8-bit binary, is 00000000. See Appendix A, "Numeric Reference Tables," for a conversion table.

Number of Hosts per Network

Calculating the number of hosts per network requires some basic binary math. First, consider a case where you have a single binary digit. How many unique values are there? There are, of course, two values: 0 and 1. With 2 bits, you can make four combinations: 00, 01, 10, and 11. As it turns out, the total combination of unique values you can make with N bits is 2^N.

Host addresses—the IP addresses assigned to hosts—must be unique. The host bits exist for the purpose of giving each host a unique IP address by virtue of having a different value in the host part of the addresses. So, with H host bits, 2^H unique combinations exist.

However, the number of hosts in a network is not 2^H; instead, it is $2^H - 2$. Each network reserves two numbers that would have otherwise been useful as host addresses, but have instead been reserved for special use: one for the network ID and one for the network broadcast address. As a result, the formula to calculate the number of host addresses per Class A, B, or C network is

$$2^H - 2$$

where H is the number of host bits.

Deriving the Network ID and Related Numbers

Each classful network has four key numbers that describe the network. You can derive these four numbers if you start with just one IP address in the network. The numbers are as follows:

- Network number
- First (numerically lowest) usable address
- Last (numerically highest) usable address
- Network broadcast address

First, consider both the network number and first usable IP address. The *network number*, also called the *network ID* or *network address*, identifies the network. By definition, the network number is the numerically lowest number in the network. However, to prevent any ambiguity, the people that made up IP addressing added the restriction that the network number cannot be assigned as an IP address. So, the lowest number in the network is the network ID. Then, the first (numerically lowest) host IP address is *one larger than* the network number.

Next, consider the network broadcast address along with the last (numerically highest) usable IP address. The TCP/IP RFCs define a network broadcast address as a special address in each network. This broadcast address could be used as the destination address in a packet, and the routers would forward a copy of that one packet to all hosts in that classful network. Numerically, a network broadcast address is always the highest (last) number in the network. As a result, the highest (last) number usable as an IP address is the address that is simply *one less than* the network broadcast address.

Simply put, if you can find the network number and network broadcast address, finding the first and last usable IP addresses in the network is easy. For the exam, you should be able to find all four values with ease; the process is as follows:

Step 1.   Determine the class (A, B, or C) based on the first octet.

Step 2.   Mentally divide the network and host octets based on the class.

Step 3.   To find the network number, change the IP address's host octets to 0.

Step 4.   To find the first address, add 1 to the fourth octet of the network ID.

Step 5.   To find the broadcast address, change the network ID's host octets to 255.

Step 6.   To find the last address, subtract 1 from the fourth octet of the network broadcast address.

The written process actually looks harder than it is. Figure 12-4 shows an example of the process, using Class A IP address 10.1.2.3, with the circled numbers matching the process.

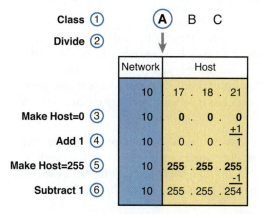

Figure 12-4   *Example of Deriving the Network ID and Other Values from 10.17.18.21*

Figure 12-4 shows the identification of the class as Class A (Step 1) and the number of network/host octets as 1 and 3, respectively. So, to find the network ID at Step 3, the figure copies only the first octet, setting the last three (host) octets to 0. At Step 4, just copy the network ID and add 1 to the fourth octet. Similarly, to find the broadcast address at Step 5, copy the network octets, but set the host octets to 255. Then, at Step 6, subtract 1 from the fourth octet to find the last (numerically highest) usable IP address.

Just to show an alternative example, consider IP address 172.16.8.9. Figure 12-5 shows the process applied to this IP address.

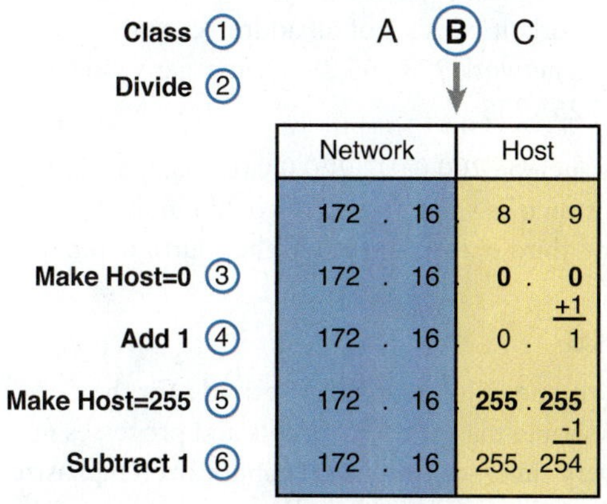

Figure 12-5   *Example Deriving the Network ID and Other Values from 172.16.8.9*

Figure 12-5 shows the identification of the class as Class B (Step 1) and the number of network/host octets as 2 and 2, respectively. So, to find the network ID at Step 3, the figure copies only the first two octets, setting the last two (host) octets to 0. Similarly, Step 5 shows the same action, but with the last two (host) octets being set to 255.

12

Unusual Network IDs and Network Broadcast Addresses

Some of the more unusual numbers in and around the range of Class A, B, and C network numbers can cause some confusion. This section lists some examples of numbers that make many people make the wrong assumptions about the meaning of the number.

For Class A, the first odd fact is that the range of values in the first octet omits the numbers 0 and 127. As it turns out, what would be Class A network 0.0.0.0 was originally reserved for some broadcasting requirements, so all addresses that begin with 0 in the first octet are reserved. What would be Class A network 127.0.0.0 is still reserved because of a special address used in software testing, called the loopback address (127.0.0.1).

For Class B (and C), some of the network numbers can look odd, particularly if you fall into a habit of thinking that 0s at the end means the number is a network ID, and 255s at the end means it's a network broadcast address. First, Class B network numbers range from 128.0.0.0 to 191.255.0.0, for a total of 2^{14} networks. However, even the very first (lowest number) Class B network number (128.0.0.0) looks a little like a Class A network number, because it ends with three 0s. However, the first octet is 128, making it a Class B network with a two-octet network part (128.0).

For another Class B example, the high end of the Class B range also might look strange at first glance (191.255.0.0), but this is indeed the numerically highest of the valid Class B network numbers. This network's broadcast address, 191.255.255.255, might look a little like a Class A broadcast address because of the three 255s at the end, but it is indeed the broadcast address of a Class B network.

Other valid Class B network IDs that look unusual include 130.0.0.0, 150.0.0.0, 155.255.0.0, and 190.0.0.0. All of these follow the convention of a value from 128 to 191 in the first octet, a value from 0 to 255 in the second octet, and two more 0s, so they are indeed valid Class B network IDs.

Class C networks follow the same general rules as Class B, but with the first three octets defining the network. The network numbers range from 192.0.0.0 to 223.255.255.0, with all addresses in a single network sharing the same value in the first three octets.

Similar to Class B networks, some of the valid Class C network numbers do look strange. For example, Class C network 192.0.0.0 looks a little like a Class A network because of the last three octets being 0, but because it is a Class C network, it consists of all addresses that begin with three octets equal to 192.0.0. Similarly, Class C network 223.255.255.0, another valid Class C network, consists of all addresses that begin 223.255.255.

Other valid Class C network IDs that look unusual include 200.0.0.0, 220.0.0.0, 205.255.255.0, and 199.255.255.0. All of these follow the convention of a value from 192 to 223 in the first octet, a value from 0 to 255 in both the second and third octets, and a 0 in the fourth octet.

Practice with Classful Networks

As with all areas of IP addressing and subnetting, you need to practice to be ready for the CCENT and CCNA exams. Before the exam, you should master the concepts and processes in this chapter and be able to get the right answer every time—with speed. I cannot overemphasize the importance of mastering IP addressing and subnetting for the exams: Know the topics, and know them well.

However, you do not need to completely master everything in this chapter right now. You should practice some now to make sure that you understand the processes, but you can use your notes, use this book, or whatever. After you practice enough to confirm you can get the right answers using any help available, you understand the topics in this chapter well enough to move to the next chapter.

Then, before the exam, practice until you master the topics in this chapter and can move pretty fast. Table 12-3 summarizes the key concepts and suggestions for this two-phase approach.

Table 12-3   Keep-Reading and Take-Exam Goals for This Chapter's Topics

Time Frame	After Reading This Chapter	Before Taking the Exam
Focus On...	Learning how	Being correct and fast
Tools Allowed	All	Your brain and a notepad
Goal: Accuracy	90% correct	100% correct
Goal: Speed	Any speed	10 seconds

Practice Deriving Key Facts Based on an IP Address

Practice finding the various facts that can be derived from an IP address, as discussed throughout this chapter. To do so, complete Table 12-4.

Table 12-4   Practice Problems: Find the Network ID and Network Broadcast

	IP Address	Class	Number of Network Octets	Number of Host Octets	Network ID	Network Broadcast Address
1	1.1.1.1					
2	128.1.6.5					
3	200.1.2.3					
4	192.192.1.1					
5	126.5.4.3					
6	200.1.9.8					
7	192.0.0.1					
8	191.255.1.47					
9	223.223.0.1					

The answers are listed in the section "Answers to Earlier Practice Problems," later in this chapter.

Practice Remembering the Details of Address Classes

Tables 12-1 and 12-2, shown earlier in this chapter, summarized some key information about IPv4 address classes. Tables 12-5 and 12-6 show sparse versions of these same tables. To practice recalling those key facts, particularly the range of values in the first octet that identifies the address class, complete these tables. Then, refer to Tables 12-1 and 12-2 to check your answers. Repeat this process until you can recall all the information in the tables.

Table 12-5   Sparse Study Table Version of Table 12-1

Class	First Octet Values	Purpose
A		
B		
C		
D		
E		

Table 12-6   Sparse Study Table Version of Table 12-2

	Class A	Class B	Class C
First octet range			
Valid network numbers			
Total networks			
Hosts per network			
Octets (bits) in network part			
Octets (bits) in host part			
Default mask			

Additional Practice

For additional practice with classful networks, consider the following:

- DVD Appendix D, "Practice for Chapter 12: Analyzing Classful IPv4 Networks," has additional practice problems. This appendix also includes explanations about how to find the answer of each problem.

- Create your own problems. You can randomly choose any IP address and try to find the same information asked for by the practice problems in this section. Then, to check your work, use any subnet calculator. Most subnet calculators list the class and network ID.

Review Activities

Chapter Summary

- IP version 4 (IPv4) defines five address classes. Three of the classes, Classes A, B, and C, consist of unicast IP addresses. Unicast addresses identify a single host or interface so that the address uniquely identifies the device. Class D addresses serve as multicast addresses, so that one packet sent to a Class D multicast IPv4 address might actually be delivered to multiple hosts. Finally, Class E addresses are experimental.

- Addresses in the classful network have a structure with two parts: the *network part* (sometimes called the *prefix*), and the *host part*.

  - The addresses in the same network have the same values in the network part.

  - The addresses in the same network have different values in the host part.

  - Each network class has an associated *default mask* that defines the size of the network and host parts of an unsubnetted Class A, B, and C network. To do so, the mask lists binary 1s for the bits considered to be in the network part and binary 0s for the bits considered to be in the host part.

- Each classful network has four key numbers that describe the network. You can derive these four numbers if you start with just one IP address in the network. The numbers are as follows:

  - Network number

  - First (numerically lowest) usable address

  - Last (numerically highest) usable address

  - Network broadcast address

Review Questions

Answer these review questions. You can find the answers at the bottom of the last page of the chapter. For thorough explanations, see DVD Appendix C, "Answers to Review Questions."

1. Which of the following are not valid Class A network IDs? (Choose two answers.)

    A. 1.0.0.0

    B. 130.0.0.0

    C. 127.0.0.0

    D. 9.0.0.0

2. Which of the following are not valid Class B network IDs?

    A. 130.0.0.0

    B. 191.255.0.0

    C. 128.0.0.0

    D. 150.255.0.0

    E. All are valid Class B network IDs

12

3. Which of the following are true about IP address 172.16.99.45's IP network? (Select two answers.)

   A. The network ID is 172.0.0.0.

   B. The network is a Class B network.

   C. The default mask for the network is 255.255.255.0.

   D. The number of host bits in the unsubnetted network is 16.

4. Which of the following are true about IP address 192.168.6.7's IP network? (Select two answers.)

   A. The network ID is 192.168.6.0.

   B. The network is a Class B network.

   C. The default mask for the network is 255.255.255.0.

   D. The number of host bits in the unsubnetted network is 16.

5. Which of the following is a network broadcast address?

   A. 10.1.255.255

   B. 192.168.255.1

   C. 224.1.1.255

   D. 172.30.255.255

6. Which of the following is a Class A, B, or C network ID?

   A. 10.1.0.0

   B. 192.168.1.0

   C. 127.0.0.0

   D. 172.20.0.1

Review All the Key Topics

Review the most important topics from this chapter, noted with the Key Topic icon. Table 12-7 lists these key topics and where each is discussed.

Table 12-7   Key Topics for Chapter 12

Key Topic Elements	Description	Page Number
Table 12-1	Address classes	295
Table 12-2	Key facts about Class A, B, and C networks	296
List	Comparisons of network and host parts of addresses in the same classful network	297
Figure 12-3	Default masks	297
Paragraph	Function to calculate the number of hosts per network	298
List	Steps to find information about a classful network	298

Complete the Tables and Lists from Memory

Print a copy of DVD Appendix M, "Memory Tables," or at least the section for this chapter, and complete the tables and lists from memory. DVD Appendix N, "Memory Tables Answer Key," includes completed tables and lists for you to check your work.

Definitions of Key Terms

After your first reading of the chapter, try to define these key terms, but do not be concerned about getting them all correct at that time. Chapter 30 directs you in how to use these terms for late-stage preparation for the exam.

network, classful network, network number, network ID, network address, network broadcast address, first address, last address, network part, host part, default mask

Practice

If you have not done so already, practice discovering the details of a classful network as discussed in this chapter. Refer to the earlier section "Practice with Classful Networks" for suggestions.

Answers to Earlier Practice Problems

Table 12-4, shown earlier, listed several practice problems. Table 12-8 lists the answers.

Table 12-8   Practice Problems: Find the Network ID and Network Broadcast

	IP Address	Class	Number of Network Octets	Number of Host Octets	Network ID	Network Broadcast
1	1.1.1.1	A	1	3	1.0.0.0	1.255.255.255
2	128.1.6.5	B	2	2	128.1.0.0	128.1.255.255
3	200.1.2.3	C	3	1	200.1.2.0	200.1.2.255
4	192.192.1.1	C	3	1	192.192.1.0	192.192.1.255
5	126.5.4.3	A	1	3	126.0.0.0	126.255.255.255
6	200.1.9.8	C	3	1	200.1.9.0	200.1.9.255
7	192.0.0.1	C	3	1	192.0.0.0	192.0.0.255
8	191.255.1.47	B	2	2	191.255.0.0	191.255.255.255
9	223.223.0.1	C	3	1	223.223.0.0	223.223.0.255

12

The class, number of network octets, and number of host octets, all require you to look at the first octet of the IP address to determine the class. If a value is between 1 and 126, inclusive, the address is a Class A address, with one network and three host octets. If a value is between 128 and 191 inclusive, the address is a Class B address, with two network and two host octets. If a value is between 192 and 223, inclusive, it is a Class C address, with three network and one host octet.

The last two columns can be found based on Table 12-2, specifically the number of network and host octets along with the IP address. To find the network ID, copy the IP address, but change the host octets to 0. Similarly, to find the network broadcast address, copy the IP address, but change the host octets to 255.

The last three problems can be confusing, and were included on purpose so that you could see an example of these unusual cases, as follows.

Answers to Practice Problem 7 (From Table 12-4)

Consider IP address 192.0.0.1. First, 192 is on the lower edge of the first octet range for Class C; as such, this address has three network and one host octet. To find the network ID, copy the address, but change the single host octet (the fourth octet) to 0, for a network ID of 192.0.0.0. It looks strange, but it is indeed the network ID.

The network broadcast address choice for problem 7 can also look strange. To find the broadcast address, copy the IP address (192.0.0.1), but change the last octet (the only host octet) to 255, for a broadcast address of 192.0.0.255. In particular, if you decide that the broadcast should be 192.255.255.255, you might have fallen into the trap of logic, like "Change all 0s in the network ID to 255s," which is not the correct logic. Instead, change all host octets in the IP address (or network ID) to 255s.

Answers to Practice Problem 8 (From Table 12-4)

The first octet of problem 8 (191.255.1.47) sits on the upper edge of the Class B range for the first octet (128–191). As such, to find the network ID, change the last two octets (host octets) to 0, for a network ID of 191.255.0.0. This value sometimes gives people problems, because they are used to thinking that 255 somehow means the number is a broadcast address.

The broadcast address, found by changing the two host octets to 255, means that the broadcast address is 191.255.255.255. It looks more like a broadcast address for a Class A network, but it is actually the broadcast address for Class B network 191.255.0.0.

Answers to Practice Problem 9 (From Table 12-4)

The last problem with IP address 223.223.0.1 is that it's near the high end of the Class C range. As a result, only the last (host) octet is changed to 0 to form the network ID 223.223.0.0. It looks a little like a Class B network number at first glance, because it ends in two octets of 0. However, it is indeed a Class C network ID (based on the value in the first octet).

Answers to Review Questions:

1 B and C **2** E **3** B and D **4** A and C **5** D **6** B

Chapter 13

Analyzing Subnet Masks

The subnet mask used in one or many subnets in an IP internetwork says a lot about the intent of the subnet design. First, the mask divides addresses into two parts: *prefix* and *host*, with the host part defining the size of the subnet. Then, the class (A, B, or C) further divides the structure of addresses in a subnet, breaking the prefix part into the *network* and *subnet* parts. The subnet part defines the number of subnets that could exist inside one classful IP network, assuming that one mask is used throughout the classful network.

The subnet mask holds the key to understanding several important subnetting design points. However, to analyze a subnet mask, you first need some basic math skills with masks. The math converts masks between the three different formats used to represent a mask:

Binary

Dotted-decimal notation (DDN)

Prefix (also called CIDR)

This chapter has two major sections. The first focuses totally on the mask formats and the math used to convert between the three formats. The second section explains how to take an IP address and its subnet mask and analyze those values. In particular, it shows how to determine the three-part format of the IPv4 address and describes the facts about the subnetting design that are implied by the mask.

This chapter covers the following exam topics:

Troubleshooting

Troubleshoot and correct common problems associated with IP addressing and host configurations.

Foundation Topics

Subnet Mask Conversion

This section describes how to convert between different formats for the subnet mask. You can then use these processes when you practice. If you already know how to convert from one format to the other, go ahead and move to the section "Practice Converting Subnet Masks," later in this chapter.

Three Mask Formats

Subnet masks can be written as 32-bit binary numbers, but not just any binary number. In particular, the binary subnet mask must follow these rules:

- The value must not interleave 1s and 0s.
- If 1s exist, they are on the left.
- If 0s exist, they are on the right.

For example, the following values would be illegal. The first is illegal because the value interleaves 0s and 1s, and the second is illegal because it lists 0s on the left and 1s on the right:

    10101010 01010101 11110000 00001111

    00000000 00000000 00000000 11111111

The following two binary values meet the requirements, in that they have all 1s on the left, followed by all 0s, with no interleaving of 1s and 0s:

    11111111 00000000 00000000 00000000

    11111111 11111111 11111111 00000000

Two alternate subnet mask formats exist so that we humans do not have to work with 32-bit binary numbers. One format, *dotted-decimal notation (DDN)*, converts each set of 8 bits into the decimal equivalent. For example, the two previous binary masks would convert to the following DDN subnet masks, because binary 11111111 converts to decimal 255, and binary 00000000 converts to decimal 0:

    255.0.0.0

    255.255.255.0

Although the DDN format has been around since the beginning of IPv4 addressing, the third mask format was added later, in the early 1990s: the *prefix* format. This format takes advantage of the rule that the subnet mask starts with some number of 1s, and then the rest of the digits are 0s. Prefix format lists a slash (/) followed by the number of binary 1s in the binary mask. Using the same two examples as earlier in this section, the prefix format equivalent masks are as follows:

    /8

    /24

Note that although the terms *prefix* or *prefix mask* can be used, the terms *CIDR mask* or *slash mask* can also be used. This newer prefix style mask was created around the same time as the *classless interdomain routing (CIDR)* specification back in the early 1990s, and the acronym CIDR grew to be used for anything related to CIDR, including prefix-style masks. Additionally, the term *slash mask* is sometimes used because the value includes a slash mark (/).

Both in real life and on the Cisco CCENT and CCNA exams, you need to be able to think about masks in different formats. The rest of this section examines how to convert between the three formats.

Converting Between Binary and Prefix Masks

Converting between binary and prefix masks should be relatively intuitive after you know that the prefix value is simply the number of binary 1s in the binary mask. For the sake of completeness, the processes to convert in each direction are

Key Topic

Binary to prefix: Count the number of binary 1s in the binary mask, and write the total, in decimal, after a /.

Prefix to binary: Write P binary 1s, where P is the prefix value, followed by as many binary 0s as required to create a 32-bit number.

Tables 13-1 and 13-2 show some examples.

Table 13-1   Example Conversions: Binary to Prefix

Binary Mask	Logic	Prefix Mask
11111111 11111111 11000000 00000000	Count 8 + 8 + 2 = 18 binary 1s	/18
11111111 11111111 11111111 11110000	Count 8 + 8 + 8 + 4 = 28 binary 1s	/28
11111111 11111000 00000000 00000000	Count 8 + 5 = 13 binary 1s	/13

Table 13-2   Example Conversions: Prefix to Binary

Prefix Mask	Logic	Binary Mask
/18	Write 18 1s, then 14 0s, total 32	11111111 11111111 11000000 00000000
/28	Write 28 1s, then 4 0s, total 32	11111111 11111111 11111111 11110000
/13	Write 13 1s, then 19 0s, total 32	11111111 11111000 00000000 00000000

Converting Between Binary and DDN Masks

By definition, a *dotted-decimal number (DDN)* used with IPv4 addressing contains four decimal numbers, separated by dots. Each decimal number represents 8 bits. So, a single DDN shows four decimal numbers that together represent some 32-bit binary number.

Conversion from a DDN mask to the binary equivalent is relatively simple to describe, but can be laborious to perform. First, to do the conversion, the process is as follows:

For each octet, perform a decimal-to-binary conversion.

However, depending on your comfort level with doing decimal-to-binary conversions, that process can be difficult or time-consuming. If you want to think about masks in binary for the exam, consider picking one of the following methods to do the conversion and practicing until you can do it quickly and accurately:

■ Do the decimal-binary conversions, but practice your decimal-binary conversions to get fast. If you choose this path, consider the Cisco Binary Game, which you can find by searching its name at the Cisco Learning Network (CLN) (http://learningnetwork.cisco.com).

■ Use the decimal-binary conversion chart in Appendix A, "Numeric Reference Tables." This lets you find the answer more quickly now, but you cannot use the chart on exam day.

■ Memorize the nine possible decimal values that can be in a decimal mask, and practice using a reference table with those values.

The third method, which is the method recommended in this book, takes advantage of the fact that any and every DDN mask octet must be one of only nine values. Why? Well, remember how a binary mask cannot interleave 1s and 0s, and the 0s must be on the right? It turns out that only nine different 8-bit binary numbers conform to these rules. Table 13-3 lists the values, along with other relevant information.

Table 13-3   Nine Possible Values in One Octet of a Subnet Mask

Binary Mask Octet	Decimal Equivalent	Number of Binary 1s
00000000	0	0
10000000	128	1
11000000	192	2
11100000	224	3
11110000	240	4
11111000	248	5
11111100	252	6
11111110	254	7
11111111	255	8

Many subnetting processes can be done with or without binary math. Some of those processes—mask conversion included—use the information in Table 13-3. You should plan to memorize the information in the table. I recommend making a copy of the table to keep handy while you practice. (You will likely memorize the contents of this table simply by practicing the conversion process enough to get both good and fast at the conversion.)

Using the table, the conversion processes in each direction with binary and decimal masks are as follows:

Binary to decimal: Organize the bits into four sets of eight. For each octet, find the binary value in the table and write down the corresponding decimal value.

Decimal to binary: For each octet, find the decimal value in the table and write down the corresponding 8-bit binary value.

Tables 13-4 and 13-5 show some examples.

Table 13-4   Example Conversions: Binary to Decimal

Binary Mask	Logic	Decimal Mask
11111111 11111111 11000000 00000000	11111111 maps to 255 11000000 maps to 192 00000000 maps to 0	255.255.192.0
11111111 11111111 11111111 11110000	11111111 maps to 255 11110000 maps to 240	255.255.255.240
11111111 11111000 00000000 00000000	11111111 maps to 255 11111000 maps to 248 00000000 maps to 0	255.248.0.0

13

Table 13-5   Example Conversions: Decimal to Binary

Decimal Mask	Logic	Binary Mask
255.255.192.0	255 maps to 11111111 192 maps to 11000000 0 maps to 00000000	11111111 11111111 11000000 00000000
255.255.255.240	255 maps to 11111111 240 maps to 11110000	11111111 11111111 11111111 11110000
255.248.0.0	255 maps to 11111111 248 maps to 11111000 0 maps to 00000000	11111111 11111000 00000000 00000000

Converting Between Prefix and DDN Masks

When learning, the best way to convert between the prefix and decimal formats is to first convert to binary. For example, to move from decimal to prefix, first convert decimal to binary and then from binary to prefix.

For the exams, set a goal to master these conversions doing the math in your head. While learning, you will likely want to use paper. To train yourself to do all this without writing it down, instead of writing each octet of binary, just write the number of binary 1s in that octet.

Figure 13-1 shows an example with a prefix-to-decimal conversion. The left side shows the conversion to binary as an interim step. For comparison, the right side shows the binary interim step in shorthand that just lists the number of binary 1s in each octet of the binary mask.

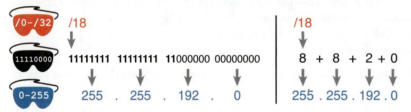

Figure 13-1   *Conversion from Prefix to Decimal: Full Binary Versus Shorthand*

Similarly, when converting from decimal to prefix, mentally convert to binary along the way, and as you improve, just think of the binary as the number of 1s in each octet. Figure 13-2 shows an example of such a conversion.

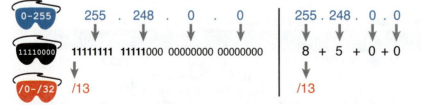

Figure 13-2   *Conversion from Decimal to Prefix: Full Binary Versus Shorthand*

Note that Appendix A has a table that lists all 33 legal subnet masks, with all three formats shown.

Practice Converting Subnet Masks

Before moving to the second half of this chapter, and thinking about what these subnet masks mean, first do some practice. Practice the processes discussed in this chapter until you get the right answer most of the time. Use any tools you want, and take all the time you need, until you meet the goal in Table 13-6 for being ready to move on to the next section. Later, before taking the exam, practice more until you master the topics in this chapter and can move pretty fast, as outlined in the right column of Table 13-6.

Table 13-6   Keep-Reading and Take-Exam Goals for This Chapter's Topics

Time Frame	Before Moving to the Next Section	Before Taking the Exam
Focus On...	Learning how	Being correct and fast
Tools Allowed	All	Your brain and a notepad
Goal: Accuracy	90% correct	100% correct
Goal: Speed	Any speed	10 seconds

Table 13-7 lists eight practice problems. The table has three columns, one for each mask format. Each row lists one mask, in one format. Your job is to find the mask's value in the other two formats for each row. Table 13-10, located in the section "Answers to Earlier Practice Problems," later in this chapter, lists the answers.

Table 13-7   Practice Problems: Find the Mask Values in the Other Two Formats

Prefix	Binary Mask	Decimal
	11111111 11111111 11000000 00000000	
		255.255.255.252
/25		
/16		
		255.0.0.0
	11111111 11111111 11111100 00000000	
		255.254.0.0
/27		

For additional practice converting subnet masks, consider the following:

- DVD Appendix E, "Practice for Chapter 13: Analyzing Subnet Masks," has some additional practice problems listed. This section also includes explanations as to how to find the answer of each problem.

- Create your own problems. Only 33 legal subnet masks exist, so pick one, and convert that mask to the other two formats. Then check your work based on Appendix A, which lists all mask values in all three formats. (Recommendation: Think of a prefix and convert it to binary and then decimal. Then, think of a DDN mask and convert it to binary and to prefix format.)

Note that many other subnetting problems will require you to do these conversions, so you will get extra practice as well.

Identifying Subnet Design Choices Using Masks

Subnet masks have many purposes. In fact, if ten experienced network engineers were independently asked, "What is the purpose of a subnet mask?" the engineers would likely give a variety of true answers. The subnet mask plays several roles.

This chapter focuses on one particular use of a subnet mask: defining the prefix part of the IP addresses in a subnet. The prefix part must be the same value for all addresses in a subnet. In fact, a single subnet can be defined as all IPv4 addresses that have the same value in the prefix part of their IPv4 addresses.

While the previous paragraph might sound a bit formal, the idea is relatively basic, as shown in Figure 13-3. The figure shows a network diagram, focusing on two subnets: a subnet of all addresses that begin with 172.16.2 and another subnet made of all addresses that begin with 172.16.3. In this example, the prefix—the part that has the same value in all the addresses in the subnet—is the first three octets.

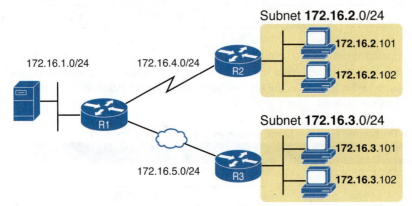

Figure 13-3 *Simple Subnet Design, with Mask /24*

While people can sit around a conference table and talk about how a prefix is three octets long, computers communicate that same concept using a subnet mask. In this case, the subnets use a subnet mask of /24, which means that the prefix part of the addresses is 24 bits (3 octets) long.

This section explains more about how to use a subnet mask to understand this concept of a prefix part of an IPv4 address, along with these other uses for a subnet mask. Note that this section discusses the first five items in the list.

- Defines the size of the prefix (combined network and subnet) part of the addresses in a subnet
- Defines the size of the host part of the addresses in the subnet
- Can be used to calculate the number of hosts in the subnet
- Provides a means for the network designer to communicate the design details—the number of subnet and host bits—to the devices in the network
- Under certain assumptions, can be used to calculate the number of subnets in the entire classful network
- Can be used in binary calculations of both the subnet ID and the subnet broadcast address

Masks Divide the Subnet's Addresses into Two Parts

The subnet mask subdivides the IP addresses in a subnet into two parts: the *prefix*, or *subnet part*, and the *host part*.

The prefix part identifies the addresses that reside in the same subnet, because all IP addresses in the same subnet have the same value in the prefix part of their addresses. The idea is much like the postal code (ZIP codes in the United States) in mailing addresses. All mailing addresses in the same town have the same postal code. Likewise, all IP addresses in the same subnet have identical values in the prefix part of their addresses.

The host part of an address identifies the host uniquely inside the subnet. If you compare any two IP addresses in the same subnet, their host parts will differ, even though the prefix parts of their addresses have the same value. To summarize these key comparisons:

Prefix (subnet) part: Equal in all addresses in the same subnet.

Host part: Different in all addresses in the same subnet.

For example, imagine a subnet that, in concept, includes all addresses whose first three octets are 10.1.1. So, the following list shows several addresses in this subnet:

10.1.1.**1**

10.1.1.**2**

10.1.1.**3**

In this list, the prefix or subnet part (the first three octets of 10.1.1) are equal. The host part (the last octet [in bold]) are different. So, the prefix or subnet part of the address identifies the group, and the host part identifies the specific member of the group.

The subnet mask defines the dividing line between the prefix and the host part. To do so, the mask creates a conceptual line between the binary 1s in the binary mask and the binary 0s in the mask. In short, if a mask has P binary 1s, the prefix part is P bits long and the rest of the bits are host bits. Figure 13-4 shows the general concept.

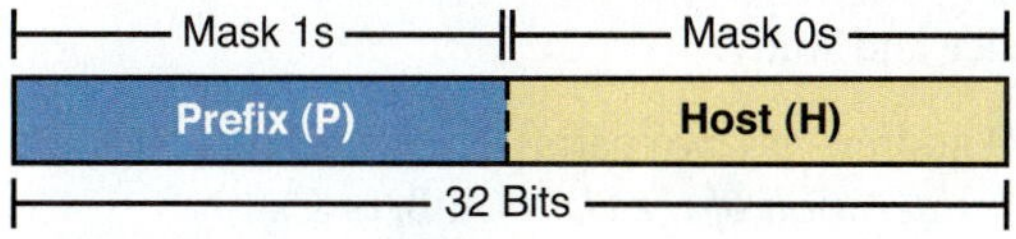

Figure 13-4   *Prefix (Subnet) and Host Parts Defined by Masks 1s and 0s*

The next figure, Figure 13-5, shows a specific example using mask 255.255.255.0. Mask 255.255.255.0 (/24) has 24 binary 1s, for a prefix length of 24 bits.

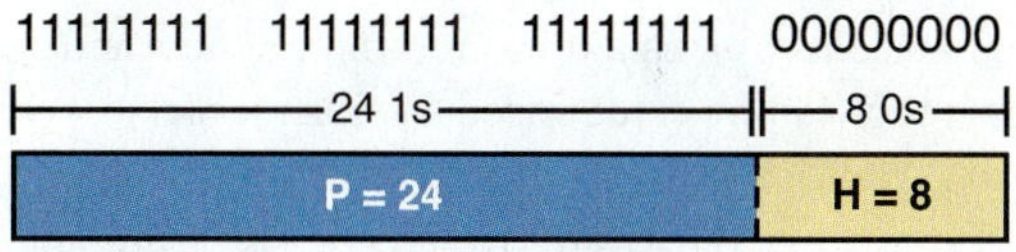

Figure 13-5   *Mask 255.255.255.0: P=24, H=8*

Masks and Class Divide Addresses into Three Parts

In addition to the two-part view of IPv4 addresses, you can also think about IPv4 addresses as having three parts. To do so, just apply Class A, B, and C rules to the address format to define the network part at the beginning of the address. This added logic divides the prefix into two parts: the *network* part and the *subnet* part. The class defines the length of the network part, with the subnet part simply being the rest of the prefix. Figure 13-6 shows the idea.

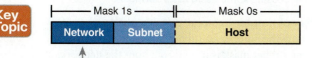

Figure 13-6   *Class Concepts Applied to Create Three Parts*

13

The combined network and subnet parts act like the prefix because all addresses in the same subnet must have identical values in the network and subnet parts. The size of the host part remains unchanged, whether viewing the addresses as having two parts or three parts.

To be complete, Figure 13-7 shows the same example as in the previous section, with the subnet of "all addresses that begin with 10.1.1." In that example, the subnet uses mask 255.255.255.0, and the addresses are all in Class A network 10.0.0.0. The class defines 8 network bits, and the mask defines 24 prefix bits, meaning that 24 − 8 = 16 subnet bits exist. The host part remains as 8 bits per the mask.

```
11111111   11111111   11111111   00000000
|————————— 24 1s —————————|—— 8 0s ——|

| N = 8 |    S = (24 - 8) = 16    |   H = 8   |
```
Based on
Class

Figure 13-7 *Subnet 10.1.1.0, Mask 255.255.255.0: N=8, S=16, H=8*

Classless and Classful Addressing

The terms *classless addressing* and *classful addressing* refer to the two different ways to think about IPv4 addresses as described so far in this chapter. Classful addressing means that you think about Class A, B, and C rules, so the prefix is separated into the network and subnet parts, as shown in Figures 13-6 and 13-7. Classless addressing means that you ignore the Class A, B, and C rules and treat the prefix part as one part, as shown in Figures 13-4 and 13-5. The following more formal definitions are listed for reference and study:

Classless addressing: The concept that an IPv4 address has two parts—the prefix part plus the host part—as defined by the mask, with *no consideration of the class* (A, B, or C).

Classful addressing: The concept that an IPv4 address has three parts—network, subnet, and host—as defined by the mask *and Class A, B, and C rules.*

> **NOTE**   The scope of the CCENT and CCNA certifications includes two other related topics that are (unfortunately) also referenced as *classless* and *classful*. In addition to the classless and classful addressing described here, each routing protocol can be categorized as either a *classless routing protocol* or a *classful routing protocol*. Additionally, the terms *classless routing* and *classful routing* refer to some details of how Cisco routers forward (route) packets using the default route in some cases (which do not happen to be within the scope of this book). As a result, these terms can be easily confused and misused. So, when you see the words *classless* and *classful*, be careful to note the context: addressing, routing, or routing protocols.

Calculations Based on the IPv4 Address Format

After you know how to break an address down using both classless and classful addressing rules, you can easily calculate a couple of important facts using some basic math formulas.

First, for any subnet, after you know the number of host bits, you can calculate the number of host IP addresses in the subnet. Next, if you know the number of subnet bits (using classful addressing concepts) and you know that only one subnet mask is used throughout the network, you can also calculate the number of subnets in the network. The formulas just require that you know the powers of 2:

Hosts in the subnet: $2^H - 2$, where H is the number of host bits.

Subnets in the network: 2^S, where S is the number of subnet bits. Only use this formula if only one mask is used throughout the network.

> **NOTE**   Chapter 11's section "Choose the Mask" details many concepts related to masks, including comments about this assumption of one mask throughout a single Class A, B, or C network.

The sizes of the parts of IPv4 addresses can also be calculated. The math is basic, but the concepts are important. Keeping in mind that IPv4 addresses are 32 bits long, the two parts with classless addressing must add up to 32 (P + H = 32), and with classful addressing, the three parts must add up to 32 (N + S + H = 32). Figure 13-8 shows the relationships.

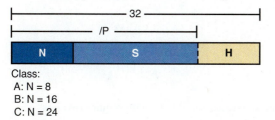

Class:
A: N = 8
B: N = 16
C: N = 24

Figure 13-8   *Relationship Between /P, N, S, and H*

You often begin with an IP address and mask, both when answering questions on the CCENT and CCNA exams and when examining problems that occur in real networks. Based on the information in this chapter and earlier chapters, you should be able to find all the information in Figure 13-8 and then calculate the number of hosts/subnet and the number of subnets in the network. For reference, the following process spells out the steps:

Step 1.   Convert the mask to prefix format (/P) as needed. (See the earlier section "Practice Converting Subnet Masks" for review.)

Step 2.   Determine N based on the class. (See Chapter 12, "Analyzing Classful IPv4 Networks," for review.)

Step 3.   Calculate S = P – N.

Step 4.   Calculate H = 32 – P.

Step 5.   Calculate hosts/subnet: $2^H - 2$.

Step 6.   Calculate number of subnet: 2^S.

For example, consider the case of IP address 8.1.4.5 with mask 255.255.0.0. Following the process:

Step 1.   255.255.0.0 = /16, so P=16.

Step 2.   8.1.4.5 is in the range 1–126 in the first octet, so it is Class A; so N=8.

Step 3.   S = P – N = 16 – 8 = 8.

Step 4.   H = 32 – P = 32 – 16 = 16.

Step 5. $2^{16} - 2 = 65,534$ hosts/subnet.

Step 6. $2^8 = 256$ subnets.

Figure 13-9 shows a visual analysis of the same problem.

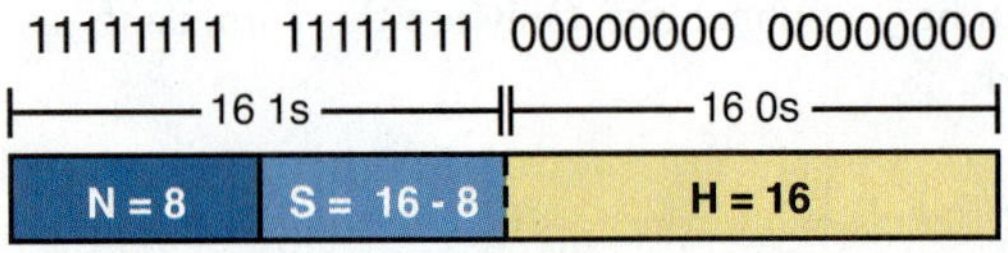

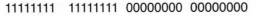

```
11111111   11111111  00000000  00000000
|———— 16 1s ————|——————— 16 0s ——————|
```

| N = 8 | S = 16 - 8 | H = 16 |

Figure 13-9 *Visual Representation of Problem: 8.1.4.5, 255.255.0.0*

For another example, consider address 200.1.1.1, mask 255.255.255.252. Following the process:

Step 1.   255.255.255.252 = /30, so P=30.

Step 2.   200.1.1.1 is in the range 192–223 in the first octet, so it is Class C; so N=24.

Step 3.   S = P – N = 30 – 24 = 6.

Step 4.   H = 32 – P = 32 – 30 = 2.

Step 5. $2^2 - 2 = 2$ hosts/subnet

Step 6. $2^6 = 64$ subnets.

This example uses a popular mask for serial links, because serial links only require two host addresses, and the mask supports only two host addresses.

Practice Analyzing Subnet Masks

Before moving to the next chapter, practice until you get the right answer most of the time, but use any tools you want and take all the time you need. Then, you can move on with your reading.

However, before taking the exam, practice until you master the topics in this chapter and can move pretty fast. As for time, you should be able to find the entire answer—the size of the three parts, plus the formulas to calculate the number of subnets and hosts—in around 15 seconds. Table 13-8 summarizes the key concepts and suggestions for this two-phase approach.

Table 13-8   Goals: To Keep Reading and to Take the Exam

Time Frame	Before Moving to the Next Chapter	Before Taking the Exam
Focus On...	Learning how	Being correct and fast
Tools Allowed	All	Your brain and a notepad
Goal: Accuracy	90% correct	100% correct
Goal: Speed	Any speed	15 seconds

On a piece of scratch paper, answer the following questions. In each case:

- Determine the structure of the addresses in each subnet based on the class and mask, using classful IP addressing concepts. In other words, find the size of the network, subnet, and host parts of the addresses.
- Calculate the number of hosts in the subnet.
- Calculate the number of subnets in the network, assuming that the same mask is used throughout.

1. 8.1.4.5, 255.255.254.0
2. 130.4.102.1, 255.255.255.0
3. 199.1.1.100, 255.255.255.0
4. 130.4.102.1, 255.255.252.0
5. 199.1.1.100, 255.255.255.224

The answers are listed in the section "Answers to Earlier Practice Problems," later in this chapter.

For additional practice analyzing subnet masks, consider the following:

■ DVD Appendix E, "Practice for Chapter 13: Analyzing Subnet Masks," has some additional practice problems listed. This section also includes explanations as to how to find the answer to each problem.

■ DVD Appendix F, "Practice for Chapter 14: Analyzing Existing Subnets," has another 25 practice problems related to this chapter. Although Appendix E focuses on the topics in this chapter, the problems in Appendix E and Appendix F both begin with an IP address and mask. So, Appendix F also includes commentary and answers for items such as the number of network, subnet, and host bits, and other topics related to this chapter.

■ Create your own problems. Many subnet calculators show the number of network, subnet, and host bits when you type in an IP address and mask, so make up an IP address and mask on paper, and then find N, S, and H. Then, to check your work, use any subnet calculator. Most subnet calculators list the class and network ID.

13

Review Activities

Chapter Summary

- Subnet masks may be written as 32-bit binary numbers, but not just any binary number. In particular, the binary subnet mask must follow these rules:
  - The value must not interleave 1s and 0s.
  - If 1s exist, they must be on the left.
  - If 0s exist, they must be on the right.

- Converting between binary and prefix masks should be relatively intuitive once you know that the prefix value is simply the number of binary 1s in the binary mask. For the sake of completeness, the following are the processes to convert in each direction:
  - **Binary to prefix:** Count the number of binary 1s in the binary mask and write the total, in decimal, after a /.
  - **Prefix to binary:** Write P binary 1s, where P is the prefix value, followed by as many binary 0s as required to create a 32-bit number.

- By definition, a dotted-decimal number (DDN) used with IPv4 addressing contains four decimal numbers separated by dots. Each decimal number represents 8 bits. So, a single DDN shows four decimal numbers that together represent some 32-bit binary number.

- The uses for a subnet mask are as follows:
  - Defines the size of the prefix (combined network and subnet) part of the addresses in a subnet
  - Defines the size of the host part of the addresses in the subnet
  - Can be used to calculate the number of hosts in the subnet
  - Provides a means for the network designer to communicate the design details—the number of subnet and host bits—to the devices in the network
  - Under certain assumptions, can be used to calculate the number of subnets in the entire classful network
  - Can be used in binary calculations of both the subnet ID and the subnet broadcast address

- The subnet mask subdivides the IP addresses in a subnet into two parts: the *prefix* or *subnet part* and the *host part*.

- The prefix part identifies the addresses that reside in the same subnet, because all IP addresses in the same subnet have the same value in the prefix part of their addresses.
  - **Prefix (subnet) part:** Equal in all addresses in the same subnet.
  - **Host part:** Different in all addresses in the same subnet.

- **Classless addressing:** The concept that an IPv4 address has two parts—the prefix part plus the host part—as defined by the mask, with *no consideration of the class* (A, B, or C).

- **Classful addressing:** The concept that an IPv4 address has three parts—network, subnet, and host—as defined by the mask *and Class A, B, and C rules.*

Review Questions

Answer these review questions. You can find the answers at the bottom of the last page of the chapter. For thorough explanations, see DVD Appendix C, "Answers to Review Questions."

1. Which of the following answers lists the prefix (CIDR) format equivalent of 255.255.254.0?

   A. /19

   B. /20

   C. /23

   D. /24

   E. /25

2. Which of the following answers lists the prefix (CIDR) format equivalent of 255.255.255.240?

   A. /26

   B. /28

   C. /27

   D. /30

   E. /29

3. Which of the following answers lists the dotted-decimal notation (DDN) equivalent of /24?

   A. 255.255.240.0

   B. 255.255.252.0

   C. 255.255.255.0

   D. 255.255.255.192

   E. 255.255.255.240

4. Which of the following answers lists the dotted-decimal notation (DDN) equivalent of /30?

   A. 255.255.255.192

   B. 255.255.255.252

   C. 255.255.255.240

   D. 255.255.254.0

   E. 255.255.255.0

5. Working at the help desk, you receive a call and learn a user's PC IP address and mask (10.55.66.77, mask 255.255.255.0). When thinking about this using classful logic, you determine the number of network (N), subnet (S), and host (H) bits. Which of the following is true in this case?

   A. N=12

   B. S=12

   C. H=8

   D. S=8

   E. N=24

6. Working at the help desk, you receive a call and learn a user's PC IP address and mask (192.168.9.1/27). When thinking about this using classful logic, you determine the number of network (N), subnet (S), and host (H) bits. Which of the following is true in this case?

    A. N=24

    B. S=24

    C. H=8

    D. H=7

7. An engineer is thinking about the following IP address and mask using classless IP addressing logic: 10.55.66.77, 255.255.255.0. Which of the following statements are true when using classless addressing logic? (Choose two.)

    A. The network part's size is 8 bits.

    B. The prefix length is 24 bits.

    C. The prefix length is 16 bits.

    D. The host part's size is 8 bits.

8. Which of the following statements is true about classless IP addressing concepts?

    A. Uses a 128-bit IP address

    B. Applies only for Class A and B networks

    C. Separates IP addresses into network, subnet, and host parts

    D. Ignores Class A, B, and C network rules

9. Which of the following masks, when used as the only mask within a Class B network, would supply enough subnet bits to support 100 subnets? (Choose two.)

    A. /24

    B. 255.255.255.252

    C. /20

    D. 255.255.252.0

Review All the Key Topics

Review the most important topics from this chapter, noted with the Key Topic icon. Table 13-9 lists these key topics and where each is discussed.

Table 13-9   Key Topics for Chapter 13

Key Topic Element	Description	Page Number
List	Rules for binary subnet mask values	309
List	Rules to convert between binary and prefix masks	310
Table 13-3	Nine possible values in a decimal subnet mask	311
List	Rules to convert between binary and DDN masks	311
List	Some functions of a subnet mask	314
List	Comparisons of IP addresses in the same subnet	315
Figure 13-4	Two-part classless view of an IP address	315
Figure 13-6	Three-part classful view of an IP address	315
List	Definitions of classful addressing and classless addressing	316
List	Formal steps to analyze masks and calculate values	317

Complete the Tables and Lists from Memory

Print a copy of DVD Appendix M, "Memory Tables," or at least the section for this chapter, and complete the tables and lists from memory. DVD Appendix N, "Memory Tables Answer Key," includes completed tables and lists for you to check your work.

Definitions of Key Terms

After your first reading of the chapter, try to define these key terms, but do not be concerned about getting them all correct at that time. Chapter 30 directs you in how to use these terms for late-stage preparation for the exam.

binary mask, dotted-decimal notation (DDN), decimal mask, prefix mask, slash mask, CIDR mask, classful addressing, classless addressing

Practice

If you have not done so already, practice converting and analyzing subnet masks as discussed in this chapter. Refer to the earlier sections "Practice Converting Subnet Masks" and "Practice Analyzing Subnet Masks" for suggestions.

13

Answers to Earlier Practice Problems

Table 13-7, shown earlier, listed several practice problems for converting subnet masks; Table 13-10 lists the answers.

Table 13-10   Answers to Problems in Table 13-7

Prefix	Binary Mask	Decimal
/18	11111111 11111111 11000000 00000000	255.255.192.0
/30	11111111 11111111 11111111 11111100	255.255.255.252
/25	11111111 11111111 11111111 10000000	255.255.255.128
/16	11111111 11111111 00000000 00000000	255.255.0.0
/8	11111111 00000000 00000000 00000000	255.0.0.0
/22	11111111 11111111 11111100 00000000	255.255.252.0
/15	11111111 11111110 00000000 00000000	255.254.0.0
/27	11111111 11111111 11111111 11100000	255.255.255.224

Table 13-11 lists the answers to the practice problems from the earlier section "Practice Analyzing Subnet Masks."

Table 13-11   Answers to Problems from Earlier in the Chapter

	Problem	/P	Class	N	S	H	2^S	$2^H - 2$
1	8.1.4.5 255.255.254.0	23	A	8	15	9	32,768	510
2	130.4.102.1 255.255.255.0	24	B	16	8	8	256	254
3	199.1.1.100 255.255.255.0	24	C	24	0	8	N/A	254
4	130.4.102.1 255.255.252.0	22	B	16	6	10	64	1022
5	199.1.1.100 255.255.255.224	27	C	24	3	5	8	30

The following list reviews the problems:

1. For 8.1.4.5, the first octet (8) is in the 1–126 range, so it is a Class A address, with 8 network bits. Mask 255.255.254.0 converts to /23, so P – N = 15, for 15 subnet bits. H can be found by subtracting /P (23) from 32, for 9 host bits.

2. 130.4.102.1 is in the 128–191 range in the first octet, making it a Class B address, with N = 16 bits. 255.255.255.0 converts to /24, so the number of subnet bits is 24 – 16 = 8. With 24 prefix bits, the number of host bits is 32 – 24 = 8.

3. The third problem purposely shows a case where the mask does not create a subnet part of the address. The address, 199.1.1.100, has a first octet between 192 and 223, making it a Class C address with 24 network bits. The prefix version of the mask is /24, so the number of subnet bits is 24 – 24 = 0. The number of host bits is 32 minus the prefix length (24), for a total of 8 host bits. So in this case, the mask shows that the network engineer is using the default mask, which creates no subnet bits and no subnets.

4. With the same address as the second problem, 130.4.102.1 is a Class B address with N = 16 bits. This problem uses a different mask, 255.255.252.0, which converts to /22. This makes the number of subnet bits 22 − 16 = 6. With 22 prefix bits, the number of host bits is 32 − 22 = 10.

5. With the same address as the third problem, 199.1.1.100 is a Class C address with N = 24 bits. This problem uses a different mask, 255.255.255.224, which converts to /27. This makes the number of subnet bits 27 − 24 = 3. With 27 prefix bits, the number of host bits is 32 − 27 = 5.

Answers to Review Questions:

1 C **2** B **3** C **4** B **5** C **6** A **7** B and D **8** D **9** A and B

13

Chapter 14

Analyzing Existing Subnets

Often, a networking task begins with the discovery of the IP address and mask used by some host. Then, to understand how the internetwork routes packets to that host, you must find key pieces of information about the subnet, specifically:

- Subnet ID
- Subnet broadcast address
- Subnet's range of usable unicast IP addresses

This chapter discusses the concepts and math to take a known IP address and mask, and then fully describe a subnet by finding the values in this list. These specific tasks might well be the most important IP skills in the entire IP addressing and subnetting topics in this book, because these tasks might be the most commonly used tasks when operating and troubleshooting real networks.

This chapter covers the following exam topics:

Troubleshooting

Troubleshoot and correct common problems associated with IP addressing and host configurations

Foundation Topics

Defining a Subnet

An IP subnet is a subset of a classful network, created by choice of some network engineer. However, that engineer cannot pick just any arbitrary subset of addresses; instead, the engineer must follow certain rules, such as the following:

- The subnet contains a set of consecutive numbers.
- The subnet holds 2^H numbers, where H is the number of host bits defined by the subnet mask.
- Two special numbers in the range cannot be used as IP addresses:
  - The first (lowest) number acts as an identifier for the subnet (*subnet ID*).
  - The last (highest) number acts as a *subnet broadcast address*.
- The remaining addresses, whose values sit between the subnet ID and subnet broadcast address, are used as *unicast IP addresses*.

This section reviews and expands the basic concepts of the subnet ID, subnet broadcast address, and range of addresses in a subnet.

An Example with Network 172.16.0.0 and Four Subnets

Imagine that you work at the customer support center, where you receive all initial calls from users who have problems with their computer. You coach the user through finding her IP address and mask: 172.16.150.41, mask 255.255.192.0. One of the first and most common tasks you will do based on that information is to find the subnet ID of the subnet in which that address resides. (In fact, this subnet ID is sometimes called the *resident subnet*, because the IP address exists in or resides in that subnet.)

Before getting into the math, examine the mask (255.255.192.0) and classful network (172.16.0.0) for a moment. From the mask, based on what you learned in Chapter 13, "Analyzing Subnet Masks," you can find the structure of the addresses in the subnet, including the number of host and subnet bits. That analysis tells you that 2 subnet bits exist, meaning that there should be four (2^2) subnets. (If these concepts are not yet clear, review Chapter 13's section "How Masks Define the Format of Addresses.") Figure 14-1 shows the idea.

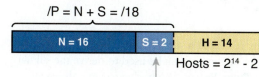

Figure 14-1 *Address Structure: Class B Network, /18 Mask*

> **NOTE** This chapter, like the others in this part of the book, assume that one mask is used throughout an entire classful network.

Because each subnet uses a single mask, all subnets of this single IP network must be the same size, because all subnets have the same structure. In this example, all four subnets will have the structure shown in the figure, so all four subnets will have $2^{14} - 2$ host addresses.

Next, consider the big picture of what happens with this example subnet design: The one Class B network now has four subnets of equal size. Conceptually, if you represent the entire Class B network as a number line, each subnet consumes one-fourth of the number line, as shown in Figure 14-2. Each subnet has a subnet ID—the numerically lowest number in the subnet—so it sits on the left of the subnet. And each subnet has a subnet broadcast address—the numerically highest number in the subnet—so it sits on the right side of the subnet.

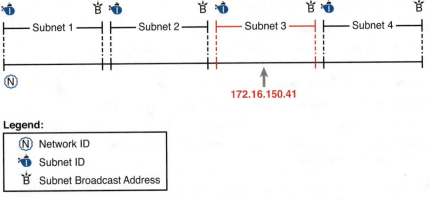

Figure 14-2   *Network 172.16.0.0, Divided into Four Equal Subnets*

The rest of this chapter focuses on how to take one IP address and mask and discover the details about that one subnet in which the address resides. In other words, you see how to find the resident subnet of an IP address. Again, using IP address 172.16.150.41 and mask 255.255.192.0 as an example, Figure 14-3 shows the resident subnet, along with the subnet ID and subnet broadcast address that bracket the subnet.

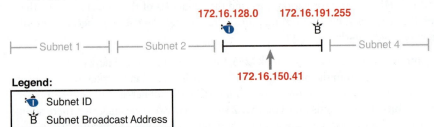

Figure 14-3   *Resident Subnet for 172.16.150.41, 255.255.192.0*

Subnet ID Concepts

A subnet ID is simply a number used to succinctly represent a subnet. When listed along with its matching subnet mask, the subnet ID identifies the subnet and can be used to derive the subnet broadcast address and range of addresses in the subnet. Rather than having to write down all these details about a subnet, you simply need to write down the subnet ID and mask, and you have enough information to fully describe the subnet.

The subnet ID appears in many places, but it is seen most often in IP routing tables. For example, when an engineer configures a router with its IP address and mask, the router calculates the subnet ID and puts a route into its routing table for that subnet. The router typically then advertises the subnet ID/mask combination to neighboring routers with some IP routing protocol. Eventually, all the routers in an enterprise learn about the subnet—again using the subnet ID and subnet mask combination—and display it in their routing tables. (You can display the contents of a router's IP routing table using the **show ip route** command.)

Unfortunately, the terminology related to subnets can sometimes cause problems. First, the terms *subnet ID*, *subnet number*, and *subnet address* are synonyms. Additionally, people sometimes simply say *subnet* when referring to both the idea of a subnet and the number that is used as the subnet ID. When talking about routing, people sometimes use the term *prefix* instead of *subnet*. The term *prefix* refers to the same idea as *subnet*; it just uses terminology from the classless addressing way to describe IP addresses, as discussed in Chapter 13's section "Classless and Classful Addressing."

The biggest terminology confusion arises between the terms *network* and *subnet*. In the real world, people often use these terms synonymously, and that is perfectly reasonable in some cases. In other cases, the specific meaning of these terms, and their differences, matter to what is being discussed.

For example, people often might say, "What is the network ID?" when they really want to know the subnet ID. In another case, they might want to know the Class A, B, or C network ID. So, when one engineer asks something like, "What's the net ID for 172.16.150.41 slash 18?" use the context to figure out whether he wants the literal classful network ID (172.16.0.0, in this case) or the literal subnet ID (172.16.128.0, in this case).

For the exams, be ready to notice when the terms *subnet* and *network* are used, and then use the context to figure out the specific meaning of the term in that case.

Table 14-1 summarizes the key facts about the subnet ID, along with the possible synonyms, for easier review and study.

Key Topic

Table 14-1   Summary of Subnet ID Key Facts

Definition	Number that represents the subnet
Numeric Value	First (smallest) number in the subnet
Literal Synonyms	Subnet number, subnet address, prefix, resident subnet
Common-Use Synonyms	Network, network ID, network number, network address
Typically Seen In...	Routing tables, documentation

Subnet Broadcast Address

The subnet broadcast address has two main roles: to be used as a destination IP address for the purpose of sending packets to all hosts in the subnet, and as a means to find the high end of the range of addresses in a subnet.

The original purpose for the subnet broadcast address was to give hosts a way to send one packet to all hosts in a subnet, and to do so efficiently. For example, a host in subnet A could send a packet with a destination address of subnet B's subnet broadcast address. The routers would forward this one packet just like a packet sent to a host in subnet B. After the packet arrives at the router connected to subnet B, that last router would then forward the packet to all hosts in subnet B, typically by encapsulating the packet in a data link layer broadcast frame. As a result, all hosts in host B's subnet would receive a copy of the packet.

The subnet broadcast address also helps you find the range of addresses in a subnet, because the broadcast address is the last (highest) number in a subnet's range of addresses. To find the low end of the range, calculate the subnet ID; to find the high end of the range, calculate the subnet broadcast address.

14

Table 14-2 summarizes the key facts about the subnet broadcast address, along with the possible synonyms, for easier review and study.

Key Topic

Table 14-2   Summary of Subnet Broadcast Address Key Facts

Definition	A reserved number in each subnet that, when used as the destination address of a packet, causes the routers to forward the packet to all hosts in that subnet
Numeric Value	Last (highest) number in the subnet
Literal Synonyms	Directed broadcast address
Broader-Use Synonyms	Network broadcast
Typically Seen In...	In calculations of the range of addresses in a subnet

Range of Usable Addresses

The engineers implementing an IP internetwork need to know the range of unicast IP addresses in each subnet. Before you can plan which addresses to use as statically assigned IP addresses, which to configure to be leased by the DHCP server, and which to reserve for later use, you need to know the range of usable addresses.

To find the range of usable IP addresses in a subnet, first find the subnet ID and the subnet broadcast address. Then, just add 1 to the fourth octet of the subnet ID to get the first (lowest) usable address, and subtract 1 from the fourth octet of the subnet broadcast address to get the last (highest) usable address in the subnet.

For example, Figure 14-3 showed subnet ID 172.16.128.0, mask /18. The first usable address is simply 1 more than the subnet ID (in this case, 172.16.128.1). That same figure showed a subnet broadcast address of 172.16.191.255, so the last usable address is 1 less, or 172.16.191.254.

Now that this section has described the concepts behind the numbers that collectively define a subnet, the rest of this chapter focuses on the math used to find these values.

Analyzing Existing Subnets: Binary

What does it mean to "analyze a subnet"? For this book, it means that you should be able to start with an IP address and mask and then define key facts about the subnet in which that address resides. Specifically, that means discovering the subnet ID, subnet broadcast address, and range of addresses. The analysis can also include the calculation of the number of addresses in the subnet as discussed in Chapter 13, but this chapter does not review those concepts.

Many methods exist to calculate the details about a subnet based on the address/mask. This section begins by discussing some calculations that use binary math, with the next section showing alternatives that use only decimal math. Although many people prefer the decimal method for going fast on the exams, the binary calculations ultimately give you a better understanding of IPv4 addressing. In particular, if you plan to move on to attain Cisco certifications beyond CCNA, you should take the time to understand the binary methods discussed in this section, even if you use the decimal methods for the exams.

Finding the Subnet ID: Binary

To start this section that uses binary, first consider a simple decimal math problem. The problem: Find the smallest three-digit decimal number that begins with 4. The answer, of course, is 400. And although most people would not have to break down the logic into steps, you know that 0 is the lowest-value digit you can use for any digit in a decimal number. You know that the first digit must be a 4, and the number is a three-digit number, so you just use the lowest value (0) for the last two digits, and find the answer: 400.

This same concept, applied to binary IP addresses, gives you the subnet ID. You have seen all the related concepts in other chapters, so if you already intuitively know how to find the subnet ID in binary, great! If not, the following key facts should help you see the logic:

All numbers in the subnet (subnet ID, subnet broadcast address, and all usable IP addresses) have the same value in the prefix part of the numbers.

The subnet ID is the lowest numeric value in the subnet, so its host part, in binary, is all 0s.

To find the subnet ID in binary, you take the IP address in binary and change all host bits to binary 0. To do so, you need to convert the IP address to binary. You also need to identify the prefix and host bits, which can be easily done by converting the mask (as needed) to prefix format. (Note that Appendix A, "Numeric Reference Tables," includes a decimal-binary conversion table.) Figure 14-4 shows the idea, using the same address/mask as in the earlier examples in this chapter: 172.16.150.41, mask /18.

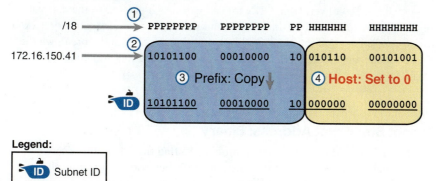

Legend:
 Subnet ID

Figure 14-4 *Binary Concept: Convert the IP Address to the Subnet ID*

Starting at the top of Figure 14-4, the format of the IP address is represented with 18 prefix (P) and 14 host (H) bits in the mask (Step 1). The second row (Step 2) shows the binary version of the IP address, converted from the dotted-decimal notation (DDN) value 172.16.150.41. (If you have not used the conversion table in Appendix A yet, it might be useful to double-check the conversion of all four octets based on the table.)

The next two steps show the action to copy the IP address's prefix bits (Step 3) and give the host bits a value of binary 0 (Step 4). This resulting number is the subnet ID (in binary).

The last step, not shown in Figure 14-4, is to convert the subnet ID from binary to decimal. This book shows that conversion as a separate step, in Figure 14-5, mainly because many people make a mistake at this step in the process. When converting a 32-bit number (like an IP address or IP subnet ID) back to an IPv4 DDN, you must follow this rule:

Convert 8 bits at a time from binary to decimal, regardless of the line between the prefix and host parts of the number.

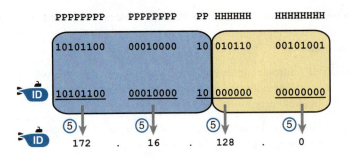

Figure 14-5   *Converting the Subnet ID from Binary to DDN*

Figure 14-5 shows this final step. Note that the third octet (the third set of 8 bits) has 2 bits in the prefix and 6 bits in the host part of the number, but the conversion occurs for all 8 bits.

> **NOTE**   You can do the numeric conversions in Figures 14-4 and 14-5 by relying on the conversion table in Appendix A. To convert from DDN to binary, for each octet, find the decimal value in the table and then write down the 8-bit binary equivalent. To convert from binary back to DDN, for each octet of 8 bits, find the matching binary entry in the table and write down the corresponding decimal value. For example, 172 converts to binary 10101100, and 00010000 converts to decimal 16.

Finding the Subnet Broadcast Address: Binary

Finding the subnet broadcast address uses a similar process. To find the subnet broadcast address, use the same binary process used to find the subnet ID, but instead of setting all the host bits to the lowest value (all binary 0s), set the host part to the highest value (all binary 1s). Figure 14-6 shows the concept.

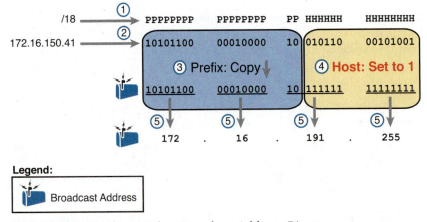

Figure 14-6   *Finding a Subnet Broadcast Address: Binary*

The process in Figure 14-6 demonstrates the same first three steps shown Figure 14-4. Specifically, it shows the identification of the prefix and host bits (Step 1), the results of converting the IP address 172.16.150.41 to binary (Step 2), and the copying of the prefix bits (first 18 bits, in this case). The difference occurs in the host bits on the right, changing all host bits (the last 14, in this case) to the largest possible value (all binary 1s). The final step converts the

32-bit subnet broadcast address to DDN format. Also, remember that with any conversion from DDN to binary or vice versa, the process always converts using 8 bits at a time. In particular, in this case, the entire third octet of binary 10111111 is converted back to decimal 191.

Binary Practice Problems

Figures 14-4 and 14-5 demonstrate a process to find the subnet ID using binary math. The following process summarizes those steps in written form for easier reference and practice:

Key Topic

Step 1. Convert the mask to prefix format to find the length of the prefix (/P) and the length of the host part (32 − P).

Step 2. Convert the IP address to its 32-bit binary equivalent.

Step 3. Copy the prefix bits of the IP address.

Step 4. Write down 0s for the host bits.

Step 5. Convert the resulting 32-bit number, 8 bits at a time, back to decimal.

The process to find the subnet broadcast address is exactly the same, except in Step 4, you set the bits to 1s, as seen in Figure 14-6.

Take a few moments and run through the following five practice problems on scratch paper. In each case, find both the subnet ID and subnet broadcast address. Also, record the prefix style mask:

1. 8.1.4.5, 255.255.0.0
2. 130.4.102.1, 255.255.255.0
3. 199.1.1.100, 255.255.255.0
4. 130.4.102.1, 255.255.252.0
5. 199.1.1.100, 255.255.255.224

Tables 14-3 through 14-7 show the results for the five different examples. The tables show the host bits in bold, and they include the binary version of the address and mask and the binary version of the subnet ID and subnet broadcast address.

Table 14-3   Subnet Analysis for Subnet with Address 8.1.4.5, Mask 255.255.0.0

Prefix Length	/16	11111111 11111111 00000000 00000000
Address	8.1.4.5	00001000 00000001 **00000100** **00000101**
Subnet ID	8.1.0.0	00001000 00000001 **00000000** **00000000**
Broadcast Address	8.1.255.255	00001000 00000001 **11111111** **11111111**

Table 14-4   Subnet Analysis for Subnet with Address 130.4.102.1, Mask 255.255.255.0

Prefix Length	/24	11111111 11111111 11111111 00000000
Address	130.4.102.1	10000010 00000100 01100110 **00000001**
Subnet ID	130.4.102.0	10000010 00000100 01100110 **00000000**
Broadcast Address	130.4.102.255	10000010 00000100 01100110 **11111111**

14

Table 14-5   Subnet Analysis for Subnet with Address 199.1.1.100, Mask 255.255.255.0

Prefix Length	/24	11111111 11111111 11111111 **00000000**
Address	199.1.1.100	11000111 00000001 00000001 **01100100**
Subnet ID	199.1.1.0	11000111 00000001 00000001 **00000000**
Broadcast Address	199.1.1.255	11000111 00000001 00000001 **11111111**

Table 14-6   Subnet Analysis for Subnet with Address 130.4.102.1, Mask 255.255.252.0

Prefix Length	/22	11111111 11111111 11111100 00000000
Address	130.4.102.1	10000010 00000100 011001**10** 00000001
Subnet ID	130.4.100.0	10000010 00000100 011001**00** 00000000
Broadcast Address	130.4.103.255	10000010 00000100 011001**11** 11111111

Table 14-7   Subnet Analysis for Subnet with Address 199.1.1.100, Mask 255.255.255.224

Prefix Length	/27	11111111 11111111 11111111 11100000
Address	199.1.1.100	11000111 00000001 00000001 011**00100**
Subnet ID	199.1.1.96	11000111 00000001 00000001 011**00000**
Broadcast Address	199.1.1.127	11000111 00000001 00000001 011**11111**

Shortcut for the Binary Process

The binary process described in this section so far requires that all four octets be converted to binary and then back to decimal. However, you can easily predict the results in at least three of the four octets, based on the DDN mask. You can then avoid the binary math in all but one octet and reduce the number of binary conversions you need to do.

First, consider an octet, and that octet only, whose DDN mask value is 255. The mask value of 255 converts to binary 11111111, which means that all 8 bits are prefix bits. Thinking through the steps in the process, at Step 2, you convert the address to some number. At Step 3, you copy the number. At Step 4, you convert the same 8-bit number back to decimal. All you did in those three steps, in this one octet, is convert from decimal to binary and convert the same number back to the same decimal value!

In short, the subnet ID (and subnet broadcast address) are equal to the IP address in octets for which the mask is 255.

For example, the resident subnet ID for 172.16.150.41, mask 255.255.192.0 is 172.16.128.0. The first two mask octets are 255. Rather than think about the binary math, you could just start by copying the address's value in those two octets: 172.16.

Another shortcut exists for octets whose DDN mask value is decimal 0, or binary 00000000. With a decimal mask value of 0, the math always results in a decimal 0 for the subnet ID, no matter the beginning value in the IP address. Specifically, just look at Steps 4 and 5 in this case: At Step 4, you would write down 8 binary 0s, and at Step 5, convert 00000000 back to decimal 0.

The following revised process steps take these two shortcuts into account. However, when the mask is neither 0 nor 255, the process requires the same conversions. At most, you have to do only one octet of the conversions. To find the subnet ID, apply the logic in these steps for each of the four octets:

Step 1. If the mask = 255, copy the decimal IP address for that octet.

Step 2. If the mask = 0, write down a decimal 0 for that octet.

Step 3. If the mask is neither 0 nor 255 in this octet, use the same binary logic as shown in the section "Finding the Subnet ID: Binary," earlier in this chapter.

Figure 14-7 shows an example of this process, again using 172.16.150.41, 255.255.192.0.

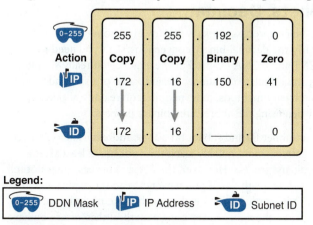

Legend:

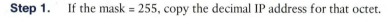

Figure 14-7 *Binary Shortcut Example*

A similar shortcut exists when finding the subnet broadcast address. For DDN mask octets equal to decimal 0, set the decimal subnet broadcast address value to 255 instead of 0, as noted in the following list:

Step 1. If the mask = 255, copy the decimal IP address for that octet.

Step 2. If the mask = 0, write down a decimal 255 for that octet.

Step 3. If the mask is neither 0 nor 255 in this octet, use the same binary logic as shown in the section "Finding the Subnet Broadcast Address: Binary," earlier in this chapter.

Brief Note About Boolean Math

So far, this chapter has described how humans can use binary math to find the subnet ID and subnet broadcast address. However, computers typically use an entirely different binary process to find the same values, using a branch of mathematics called *Boolean Algebra*. Computers already store the IP address and mask in binary form, so they do not have to do any conversions to and from decimal. Then, certain Boolean operations allow the computers to calculate the subnet ID and subnet broadcast address with just a few CPU instructions.

You do not need to know Boolean math to have a good understanding of IP subnetting. However, in case you are interested, computers use the following Boolean logic to find the subnet ID and subnet broadcast address, respectively:

Perform a *Boolean AND* of the IP address and mask. This process converts all host bits to binary 0.

Invert the mask, and then perform a *Boolean OR* of the IP address and inverted subnet mask. This process converts all host bits to binary 1s.

14

Finding the Range of Addresses

Finding the range of usable addresses in a subnet, after you know the subnet ID and subnet broadcast address, requires only simple addition and subtraction. To find the first (lowest) usable IP address in the subnet, simply add 1 to the fourth octet of the subnet ID. To find the last (highest) usable IP address, simply subtract 1 from the fourth octet of the subnet broadcast address.

Analyzing Existing Subnets: Decimal

Analyzing existing subnets using the binary process works well. However, some of the math takes time for most people, particularly the decimal-binary conversions. And you need to do the math quickly for the Cisco CCENT and CCNA exams. For the exams, you really should be able to take an IP address and mask, and calculate the subnet ID and range of usable addresses within about 15 seconds. When using binary methods, most people require a lot of practice to be able to find these answers, even when using the abbreviated binary process.

This section discusses how to find the subnet ID and subnet broadcast address using only decimal math. Most people can find the answers more quickly using this process, at least after a little practice, as compared with the binary process. However, the decimal process does not tell you anything about the meaning behind the math. So, if you have not read the earlier section "Analyzing Existing Subnets: Binary," it is worthwhile to read it for the sake of understanding subnetting. This section focuses on getting the right answer using a method that, after you have practiced, should be faster.

Analysis with Easy Masks

With three easy subnet masks in particular, finding the subnet ID and subnet broadcast address requires only easy logic and literally no math. Three easy masks exist:

255.0.0.0

255.255.0.0

255.255.255.0

These easy masks have only 255 and 0 in decimal. In comparison, difficult masks have one octet that has neither a 255 nor a 0 in the mask, which makes the logic more challenging.

> **NOTE** The terms *easy mask* and *difficult mask* are terms created for use in this book to describe the masks and the level of difficulty when working with each.

When the problem uses an easy mask, you can quickly find the subnet ID based on the IP address and mask in DDN format. Just use the following process for each of the four octets to find the subnet ID:

Step 1.   If the mask octet = 255, copy the decimal IP address.

Step 2.   If the mask octet = 0, write a decimal 0.

A similar simple process exists to find the subnet broadcast address, as follows:

Step 1.   If the mask octet = 255, copy the decimal IP address.

Step 2.   If the mask octet = 0, write a decimal 255.

Before moving to the next section, take some time to fill in the blanks in Table 14-8. Check your answers against Table 14-13 in the section "Answers to Earlier Practice Problems," later in this chapter. Complete the table by listing the subnet ID and subnet broadcast address.

Table 14-8   Practice Problems: Find Subnet ID and Broadcast, Easy Masks

	IP Address	Mask	Subnet ID	Broadcast Address
1	10.77.55.3	255.255.255.0		
2	172.30.99.4	255.255.255.0		
3	192.168.6.54	255.255.255.0		
4	10.77.3.14	255.255.0.0		
5	172.22.55.77	255.255.0.0		
6	1.99.53.76	255.0.0.0		

Predictability in the Interesting Octet

Although three masks are easier to work with (255.0.0.0, 255.255.0.0, and 255.255.255.0), the rest make the decimal math a little more difficult, so we call these masks difficult masks. With difficult masks, one octet is neither a 0 nor a 255. The math in the other three octets is easy and boring, so this book calls the one octet with the more difficult math the *interesting octet*.

If you take some time to think about different problems and focus on the interesting octet, you will begin to see a pattern. This section takes you through that examination so that you can learn how to predict the pattern, in decimal, and find the subnet ID.

First, the subnet ID value has a predictable decimal value because of the assumption that a single subnet mask is used for all subnets of a single classful network. The chapters in this part of the book assume that, for a given classful network, the design engineer chooses to use a single subnet mask for all subnets. (Refer to Chapter 11's section "One Size Subnet Fits All—Or Not" for more details.)

To see that predictability, consider some planning information written down by a network engineer, as shown in Figure 14-8. The figure shows four different masks the engineer is considering using in an IPv4 network, along with Class B network 172.16.0.0. The figure shows the third-octet values for the subnet IDs that would be created when using mask 255.255.128.0, 255.255.192.0, 255.255.224.0, and 255.255.240.0, from top to bottom in the figure.

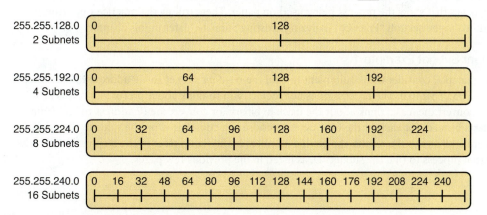

Figure 14-8 *Numeric Patterns in the Interesting Octet*

First, to explain the figure further, look at the top row of the figure. If the engineer uses 255.255.128.0 as the mask, the mask creates two subnets, with subnet IDs 172.16.0.0 and 172.16.128.0. If the engineer uses mask 255.255.192.0, the mask creates four subnets, with subnet IDs 172.16.0.0, 172.16.64.0, 172.16.128.0, and 172.16.192.0.

If you take the time to look at the figure, the patterns become obvious. In this case:

Mask: 255.255.128.0   Pattern: Multiples of 128

Mask: 255.255.192.0   Pattern: Multiples of 64

Mask: 255.255.224.0   Pattern: Multiples of 32

Mask: 255.255.240.0   Pattern: Multiples of 16

To find the subnet ID, you just need a way to figure out what the pattern is. If you start with an IP address and mask, just find the subnet ID closest to the IP address, without going over, as discussed in the next section.

Finding the Subnet ID: Difficult Masks

The following written process lists all the steps for find the subnet ID, using only decimal math. This process adds to the earlier process used with easy masks. For each octet:

Step 1.   If the mask octet = 255, copy the decimal IP address.

Step 2.   If the mask octet = 0, write a decimal 0.

Step 3.   If the mask is neither, refer to this octet as the *interesting octet*:

   A.   Calculate the *magic number* as 256 – mask.

   B.   Set the subnet ID's value to the multiple of the magic number that is closest to the IP address without going over.

The process uses two new terms created for this book: *magic number* and *interesting octet*. The term *interesting octet* refers to the octet identified at Step 3 in the process; in other words, it is the octet with the mask that is neither 255 nor 0. Step 3A then uses the term *magic number*, which is derived from the DDN mask. Conceptually, the magic number is the number you add to one subnet ID to get the next subnet ID in order, as shown in Figure 14-8. Numerically, it can be found by subtracting the DDN mask's value, in the interesting octet, from 256, as mentioned in Step 3A.

The best way to learn this process is to see it happen. In fact, if you can, stop reading now, use the DVD accompanying this book, and watch the videos about finding the subnet ID with a difficult mask. These videos demonstrate this process. You can also use the examples on the next few pages that show the process being used on paper. Then, follow the practice opportunities outlined in the section "Practice Analyzing Existing Subnets," later in this chapter.

Resident Subnet Example 1

For example, consider the requirement to find the resident subnet for IP address 130.4.102.1, mask 255.255.240.0. The process does not require you to think about prefix bits versus host bits, convert the mask, think about the mask in binary, or convert the IP address to and from binary. Instead, for each of the four octets, choose an action based on the value in the mask. Figure 14-9 shows the results; the circled numbers in the figure refer to the step numbers in the written process to find the subnet ID, as listed in the previous few pages.

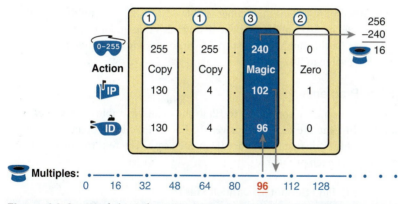

Figure 14-9 *Find the Subnet ID: 130.4.102.1, 255.255.240.0*

First, examine the three uninteresting octets (1, 2, and 4, in this example). The process keys on the mask, and the first two octets have a mask value of 255, so simply copy the IP address to the place where you intend to write down the subnet ID. The fourth octet has a mask value 0, so write down a 0 for the fourth octet of the subnet ID.

The most challenging logic occurs in the interesting octet, which is the third octet in this example, because of the mask value 240 in that octet. For this octet, Step 3A asks you to calculate the magic number as 256 – mask. That means you take the mask's value in the interesting octet (240, in this case) and subtract it from 256: 256 – 240 = 16. The subnet ID's value in this octet must be a multiple of decimal 16, in this case.

Step 3B then asks you to find the multiples of the magic number (16, in this case) and choose the one closest to the IP address without going over. Specifically, that means that you should mentally calculate the multiples of the magic number, starting at 0. (Do not forget to start at 0!) Counting, starting at 0: 0, 16, 32, 48, 64, 80, 96, 112, and so on. Then, find the multiple closest to the IP address value in this octet (102, in this case), without going over 102. So, as shown in Figure 14-9, you make the third octet's value 96 to complete the subnet ID of 130.4.96.0.

Resident Subnet Example 2

Consider another example: 192.168.5.77, mask 255.255.255.224. Figure 14-10 shows the results.

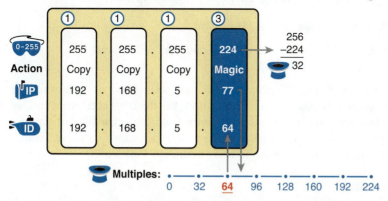

Figure 14-10 *Resident Subnet for 192.168.5.77, 255.255.255.224*

The three uninteresting octets (1, 2, and 3, in this case) require only a little thought. For each octet, each with a mask value of 255, just copy the IP address.

14

For the interesting octet, at Step 3A, the magic number is 256 – 224 = 32. The multiples of the magic number are 0, 32, 64, 96, and so on. Because the IP address value in the fourth octet is 77, in this case, the multiple must be the number closest to 77 without going over; therefore, the subnet ID ends with 64, for a value of 192.168.5.64.

Resident Subnet Practice Problems

Before moving to the next section, take some time to fill in the blanks in Table 14-9. Check your answers against Table 14-14 in the section "Answers to Earlier Practice Problems," later in this chapter. Complete the table by listing the subnet ID in each case. The text following Table 14-14 also lists explanations for each problem.

Table 14-9   Practice Problems: Find Subnet ID, Difficult Masks

Problem	IP Address	Mask	Subnet ID
1	10.77.55.3	255.248.0.0	
2	172.30.99.4	255.255.192.0	
3	192.168.6.54	255.255.255.252	
4	10.77.3.14	255.255.128.0	
5	172.22.55.77	255.255.254.0	
6	1.99.53.76	255.255.255.248	

Finding the Subnet Broadcast Address: Difficult Masks

To find a subnet's broadcast address, a similar process can be used. For simplicity, this process begins with the subnet ID, rather than the IP address. If you happen to start with an IP address instead, use the processes in this chapter to first find the subnet ID, and then use the following process to find the subnet broadcast address for that same subnet. For each octet:

Step 1.   If the mask octet = 255, copy the subnet ID.

Step 2.   If the mask octet = 0, write a 255.

Step 3.   If the mask is neither, identify this octet as the *interesting octet*:

    A. Calculate the *magic number* as 256 – mask.

    B. Take the subnet ID's value, add the magic number, and subtract 1 (ID + magic – 1).

As with the similar process used to find the subnet ID, you have several options for how to best learn and internalize the process. If you can, stop reading now, use the DVD accompanying this book, and watch the videos about finding the subnet broadcast address with a difficult mask. Also, look at the examples in this section, which show the process being used on paper. Then, follow the practice opportunities outlined in the section "Additional Practice."

Subnet Broadcast Example 1

The first example continues the first example from the section "Finding the Subnet ID: Difficult Masks," earlier in this chapter, as demonstrated in Figure 14-9. That example started with the IP address/mask of 130.4.102.1, 255.255.240.0, and showed how to find subnet ID 130.4.96.0. Figure 14-11 now begins with that subnet ID and the same mask.

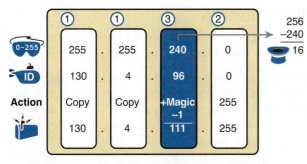

Figure 14-11   *Find the Subnet Broadcast: 130.4.96.0, 255.255.240.0*

First, examine the three uninteresting octets (1, 2, and 4). The process keys on the mask, and the first two octets have a mask value of 255, so simply copy the subnet ID to the place where you intend to write down the subnet broadcast address. The fourth octet has a mask value 0, so write down a 255 for the fourth octet.

The logic related to the interesting octet occurs in the third octet in this example, because of the mask value 240. First, Step 3A asks you to calculate the magic number, as 256 − mask. (If you had already calculated the subnet ID using the decimal process in this book, you should already know the magic number.) At Step 3B, you take the subnet ID's value (96), add magic (16), and subtract 1, for a total of 111. That makes the subnet broadcast address 130.4.111.255.

Subnet Broadcast Example 2

Again, this example continues an earlier example, from the section "Resident Subnet Example 2," as demonstrated in Figure 14-10. That example started with the IP address/mask of 192.168.5.77, mask 255.255.255.224 and showed how to find subnet ID 192.168.5.64. Figure 14-12 now begins with that subnet ID and the same mask.

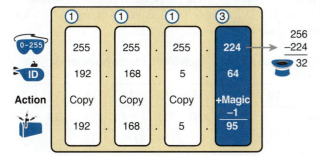

Figure 14-12   *Find the Subnet Broadcast: 192.168.5.64, 255.255.255.224*

First, examine the three uninteresting octets (1, 2, and 3). The process keys on the mask, and the first three octets have a mask value of 255, so simply copy the subnet ID to the place where you intend to write down the subnet broadcast address.

The interesting logic occurs in the interesting octet, the fourth octet in this example, because of the mask value 224. First, Step 3A asks you to calculate the magic number, as 256 − mask. (If you had already calculated the subnet ID, it is the same magic number, because the same mask is used.) At Step 3B, you take the subnet ID's value (64), add magic (32), and subtract 1, for a total of 95. That makes the subnet broadcast address 192.168.5.95.

Subnet Broadcast Address Practice Problems

Before moving to the next section, take some time to do several practice problems on a scratch piece of paper. Go back to Table 14-9, which lists IP addresses and masks, and practice by finding the subnet broadcast address for all the problems in that table. Then check your answers against Table 14-15 in the section "Answers to Earlier Practice Problems," later in this chapter.

14

Practice Analyzing Existing Subnets

Before moving to the next chapter, practice until you get the right answer most of the time—but use any tools you want and take all the time you need. Then, you can move on with your reading.

However, before taking the exam, practice until you master the topics in this chapter and can move pretty fast. As for time, you should be able to find the subnet ID, based on an IP address and mask, in around 15 seconds. You should also strive to start with a subnet ID/mask, and find the broadcast address and range of addresses, in another 10–15 seconds. Table 14-10 summarizes the key concepts and suggestions for this two-phase approach.

Table 14-10   Keep-Reading and Take-Exam Goals for This Chapter's Topics

Time Frame	Before Moving to the Next Chapter	Before Taking the Exam
Focus On...	Learning how	Being correct and fast
Tools Allowed	All	Your brain and a notepad
Goal: Accuracy	90% correct	100% correct
Goal: Speed	Any speed	20–30 seconds

A Choice: Memorize or Calculate

As described in this chapter, the decimal processes to find the subnet ID and subnet broadcast address do require some calculation, including the calculation of the magic number (256 – mask). The processes also use a DDN mask, so if an exam question gives you a prefix-style mask, you need to convert to DDN format before using the process in this book.

Over the years, some people have told me they prefer to memorize a table to find the magic number. These tables could list the magic number for different DDN masks and prefix masks, so you avoid converting from the prefix mask to DDN. Table 14-11 shows an example of such a table. Feel free to ignore this table, use it, or make your own.

Table 14-11   Reference Table: DDN Mask Values, Binary Equivalent, Magic Numbers, and Prefixes

Prefix, interesting octet 2	/9	/10	/11	/12	/13	/14	/15	/16
Prefix, interesting octet 3	/17	/18	/19	/20	/21	/22	/23	/24
Prefix, interesting octet 4	/25	/26	/27	/28	/29	/30		
Magic number	128	64	32	16	8	4	2	1
DDN mask in the interesting octet	128	192	224	240	248	252	254	255

Additional Practice

This section lists several options for additional practice:

- DVD Appendix F, "Practice for Chapter 14: Analyzing Existing Subnets," has some additional practice problems. This appendix also includes explanations about how to find the answer of each problem.

- Create your own problems. Many subnet calculators list the number of network, subnet, and host bits when you type in an IP address and mask, so make up an IP address and mask on paper, and find the subnet ID and range of addresses. Then, to check your work, use any subnet calculator. (Check the author's web pages for this book, as listed in the Introduction, for some suggested calculators.)

Review Activities

Chapter Summary

- An IP subnet is a subset of a classful network created by choice of some network engineer. The engineer must follow these rules:

  - The subnet must contain a set of consecutive numbers.

  - The subnet must hold the number of host bits defined by the subnet mask.

  - Two special numbers in the range cannot be used as IP addresses:

    - The first (lowest) number acts as an identifier for the subnet (*subnet ID*).

    - The last (highest) number acts as a *subnet broadcast address*.

  - The remaining addresses, whose values sit between the subnet ID and subnet broadcast address, are used as *unicast IP addresses*.

- A subnet ID is a number used to succinctly represent a subnet. When listed along with its matching subnet mask, the subnet ID identifies the subnet and can be used to derive the subnet broadcast address and range of addresses in the subnet.

- The subnet ID appears in many places but it is seen most often in IP routing tables.

- The terms *subnet ID*, *subnet number*, and *subnet address* are synonyms.

- The subnet broadcast address has two main roles: to be used as a destination IP address for the purpose of sending packets to all hosts in the subnet, and as a means to finding the high end of the range of addresses in a subnet.

- To find the range of usable IP addresses in a subnet, first find the subnet ID and the subnet broadcast address. Then, just add 1 to the fourth octet of the subnet ID to get the first (lowest) usable address, and subtract 1 from the fourth octet of the subnet broadcast address to get the last (highest) usable address in the subnet.

- All numbers in the subnet (subnet ID, subnet broadcast address, and all usable IP addresses) have the same value in the prefix part of the numbers.

- The subnet ID is the lowest numeric value in the subnet, so its host part, in binary, is all 0s.

- The following process summarizes a process to find the subnet ID using binary math:

  1. Convert the mask to prefix format to find the length of the prefix (/P) and the length of the host part (32 − P).

  2. Convert the IP address to its 32-bit binary equivalent.

  3. Copy the prefix bits of the IP address.

  4. Write down 0s for the host bits.

  5. Convert the resulting 32-bit number, 8 bits at a time, back to decimal.

- The process of finding the subnet broadcast address is exactly the same, except in Step 4, set the bits to 1s.

14

Review Questions

Answer these review questions. You can find the answers at the bottom of the last page of the chapter. For thorough explanations, see DVD Appendix C, "Answers to Review Questions."

1. When thinking about an IP address using classful addressing rules, an address can have three parts: network, subnet, and host. If you examined all the addresses in one subnet, in binary, which of the following answers correctly states which of the three parts of the addresses will be equal among all addresses? Pick the best answer.

   A. Network part only

   B. Subnet part only

   C. Host part only

   D. Network and subnet parts

   E. Subnet and host parts

2. Which of the following statements are true regarding the binary subnet ID, subnet broadcast address, and host IP address values in any single subnet? (Choose two.)

   A. The host part of the broadcast address is all binary 0s.

   B. The host part of the subnet ID is all binary 0s.

   C. The host part of a usable IP address can have all binary 1s.

   D. The host part of any usable IP address must not be all binary 0s.

3. Which of the following is the resident subnet ID for IP address 10.7.99.133/24?

   A. 10.0.0.0

   B. 10.7.0.0

   C. 10.7.99.0

   D. 10.7.99.128

4. Which of the following is the resident subnet for IP address 192.168.44.97/30?

   A. 192.168.44.0

   B. 192.168.44.64

   C. 192.168.44.96

   D. 192.168.44.128

5. Which of the following is the subnet broadcast address for the subnet in which IP address 172.31.77.201/27 resides?

   A. 172.31.201.255

   B. 172.31.255.255

   C. 172.31.77.223

   D. 172.31.77.207

6. A fellow engineer tells you to configure the DHCP server to lease the last 100 usable IP addresses in subnet 10.1.4.0/23. Which of the following IP addresses could be leased as a result of your new configuration?

   A. 10.1.4.156

   B. 10.1.4.254

   C. 10.1.5.200

   D. 10.1.7.200

   E. 10.1.255.200

7. A fellow engineer tells you to configure the DHCP server to lease the first 20 usable IP addresses in subnet 192.168.9.96/27. Which of the following IP addresses could be leased as a result of your new configuration?

   A. 192.168.9.126

   B. 192.168.9.110

   C. 192.168.9.1

   D. 192.168.9.119

Review All the Key Topics

Review the most important topics from this chapter, noted with the Key Topic icon. Table 14-12 lists these key topics and where each is discussed.

Table 14-12   Key Topics for Chapter 14

Key Topic Element	Description	Page Number
List	Definition of a subnet's key numbers	327
Table 14-1	Key facts about the subnet ID	329
Table 14-2	Key facts about the subnet broadcast address	330
List	Steps to use binary math to find the subnet ID	333
List	General steps to use binary and decimal math to find the subnet ID	335
List	Steps to use decimal and binary math to find the subnet broadcast address	335
List	Steps to use only decimal math to find the subnet ID	338
List	Steps to use only decimal math to find the subnet broadcast address	340

Complete the Tables and Lists from Memory

Print a copy of DVD Appendix M, "Memory Tables," or at least the section for this chapter, and complete the tables and lists from memory. DVD Appendix N, "Memory Tables Answer Key," includes completed tables and lists for you to check your work.

Definitions of Key Terms

After your first reading of the chapter, try to define these key terms, but do not be concerned about getting them all correct at that time. Chapter 30 directs you in how to use these terms for late-stage preparation for the exam.

resident subnet, subnet ID, subnet number, subnet address, subnet broadcast address

Practice

If you have not done so already, practice finding the subnet ID, range of addresses, and subnet broadcast address associated with an IP address and mask. Refer to the earlier section "Practice Analyzing Existing Subnets" for suggestions.

Answers to Earlier Practice Problems

This chapter includes practice problems spread around different locations in the chapter. The answers are located in Tables 14-13, 14-14, and 14-15.

Table 14-13   Answers to Problems in Table 14-8

	IP Address	Mask	Subnet ID	Broadcast Address
1	10.77.55.3	255.255.255.0	10.77.55.0	10.77.55.255
2	172.30.99.4	255.255.255.0	172.30.99.0	172.30.99.255
3	192.168.6.54	255.255.255.0	192.168.6.0	192.168.6.255
4	10.77.3.14	255.255.0.0	10.77.0.0	10.77.255.255
5	172.22.55.77	255.255.0.0	172.22.0.0	172.22.255.255
6	1.99.53.76	255.0.0.0	1.0.0.0	1.255.255.255

Table 14-14   Answers to Problems in Table 14-9

	IP Address	Mask	Subnet ID
1	10.77.55.3	255.248.0.0	10.72.0.0
2	172.30.99.4	255.255.192.0	172.30.64.0
3	192.168.6.54	255.255.255.252	192.168.6.52
4	10.77.3.14	255.255.128.0	10.77.0.0
5	172.22.55.77	255.255.254.0	172.22.54.0
6	1.99.53.76	255.255.255.248	1.99.53.72

The following list explains the answers for Table 14-14:

1. The second octet is the interesting octet, with magic number 256 − 248 = 8. The multiples of 8 include 0, 8, 16, 24, ..., 64, 72, and 80. 72 is closest to the IP address value in that same octet (77) without going over, making the subnet ID 10.72.0.0.

2. The third octet is the interesting octet, with magic number 256 − 192 = 64. The multiples of 64 include 0, 64, 128, and 192. 64 is closest to the IP address value in that same octet (99) without going over, making the subnet ID 172.30.64.0.

3. The fourth octet is the interesting octet, with magic number 256 − 252 = 4. The multiples of 4 include 0, 4, 8, 12, 16, ..., 48, and 52, 56. 52 is the closest to the IP address value in that same octet (54) without going over, making the subnet ID 192.168.6.52.

4. The third octet is the interesting octet, with magic number 256 − 128 = 128. Only two multiples exist that matter: 0 and 128. 0 is the closest to the IP address value in that same octet (3) without going over, making the subnet ID 10.77.0.0.

5. The third octet is the interesting octet, with magic number 256 − 254 = 2. The multiples of 2 include 0, 2, 4, 6, 8, and so on—essentially all even numbers. 54 is closest to the IP address value in that same octet (55) without going over, making the subnet ID 172.22.54.0.

6. The fourth octet is the interesting octet, with magic number 256 − 248 = 8. The multiples of 8 include 0, 8, 16, 24, ..., 64, 72, and 80. 72 is closest to the IP address value in that same octet (76) without going over, making the subnet ID 1.99.53.72.

Table 14-15 Answers to Problems in the Section "Subnet Broadcast Address Practice Problems"

	Subnet ID	Mask	Broadcast Address
1	10.72.0.0	255.248.0.0	10.79.255.255
2	172.30.64.0	255.255.192.0	172.30.127.255
3	192.168.6.52	255.255.255.252	192.168.6.55
4	10.77.0.0	255.255.128.0	10.77.127.255
5	172.22.54.0	255.255.254.0	172.22.55.255
6	1.99.53.72	255.255.255.248	1.99.53.79

The following list explains the answers for Table 14-15:

1. The second octet is the interesting octet. Completing the three easy octets means that the broadcast address in the interesting octet will be 10.____.255.255. With a magic number 256 − 248 = 8, the second octet will be 72 (from the subnet ID), plus 8, minus 1, or 79.

2. The third octet is the interesting octet. Completing the three easy octets means that the broadcast address in the interesting octet will be 172.30.____.255. With magic number 256 − 192 = 64, the interesting octet will be 64 (from the subnet ID), plus 64 (the magic number), minus 1, for 127.

3. The fourth octet is the interesting octet. Completing the three easy octets means that the broadcast address in the interesting octet will be 192.168.6.____. With magic number 256 − 252 = 4, the interesting octet will be 52 (the subnet ID value), plus 4 (the magic number), minus 1, or 55.

4. The third octet is the interesting octet. Completing the three easy octets means that the broadcast address will be 10.77.____.255. With magic number 256 − 128 = 128, the interesting octet will be 0 (the subnet ID value), plus 128 (the magic number), minus 1, or 127.

5. The third octet is the interesting octet. Completing the three easy octets means that the broadcast address will be 172.22.____.255. With magic number 256 − 254 = 2, the broadcast address in the interesting octet will be 54 (the subnet ID value), plus 2 (the magic number), minus 1, or 55.

6. The fourth octet is the interesting octet. Completing the three easy octets means that the broadcast address will be 1.99.53.____. With magic number 256 − 248 = 8, the broadcast address in the interesting octet will be 72 (the subnet ID value), plus 8 (the magic number), minus 1, or 79.

Answers to Review Questions:

1 D **2** B and D **3** C **4** C **5** C **6** C **7** B

14

Part III Review

Keep track of your part review progress with the checklist in Table P3-1. Details on each task follow the table.

Table P3-1 Part III Part Review Checklist

Activity	First Date Completed	Second Date Completed
Repeat all Chapter Review Questions		
Answer Part Review Questions		
Review Key Topics		
Create Subnet Terms Mind Map A		
Create Subnet Math Mind Map B		

Repeat All Chapter Review Questions

For this task, answer the chapter review questions again for the chapters in this part of the book, using the PCPT software. Refer to the Introduction to this book, heading "How to View Only Chapter Review Questions by Part," for help with how to make the PCPT software show you chapter review questions for this part only.

Answer Part Review Questions

For this task, answer the Part Review questions for this part of the book, using the PCPT software. Refer to the Introduction to this book, heading "How to View Only Part Review Questions by Part," for help with how to make the PCPT software show you Part Review questions for this part only.

Review Key Topics

Browse back through the chapters, and look for the Key Topic icons. If you do not remember some details, take the time to reread those topics.

Create Terminology Mind Map

The topic of IPv4 addressing and subnetting happens to have many terms that are literal synonyms, many terms with similar meanings, along with terms that describe something about another term. This first Part Review mind map (Part III, Mind Map A) asks you to organize all IP addressing and subnetting terms you remember into four topic areas, but inside each area, subdivide terms as to whether they are either a synonym, a similar term, or a description.

Figure P3-1 shows the beginnings of one branch of the mind map to give you the general idea. For this branch, you would just remember any terms related to "IP address" and place them into one of these three categories. Your map can of course look different. As usual, first do this exercise without the book or your notes. Later, when you do look at the book again, make sure that you have at least included all the key terms from the ends of the chapters.

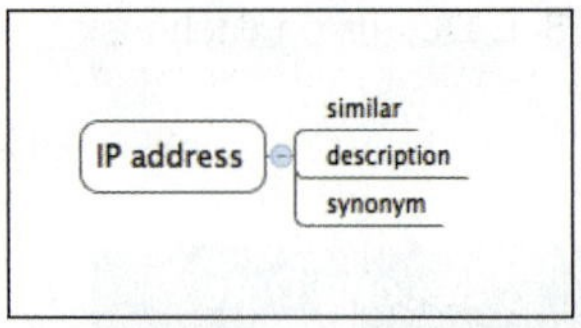

```
              similar
IP address ─┤ description
              synonym
```

Figure P3-1   *Sample Beginning Point for Part III Mind Map A*

> **NOTE**   For more information on mind mapping, refer to the Introduction, in the section "About Mind Maps."

Create Subnet Math Mind Maps

This book part explains several types of subnetting problems that you can analyze and solve. The next mind map exercise helps to review the big ideas of what each type of problem does. This review does not focus on the details of how to find the answer to any one problem, leaving that for all the other practice suggestions included near the end of Chapters 12, 13, and 14. Those chapters discussed four major types of problems that can be solved with some arithmetic:

■ **Classful Facts:** Based on an IP address, find many facts about the associated classful IP network.

■ **Mask Conversion:** Given a subnet mask, find the equivalent mask in the other two mask formats.

■ **Mask Analysis:** Given a subnet mask, address, and an assumption, find the number of hosts per subnet and the number of subnets.

■ **Subnet Analysis:** Given a subnet mask and address, find the numbers that define the resident subnet (the subnet ID, subnet broadcast address, and range of usable IP addresses).

Create a mind map with four branches, one for each topic in the list. For each branch, begin with the core concept, and branch into three subtopics:

■ **Given:** The information you have and the assumptions you make to start the problem.

■ **Process:** The information or terms used during the process. Do not write the specific steps of the process; the goal here is just to make memory connections so that you know it is this process, and not some other process.

■ **Result:** The facts you determine by doing the problem.

Figure P3-2 shows an example (incomplete) map for the classful facts problem, just to show the basic idea.

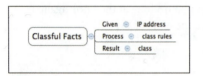

Figure P3-2   *Sample Mind Map for Part III Mind Map B*

If you do choose to use mind map software, rather than paper, you might want to remember where you stored your mind map files; Table P3-2 lists the mind maps for this part review and a place to record those filenames.

Table P3-2   Configuration Mind Maps for Part III Review

Map	Description	Where You Saved It
1	Mind Map A: Subnetting Terms	
2	Mind Map B: Subnetting Math	

Appendix O, "Mind Map Solutions," lists sample mind map answers, but as usual, your mind maps can and will look different.

Implementing IPv4 in a network begins with the configuration of IPv4 addresses on hosts and routers, along with IPv4 routing protocols that learn routes to the subnets in that network. Part IV walks you through these details. Chapter 15 focuses on Cisco routers as an end to themselves, with Chapter 16 focusing on router IPv4 address and static IPv4 route configuration. With those details configured, Chapter 17 focuses on adding OSPF configuration to the routers so that the routers learn routes. The final chapter in this part (18) then discusses implementing IPv4 on hosts and describes how hosts think about IPv4, with some discussion of basic testing tools to test all the features discussed in this part.

Part IV

Implementing IP Version 4

Chapter 15

Operating Cisco Routers

This chapter focuses on how to install an enterprise-class Cisco router, with just enough configuration to get the router working. You might recall, when you buy a Cisco LAN switch, you can just plug in all the Ethernet cables, power on the switch, and by default, the switch works. However, the Cisco routers used by companies require at least some configuration before the router will start routing IPv4 packets. In particular, the router needs to be told what interfaces to use and what IP address to use on each of those interfaces.

This chapter breaks the topics into two major headings. The first discusses the physical installation of an enterprise-class Cisco router. The second section looks at the command-line interface (CLI) on a Cisco router, which has the same look and feel as the Cisco switch CLI. This section first lists the similarities between a switch and router CLI, and then introduces the configuration required to make the router start forwarding IP packets on its interfaces.

This chapter covers the following exam topics:

Operation of IP Data Networks

Recognize the purpose and functions of various network devices such as Routers, Switches, Bridges, and Hubs.

Select the components required to meet a given network specification.

Identify the appropriate media, cables, ports, and connectors to connect Cisco network devices to other network devices and hosts in a LAN

IP Routing Technologies

Configure and verify utilizing the CLI to set basic Router configuration

Network Device Security

Configure and verify network device security features such as

Device password security

Enable secret vs enable

Troubleshooting

Troubleshoot and correct common problems associated with IP addressing and host configurations.

Installing Cisco Routers

Routers collectively provide the main feature of the network layer—the capability to forward packets end to end through a network. As introduced in Chapter 4, "Fundamentals of IPv4 Addressing and Routing," routers forward packets by connecting to various physical network links, like Ethernet, serial links, and Frame Relay, and then using Layer 3 routing logic to choose where to forward each packet. As a reminder, Chapter 2, "Fundamentals of Ethernet LANs," covered the details of making those physical connections to Ethernet networks, while Chapter 3, "Fundamentals of WANs," covered the basics of cabling with WAN links.

This section examines some of the details of router installation and cabling, first from the enterprise perspective and then from the perspective of connecting a typical small office/home office (SOHO) to an ISP using high-speed Internet.

Installing Enterprise Routers

A typical enterprise network has a few centralized sites as well as lots of smaller remote sites. To support devices at each site (the computers, IP phones, printers, and other devices), the network includes at least one LAN switch at each site. Additionally, each site has a router, which connects to the LAN switch and to some WAN link. The WAN link provides connectivity from each remote site, back to the central site, and to other sites through the connection to the central site.

Figures 15-1 and 15-2 show contrasting ways to draw parts of an enterprise network. Both show a typical branch office on the left, with a router and some end-user PCs. The central site, on the right, has basically the same components, plus some servers. The sites connect using a point-to-point serial link connecting the two routers. The first figure omits many of the cabling details, making the figure more useful when you want to discuss general Layer 3 concepts; the second figure shows the cabling details.

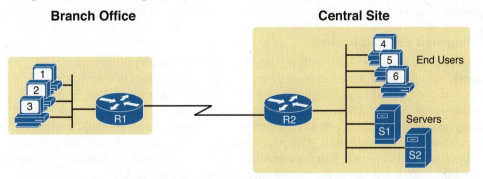

Figure 15-1 *Generic Enterprise Network Diagram*

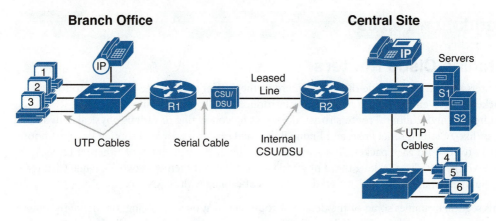

Figure 15-2 *More Detailed Cabling Diagram for the Same Enterprise Network*

The Ethernet cables in Figure 15-2 should be familiar. In particular, routers use the same Ethernet cabling pinouts as PCs, so each router uses a UTP cable with a straight-through pinout.

Next, consider the hardware on the ends of the serial link, in particular where the channel service unit/data service unit (CSU/DSU) hardware resides on each end of the serial link. It sits either outside the router as a separate device (as shown on the left) or integrated into the router's serial interface hardware (as shown on the right). Most new installations today include the CSU/DSU in the router's serial interface.

Finally, the serial link requires some cabling inside the same wiring closet or other space between where the telco serial line terminates and where the router sits on a shelf or in a rack. The WAN cable installed by the telco typically has an RJ-48 connector, which is the same size and shape as an RJ-45 connector. The telco cable with the RJ-48 connector inserts into the CSU/DSU. In the example of Figure 15-2, at the central site, the telco cable connects directly into the router's serial interface. At the branch office router, the cable connects to the external CSU/DSU, which then connects to the router serial interface using some other serial cable. (As a reminder, Chapter 3's section "Leased Line Cabling" introduced the basics of this cabling.)

Cisco Integrated Services Routers

Product vendors, including Cisco, typically provide several different types of router hardware, including some routers that just do routing, with other routers that serve other functions in addition to routing. A typical enterprise branch office needs a router for WAN/LAN connectivity, and a LAN switch to provide a high-performance local network and connectivity into the router and WAN. Many branches also need Voice over IP (VoIP) services and several security services as well. (One popular security service, Virtual Private Networking [VPN], is covered in Chapter 5, "Fundamentals of TCP/IP Transport and Applications.") Rather than require multiple separate devices at one site, as shown in Figure 15-2, Cisco offers single devices that act as both router and switch, and provide other functions as well.

Following that concept further, Cisco offers several router model series in which the routers support many other functions. In fact, Cisco has several router product series called Integrated Services Routers (ISR), with the name emphasizing the fact that many functions are integrated into a single device. However, for the sake of learning and understanding the different functions, the CCENT and CCNA exams focus on using a separate switch and separate router, which provides a much cleaner path for learning the basics.

Figure 15-3 shows a couple of pictures of the Cisco 2901 ISR, with some of the more important features highlighted. The top part of the figure shows a full view of the back of the router.

This model comes with two built-in Gigabit Ethernet interfaces and four modular slots that allow you to add small cards called WAN interface cards (WIC) that add other interfaces. The bottom of the figure shows one example WIC, which would take one of the four slots after it is installed. The router has other items as well, including both an RJ-45 and USB console port.

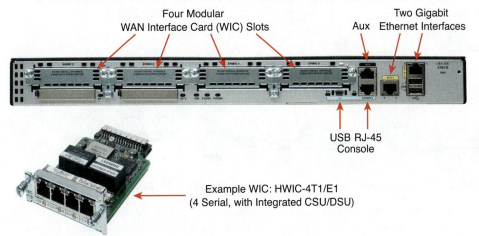

Four Modular
WAN Interface Card (WIC) Slots

Two Gigabit
Aux Ethernet Interfaces

USB RJ-45
Console

Example WIC: HWIC-4T1/E1
(4 Serial, with Integrated CSU/DSU)

Figure 15-3 *Photos of a Model 2901 Cisco Integrated Services Router (ISR)*

Physical Installation

Armed with the cabling details in figures like Figure 15-2, and the router hardware details in figures like Figure 15-3, you can physically install a router. To install a router, follow these steps:

Step 1. Connect any LAN cables to the LAN ports.

Step 2. If using an external CSU/DSU, connect the router's serial interface to the CSU/DSU and the CSU/DSU to the line from the telco.

Step 3. If using an internal CSU/DSU, connect the router's serial interface to the line from the telco.

Step 4. Connect the router's console port to a PC (using a rollover cable), as needed, to configure the router.

Step 5. Connect a power cable from a power outlet to the power port on the router.

Step 6. Power on the router.

Note that the steps for router installation match those for a switch, except that Cisco enterprise routers typically have an on/off switch, while switches do not.

Installing Internet Access Routers

Routers play a key role in SOHO networks, connecting the LAN-attached end-user devices to a high-speed Internet access service. After they are connected to the Internet, SOHO users can send packets to and from their enterprise network at their company or school.

Vendors like Cisco offer router products that primarily act as routers and other products that combine routing functions with many other functions. However, to make learning each function more obvious, this section first shows each function as a separate device and later shows a more typical example with many functions combined into one integrated networking device.

15

A SOHO Installation with a Separate Switch, Router, and Cable Modem

Figure 15-4 shows an example of the devices and cables used in a SOHO network to connect to the Internet using cable TV (CATV) as the high-speed Internet service. For now, keep in mind that the figure shows one alternative for the devices and cables, whereas many variations are possible.

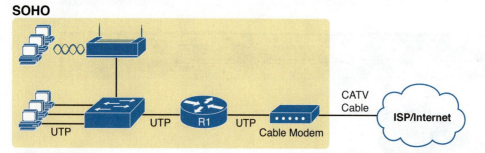

Figure 15-4   *Devices in a SOHO Network with High-Speed CATV Internet*

This figure has many similarities to Figure 15-2, which shows a typical enterprise branch office. Some end-user PCs still connect to a switch, and the switch still connects to a router's Ethernet interface. Other end-user devices use a wireless LAN, with a wireless access point, that also connects to the Ethernet LAN. For both the wired and wireless devices, the router still provides routing services, forwarding IP packets.

The main differences between the SOHO connection in Figure 15-4 and the enterprise branch in Figure 15-2 relate to the connection into the Internet. An Internet connection that uses CATV or digital subscriber line (DSL) needs a device that converts between the Layer 1 and 2 standards used on the CATV cable or DSL line and the Ethernet used by the router. These devices, commonly called *cable modems* and *DSL modems*, respectively, convert electrical signals between an Ethernet cable and either CATV or DSL.

In fact, while the details differ greatly, the purpose of the cable modem and DSL modem is similar to a CSU/DSU on a serial link. A CSU/DSU converts between the Layer 1 standards used on a telco's WAN circuit and a serial cable's Layer 1 standards. Similarly, a cable modem converts between CATV signals and a Layer 1 (and Layer 2) standard usable by a router—namely, Ethernet. Similarly, DSL modems convert between the DSL signals over a home telephone line and Ethernet.

To physically install a SOHO network with the devices shown in Figure 15-4, you basically need the correct UTP cables for the Ethernet connections, and either the CATV cable (for cable Internet services) or a phone line (for DSL services). Note that the router used in Figure 15-4 simply needs to have two Ethernet interfaces—one to connect to the LAN switch and one to connect to the cable modem. Thinking specifically just about the router installation, you would need to use the following steps to install this SOHO router:

Step 1.   Connect a UTP straight-through cable from the router to the switch.

Step 2.   Connect a UTP straight-through cable from the router to the cable modem.

Step 3.   Connect the router's console port to a PC (using a rollover cable), as needed, to configure the router.

Step 4.   Connect a power cable from a power outlet to the power port on the router.

Step 5.   Power on the router.

A SOHO Installation with an Integrated Switch, Router, and DSL Modem

Today, most new SOHO installations use an integrated device rather than the separate devices shown in Figure 15-4. In fact, you can buy a single SOHO device today that includes all of these functions:

- Router
- Switch
- Cable or DSL modem
- Wireless access point
- Hardware-enabled encryption

A newly installed high-speed SOHO Internet connection today probably looks more like Figure 15-5, with an integrated device. In fact, when you go to a typical office supply store today and look at consumer devices called a "router," it is likely one of these integrated devices that does many functions.

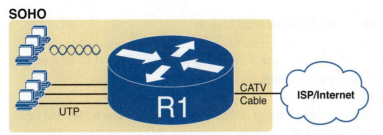

Figure 15-5 *SOHO Network, Using Cable Internet and an Integrated Device*

Enabling IPv4 Support on Cisco Routers

Routers support a relatively large number of features, with a large number of configuration and EXEC commands to support those features. This section introduces the most commonly used commands: a variety of administrative commands, plus the commands used to enable IPv4 processing on LAN and WAN interfaces.

> **NOTE**   For perspective, the Cisco router documentation includes a command reference, with an index to every single router command. A quick informal count of a recent IOS version listed around 5000 CLI commands.

Thankfully, learning router administrative commands requires only a little work, because many Cisco router and Cisco switch administrative features use the exact same commands. For example, the console, vty, and enable passwords all work the same. This section begins with a review of the CLI features you have already learned from Part II of this book and reviews which ones do indeed work the same way on Cisco routers and switches.

The rest of this section focuses on the basic commands related to router interfaces. In particular, this section explains the configuration required to enable IPv4 processing on a router interface.

Comparisons Between the Switch CLI and Router CLI

The following list details the many items covered in Chapter 8, "Configuring Ethernet Switching," for which the router CLI behaves the same. If these details are not fresh in your memory, it might be worthwhile to spend a few minutes briefly reviewing Chapter 8.

The configuration commands used for the following features are the same on both routers and switches:

- User and Enable (privileged) mode
- Entering and exiting configuration mode, using the **configure terminal**, **end**, and **exit** commands and the Ctrl+Z key sequence
- Configuration of console, Telnet, and enable secret passwords
- Configuration of SSH encryption keys and username/password login credentials
- Configuration of the hostname and interface description
- Configuration of Ethernet interfaces that can negotiate speed, using the **speed** and **duplex** commands
- Configuring an interface to be administratively disabled (**shutdown**) and administratively enabled (**no shutdown**)
- Navigation through different configuration mode contexts using commands like **line console 0** and **interface**
- CLI help, command editing, and command recall features
- The use of the **debug** command's many options to create log messages about certain events, so that any user can monitor those messages using the **terminal monitor** EXEC command
- Setup mode, used to guide the user through a set of questions to create a simple initial configuration
- The meaning and use of the startup config (in NVRAM), running config (in RAM), and external servers (like TFTP), along with how to use the **copy** command to copy the configuration files and IOS images

At first glance, this list seems to cover most everything covered in Chapter 8—and it does cover most of the details. However, a couple of topics covered in Chapter 8 do work differently with the router CLI as compared to the switch CLI, namely:

- The configuration of IP addresses differs in some ways.
- Routers have an auxiliary (Aux) port, intended to be connected to an external modem and phone line to allow remote users to dial in to the router, and access the CLI, by making a phone call.

Beyond these two items from Chapter 8, the router CLI does differ from a switch CLI just because switches and routers do different things. For example, Cisco Layer 2 switches support the **show mac address-table** command, but these Layer 2–only devices do not support the **show ip route** command, which lists IP routes. Some Cisco routers can do IP routing but not Layer 2 switching, so they support the **show ip route** command but not the **show mac address-table** command.

Router Interfaces

One minor difference between Cisco switches and routers is that routers support a much wider variety of interfaces. Today, LAN switches support Ethernet LAN interfaces of various speeds. Routers support a variety of other types of interfaces, including serial interfaces, cable TV, DSL, and others not mentioned in this book.

Most Cisco routers have at least one Ethernet interface of some type. Many of those Ethernet interfaces support multiple speeds and use autonegotiation, so for consistency, the router IOS refers to these interfaces based on the fastest speed. For example, a 10-Mbps-only Ethernet interface would be configured with the **interface ethernet** *number* configuration command, a 10/100 interface with the **interface fastethernet** *number* command, and a 10/100/1000 interface with the **interface gigabitethernet** *number* command.

Serial interfaces make up the second most common type of router interface shown in this book. As you might recall from Chapter 3, Cisco routers use serial interfaces to connect to a serial link. Each point-to-point serial link can then use High-Level Data Link Control (HDLC, the default) or Point-to-Point Protocol (PPP).

Routers refer to interfaces in many commands, first by the type of interface (Ethernet, Fast Ethernet, Serial, and so on) and then with a unique number of that router. On routers, the interface numbers might be a single number, two numbers separated by a slash, or three numbers separated by slashes. For example, all three of the following configuration commands are correct on at least one model of Cisco router:

```
interface ethernet 0
interface fastEthernet 0/1
interface gigabitethernet 0/0
interface serial 1/0/1
```

Two of the most common commands to display the interfaces, and their status, are the **show ip interface brief** and **show interfaces** commands. The first of these commands displays a list with one line per interface, with some basic information, including the interface IP address and interface status. The second command lists the interfaces, but with a large amount of information per interface. Example 15-1 shows a sample of each command.

Example 15-1 *Listing the Interfaces in a Router*

```
R1# show ip interface brief
Interface                  IP-Address      OK? Method Status                Protocol
Embedded-Service-Engine0/0 unassigned      YES NVRAM  administratively down  down
GigabitEthernet0/0         172.16.1.1      YES NVRAM  down                   down
GigabitEthernet0/1         unassigned      YES manual administratively down  down
Serial0/0/0                172.16.4.1      YES NVRAM  up                     up
Serial0/0/1                172.16.5.1      YES NVRAM  up                     up
Serial0/1/0                unassigned      YES NVRAM  up                     up
Serial0/1/1                unassigned      YES NVRAM  administratively down  down


R1# show interfaces serial 0/0/0
Serial0/0/0 is up, line protocol is up
  Hardware is WIC MBRD Serial
  Description: Link in lab to R2's S0/0/1
  Internet address is 172.16.4.1/24
  MTU 1500 bytes, BW 1544 Kbit/sec, DLY 20000 usec,
     reliability 255/255, txload 1/255, rxload 1/255
  Encapsulation HDLC, loopback not set
  Keepalive set (10 sec)
  Last input 00:00:03, output 00:00:06, output hang never
  Last clearing of "show interface" counters never
  Input queue: 0/75/0/0 (size/max/drops/flushes); Total output drops: 0
  Queueing strategy: fifo
  Output queue: 0/40 (size/max)
  5 minute input rate 0 bits/sec, 0 packets/sec
  5 minute output rate 0 bits/sec, 0 packets/sec
     42 packets input, 3584 bytes, 0 no buffer
     Received 42 broadcasts (0 IP multicasts)
     0 runts, 0 giants, 0 throttles
     0 input errors, 0 CRC, 0 frame, 0 overrun, 0 ignored, 0 abort
```

15

```
41 packets output, 3481 bytes, 0 underruns

0 output errors, 0 collisions, 4 interface resets

3 unknown protocol drops

0 output buffer failures, 0 output buffers swapped out

0 carrier transitions

DCD=up  DSR=up  DTR=up  RTS=up  CTS=up
```

> **NOTE** Commands that refer to router interfaces can be significantly shortened by truncating the words. For example, **sh int fa0/0** can be used instead of **show interfaces fastethernet 0/0**. In fact, many network engineers, when looking over someone's shoulder, would say something like "just do a show int F-A-oh-oh command" in this case, rather than speaking the long version of the command.

Also, note that **show interfaces** command lists a text interface description on about the 3rd line, if configured. In this case, interface S0/0/0 had been previously configured with the **description Link in lab to R2's S0/0/1** command in interface configuration mode for interface S0/0/0. The **description** interface subcommand provides an easy way to keep small notes about what router interfaces connect to which neighboring devices, with the **show interfaces** command listing that information.

Interface Status Codes

Each interface has two *interface status codes*. To be usable, the two interface status codes must be in an "up" state. The first status code refers essentially to whether Layer 1 is working, and the second status code mainly (but not always) refers to whether the data link layer protocol is working. Table 15-1 summarizes these two status codes.

Table 15-1 Interface Status Codes and Their Meanings

Name	Location	General Meaning
Line status	First status code	Refers to the Layer 1 status—for example, is the cable installed, is it the right/wrong cable, is the device on the other end powered on?
Protocol status	Second status code	Refers generally to the Layer 2 status. It is always down if the line status is down. If the line status is up, a protocol status of down is usually caused by a mismatched data link layer configuration.

Several combinations of interface status codes exist, as summarized in Table 15-2. The table lists the status codes in order, from being disabled on purpose by the configuration to a fully working state.

Table 15-2 Typical Combinations of Interface Status Codes

Line Status	Protocol Status	Typical Reasons
Administratively down	Down	The interface has a **shutdown** command configured on it.
Down	Down	The interface is not **shutdown**, but the physical layer has a problem. For example, no cable has been attached to the interface, or with Ethernet, the switch interface on the other end of the cable is shut down or the switch is powered off.

Line Status	Protocol Status	Typical Reasons
Up	Down	Almost always refers to data link layer problems, most often configuration problems. For example, serial links have this combination when one router was configured to use PPP and the other defaults to use HDLC.
Up	Up	Layer 1 and Layer 2 of this interface are functioning.

For some examples, look back at Example 15-1's **show ip interface brief** command, to the three interfaces in the following list. The interfaces in this list each have a different combination of interface status codes; the list details the specific reasons for this status code in the lab used to create this example for the book.

G0/0: The interface is down/down, in this case because no cable was connected to the interface.

G0/1: The interface is administratively down/down, because the configuration includes the **shutdown** command under the G0/1 interface.

S0/0/0: The interface is up/up because a serial cable is installed, connected to another router in a lab, and is working.

Router Interface IP Addresses

Cisco enterprise routers require at least some configuration beyond the default configuration before they will do their primary job: routing IP packets. The following facts tell us that to make a router ready to route IPv4 packets on an interface, you need to enable the interface and assign it an IPv4 address:

■ Most Cisco router interfaces default to a disabled (**shutdown**) state and should be enabled with the **no shutdown** interface subcommand.

■ Cisco routers do not route IP packets in or out an interface until an IP address and mask have been configured; by default, no interfaces have an IP address and mask.

■ Cisco routers attempt to route IP packets for any interfaces that are in an up/up state and that have an IP address/mask assigned. (Routers enable IPv4 routing by default due to a default **ip routing** global configuration command.)

To configure the address and mask, simply use the **ip address** *address mask* interface subcommand. Figure 15-6 shows a simple IPv4 network, the same network used in several of the subnetting examples in Part III of this book. The figure shows the IPv4 addresses on Router R1, with Example 15-2 showing the matching configuration.

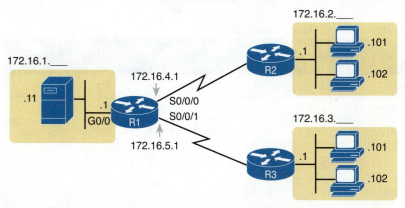

Figure 15-6 *IPv4 Addresses Used in Example 15-2*

15

Example 15-2 *Configuring IP Addresses on Cisco Routers*

```
R1# configure terminal
Enter configuration commands, one per line.  End with CNTL/Z.
R1config)# interface G0/0
R1(config-if)# ip address 172.16.1.1 255.255.255.0
R1(config-if)# no shutdown
R1(config-if)# interface S0/0/0
R1(config-if)# ip address 172.16.4.1 255.255.255.0
R1(config-if)# no shutdown
R1(config-if)# interface S0/0/1
R1(config-if)# ip address 172.16.5.1 255.255.255.0
R1(config-if)# no shutdown
R1(config-if)# ^Z
R1#
```

Example 15-3 shows the output of the **show protocols** command. This command confirms the state of each of the three R1 interfaces in Figure 15-6 and the IP address and mask configured on those same interfaces.

Example 15-3 *Verifying IP Addresses on Cisco Routers*

```
R1# show protocols
Global values:
  Internet Protocol routing is enabled
Embedded-Service-Engine0/0 is administratively down, line protocol is down
GigabitEthernet0/0 is up, line protocol is up
  Internet address is 172.16.1.1/24
GigabitEthernet0/1 is administratively down, line protocol is down
Serial0/0/0 is up, line protocol is up
  Internet address is 172.16.4.1/24
Serial0/0/1 is up, line protocol is up
  Internet address is 172.16.5.1/24
Serial0/1/0 is administratively down, line protocol is down
Serial0/1/1 is administratively down, line protocol is down
```

One of the first actions to take when verifying whether a router is working is to find the interfaces, check the interface status, and check to see whether the correct IP addresses and masks are used. Examples 15-1 and 15-3 showed samples of the key **show** commands, while Table 15-3 summarizes those commands and the types of information they display.

Table 15-3 Key Commands to List Router Interface Status

Command	Lines of Output per Interface	IP Configuration Listed	Interface Status Listed?
show ip interface brief	1	Address	Yes
show protocols [*type number*]	1 or 2	Address/mask	Yes
show interfaces [*type number*]	Many	Address/mask	Yes

Bandwidth and Clock Rate on Serial Interfaces

Cisco happens to leave most of the details about WAN technologies out of CCENT, with the ICND2 exam and CCNA R/S discussing more details. However, if you decide to build your own study lab with real gear, you need to know just a little more information about serial links. This last topic in the chapter discusses those details.

As mentioned back in Chapter 3, WAN links can run at a wide variety of speeds. To deal with the wide range of speeds, routers physically slave themselves to the speed as dictated by the CSU/DSU through a process called *clocking*. As a result, routers can use serial links without the need for additional configuration or autonegotiation to sense the serial link's speed. The CSU/DSU knows the speed, the CSU/DSU sends clock pulses over the cable to the router, and the router reacts to the clocking signal.

To build a serial link in a home lab, the routers can use serial interface cards that normally use an external CSU/DSU, and make a serial link, without requiring the expense of two CSU/DSUs. Chapter 3's Figure 3-5 introduced this concept, and it is repeated here as Figure 15-7. To make it work, the link uses two serial cables—one a DTE cable and the other a DCE cable—which swap the transmit and receive pair on the cables.

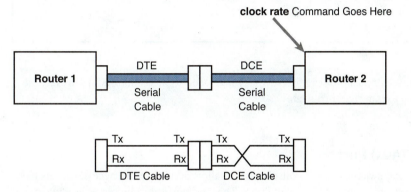

Figure 15-7 *Serial Link in Lab*

Using the correct cabling works, as long as you add one command: the **clock rate** interface subcommand. This command tells that router the speed at which to transmit bits on a serial link like the one shown in Figure 15-7. The **clock rate** command is not needed on real serial links, because the CSU/DSU provides the clocking. Without any real CSU/DSUs on the link, the router with the DCE cable must supply that clocking function, and the **clock rate** command tells the router to provide it.

> **NOTE** Some versions of IOS will automatically implement a default **clock rate 2000000** command on serial interfaces that have a DCE cable connected to them. While helpful, this speed might be too high for some types of back-to-back serial cables, so consider using a lower speed in lab.

Example 15-4 shows the configuration of the **clock rate** command using the same Router R1 used in the earlier Example 15-2. The end of the example verifies that this router can use the **clock rate** command with the **show controllers** command. This command confirms that R1 has a V.35 DCE cable connected.

> **NOTE** Example 15-4 omits some of the output of the **show running-config** command, specifically the parts that do not matter to the information covered here.

15

Example 15-4   *Router R1 Configuration with the* **clock rate** *Command*

```
R1# show running-config
! lines omitted for brevity
interface Serial0/0/0
 ip address 172.16.4.1 255.255.255.0
 clock rate 2000000
!
interface Serial0/0/1
 ip address 172.16.5.1 255.255.255.0
 clock rate 128000

! lines omitted for brevity


R1# show controllers serial 0/0/1
Interface Serial0
Hardware is PowerQUICC MPC860
DCE V.35, clock rate 128000
idb at 0x8169BB20, driver data structure at 0x816A35E4
! Lines omitted for brevity
```

NOTE The **clock rate** command does not allow just any speed to be configured. However, the list of speeds does vary from router to router.

Router Auxiliary (Aux) Port

While both routers and switches have a console port to allow administrative access, routers have an extra physical port called an auxiliary (Aux) port. The Aux port typically serves as a means to make a phone call to connect into the router to issue commands from the CLI.

The Aux port works like the console line, except that the Aux port is typically connected through a cable to an external analog modem, which in turn connects to a phone line. Then, the engineer uses a PC, terminal emulator, and modem to call the remote router. After being connected, the engineer can use the terminal emulator to access the router CLI, starting in user mode as usual.

Aux ports can be configured beginning with the **line aux 0** command to reach aux line configuration mode. From there, all the commands for the console line, covered mostly in Chapter 8, can be used. For example, the **login** and **password** *password* commands could be used to set up simple password checking when a user dials in.

Operational Status with the show version Command

Finally, one more command, the **show version** command, identifies a large number of important base features about a router. It does list the IOS version currently used by the router. However, it lists other important details as well: how long the router has been running, why the IOS was last reloaded, what file was used to load the IOS, and what interfaces are installed in the router. It also lists details about the amounts of NVRAM, RAM, and flash memory installed.

Example 15-5 shows an example, with the highlighted lines pointing out some of the more interesting features.

Example 15-5 *Displaying IOS Version and Other Details with the* **show version** *Command*

```
R1# show version
Cisco IOS Software, C2900 Software (C2900-UNIVERSALK9-M), Version 15.2(4)M1, RELEASE
SOFTWARE (fc1)
Technical Support: http://www.cisco.com/techsupport
Copyright (c) 1986-2012 by Cisco Systems, Inc.
Compiled Thu 26-Jul-12 20:54 by prod_rel_team


ROM: System Bootstrap, Version 15.0(1r)M15, RELEASE SOFTWARE (fc1)


R1 uptime is 3 days, 4 hours, 19 minutes
System returned to ROM by reload at 14:00:46 UTC Sat Oct 13 2012
System image file is "flash:c2900-universalk9-mz.SPA.152-4.M1.bin"
Last reload type: Normal Reload
Last reload reason: Reload Command



! Legal notices omitted for brevity

If you require further assistance please contact us by sending email to
export@cisco.com.

Cisco CISCO2901/K9 (revision 1.0) with 483328K/40960K bytes of memory.
Processor board ID FTX1628838P
2 Gigabit Ethernet interfaces
4 Serial(sync/async) interfaces
1 terminal line
DRAM configuration is 64 bits wide with parity enabled.
255K bytes of non-volatile configuration memory.
3425968K bytes of USB Flash usbflash1 (Read/Write)
250880K bytes of ATA System CompactFlash 0 (Read/Write)


License Info:

! License information omitted for brevity

Configuration register is 0x2102
```

15

Review Activities

Chapter Summary

- Routers collectively provide the main feature of the network layer—the capability to forward packets end to end through a network.

- A typical enterprise branch office needs a router for WAN/LAN connectivity and a LAN switch to provide a high-performance local network and connectivity into the router and WAN.

- Many branches also need Voice over IP (VoIP) services and several security services.

- To install a router, follow these steps:

    Step 1.   Connect any LAN cables to the LAN ports.

    Step 2.   If using an external CSU/DSU, connect the router's serial interface to the CSU/DSU and the CSU/DSU to the line from the telco.

    Step 3.   If using an internal CSU/DSU, connect the router's serial interface to the line from the telco.

    Step 4.   Connect the router's console port to a PC (using a rollover cable), as needed, to configure the router.

    Step 5.   Connect a power cable from a power outlet to the power port on the router.

    Step 6.   Power on the router.

- You can buy a single SOHO device today that includes all of these functions:

    - Router
    - Switch
    - Cable or DSL modem
    - Wireless access point
    - Hardware-enabled encryption

- The configuration commands used for the following features are the same on both routers and switches:

    - User and Enable (privileged) mode
    - Entering and exiting configuration mode, using the **configure terminal**, **end**, and **exit** commands and the Ctrl+Z key sequence
    - Configuration of console, Telnet, and enable secret passwords
    - Configuration of SSH encryption keys and username/password login credentials
    - Configuration of the host name and interface description
    - Configuration of Ethernet interfaces that can negotiate speed, using the **speed** and **duplex** commands
    - Configuring an interface to be administratively disabled (**shutdown**) and administratively enabled (**no shutdown**)
    - Navigation through different configuration mode contexts using commands such as **line console 0** and **interface**
    - CLI help, command editing, and command recall features

- The use of the **debug** command's many options to create log messages about certain events, so any user can monitor those messages using the **terminal monitor** exec command

- Setup mode, used to guide the user through a set of questions to create a simple initial configuration

- The meaning and use of the startup-config (in NVRAM), running-config (in RAM), and external servers (such as TFTP), along with how to use the **copy** command to copy the configuration files and IOS images

- One minor difference between Cisco switches and routers is that routers support a much wider variety of interfaces. Today, LAN switches support Ethernet LAN interfaces of various speeds. Routers support a variety of other types of interfaces, including serial interfaces, cable TV, DSL, and others not mentioned in this book.

- Each interface has two *interface status codes*. To be usable, the two interface status codes must be in an up state.

  - The first status code is the line status. It refers to the Layer 1 status; for example, is the cable installed, is it the right/wrong cable, is the device on the other end powered on?

  - The second status code is the protocol status. It refers generally to the Layer 2 status. It is always down if the line status is down. If the line status is up, a protocol status of down usually is caused by mismatched data link layer configuration.

- The following facts tell you that to make a router ready to route IPv4 packets on an interface, you must enable the interface and assign it an IPv4 address:

  - Most Cisco router interfaces default to a disabled (**shutdown**) state, and should be enabled with the **no shutdown** interface subcommand.

  - Cisco routers do not route IP packets in or out of an interface until an IP address and mask have been configured; by default, no interfaces have an IP address and mask.

  - Cisco routers attempt to route IP packets for any interfaces that are in an up/up state and that have an IP address/mask assigned. (IPv4 routing is enabled based on the default use of the **ip routing** global configuration command.)

- Although both routers and switches have a console port to allow administrative access, routers have an extra physical port called an auxiliary (Aux) port. The Aux port usually serves as a means to make a phone call to connect into the router to issue commands from the CLI.

Review Questions

Answer these review questions. You can find the answers at the bottom of the last page of the chapter. For thorough explanations, see DVD Appendix C, "Answers to Review Questions."

1. Which of the following installation steps are typically required on a Cisco router, but not typically required on a Cisco switch? (Choose two answers.)

   A. Connect Ethernet cables

   B. Connect serial cables

   C. Connect to the console port

   D. Connect the power cable

   E. Turn the on/off switch to "on"

2. Which of the following commands might you see associated with the router CLI, but not with the switch CLI?

   A. The **clock rate** command

   B. The **ip address** *address mask* command

   C. The **ip address dhcp** command

   D. The **interface vlan 1** command

3. You just bought two Cisco routers for use in a lab, connecting each router to a different LAN switch with their Fa0/0 interfaces. You also connected the two routers' serial interfaces using a back-to-back cable. Which of the following steps are not required to be able to forward IPv4 packets on both routers' interfaces? (Choose two answers.)

   A. Configuring an IP address on each router's Fast Ethernet and serial interfaces

   B. Configuring the **bandwidth** command on one router's serial interface

   C. Configuring the **clock rate** command on one router's serial interface

   D. Setting the interface **description** on both the Fast Ethernet and serial interface of each router

4. The output of the **show ip interface brief** command on R1 lists interface status codes of "down" and "down" for interface Serial 0/0. Which of the following could be true?

   A. The **shutdown** command is currently configured for that interface.

   B. R1's serial interface has been configured to use Frame Relay, but the router on the other end of the serial link has been configured to use PPP.

   C. R1's serial interface does not have a serial cable installed.

   D. Both routers have been cabled to a working serial link (CSU/DSUs included), but only one router has been configured with an IP address.

5. Which of the following commands do not list the IP address and mask of at least one interface? (Choose two answers.)

   A. show running-config

   B. show protocols *type number*

   C. show ip interface brief

   D. show interfaces

   E. show version

6. Which of the following is different on the Cisco switch CLI as compared with the Cisco router CLI?

   A. The commands used to configure simple password checking for the console

   B. The number of IP addresses configured

   C. The configuration of the device's host name

   D. The configuration of an interface description

Review All the Key Topics

Review the most important topics from this chapter, noted with the Key Topic icon. Table 15-4 lists these key topics and where each is discussed.

Table 15-4   Key Topics for Chapter 15

Key Topic	Description	Page Number
List	Steps required to install a router	357
List	Similarities between a router CLI and a switch CLI	360
List	Items covered for switches in Chapter 8 that differ in some way on routers	360
Table 15-1	Router interface status codes and their meanings	362
Table 15-2	Combinations of the two interface status codes and the likely reasons for each combination	362

Complete the Tables and Lists from Memory

Print a copy of DVD Appendix M, "Memory Tables," or at least the section for this chapter, and complete the tables and lists from memory. DVD Appendix N, "Memory Tables Answer Key," includes completed tables and lists for you to check your work.

Definitions of Key Terms

After your first reading of the chapter, try to define these key terms, but do not be concerned about getting them all correct at that time. Chapter 30 directs you in how to use these terms for late-stage preparation for the exam.

bandwidth, clock rate, IOS image

Command References

Although you should not necessarily memorize the information in the tables in this section, this section does include a reference for the configuration commands (Table 15-5) and EXEC commands (Table 15-6) covered in this chapter. Practically speaking, you should memorize the commands as a complement to reading the chapter and doing all the activities in this exam preparation section. To check to see how well you have memorized the commands, cover the left side of the table with a piece of paper, read the descriptions on the right side, and see whether you remember the command.

Table 15-5   Chapter 15 Configuration Command Reference

Command	Description
interface *type number*	Global command that moves the user into configuration mode of the named interface.
ip address *address mask*	Interface subcommand that sets the router's IPv4 address and mask.
[no] shutdown	Interface subcommand that enables (**no shutdown**) or disables (**shutdown**) the interface.
duplex{ full | half | auto }	Interface command that sets the duplex, or sets the use of IEEE autonegotiation, for router LAN interfaces that support multiple speeds.
speed { 10 | 100 | 1000 }	Interface command for router Gigabit (10/100/1000) interfaces that sets the speed at which the router interface sends and receives data.
clock rate *rate*	Interface command that sets the speed at which the router supplies a clocking signal, applicable only when the router has a DCE cable installed. The unit is bits/second.
description *text*	An interface subcommand with which you can type a string of text to document information about that particular interface.

Table 15-6   Chapter 15 EXEC Command Reference

Command	Purpose
show interfaces *[type number]*	Lists a large set of informational messages about each interface, or about the one specifically listed interface.
show ip interface brief	Lists a single line of information about each interface, including the IP address, line and protocol status, and the method with which the address was configured (manual or DHCP).
show protocols *type number*	Lists information about the listed interface, including the IP address, mask, and line/protocol status.
show controllers *[type number]*	Lists many lines of information per interface, or for one interface, for the hardware controller of the interface. On serial interfaces, this command identifies the cable as either a DCE or DTE cable.
show version	Lists the version of IOS currently running in the router, plus a variety of other facts about the currently installed hardware and software in the router.

Answers to Review Questions:

1 B and E **2** A **3** B and D **4** C **5** C and E **6** B

Chapter 16

Configuring IPv4 Addresses and Routes

Routers route IPv4 packets. That simple statement actually carries a lot of hidden meaning. For routers to route packets, routers follow a routing process. That routing process relies on information called IP routes. Each IP route lists a destination—an IP network, IP subnet, or some other group of IP addresses. Each route also lists instructions that tell the router where to forward packets sent to addresses in that IP network or subnet. For routers to do a good job of routing packets, routers need to have a detailed accurate list of IP routes.

Routers use three methods to add IPv4 routes to their IPv4 routing tables. Routers first learn *connected routes*, which are routes for subnets attached to a router interface. Routers can also use *static routes*, which are routes created through a configuration command (**ip route**) that tells the router what route to put in the IPv4 routing table. And routers can use a routing protocol, in which routers tell each other about all their known routes, so that all routers can learn and build routes to all networks and subnets.

This chapter begins by reintroducing the IP routing process that relies on these routes. This IP routing discussion both reviews the concepts from Chapter 4, "Fundamentals of IPv4 Addressing and Routing," plus takes the concepts deeper, including showing information needed in a single IP route. Then, the second major heading in this chapter discusses connected routes, including variations of connected routes to VLANs connected to a router's VLAN trunk, and for connected routes on Layer 3 switches.

The final major section then looks at static routes, which let the engineer tell the router what route(s) to add to the router's IP routing table. The static route section also shows how to configure a static default route that is used when no other route matches an IP packet. Dynamic routing, using the Open Shortest Path First (OSPF) routing protocol, awaits in Chapter 17, "Learning IPv4 Routes with OSPFv2."

This chapter covers the following exam topics:

Operation of IP Data Networks

Predict the data flow between two hosts across a network.

IP Routing Technologies

Describe basic routing concepts:

CEF

Packet forwarding

Router lookup process

Configure and verify utilizing the CLI to set basic Router configuration:

Cisco IOS commands to perform basic router setup

Configure and verify operation status of an ethernet interface

Verify router configuration and network connectivity

Cisco IOS commands to review basic router information and network connectivity

Configure and verify routing configuration for a static or default route given specific routing requirements

Differentiate methods of routing and routing protocols:

next hop

ip routing table

Configure and verify interVLAN routing (Router on a stick)

sub interfaces

upstream routing

encapsulation

Configure SVI interfaces

Foundation Topics

IP Routing

IP routing—the process of forwarding IP packets—delivers packets across entire TCP/IP networks, from the device that originally builds the IP packet to the device that is supposed to receive the packet. In other words, IP routing delivers IP packets from the sending host to the destination host.

The complete end-to-end routing process relies on network layer logic on hosts and on routers. The sending host uses Layer 3 concepts to create an IP packet, forwarding the IP packet to the host's default gateway (default router). The process requires Layer 3 logic on the routers as well, by which the routers compare the destination address in the packet to their routing tables, to decide where to forward the IP packet next.

The routing process also relies on data link and physical details at each link. IP routing relies on serial links, Ethernet LANs, wireless LANs, and many other networks that implement data link and physical layer standards. These lower-layer devices and protocols move the IP packets around the TCP/IP network by encapsulating and transmitting the packets inside data link layer frames.

Those previous two paragraphs summarize the key concepts about IP routing as introduced back in Chapter 4. Next, this section reviews IP routing, while taking the discussion another step or two deeper, taking advantage of the additional depth of knowledge discussed in Parts II and III of this book.

> **NOTE**   Some references also incorrectly claim that the term "IP routing" includes the function of dynamically learning routes with IP routing protocols. While IP routing protocols play an important role, the term "IP routing" refers to the packet-forwarding process only.

IPv4 Routing Process Reference

Because you have already seen the basics back in Chapter 4, this section collects the routing process into steps for reference. The steps use many specific terms discussed in Parts II and III of this book. The upcoming descriptions and example then discuss these summaries of routing logic to make sure that each step is clear.

The routing process starts with the host that creates the IP packet. First, the host asks the question: Is the destination IP address of this new packet in my local subnet? The host uses its own IP address/mask to determine the range of addresses in the local subnet. Based on its own opinion of the range of addresses in the local subnet, a LAN-based host acts as follows:

Step 1.   If the destination is local, send directly:

    A.   Find the destination host's MAC address. Use the already-known Address Resolution Protocol (ARP) table entry, or use ARP messages to learn the information.

    B.   Encapsulate the IP packet in a data link frame, with the destination data link address of the *destination host*.

Step 2. If the destination is not local, send to the default gateway:

    A. Find the default gateway's MAC address. Use the already-known ARP table entry, or use ARP messages to learn the information.

    B. Encapsulate the IP packet in a data link frame, with the destination data link address of the *default gateway*.

Figure 16-1 summarizes these same concepts. In the figure, host A sends a local packet directly to host D. However, for packets to host B, on the other side of a router and therefore in a different subnet, host A sends the packet to its default router (R1). (As a reminder, the terms *default gateway* and *default router* are synonyms.)

Local Subnet

Figure 16-1 *Host Routing Logic Summary*

Routers have a little more routing work to do as compared with hosts. While the host logic began with an IP packet sitting in memory, a router has some work to do before getting to that point. With the following five-step summary of a router's routing logic, the router takes the first two steps just to receive the frame and extract the IP packet, before thinking about the packet's destination address at Step 3. The steps are as follows:

1. For each received data link frame, choose whether or not to process the frame. Process it if:

    A. The frame has no errors (per the data link trailer Frame Check Sequence, or FCS, field)

    B. The frame's destination data link address is the router's address (or an appropriate multicast or broadcast address).

2. If choosing to process the frame at Step 1, deencapsulate the packet from inside the data link frame.

3. Make a routing decision. To do so, compare the packet's destination IP address to the routing table and find the route that matches the destination address. This route identifies the outgoing interface of the router and possibly the next-hop router.

4. Encapsulate the packet into a data link frame appropriate for the outgoing interface. When forwarding out LAN interfaces, use ARP as needed to find the next device's MAC address.

5. Transmit the frame out the outgoing interface, as listed in the matched IP route.

NOTE The fact that this list has five steps, instead of breaking the logic into some other number of steps, does not matter. The concepts inside each step matter a lot—know them—but for the exams, there is no need to memorize which piece of logic goes with a particular step number.

This routing process summary lists many details, but sometimes you can think about the routing process in simpler terms. For example, leaving out some details, this paraphrase of the step list details the same big concepts:

> The router receives a frame, removes the packet from inside the frame, decides where to forward the packet, puts the packet into another frame, and sends the frame.

To give you a little more perspective on these steps, Figure 16-2 breaks down the same five-step routing process as a diagram. The figure shows a packet arriving from the left, entering a router Ethernet interface, with an IP destination of host C. The figure shows the packet arriving, encapsulated inside an Ethernet frame (both header and trailer).

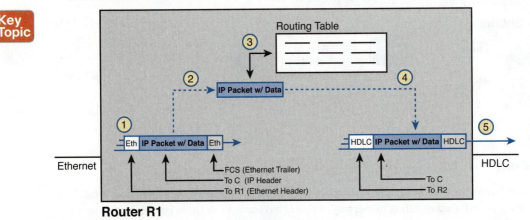

Figure 16-2 *Router Routing Logic Summary*

Router R1 processes the frame and packet as shown with the numbers in the figure, matching the same five-step process describe just before the figure, as follows:

1. Router R1 notes that the received Ethernet frame passes the FCS check, and that the destination Ethernet MAC address is R1's MAC address, so R1 processes the frame.

2. R1 deencapsulates the IP packet from inside the Ethernet frame's header and trailer.

3. R1 compares the IP packet's destination IP address to R1's IP routing table.

4. R1 encapsulates the IP packet inside a new data link frame, in this case, inside a High-Level Data Link Control (HDLC) header and trailer.

5. R1 transmits the IP packet, inside the new HDLC frame, out the serial link on the right.

> **NOTE** This chapter uses several figures that show an IP packet encapsulated inside a data link layer frame. These figures often show both the data link header as well as the data link trailer, with the IP packet in the middle. The IP packets all include the IP header, plus any encapsulated data.

An Example of IP Routing

The next several pages walk you through an example that discusses each routing step, in order, through multiple devices. That example uses a case in which host A (172.16.1.9) sends a packet to host B (172.16.2.9), with host routing logic and the five steps showing how R1 forwards the packet.

Figure 16-3 shows a typical IP addressing diagram for an IPv4 network with typical address abbreviations. The diagram can get a little too messy if it lists the full IP address for every router interface. When possible, these diagrams usually list the subnet, and then the last octet or two of the individual IP addresses—just enough so that you know the IP address, but with less clutter. For example, host A uses IP address 172.16.1.9, taking from subnet 172.16.1.0/24 (in which all addresses begin 172.16.1), and the ".9" beside the host A icon. As another example, R1 uses address 172.16.1.1 on its LAN interface, 172.16.4.1 on one serial interface, and 172.16.5.1 on the other serial interface.

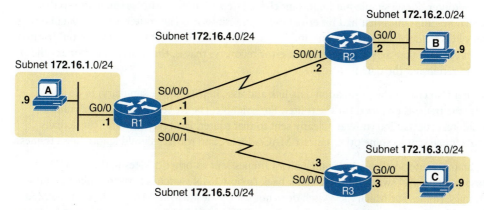

Figure 16-3 *IPv4 Network Used to Show Five-Step Routing Example*

Now on to the example, with host A (172.16.1.9) sending a packet to host B (172.16.2.9).

Host Forwards the IP Packet to the Default Router (Gateway)

In this example, host A uses some application that sends data to host B (172.16.2.9). After host A has the IP packet sitting in memory, host A's logic reduces to the following:

- My IP address/mask is 172.16.1.9/24, so my local subnet contains numbers 172.16.1.0–172.16.1.255 (including the subnet ID and subnet broadcast address).

- The destination address is 172.16.2.9, which is clearly not in my local subnet.

- Send the packet to my default gateway, which is set to 172.16.1.1.

- To send the packet, encapsulate it in an Ethernet frame. Make the destination MAC address be R1's G0/0 MAC address (host A's default gateway).

Figure 16-4 pulls these concepts together, showing the destination IP address and destination MAC address in the frame and packet sent by host A in this case.

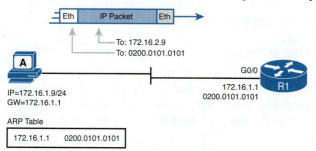

Figure 16-4 *Host A Sends Packet to Host B*

Note that the figure shows the Ethernet LAN as simple lines, but the LAN can include any of the devices discussed in Part II of this book. The LAN could be a single cable between host A and R1, or it could be 100 LAN switches connected across a huge campus of buildings. Regardless, host A and R1 sit in the same VLAN, and the Ethernet LAN then delivers the Ethernet frame to R1's G0/0 interface.

Routing Step 1: Decide Whether to Process the Incoming Frame

Routers receive many frames in an interface, particular LAN interfaces. However, a router can and should ignore some of those frames. So, the first step in the routing process begins with a decision of whether a router should process the frame or silently discard (ignore) the frame.

First, the router does a simple but important check (Step 1A in the process summary) so that the router ignores all frames that had bit errors during transmission. The router uses the data link header's FCS field to check the frame, and if errors occurred in transmission, the router discards the frame. (The router makes no attempt at error recovery; that is, the router does not ask the sender to retransmit the data.)

The router also checks the destination data link address (Step 1B in the summary) to decide whether the frame is intended for the router. For example, frames sent to the router's unicast MAC address for that interface are clearly sent to that router. However, a router can actually receive a frame sent to some other unicast MAC address, and routers should ignore these frames.

For example, routers will receive some unicast frames sent to other devices in the VLAN just because of how LAN switches work. Think back to how LAN switches forward unknown unicast frames: frames for which the switch does not list the destination MAC address in the MAC address table. The LAN switch floods those frames. The result? Routers sometimes receive frames destined for some other device, with some other device's MAC address listed as the destination MAC address. Routers should ignore those frames.

In this example, host A sends a frame destined for R1's MAC address. So, after the frame is received, and after R1 confirms with the FCS that no errors occurred, R1 confirms that the frame is destined for R1's MAC address (0200.0101.0101 in this case). All checks have been passed, so R1 will process the frame, as shown in Figure 16-5. (Note that the large rectangle in the figure represents the internals of Router R1.)

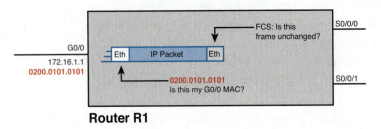

Router R1

Figure 16-5   *Routing Step 1, on Router R1: Checking FCS and Destination MAC*

Routing Step 2: Deencapsulation of the IP Packet

After the router knows that it ought to process the received frame (per Step 1), the next step is a relatively simple step: deencapsulating the packet. In router memory, the router no longer needs the original frame's data link header and trailer, so the router removes and discards them, leaving the IP packet, as shown in Figure 16-6. Note that the destination IP address remains unchanged (172.16.2.9).

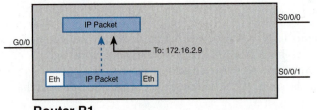

Router R1

Figure 16-6   *Routing Step 2 on Router R1: Deencapsulating the Packet*

Routing Step 3: Choosing Where to Forward the Packet

While routing Step 2 required little thought, Step 3 requires the most thought of all the steps. At this point, the router needs to make a choice about where to forward the packet next. That process uses the router's IP routing table, with some matching logic to compare the packet's destination address with the table.

First, an IP routing table lists multiple routes. Each individual route contains several facts, which in turn can be grouped as shown in Figure 16-7. Part of each route is used to match the destination address of the packet, while the rest of the route lists forwarding instructions: where to send the packet next.

Router R1

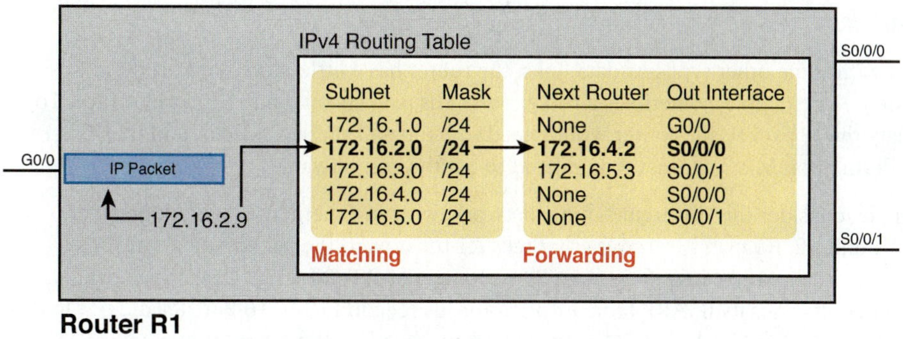

Figure 16-7 *Routing Step 3 on Router R1: Matching the Routing Table*

Focus on the entire routing table for a moment, and notice the fact that it lists five routes. Earlier, Figure 16-3 shows the entire example network, with five subnets, so R1 has a route for each of the five subnets.

Next, look at the part of the five routes that Router R1 will use to match packets. To fully define each subnet, each route lists both the subnet ID and the subnet mask. When matching the IP packet's destination with the routing table, the router looks at the packet's destination IP address (172.16.2.9) and compares it to the range of addresses defined by each subnet. Specifically, the router looks at the subnet and mask information, which with a little math, the router can figure out in which of those subnets 172.16.2.9 resides (the route for subnet 172.16.2.0/24).

Finally, look to the right side of the figure, to the forwarding instructions for these five routes. After the router matches a specific route, the router uses the forwarding information in the route to tell the router where to send the packet next. In this case, the router matched the route for subnet 172.16.2.0/24, so R1 will forward the packet out its own interface S0/0/0, to Router R2 next, listed with its next-hop router IP address of 172.16.4.2.

> **NOTE** Routes for remote subnets typically list both an outgoing interface and next-hop router IP address. Routes for subnets that connect directly to the router list only the outgoing interface, because packets to these destinations do not need to be sent to another router.

Routing Step 4: Encapsulating the Packet in a New Frame

At this point, the router knows how it will forward the packet. However, routers cannot forward a packet without first wrapping a data link header and trailer around it (encapsulation).

Encapsulating packets for serial links does not require a lot of thought, because of the simplicity of the HDLC and PPP protocols. As discussed back in Chapter 3, "Fundamentals of WANs," because serial links have only two devices on the link—the sender and the then-obvious receiver—the data link addressing does not matter. In this example, R1 forwards the packet out S0/0/0, after encapsulating the packet inside an HDLC frame, as shown in Figure 16-8.

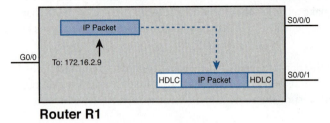

Router R1

Figure 16-8   *Routing Step 4 on Router R1: Encapsulating the Packet*

Note that with some other types of data links, the router has a little more work to do at this routing step. For example, sometimes a router forwards packets out an Ethernet interface. To encapsulate the IP packet, the router would need to build an Ethernet header, and that Ethernet header's destination MAC address would need to list the correct value.

For example, consider this different sample network, with an Ethernet WAN link between Routers R1 and R2. R1 matches a route that tells R1 to forward the packet out R1's G0/1 Ethernet interface to 172.16.6.2 (R2) next. R1 needs to put R2's MAC address in the header, and to do that, R1 uses its IP ARP table information, as seen in Figure 16-9. If R1 did not have an ARP table entry for 172.16.6.2, R1 would first have to use ARP to learn the matching MAC address.

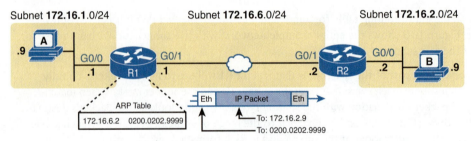

Figure 16-9   *Routing Step 4 on Router R1 with a LAN Outgoing Interface*

Routing Step 5: Transmitting the Frame

After the frame has been prepared, the router simply needs to transmit the frame. The router might have to wait, particularly if other frames are already waiting their turn to exit the interface.

Internal Processing on Cisco Routers

The discussion so far in this chapter explains one way to think about how a host and a router do their work internally. However, for Cisco to compete well in the router marketplace, it must be ready to make its routers perform that routing process well, and quickly, in all kinds of environments. If not, Cisco competitors could argue that their routers performed better, could route more packets per second (pps), and could win business away from Cisco.

This next topic looks a little deeper at how Cisco actually implements IP routing internal to a router. The discussion so far in this chapter was fairly generic, but it matches an early type of internal processing on Cisco routers called *process switching*. This section discusses the issues that drove Cisco to improve the internal routing process, while having the same result: A packet arrives inside one frame, a choice is made, and it exits the router inside another frame.

Potential Routing Performance Issues

When learning about IP routing, it helps to think through all the particulars of the routing process, as discussed over the last five or so pages. However, routers barely spend any processing time to route a single IP packet. In fact, even slower routers need to forward tens of thousands of packets per second (pps); to do that, the routers cannot spend a lot of effort processing each packet.

The process of matching a packet's destination address with the IP routing table can actually take a lot of CPU time. The example in this chapter (Figure 16-7) listed only five routes, but enterprise networks routinely have thousands of IP routes, while routers in the core of the Internet have hundreds of thousands of routes. Now think about a router CPU that needs to search a list 100,000 entries long, for every packet, for a router that needed to forward hundreds of thousands of packets per second! And what if the router had to do subnetting math each time, calculating the range of addresses in each subnet for each route? Those actions would take too many CPU cycles.

Over the years, Cisco has created several ways to optimize the internal process of how routers forward packets. Some methods tie to a specific model series of router. Layer 3 switches do the forwarding in Application Specific Integrated Circuits (ASIC), which are computer chips built for the purpose of forwarding frames or packets. All these optimizations take the basic logic from the five-step list here in the book, but work differently inside the router hardware and software, in an effort to use fewer CPU cycles and reduce the overhead of forwarding IP packets.

Cisco Router Fast Switching and CEF

Historically speaking, Cisco has had three major variations of internal routing logic that apply across the entire router product family. First, Cisco routers used internal logic called *process switching* in the early days of Cisco routers, dating back to the late 1980s and early 1990s. Process switching works basically like the routing process detailed so far in this chapter, without any of the extra optimizations.

Next, in the early 1990s, Cisco introduced alternate internal routing logic called *fast switching*. Fast switching made a couple of optimizations compared to the older process-switching logic. First, it kept another list in addition to the routing table, listing specific IP addresses for recently forwarded packets. This fast-switching cache also kept a copy of the new data link headers used when forwarding packets to each destination, so rather than build a new data link header for each packet destined for a particular IP address, the router saved a little effort by copying the old data link header.

Cisco improved over fast switching with the introduction of Cisco Express Forwarding (CEF) later in the 1990s. Like fast switching, CEF uses additional tables for faster searches, and it saves outgoing data link headers. However, CEF organizes its tables for all routing table destinations, ahead of time, not just for some of the specific destination IP addresses. CEF also uses much more sophisticated search algorithms and binary tree structures as compared to fast switching. As a result, the CEF table lookups that replace the routing table matches take even less time than with fast switching. And it caches the data link headers as well.

Today, current models of Cisco routers, and current IOS versions, use CEF by default. Table 16-1 lists a summary of the key comparison points between process switching, fast switching, and CEF.

Table 16-1   Comparisons of Packet Switching, Fast Switching, and CEF

Improves Routing Efficiency By...	Process Switching	Fast Switching	CEF
...saving data link headers used for encapsulating packets	No	Yes	Yes
...using other tables, with faster lookup time, before looking at the routing table	No	Yes	Yes
...organizing the tables using tree structures for very fast searches and less time to route packets	No	No	Yes

Configuring Connected Routes

Cisco routers enable IPv4 routing globally, by default. Then, to make the router be ready to route packets on a particular interface, the router must be configured with an IP address and the interface must be configured such that it comes up, reaching a "line status up, line protocol up" state. Only at that point can routers route IP packets in and out a particular interface.

After a router can route IP packets out one or more interfaces, the router needs some routes. Routers can add routes to their routing tables through three methods:

Connected routes: Added because of the configuration of the **ip address** interface subcommand on the local router

Static routes: Added because of the configuration of the **ip route** global command on the local router

Routing protocols: Added as a function by configuration on all routers, resulting in a process by which routers dynamically tell each other about the network so that they all learn routes

This second of three sections discusses several variations on how to configure connected routes, while the last major section discusses static routes.

Connected Routes and the ip address Command

A Cisco router automatically adds a route to its routing table for the subnet connected to each interface, assuming that the following two facts are true:

■ The interface is in a working state—in other words, the interface status in the **show interfaces** command lists a line status of up and a protocol status of up.

■ The interface has an IP address assigned through the **ip address** interface subcommand.

The concept of connected routes is relatively basic. The router of course needs to know the subnet number used on the physical network connected to each of its interfaces, so the router can route packets to that subnet. The router can simply do the math, taking the interface IP address and mask, and calculate the subnet ID. However, the router only needs that route when the interface is up and working, so the router includes a connected route in the routing table only when the interface is working.

Example 16-1 shows the connected routes on Router R1 in Figure 16-10. The figure repeats the same IP network shown earlier in the routing example. The first part of the example shows the configuration of IP addresses on all three of R1's interfaces. The end of the examples lists the output from the **show ip route** command, which lists these routes with a *c* as the route code, meaning *connected*.

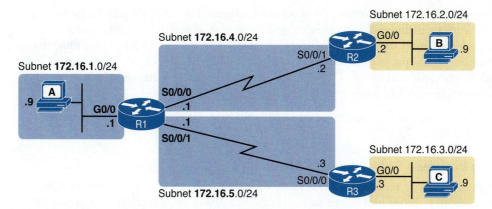

Figure 16-10   *Sample Network to Show Connected Routes*

Example 16-1   *Connected and Local Routes on Router R1*

```
! Excerpt from show running-config follows...
!
interface GigabitEthernet0/0
 ip address 172.16.1.1 255.255.255.0
!
interface Serial0/0/0
 ip address 172.16.4.1 255.255.255.0
!
interface Serial0/0/1
 ip address 172.16.5.1 255.255.255.0


R1# show ip route
Codes: L - local, C - connected, S - static, R - RIP, M - mobile, B - BGP
       D - EIGRP, EX - EIGRP external, O - OSPF, IA - OSPF inter area
       N1 - OSPF NSSA external type 1, N2 - OSPF NSSA external type 2
       E1 - OSPF external type 1, E2 - OSPF external type 2
       i - IS-IS, su - IS-IS summary, L1 - IS-IS level-1, L2 - IS-IS level-2
       ia - IS-IS inter area, * - candidate default, U - per-user static route
       o - ODR, P - periodic downloaded static route, H - NHRP, l - LISP
       + - replicated route, % - next hop override


Gateway of last resort is not set


      172.16.0.0/16 is variably subnetted, 6 subnets, 2 masks
C        172.16.1.0/24 is directly connected, GigabitEthernet0/0
L        172.16.1.1/32 is directly connected, GigabitEthernet0/0
C        172.16.4.0/24 is directly connected, Serial0/0/0
L        172.16.4.1/32 is directly connected, Serial0/0/0
C        172.16.5.0/24 is directly connected, Serial0/0/1
L        172.16.5.1/32 is directly connected, Serial0/0/1
```

Take a moment to look closely at each of the three highlighted routes in the output of **show ip route**. Each lists a C in the first column, and each has text that says "directly connected"; both identify the route as connected to the router. The early part of each route lists the matching parameters (subnet ID and mask), as shown in the earlier example in Figure 16-7. The end of each of these routes lists the outgoing interface.

Note that the router also automatically produces a different kind of route, called a *local route*. The local routes define a route for the one specific IP address configured on the router interface. Each local route has a /32 prefix length, defining a *host route*, which defines a route just for that one IP address. For example, the last local route, for 172.16.5.1/32, defines a route that matches only the IP address of 172.16.5.1. Routers use these local routes that list their own local IP addresses to more efficiently forward packets sent to the router itself.

After a router has added these connected routes, the router can route IPv4 packets between those subnets.

Routing Between Subnets on VLANs

Almost all enterprise networks use VLANs. To route IP packets in and out of those VLANs—or more accurately, the subnets that sit on each those VLANs—some router needs to have an IP address in each subnet and have a connected route to each of those subnets. Then the hosts in each subnet can use the router IP addresses as their default gateways, respectively.

Three options exist for connecting a router to each subnet on a VLAN. However, the first option requires too many interfaces and links, and is only mentioned to make the list complete:

- Use a router, with one router LAN interface and cable connected to the switch for each and every VLAN (typically not used).
- Use a router, with a VLAN trunk connecting to a LAN switch.
- Use a Layer 3 switch.

Figure 16-11 shows an example network where the second and third options both happen to be used. The figure shows a central site campus LAN on the left, with 12 VLANs. At the central site, two of the switches act as Layer 3 switches, combining the functions of a router and a switch, routing between all 12 subnets/VLANs. The remote branch sites on the right side of the figure each use two VLANs; each router uses a VLAN trunk to connect to and route for both VLANs.

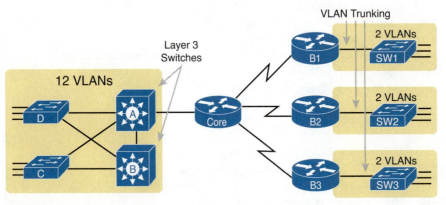

Figure 16-11 *Subinterfaces on Router R1*

Note that Figure 16-11 just shows an example. The engineer could use Layer 3 switching at each site, or routers with VLAN trunking at each site. This chapter focuses more on the details of how to configure the features, as discussed in the next few pages.

Configuring Routing to VLANs using 802.1Q on Routers

This next topic discusses how to route packets to subnets associated with VLANs connected to a router 802.1Q trunk. That long description can be a bit of a chore to repeat each time someone wants to discuss this feature, so over time, the networking world has instead settled on a shorter and more interesting name for this feature: Router on a Stick (ROAS).

ROAS uses router VLAN trunking configuration to give the router a logical router interface connected to each VLAN, and therefore each subnet that sits on a separate VLAN. That trunking configuration revolves around *subinterfaces*. The router needs to have an IP address/mask associated with each VLAN on the trunk. However, the router uses only one physical interface on which to configure the **ip address** command. Cisco solves this problem by creating multiple virtual router interfaces, one associated with each VLAN on that trunk (at least for each VLAN that you want the trunk to support). Cisco calls these virtual interfaces *subinterfaces*.

The ROAS configuration creates a subinterface for each VLAN on the trunk, and the router then treats all frames tagged with that associated VLAN ID as if they came in or out of that subinterface. Figure 16-12 shows the concept with Router B1, one of the branch routers from Figure 16-11. Because this router needs to route between only two VLANs, the figure also shows two subinterfaces, named G0/0.10 and G0/0.20, which create a new place in the configuration where the per-VLAN configuration settings can be made. The router treats frames tagged with VLAN 10 as if they came in or out of G0/0.10, and frames tagged with VLAN 20 as if they came in or out G0/0.20.

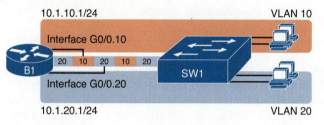

Figure 16-12 *Subinterfaces on Router B1*

Additionally, note that Cisco routers do not attempt to negotiate trunking, so both the router and switch need to manually configure trunking. This chapter discusses the router side of that trunking configuration; the matching switch interface would need to be configured with the **switchport mode trunk** command.

Example 16-2 shows a full example of the 802.1Q trunking configuration required on Router B1 in the figure. More generally, these steps detail how to configure 802.1Q trunking on a router:

Step 1.   Create a unique subinterface for each VLAN that needs to be routed (**interface** *type number.subint*).

Step 2.   Enable 802.1Q, and associate one specific VLAN with the subinterface in subinterface config mode (**encapsulation dot1q** *vlan_id*).

Step 3.   Configure IP settings (address and mask) in subinterface config mode (**ip address** *address mask*).

Example 16-2   *Router Configuration for the 802.1Q Encapsulation Shown in Figure 16-12*

```
B1# show running-config
! Only pertinent lines shown
interface gigabitethernet 0/0
! No IP address up here! No encapsulation up here!
!
interface gigabitethernet 0/0.10
 encapsulation dot1q 10
 ip address 10.1.10.1 255.255.255.0
!
interface gigabitethernet 0/0.20
 encapsulation dot1q 20
 ip address 10.1.20.1 255.255.255.0
!
B1# show ip route
Codes: L - local, C - connected, S - static, R - RIP, M - mobile, B - BGP
! Lines omitted for brevity


     10.0.0.0/8 is variably subnetted, 4 subnets, 2 masks
C        10.1.10.0/24 is directly connected, GigabitEthernet0/0.10
L        10.1.10.1/32 is directly connected, GigabitEthernet0/0.10
C        10.1.20.0/24 is directly connected, GigabitEthernet0/0.20
L        10.1.20.1/32 is directly connected, GigabitEthernet0/0.20
```

First, look at the subinterface numbers. The subinterface number begins with the period, like .10 and .20 in this case. These numbers can be any number from 1 up through a very large number (over 4 billion). The number just needs to be unique among all subinterfaces associated with this one physical interface. In fact, the subinterface number does not even have to match the associated VLAN ID. (The **encapsulation** command, and not the subinterface number, defines the VLAN ID associated with the subinterface.)

NOTE   While not required, most sites do choose to make the subinterface number match the VLAN ID, as shown in Example 16-2, just to avoid confusion.

Each subinterface configuration lists two subcommands. One command (**encapsulation**) enables trunking and defines the VLAN whose frames are considered to be coming in and out of the subinterface. The **ip address** command works the same way it does on any other interface. Note that if the physical Ethernet interface reaches an up/up state, the subinterface should as well, which would then let the router add the connected routes shown at the bottom of the example.

Now that the router has a working interface, with IPv4 addresses configured, the router can route IPv4 packets on these subinterfaces. That is, the router treats these subinterfaces like any physical interface in terms of adding connected routes, matching those routes and forwarding packets to/from those connected subnets.

NOTE   As a brief aside, while Example 16-2 shows 802.1Q configuration, the ISL configuration on the same router would be practically identical. Just substitute the keyword **isl** instead of **dot1q** in each case.

While Example 16-2 shows one way to configure ROAS on a router, that particular example avoids using the native VLAN. However, each 802.1Q trunk has one native VLAN, and when used, the configuration to use that native VLAN differs, with two options for the router side of the configuration:

- Configure the **ip address** command on the physical interface, but without an **encapsulation** command; the router considers this physical interface to be using the native VLAN.

- Configure the **ip address** command on a subinterface, and use the **encapsulation...native** subcommand.

Example 16-3 shows both configuration options with a small change to the same configuration in Example 16-2. In this case, VLAN 10 becomes the native VLAN. The top part of the example shows the option to configure the router to use native VLAN 10, assuming that the switch also has been configured to use native VLAN 10 as well. The second half of the example shows how to configure that same native VLAN on a subinterface.

Example 16-3 *Router Configuration Using Native VLAN 10 on Router B1*

```
! First option: put the native VLAN IP address on the
! physical interface
interface gigabitethernet 0/0
 ip address 10.1.10.1 255.255.255.0
!
interface gigabitethernet 0/0.20
 encapsulation dot1q 20
 ip address 10.1.20.1 255.255.255.0
```
```
! Second option: like normal, but add the native keyword
interface gigabitethernet 0/0.10
 encapsulation dot1q 10 native
 ip address 10.1.10.1 255.255.255.0
!
interface gigabitethernet 0/0.20
 encapsulation dot1q 20
 ip address 10.1.20.1 255.255.255.0
```

Besides just scanning the configuration, the **show vlans** command on a router spells out which router trunk interfaces use which VLANs, which VLAN is the native VLAN, plus some packet statistics. Example 16-4 shows a sample, based on the Router B1 configuration in Example 16-3 (bottom half), in which native VLAN 10 is configured on subinterface G0/0.10. Note that the output identifies VLAN 1 associated with the physical interface, VLAN 10 as the native VLAN associated with G0/0.10, and VLAN 20 associated with G0/0.20.

Example 16-4 *Sample* **show vlans** *Command to Match Sample Router Trunking Configuration*

```
R1# show vlans

Virtual LAN ID:  1 (IEEE 802.1Q Encapsulation)

   vLAN Trunk Interface:    GigabitEthernet0/0

   Protocols Configured:   Address:          Received:      Transmitted:
        Other                                        0                 83
```

```
      69 packets, 20914 bytes input
      147 packets, 11841 bytes output


Virtual LAN ID:  10 (IEEE 802.1Q Encapsulation)


  vLAN Trunk Interface:   GigabitEthernet0/0.10


 This is configured as native Vlan for the following interface(s) :
GigabitEthernet0/0

    Protocols Configured:    Address:           Received:         Transmitted:
          IP              10.1.10.1              2                 3
       Other                                     0                 1


    3 packets, 722 bytes input
    4 packets, 264 bytes output


Virtual LAN ID:  20 (IEEE 802.1Q Encapsulation)


  vLAN Trunk Interface:   GigabitEthernet0/0.20


    Protocols Configured:    Address:           Received:         Transmitted:
          IP              10.1.20.1              0                 134
       Other                                     0                 1


    0 packets, 0 bytes input
    135 packets, 10498 bytes output
```

Finally, for those of you paying close attention to the exam topics, note that the subtopics about inter-VLAN routing and ROAS mention "upstream routing." This topic refers to a basic concept: The router that uses ROAS might only need to route between those subnets off the VLAN trunk, but more than likely, the router will also need to route packets to other subnets in other parts of the enterprise network. This "upstream routing" topic simply reminds us to not forget about the need to configure other router interfaces, static routes, a routing protocol, and so on, so that the router can forward packets to other "upstream" destinations.

Configuring Routing to VLANs Using a Layer 3 Switch

The other option for routing traffic to VLANs uses a device called a Layer 3 switch or multi-layer switch. As introduced back in Chapter 9, "Implementing Ethernet Virtual LANs," a Layer 3 switch is one device that does two primary functions: Layer 2 LAN switching and Layer 3 IP routing. The Layer 2 switch function forwards frames inside each VLAN, but it will not forward frames between VLANs. The Layer 3 forwarding logic—routing—forwards IP packets between VLANs.

The configuration of a Layer 3 switch mostly looks like the Layer 2 switching configuration shown back in Part II of this book, with a small bit of configuration added for the Layer 3 functions. The Layer 3 switching function needs a virtual interface connected to each VLAN internal to the switch. These *VLAN interfaces* act like router interfaces, with an IP address and mask. The Layer 3 switch has an IP routing table, with connected routes off each of these VLAN interfaces. (These interfaces are also referred to as Switched Virtual Interfaces [SVI].)

To show the concept, Figure 16-13 shows the design changes and configuration concept for the same branch office used in Figures 16-11 and 16-12. The figure shows the Layer 3 switch function with a router icon inside the switch, to emphasize that the switch routes the packets. The branch still has two user VLANs, so the Layer 3 switch needs one VLAN interface for each VLAN. Additionally, the traffic still needs to get to the router to access the WAN, so the switch uses a third VLAN (VLAN 30 in this case) for the link to Router B1. This link would not be a trunk, but would be an access link.

Key Topic

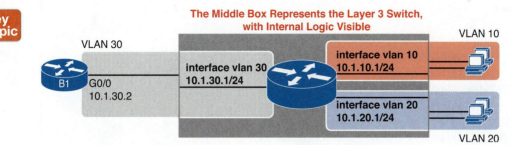

Figure 16-13 *Routing on VLAN Interfaces in a Layer 3 Switch*

The following steps show how to configure Layer 3 switching. Note that on some switches, like the 2960 switches used for the examples in this book, the ability to route IPv4 packets must be enabled first, with a **reload** of the switch required to enable the feature. The rest of the steps after Step 1 would apply to all models of Cisco switches that are capable of doing Layer 3 switching.

Key Topic

Step 1. Enable hardware support for IPv4 routing. For example, on 2960 switches, configure the **sdm prefer lanbase-routing** global command and **reload** the switch.

Step 2. Enable IPv4 routing globally (**ip routing**).

Step 3. Create VLAN interfaces for each VLAN for which the Layer 3 switch is routing packets (**interface vlan** *vlan_id*).

Step 4. Configure an IP address and mask on the VLAN interface (in interface configuration mode for that interface), enabling IPv4 on that VLAN interface (**ip address** *address mask*).

Step 5. If the switch defaults to place the VLAN interface in a disabled (shutdown) state, enable the interface (**no shutdown**).

Example 16-5 shows the configuration to match Figure 16-13. In this case, switch SW1, a 2960, has already used the **sdm prefer lanbase-routing** global command and been reloaded. The example shows the related configuration on all three VLAN interfaces.

Example 16-5 *VLAN Interface Configuration for Layer 3 Switching*

```
ip routing
!
interface vlan 10
 ip address 10.1.10.1 255.255.255.0
!
interface vlan 20
 ip address 10.1.20.1 255.255.255.0
!
interface vlan 30
 ip address 10.1.30.1 255.255.255.0
```

With the VLAN configuration shown here, the switch is ready to route packets between the VLANs as shown in Figure 16-13. To support the routing of packets, the switch adds connected IP routes, as shown in Example 16-6; note that each route is listed as being connected to a different VLAN interface.

Example 16-6 *Connected Routes on a Layer 3 Switch*

```
SW1# show ip route
! legend omitted for brevity

        10.0.0.0/8 is variably subnetted, 6 subnets, 2 masks
C       10.1.10.0/24 is directly connected, Vlan10
L       10.1.10.1/32 is directly connected, Vlan10
C       10.1.20.0/24 is directly connected, Vlan20
L       10.1.20.1/32 is directly connected, Vlan20
C       10.1.30.0/24 is directly connected, Vlan30
L       10.1.30.1/32 is directly connected, Vlan30
```

The switch would also need additional routes to the rest of the network shown in Figure 16-11, possibly using static routes as discussed in the final major section of this chapter.

Secondary IP Addressing

Most networks today make use of either routers with VLAN trunks or Layer 3 switches. This next topic moves to an interesting, but frankly less commonly used, feature that helps overcome some growing pains with an IP network.

Imagine that you planned your IP addressing scheme for a network. Later, a particular subnet grows, and you have used all the valid IP addresses in the subnet. What should you do? Three main options exist:

■ Make the existing subnet larger, by choosing a mask with more host bits. Existing hosts have to change their subnet mask settings, and new hosts can use IP addresses from the expanded address range.

■ Migrate to a completely new (larger) subnet. All existing devices change their IP addresses.

■ Add a second subnet in the same location, using secondary addressing.

The first options works well, as long as the new subnet does not overlap with existing subnets. For example, if the design used 172.16.2.0/24, and it ran out of addresses, the engineer could try to use mask /23 instead. That creates a subnet 172.16.2.0/23, with a range of addresses from 172.16.2.1 to 172.16.3.254. However, if subnet 172.16.3.0/24 had already been assigned to some other part of the network, space would not exist in the addressing plan to make the existing subnet larger.

The second option is more likely to work. The engineer looks at the unused IP addresses in that IP network and picks a new subnet. However, all the existing IP addresses would need to be changed. This is a relatively simple process if most or all hosts use DHCP, but potentially laborious if many hosts use statically configured IP addresses.

The third option uses a Cisco router feature called *secondary IP addressing*. Secondary addressing uses multiple networks or subnets on the same data link. (This feature actually breaks the subnetting rules discussed earlier in this book, but it works.) By using more than one subnet in the same Layer 2 broadcast domain, you increase the number of available IP addresses.

Figure 16-14 shows the ideas behind secondary addressing. Hosts A and B sit on the same LAN, in fact, in the same VLAN. So does R1. No trunking needs to occur, either. In fact, if you ignore the numbers, normally, A, B, and R1 would all be part of the same subnet.

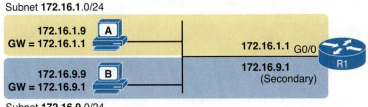

Subnet **172.16.1**.0/24

Subnet **172.16.9**.0/24

Figure 16-14 *TCP/IP Network with Secondary Addresses*

Secondary addressing allows some hosts to have addresses in one IP subnet, others to have addresses in a second IP subnet, and the router to have addresses in both. Both IP subnets would be in the same Layer 2 broadcast domain (VLAN). As a result, the router will have connected routes for both the subnets, so the router can route packets to both subnets and even between both subnets.

Example 16-7 shows the configuration on R1 to match the example shown in Figure 16-14. Note that the second **ip address** command must have the **secondary** keyword, implementing secondary addressing, which tells router to add this as an additional IP address. Without this keyword, the router would replace the other IP address.

Example 16-7 *Secondary IP Addressing Configuration and the* **show ip route** *Command*

```
! Excerpt from show running-config follows...
interface gigabitethernet 0/0
 ip address 172.16.9.1  255.255.255.0 secondary
 ip address 172.16.1.1  255.255.255.0


R1# show ip route connected
! lines omitted for brevity
      172.16.0.0/16 is variably subnetted, 8 subnets, 2 masks
C        172.16.1.0/24 is directly connected, GigabitEthernet0/0
L        172.16.1.1/32 is directly connected, GigabitEthernet0/0
C        172.16.9.0/24 is directly connected, GigabitEthernet0/0
L        172.16.9.1/32 is directly connected, GigabitEthernet0/0
```

Secondary addressing does have one negative: Traffic between hosts on the same VLAN, but in different subnets, requires a trip through the router. For example, in Figure 16-14, when host A in subnet 172.16.1.0 sends a packet to host B, in subnet 172.16.9.0, host A's logic is to send the packet to its default gateway. So, the sending host sends the packet to the router, which then sends the packet to host B, which is in the other IP subnet but in the same Layer 2 VLAN.

Supporting Connected Routes to Subnet Zero

The other features discussed in this section—configuring IP addresses on physical interfaces, using ROAS, Layer 3 switching, and even secondary addressing—all give network engineers some options for how to connect routers to local subnets so that the router can route packets to and from those subnets. This last topic in the second major section of the chapter looks at a router feature that has been around for a long time to overcome some early problems in the history of IPv4, but today, you would not seek to use this feature as a means to an end.

IOS can restrict a router from configuring an **ip address** command with an address inside the zero subnet. The *zero subnet* (or *subnet zero*) is the one subnet in each classful network that has all binary 0s in the subnet part of the binary version of the subnet number. In decimal, the zero subnet happens to be the same number as the classful network number.

> **NOTE**   Chapter 19, "Subnet Design," discusses the concept around zero subnets in a little more detail.

IOS allows the network engineer to tell a router to either allow addresses in the zero subnet or not. The motivation has to do with some older IP routing protocols that did not support the use of the zero subnet. Basically, with the **ip subnet-zero** command configured, IOS allows the zero subnet with no restrictions. With the **no ip subnet-zero** command configured, the router rejects any **ip address** command that uses an address/mask combination for the zero subnet. For many of the more recent IOS versions, IOS allows the use of the zero subnet.

Example 16-8 shows how a router accepts the interface subcommand **ip address 10.0.0.1 255.255.255.0** at first, with the default setting, but later rejects the command after changing to use **no ip subnet-zero**. Note that the error message does not mention the zero subnet, instead simply stating "bad mask."

Example 16-8   *Effects of* [no] ip subnet-zero *on a Local Router*

```
R1# configure terminal
Enter configuration commands, one per line.  End with CNTL/Z.
R1(config)# interface g0/1
R1(config-if)# ip address 10.0.0.1 255.255.255.0
R1(config-if)# no ip address
R1(config-if)# exit
R1(config)# no ip subnet-zero
R1(config)# interface g0/1
R1(config-if)# ip address 10.0.0.1 255.255.255.0
Bad mask /24 for address 10.0.0.1
```

Note that the **no ip subnet-zero** command affects the local router's **ip address** commands, as well as the local router's **ip route** commands (which define static routes). However, it does not affect the local router's routes as learned with a routing protocol. For example, R1 could be configured with **no ip subnet-zero**, but still learn a route for a zero subnet using a routing protocol.

Configuring Static Routes

All routers add connected routes, as discussed in the previous section. Then, most networks use dynamic routing protocols to cause each router to learn the rest of the routes in an internetwork. Networks use static routes—routes added to a routing table through direct configuration—much less often than dynamic routing. However, static routes can be useful at times, and they happen to be useful learning tools as well. This last of three major sections in the chapter discusses static routes.

Static Route Configuration

IOS allows the definition of individual static routes using the **ip route** global configuration command. Every **ip route** command defines a destination that can be matched, usually with a subnet ID and mask. The command also lists the forwarding instructions, typically listing either the outgoing interface or the next-hop router's IP address. IOS then takes that information and adds that route to the IP routing table.

As an example, Figure 16-15 shows a small IP network. The diagram actually holds a subset of Figure 16-3, from earlier in this chapter, with some of the unrelated details removed. The figure shows only the details related to a static route on R1, for subnet 172.16.2.0/24, which sits on the far right. To create that static route on R1, R1 will configure the subnet ID and mask, and either R1's outgoing interface (S0/0/0), or R2 as the next-hop router IP address (172.16.4.2).

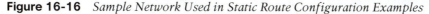
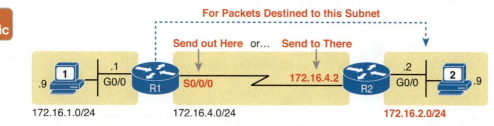

Figure 16-15 *Static Route Configuration Concept*

Example 16-9 shows the configuration of a couple of sample static routes. In particular, it shows routes on Router R1 in Figure 16-16, for the two subnets on the right side of the figure.

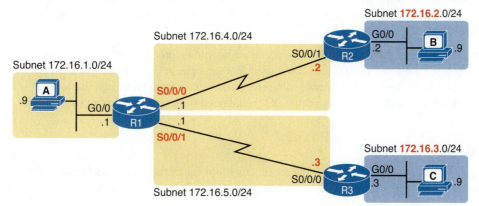

Figure 16-16 *Sample Network Used in Static Route Configuration Examples*

Example 16-9 *Static Routes Added to R1*

```
ip route 172.16.2.0 255.255.255.0 172.16.4.2
ip route 172.16.3.0 255.255.255.0 S0/0/1
```

The two example **ip route** commands show the two different styles. The first command shows subnet 172.16.2.0, mask 255.255.255.0, which sits on a LAN near Router R2. That same first command lists 172.16.4.2, R2's IP address, as the next-hop router. This route basically says this: To send packets to the subnet off Router R2, send them to R2.

The second route has the same kind of logic, but instead of identifying the next router by IP address, it lists the local router's outgoing interface. This route basically states: To send packets to the subnet off Router R3, send them out my own local S0/0/1 interface (which happens to connect to R3).

The routes created by these two **ip route** commands actually look a little different in the IP routing table. Both are static routes. However, the route that used the outgoing interface configuration is also noted as a connected route; this is just a quirk of the output of the **show ip route** command.

Example 16-10 lists these two routes using the **show ip route static** command. This command lists the details of static routes only, but it also lists a few statistics about all IPv4 routes. For example, the example shows two lines, for the two static routes configured in Example 16-9, but statistics state that this routes has routes for ten subnets.

Example 16-10 *Static Routes Added to R1*

```
R1# show ip route static
Codes: L - local, C - connected, S - static, R - RIP, M - mobile, B - BGP
! lines omitted for brevity
Gateway of last resort is not set

      172.16.0.0/16 is variably subnetted, 10 subnets, 2 masks
S        172.16.2.0/24 [1/0] via 172.16.4.2
S        172.16.3.0/24 is directly connected, Serial0/0/1
```

IOS adds and removes these static routes dynamically over time, based on whether the outgoing interface is working or not. For example, in this case, if R1's S0/0/1 interface fails, R1 removes the static route to 172.16.3.0/24 from the IPv4 routing table. Later, when the interface comes up again, IOS adds the route back to the routing table. Also, note that the **ip route** command also supports the **permanent** keyword, which tells IOS to leave the static route in the routing table, even when the associated interface fails.

Finally, if using static routes, and not using any dynamic routing protocols at all, all routers would need to have some static routes configured. For example, at this point, in the network if Figure 16-16, PC A would not be able to receive packets back from PC B, because Router R2 does not have a route for PC A's subnet. R2 would need static routes for other subnets, as would R3.

Static Default Routes

When a router tries to route a packet, the router might not match the packet's destination IP address with any route. When that happens, the router normally just discards the packet.

Routers can be configured so that they use either a statically configured or dynamically learned default route. The default route matches all packets, so that if a packet does not match any other more specific route in the routing table, the router can at least forward the packet based on the default route.

One classic example in which companies might use static default routes in their enterprise TCP/IP networks is when the company has many remote sites, each with a single, relatively slow WAN connection. Each remote site has only one possible physical route to use to send packets to the rest of the network. So, rather than use a routing protocol, which sends messages over the WAN and uses precious WAN bandwidth, each remote route might use a default route that sends all traffic to the central site, as shown in Figure 16-17.

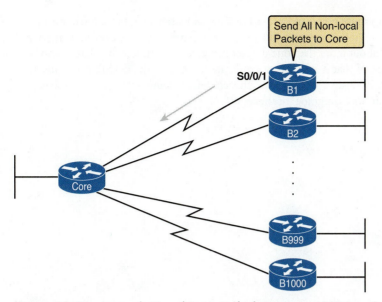

Figure 16-17 *Example Use of Static Default Routes at 1000 Low-Speed Remote Sites*

IOS allows the configuration of a static default route by using special values for the subnet and mask fields in the **ip route** command: 0.0.0.0 and 0.0.0.0. For example, the command **ip route 0.0.0.0 0.0.0.0 S0/0/1** creates a static default route on Router B1—a route that matches all IP packets—and sends those packets out interface S0/0/1.

Example 16-11 shows an example of a static default route, using Router R2 from recent Figure 16-16. Earlier, that figure, along with example 16-9, showed R1 with static routes to the two subnets on the right side of the figure. Example 16-11 shows R2, on the right, using a static default route to route packets back to the left side of the figure.

Example 16-11 *Adding a Static Default Route on R2 (Figure 16-16)*

```
R2# configure terminal
Enter configuration commands, one per line.  End with CNTL/Z.
R2(config)# ip route 0.0.0.0 0.0.0.0 s0/0/1
R2(config)# ^Z
R2# show ip route
Codes: L - local, C - connected, S - static, R - RIP, M - mobile, B - BGP
       D - EIGRP, EX - EIGRP external, O - OSPF, IA - OSPF inter area
       N1 - OSPF NSSA external type 1, N2 - OSPF NSSA external type 2
       E1 - OSPF external type 1, E2 - OSPF external type 2
       i - IS-IS, su - IS-IS summary, L1 - IS-IS level-1, L2 - IS-IS level-2
       ia - IS-IS inter area, * - candidate default, U - per-user static route
       o - ODR, P - periodic downloaded static route, H - NHRP, l - LISP
       + - replicated route, % - next hop override

Gateway of last resort is 0.0.0.0 to network 0.0.0.0

S*     0.0.0.0/0 is directly connected, Serial0/0/1
       172.16.0.0/16 is variably subnetted, 4 subnets, 2 masks
C         172.16.2.0/24 is directly connected, GigabitEthernet0/0
L         172.16.2.2/32 is directly connected, GigabitEthernet0/0
C         172.16.4.0/24 is directly connected, Serial0/0/1
L         172.16.4.2/32 is directly connected, Serial0/0/1
```

The output of the **show ip route** command lists a few new and interesting facts. First, it lists the route with a code of "S," meaning static, but also with a *, meaning it is a *candidate default route*. A router can learn about more than one default route, and the router then has to choose which one to use; the * means that it is at least a candidate to become the default route. Just above, the "Gateway of Last Resort" refers to the chosen default route, which in this case is the just-configured static route with outgoing interface S0/0/1.

Review Activities

Chapter Summary

- IP routing—the process of forwarding IP packets—delivers packets across entire TCP/IP networks, from the device that originally builds the IP packet to the device that is supposed to receive the packet. In other words, IP routing delivers IP packets from the sending host to the destination host.

- The routing process starts with the host that creates the IP packet. First, the host asks the question, is the destination IP address of this new packet in my local subnet? The host uses its own IP address/mask to determine the range of addresses in the local subnet. Based on its own opinion of the range of addresses in the local subnet, a LAN-based host acts as follows:

  - If the destination is local, send directly:

    - Find the destination host's MAC address. Use the already known Address Resolution Protocol (ARP) table entry, or use ARP messages to learn the information.

    - Encapsulate the IP packet in a data link frame, with the destination data link address of the destination host.

  - If the destination is not local, send to the default gateway:

    - Find the default gateway's MAC address. Use the already known ARP table entry, or use ARP messages to learn the information.

    - Encapsulate the IP packet in a data link frame, with the destination data link address of the default gateway.

- Routers have a little more routing work to do compared to hosts. While the host logic began with an IP packet sitting in memory, a router has some work to do before getting to that point. With the following five-step summary of a router's routing logic, the router takes the first two steps just to receive the frame and extract the IP packet, before thinking about the packet's destination address at Step 3.

  Step 1. For each received data link frame, choose whether to process the frame. Process it if

  - The frame has no errors (per the data-link trailer frame check sequence or FCS field)

  - The frame's destination data link address is the router's address (or an appropriate multicast or broadcast)

  Step 2. If choosing to process the frame at Step 1, deencapsulate the packet from inside the data link frame.

  Step 3. Make a routing decision. To do so, compare the packet's destination IP address to the routing table and find the route that matches the destination address. This route identifies the outgoing interface of the router and possibly the next-hop router.

  Step 4. Encapsulate the packet into a data link frame appropriate for the outgoing interface. When forwarding out LAN interfaces, this requires the use of ARP.

  Step 5. Transmit the frame out the outgoing interface, as listed in the matched IP route.

- To summarize the routing process, the router receives a frame, removes the packet from inside the frame, decides where to forward the packet, puts the packet into another frame, and sends the frame.

- When a router can route IP packets out one or more interfaces, the router needs some routes. Routers can add routes to their routing tables through three methods:

- **Connected routes:** Added due to the configuration of the **ip address** interface subcommand on the local router

- **Static routes:** Added due to the configuration of the **ip route** global command on the local router

- **Routing protocols:** Added as a function by configuration on all routers, resulting in a process by which routers dynamically tell each other about the network so that they all learn routes

- Cisco IOS can restrict a router from configuring an **ip address** command with an address inside the zero subnet. The *zero subnet* (or *subnet zero*) is the one subnet in each classful network that has all binary 0s in the subnet part of the binary version of the subnet number. In decimal, the zero subnet happens to be the same number as the classful network number.

- When a router tries to route a packet, the router might not match the packet's destination IP address with any route at all. When that happens, the router normally just discards the packet.

- Routers can be configured so that they use either a statically configured or dynamically learned default route. The default route matches all packets, so that if a packet does not match any other more specific route in the routing table, the router can at least forward the packet based on the default route.

Review Questions

Answer these review questions. You can find the answers at the bottom of the last page of the chapter. For thorough explanations, see DVD Appendix C, "Answers to Review Questions."

1. A PC opens a command prompt and uses the **ipconfig** command to see that the PC's IP address and mask are 192.168.4.77 and 255.255.255.224. The user then runs a test using the **ping 192.168.4.117** command. Which of the following answers is the most likely to happen?

    A. The PC sends packets directly to the host with address 192.168.4.117.

    B. The PC sends packets to its default gateway.

    C. The PC sends a DNS query for 192.168.4.117.

    D. The PC sends an ARP looking for the MAC address of the DHCP server.

2. Router R1 lists a route in its routing table. Which of the following answers list a fact from a route, that the router then compares to the packet's destination address? (Choose 2 answers.)

    A. Mask

    B. Next-hop router

    C. Subnet ID

    D. Outgoing interface

3. Router 1 has a Fast Ethernet interface 0/0 with IP address 10.1.1.1. The interface is connected to a switch. This connection is then migrated to use 802.1Q trunking. Which of the following commands could be part of a valid configuration for Router 1's Fa0/0 interface? (Choose two answers.)

   A. interface fastethernet 0/0.4

   B. dot1q enable

   C. dot1q enable 4

   D. trunking enable

   E. trunking enable 4

   F. encapsulation dot1q 4

4. A router is configured with the **no ip subnet-zero** global configuration command. Which of the following interface subcommands would not be accepted by this router?

   A. ip address 10.1.1.1 255.255.255.0

   B. ip address 10.0.0.129 255.255.255.128

   C. ip address 10.1.2.2 255.254.0.0

   D. ip address 10.0.0.5 255.255.255.252

5. A Layer 3 switch has been configured to route IP packets between VLANs 1, 2, and 3, which connect to subnets 172.20.1.0/25, 172.20.2.0/25, and 172.20.3.0/25, respectively. The engineer issues a **show ip route** command on the Layer 3 switch, listing the connected routes. Which of the following answers lists a piece of information that should be in at least one of the routes?

   A. Interface Gigabit Ethernet 0/0.3

   B. Next-hop router 172.20.4.1

   C. Interface VLAN 2

   D. Mask 255.255.255.0

6. An engineer configures a static IPv4 route on Router R1. Which of the following pieces of information should not be listed as a parameter in the configuration command that creates this static IPv4 route?

   A. The destination subnet's subnet ID

   B. The next-hop router's IP address

   C. The next-hop router's neighboring interface

   D. The subnet mask

7. Which of the following commands correctly configures a static route?

   A. ip route 10.1.3.0 255.255.255.0 10.1.130.253

   B. ip route 10.1.3.0 serial 0

   C. ip route 10.1.3.0 /24 10.1.130.253

   D. ip route 10.1.3.0 /24 serial 0

Review All the Key Topics

Review the most important topics from this chapter, noted with the Key Topic icon. Table 16-2 lists these key topics and where each is discussed.

Table 16-2   Key Topics for Chapter 16

Key Topic Element	Description	Page Number
List	Steps taken by a host when forwarding IP packets	376
List	Steps taken by a router when forwarding IP packets	377
Figure 16-2	Diagram of five routing steps taken by a router	378
Figure 16-7	Breakdown of IP routing table with matching and forwarding details	381
List	Three common sources from which routers build IP routes	384
List	Rules regarding when a router creates a connected route	384
List	Three options for connecting a router to each VLAN	386
Figure 16-12	Concept of VLAN subinterfaces on a router	387
List	802.1Q configuration checklist	387
List	802.1 native VLAN configuration checklist	389
Figure 16-13	Layer 3 switching concept and configuration	391
List	Layer 3 switching configuration	391
Figure 16-15	Static route configuration concept	395

Complete the Tables and Lists from Memory

Print a copy of DVD Appendix M, "Memory Tables," or at least the section for this chapter, and complete the tables and lists from memory. DVD Appendix N, "Memory Tables Answer Key," includes completed tables and lists for you to check your work.

Definitions of Key Terms

After your first reading of the chapter, try to define these key terms, but do not be concerned about getting them all correct at that time. Chapter 30 directs you in how to use these terms for late-stage preparation for the exam.

default gateway/router, ARP table, routing table, next-hop router, outgoing interface, subinterface, VLAN interface, Layer 3 switch, Cisco Express Forwarding (CEF), connected route, static route, default route, zero subnet

Command Reference to Check Your Memory

Although you should not necessarily memorize the information in the tables in this section, this section does include a reference for the configuration and EXEC commands covered in this chapter. Practically speaking, you should memorize the commands as a side effect of reading the chapter and doing all the activities in this exam preparation section. To check to see how well you have memorized the commands as a side effect of your other studies, cover the left side of the table with a piece of paper, read the descriptions on the right side, and see whether you remember the command.

Table 16-3 Chapter 16 Configuration Command Reference

Command	Description
ip address *ip-address mask* [secondary]	Interface subcommand that assigns the interface's IP address and optionally makes the address a secondary address
interface *type number.subint*	Global command to create a subinterface and to enter configuration mode for that subinterface
encapsulation dot1q *vlan-id* [native]	A subinterface subcommand that tells the router to use 802.1Q trunking, for a particular VLAN, and with the **native** keyword, to not encapsulate in a trunking header
encapsulation isl *vlan-identifier*	A subinterface subcommand that tells the router to use ISL trunking for a particular VLAN
sdm prefer lanbase-routing	A command on Cisco switches that enables the switch to support IP routing if configured
[no] ip routing	Global command that enables (**ip routing**) or disables (**no ip routing**) the routing of IPv4 packets on a router or Layer 3 switch
interface vlan *vlan_id*	Global command on a Layer 3 switch to create a VLAN interface and to enter configuration mode for that VLAN interface
[no] ip subnet-zero	Global command that allows (**ip subnet-zero**) or disallows (**no ip subnet-zero**) the configuration of an interface IP address in a zero subnet
ip route *prefix mask* {*ip-address* | *interface-type interface-number*} [*distance*] [permanent]	Global configuration command that creates a static route
ip default-network *network-number*	Global command that creates a default route based on the router's route to reach the classful network listed in the command

Table 16-4 Chapter 16 EXEC Command Reference

Command	Description
show ip route	Lists the router's entire routing table
show ip route [connected | static | ospf]	Lists a subnet of the IP routing table
show ip route *ip-address*	Lists detailed information about the route that a router matches for the listed IP address
show vlans	Lists VLAN configuration and statistics for VLAN trunks configured on routers

Answers to Review Questions:

1 B **2** A and C **3** A and F **4** C **5** C **6** C **7** A

Chapter 17

Learning IPv4 Routes with OSPFv2

The Open Shortest Path First (OSPF) routing protocol can be used by each router such that all routers learn routes to all subnets in an enterprise IPv4 network. In fact, with a relatively simple OSPF design, the routers could all use the same exact OSPF configuration, with two commands: **router ospf 1** and **network 0.0.0.0 255.255.255.255 area 0**. If your only goal was to get OSPF working right now, ignoring any desire to understand it, you could just skip the chapter, configure all the routers, and be finished. (Tempting, isn't it?)

Of course, both for real networking jobs and for the CCENT and CCNA exams, it helps to both understand the concepts and to know the configuration options. This chapter walks you through the entire process, all in one chapter. It starts with a major section that compares different routing protocols, and different concepts related to routing protocols, to introduce the topic. The middle of the three major sections looks at the theory behind link-state routing protocols, because OSPF uses link-state principles. The last section shows how to configure OSPF using basic parameters, with the corresponding **show** commands.

Note that OSPF version 2 (OSPFv2) happens to be the long-established version of OSPF used for IPv4, while OSPF version 3 (OSPFv3) was defined specifically to support IPv6. So, this chapter discusses routing protocols for IPv4 only, so all references to OSPF refer to OSPFv2. Chapter 29, "Implementing IPv6 Routing," discusses OSPF's use with IPv6.

This chapter covers the following exam topics:

IP Routing Technologies

Configure and verify utilizing the CLI to set basic Router configuration

  Cisco IOS commands to perform basic router setup

Verify router configuration and network connectivity

  Cisco IOS commands to review basic router information and network connectivity

Differentiate methods of routing and routing protocols

  Static vs. Dynamic

  Link state vs. Distance Vector

  Passive interfaces

Configure and verify OSPF (single area)

  Benefit of single area

  Configure OSPF v2

  Router ID

  Passive interface

Foundation Topics

Comparing Dynamic Routing Protocol Features

Routers add IP routes to their routing tables using three methods: connected routes, static routes, and routes learned by using dynamic routing protocols. Before we get too far into the discussion, however, it is important to define a few related terms and clear up any misconceptions about the terms *routing protocol*, *routed protocol*, and *routable protocol*. The concepts behind these terms are not that difficult, but because the terms are so similar, and because many documents pay poor attention to when each of these terms is used, they can be a bit confusing. These terms are generally defined as follows:

- **Routing protocol:** A set of messages, rules, and algorithms used by routers for the overall purpose of learning routes. This process includes the exchange and analysis of routing information. Each router chooses the best route to each subnet (path selection) and finally places those best routes in its IP routing table. Examples include RIP, EIGRP, OSPF, and BGP.

- **Routed protocol and routable protocol:** Both terms refer to a protocol that defines a packet structure and logical addressing, allowing routers to forward or route the packets. Routers forward packets defined by routed and routable protocols. Examples include IP Version 4 (IPv4) and IP Version 6 (IPv6).

> **NOTE** The term *path selection* sometimes refers to part of the job of a routing protocol, in which the routing protocol chooses the best route.

Even though routing protocols (such as OSPF) are different from routed protocols (such as IP), they do work together very closely. The routing process forwards IP packets, but if a router does not have any routes in its IP routing table that match a packet's destination address, the router discards the packet. Routers need routing protocols so that the routers can learn all the possible routes and add them to the routing table, so that the routing process can forward (route) routable protocols such as IP.

Routing Protocol Functions

Cisco IOS software supports several IP routing protocols, performing the same general functions:

1. Learn routing information about IP subnets from other neighboring routers.

2. Advertise routing information about IP subnets to other neighboring routers.

3. If more than one possible route exists to reach one subnet, pick the best route based on a metric.

4. If the network topology changes—for example, a link fails—react by advertising that some routes have failed and pick a new currently best route. (This process is called convergence.)

> **NOTE** A neighboring router connects to the same link as another router, for example, the same WAN link or the same Ethernet LAN.

Figure 17-1 shows an example of three of the four functions in the list. Both R1 and R3 learn about a route to subnet 172.16.3.0/24 from R2 (function 1). After R3 learns about the route to 172.16.3.0/24 from R2, R3 advertises that route to R1 (function 2). Then R1 must make a decision about the two routes it learned about for reaching subnet 172.16.3.0/24: one with metric 1 from R2 and one with metric 2 from R3. R1 chooses the lower metric route through R2 (function 3).

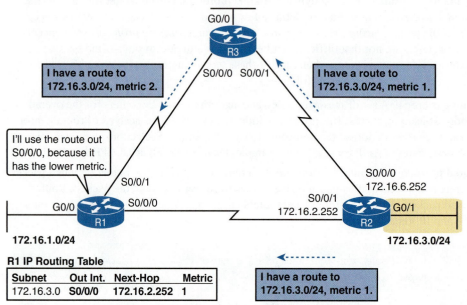

Figure 17-1 *Three of the Four Basic Functions of Routing Protocols*

Convergence is the fourth routing protocol function listed here. The term *convergence* refers to a process that occurs when the topology changes—that is, when either a router or link fails or comes back up again. When something changes, the best routes available in the network can change. Convergence simply refers to the process by which all the routers collectively realize something has changed, advertise the information about the changes to all the other routers, and all the routers then choose the currently best routes for each subnet. The ability to converge quickly, without causing loops, is one of the most important considerations when choosing which IP routing protocol to use.

In Figure 17-1, convergence might occur if the link between R1 and R2 failed. In that case, R1 should stop using its old route for subnet 172.16.3.0/24 (directly through R2) and begin sending packets to R3.

Interior and Exterior Routing Protocols

IP routing protocols fall into one of two major categories: *interior gateway protocols (IGP)* or *exterior gateway protocols (EGP)*. The definitions of each are as follows:

- **IGP:** A routing protocol that was designed and intended for use inside a single autonomous system (AS)

- **EGP:** A routing protocol that was designed and intended for use between different autonomous systems

> **NOTE**   The terms IGP and EGP include the word gateway because routers used to be called gateways.

These definitions use another new term: autonomous system (AS). An AS is a network under the administrative control of a single organization. For example, a network created and paid for by a single company is probably a single AS, and an network created by a single school system is probably a single AS. Other examples include large divisions of a state or national government, where different government agencies might be able to build their own networks. Each ISP is also typically a single different AS.

Some routing protocols work best inside a single AS by design, so these routing protocols are called IGPs. Conversely, routing protocols designed to exchange routes between routers in different autonomous systems are called EGPs. Today, Border Gateway Protocol (BGP) is the only EGP used.

Each AS can be assigned a number called (unsurprisingly) an *AS number (ASN)*. Like public IP addresses, the Internet Assigned Numbers Authority (IANA, www.iana.org) controls the worldwide rights to assigning ASNs. It delegates that authority to other organizations around the world, typically to the same organizations that assign public IP addresses. For example, in North America, the American Registry for Internet Numbers (ARIN, www.arin.net) assigns public IP address ranges and ASNs.

Figure 17-2 shows a small view of the worldwide Internet. The figure shows two enterprises and three ISPs using IGPs (OSPF and EIGRP) inside their own networks and with BGP being used between the ASNs.

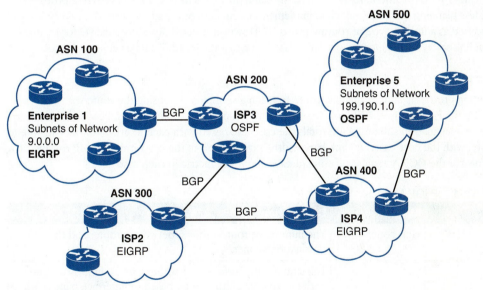

Figure 17-2 *Comparing Locations for Using IGPs and EGPs*

Comparing IGPs

Organizations have several options when choosing an IGP for their enterprise network, but most companies today use either OSPF or EIGRP. This book discusses OSPF in some depth, with the ICND2 book discussing more about OSPF and also introducing EIGRP. While these books will compare and contrast these most common IGPs, this section first discusses some of the main goals of every IGP, comparing OSPF, EIGRP, plus a few other IPv4 routing protocols.

IGP Routing Protocol Algorithms

A routing protocol's underlying algorithm determines how the routing protocol does its job. The term *routing protocol algorithm* simply refers to the logic and processes used by different routing protocols to solve the problem of learning all routes, choosing the best route to each subnet, and converging in reaction to changes in the internetwork. Three main branches of routing protocol algorithms exist for IGP routing protocols:

- Distance vector (sometimes called Bellman-Ford after its creators)
- Advanced distance vector (sometimes called "balanced hybrid")
- Link-state

Historically speaking, distance vector protocols were invented first, mainly in the early 1980s. Routing Information Protocol (RIP) was the first popularly used IP distance vector protocol, with the Cisco-proprietary Interior Gateway Routing Protocol (IGRP) being introduced a little later.

By the early 1990s, distance vector protocols' somewhat slow convergence and potential for routing loops drove the development of new alternative routing protocols that used new algorithms. Link-state protocols—in particular, Open Shortest Path First (OSPF) and Integrated Intermediate System to Intermediate System (IS-IS)—solved the main issues. They also came with a price: They required extra CPU and memory on routers, with more planning required from the network engineers.

Around the same time as the introduction of OSPF, Cisco created a proprietary routing protocol called Enhanced Interior Gateway Routing Protocol (EIGRP), which used some features of the earlier IGRP protocol. EIGRP solved the same problems as did link-state routing protocols, but less planning was required when implementing the network. As time went on, EIGRP was classified as a unique type of routing protocol. However, it used more distance vector features than link-state, so it is more commonly classified as an advanced distance vector protocol.

Metrics

Routing protocols choose the best route to reach a subnet by choosing the route with the lowest metric. For example, RIP uses a counter of the number of routers (hops) between a router and the destination subnet. OSPF totals the cost associated with each interface in the end-to-end route, with the cost based on link bandwidth. Table 17-1 lists the most important IP routing protocols for the CCNA exams and some details about the metric in each case.

Table 17-1 IP IGP Metrics

IGP	Metric	Description
RIP-2	Hop count	The number of routers (hops) between a router and the destination subnet.
OSPF	Cost	The sum of all interface cost settings for all links in a route, with the cost defaulting to be based on interface bandwidth.
EIGRP	Composite of bandwidth and delay	Calculated based on the route's slowest link and the cumulative delay associated with each interface in the route.

While today's CCENT and CCNA R/S exams ignore RIP, a brief comparison of the metric used by the older RIP, versus the metric used by EIGRP, shows some insight into why OSPF and EIGRP surpassed RIP. Figure 17-3 shows an example in which Router B has two possible routes to subnet 10.1.1.0 on the left side of the network: a shorter route over a very slow 64-Kbps link, or a longer route over two higher-speed (T1) links.

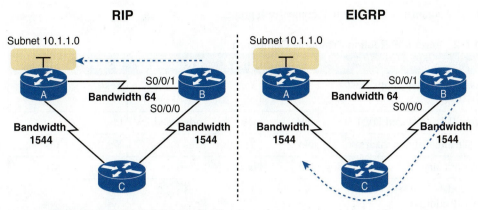

Figure 17-3 *RIP and EIGRP Metrics Compared*

The left side of the figure shows the results of RIP in this network. Using hop count, Router B learns of a 1-hop route directly to Router A through B's S0/0/1 interface. B also learns a two-hop route through Router C, through B's S0/0/0 interface. Router B chooses the lower hop count route, which happens to go over the slow speed link.

The right side of the figure shows the arguably better choice made by EIGRP based on its better metric.

To cause EIGRP to make the right choice, the engineer correctly configured the interface bandwidth to match the actual link speeds, thereby allowing EIGRP to choose the faster route. (The **bandwidth** interface subcommand does not change the actual physical speed of the interface. It just tells the IOS what speed to assume the interface is using.)

Other IGP Comparisons

Some other IGP comparisons can be made. However, some topics require more fundamental knowledge of specific routing protocols, or other features not yet covered in this book. For now, this section introduces a few more comparison points, and leaves the details until later in the book.

First, routing protocols differ based on whether they are classless routing protocols (thereby supporting VLSM), or classful, which means they do not support VLSM. VLSM, as discussed at length in Chapter 20, "Variable Length Subnet Masks," is a subnetting design that uses more than one mask in different subnets of the same Class A, B, or C network. *Classless routing protocols* support VLSM by sending Updates with subnet masks in the message, whereas the generally older classful routing protocols do not send masks in the routing update messages.

Routing protocols also differ in how they support route summarization. Chapter 21, "Route Summarization," discusses these features in some depth, but for now, know that modern networks want to be able to use manual route summarization, and all the IGP routing protocols mentioned in this book, except the truly old RIP Version 1 (RIP-1), supports manual route summarization.

Table 17-2 summarizes the key IGP comparison points.

Table 17-2   Interior IP Routing Protocols Compared

Feature	RIP-1	RIP-2	EIGRP	OSPF	IS-IS
Classless/sends mask in updates/ supports VLSM	No	Yes	Yes	Yes	Yes
Algorithm (DV, advanced DV, LS)	DV	DV	advanced DV	LS	LS
Supports manual summarization	No	Yes	Yes	Yes	Yes
Cisco-proprietary	No	No	Yes[1]	No	No
Routing updates are sent to a multicast IP address	No	Yes	Yes	Yes	—
Convergence	Slow	Slow	Fast	Fast	Fast

[1] Although Cisco created EIGRP, and has kept it as a proprietary protocol for many years, Cisco happened to choose to publish EIGRP as an informational RFC around the time this book was published in early 2013. This choice allows other vendors to implement EIGRP, while Cisco retains the rights to the protocol.

Administrative Distance

Many companies and organizations use a single routing protocol. However, in some cases, a company needs to use multiple routing protocols. For example, if two companies connect their networks so that they can exchange information, they need to exchange some routing information. If one company uses OSPF, and the other uses EIGRP, on at least one router, both OSPF and EIGRP must be used. Then, that router can take routes learned by OSPF and advertise them into EIGRP, and vice versa, through a process called *route redistribution*.

Depending on the network topology, the two routing protocols might learn routes to the same subnets. When a single routing protocol learns multiple routes to the same subnet, the metric tells it which route is best. However, when two different routing protocols learn routes to the same subnet, because each routing protocol's metric is based on different information, IOS cannot compare the metrics. For example, OSPF might learn a route to subnet 10.1.1.0 with metric 101, and EIGRP might learn a route to 10.1.1.0 with metric 2,195,416, but the EIGRP might be the better route—or it might not. There is simply no basis for comparison between the two metrics.

When IOS must choose between routes learned using different routing protocols, IOS uses a concept called *administrative distance*. Administrative distance is a number that denotes how believable an entire routing protocol is on a single router. The lower the number, the better, or more believable, the routing protocol. For example, RIP has a default administrative distance of 120, OSPF uses a default of 110, and EIGRP defaults to 90. When using OSPF and EIGRP, the router will believe the EIGRP route instead of the OSPF route (at least by default). The administrative distance values are configured on a single router and are not exchanged with other routers. Table 17-3 lists the various sources of routing information, along with the default administrative distances.

Key Topic

Table 17-3   Default Administrative Distances

Route Type	Administrative Distance
Connected	0
Static	1
BGP (external routes)	20
EIGRP (internal routes)	90
IGRP	100
OSPF	110
IS-IS	115
RIP	120
EIGRP (external routes)	170
BGP (internal routes)	200
Unusable	255

17

NOTE   The **show ip route** command lists each route's administrative distance as the first of the two numbers inside the brackets. The second number in brackets is the metric.

The table shows the default administrative distance values, but IOS can be configured to change the administrative distance of a particular routing protocol, a particular route, or even a static route. For example, the command **ip route 10.1.3.0 255.255.255.0 10.1.130.253** defines a static route with a default administrative distance of 1, but the command **ip route 10.1.3.0 255.255.255.0 10.1.130.253 210** defines the same static route with an administrative distance of 210. So, you can actually create a static route that is only used when the routing protocol does not find a route, just by giving the static route a higher administrative distance.

Understanding the OSPF Link-State Routing Protocol

Routing protocols basically exchange information so routers can learn routes. The routers learn information about subnets, routes to those subnets, and metric information about how good each route is compared to others. The routing protocol can then choose the currently best route to each subnet, building the IP routing table.

This next (second) major section continues to look at routing protocol concepts, now by narrowing the focus to only link-state protocols, specifically OSPF. This section begins by discussing how OSPF routers learn information and choose what routes to add to the routing table. Then, the discussion backs up a bit to a fundamental part of the process: How OSPF routers use neighbor relationships, and how routers must be neighbors before they ever exchange routing information and learn routes. This section ends with some design discussions about how OSPF scales to larger and larger enterprise designs, and how that impacts the details of how link-state protocols work.

Building the LSDB and Creating IP Routes

Link-state protocols build IP routes with a couple of major steps. First, the routers together build a lot of information about the network: routers, links, IP address, status information, and so on. Then the routers flood the information, so all routers know the same information. At that point, each router can calculate routes to all subnets, but from each router's own perspective.

Topology Information and LSAs

Routers using link-state routing protocols need to collectively advertise practically every detail about the internetwork to all the other routers. At the end of the process of *flooding* the information to all routers, every router in the internetwork has the exact same information about the internetwork. Flooding a lot of detailed information to every router sounds like a lot of work, and relative to distance vector routing protocols, it is.

Open Shortest Path First (OSPF), the most popular link-state IP routing protocol, organizes topology information using link-state advertisements (LSA) and the link-state database (LSDB). Figure 17-4 represents the ideas. Each LSA is a data structure with some specific information about the network topology; the LSDB is simply the collection of all the LSAs known to a router. When sitting at the CLI of a router that uses OSPF, the **show ip ospf database** command lists information about the LSDB on that router by listing some of the information in each of the LSAs in the LSDB.

Link State Database (LSDB)

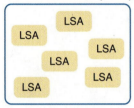

Figure 17-4   *LSA and LSDB Relationship*

Figure 17-5 shows the general idea of the flooding process, with R8 creating and flooding its router LSA. The router LSA for Router R8 describes the router itself, including the existence of subnet 172.16.3.0/24, as seen on the right side of the figure. (Note that Figure 17-5 actually shows only a subset of the information in R8's router LSA.)

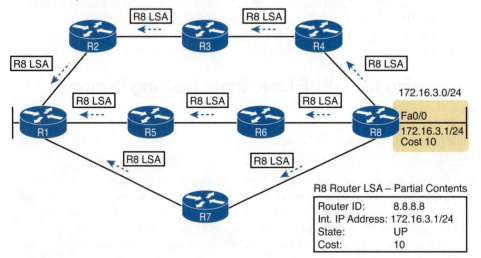

Figure 17-5   *Flooding LSAs Using a Link-State Routing Protocol*

Figure 17-5 shows the rather basic flooding process, with R8 sending the original LSA for itself, and the other routers flooding the LSA by forwarding it until every router has a copy. The flooding process has a way to prevent loops so that the LSAs do not get flooded around in circles. Basically, before sending an LSA to yet another neighbor, routers communicate, and ask "do you already have this LSA?," and then they avoid flooding the LSA to neighbors that already have it.

Once flooded, routers do occasionally reflood a particular LSA. Routers reflood an LSA when some information changes, for example, when a link goes up or comes down. They also reflood each LSA based on each LSA's separate aging timer (default 30 minutes).

Applying Dijkstra SPF Math to Find the Best Routes

The link-state flooding process results in every router having an identical copy of the LSDB in memory, but the flooding process alone does not cause a router to learn what routes to add to the IP routing table. Although incredibly detailed and useful, the information in the LSDB does not explicitly state each router's best route to reach a destination.

To build routes, link-state routers have to do some math. Thankfully, you and I do not have to know the math! However, all link-state protocols use a type of math algorithm, called the Dijkstra Shortest Path First (SPF) algorithm, to process the LSDB. That algorithm analyzes (with math) the LSDB, and builds the routes that the local router should add to the IP routing table—routes that list a subnet number and mask, an outgoing interface, and a next-hop router IP address.

The ICND2 book discusses the SPF process more, at least to the depth needed to plan OSPF configuration. In particular, that book looks at how to choose OSPF metrics, so changes the decisions made by SPF, allowing an engineer to influence which routes a router chooses as the best route.

Using OSPF Neighbor Relationships

OSPF uses three major categories of internal operation to eventually build routes:

Neighbors: A relationship between two routers that connect to the same data link, created so that the neighboring routers have a means to exchange their LSDBs.

Database exchange: The process of sending LSAs to neighbors so that all routers learn the same LSAs.

Adding the best routes: The process of each router independently running SPF, on their local copy of the LSDB, calculating the best routes, and adding those to the IPv4 routing table.

The previous few pages already discussed the last two items in the list, but neither of those happen until a router has some OSPF neighbor relationships with other routers. In fact, much of the verification and troubleshooting of OSPF revolves around the OSPF neighbor relationship. This section discusses the fundamentals.

The Basics of OSPF Neighbors

OSPF neighbors are routers that both use OSPF and both sit on the same data link. With the data link technology discussed so far in this book, that means two routers connected to the same VLAN become OSPF neighbors, or two routers on the ends of a serial link become OSPF neighbors.

Two routers need to do more than simply exist on the same link to become OSPF neighbors; they must send OSPF messages and agree to become neighbors. To do so, the routers send OSPF Hello messages, introducing themselves to the neighbor. Assuming the two neighbors have compatible OSPF parameters, the two form a neighbor relationship, and would be displayed in the output of the **show ip ospf neighbors** command.

The OSPF neighbor relationship also lets OSPF know when a neighbor might not be a good option for routing packets right now. Imagine R1 and R2 form a neighbor relationship, learn LSAs, and calculate routes that send packets through the other router. Months later, R1 notices that the neighbor relationship with R2 fails. That failed neighbor connection to R2 makes R1 react: R1 refloods LSAs that formerly relied on the link from R1 to R2, and R1 runs SPF to recalculate its own routes.

Finally, the OSPF neighbor model allows new routers to be dynamically discovered. That means new routers can be added to a network without requiring every router to be reconfigured. Instead, the configuration enables OSPF on a router's interfaces, and then the router reacts to any Hello messages from new neighbors, whenever those neighbors happen to be installed.

Meeting Neighbors and Learning Their Router ID

The OSPF Hello process, by which new neighbor relationships are formed, works somewhat like when you move to a new house and meet your various neighbors. When you see each other outside, you might walk over, say hello, and learn each others' names. After talking a bit, you form a first impression, particularly as to whether you think you'll enjoy chatting with this neighbor occasionally, or whether you can just wave and not take the time to talk the next time you see him outside.

Similarly, with OSPF, the process starts with messages called OSPF Hello messages. The Hellos in turn list each router's *Router ID (RID)*, which serves as each router's unique name or identifier for OSPF. Finally, OSPF does several checks of the information in the Hello messages to ensure that the two routers should become neighbors.

OSPF RIDs are 32-bit numbers. As a result, most command output lists these as dotted decimal numbers. Additionally, by default, IOS chooses its OSPF RID based on an interface IPv4 address, because those are some nearby convenient 32-bit numbers as well. However, the OSPF RID can be directly configured, as covered in the later section "Configuring the OSPF Router ID."

As soon as a router has chosen its OSPF RID and some interfaces come up, the router is ready to meet its OSPF neighbors. OSPF routers can become neighbors if they are connected to the same subnet (and in some other special cases not covered on the CCENT and CCNA exams). To discover other OSPF-speaking routers, a router sends multicast OSPF Hello packets to each interface and hopes to receive OSPF Hello packets from other routers connected to those interfaces. Figure 17-6 outlines the basic concept.

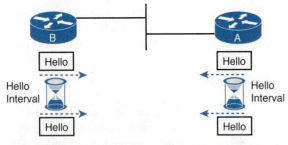

Figure 17-6 *OSPF Hello Packets*

Routers A and B both send Hello messages onto the LAN. They continue to send Hellos at a regular interval based on their Hello Timer settings. The Hello messages themselves have the following features:

- The Hello message follows the IP packet header, with IP protocol type 89.
- Hello packets are sent to multicast IP address 224.0.0.5, a multicast IP address intended for all OSPF-speaking routers.
- OSPF routers listen for packets sent to IP multicast address 224.0.0.5, in part hoping to receive Hello packets and learn about new neighbors.

The Hello messages contain a variety of OSPF parameters. These details let each router know something about their potential neighbor, including whether the two routers should or should not become neighbors. For example, two OSPF routers will not become neighbors if their interface IPv4 addresses are in different subnets. So, just because two routers happen to hear a Hello from a neighbor does not mean that the two routers will become neighbors. However, if routers do become neighbors, the routers begin to exchange their LSDBs and then calculate any new IP routes.

> **NOTE** The ICND2 book discusses routing protocol troubleshooting, with a fair amount of focus on the reasons why OSPF and EIGRP routers might not become neighbors.

Scaling OSPF Through Hierarchical Design

OSPF can be used in some networks with very little thought about design issues. You just turn on OSPF in all the routers, and it works! However, in large networks, engineers need to think about and plan how to use several OSPF features that allow it to scale well. For instance, the OSPF design in Figure 17-7 uses a single OSPF area, because this small internetwork does not need the scalability benefits of OSPF areas.

Area 0 (Backbone)

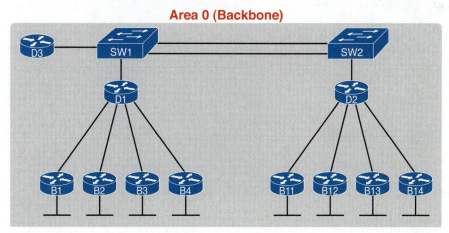

Figure 17-7 *Single-Area OSPF*

Using a single OSPF area for smaller internetworks, as in Figure 17-7, works well. The configuration is simple, and some of the hidden details in how OSPF works remain simple. In fact, with a small OSPF internetwork, you can just enable OSPF, with all interfaces in the same area, and mostly ignore the idea of an OSPF area.

Now imagine a network with 900 routers instead of only 11, and several thousand subnets. In that size of network, the sheer amount of processing required to run the complex SPF algorithm might cause convergence time to be slow just because of the time it takes each router to process all the math. Also, the routers might experience memory shortages. The problems can be summarized as follows:

- A larger topology database requires more memory on each router.

- Processing the larger-topology database with the SPF algorithm requires processing power that grows exponentially with the size of the topology database.

- A single interface status change (up to down, or down to up) forces every router to run SPF again!

OSPF breaks up the large and complex task of running SPF on a large LSDB by using areas. The engineer places some links one one area, some in another, others in yet a third area, and so on. OSPF then creates a smaller LSDB per-area, rather than one huge LSDB for all links and routers in the internetwork. With smaller topology databases, routers consume less memory and take less processing time to run SPF.

Although there is no exact definition of "large" in this context, networks larger than a few dozen routers benefit from using multiple areas, while even larger networks suffer unless they use multiple areas. (Some documents over the years have listed 50 routers as the most that should be in the same area.) However, note that these numbers of routers are gross generalizations. They depend largely on the network design, the power of the router CPU, the amount of RAM, and so on.

OSPF multiarea design puts all of link—a serial link, and VLAN, and so on—inside an area. To make that work, some routers (Area Border Routers, or ABRs) sit at the border between multiple areas. Routers D1 and D2 serve as ABRs in the area design shown in Figure 17-8, which shows the same network as Figure 17-8, but with three OSPF areas (0, 1, and 2).

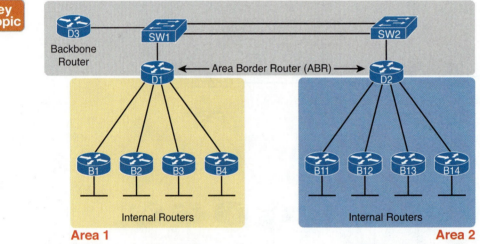

Figure 17-8 *Three-Area OSPF*

While Figure 17-8 shows a sample area design and some terminology related to areas, it does not show the power and benefit of the areas. By using areas, the OSPF SPF algorithm ignores the details of the topology in the other areas. For example, OSPF on Router B1 (area 1), when doing the complex SPF math processing, ignores the topology information about area 0 and area 2. Each router has far less SPF work to do, so each router more quickly finishes its SPF work, finding the currently-best OSPF routes.

The ICND2 book looks more closely at how SPF works, particularly with more information about LSA types. For now, just know that single-area works great for smaller networks, while multiarea designs overcome the scaling problems that occur as a network grows.

OSPF Configuration

OSPF configuration includes only a few required steps, but it has many optional steps. After an OSPF design has been chosen—a task that can be complex in larger IP internetworks—the configuration can be as simple as enabling OSPF on each router interface and placing that interface in the correct OSPF area.

This section shows several configuration examples, all with a single-area OSPF internetwork. Following those examples, the text goes on to cover several of the additional optional configuration settings. For reference, the following list outlines the configuration steps covered in this chapter, as well as a brief reference to the required commands:

Key Topic

Step 1.   Enter OSPF configuration mode for a particular OSPF process using the **router ospf** *process-id* global command.

Step 2.   (Optional) Configure the OSPF router ID by:

   A.   Configuring the **router-id** *id-value* router subcommand

   B.   Configuring an IP address on a loopback interface

Step 3.   Configure one or more **network** *ip-address wildcard-mask* **area** *area-id* router subcommands, with any matched interfaces being added to the listed area.

For a more visual perspective on OSPFv2 configuration, Figure 17-9 shows the relationship between the key OSPF configuration commands. Note that the configuration creates a routing process in one part of the configuration, and then indirectly enables OSPF on each interface. The configuration does not name the interfaces on which OSPF is enabled, instead requiring IOS to apply some logic by comparing the OSPF **network** command to the interface **ip address** commands. The upcoming example discusses more about this logic.

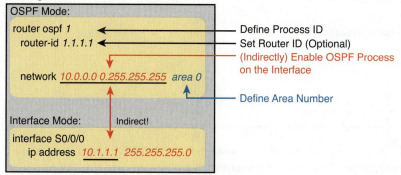

Figure 17-9   *Organization of OSPFv2 Configuration*

OSPF Single-Area Configuration

Figure 17-10 shows a sample network that will be used for OSPF configuration. All links sit in area 0. It has four routers, each connected to one or two LANs. However, note that routers R3 and R4, at the top of the figure, connect to the same two VLANs/subnets, so they will form neighbor relationships with each other over each of those VLANs as well.

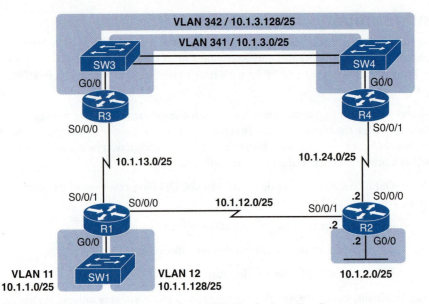

Figure 17-10 *Sample Network for OSPF Single-Area Configuration*

Example 17-1 shows the IPv4 addressing configuration on Router R3, before getting into the OSPF detail. The configuration enables 802.1Q trunking on R3's G0/0 interface, and assigns an IP address to each. (Not shown, switch S3 has configured trunking on the other side of that Ethernet link.)

Example 17-1 *IPv4 Address Configuration on R3 (Including VLAN Trunking)*

```
interface gigabitethernet 0/0.341
 encapsulation dot1q 341
 ip address 10.1.3.1 255.255.255.128
!
interface gigabitethernet 0/0.342
 encapsulation dot1q 342
 ip address 10.1.3.129 255.255.255.128
!
interface serial 0/0/0
 ip address 10.1.13.3 255.255.255.128
```

The beginning single-area configuration on R3, as shown in Example 17-2, enables OSPF on all the interfaces shown in Figure 17-9. First, the **router ospf 1** global command puts the user in OSPF configuration mode, and sets the OSPF *process-id*. This number just needs to be unique on the local router, allowing the router to support multiple OSPF processes in a single router by using different process IDs. (The **router** command uses the *process-id* to distinguish between the processes.) The *process-id* does not have to match on each router, and it can be any integer between 1 and 65,535.

Example 17-2 *OSPF Single-Area Configuration on R3 Using One* **network** *Command*

```
router ospf 1
 network 10.0.0.0 0.255.255.255 area 0
```

Speaking generally rather than about this example, the OSPF **network** command tells a router to find its local interfaces that match the first two parameters on the **network** command. Then, for each matched interface, the router enables OSPF on those interfaces, discovers neighbors, creates neighbor relationships, and assigns the interface to the area listed in the **network** command.

For the specific command in Example17-2, any matched interfaces are assigned to area 0. However, the first two parameters—the *ip_address* and *wildcard_mask* parameter values of 10.0.0.0 and 0.255.255.255—need some explaining. In this case, the command matches all three interfaces shown for router R3; the next topic explains why.

Matching with the OSPF **network** Command

The OSPF **network** command compares the first parameter in the command to each interface IP address on the local router, trying to find a match. However, rather than comparing the entire number in the **network** command to the entire IPv4 address on the interface, the router can compare a subset of the octets, based on the wildcard mask, as follows:

Wildcard 0.0.0.0: Compare all 4 octets. In other words, the numbers must exactly match.

Wildcard 0.0.0.255: Compare the first 3 octets only. Ignore the last octet when comparing the numbers.

Wildcard 0.0.255.255: Compare the first 2 octets only. Ignore the last 2 octets when comparing the numbers.

Wildcard 0.255.255.255: Compare the first octet only. Ignore the last 3 octets when comparing the numbers.

Wildcard 255.255.255.255: Compare nothing—this wildcard mask means that all addresses will match the **network** command.

Basically, a wildcard mask value of 0 in an octet tells IOS to compare to see if the numbers match, and a value of 255 tells IOS to ignore that octet when comparing the numbers.

The **network** command provides many flexible options because of the wildcard mask. For example, in router R3, many **network** commands could be used, with some matching all interfaces, and some matching a subset of interfaces. Table 17-4 shows a sampling of options, with notes.

Table 17-4   Example OSPF **network** Commands on R3, with Expected Results

Command	Logic in Command	Matched Interfaces
network 10.1.0.0 0.0.255.255	Match interface IP addresses that begin with 10.1	G0/0.341 G0/0.342 S0/0/0
network 10.0.0.0 0.255.255.255	Match interface IP addresses that begin with 10.	G0/0.341 G0/0.342 S0/0/0
network 0.0.0.0 255.255.255.255	Match all interface IP addresses	G0/0.341 G0/0.342 S0/0/0
network 10.1.13.0 0.0.0.255	Match interface IP addresses that begin with 10.1.13	S0/0/0
network 10.1.3.1 0.0.0.0	Match one IP address: 10.1.3.1	G0/0.341

The wildcard mask gives the local router its rules for matching its own interfaces. For example, Example 17-2 shows R3 using the **network 10.0.0.0 0.255.255.255 area 0** command. In that same internetwork, Routers R1 and R2 would use the configuration shown in Example 17-3, with two other wildcard masks. In both routers, OSPF is enabled on all the interfaces shown in Figure 17-10.

Example 17-3   *OSPF Configuration on Routers R1 and R2*

```
! R1 configuration next - one network command enables OSPF
! on all three interfaces
router ospf 1
 network 10.1.0.0 0.0.255.255 area 0
```
```
! R2 configuration next - One network command per interface
router ospf 1
 network 10.1.12.2 0.0.0.0 area 0
 network 10.1.24.2 0.0.0.0 area 0
 network 10.1.2.2 0.0.0.0 area 0
```

Finally, note that other wildcard mask values can be used as well, so that the comparison happens between specific bits in the 32-bit numbers. Chapter 22, "Basic IPv4 Access Control Lists," discusses wildcard masks in more detail, including these other mask options.

NOTE   The **network** command uses another convention for the first parameter (the address): if an octet will be ignored because of the wildcard mask octet value of 255, the address parameter should be a 0. However, IOS will actually accept a **network** command that breaks this rule, but then IOS will change that octet of the address to a 0 before putting it into the running configuration file. For example, IOS will change a typed command that begins with **network 1.2.3.4 0.0.255.255** to **network 1.2.0.0 0.0.255.255.**

Verifying OSPF

As mentioned earlier, OSPF routers use a three-step process. First, they create neighbor relationships. Then they build and flood LSAs, so each router in the same area has a copy of the same LSDB. Finally, each router independently computes its own IP routes and adds them to its routing table.

The show **ip ospf neighbor**, show **ip ospf database**, and show **ip route** commands display information for each of these three steps, respectively. To verify OSPF, you can use the same sequence. Or, you can just go look at the IP routing table, and if the routes look correct, OSPF probably worked.

First, examine the list of neighbors known on Router R3. R3 should have one neighbor relationship with R1, over the serial link. It also has two neighbor relationships with R4, over the two different VLANs to which both routers connect. Example 17-4 shows all three.

Example 17-4   *OSPF Neighbors on Router R3 from Figure 17-10*

```
R3# show ip ospf neighbor

Neighbor ID     Pri   State       Dead Time   Address       Interface
1.1.1.1           0   FULL/  -    00:00:33    10.1.13.1     Serial0/0/0
10.1.24.4         1   FULL/DR     00:00:35    10.1.3.130    GigabitEthernet0/0.342
10.1.24.4         1   FULL/DR     00:00:36    10.1.3.4      GigabitEthernet0/0.341
```

The detail in the output mentions several important facts, and for most people, working right to left works best. For example, looking at the headings:

Interface: This is the local router's interface connected to the neighbor. For example, the first neighbor in the list is reachable through R3's S0/0/0 interface.

Address: This is the neighbor's IP address on that link. Again, for this first neighbor, the neighbor, which is R1, uses IP address 10.1.13.1.

State: While many possible states exist, for the details discussed in this chapter, FULL is the correct and fully-working state in this case.

Neighbor ID: This is the router ID of the neighbor.

Next, Example 17-5 shows the contents of the LSDB on router R3. Interestingly, when OSPF is working correctly in an internetwork with a single area design, all the routers will have the same LSDB contents. So, the **show ip ospf database** command in Example 17-5 should list the same exact information, no matter which of the four routers on which it is issued.

Example 17-5 *OSPF Database on Router R3 from Figure 17-10*

```
R3# show ip ospf database

            OSPF Router with ID (10.1.13.3) (Process ID 1)


            Router Link States (Area 0)


Link ID         ADV Router      Age       Seq#        Checksum Link count
1.1.1.1         1.1.1.1         498       0x80000006  0x002294 6
2.2.2.2         2.2.2.2         497       0x80000004  0x00E8C6 5
10.1.13.3       10.1.13.3       450       0x80000003  0x001043 4
10.1.24.4       10.1.24.4       451       0x80000003  0x009D7E 4


            Net Link States (Area 0)


Link ID         ADV Router      Age       Seq#        Checksum
10.1.3.4        10.1.24.4       451       0x80000001  0x0045F8
10.1.3.130      10.1.24.4       451       0x80000001  0x00546B
```

For the purposes of this book, do not be concerned about the specifics in the output of this command. However, for perspective, note that the LSDB should list one "Router Link State" (Type 1 Router LSA) for each of the four routers in the design, as highlighted in the example.

Next, Example 17-6 shows R3's IPv4 routing table with the **show ip route** command. Note that it lists connected routes as well as OSPF routes. Take a moment to look back at Figure 17-10, and look for the subnets that are not locally connected to R3. Then look for those routes in the output in Example 17-5.

Example 17-6 *IPv4 Routes Added by OSPF on Router R3 from Figure 17-10*

```
R3# show ip route
Codes: L - local, C - connected, S - static, R - RIP, M - mobile, B - BGP
       D - EIGRP, EX - EIGRP external, O - OSPF, IA - OSPF inter area
       N1 - OSPF NSSA external type 1, N2 - OSPF NSSA external type 2
       E1 - OSPF external type 1, E2 - OSPF external type 2
! Legend lines omitted for brevity
```

```
        10.0.0.0/8 is variably subnetted, 11 subnets, 2 masks
O         10.1.1.0/25 [110/65] via 10.1.13.1, 00:13:28, Serial0/0/0
O         10.1.1.128/25 [110/65] via 10.1.13.1, 00:13:28, Serial0/0/0
O         10.1.2.0/25 [110/66] via 10.1.3.130, 00:12:41, GigabitEthernet0/0.342
                      [110/66] via 10.1.3.4, 00:12:41, GigabitEthernet0/0.341
C         10.1.3.0/25 is directly connected, GigabitEthernet0/0.341
L         10.1.3.1/32 is directly connected, GigabitEthernet0/0.341
C         10.1.3.128/25 is directly connected, GigabitEthernet0/0.342
L         10.1.3.129/32 is directly connected, GigabitEthernet0/0.342
O         10.1.12.0/25 [110/128] via 10.1.13.1, 00:13:28, Serial0/0/0
C         10.1.13.0/25 is directly connected, Serial0/0/0
L         10.1.13.3/32 is directly connected, Serial0/0/0
O         10.1.24.0/25
             [110/65] via 10.1.3.130, 00:12:41, GigabitEthernet0/0.342
             [110/65] via 10.1.3.4, 00:12:41, GigabitEthernet0/0.341
```

First, take a look at the bigger ideas confirmed by this output. The code of "O" on the left identifies a route as being learned by OSPF. The output lists five such IP routes. From the figure, five subnets exist that do not happen to be connected subnets off router R3. Looking for a quick count of OSPF routes, versus nonconnected routes in the diagram, gives a quick check whether OSPF learned all routes.

Next, take a look at the first route (to subnet 10.1.1.0/25). It lists the subnet ID and mask, identifying the subnet. It also lists two numbers in brackets. The first, 110, is the administrative distance of the route. All the OSPF routes in this example use the default of 110. The second number, 65, is the OSPF metric for this route.

Additionally, the **show ip protocols** command is also popular as a quick look at how any routing protocol works. This command lists a group of messages for each routing protocol running on a router. Example 17-7 shows a sample, this time taken from router R3.

Example 17-7   *The* show ip protocols *Command on R3*

```
R3# show ip protocols
*** IP Routing is NSF aware ***

Routing Protocol is "ospf 1"
  Outgoing update filter list for all interfaces is not set
  Incoming update filter list for all interfaces is not set
  Router ID 10.1.13.3
  Number of areas in this router is 1. 1 normal 0 stub 0 nssa
  Maximum path: 4
  Routing for Networks:
    10.0.0.0 0.255.255.255 area 0
  Routing Information Sources:
    Gateway         Distance      Last Update
    1.1.1.1              110      06:26:17
    2.2.2.2              110      06:25:30
    10.1.24.4            110      06:25:30
  Distance: (default is 110)
```

The output shows several interesting facts. The first highlighted line repeats the parameters on the **router ospf 1** global configuration command. The second highlighted item points out R3's router ID, as discussed further in the next section. The third highlighted line repeats more configuration, listing the parameters of the **network 10.0.0.0 0.255.255.255 area 0** OSPF subcommand. Finally, the last highlighted item in the example acts as a heading before a list of known OSPF routers, by router ID.

Configuring the OSPF Router ID

While OSPF has many other optional features, most enterprise networks that use OSPF choose to configure each router's OSPF router ID. OSPF-speaking routers must have a Router ID (RID) for proper operation. By default, routers will choose an interface IP address to use as the RID. However, many network engineers prefer to choose each router's router ID, so command output from commands like **show ip ospf neighbor** lists more recognizable router IDs.

To find its RID, a Cisco router uses the following process when the router reloads and brings up the OSPF process. Note that when one of these steps identifies the RID, the process stops.

1. If the **router-id** *rid* OSPF subcommand is configured, this value is used as the RID.

2. If any loopback interfaces have an IP address configured, and the interface has an interface status of up, the router picks the highest numeric IP address among these loopback interfaces.

3. The router picks the highest numeric IP address from all other interfaces whose interface status code (first status code) is up. (In other words, an interface in up/down state will be included by OSPF when choosing its router ID.)

The first and third criteria should make some sense right away: the RID is either configured or is taken from a working interface's IP address. However, this book has not yet explained the concept of a *loopback interface*, as mentioned in Step 2.

A loopback interface is a virtual interface that can be configured with the **interface loopback** *interface-number* command, where *interface-number* is an integer. Loopback interfaces are always in an "up and up" state unless administratively placed in a shutdown state. For example, a simple configuration of the command **interface loopback 0**, followed by **ip address 2.2.2.2 255.255.255.0**, would create a loopback interface and assign it an IP address. Because loopback interfaces do not rely on any hardware, these interfaces can be up/up whenever IOS is running, making them good interfaces on which to base an OSPF RID.

Example 17-8 shows the configuration that existed in Routers R1 and R2 before the creation of the **show** command output in examples 17-4, 17-5, and 17-6. R1 set its router ID using the direct method, while R2 used a loopback IP address.

Example 17-8 *OSPF Router ID Configuration Examples*

```
! R1 Configuration first
router ospf 1
 router-id 1.1.1.1
 network 10.1.0.0 0.0.255.255 area 0
 network 10.0.0.0 0.255.255.255 area 0
! R2 Configuration next
!
interface Loopback2
 ip address 2.2.2.2 255.255.255.255
```

Each router chooses its OSPF RID when OSPF is initialized, which happens when the router boots or when a CLI user stops and restarts the OSPF process (with the **clear ip ospf process** command). So, if OSPF comes up, and later, the configuration changes in a way that would impact the OSPF RID, OSPF does not change the RID immediately. Instead, IOS waits until the next time the OSPF process is restarted.

Example 17-9 shows the output of the **show ip ospf** command on R1, after the configuration of Example 17-8 was made, and after the router was reloaded, which made the OSPF router ID change.

Example 17-9   *Confirming the Current OSPF Router ID*

```
R1# show ip ospf
Routing Process "ospf 1" with ID 1.1.1.1
! lines omitted for brevity
```

Miscellaneous OSPF Configuration Settings

These last few topics in the chapter discuss a few unrelated and optional OSPF configuration settings, namely how to make a router interface passive for OSPF, and how to originate and flood a default route using OSPF.

OSPF Passive Interfaces

Once OSPF has been enabled on an interface, the router tries to discover neighboring OSPF routers and form a neighbor relationship. To do so, the router sends OSPF Hello messages on a regular time interval (called the Hello interval). The router also listens for incoming Hello messages from potential neighbors.

Sometimes, a router does not need to form neighbor relationships with neighbors on an interface. Often times, no other routers exist on a particular link, so the router has no need to keep sending those repetitive OSPF Hello messages.

When a router does not need to discover neighbors off some interface, the engineer has a couple of configuration options. First, by doing nothing, the router keeps sending the messages, wasting some small bit of CPU cycles and effort. Alternately, the engineer can configure the interface as an OSPF passive interface, telling the router to do the following:

- Quit sending OSPF Hellos on the interface
- Ignore received Hellos on the interface
- Do not form neighbor relationships over the interface

By making an interface passive, OSPF does not form neighbor relationships over the interface, but it does still advertise about the subnet connected to that interface. That is, the OSPF configuration enables OSPF on the interface (using the **network** router subcommand), and then makes the interface passive (using the **passive-interface** router subcommand).

To configure an interface as passive, two options exist. First, you can add the following command to the configuration of the OSPF process, in router configuration mode:

    passive-interface *type number*

Alternately, the configuration can change the default setting so that all interfaces are passive by default, and then add a **no passive-interface** command for all interfaces that need to not be passive:

    passive-interface default

    no passive interface *type number*

For example, in the sample internetwork in Figure 17-10, Router R1, at the bottom left of the figure, has a LAN interface configured for VLAN trunking. The only router connected to both VLANs is Router R1, so R1 will never discover an OSPF neighbor on these subnets. Example 17-10 shows two alternative configurations make the two LAN subinterfaces passive to OSPF.

Example 17-10 *Configuring Passive Interfaces on R1 and R2 from Figure 17-10*

```
! First, make each subinterface passive directly
router ospf 1
 passive-interface gigabitethernet0/0.11
 passive-interface gigabitethernet0/0.12

! Or, change the default to passive, and make the other interfaces
! not be passive

router ospf 1
 passive-interface default
 no passive-interface serial0/0/0
 no passive-interface serial0/0/1
```

In real internetworks, the choice of configuration style reduces to which option requires the least number of commands. For example, a router with 20 interfaces, 18 of which are passive to OSPF, has far fewer configuration commands when using the **passive-interface default** command to change the default to passive. If only two of those 20 interfaces need to be passive, use the default setting, in which all interfaces are not passive, to keep the configuration shorter.

Interestingly, OSPF makes it a bit of a challenge to use **show** commands to find whether or not an interface is passive. The **show running-config** command lists the configuration directly, but if you cannot get into enable mode to use this command, note these two facts:

The **show ip ospf interface brief** command lists all interfaces on which OSPF is enabled, *including passive interfaces.*

The **show ip ospf interface** command lists a single line that mentions that the interface is passive.

Example 17-11 shows these two commands on Router R1, with the configuration shown in the top of Example 17-10. Note that subinterfaces G0/0.11 and G0/0.12 both show up in the output of **show ip ospf interface brief**.

Example 17-11 *Displaying Passive Interfaces*

```
R1# show ip ospf interface brief
Interface   PID   Area        IP Address/Mask   Cost   State   Nbrs F/C
Gi0/0.12    1     0           10.1.1.129/25     1      DR      0/0
Gi0/0.11    1     0           10.1.1.1/25       1      DR      0/0
Se0/0/0     1     0           10.1.12.1/25      64     P2P     0/0
Se0/0/1     1     0           10.1.13.1/25      64     P2P     0/0

R1# show ip ospf interface g0/0.11
GigabitEthernet0/0.1 is up, line protocol is up
  Internet Address 10.1.1.1/25, Area 0, Attached via Network Statement
  Process ID 1, Router ID 10.1.1.129, Network Type BROADCAST, Cost: 1
  Topology-MTID   Cost   Disabled   Shutdown   Topology Name
        0          1        no         no         Base
  Transmit Delay is 1 sec, State DR, Priority 1
```

```
 Designated Router (ID) 10.1.1.129, Interface address 10.1.1.1
 No backup designated router on this network
 Timer intervals configured, Hello 10, Dead 40, Wait 40, Retransmit 5
   oob-resync timeout 40
   No Hellos (Passive interface)
! Lines omitted for brevity
```

OSPF Default Routes

As discussed in Chapter 16, "Configuring IPv4 Addresses and Routes," in some cases, routers benefit from using a default route. Chapter 16 shows how to configure a router to know a static default route that only that one router uses. This final topic of the chapter looks a different strategy for using default IP routes, one in which an OSPF router creates a default route and also advertises it with OSPF, so that other routers learn default routes dynamically.

The most classic case for using a routing protocol to advertise a default route has to do with an enterprise's connection to the Internet. As a strategy, the enterprise engineer uses these design goals:

- All routers learn specific routes for subnets inside the company; a default route is not needed when forwarding packets to these destinations.

- One router connects to the Internet, and it has a default route that points toward the Internet.

- All routers should dynamically learn a default route, used for all traffic going to the Internet, so that all packets destined to locations in the Internet go to the one router connected to the Internet.

Figure 17-11 shows the idea of how OSPF advertises the default route, with the specific OSPF configuration. In this case, a company connects to an ISP with their Router R1. That router uses the OSPF **default-information originate** command (Step 1). As a result, the router advertises a default route using OSPF (Step 2) to the remote routers (B1, B2, and B3).

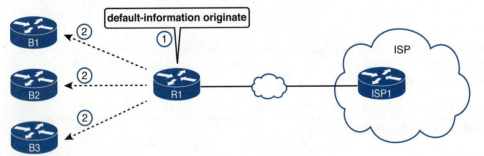

Figure 17-11 *Using OSPF to Create and Flood a Default Route*

Figure 17-12 shows the default routes that result from OSPF's advertisements in Figure 17-11. On the far left, the three branch routers all have OSPF-learned default routes, pointing to R1. R1 itself also needs a default route, pointing to the ISP router, so that R1 can forward all Internet-bound traffic to the ISP.

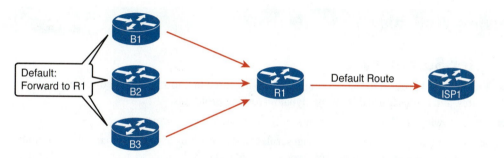

Figure 17-12 *Default Routes Resulting from the* **default-information originate** *Command*

Finally, this feature gives the engineer control over when the router originates this default route. First, R1 needs a default route, either defined as a static default route or learned from the ISP. The **default-information originate** command then tells the R1 to advertise a default route when its own default route is working, and to advertise it as down when its own default route fails.

> **NOTE** Interestingly, the **default-information originate always** router subcommand tells the router to always advertise the default route, no matter whether the router's default route is working or not.

Review Activities

Chapter Summary

- Routers add IP routes to their routing tables using three methods: connected routes, static routes, and routes learned by using dynamic routing protocols.

- The following are definitions of commonly confused routing terms:

    - **Routing protocol:** A set of messages, rules, and algorithms used by routers for the overall purpose of learning routes. This process includes the exchange and analysis of routing information. Each router chooses the best route to each subnet (path selection) and finally places those best routes in its IP routing table. Examples include RIP, EIGRP, OSPF, and BGP.

    - **Routed protocol and routable protocol:** Both terms refer to a protocol that defines a packet structure and logical addressing, enabling routers to forward or route the packets. Routers forward packets defined by routed and routable protocols. Examples include IP version 4 (IPv4) and IP version 6 (IPv6).

- Cisco IOS software supports several IP routing protocols, performing the same general functions:

    1. Learn routing information about IP subnets from other neighboring routers.

    2. Advertise routing information about IP subnets to other neighboring routers.

    3. If more than one possible route exists to reach one subnet, pick the best route based on a metric.

    4. If the network topology changes—for example, a link fails—react by advertising that some routes have failed and pick a new currently best route. (This process is called convergence.)

- The term *convergence* refers to a process that occurs when the topology changes—that is, when either a router or link fails or comes back up again. When something changes, the best routes available in the network might change. Convergence simply refers to the process by which all the routers collectively realize something has changed, advertise the information about the changes to all the other routers, and all the routers then choose the currently best routes for each subnet. The capability to converge quickly, without causing loops, is one of the most important considerations when choosing which IP routing protocol to use.

- IP routing protocols fall in to one of two major categories: Interior Gateway Protocols (IGP) or Exterior Gateway Protocols (EGP). The definitions of each are as follows:

    - **IGP:** A routing protocol that was designed and intended for use inside a single autonomous system (AS)

    - **EGP:** A routing protocol that was designed and intended for use between different autonomous systems

- An AS is a network under the administrative control of a single organization. For example, a network created and paid for by a single company is probably a single AS, and a network created by a single school system is probably a single AS.

- Each AS can be assigned a number called (unsurprisingly) an AS number (ASN). Like public IP addresses, the Internet Assigned Numbers Authority (IANA, http://www.iana.org) controls the worldwide rights to assigning ASNs.

- Organizations have several options when choosing an IGP for their enterprise network, but most companies today use either OSPF or EIGRP.

- A routing protocol's underlying algorithm determines how the routing protocol does its job. The term *routing protocol algorithm* simply refers to the logic and processes used by different routing protocols to solve the problem of learning all routes, choosing the best route to each subnet, and converging in reaction to changes in the internetwork.

- Three main branches of routing protocol algorithms exist for IGP routing protocols:

  - Distance vector (sometimes called Bellman-Ford after its creators)

  - Advanced distance vector (sometimes called balanced hybrid)

  - Link-state

- Routing protocols choose the best route to reach a subnet by choosing the route with the lowest metric. For example, RIP counts the number of routers (hops) between a router and the destination subnet. OSPF totals the cost associated with each interface in the end-to-end route, with the cost based on link bandwidth.

- Administrative distance is a number that denotes how believable an entire routing protocol is on a single router. The lower the number, the better, or more believable, the routing protocol.

- Link-state protocols build IP routes with a couple of major steps. First, the routers together build a lot of information about the network: routers, links, IP address, status information, and so on. Then the routers flood the information, so all routers know the same information. At that point, each router can calculate routes to all subnets but from each router's own perspective.

- Open Shortest Path First (OSPF), the most popular link-state IP routing protocol, organizes topology information using link-state advertisements (LSA) and the link state database (LSDB).

- To build routes, link-state routers must do some math. Thankfully, you do not have to know the math! However, all link state protocols use a type of math algorithm, called the Dijkstra Shortest Path First (SPF) algorithm, to process the LSDB.

- OSPF uses three major categories of internal operation to eventually build routes:

  - **Neighbors:** A relationship between two routers that connect to the same data link, created so that the neighboring routers have a means to exchange their LSDBs.

  - **Database Exchange:** The process of sending LSAs to neighbors so that all routers learn the same LSAs.

  - **Adding the best routes:** The process of each router independently running SPF algorithm on their local copy of the LSDB, calculating the best routes, and adding them to the IPv4 routing table.

- The following are the basic steps to configuring OSPF:

  Step 1.   Enter OSPF configuration mode for a particular OSPF process using the **router ospf** *process-id* global command.

  Step 2.   (Optional) Configure the OSPF router ID by

  - Configuring the **router-id** *id-value* router subcommand

  - Configuring an IP address on a loopback interface

  Step 3.   Configure one or more **network** *ip-address wildcard-mask* **area** *area-id* router subcommands, with any matched interfaces being added to the listed area.

- OSPF-speaking routers must have a router ID (RID) for proper operation. By default, routers will choose an interface IP address to use as the RID. However, many network engineers prefer to choose each router's router ID, so that reading command output from commands like **show ip ospf neighbor** lists more recognizable router IDs.

- To find its RID, a Cisco router uses the following process when the router reloads and brings up the OSPF process. Note that when one of these steps identifies the RID, the process stops.
  - If the **router-id** *rid* OSPF subcommand is configured, this value is used as the RID.
  - If any loopback interfaces have an IP address configured and the interface has an interface status of up, the router picks the highest numeric IP address among these loopback interfaces.
  - The router picks the highest numeric IP address from all other interfaces whose interface status code (first status code) is up. (In other words, an interface in up/down state will be included by OSPF when choosing its router ID.)

Review Questions

Answer these review questions. You can find the answers at the bottom of the last page of the chapter. For thorough explanations, see DVD Appendix C, "Answers to Review Questions."

1. Which of the following routing protocols are considered to use link-state logic? (Choose two answers.)

   A. RIP-1

   B. RIP-2

   C. EIGRP

   D. OSPF

   E. Integrated IS-IS

2. Which of the following routing protocols use a metric that is, by default, at least partially affected by link bandwidth? (Choose two answers.)

   A. RIP-1

   B. RIP-2

   C. EIGRP

   D. OSPF

3. Which of the following interior routing protocols support VLSM? (Choose four answers.)

   A. RIP-1

   B. RIP-2

   C. EIGRP

   D. OSPF

   E. Integrated IS-IS

4. Which of the following is true about how a router using a link-state routing protocol chooses the best route to reach a subnet?

   A. The router finds the best route in the link-state database.

   B. The router calculates the best route by running the SPF algorithm against the information in the link-state database.

   C. The router compares the metrics listed for that subnet in the updates received from each neighbor and picks the best (lowest) metric route.

   D. The router uses the path that has the lowest hop count.

5. OSPF runs an algorithm to calculate the currently best route. Which of the following terms refer to that algorithm? (Choose two answers.)

   A. SPF

   B. DUAL

   C. Feasible successor

   D. Dijkstra

   E. Good old common sense

6. Which of the following **network** commands, following the command **router ospf 1**, tells this router to start using OSPF on interfaces whose IP addresses are 10.1.1.1, 10.1.100.1, and 10.1.120.1?

   A. network 10.0.0.0 255.0.0.0 area 0

   B. network 10.0.0.0 0.255.255.255 area 0

   C. network 10.0.0.1 0.0.0.255 area 0

   D. network 10.0.0.1 0.0.255.255 area 0

7. Which of the following **network** commands, following the command **router ospf 1**, tells this router to start using OSPF on interfaces whose IP addresses are 10.1.1.1, 10.1.100.1, and 10.1.120.1?

   A. network 0.0.0.0 255.255.255.255 area 0

   B. network 10.0.0.0 0.255.255.0 area 0

   C. network 10.1.1.0 0.x.1x.0 area 0

   D. network 10.1.1.0 255.0.0.0 area 0

   E. network 10.0.0.0 255.0.0.0 area 0

8. Which of the following commands list the OSPF neighbors off interface serial 0/0? (Choose two answers.)

   A. show ip ospf neighbor

   B. show ip ospf interface brief

   C. show ip neighbor

   D. show ip interface

   E. show ip ospf neighbor serial 0/0

Review All the Key Topics

Review the most important topics from this chapter, noted with the Key Topic icon. Table 17-5 lists these key topics and where each is discussed.

Table 17-5   Key Topics for Chapter 17

Key Topic Element	Description	Page Number
List	List of the main functions of a routing protocol	405
List	Definitions of IGP and EGP	406
List	Three types of IGP routing protocol algorithms	408
Table 17-1	IGP metric comparisons	408
Table 17-2	More comparisons between IGPs	410
Table 17-3	List of routing information sources and their respective administrative distance	411
Figure 17-8	OSPF multi-area terminology	416
List	Configuration checklist for OSPF	417
List	Example OSPF wildcard masks and their meaning	419
List	Rules for setting the Router ID	423
List	Actions IOS takes when an OSPF interface is passive.	424

Complete the Tables and Lists from Memory

Print a copy of DVD Appendix M, "Memory Tables," or at least the section for this chapter, and complete the tables and lists from memory. DVD Appendix N, "Memory Tables Answer Key," includes completed tables and lists for you to check your work.

Definitions of Key Terms

After your first reading of the chapter, try to define these key terms, but do not be concerned about getting them all correct at that time. Chapter 30 directs you in how to use these terms for late-stage preparation for the exam.

convergence, Shortest Path First (SPF) algorithm, distance vector, interior gateway protocol (IGP), link-state, link-state advertisement (LSA), link-state database (LSDB), metric, routed protocol, routing protocol, Area Border Router (ABR), neighbor, router ID (RID)

Command Reference to Check Your Memory

Although you should not necessarily memorize the information in the tables in this section, this section does include a reference for the configuration and EXEC commands covered in this chapter. Practically speaking, you should memorize the commands as a side effect of reading the chapter and doing all the activities in this exam preparation section. To check to see how well you have memorized the commands as a side effect of your other studies, cover the left side of the table with a piece of paper, read the descriptions on the right side, and see whether you remember the command.

Table 17-6 Chapter 17 Configuration Command Reference

Command	Description
router ospf *process-id*	Enters OSPF configuration mode for the listed process.
network *ip-address wildcard-mask* area *area-id*	Router subcommand that enables OSPF on interfaces matching the address/wildcard combination and sets the OSPF area.
auto-cost reference- bandwidth *number*	Router subcommand that tells OSPF the numerator in the *Ref-BW/Int-BW* formula used to calculate the OSPF cost based on the interface bandwidth.
router-id *id*	OSPF subcommand that statically sets the router ID.
passive-interface *type number*	OSPF subcommand that tells OSPF to be passive on that interface or subinterface.
passive-interface default	OSPF subcommand that changes the OSPF default for interfaces to be passive instead of active (not passive).
no passive-interface *type number*	OSPF subcommand that tells OSPF to be active (not passive) on that interface or subinterface.
Default-information originate [always]	OSPF subcommand to tell OSPF to create and advertise an OSPF default route, as long as the router has some default route (or to always advertise a default, if the **always** option is configured).

Table 17-7 Chapter 17 EXEC Command Reference

Command	Description
show ip route [ospf]	Lists routes in the routing table learned by OSPF.
show ip ospf interface [*type number*]	Lists a large group of messages per interface (or just for the one listed interface), with many facts: the area in which the interface resides, neighbors adjacent on this interface, and Hello and dead timers.
show ip ospf interface brief	Lists one line per interface on which OSPF is enabled, for all interfaces (including passive interfaces) on which OSPF is enabled.
show ip ospf neighbor [*neighbor-RID*]	Lists neighbors and current status with neighbors, per interface, and optionally lists details for the router ID listed in the command.
show ip ospf database	Lists a summary of the LSAs in the local router's LSDB, listing one line for each LSA.
show ip ospf	Lists a variety of facts about the local router's OSPF process, notably with the first line listing the router's router ID.
show ip protocols	Lists a group of messages for every instance of every routing protocol running in the router, restating many configuration parameters, default configuration settings when used, and listing the known OSPF routers in that area.

Answers to Review Questions:
1 D and E 2 C and D 3 B, C, D, and E 4 B 5 A and D 6 B 7 A 8 A and E

Chapter 18

Configuring and Verifying Host Connectivity

In the world of TCP/IP, the word *host* refers to any device with an IP address: your phone, your tablet, a PC, a router, a switch, or a wireless access point. Hosts even include some less obvious devices as well: the electronic advertising video screen at the mall, your electrical power meter that uses the same technology as mobile phones to submit your electrical usage information for billing, your new car.

No matter the type of host, any host that uses IPv4 needs four IPv4 settings to work properly:

- IP address
- Subnet mask
- Default router(s)
- DNS server IP address(es)

This last chapter in this part of the book completes the discussion of how to build a basic IPv4 network by focusing on the IPv4 settings on hosts. In particular, this chapter begins by discussing how a host can dynamically learn these four settings using the Dynamic Host Configuration Protocol, or DHCP. The middle section of the chapter then discusses some tips for how to verify that a host has all four of these IPv4 settings. The third and final section of this chapter then looks at three testing and verification tools—ping, traceroute, and Telnet—to learn how they can help verify whether the IP settings that do exist actually work.

This chapter covers the following exam topics:

LAN Switching Technologies

Verify network status and switch operation using basic utilities such as ping, telnet and ssh.

IP Routing Technologies

Configure and verify utilizing the CLI to set basic Router configuration

Cisco IOS commands to perform basic router setup

Verify router configuration and network connectivity

Cisco IOS commands to review basic router information and network connectivity

IP Services

Configure and verify DHCP (IOS Router)

configuring router interfaces to use DHCP

DHCP options

excluded addresses

lease time

Troubleshooting

Troubleshoot and correct common problems associated with IP addressing and host configurations.

Foundation Topics

Configuring Routers to Support DHCP

Dynamic Host Configuration Protocol (DHCP) is one of the most commonly used protocols in a TCP/IP network. The vast majority of hosts in a TCP/IP network are user devices, and the vast majority of user devices learn their IPv4 settings using DHCP.

Using DHCP has several advantages over using manually or statically configured IPv4 settings. The configuration of host IP settings sits in a DHCP server, with the client learning these settings using DHCP messages. As a result, the host IP configuration is controlled by the IT staff, which cuts down on user errors. DHCP allows both the permanent assignment of host addresses, but more commonly, DHCP assigns a temporary lease of IP addresses. With these leases, the DHCP server can reclaim IP addresses when a device is removed from the network, making better use of the available addresses.

DHCP also enables mobility. For example, every time a user moves to a new location with a tablet computer—to a coffee shop, a client location, or back at the office—the user's device can connect to the wireless LAN, use DHCP to lease a new IP address, and begin working on the new network. Without DHCP, the user would have to ask for information about the local network, configure settings manually, with more than a few users making mistakes.

Although DHCP works automatically for user hosts, it does require some preparation from the network, with some configuration on routers. In some enterprise networks, that router configuration can be a single command on many of the router's LAN interfaces (**ip helper-address** *server-ip*), which identifies the DHCP server by its IP address. In other cases, the router actually plays the role of the DHCP server. Regardless, the routers have some role to play.

This first major section of the chapter begins with a look at the DHCP protocols that run between a DHCP client (any host) and the DHCP server. The next topic looks at the minimum router configuration option, which uses a separate appliance or server as the DHCP server. The final part of this section looks at how to configure a Cisco router to be that DHCP server.

DHCP Protocol Messages and Addresses

Sit back for a moment, and think about the role of DHCP for a host computer. The host acts as a DHCP client. As DHCP client, the host begins with no IPv4 settings: no IPv4 address, no mask, no default router, and no DNS server IP addresses. But a DHCP client does have knowledge of the DHCP protocol, so the client can use that protocol to (a) discover a DHCP server and (b) request to lease an IPv4 address.

The DHCP process to lease an IP address uses the following four messages between the client and server. (Also, as a way to help remember the messages, note that the first letters spell DORA):

Discover: Sent by the DHCP client to find a willing DHCP server

Offer: Sent by a DHCP server to offer to lease to that client a specific IP address (and inform the client of its other parameters)

Request: Sent by the DHCP client to ask the server to lease the IPv4 address listed in the Offer message

Acknowledgment: Sent by the DHCP Server to assign the address, and to list the mask, default router, and DNS server IP addresses

DHCP clients, however, have a somewhat unique problem: they do not have an IP address yet, but they need to send IP packets. To make that work, DHCP messages make use of two special IPv4 addresses that allow a host that has no IP address still be able to send and receive messages on the local subnet:

Key Topic

0.0.0.0: An address reserved for use as a source IPv4 address for hosts that do not yet have an IP address.

255.255.255.255: The address reserved as a local subnet broadcast address. Packets sent to this destination address are broadcast on the local data link, but routers do not forward them to other subnets.

To see how these addresses work, Figure 18-1 shows an example of the IP addresses used between a host (A) and a DHCP server on the same LAN. Host A, a client, sends a Discover message, with source IP address of 0.0.0.0 because host A does not have an IP address to use yet. Host A sends the packet to destination 255.255.255.255, which is sent in a LAN broadcast frame, reaching all hosts in the subnet. The client hopes that there is a DHCP server on the local subnet. Why? Packets sent to 255.255.255.255 only go to hosts in the local subnet; Router R1 will not forward this packet.

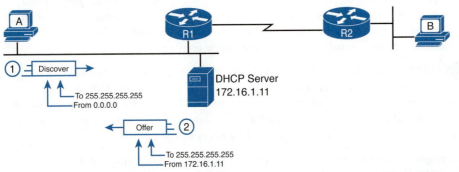

Figure 18-1   *DHCP Discover and Offer*

> **NOTE**   Figure 18-1 shows just one example of the addresses that can be used, specifically when the DHCP client chooses to use a DHCP option called the broadcast flag. This chapter does not attempt to show every variation of addresses used by the DHCP protocols; instead, the goal is to show one typical example, so you see the need for a particular function on the router, called DHCP Relay. However, note that all the DHCP examples in this chapter show the addresses used if client uses the DHCP broadcast flag.

Now look at the Offer message sent back by the DHCP server. The server sets the destination IP address to 255.255.255.255 again. Why? Host A still does not have an IP address, so the server cannot send a packet directly to host A. So, the server sends the packet to "all hosts on the local subnet" (255.255.255.255), a packet that is also encapsulated in an Ethernet broadcast frame. Host A will be able to receive and process the message. (Other hosts receive and ignore the message.)

The DHCP messages work well, as shown in the figure, when the DHCP client and server sit in the same subnet. Once the four messages are complete, the DHCP client has an IP address, plus its other IPv4 settings, and it can send unicast IP packets as normal.

Supporting DHCP for Remote Subnets with DHCP Relay

Network engineers have a major design choice to make with DHCP: Do they put a DHCP server in every LAN subnet, or locate a DHCP server in a central site? With a DHCP server in every subnet, the protocols work as shown in Figure 18-1, and the router can ignore DHCP completely. However, with a centralized DHCP server, many DHCP clients sit in a different subnet than the DHCP server. So far in this section, it appears that the DHCP message would never reach the DHCP server, because routers do not route (forward) IPv4 packets sent to destination IP address 255.255.255.255.

Many enterprise networks use a couple of DHCP servers at a centralized site, supporting DHCP services to all remote subnets. The routers need to somehow forward those DHCP messages between clients and the DHCP server. To make that work, the routers connected to the remote LAN subnets need an interface subcommand: the **ip helper-address** *server-ip* command.

The **ip helper-address** *server-ip* subcommand tells the router to do the following for the messages coming in an interface, from a DHCP client:

Key Topic

1. Watch for incoming DHCP messages, with destination IP address 255.255.255.255.

2. Change that packet's source IP address to the router's incoming interface IP address.

3. Change that packet's destination IP address to the address of the DHCP server (as configured in the **ip helper-address** command).

4. Route the packet to the DHCP server.

This command gets around the "do not route packets sent to 255.255.255.255" rule by changing the destination IP address. Once the destination has been set to match the DHCP server's IP address, the network can route the packet to the server.

> **NOTE**   This feature, by which a route relays DHCP messages by changing the IP addresses in the packet header, is called *DHCP relay*.

Figure 18-2 shows an example of the process. Host A sits on the left, as a DHCP client. The DHCP server (172.16.2.11) sits on the right. R1 has an **ip helper-address 172.16.2.11** command configured, under its G0/0 interface. At Step 1, Router R1 notices the incoming DHCP packet destined for 255.255.255.255. Step 2 shows the results of changing both the source and destination IP address, with R1 routing the packet.

Key Topic

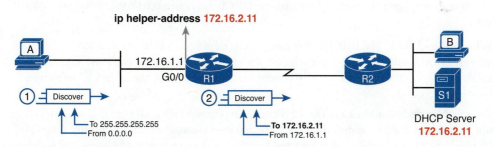

Figure 18-2   *IP Helper Address Effect*

The router uses a similar process for the return DHCP messages from the server. First, for the return packet from the DHCP server, the server simply reverses the source and destination IP address of the packet received from the router (relay agent). For example, in Figure 18-2, the Discover message lists source IP address 172.16.1.1, so the server sends the Offer message back to destination IP address 172.16.1.1.

When a router receives a DHCP message, addressed to one of the router's own IP addresses, the router realized the packet might be part of the DHCP relay feature. When that happens, the DHCP relay agent (Router R1) needs to change the destination IP address, so that the real DHCP client (host A), which does not have an IP address yet, can receive and process the packet. Figure 18-3 shows one example of how these addresses work, when R1 receives the DHCP Offer message sent to R1's own 172.16.1.1 address. R1 changes the packet's destination to 255.255.255.255, and forwards it out G0/0, knowing that all hosts (including the DHCP client A) will receive the message.

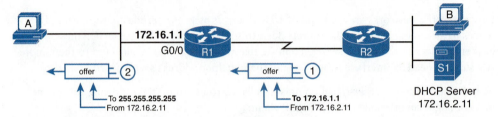

Figure 18-3   *IP Helper Address for the Offer Message Returned from the DHCP Server*

Many enterprise networks use a centralized DHCP server, so the normal router configuration includes an **ip helper-address** command on every LAN interface/subinterface. With that standard configuration, user hosts off any router LAN interface can always reach the DHCP server and lease an IP address.

Information Stored at the DHCP Server

A DHCP server might sound like some large piece of hardware, sitting in a big locked room with lots of air conditioning to keep the hardware cool. However, like most servers, the server is actually software, running on some server OS. The DHCP server could be a piece of software downloaded for free and installed on an old PC. However, because the server needs to be available all the time, to support new DHCP clients, most companies install the software on a very stable and highly available server environment, but the DHCP service is still created by software.

To be ready to answer DHCP clients, and to supply them with an IPv4 address and other information, the DHCP server (software) needs information. DHCP servers typically organize these IPv4 settings per subnet, because the information the server tells the client is usually the same for all hosts in the same subnet. For example, IP addressing rules tell us that all hosts on the same subnet should use the same mask.

The following list shows the types of settings the DHCP server needs to know to support DHCP clients:

Subnet ID and mask: The DHCP server can use this information to know all addresses in the subnet. Usually, unless reserved or excluded, the server believes that it can lease any and all valid addresses in the subnet. (The DHCP server knows to not lease the subnet ID or subnet broadcast address.)

Reserved (excluded) addresses: The server needs to know which addresses in the subnet to *not* lease. This list allows some addresses to be reserved for assignment as statically assigned IP addresses. For example, most router and switch IP addresses, server addresses, and addresses of most anything other than user devices use a statically assigned IP address. Most of the time, engineers use the same convention for all subnets, either reserving the lowest IP addresses in all subnets, or reserving the highest IP addresses in all subnets.

Default router(s): This is the IP address of the router on that subnet.

DNS IP address(es): This is a list of DNS server IP addresses

Figure 18-4 shows the concept behind the preconfiguration on a DHCP server for two LAN-based subnets, 172.16.1.0/24 and 172.16.2.0/24. The DHCP server sits on the right. For each subnet, the server defines all the items in the list. In this case, the configuration reserves the lowest IP addresses in the subnet to be used as static addresses.

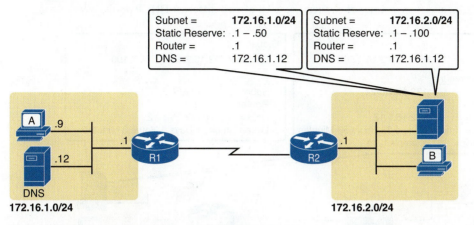

Figure 18-4 *Preconfiguration on a DHCP Server*

The configuration can list other parameters as well. For example, it can set the time limit for leasing an IP address. The server leases an address for a time (usually a number of days), and then the client can ask to renew the lease. If the client does not renew, the server can reclaim the IP address and put it back in the pool of available IP addresses. The server configuration sets the maximum time for the lease.

DHCP Server Configuration and Verification on Routers

A quick Google search on "DHCP server products" reveals that many companies offer DHCP server software. Cisco routers (and some Cisco switches) can also act as a DHCP server with just a little added configuration. This last topic in DHCP shows how to configure and verify the operation of DHCP on a Cisco router.

IOS DHCP Server Configuration

The previous page or two should have prepared you for the kinds of information that a server needs to configure. The Cisco DHCP server is no different. The configuration groups most of the parameters into a new configuration area, one per subnet, called a *DHCP pool*. The only DHCP command that sits outside the pool is the command that defines the list of addresses excluded from being leased by DHCP.

The Cisco IOS DHCP server configuration steps are as follows:

Key Topic

Step 1. Exclude addresses from being assigned by DHCP: **ip dhcp excluded-address** *first last*

Step 2. Create a DHCP pool and go to pool configuration mode: **ip dhcp pool** *name*

A. Define subnet that the DHCP server should support: **network** *subnet-ID mask* or **network** *subnet-ID prefix-length*

B. Define default router IP address(es) in that subnet: **default-router** *address1 address2…*

C. Define list of DNS server IP addresses: **dns-server** *address1 address2…*

D. Define length of lease, in days, hours, and minutes: **lease** *days hours minutes*

E. Define the DNS domain name: **domain-name** *name*

Of course, an example can help, particularly with so many configuration commands required. Figure 18-5 shows the organization of the configuration, while sticking to pseudocode rather than the specific configuration commands. (Upcoming Example 18-1 shows a matching configuration.) Note that for each of the two LAN subnets, there is a global command to exclude addresses, and then a group of settings for each of two different DHCP pools.

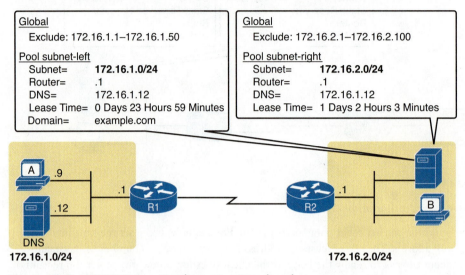

Figure 18-5 *DHCP Server Configuration Pseudocode*

Example 18-1 *R2 as a DHCP Server Per the Concepts in Figure 18-5*

```
ip dhcp excluded-address 172.16.1.1 172.16.1.50
ip dhcp excluded-address 172.16.2.1 172.16.2.100
!
ip dhcp pool subnet-left
 network 172.16.1.0 255.255.255.0
 dns-server 172.16.1.12
 default-router 172.16.1.1
 lease 0 23 59
 domain-name example.com
!
ip dhcp pool subnet-right
 network 172.16.2.0 /24
 dns-server 172.16.1.12
 default-router 172.16.2.1
 lease 1 2 3
```

Focus on subnet 172.16.1.0/24 for a moment: the subnet configured as pool subnet-left. The subnet ID and mask match the subnet ID chosen for that subnet. Then, the global **ip dhcp excluded-address** command, just above, reserves 172.16.1.1 through 172.16.1.50, so that this DHCP server will not lease these addresses. The server will automatically exclude the subnet ID (172.16.1.0) as well, so this DHCP server will begin leasing IP addresses starting with the .51 address.

Finally, note that configuring a router as a DHCP server does not remove the need for the **ip helper-address** command. If DHCP clients still exist on LANs that do not have a DHCP server, then the routers connected to those LANs still need the **ip helper-address** command. For example, in Figure 18-5, R1 would still need the **ip helper-address** command on its LAN interface.

IOS DHCP Server Verification

The IOS DHCP server function has several different **show** commands. These three commands list most of the details:

show ip dhcp binding: Lists state information about each IP address currently leased to a client

show ip dhcp pool [*poolname*]: Lists the configured range of IP addresses, plus statistics for the number of currently leased addresses and the high-water mark for leases from each pool

show ip dhcp server statistics: Lists DHCP server statistics

Example 18-2 shows sample output from two of these commands, based on the configuration from Figure 18-5 and Example 18-1. In this case, the DHCP server leased one IP address from each of the pools, one for host A, and one for host B, as seen in the highlighted portions of the output.

Example 18-2 *Verifying Current Operation of a Router-Based DHCP Server*

```
R2# show ip dhcp binding
Bindings from all pools not associated with VRF:
IP address          Client-ID/            Lease expiration        Type
                    Hardware address/
                    User name
172.16.1.51         0063.6973.636f.2d30.   Oct 12 2012 02:56 AM    Automatic
                    3230.302e.3131.3131.
                    2e31.3131.312d.4661.
                    302f.30
172.16.2.101        0063.6973.636f.2d30.   Oct 12 2012 04:59 AM    Automatic
                    3230.302e.3232.3232.
                    2e32.3232.322d.4769.
                    302f.30
R2# show ip dhcp pool subnet-right
Pool subnet-right :
 Utilization mark (high/low)    : 100 / 0
 Subnet size (first/next)       : 0 / 0
 Total addresses                : 254
 Leased addresses               : 1
 Pending event                  : none
 1 subnet is currently in the pool :
 Current index        IP address range              Leased addresses
 172.16.2.102         172.16.2.1     - 172.16.2.254      1
```

Note that the output in Example 18-2 does not happen to list the excluded addresses, but it does show the affects. The addresses assigned to the clients end with .51 (host A, subnet 172.16.1.0) and .101 (host B, subnet 172.16.2.0), proving that the server did exclude the addresses as shown in the configuration in Example 18-1. The server avoided the .1 through .50 addresses in subnet 172.16.1.0, and the .1 through .100 addresses in subnet 172.16.2.0.

> **NOTE** The DHCP server keeps status (state) information about each DHCP client that leases an address. Specifically, it remembers the DHCP client ID, and the IP address leased to the client. As a result, an IPv4 DHCP server can be considered to be a stateful DHCP server. This description will be useful when reading about DHCP for IPv6 in Chapter 28, "Implementing IPv6 Addressing on Hosts."

Detecting Conflicts with Offered Versus Used Addresses

The Cisco IOS DHCP server also looks for potential conflicts between addresses it leases and statically configured addresses. Although the DHCP server configuration clearly lists the addresses in the pool, plus those to be excluded from the pool, hosts can still statically configure addresses from the range inside the DHCP pool. In other words, no protocols prevent a host from statically configuring and using an IP address from within the range of addresses used by the DHCP server.

Knowing that some host might have statically configured an address from within the range of addresses in the DHCP pool, both DHCP servers and clients try to detect such problems, called conflicts, before the client uses a newly leased address.

DHCP servers detect conflicts by using pings. Before offering a new IP address to a client, the DHCP server first pings the address. If the server receives a response to the ping, some other host must already be using the address, which lets the server know a conflict exists. The server notes that particular address as being in conflict, and the server does not offer the address, moving on to the next address in the pool.

The DHCP client can also detect conflicts, but instead of using ping, it uses ARP. In the client case, when the DHCP client receives from the DHCP server an offer to use a particular IP address, the client sends an ARP for that address. If another host replies, the DHCP client has found a conflict.

Example 18-3 lists output from the router-based DHCP server on R2, after host B detected a conflict using ARP. Behind the scenes, host B used DHCP to request a lease, with the process working normally until host B used ARP and found some other device already used 172.16.2.102. At that point, host B then sent a DHCP message back to the server, rejecting the use of address 172.16.2.102. The example shows the router's log message related to host B's discovery of the conflict, and a **show** command that lists all conflicted addresses.

Example 18-3 *Displaying Information About DHCP Conflicts in IOS*

```
*Oct 16 19:28:59.220: %DHCPD-4-DECLINE_CONFLICT: DHCP address conflict:  client
0063.6973.636f.2d30.3230.302e.3034.3034.2e30.3430.342d.4769.302f.30 declined
172.16.2.102.
R2# show ip dhcp conflict
IP address        Detection method   Detection time          VRF
172.16.2.102      Gratuitous ARP     Oct 16 2012 07:28 PM
```

The **show ip dhcp conflict** command lists the method through which the server added each address to the conflict list: either gratuitous ARP, as detected by the client, or ping, as detected by the server. The server avoids offering these conflicted addresses to any future clients, until the engineer uses the **clear ip dhcp conflict** command to clear the list.

Verifying Host IPv4 Settings

Some hosts use DHCP to learn their IPv4 settings. Others manually set all their settings. Other hosts actually allow you to make some settings manually, and learn other settings with DHCP.

Regardless of how a given host builds its IPv4 configuration, that host will either work, or have problems. And if it has problems, someone needs to be ready and able to jump in and help solve the problem. On hosts, that means someone needs to be able to find the IPv4 settings, make sure they are correct, and troubleshoot problems related to the host IP settings.

This short section brushes the surface of how to verify IPv4 settings on hosts. This section touches on each of the settings, showing some host commands used to confirm each setting, as well as giving a few related hints on how to confirm if it is working or not. Note that the CCNA and ICND2 exams take a closer look at end-to-end troubleshooting.

IP Address and Mask Configuration

Most every OS in the world—certainly the more common OSs people work with every day— have a fairly easy-to-reach window that lists most if not all the IPv4 settings in one place. For example, Figure 18-6 shows the Network configuration screen from a user host OS (Mac OS X in this case), with all the IPv4 settings. This particular example shows the big four settings: address, mask, router, and DNS.

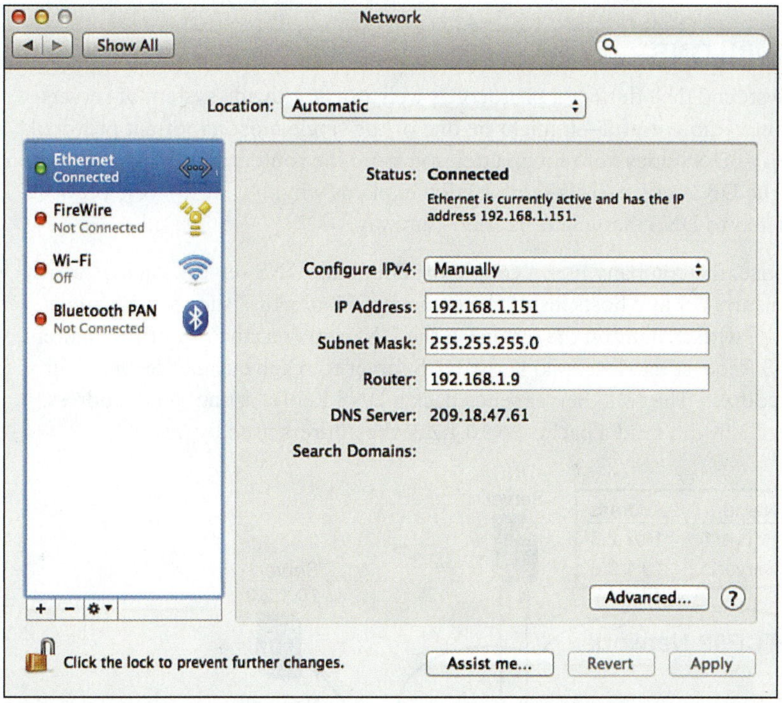

Figure 18-6 *IP Address, Mask, and Default Router Settings on Mac OS*

However, beyond these windows into the graphical user interface (GUI) of any OS, most OSs have a variety of networking commands available from a command line. Interestingly, some of the commands are the same across many different OSs, even between Microsoft Windows versions and other OSs.

For example, to verify the IP address, mask, default router, and other settings, OSs typically support either the **ipconfig** (Windows) or **ifconfig** (Linux and Mac OS) commands. Both commands have several options that can be seen by adding a **-?** to the end. Example 18-4 shows a sample from a Windows PC.

Example 18-4   ipconfig /all *(Windows)*

```
C:\DOCUME1\OWNER> ipconfig /all
Windows IP Configuration


Ethernet adapter Wireless Network Connection 3:

        Connection-specific DNS Suffix  . : Belkin
        Description . . . . . . . . . . . : Linksys WUSB600N Dual-Band Wireless-N USB
Network Adapter
        Physical Address. . . . . . . . . : 00-1E-E5-D8-CB-E4
```

```
Dhcp Enabled. . . . . . . . . . . : Yes
Autoconfiguration Enabled . . . . : Yes
IP Address. . . . . . . . . . . . : 192.168.2.13
Subnet Mask . . . . . . . . . . . : 255.255.255.0
Default Gateway . . . . . . . . . : 192.168.2.1
DHCP Server . . . . . . . . . . . : 192.168.2.1
DNS Servers . . . . . . . . . . . : 192.168.2.1
Lease Obtained. . . . . . . . . . : Wednesday, October 10, 2012 3:25:00AM
Lease Expires . . . . . . . . . . : Monday, January 18, 2013 11:14:07 PM
```

Name Resolution with DNS

The Domain Name System (DNS) defines a protocol as well as a worldwide system of servers that use DNS. While incredibly useful—it might be one of the single most important protocols in the world of TCP/IP—DNS does not require attention from the routers and switches between the user devices and the DNS servers. This short section explains why, but shows you a few router commands related to DNS that might be handy anyway.

Inside a single enterprise, the company uses a couple of redundant DNS servers, each of which can resolve any host names for any hosts inside the company. Figure 18-7 shows an example using a single company, with a client on the left using the DNS server at the top of the figure. Step 1 shows the DNS Request message, asking the DNS server to resolve name "Server1" into its corresponding IP address. The DNS Server sends back a DNS Reply, listing the IP address. Finally, at Step 3, the client can send a packet to 10.1.2.3, the address used by Server1.

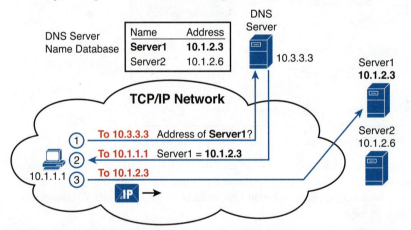

Figure 18-7   *Host Resolves Name to IP Address Before Sending Packet to Server1*

Now stop for a moment, and focus on the "To:" part of the three messages. Each packet has a known unicast destination address. The routers in the TCP/IP network can simply forward those packets. No need for any special configuration, no need for a command and function like the **ip helper-address** command used with DHCP. In short, the routers and switches have no extra work to do, and no extra configuration required, to support DNS between a host and the DNS servers.

When looking at problems with hosts, you can and should check the DNS settings to find out what DNS server addresses the host tries to use. At the same time, the user at the host can make the host try and use DNS. For example:

- Open a web browser and type in the name of the web server. DNS resolves the name that sits between the // and the first /.

- Use a command like **nslookup** *hostname*, supported on most PC OSs, which sends a DNS Request to the DNS server, showing the results.

Example 18-5 shows an example of the **nslookup** command that confirms that the host's DNS server is set to 209.18.47.61, with the end of the output showing that the DNS request worked.

Example 18-5   nslookup *Command (Mac)*

```
Wendell-Odoms-iMac: wendellodom$ nslookup www.certskills.com
Server:            209.18.47.61
Address:           209.18.47.61#53

Non-authoritative answer:
www.certskills.com    canonical name = certskills.com.
Name:    certskills.com
Address: 173.227.251.150
```

And as a brief aside, note that routers and switches do have some settings related to DNS. However, these router and switch DNS settings only allow the router or switch to act as a DNS resolver (client). That is, the router and switch will use DNS messages to ask the DNS server to resolve the name into its matching IP address. The commands to configure how a router or switch will resolve host names into their matching addresses (all global commands) are

ip name-server *server_IP...*: Configure the IP addresses of up to six DNS servers in this one command.

ip host *name address*: Statically configure one name and matching IP address, on this one router or switch. The local router/switch only will use this IP address if a command refers to the name.

no ip domain-lookup: Disable the DNS resolver function, so that the router or switch does not attempt to ask a DNS server to resolve names. (The **ip domain-lookup** command, a default setting, enables the router to use a DNS server.)

Default Routers

As discussed in some detail back in Chapter 16, "Configuring IPv4 Addresses and Routes," IPv4 host routing logic reduces to a basic two-part choice. For packets destined for a host in the same subnet, the local host sends the packet directly, ignoring any routers. For packets destined for a host in a different subnet, the local host next sends the packet to its default gateway (also known as the default router), expecting that router to forward the packet.

Interestingly, a couple of simple errors can occur between any LAN-based host and their default router. For a LAN-based host's default router setting to work, the following must be true:

- The host link to the LAN and the default router link to the LAN must be in the same VLAN.

- The host and default router IP addresses must be in the same subnet.

- The host default router setting must refer to the same IP address configured on the router. (In other words, if the host claims the default router is 10.1.1.1, make sure the router interface IP address is not 10.1.1.2.)

- The LAN switches must not discard the frame because of the port security configuration.

All of the above settings and choices can be mismatched between a host and the default router. On the router, the settings can be checked with the usual CLI commands: **show interfaces, show ip interface brief, show protocols,** and **show running-config.** On the switch, to check the VLAN assignments, use **show interfaces status, show vlan,** and **show interfaces switchport.**

On the host, the methods to check the default router setting of course differ depending on the OS. A look at the settings using the GUI simply lists the default router. However, common command on most user host OSs is the **netstat -rn** command, which lists the default gateway as the route for destination 0.0.0.0. Example 18-6 shows an example **netstat -rn** command from a PC running windows, with the default router setting highlighted.

Example 18-6   netstat -rn *Command (Windows)*

```
C:\DOCUME1\OWNER> netstat -rn
Interface List
0x1 ......................... MS TCP Loopback interface
0x2 ...00 11 2f 16 c4 7a ...... NVIDIA nForce Networking Controller - Packet Scheduler
Miniport
0x3 ...00 1e e5 d8 cb e4 ...... Linksys WUSB600N Dual-Band Wireless-N USB Network Adapter
- Packet Scheduler Miniport
===========================================================================
===========================================================================
Active Routes:
Network Destination        Netmask          Gateway        Interface  Metric
          0.0.0.0          0.0.0.0      192.168.2.1    192.168.2.13      25
        127.0.0.0        255.0.0.0        127.0.0.1       127.0.0.1       1
      169.254.0.0      255.255.0.0    192.168.2.13    192.168.2.13      20
      192.168.2.0    255.255.255.0    192.168.2.13    192.168.2.13      25
     192.168.2.13  255.255.255.255        127.0.0.1       127.0.0.1      25
    192.168.2.255  255.255.255.255    192.168.2.13    192.168.2.13      25
        224.0.0.0        240.0.0.0    192.168.2.13    192.168.2.13      25
  255.255.255.255  255.255.255.255    192.168.2.13               2       1
  255.255.255.255  255.255.255.255    192.168.2.13    192.168.2.13       1
Default Gateway:       192.168.2.1
===========================================================================
```

Another good step to take to verify the default router is to find out if ARP works for the default router. For example, host A in Figure 18-8, when sending packets to host D, in the same subnet, will send the packet directly to host D. So, host A will first need an ARP entry for host D. Similarly, before sending a packet to server B, which sits on another subnet, host A will need an ARP entry for R1's MAC address.

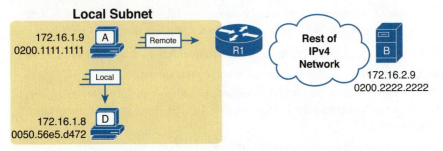

Figure 18-8   *Host IP and MAC Addresses in the Next Two ARP Examples*

The **arp -a** command happens to be another common command on many user OSs. listing the host's ARP table. The same in Example 18-7 shows host A's ARP table after host A successful sent a packet to both server B and host D. Note that server B's IP address of 172.16.2.9 is not listed, because the ARP table lists IP addresses for IP addresses on the same subnet, and not those on remote subnets.

Example 18-7 *ARP Table on Host A (Windows)*

```
C:\Users\wodom> arp -a

Interface: 172.16.1.9 --- 0xa
  Internet Address      Physical Address      Type
  172.16.1.1            02-00-01-01-01-01      dynamic
  172.16.1.8            00-50-56-e5-d4-72      dynamic
```

Routers also need to keep an ARP table, so they can encapsulate IP packets into LAN frames. Example 18-8 shows the output of the **show arp** command on Router R1, which lists an entry for host A (172.16.1.9), and for the router itself (172.16.1.1). (Note that hosts typically do not list their own IP addresses in their own ARP cache, but the Cisco router ARP cache does.)

Example 18-8 *ARP Table on Router R1*

```
R1# show arp
Protocol  Address         Age (min)  Hardware Addr   Type   Interface
Internet  172.16.1.1          -       0200.0101.0101  ARPA   GigabitEthernet0/0
Internet  172.16.1.9          2       0200.1111.1111  ARPA   GigabitEthernet0/0
```

Testing Connectivity with ping, traceroute, and telnet

While checking a host's IPv4 settings can be important, the final true test for hosts is whether the host applications can communicate like they should. Can the user open a web browser and connect to web sites? Does email work? Can all those apps on a smart phone connect through the Internet?

This last section of the chapter looks at some connectivity testing tools that ask a simpler but cleaner question: Can a host send packets to another host, and can that host send packets back? The user applications cannot work until the two hosts can send packets back and forth. If the tools show that IPv4 packets can indeed flow from between two hosts, but an application does not work, then the troubleshooting process can next look at why the application might be having problems. However, if the hosts cannot send packets to each other, the troubleshooting process points to some network problem that prevents the packets from being forwarded correctly.

Specifically, this section looks at the **ping** and **traceroute** commands. **ping** answers the basic question of whether two hosts can send packets back and forth to each other or not. **traceroute** takes a more diagnostic approach, so that if the hosts cannot send packets, this command helps a network engineer determine where the problem is occurring.

This section ends with some details about how to use Telnet to move around between Cisco routers so that network engineers can make better use of commands like **ping** and **traceroute**.

The ping Command

The **ping** command exists to test connectivity. It sends a series of packets to one destination IP address. The packets mean basically "if you get this packet, send a reply back." Each time the sender sends the request, and the other host sends a reply, the **ping** command knows a packet made it from the source host, to the destination, and back.

More formally, the **ping** command uses the Internet Control Message Protocol (ICMP), specifically the ICMP Echo Request and ICMP Echo Reply messages. ICMP defines many other messages as well, but these two messages were made specifically for connectivity testing by commands like **ping**. As a protocol, ICMP does not rely on a transport layer protocol like TCP or UDP, and it does not use any application layer protocol. It exists to assist IP by helping manage the IP network functions.

Figure 18-9 shows the ICMP messages, with IP headers, in an example. In this case, the user at host A opens a command prompt and issues the **ping 172.16.2.101** command, testing connectivity to host B. The command sends one Echo Request, and waits (Step 1); host B receives the messages, and sends back an Echo Reply (Step 2). At that point, the ping command can issue a message to the user, confirming that the ping worked.

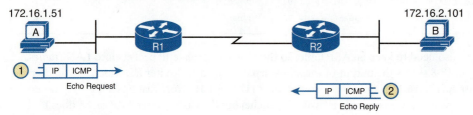

Figure 18-9 *Concept Behind ping 172.16.2.101 on Host A*

The **ping** command is supported on many different devices and many common OSs. The command has many options: the name or IP address of the destination, how many times the command should send an Echo Request, how long it should wait (timeout) for an Echo Reply, how big to make the packets, and many others. Example 18-9 shows a sample from host A, with the same command that matches the concept in Figure 18-9: a **ping 172.16.2.101** command on host A.

Example 18-9 *Sample Output from Host A's ping 172.16.2.101 Command*

```
Wendell-Odoms-iMac: wendellodom$ ping 172.16.2.101
PING 172.16.2.101 (172.16.2.101): 56 data bytes
64 bytes from 172.16.2.101: icmp_seq=0 ttl=64 time=1.112 ms
64 bytes from 172.16.2.101: icmp_seq=1 ttl=64 time=0.673 ms
64 bytes from 172.16.2.101: icmp_seq=2 ttl=64 time=0.631 ms
64 bytes from 172.16.2.101: icmp_seq=3 ttl=64 time=0.674 ms
64 bytes from 172.16.2.101: icmp_seq=4 ttl=64 time=0.642 ms
64 bytes from 172.16.2.101: icmp_seq=5 ttl=64 time=0.656 ms
^C
--- 172.16.2.101 ping statistics ---
6 packets transmitted, 6 packets received, 0.0% packet loss
round-trip min/avg/max/stddev = 0.631/0.731/1.112/0.171 ms
```

Testing IP Routes with **ping** on a Router

Today, many tools exist so that support personnel can view and take over the desktop GUI of a remote user device. Customer support representatives (CSR) can sit at their desks in one city, receive a phone call from a customer, and connect to look at the user's desktop GUI in a matter of a few clicks—as long as the problem is not a network problem. However, if a network problem exists, the remote connection to the user's device can fail, and the CSR has to troubleshoot the IP connectivity problem without access to the user device.

In some cases, talking a user through typing the right commands and making the right clicks on their machines can be a problem. Or, the user just might not be available. In those cases, the CSR could connect to a nearby router (with Telnet or SSH) and use the router **ping** command to test the host connectivity.

For example, in Figure 18-9, imagine that the user of host A had called IT support with a problem related to sending packets to host B (in Figure 18-9). The CSR tries, but fails, to remotely connect to host A's desktop. So, the CSR Telnets to Router R1, the router nearest to host A, and pings host B from there, as seen in Example 18-10.

Example 18-10   *Router R2 Pings Host B (Two Commands)*

```
R1# ping 172.16.2.101
Type escape sequence to abort.
Sending 5, 100-byte ICMP Echos to 172.16.2.101, timeout is 2 seconds:
.!!!!
Success rate is 80 percent (4/5), round-trip min/avg/max = 1/2/4 ms
R1# ping 172.16.2.101
Type escape sequence to abort.
Sending 5, 100-byte ICMP Echos to 172.16.2.101, timeout is 2 seconds:
!!!!!
Success rate is 100 percent (5/5), round-trip min/avg/max = 1/2/4 ms
```

Focus on the first command for a moment. The Cisco IOS **ping** command sends five Echo messages, with a timeout of 2 seconds. If the command does not receive an Echo Reply within two seconds, the command considers that message to be a failure, and it sends the next one. So each **ping** command, when getting no responses at all, takes about 10 seconds to complete. The command lists a period for each unanswered Echo Request, while success—the arrival of an Echo Reply within two seconds—shows up as an exclamation point. In this case, the first one failed, and the others worked.

Interestingly, the two **ping** commands in the sample show a common occurrence: the first **ping** command shows failures for a few messages, but then the rest of the messages work. This usually happens because some device in the end-to-end route is missing an ARP table entry, and must first complete the ARP process before being ready to forward the packet. (For this test, I first used the **clear ip arp 172.16.2.101** command on R2 to clear its ARP cache, so that the test would show at least one failure.)

Controlling the Source IP Address with Extended **ping**

The **ping** command on Router R1 in Example 18-10 tests many parts of the connectivity from host A to host B, but not all. In fact it has a subtle problem in what this command actually tests. Thankfully, the IOS **ping** command allows us to overcome the problem using a function called an extended ping.

First, to see the problem—or really a missed opportunity—consider again the **ping 172.16.2.101** command on Router R1, as shown in Example 18-10. The command does confirm that many parts of the network works correctly. It clearly tests the physical and data link functions between R1 and R2, as well as between R2 and host B. It tests the network layer routes towards 172.16.2.101 (the forward route). However, the not-so-obvious problem is that it does not test the reverse route towards host A.

The **ping** in Example 18-9 does not properly test the reverse route back toward host A because of how the router chooses the source IP address for the **ping** command's packets. Figure 18-10 shows the default behavior of the router **ping** command. It has to pick a source IP address to use for the Echo Request, and routers choose the *IP address of the outgoing interface*. The Echo Request, from R1 to host B, flows with source IP address 172.16.4.1 (R1's S0/0/0 IP address), and of course destination IP address 172.16.2.101.

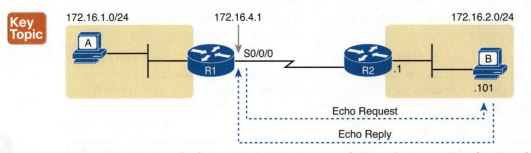

Figure 18-10 *Standard* **ping 172.6.2.101** *Command Using the Source Interface IP Address*

The ICMP Echo Reply packet shows the missed opportunity. It flows to an IP address in subnet 172.16.4.0/24, and not to an IP address in host A's subnet of 172.16.1.0/24. So, the ICMP Echo Reply does not test the route back to host A's subnet. A better test would be to use R1's LAN IP address as the source of the Echo Request, so that the Echo Reply messages would flow back to host A's subnet, testing routes to that subnet, as shown in Figure 18-11.

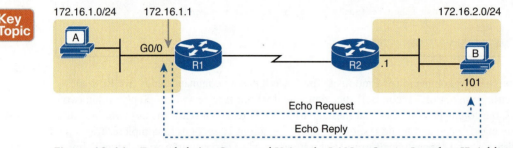

Figure 18-11 *Extended* **ping** *Command Using the LAN as Source Interface IP Address*

The router extended **ping** command allows the user to choose from several additional parameters on the **ping** command as compared to the standard **ping** command. As you would guess by now, this command does let the user choose the source IP address as any of the local router's own IP addresses. The command can refer to the IP address directly, or to the router interface.

While the extended **ping** command allows the user to type all the parameters on a potentially long command, it also allows users to simply issue the **ping** command, press Enter, with IOS then asking the user to answer questions to complete the command, as shown in Example 18-11. The example shows the **ping** command on R1 that matches the logic in Figure 18-11.

Example 18-11 *Creating a Better Test Using the Extended* **ping** *Command*

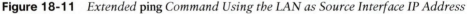

```
R1# ping
Protocol [ip]:
Target IP address: 172.16.2.101
Repeat count [5]:
Datagram size [100]:
Timeout in seconds [2]:
Extended commands [n]: y
Source address or interface: 172.16.1.1
Type of service [0]:
Set DF bit in IP header? [no]:
Validate reply data? [no]:
```

```
Data pattern [0xABCD]:
Loose, Strict, Record, Timestamp, Verbose[none]:
Sweep range of sizes [n]:
Type escape sequence to abort.
Sending 5, 100-byte ICMP Echos to 172.16.2.101, timeout is 2 seconds:
Packet sent with a source address of 172.16.1.1
!!!!!
Success rate is 100 percent (5/5), round-trip min/avg/max = 1/2/4 ms
```

Reading from the top down, the first two highlighted lines show where the extended ping options start. If the user had answered "n" or "no" on the "Extended commands" option, IOS would not have asked the remaining questions for the extended version of the command. By answering yes, IOS asks the extra questions, including the "Source address or interface" question used to supply 172.16.1.1 as the source IP address in this case.

The last highlighted line confirms the source IP address used for this test. Note that IOS only lists this line of output when the extended ping command happens to specify the source IP address to use.

NOTE   The extended **ping** command does allow you to refer to the interface, but it must be the full spelled-out interface name, for example, gigabitethernet0/0.

The extended version of the **ping** command, using the source interface option, creates a much more realistic connectivity test. Comparing the standard and extended **ping** examples in this section, both do the same job in testing connectivity and links from R1 toward host B. However, the extended **ping** tests the likely route back to the user host (host A), while the standard ping does not.

The traceroute Command

Imagine some network engineer or CSR starts to troubleshoot some problem. They ping from the user's host, ping from a nearby router, and after a few commands, convince themselves that the host can indeed send and receive IP packets. The problem might not be solved yet, but the problem does not appear to be a problem with packet delivery between the user's device and the rest of the network.

Now imagine the next problem comes along, and for that devices, pings fail. It appears that some problem does exist in the IP network. Where is the problem? Where should the engineer look more closely? While **ping** can be helpful in answering these questions, isolating the source of the problem, the **traceroute** command might be a better option. The **traceroute** command systematically helps pinpoint problems by showing how far a packet goes through an IP network before being discarded.

The **traceroute** command that fully completes identifies the routers in the path from source host to destination host. Specifically, it lists the next-hop IP address of each router that would be in each of the individual routes. For example, a **traceroute 172.16.2.101** command on host A in Figure 18-12 would identify an IP address on Router R1, another on Router R2, and then host B, as shown in the figure. Example 18-12 that follows lists the output of the command, taken from host A.

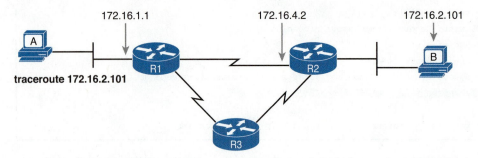

Figure 18-12 *IP Addresses Identified by a Successful* **traceroute 172.16.2.101** *Command on Host A*

Example 18-12 *Example Output from* **traceroute 172.16.2.101** *on Host A*

```
Wendell-Odoms-iMac: wendellodom$ traceroute 172.16.2.101
traceroute to 172.16.2.101, 64 hops max, 52 byte packets
 1  172.16.1.1 (172.16.1.1)  0.870 ms  0.520 ms  0.496 ms
 2  172.16.4.2 (172.16.4.2) 8.263 ms  7.518 ms  9.319 ms
 3  172.16.2.101 (172.16.2.101) 16.770 ms  9.819 ms  9.830 ms
```

How the **traceroute** Command Works

The **traceroute** command gathers this information about each router by relying on an ICMP message that was originally meant for other purposes: The ICMP Time-to-Live Exceeded (TTL Exceeded) message.

Before discussing traceroute, you need a little background on TTL and the TTL Exceeded message. In an IP network, the routers can create a loop. A routing loop is something to be avoided, because the routers keep forwarding packets around and around, never delivering them to the correct destination. For example, R1 sends the packet to R2, which sends it to R3, which sends it to R1 again, over and over again, with the same packets going around and around between these three routers.

IPv4 routers deal with one bad side effect of routing loops—the fact that packets keep looping around the network—by discarding looping IP packets. To do so, the IPv4 header holds a field called Time To Live (TTL). The original host sets this value. Then, each router that forwards the packet decrements the TTL value by 1. When a router decrements the TTL to 0, the router perceives the packet is looping around, and the router discards the packet. The router also notifies the host that sent the discarded packet by sending an ICMP TTL Exceeded message.

Now back to **traceroute. traceroute** sends messages to make the routers send back a TTL exceeded message, but without a routing loop existing in the network. As a result, the **traceroute** command can identify the router based on the source IP address of the packet holding the ICMP TTL exceeded message.

Specifically, a **traceroute** command begins by sending several packets (usually 3), each with the header TTL field equal to 1. When that packet arrives at the next router—host A's default Router R1 in this example—the router decrements TTL to 0, and discards the packet. The router then sends host A the TTL Exceeded message, which identifies the router's IP address to the **traceroute** command. Figure 18-13 shows one such packet and TTL Exceeded message.

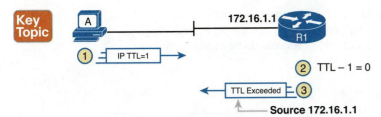

Figure 18-13 *How* **traceroute** *Identifies the First Router in the Route*

The **traceroute** command sends several TTL=1 packets, checking them to see if the TTL Exceeded messages flow from the same router, based on the source IP address of the TTL Exceeded message. Assuming the messages come from the same router, the **traceroute** command lists that IP address as the next line of output on the command. Routers have a choice of IP addresses to use, but as you might guess at this point, routers use the IP address of the outgoing interface. In this case, R1's outgoing interface for the message is 172.16.1.1.

To find all the routers in the path, and finally confirm that packets flow all the way to the destination host, the **traceroute** command sends packets with TTL=2, then 3, 4, and so on, until the destination host actually replies. Figure 18-14 shows the first packet with TTL=2, to show how R1 actually forwards the packet, while R2 decrements the TTL to 0, causing R2 to send a TTL Exceeded message being sent back to host A.

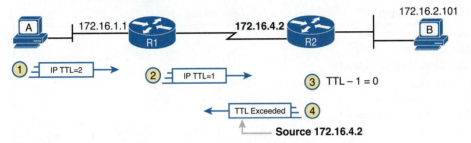

Figure 18-14 *TTL=2 Message Sent by* **traceroute**

The figure shows these four steps:

Step 1.   The **traceroute** command sends a packet, with TTL=2.

Step 2.   Router R1 processes the packet, and decrements TTL to 1. R1 forwards the packet.

Step 3.   Router R2 processes the packet, and decrements TTL to 0. R2 discards the packet.

Step 4.   R2 notifies the sending host of the discarded packet by sending a TTL Exceeded ICMP message. The source IP address of that message is R2's outgoing interface for the message, in this case, 172.16.4.2.

If the **traceroute** command completes, listing the destination host's IP address on a final line, great! In that case, the command has confirmed that connectivity exists from source to destination and back. However, if an IP routing problem exists, the command might either keep running until the user cancels it, or the command finishes but lists codes meaning that the command failed at that point.

When the **traceroute** command cannot complete, or it fails, the last few lines of output tell us where to spend time troubleshooting. When that happens, the problem most likely exists either in the last router listed in the **traceroute** output, or in the next router that should be listed in the output.

For example, if the earlier **traceroute 172.16.2.101** command listed R1 (172.16.1.1), but no other routers, the next troubleshooting steps should happen at R1 and R2. In a large network, narrowing down a problem to a couple of routers can be a great early step to troubleshoot a routing problem.

traceroute and Similar Commands

Both the **ping** and **traceroute** commands exist on most OSs, including Cisco IOS. However, some OSs use a slightly different syntax for **traceroute**. For example, most Windows OSs support **tracert** and **pathping**, and not **traceroute**. Linux and MAC OS X support the **traceroute** command.

Cisco IOS supports the **traceroute** command, with the memorable abbreviation **trace**. Like **ping**, **traceroute** can be issued with all parameters on one command line, or by letting IOS prompt the user to answer questions. And like the extended **ping** command, an extended **traceroute** command exists, allowing the network engineer to choose the source IP address, for the same good reasons as done with the **ping** command.

Example 18-13 lists the output of two **traceroute** commands on Router R1. The first, a standard **traceroute** command, uses the default source interface as chosen by R1. The second uses the prompting method by IOS, and shows the user choosing a different source IP address (172.16.1.1).

Example 18-13   *Example Standard and Extended* **traceroute** *on R1*

```
R1# traceroute 172.16.2.101
Type escape sequence to abort.
Tracing the route to 172.16.2.101
VRF info: (vrf in name/id, vrf out name/id)
  1 172.16.4.2 0 msec 0 msec 0 msec
  2 172.16.2.101 0 msec 0 msec *


R1# traceroute
Protocol [ip]:
Target IP address: 172.16.2.101
Source address: 172.16.1.1
Numeric display [n]:
Timeout in seconds [3]:
Probe count [3]:
Minimum Time to Live [1]:
Maximum Time to Live [30]:
Port Number [33434]:
Loose, Strict, Record, Timestamp, Verbose[none]:
Type escape sequence to abort.
Tracing the route to 172.16.2.101
VRF info: (vrf in name/id, vrf out name/id)
  1 172.16.4.2 0 msec 0 msec 0 msec
  2 172.16.2.101 0 msec 0 msec *
```

NOTE Host OS **traceroute** commands typically create ICMP Echo Requests. The Cisco IOS **traceroute** command instead creates IP packets with a UDP header. This bit of information might seem trivial at this point. However, when learning about IP access control lists (ACL), note that an ACL can actually filter the traffic from a host's **traceroute** messages, but not the router **traceroute** command, or vice versa.

Telnet and Suspend

Many engineers troubleshoot network problems sitting at their desks. To get access to a router or switch, the engineer just needs to use Telnet or SSH on their desktop PC to connect to each router or switch, often opening multiple Telnet or SSH windows to connect to multiple devices.

As an alternative, the engineer could connect to one router or switch using a Telnet or SSH client on their desktop computer, and then use the **telnet** or **ssh** Cisco IOS EXEC commands to connect to other routers and switches. These commands act as a Telnet or SSH client, respectively, so that you can easily connect to other devices when troubleshooting. When finished, the user could just use the **exit** command to disconnect the Telnet or SSH session.

One of the most important advantages of using the Cisco IOS **telnet** and **ssh** commands is the suspend feature. The suspend feature allows a Telnet or SSH connection to remain active while creating another Telnet or SSH connection, so that you can make many concurrent connections, and then easily switch between the connections. Figure 18-15 shows a sample internetwork with which the text will demonstrate the suspend feature and its power.

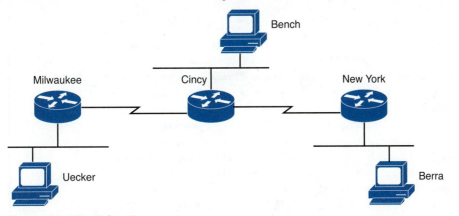

Figure 18-15 *Telnet Suspension*

The router administrator is using the PC named Bench to telnet into the Cincy router. When connected to the Cincy CLI, the user telnets to router Milwaukee. When in Milwaukee, the user suspends the Telnet session by pressing Ctrl-Shift-6, followed by pressing the letter x. (Note that Ctrl-Shift-6 sends a break character and some international keyboards might map a different key sequence to send a break character.) The user then telnets from the Cincy CLI to New York and again suspends the connection. At the end of the example, the user is concurrently connected to all three routers in one window, with the ability to switch between the connections with just a few keystrokes. Example 18-14 shows example output, with annotations to the side.

Example 18-14   *Telnet Suspensions*

```
Cincy# telnet milwaukee                (User issues command to Telnet to Milwaukee)
Trying Milwaukee (10.1.4.252)... Open


User Access Verification


Password:                  (User plugs in password, can type commands at Milwaukee)
Milwaukee>
Milwaukee>
Milwaukee>
                         (Note: User pressed Ctrl-Shift-6 and then x)
Cincy# telnet NewYork          (User back at Cincy because Telnet was suspended)
Trying NewYork (10.1.6.253)... Open
                    (User is getting into New York now, based on telnet NewYork command)



User Access Verification



Password:
NewYork>                                (User can now type commands on New York)
NewYork>
NewYork>
NewYork>
                     (Note: User pressed Ctrl-Shift-6 and then x)
                     (Note: User is now back at router Cincy as a result)
Cincy# show sessions              (This command lists suspended Telnet sessions)
Conn Host              Address             Byte   Idle Conn Name
   1 Milwaukee         10.1.4.252             0      0 Milwaukee
*  2 NewYork           10.1.6.253             0      0 NewYork

Cincy# where                      (where does the same thing as show sessions)
Conn Host              Address             Byte   Idle Conn Name
   1 Milwaukee         10.1.4.252             0      0 Milwaukee
*  2 NewYork           10.1.6.253             0      0 NewYork

Cincy# resume 1        (Resume connection 1 (see show session) to Milwaukee)
[Resuming connection 1 to milwaukee ... ]

Milwaukee>                         (User can type commands on Milwaukee)
Milwaukee>
Milwaukee>
! (Note: User pressed Ctrl-Shift-6 and then x, because the user wants to
!  go back to Cincy)

Cincy#          (WOW! User just pressed Enter and resumes the last Telnet)
 [Resuming connection 1 to milwaukee ... ]

Milwaukee>
Milwaukee>
Milwaukee>
```

```
                              (Note: User pressed Ctrl-Shift-6 and then x)
                              (Note: User is now back at router Cincy as a result)
Cincy# disconnect 1           (No more need to use Milwaukee  Telnet terminated!)
Closing connection to milwaukee [confirm]        (User presses Enter to confirm)
Cincy#
[Resuming connection 2 to NewYork ... ]
                    (Pressing Enter resumes most recently suspended active Telnet)


NewYork>
NewYork>
NewYork>
                              (Note: User pressed Ctrl-Shift-6 and then x)
                              (Note: User is now back at router Cincy as a result)
Cincy# disconnect 2                      (Done with New York, terminate Telnet)
Closing connection to NewYork [confirm]        (Just press Enter to confirm)
Cincy#
```

The play-by-play notes in the example explain most of the details. Example 18-14 begins with the Cincy command prompt that would be seen in the Telnet window from host Bench. After telnetting to Milwaukee, the Telnet connection was suspended because the user pressed Ctrl-Shift-6, let go, and then pressed x and let go. Then, after establishing a Telnet connection to New York, that connection was suspended with the same key sequence.

The two connections can be suspended or resumed easily. The **resume** command can be used to resume any suspended connection. To reconnect to a particular session, the **resume** command can list a connection ID, which is shown in the **show sessions** command. (The **where** command provides the same output.) If the **resume** command is used without a connection ID, the command reconnects the user to the most recently suspended connection. Also, instead of using the **resume** command, you can just use the session number as a command. For example, just typing the command **2** does the same thing as typing the command **resume 2**.

The interesting and potentially dangerous nuance here is that if a Telnet session is suspended and you simply press Enter, Cisco IOS Software resumes the connection to the most recently suspended Telnet connection. That is fine, until you realize that you tend to press the Enter key occasionally to clear some of the clutter from the screen. With a suspended Telnet connection, pressing Enter a few times to unclutter the screen reconnects to another router. This is particularly dangerous when you are changing the configuration or using potentially damaging EXEC commands, so be careful about what router you are actually using when you have suspended Telnet connections.

If you want to know which session has been suspended most recently, look for the session listed in the **show sessions** command that has an asterisk (*) to the left of the entry. The asterisk marks the most recently suspended session.

In addition to the commands in Example 18-14 that show how to suspend and resume Telnet and SSH connections, two other commands can list useful information about sessions for users logged into a router. The **show users** command lists all users logged in to the router on which the command is used. This command lists all sessions, including users at the console, and those connecting using both Telnet and SSH. The **show ssh** command lists the same kind of information, but only for users that connected using SSH. Note that these commands differ from the **show sessions** command, which lists suspended Telnet/SSH sessions from the local router to other devices.

Review Activities

Chapter Summary

- Dynamic Host Configuration Protocol (DHCP) is one of the most commonly used protocols in a TCP/IP network. The vast majority of hosts in a TCP/IP network are user devices, and the vast majority of user devices learn their IPv4 settings using DHCP.

- The DHCP process to lease an IP address uses the following four messages between the client and the server. (To remember the messages, note that the first letters spell DORA.)

  - **Discover:** Sent by the DHCP client to find a willing DHCP server

  - **Offer:** Sent by a DHCP server to offer to lease to that client a specific IP address (and inform the client of its other parameters)

  - **Request:** Sent by the DHCP client to ask the server to lease the IPv4 address listed in the Offer message

  - **Acknowledgement:** Sent by the DHCP Server to assign the address and list the mask, default router, and DNS server IP addresses

- DHCP clients, however, have a somewhat unique problem: They do not have an IP address yet but they need to send IP packets. To make that work, DHCP messages use two special IPv4 addresses that enable a host that has no IP address to be able to send and receive messages on the local subnet:

  - **0.0.0.0:** An address reserved for use as a source IPv4 address for hosts that do not yet have an IP address.

  - **255.255.255.255:** The address reserved as a local subnet broadcast address. Packets sent to this destination address are broadcast on the local data link, but routers do not forward them to other subnets.

- Many enterprise networks use a couple of DHCP servers at a centralized site that support DHCP services to all remote subnets. The routers need to somehow forward those DHCP messages between clients and the DHCP server. To make that work, the routers connected to the remote LAN subnets need an interface subcommand: the **ip helper-address** *server_IP* command.

- The following list shows the types of settings the DHCP server needs to know to support DHCP clients:

  - **Subnet ID and Mask:** The DHCP server can use this information to know all addresses in the subnet. Usually, unless reserved or excluded, the server believes that it can lease all valid addresses in the subnet. (The DHCP server knows to not lease the subnet ID or subnet broadcast address.)

  - **Reserved (excluded) addresses:** The server needs to know which addresses in the subnet to not lease. This list enables some addresses to be reserved for assignment as statically assigned IP addresses. For example, most router and switch IP addresses, server addresses, and addresses of almost anything other than user devices use a statically assigned IP address. Most of the time, engineers use the same convention for all subnets, either reserving the lowest IP addresses in all subnets or reserving the highest IP addresses in all subnets.

  - **Default router(s):** This is the IP address of the router on that subnet.

  - **DNS IP Address(es):** This is a list of DNS server IP addresses.

- The following are the Cisco IOS DHCP server configuration steps:

  Step 1.   Exclude addresses from being assigned by DHCP: **ip dhcp excluded-address** *first last*.

Step 2.   Create DHCP pool and go to pool configuration mode: **ip dhcp pool** *name*.

- **A.**   Define the subnet that the DHCP server should support: **network** *subnet_ID mask* or **network** *subnet_ID prefix_length*

- **B.**   Define the default router IP address(es) in that subnet: **default-router** *address1 address2…*

- **C.**   Define the list of DNS server IP addresses: **dns-server** *address1 address2…*

- **D.**   Define the length of lease, in days, hours, and minutes: **lease** *days hours minutes*

- **E.**   Define the DNS domain name: **domain-name** *name*

- The Cisco IOS DHCP server function has several different **show** commands. These three commands list most of the details:

  - **show ip dhcp binding:** Lists the state information about each IP address currently leased to a client.

  - **show ip dhcp pool** [*poolname*]: Lists the configured range of IP addresses, plus statistics for the number of currently leased addresses and the high-water mark for leases from each pool.

  - **show ip dhcp server statistics:** Lists DHCP server statistics.

- For a LAN-based host's default router setting to work, the following must be true:

  - The host link to the LAN and the default router link to the LAN must be in the same VLAN.

  - The host and default router IP addresses must be in the same subnet.

  - The host default router setting must match the IP address configured on the router.

  - The LAN switches must not discard the frame due to the port security configuration.

- The **ping** command exists to test connectivity. It sends a series of packets to one destination IP address. The packets mean basically, "If you get this packet, send a reply back." Each time the sender sends the request and the other host sends a reply, the **ping** command knows a packet made it from the source host to the destination and back.

- The **traceroute** command's output, when the command successfully completes, identifies the routers in the path between the source and destination host. Specifically, it lists the next-hop IP address of each router that would be in each of the individual routes.

Review Questions

Answer these review questions. You can find the answers at the bottom of the last page of the chapter. For thorough explanations, see DVD Appendix C, "Answers to Review Questions."

1. A PC connects to a LAN and uses DHCP to lease an IP address for the first time. Of the usual four DHCP messages that flow between the PC and the DHCP server, which ones do the client send? (Choose 2 answers.)

   A. Acknowledgment

   B. Discover

   C. Offer

   D. Request

2. An enterprise puts the DHCP and DNS servers on VLAN 10/subnet 10 in Atlanta, using IP address 10.1.10.1 for the DHCP server and 10.1.10.2 for the DNS server. A remote router sits in Boston, with devices on the Boston LAN using the DHCP and DNS servers in Atlanta. Which of the following needs to be configured in the routers in this enterprise to support DHCP and DNS?

    A. The **ip helper-address 10.1.10.1** command in the Atlanta router

    B. The **ip helper-address 10.1.10.2** command in the Boston router

    C. The **ip name-server 10.1.10.2** command in the Atlanta router

    D. The **ip dhcp-server 10.1.10.1** command in the Boston router

    E. None of the other answers is correct.

3. Fred decides to migrate from an old DHCP server platform to use a Cisco router at the headquarters building. This DHCP server, created with configuration in IOS on a Cisco router, supports 200 remote subnets. Which of the following settings are made outside of a per-subnet pool of addresses?

    A. Client IP address

    B. Addresses in that subnet excluded from being leased by the server

    C. Default router

    D. DNS server

    E. Length of address lease

4. PC1 uses manual (static) IPv4 configuration associated with its Ethernet NIC. Which of the following IPv4 settings will the PC list in the IPv4 configuration? (Choose 2 answers.)

    A. A DHCP server address

    B. A DNS server address

    C. A traceroute server address

    D. The PC's own IP address

Use the following figure to answer Questions 5 and 6:

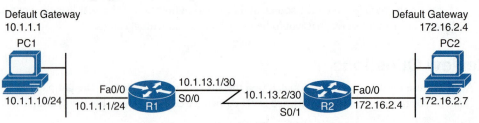

5. A new network engineer is trying to troubleshoot a problem for the user of PC1. Which of the following tasks and results would most likely point to a Layer 1 or 2 Ethernet problem on the LAN on the left side of the figure?

    A. A **ping 10.1.1.1** command on PC1 did not succeed.

    B. A **ping 10.1.13.2** command from PC1 succeeded, but a **ping 172.16.2.4** did not.

    C. A **ping 10.1.1.1** command from PC1 succeeded, but a **ping 10.1.13.1** did not.

    D. A **ping 10.1.1.10** command from PC1 succeeded.

6. The PC2 user issues the **tracert 10.1.1.10** command. Which of the following IP addresses could be shown in the command output? (Choose three answers.)

    A. 10.1.1.10

    B. 10.1.1.1

    C. 10.1.13.1

    D. 10.1.13.2

    E. 172.16.2.4

7. Examine the following command output. If the user typed the **resume** command, what would happen?

```
R1# show sessions
Conn Host              Address          Byte  Idle Conn Name
    1 Fred             10.1.1.1         0     0    Fred
*   2 Barney           10.1.2.1         0     0    Barney
```

    A. The command would be rejected, and the R1 CLI command prompt would be displayed again.

    B. The CLI user would be connected to a suspended Telnet connection to the router with IP address 10.1.1.1.

    C. The CLI user would be connected to a suspended Telnet connection to the router with IP address 10.1.2.1.

    D. The result cannot be accurately predicted from the information shown.

Review All the Key Topics

Review the most important topics from this chapter, noted with the Key Topic icon. Table 18-1 lists these key topics and where each is discussed.

Table 18-1   Key Topics for Chapter 18

Key Topic Element	Description	Page Number
List	The four DHCP messages used to lease a new IP address (DORA)	435
List	Definitions of special IPv4 addresses 0.0.0.0 and 255.255.255.255	436
List	Four logic steps created by the **ip helper-address** command	437
Figure 18-2	What the **ip helper-address** command changes in a DHCP Discover message	437
List	IOS DHCP server configuration checklist	439
List	Verification checklist for comparing host IPv4 settings with default router IPv4 settings	445
Figure 18-10	Example of how a router chooses the source IP address for an ICMP Echo Request message (for the **ping** command)	450
Figure 18-11	Example of how a router uses extended ping to choose a different source IP address for an ICMP Echo Request message (for the **ping** command)	450
Figure 18-13	Concept of how the **traceroute** command uses TTL and the TTL exceeded ICMP message	453

Definitions of Key Terms

After your first reading of the chapter, try to define these key terms, but do not be concerned about getting them all correct at that time. Chapter 30 directs you in how to use these terms for late-stage preparation for the exam.

DHCP client, DHCP server, local subnet broadcast address, ping, traceroute, DHCP relay, ICMP

Command Reference to Check Your Memory

Although you should not necessarily memorize the information in the tables in this section, this section does include a reference for the configuration and EXEC commands covered in this chapter. This section also includes a table of the host networking commands mentioned in this chapter. Practically speaking, you should memorize the commands as a side effect of reading the chapter and doing all the activities in this exam preparation section. To check to see how well you have memorized the commands as a side effect of your other studies, cover the left side of the table with a piece of paper, read the descriptions on the right side, and see whether you remember the command.

Table 18-2   Chapter 18 Configuration Command Reference

Command	Description
ip dhcp exclude-address *first last*	A global command that reserves an inclusive range of addresses, so that the DHCP server function does not lease out these addresses.
ip dhcp pool *pool-name*	A global command that creates a pool, by name, and moves the user to DHCP server pool configuration mode.
network *subnet-id {ddn-mask	/prefix-length}*	A DHCP pool mode subcommand that defines a network or subnet causing the DHCP server will lease out IP addresses in that subnet.
default-router *address1 address2...*	A DHCP pool mode subcommand that defines one or more routers as default routers, with that information passed for clients server by this pool.
dns-server *address1 address2...*	A DHCP pool mode subcommand that defines the list of DNS servers that the DHCP server will list for clients server by this pool.
lease *days hours minutes*	A DHCP pool mode subcommand that defines the length of time for a DHCP lease, for clients server by this pool.
ip helper-address *IP-address*	An interface subcommand that tells the router to notice local subnet broadcasts (to 255.255.255.255), and change the source and destination IP address, enabling DHCP servers to sit on a remote subnet.
ip name-server *address1...*	Global command that defines to a router or switch a list of DNS server IP addresses, which then lets users of the CLI of that router or switch resolve host names using DNS.
ip host *name address*	Global command to configure a static host name–to–IP address mapping, so the router or switch does not have to ask DNS to resolve that name.
[no] ip domain-lookup	Global command that enables or disables (with **no** in the front) the DNS resolver function on a router or switch.
ip address *ip-address mask* [secondary]	Interface subcommand that assigns the interface's IP address and optionally makes the address a secondary address.

Table 18-3   Chapter 18 EXEC Command Reference

Command	Description
show arp, show ip arp	Lists the router's IPv4 ARP table.
show ip dhcp binding	Lists the currently leased IP addresses on a DHCP server, along with the client identifier and lease time information.
show ip dhcp pool *name*	Lists the configured range of addresses in the pool, along with usage statistics and utilization high/low water marks.
show ip dhcp server statistics	Lists statistics about the requests served by the DHCP server.
show ip dhcp conflict	Lists IP addresses that the DHCP server found were already in use when the server tried to lease the address to a host.
clear ip dhcp conflict	Removes all entries from the DHCP server's conflict list.
ping {*host-name* | *ip-address*}	Tests IP routes by sending an ICMP packet to the destination host
traceroute {*host-name* | *ip-address*}	Tests IP routes by discovering the IP addresses of the routes between a router and the listed destination
telnet {*host-name* | *ip-address*}	Creates a Telnet connection from the local router or switch to the host listed in the command.
show sessions where	Lists Telnet or SSH connections from the local router, made to another device, and currently suspended. Users list the suspended connections and can then select one to resume the connection.
resume *session_number*	Reconnects to a previously-suspended Telnet or SSH connection from some router or switch to another device.
disconnect s*ession_ number*	Disconnects to a previously suspended Telnet or SSH connection from some router or switch to another device.
show users	Lists all users currently logged in to a router or switch.

Table 18-4   Chapter 18 Generic Host Networking Command Reference

Command	Description
ipconfig, ifconfig	Lists IP settings for the interface (NIC).
nslookup *name*	Performs a name resolution request for the name, and lists the results.
netstat -rn	Lists the hosts routing table, often listing the default router with a route to 0.0.0.0.
arp -a	Lists the host's ARP table.
ping {*host-name* | *ip-address*}	Tests IP routes by sending an ICMP packet to the destination host.
traceroute | tracert | pathping {*host-name* | *ip-address*}	Tests IP routes by discovering the IP addresses of the routes between a router and the listed destination.

Answers to Review Questions::

1 B and D **2** E **3** B **4** B and D **5** A **6** A, C, and E **7** C

Part IV Review

Keep track of your part review progress with the checklist in Table P4-1. Details on each task follow the table.

Table P4-1 Part IV Part Review Checklist

Activity	First Date Completed	Second Date Completed
Repeat All Chapter Review Questions		
Answer Part Review Questions		
Review Key Topics		
Create Command Mind Map by Category		

Repeat All Chapter Review Questions

For this task, answer the chapter review questions again for the chapters in this part of the book, using the PCPT software. Refer to the Introduction to this book, heading "How to View Only Chapter Review Questions by Part," for help with how to make the PCPT software show you chapter review questions for this part only.

Answer Part Review Questions

For this task, answer the Part Review questions for this part of the book, using the PCPT software. Refer to the Introduction to this book, heading "How to View Only Part Review Questions by Part," for help with how to make the PCPT software show you Part Review questions for this part only.

Review Key Topics

Browse back through the chapters, and look for the Key Topics icons. If you do not remember some details, take the time to reread those topics.

Create Command Mind Map by Category

Like Part II of this book, Part IV introduced more than a few CLI commands, this time on routers. The sheer number of commands can be a bit overwhelming, so it helps to take a step back from the details and let your brain sift through what you remember, and what it thinks go together, so that you can then realize which commands you need to review so that you remember them better.

The goal with this mind map exercise is to help you remember the commands. This exercise does not focus on the details, every single parameter of every command, or even their meaning. The goal is to help you organize the commands internally so that you know which commands to consider when faced with a real-life problem or an exam question.

Similar to Part II's mind map, create a mind map with the following categories of commands from this part of the book:

> Interface commands that affect Layers 1 and 2, IP addressing, static and default routing, router trunking and Layer 3 switching, OSPF, DHCP server, connectivity testing, host networking commands, and miscellaneous

Additionally, for more review, you can also include three categories for commands that apply to both routers and switches. These includes the commands that Chapter 15, "Operating Cisco Routers," only briefly reviewed, but were explained back in Part II of this book: Console and VTY, SSH, and router (switch) administration.

In this mind map, for each category, think of all configuration commands and all EXEC commands (mostly show commands). For each category, group the configuration commands separately from the EXEC commands. Figure P4-1 shows a sample for the CDP branch of the commands.

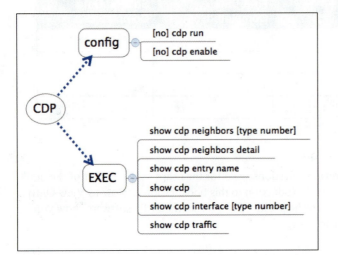

Figure P4-1   *Sample Mind Map from the CDP Branch*

> **NOTE**   For more information on mind mapping, refer to the Introduction, in the section "About Mind Maps."

Finally, keep the following important points in mind when working on this project:

- Most of the learning with this exercise happens when you do it. Reading some other mind map, or just rereading command tables, does not work as well for helping you remember for yourself.

- Do this activity without notes and without looking at the book.

- After you finish, review it versus the command summary tables at the ends of the chapters and note which commands you had originally forgotten.

- Do not worry about every last parameter, or the exact syntax; just write down the first few words of the command.

- For later study, make a note about which commands you feel you truly understand and which ones about which you feel less confident.

- Repeat this exercise when you have ten spare minutes, as a way to see what you remember (again without your notes).

DVD Appendix O, "Mind Map Solutions," lists a sample mind map answer, but as usual, your mind map can and will look different.

Table P4-2   Configuration Mind Maps for Part IV Review

Map	Description	Where You Saved It
1	Commands Mind Map	

The first four parts of this book provide enough information so that anyone can implement a small IPv4 network. The next two parts take the discussion a little deeper into IPv4 topics. In particular, Part V focuses on several IPv4 topics that have a lot to do with concepts, but with only a little configuration related to each feature.

All three chapters in this part discuss design choices an engineer can make about an IPv4 network, and describe the meaning of those design choices on how you operate the network. In particular, Chapter 19 discusses subnet design when using a single mask, while Chapter 20 discusses the implications of using multiple subnet masks in one classful network (VLSM). Chapter 21 ends this part by showing you how to reduce the size of IP routing tables using route summarization.

Part V

Advanced IPv4 Addressing Concepts

Chapter 19

Subnet Design

So far in this book, most of the discussion about IPv4 used examples with the addresses and masks already given. This book has shown many examples already, but the examples so far do not ask you to pick the IP address or pick the mask. Instead, as discussed back in Chapter 11, "Perspectives on IPv4 Subnetting," this book so far has assumed that someone else designed the IP addressing and subnetting plan, and this book shows how to implement it.

This chapter turns that model around. It goes back to the progression of building and implementing IPv4, as discussed in Chapter 11, as shown in Figure 19-1. This chapter picks up the story right after some network engineer has chosen a Class A, B, or C network to use for the enterprise's IPv4 network. And then this chapter discusses the design choices related to picking one subnet mask to use for all subnets (the first major section) and what subnet IDs that choice creates (the second major section).

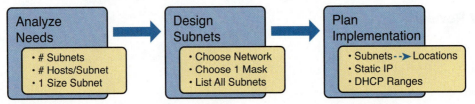

Figure 19-1 *Subnet Design and Implementation Process from Chapter 11*

Note that Chapter 20, "Variable-Length Subnet Masks," then changes the design choice of using a single mask, instead allowing any mask for each subnet, through the use of variable-length subnet masks (VLSM).

This chapter covers the following exam topics:

IP addressing (IPv4 / IPv6)

Identify the appropriate IPv4 addressing scheme using VLSM and summarization to satisfy addressing requirements in a LAN/WAN environment.

Troubleshooting

Troubleshoot and correct common problems associated with IP addressing and host configurations.

Foundation Topics

Choosing the Mask(s) to Meet Requirements

This first major section examines how to find all the masks that meet the stated requirements for the number of subnets and the number of hosts per subnet. To that end, the text assumes that the designer has already determined these requirements and has chosen the network number to be subnetted. The designer has also made the choice to use a single subnet mask value throughout the classful network.

Armed with the information in this chapter, you can answer questions such as the following, a question that matters both for real engineering jobs and the Cisco exams:

> You are using Class B network 172.16.0.0. You need 200 subnets and 200 hosts/subnet. Which of the following subnet mask(s) meet the requirements? (This question is then followed by several answers that list different subnet masks.)

To begin, this section reviews the concepts in Chapter 11's section "Choose the Mask." That section introduced the main concepts about how an engineer, when designing subnet conventions, must choose the mask based on the requirements.

After reviewing the related concepts from Chapter 11, this section examines this topic in more depth. In particular, this chapter looks at three general cases:

■ No masks meet the requirements.

■ One and only one mask meets the requirements.

■ Multiple masks meet the requirements.

For this last case, the text discusses how to determine all masks that meet the requirements and the trade-offs related to choosing which one mask to use.

Review: Choosing the Minimum Number of Subnet and Host Bits

The network designer must examine the requirements for the number of subnets and number of hosts/subnet, and then choose a mask. As discussed in detail in Chapter 13, "Analyzing Subnet Masks," a classful view of IP addresses defines the three-part structure of an IP address: network, subnet, and host. The network designer must choose the mask so that the number of subnet and host bits (S and H, respectively, in Figure 19-2) meet the requirements.

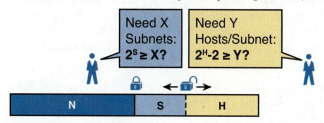

Figure 19-2 *Choosing the Number of Subnet and Host Bits*

Basically, the designer must choose S subnet bits so that the number of subnets that can be uniquely numbered with S bits (2^S) is at least as large as the required number of subnets. The designer applies similar logic to the number of host bits H, while noting that the formula is $2^H - 2$, because of the two reserved numbers in each subnet. So, keeping the powers of 2 handy, as shown in Table 19-1, will be useful when working through these problems.

Table 19-1   Powers of 2 Reference for Designing Masks

Number of Bits	2^X	Number of Bits	2^X	Number of Bits	2^X	Number of Bits	2^X
1	2	5	32	9	512	13	8192
2	4	6	64	10	1024	14	16,384
3	8	7	128	11	2048	15	32,768
4	16	8	256	12	4096	16	65,536

More formally, the process must determine the minimum values for both S and H that meet the requirements. The following list summarizes the initial steps to choose the mask:

Step 1.   Determine the number of network bits (N) based on the class.

Step 2.   Determine the smallest value of S, so that 2^S => X, where X represents the required number of subnets.

Step 3.   Determine the smallest value of H, so that $2^H - 2$ => Y, where Y represents the required number of hosts/subnet.

The next three sections examine how to use these initial steps to choose a subnet mask.

No Masks Meet Requirements

After you determine the required number of subnet and host bits, those bits might not fit into a 32-bit IPv4 subnet mask. Remember, the mask always has a total of 32 bits, with binary 1s in the network and subnet parts and binary 0s in the host part. For the exam, a question might provide a set of requirements that simply cannot be met with 32 total bits.

For example, consider the following sample exam question:

> A network engineer is planning a subnet design. The engineer plans to use Class B network 172.16.0.0. The network has a need for 300 subnets and 280 hosts per subnet. Which of the following masks could the engineer choose?

The three-step process shown in the previous section shows that these requirements mean that a total of 34 bits will be needed, so no mask meets the requirements. First, as a Class B network, 16 network bits exist, with 16 host bits from which to create the subnet part and to leave enough host bits to number the hosts in each subnet. For the number of subnet bits, S=8 does not work, because $2^8 = 256 < 300$. However, S=9 works, because $2^9 = 512$ => 300. Similarly, because $2^8 - 2 = 254$, which is less than 300, 8 host bits are not enough, but 9 host bits ($2^9 - 2 = 510$) are just enough.

These requirements do not leave enough space to number all the hosts and subnet, because the network, subnet, and host parts add up to more than 32:

N=16, because as a Class B network, 16 network bits exist.

The minimum S=9, because S=8 provides too few subnets ($2^8 = 256 < 300$), but S=9 provides $2^9 = 512$ subnets.

The minimum H=9, because H=8 provides too few hosts ($2^8 - 2 = 254 < 280$), but H=9 provides $2^9 - 2 = 510$ hosts/subnet.

Figure 19-3 shows the resulting format for the IP addresses in this subnet, after the engineer has allocated 9 subnet bits on paper. Only 7 host bits remain, but the engineer needs 9 host bits.

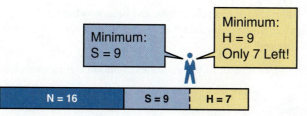

Figure 19-3 *Too Few Bits for the Host Part, Given the Requirements*

One Mask Meets Requirements

The process discussed in this chapter in part focuses on finding the smallest number of subnet bits and the smallest number of host bits to meet the requirements. If the engineer tries to use these minimum values, and the combined network, subnet, and host parts add up to exactly 32 bits, exactly one mask meets the requirements.

For example, consider a revised version of the example in the previous section, with smaller numbers of subnet and hosts, as follows:

> A network engineer is planning a subnet design. The engineer plans to use Class B network 172.16.0.0. The network has a need for 200 subnets and 180 hosts per subnet. Which of the following masks could the engineer choose?

The three-step process to determine the numbers of network, minimum subnet, and minimum host bits results in a need for 16, 8, and 8 bits, respectively. As before, with a Class B network, 16 network bits exist. With a need for only 200 hosts, S=8 does work, because $2^8 = 256 \Rightarrow 200$; 7 subnet bits would not supply enough subnets ($2^7 = 128$). Similarly, because $2^8 - 2 = 254 \Rightarrow 180$, 8 host bits meet the requirements; 7 host bits (for 126 total hosts/subnet) would not be enough.

Figure 19-4 shows the resulting format for the IP addresses in this subnet.

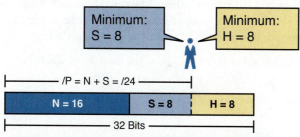

Figure 19-4 *One Mask That Meets Requirements*

Figure 19-4 shows the mask conceptually. To find the actual mask value, simply record the mask in prefix format (/P), where P = N + S or, in this case, /24.

Multiple Masks Meet Requirements

Depending on the requirements and choice of network, several masks might meet the requirements for the numbers of subnets and hosts/subnet. In these cases, you need to find all the masks that could be used. Then, you have a choice, but what should you consider when choosing one mask among all those that meet your requirements? This section shows how to find all the masks, as well as the facts to consider when choosing one mask from the list.

Finding All the Masks: Concepts

To help you better understand how to find all the subnet masks in binary, this section uses two major steps. In the first major step, you build the 32-bit binary subnet mask on paper. You write down binary 1s for the network bits, binary 1s for the subnet bits, and binary 0s for the host bits, just as always. However, you will use the minimum values for S and H. And when you write down these bits, you will not have 32 bits yet!

For example, consider the following problem, similar to the earlier examples in this chapter, but with some changes in the requirements:

> A network engineer is planning a subnet design. The engineer plans to use Class B network 172.16.0.0. The network has a need for 50 subnets and 180 hosts per subnet. Which of the following masks could the engineer choose?

This example is similar to an earlier example, except that only 50 subnets are needed in this case. Again, the engineer is using private IP network 172.16.0.0, meaning 16 network bits. The design requires only 6 subnet bits in this case, because $2^6 = 64 => 50$, and with only 5 subnet bits, $2^5 = 32 < 50$. The design then requires a minimum of 8 host bits.

One way to discuss the concepts and find all the masks that meet these requirements is to write down the bits in the subnet mask: binary 1s for the network and subnet parts and binary 0s for the host part. However, think of the 32-bit mask as 32-bit positions, and when writing the binary 0s, *write them on the far right*. Figure 19-5 shows the general idea.

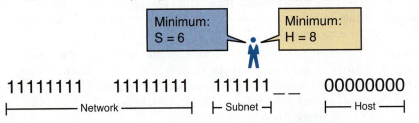

Figure 19-5 *Incomplete Mask with N=16, S=6, and H=8*

Figure 19-5 shows 30 bits of the mask, but the mask must have 32 bits. The 2 remaining bits might become subnet bits, being set to binary 1. Alternately, these 2 bits could be made host bits, being set to binary 0. The engineer simply needs to choose based on whether he would like more subnet bits, to number more subnets, or more host bits, to number more hosts/subnet.

However, the engineer cannot just choose any value for these 2 bits. The mask must still follow this rule:

> A subnet mask begins with all binary 1s, followed by all binary 0s, with no interleaving of 1s and 0s.

With the example shown in Figure 19-5, with 2 open bits, one value (binary 01) breaks this rule. However, the other three combinations of 2 bits (00, 10, and 11) do not break the rule. As a result, three masks meet the requirements in this example, as shown in Figure 19-6.

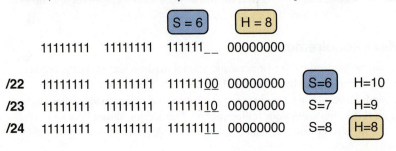

Figure 19-6 *Three Masks That Meet the Requirements*

In the three masks, the first has the least number of subnet bits among the three masks, but therefore has the most number of host bits. So, the first mask maximizes the number of hosts/subnet. The last mask uses the minimum value for the number of host bits, therefore using the most number of subnet bits allowed while still meeting the requirements. As a result, the last mask maximizes the number of subnets allowed.

Finding All the Masks: Math

Although the concepts related to the example shown in Figures 19-5 and 19-6 are important, you can find the range of masks that meets the requirements more easily just using some simple math. The process to find the masks just requires a few steps, after you know N and the minimum values of S and H. The process finds the value of /P when using the least number of subnet bits, and when using the least number of host bits, as follows:

Key Topic

Step 1. Calculate the shortest prefix mask (/P) based on the *minimum value of S*, where P = N + S.

Step 2. Calculate the longest prefix mask (/P) based on the *minimum value of H*, where P = 32 − H.

Step 3. The range of valid masks includes all /P values between the two values calculated in the previous steps.

For example, in the example shown in Figure 19-6, N = 16, the minimum S = 6, and the minimum H = 8. The first step identifies the shortest prefix mask (the /P with the smallest value of P) of /22 by adding N and S (16 + 6). The second step identifies the longest prefix mask that meets the requirements by subtracting the smallest possible value for H (8, in this case) from 32, for a mask of /24. The third step reminds us that the range is from /22 to /24, meaning that /23 is also an option.

Choosing the Best Mask

When multiple possible masks meet the stated requirements, the engineer has a choice of masks. That, of course, begs some questions: Which mask should you choose? Why would one mask be better than the other? The reasons can be summarized into three main options:

Key Topic

To maximize the number of hosts/subnet: To make this choice, use the shortest prefix mask (that is, the mask with the smallest /P value), because this mask has the largest host part.

To maximize the number of subnets: To make this choice, use the longest prefix mask (that is, the mask with the largest /P value), because this mask has the largest subnet part.

To increase both the numbers of supported subnets and hosts: To make this choice, choose a mask in the middle of the range, which gives you both more subnet bits and more host bits.

For example, in Figure 19-6, the range of masks that meet the requirements is /22 – /24. The shortest mask, /22, has the least subnet bits but the largest number of host bits (10) of the three answers, maximizing the number of hosts/subnet. The longest mask, /24, maximizes the number of subnet bits (8), maximizing the number of subnets, at least among the options that meet the original requirements. The mask in the middle, /23, provides some growth in both subnets and hosts/subnet.

The Formal Process

Although this chapter has explained various steps in finding a subnet mask to meet the design requirements, it has not yet collected these concepts into a list for the entire process. The following list collects all these steps into one place for reference. Note that this list does not introduce any new concepts compared to the rest of this chapter—it just puts all the ideas in one place:

Key Topic

Step 1.   Find the number of network bits (N) per class rules.

Step 2.   Calculate the minimum number of subnet bits (S) so that $2^S =>$ the number of required subnets.

Step 3.   Calculate the minimum number of host bits (H) so that $2^H - 2 =>$ the number of required hosts/subnet.

Step 4.   If $N + S + H > 32$, no mask meets the need.

Step 5.   If $N + S + H = 32$, one mask meets the need. Calculate the mask as /P, where $P = N + S$.

Step 6.   If $N + S + H < 32$, multiple masks meet the need:

   A. Calculate mask /P based on the minimum value of S, where $P = N + S$. This mask maximizes the number of hosts/subnet.

   B. Calculate mask /P based on the minimum value of H, where $P = 32 - H$. This mask maximizes the number of possible subnets.

   C. Note that the complete range of masks includes all prefix lengths between the two values calculated in Steps 6A and 6B.

Practice Choosing Subnet Masks

Before moving on to the next section, practice until you get the right answer most of the time—but use any tools you want and take all the time you need. Then, you can move on with your reading.

However, before taking the exam, practice until you master the topics in this chapter and can move pretty fast. As for time, you should try to find the entire answer—all the masks that meet the requirements, which maximizes the number of subnets, and which maximizes the number of hosts—in around 15 seconds. Table 19-2 summarizes the key concepts and suggestions for this two-phase approach.

Table 19-2   Keep-Reading and Take-Exam Goals for Choosing a Subnet Mask

Time Frame	Before Moving to the Next Chapter	Before Taking the Exam
Focus On...	Learning how	Being correct and fast
Tools Allowed	All	Your brain and a notepad
Goal: Accuracy	90% correct	100% correct
Goal: Speed	Any speed	15 seconds

Practice Problems for Choosing a Subnet Mask

The following list shows three separate problems, each with a classful network number and a required number of subnets and hosts/subnet. For each problem, determine the minimum number of subnet and host bits that meet the requirements. If more than one mask exists, note which mask maximizes the number of hosts/subnet and which maximizes the number of subnets. If only one mask meets the requirements, simply list that mask. List the masks in prefix format:

1. Network 10.0.0.0, need 1500 subnets, need 300 hosts/subnet
2. Network 172.25.0.0, need 130 subnets, need 127 hosts/subnet
3. Network 192.168.83.0, need 8 subnets, need 8 hosts/subnet

Table 19-5, found in the later section "Answers to Earlier Practice Problems," lists the answers.

Additional Practice for Choosing the Subnet Mask

This section lists several options for additional practice:

- Appendix G, "Practice for Chapter 19: Subnet Design," has some additional practice problems listed with explanations.
- Create your own problems. Many subnet calculators let you type the Class A, B, or C network and choose the mask, and the calculator then lists the number of subnets and hosts/subnet created by that network/mask. Make up a network number and required numbers of subnets and hosts, derive the answers, and check the math with the calculator. This can take a little more work with a calculator as compared with some of the other subnetting chapters in this book.

Finding All Subnet IDs

After the person designing the IP subnetting plan has chosen the one mask to use throughout the Class A, B, or C network, he will soon need to start assigning specific subnet IDs for use in specific VLANs, serial links, and other places in the internetwork that need a subnet. But what are those subnet IDs? As it turns out, after the network ID and one subnet mask for all subnets have been chosen, finding all the subnet IDs just requires doing a little math. This second major section of this chapter focuses on that math, which focuses on a single question:

Given a single Class A, B, or C network, and the single subnet mask to use for all subnets, what are all the subnet IDs?

When learning how to answer this question, you can think about the problem in either binary or decimal. This chapter approaches the problem using decimal. Although the process itself requires only simple math, the process requires practice before most people can confidently answer this question.

The decimal process begins by identifying the first, or numerically lowest, subnet ID. After that, the process identifies a pattern in all subnet IDs for a given subnet mask so that you can find each successive subnet ID through simple addition. This section examines the key ideas behind this process first; then you are given a formal definition of the process.

> **NOTE** Some videos included on the accompanying DVD describe the same fundamental processes to find all subnet IDs. You can view those videos before or after reading this section, or even instead of reading this section, as long as you learn how to independently find all subnet IDs. The process step numbering in the videos might not match the steps shown in this edition of the book.

First Subnet ID: The Zero Subnet

The first step in finding all subnet IDs of one network is incredibly simple: Copy the network ID. That is, take the Class A, B, or C network ID—in other words, the classful network ID—and write it down as the first subnet ID. No matter what Class A, B, or C network you use, and no matter what subnet mask you use, the first (numerically lowest) subnet ID is equal to the network ID.

For example, if you begin with classful network 172.20.0.0, no matter what the mask is, the first subnet ID is 172.20.0.0.

This first subnet ID in each network goes by two special names: either *subnet zero* or the *zero subnet*. The origin of these names is related to the fact that a network's zero subnet, when viewed in binary, has a subnet part of all binary 0s. In decimal, the zero subnet can be easily identified, because the zero subnet always has the exact same numeric value as the network ID itself.

NOTE In years past, IP subnet designs typically avoided the use of the zero subnet because of the confusion that might arise with a network ID and subnet ID that were the exact same numbers.

Finding the Pattern Using the Magic Number

Subnet IDs follow a predictable pattern, at least when using our assumption of a single subnet mask for all subnets of a network. The pattern uses the *magic number*, as discussed in Chapter 14, "Analyzing Existing Subnets." To review, the magic number is 256, minus the mask's decimal value, in a particular octet that this book refers to as the *interesting octet*.

Figure 19-7 shows four examples of these patterns with four different masks. For example, just look at the top of the figure to start. It lists mask 255.255.128.0 on the left. The third octet is the interesting octet, with a mask value other than 0 or 255 in that octet. The left side shows a magic number calculated as 256 – 128 = 128. So, the pattern of subnet IDs is shown in the high-lighted number line; that is, the subnet IDs when using this mask will have either a 0 or 128 in the third octet. For example, if using network 172.16.0.0, the subnet IDs would be 172.16.0.0 and 172.16.128.0.

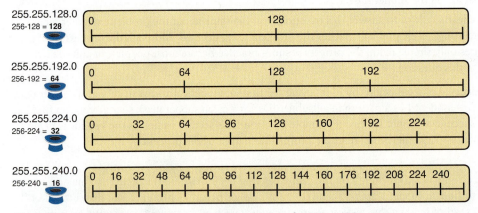

Figure 19-7   *Patterns with Magic Numbers for Masks /17 – /20*

Now focus on the second row, with another example, with mask 255.255.192.0. This row shows a magic number of 64 (256 – 192 = 64), so the subnet IDs will use a value of 0, 64, 128, or 192 (multiples of 64) in the third octet. For example, if used with network 172.16.0.0, the subnet IDs would be 172.16.0.0, 172.16.64.0, 172.16.128.0, and 172.16.192.0.

Looking at the third row/example, the mask is 255.255.224.0, with a magic number of 256 – 224 = 32. So, as seen in the center of the figure, the subnet ID values will be multiples of 32. For example, if used with network 172.16.0.0 again, this mask would tell us that the subnet IDs are 172.16.0.0, 172.16.32.0, 172.16.64.0, 172.16.96.0, and so on.

Finally, for the bottom example, mask 255.255.240.0 makes the magic number, in the third octet, be 16. So, all the subnet IDs will be a multiple of 16 in the third octet, with those values shown in the middle of the figure.

A Formal Process with Less Than 8 Subnet Bits

Although it can be easy to see the patterns in Figure 19-7, it might not be as obvious exactly how to apply those concepts to find all the subnet IDs in every case. This section outlines a specific process to find all the subnet IDs.

To simplify the explanations, this section assumes that less than 8 subnet bits exist. Later, the section "Finding All Subnets with More Than 8 Subnet Bits," describes the full process that can be used in all cases.

First, to organize your thoughts, you might want to organize the data into a table like Table 19-3. This book refers to this chart as the list-all-subnets chart.

Table 19-3   Generic List-All-Subnets Chart

Octet	1	2	3	4
Mask				
Magic Number				
Network Number/Zero Subnet				
Next Subnet				
Next Subnet				
Next Subnet				
Broadcast Subnet				
Out of Range—Used by Process				

A formal process to find all subnet IDs, given a network and a single subnet mask, is as follows:

Step 1.   Write down the subnet mask, in decimal, in the first empty row of the table.

Step 2.   Identify the interesting octet, which is the one octet of the mask with a value other than 255 or 0. Draw a rectangle around the column of the interesting octet.

Step 3.   Calculate and write down the magic number by subtracting the *subnet mask's interesting octet* from 256.

Step 4.   Write down the classful network number, which is the same number as the zero subnet, in the next empty row of the list-all-subnets chart.

Step 5.   To find each successive subnet number:

  A.   For the three uninteresting octets, copy the previous subnet number's values.

  B.   For the interesting octet, add the magic number to the previous subnet number's interesting octet.

Step 6.   When the sum calculated in Step 5B reaches 256, stop the process. The number with the 256 in it is out of range, and the previous subnet number is the broadcast subnet.

Although the written process is long, with practice, most people can find the answers much more quickly with this decimal-based process than by using binary math. As usual, most people learn this process best by seeing it in action, exercising it, and then practicing it. To that end, review the two following examples and watch any videos that came with this book that show additional examples.

Example 1: Network 172.16.0.0, Mask 255.255.240.0

To begin this example, focus on the first four of the six steps, when subnetting network 172.16.0.0 using mask 255.255.240.0. Figure 19-8 shows the results of these first four steps:

Step 1. Record mask 255.255.240.0, which was given as part of the problem statement. (Figure 19-8 also shows the network ID, 172.16.0.0, for easy reference.)

Step 2. The mask's third octet is neither 0 nor 255, which makes the third octet interesting.

Step 3. Because the mask's value in the third octet is 240, the magic number = 256 − 240 = 16.

Step 4. Because the network ID is 172.16.0.0, the first subnet ID, the zero subnet, is also 172.16.0.0.

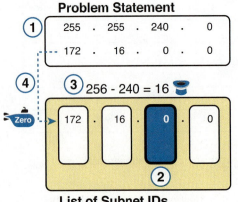

Figure 19-8 *Results of First Four Steps: 172.16.0.0, 255.255.240.0.*

These first four steps discover the first subnet (the zero subnet) and get you ready to do the remaining steps by identifying the interesting octet and the magic number. Step 5 in the process tells you to copy the three boring octets and add the magic number (16, in this case) in the interesting octet (octet 3, in this case). Keep repeating this step until the interesting octet value equals 256 (per Step 6). When the total is 256, you have listed all the subnet IDs, and the line with 256 on it is not a correct subnet ID. Figure 19-9 shows the results of these steps.

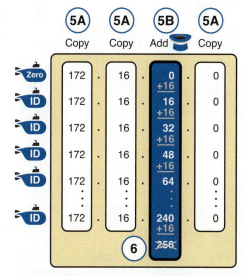

Figure 19-9 *List of Subnet IDs: 172.16.0.0, 255.255.240.0*

> **NOTE** In any list of all the subnet IDs of a network, the numerically highest subnet ID is called the *broadcast subnet*. Decades ago, engineers avoided using the broadcast subnet. However, using the broadcast subnet causes no problems. The term *broadcast subnet* has its origins in the fact that if you determine the subnet broadcast address inside the broadcast subnet, it has the same numeric value as the network-wide broadcast address.

> **NOTE** People sometimes confuse the terms *broadcast subnet* and *subnet broadcast address*. The *broadcast subnet* is one subnet, namely the numerically highest subnet; only one such subnet exists per network. The term *subnet broadcast address* refers to the one number in each and every subnet that is the numerically highest number in that subnet.

Example 2: Network 192.168.1.0, Mask 255.255.255.224

With a Class C network and a mask of 255.255.255.224, this example makes the fourth octet the interesting octet. However, the process works the same, with the same logic, just with the interesting logic applied in a different octet. As with the previous example, the following list outlines the first four steps, with Figure 19-10 showing the results of the first four steps:

Step 1. Record mask 255.255.255.224, which was given as part of the problem statement, and optionally record the network number (192.168.1.0).

Step 2. The mask's fourth octet is neither 0 nor 255, which makes the fourth octet interesting.

Step 3. Because the mask's value in the fourth octet is 224, the magic number = 256 − 224 = 32.

Step 4. Because the network ID is 192.168.1.0, the first subnet ID, the zero subnet, is also 192.168.1.0.

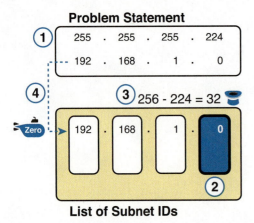

Figure 19-10 *Results of First Four Steps: 192.168.1.0, 255.255.255.224*

From this point, Step 5 in the process tells you to copy the values in the first three octets and then add the magic number (32, in this case) in the interesting octet (octet 4, in this case). Keep doing so until the interesting octet value equals 256 (per Step 6). When the total is 256, you have listed all the subnet IDs, and the line with 256 on it is not a correct subnet ID. Figure 19-11 shows the results of these steps.

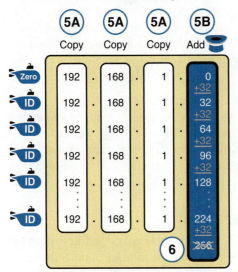

Figure 19-11 *List of Subnet IDs: 192.168.1.0, 255.255.255.224*

Finding All Subnets with Exactly 8 Subnet Bits

The formal process in the earlier section "A Formal Process with Less Than 8 Subnet Bits" identified the interesting octet as the octet whose mask value is neither a 255 nor a 0. If the mask defines exactly 8 subnet bits, you have to use a different logic to identify the interesting octet; otherwise, the same process can be used. In fact, the actual subnet IDs can be a little more intuitive.

Only two cases exist with exactly 8 subnet bits:

A Class A network with mask 255.255.0.0; the entire second octet contains subnet bits.

A Class B network with mask 255.255.255.0; the entire third octet contains subnet bits.

In each case, use the same process as with less than 8 subnet bits, but identify the interesting octet as the one octet that contains subnet bits. Also, because the mask's value is 255, the magic number will be 256 − 255 = 1, so the subnet IDs are each 1 larger than the previous subnet ID.

For example, for 172.16.0.0, mask 255.255.255.0, the third octet is the interesting octet and the magic number is 256 − 255 = 1. You start with the zero subnet, equal in value to network number 172.16.0.0, and then add 1 in the third octet. For example, the first four subnets are as follows:

172.16.0.0 (zero subnet)

172.16.1.0

172.16.2.0

172.16.3.0

Finding All Subnets with More Than 8 Subnet Bits

Earlier, the section "A Formal Process with Less Than 8 Subnet Bits" assumed less than 8 subnet bits for the purpose of simplifying the discussions while you learn. In real life, you need to be able to find all subnet IDs with any valid mask, so you cannot assume less than 8 subnet bits.

The examples that have at least 9 subnet bits have a minimum of 512 subnet IDs, so writing down such a list would take a lot of time. To conserve space, the examples will use shorthand, rather than list hundreds or thousands of subnet IDs.

The process with less than 8 subnet bits told you to count in increments of the magic number in one octet. With more than 8 subnet bits, the new expanded process must tell you how to count in multiple octets. So, this section breaks down two general cases: (a) when 9–16 subnet bits exist, which means that the subnet field exists in only two octets, and (b) cases with 17 or more subnet bits, which means that the subnet field exists in three octets.

Process with 9–16 Subnet Bits

To understand the process, you need to know a few terms that the process will use. Figure 19-12 shows the details, with an example that uses Class B network 130.4.0.0 and mask 255.255.255.192. The lower part of the figure details the structure of the addresses per the mask: a network part of two octets because it is a Class B address, a 10-bit subnet part per the mask (/26), and 6 host bits.

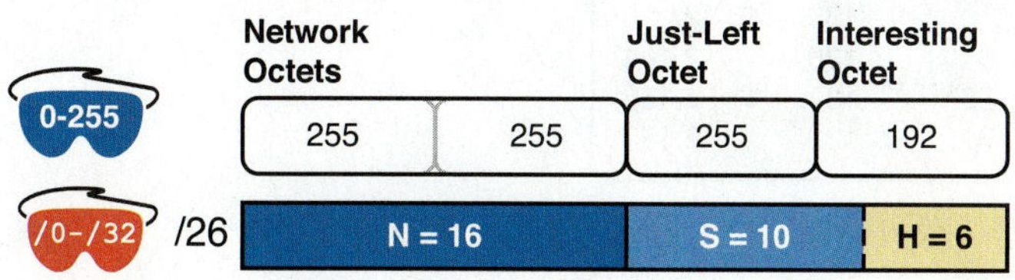

Figure 19-12 *Fundamental Concepts and Terms for the >8 Subnet Bit Process*

In this case, subnet bits exist in two octets: octets 3 and 4. For the purposes of the process, the rightmost of these octets is the interesting octet, and the octet just to the left is the cleverly named *just-left* octet.

The updated process tells you to count in increments of the magic number in the interesting octet, but count by 1s in the just-left octet. Formally:

Key Topic

Step 1.   Calculate subnet IDs using the 8-subnet-bits-or-less process. However, when the total adds up to 256, move to the next step; consider the subnet IDs listed so far as a *subnet block*.

Step 2. Copy the previous subnet block, but add 1 to the just-left octet in all subnet IDs in the new block.

Step 3. Repeat Step 2 until you create the block with a just-left octet of 255, but go no further.

To be honest, the formal concept can cause you problems until you work through some examples, so even if the process remains a bit unclear in your mind, you should work through the following examples instead of rereading the formal process.

First, consider an example based on Figure 19-12, with network 130.4.0.0 and mask 255.255.255.192. Figure 19-12 already showed the structure, and Figure 19-13 shows the subnet ID block created at Step 1.

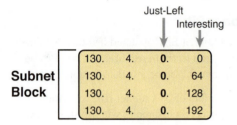

Figure 19-13   *Step 1: Listing the First Subnet ID Block*

The logic at Step 1, to create this subnet ID block of four subnet IDs, follow the same magic number process seen before. The first subnet ID, 130.4.0.0, is the zero subnet. The next three subnet IDs are each 64 bigger, because the magic number, in this case, is 256 – 192 = 64.

Steps 2 and 3 from the formal process tell you how to create 256 subnet blocks, and by doing so, you will list all 1024 subnet IDs. To do so, create 256 total subnet blocks: one with a 0 in the just-left octet, one with a 1 in the just-left octet, and another with a 2 in the just-left octet, up through 255. The process continues through the step at which you create the subnet block with 255 in the just-left octet (third octet, in this case). Figure 19-14 shows the idea, with the addition of the first few subnet blocks.

Figure 19-14   *Step 2: Replicating the Subnet Block with +1 in the Just-Left Octet*

This example, with 10 total subnet bits, creates 256 blocks of four subnets each, for a total of 1024 subnets. This math matches the usual method of counting subnets, because 2^{10} = 1024.

Process with 17 or More Subnet Bits

To create a subnet design that allows 17 or more subnet bits to exist, the design must use a Class A network. Additionally, the subnet part will consist of the entire second and third octets, plus part of the fourth octet. That means a lot of subnet IDs: at least 2^{17} (or 131,072) subnets. Figure 19-15 shows an example of just such a structure, with a Class A network and a /26 mask.

Network Octet
Subnet Octets
Interesting Octet
0-255
255
255
255
192
/0-/32
/26
N = 8
S = 18
H = 6

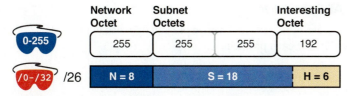

Figure 19-15 *Address Structure with 18 Subnet Bits*

To find all the subnet IDs in this example, you use the same general process as with 9–16 subnet bits, but with many more subnet blocks to create. In effect, you have to create a subnet block for all combinations of values (0–255, inclusive) in both the second and third octet. Figure 19-16 shows the general idea. Note that with only 2 subnet bits in the fourth octet in this example, the subnet blocks will have four subnets each.

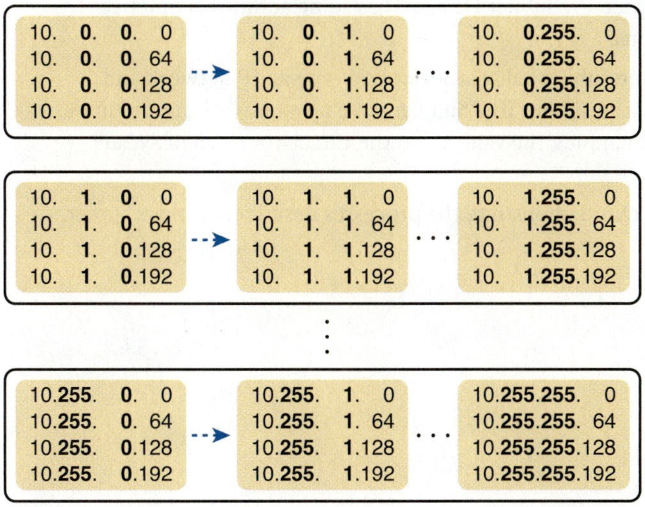

10. 0. 0. 0
10. 0. 0. 64
10. 0. 0.128
10. 0. 0.192
10. 0. 1. 0
10. 0. 1. 64
10. 0. 1.128
10. 0. 1.192
10. 0.255. 0
10. 0.255. 64
10. 0.255.128
10. 0.255.192
10. 1. 0. 0
10. 1. 0. 64
10. 1. 0.128
10. 1. 0.192
10. 1. 1. 0
10. 1. 1. 64
10. 1. 1.128
10. 1. 1.192
10. 1.255. 0
10. 1.255. 64
10. 1.255.128
10. 1.255.192
10.255. 0. 0
10.255. 0. 64
10.255. 0.128
10.255. 0.192
10.255. 1. 0
10.255. 1. 64
10.255. 1.128
10.255. 1.192
10.255.255. 0
10.255.255. 64
10.255.255.128
10.255.255.192

Figure 19-16 *256 Times 256 Subnet Blocks of Four Subnets*

Practice Finding All Subnet IDs

Before moving to the next chapter, practice until you get the right answer most of the time—but use any tools you want and take all the time you need. Then, you can move on with your reading.

However, before taking the exam, practice until you master the topics in this chapter. Gauging a reasonable speed goal is difficult, because some combinations of network ID and mask can yield hundreds or thousands of subnets, while others can yield a much smaller number. So, for speed, before the exam, you should be able to do the first four subnets, which include the zero subnet, in 45 seconds. Table 19-4 summarizes the key concepts and suggestions for this two-phase approach.

Table 19-4 Keep-Reading and Take-Exam Goals for This Chapter's Topics

Time Frame	Before Moving to the Next Chapter	Before Taking the Exam
Focus On...	Learning how	Being correct and fast
Tools Allowed	All	Your brain and a notepad
Goal: Accuracy	90% correct	100% correct
Goal: Speed	Any speed	45 seconds

Practice Problems for Finding All Subnet IDs

The following list shows three separate problems, each with a classful network number and prefix-style mask. Find all subnet IDs for each problem:

1. 192.168.9.0/27
2. 172.30.0.0/20
3. 10.0.0.0/17

The section "Answers to Earlier Practice Problems," later in this chapter, lists the answers.

Additional Practice for Finding All Subnet IDs

This section lists several options for additional practice:

■ Appendix G, "Practice for Chapter 19: Subnet Design," has some additional practice problems listed with explanations.

■ Create your own problems. Some subnet calculators let you type an IP network and mask, and the calculator lists all the subnet IDs. Simply make up a network ID and mask, find the answer on paper, and then plug the values into the calculator to check your work.

■ Watch the videos on the DVD that demonstrate the processes described in this chapter.

Review Activities

Chapter Summary

- The network designer must examine the requirements for the number of subnets and number of hosts/subnet, and then choose a mask. A classful view of IP addresses defines the three-part structure of an IP address: network, subnet, and host. The network designer must choose the mask such that the number of subnet and host bits meet the requirements.

- There are three possibilities with subnet design:
    - No mask meets the requirements
    - One mask meets the requirements
    - Multiple masks meet the requirements

- When multiple possible masks meet the stated requirements, the engineer has a choice of masks. That, of course, begs some questions: Which mask should you choose? Why would one mask be better than the other? The reasons can be summarized into three main options:

    - **To maximize the number of hosts/subnet:** To make this choice, use the shortest prefix mask (that is, the mask with the smallest /P value), because this mask has the largest host part.

    - **To maximize the number of subnets:** To make this choice, use the longest prefix mask (that is, the mask with the largest /P value), because this mask has the largest subnet part.

    - **To increase both the numbers of supported subnets and hosts:** To make this choice, choose a mask in the middle of the range, which gives you both more subnet bits and more host bits.

Review Questions

Answer these review questions. You can find the answers at the bottom of the last page of the chapter. For thorough explanations, see DVD Appendix C, "Answers to Review Questions."

1. An IP subnetting design effort is under way at a company. So far, the senior engineer has decided to use Class B network 172.23.0.0. The design calls for 100 subnets, with the largest subnet needing 500 hosts. Management requires that the design accommodate 50 percent growth in the number of subnets and the size of the largest subnet. The requirements also state that a single mask must be used throughout the Class B network. How many masks meet the requirements?

    A. 0

    B. 1

    C. 2

    D. 3+

2. An IP subnetting design requires 200 subnets and 120 hosts/subnet for the largest subnets, and requires that a single mask be used throughout the one private IP network that will be used. The design also requires planning for 20 percent growth in the number of subnets and number of hosts/subnet in the largest subnet. Which of the following answers lists a private IP network and mask that, if chosen, would meet the requirements?

    A. 10.0.0.0/25

    B. 10.0.0.0/22

    C. 172.16.0.0/23

    D. 192.168.7.0/24

3. An engineer has planned to use Class B network 172.19.0.0 and a single subnet mask throughout the network. The answers list the masks considered by the engineer. Choose the mask that, among the answers, supplies the largest number of hosts per subnet, while also supplying enough subnet bits to support 1000 subnets.

   A. 255.255.255.0

   B. /26

   C. 255.255.252.0

   D. /28

4. A subnet design uses Class A network 10.0.0.0, and the engineer must choose a single mask to use throughout the network. The design requires 1000 subnets, with the largest subnet needing 200 hosts. Which of the following masks meets the requirements and also maximizes the number of subnets?

   A. /18

   B. /20

   C. /22

   D. /24

5. An engineer has calculated the list of subnet IDs, in consecutive order, for network 172.30.0.0/22, assuming that the /22 mask is used throughout the network. Which of the following are true? (Choose two answers.)

   A. Any two consecutive subnet IDs differ by a value of 22 in the third octet.

   B. Any two consecutive subnet IDs differ by a value of 16 in the fourth octet.

   C. The list contains 64 subnet IDs.

   D. The last subnet ID is 172.30.252.0.

6. Which of the following are valid subnet IDs for network 192.168.9.0, using mask /29, assuming that mask /29 is used throughout the network?

   A. 192.168.9.144

   B. 192.168.9.58

   C. 192.168.9.242

   D. 192.168.9.9

7. Which of the following is not a valid subnet ID for network 172.19.0.0, using mask /24, assuming that mask /24 is used throughout the network?

   A. 172.19.0.0

   B. 172.19.1.0

   C. 172.19.255.0

   D. 172.19.0.16

8. Which of the following is not a valid subnet ID for network 10.0.0.0, using mask /25, assuming that this mask is used throughout the network?

   A. 10.0.0.0

   B. 10.255.255.0

   C. 10.255.127.128

   D. 10.1.1.192

Review All the Key Topics

Review the most important topics from this chapter, noted with the Key Topic icon. Table 19-5 lists these key topics and where each is discussed.

Table 19-5 Key Topics for Chapter 19

Key Topic Element	Description	Page Number
Definition	Facts about binary values in subnet masks	474
List	The shorter three-step process to find all prefix masks that meet certain requirements	475
List	Reasons to choose one subnet mask versus another	475
List	The complete process for finding and choosing masks to meet certain requirements	476
Step list	Formal steps to find all subnet IDs when less than 8 subnet bits exist	479
Figure 19-9	An example of adding the magic number in the interesting octet to find all subnet IDs	481
Step list	Formal steps to find all subnet IDs when more than 8 subnet bits exist	483

Definitions of Key Terms

After your first reading of the chapter, try to define these key terms, but do not be concerned about getting them all correct at that time. Chapter 30 directs you in how to use these terms for late-stage preparation for the exam.

zero subnet, subnet zero, broadcast subnet

Practice

If you have not done so already, practice finding all subnet masks, based on requirements, as discussed in this chapter. Refer to the earlier section "Practice Choosing Subnet Masks" for suggestions.

Answers to Earlier Practice Problems

Answers to Practice Choosing Subnet Masks

The earlier section "Practice Choosing Subnet Masks" listed three practice problems. The answers are listed here so that the answers are nearby, but not visible from the list of problems. Table 19-6 lists the answers, with notes related to each problem following the table.

Table 19-6   Practice Problems: Find the Masks That Meet Requirements

Problem	Class	Minimum Subnet Bits	Minimum Host Bits	Prefix Range	Prefix to Maximize Subnets	Prefix to Maximize Hosts
1	A	11	9	/19 – /23	/23	/19
2	B	8	8	/16	—	—
3	C	3	4	/27 – /28	/28	/27

1.   N=8, because the problem lists Class A network 10.0.0.0. With a need for 1500 subnets, 10 subnet bits supply only 1024 subnets (per Table 19-1), but 11 subnet bits (S) would provide 2048 subnets—more than the required 1500. Similarly, the smallest number of host bits would be 9, because $2^8 - 2 = 254$, and the design requires 300 hosts/subnet. The shortest prefix mask would then be /19, found by adding N (8) and the smallest usable number of subnet bits S (11). Similarly, with a minimum H value of 9, the longest prefix mask, maximizing the number of subnets, is 32 – H = /23.

2.   N=16, because the problem lists Class B network 172.25.0.0. With a need for 130 subnets, 7 subnet bits supply only 128 subnets (per Table 19-1), but 8 subnet bits (S) would provide 256 subnets—more than the required 130. Similarly, the smallest number of host bits would be 8, because $2^7 - 2 = 126$—close to the required 127, but not quite enough, making H = 8 the smallest number of host bits that meets requirements. Note that the network, minimum subnet bits, and minimum host bits add up to 32, so only one mask meets the requirements, namely /24, found by adding the number of network bits (16) to the minimum number of subnet bits (8).

3.   N=24, because the problem lists Class C network 192.168.83.0. With a need for eight subnets, 3 subnet bits supply enough, but just barely. The smallest number of host bits would be 4, because $2^3 - 2 = 6$, and the design requires 8 hosts/subnet. The shortest prefix mask would then be /27, found by adding N (24) and the smallest usable number of subnet bits S (3). Similarly, with a minimum H value of 4, the longest prefix mask, maximizing the number of subnets, is 32 – H = /28.

Answers to Practice Finding All Subnet IDs

The earlier section "Practice Finding All Subnet IDs" listed three practice problems. The answers are listed here so that they are not visible from the same page as the list of problems.

Answer, Practice Problem 1

Problem 1 lists network 192.168.9.0, mask /27. The mask converts to DDN mask 255.255.255.224. When used with a Class C network, which has 24 network bits, only 3 subnet bits exist, and they all sit in the fourth octet. So, this problem is a case of less than 8 subnet bits, with the fourth octet as the interesting octet.

To get started listing subnets, first write down the zero subnet and then start adding the magic number in the interesting octet. The zero subnet equals the network ID (192.168.9.0, in this case). The magic number, calculated as 256 − 224 = 32, should be added to the previous subnet ID's interesting octet. Table 19-7 lists the results.

Table 19-7   List-All-Subnets Chart: 192.168.9.0/27

Octet	1	2	3	4
Mask	255	255	255	224
Magic Number	—	—	—	32
Classful Network/Subnet Zero	192	168	9	0
First Nonzero Subnet	192	168	9	32
Next Subnet	192	168	9	64
Next Subnet	192	168	9	96
Next Subnet	192	168	9	128
Next Subnet	192	168	9	160
Next Subnet	192	168	9	192
Broadcast Subnet	192	168	9	224
Invalid—Used by Process	192	168	9	256

Answer, Practice Problem 2

Problem 2 lists network 172.30.0.0, mask /20. The mask converts to DDN mask 255.255.240.0. When used with a Class B network, which has 16 network bits, only 4 subnet bits exist, and they all sit in the third octet. So, this problem is a case of less than 8 subnet bits, with the third octet as the interesting octet.

To get started listing subnets, first write down the zero subnet and then start adding the magic number in the interesting octet. The zero subnet equals the network ID (or 172.30.0.0, in this case). The magic number, calculated as 256 − 240 = 16, should be added to the previous subnet ID's interesting octet. Table 19-8 lists the results.

Table 19-8   List-All-Subnets Chart: 172.30.0.0/2

Octet	1	2	3	4
Mask	255	255	240	0
Magic Number	—	—	16	—
Classful Network/Subnet Zero	172	30	0	0
First Nonzero Subnet	172	30	16	0
Next Subnet	172	30	32	0
Next Subnet	172	30	48	0
Next Subnet	172	30	64	0
Next Subnet	172	30	Skipping…	0
Next Subnet	172	30	224	0
Broadcast Subnet	172	30	240	0
Invalid—Used by Process	172	30	256	0

Answer, Practice Problem 3

Problem 3 lists network 10.0.0.0, mask /17. The mask converts to DDN mask 255.255.128.0. When used with a Class A network, which has 8 network bits, 9 subnet bits exist. Using the terms unique to this chapter, octet 3 is the interesting octet, with only 1 subnet bit in that octet, and octet 2 is the just-left octet, with 8 subnet bits.

In this case, begin by finding the first subnet block. The magic number is 256 − 128 = 128. The first subnet (zero subnet) equals the network ID. So, the first subnet ID block includes the following:

10.0.0.0

10.0.128.0

Then, you create a subnet block for all 256 possible values in the just-left octet, or octet 2 in this case. The following list shows the first three subnet ID blocks, plus the last subnet ID block, rather than listing page upon page of subnet IDs:

10.0.0.0 (zero subnet)

10.0.128.0

10.1.0.0

10.1.128.0

10.2.0.0

10.2.128.0

...

10.255.0.0

10.255.128.0 (broadcast subnet)

Answers to Review Questions:

1 A **2** B **3** B **4** D **5** C and D **6** A **7** D **8** D

Chapter 20

Variable-Length Subnet Masks

IPv4 addressing and subnetting use a lot of terms, a lot of small math steps, and a lot of concepts that fit together. While learning those concepts, it helps to keep things as simple as possible. One way this book has kept the discussion simpler so far was to show examples that use one mask only inside a single Class A, B, or C network.

This chapter removes that restriction by introducing variable-length subnet masks (VLSM). VLSM simply means that the subnet design uses more than one mask in the same classful network. VLSM has some advantages and disadvantages, but when learning, the main challenge is that a subnetting design that uses VLSM requires more math, and it requires that you think about some other issues as well. This chapter walks you through the concepts, the issues, and the math.

This chapter covers the following exam topics:

IP addressing (IPv4/IPv6)

Identify the appropriate IPv4 addressing scheme using VLSM and summarization to satisfy addressing requirements in a LAN/WAN environment.

Troubleshooting

Troubleshoot and correct common problems associated with IP addressing and host configurations.

Foundation Topics

VLSM Concepts and Configuration

VLSM occurs when an internetwork uses more than one mask for different subnets of a single Class A, B, or C network. Figure 20-1 shows an example of VLSM used in Class A network 10.0.0.0.

Figure 20-1   *VLSM in Network 10.0.0.0: Masks /24 and /30*

Figure 20-1 shows a typical choice of using a /30 prefix (mask 255.255.255.252) on point-to-point serial links, with mask /24 (255.255.255.0) on the LAN subnets. All subnets are of Class A network 10.0.0.0, with two masks being used, therefore meeting the definition of VLSM.

Oddly enough, a common mistake occurs when people think that VLSM means "using more than one mask in some internetwork" rather than "using more than one mask *in a single classful network*." For example, if in one internetwork diagram, all subnets of network 10.0.0.0 use a 255.255.240.0 mask, and all subnets of network 11.0.0.0 use a 255.255.255.0 mask, the design uses two different masks. However, Class A network 10.0.0.0 uses only one mask, and Class A network 11.0.0.0 uses only one mask. In that case, the design does not use VLSM.

VLSM provides many benefits for real networks, mainly related to how you allocate and use your IP address space. Because a mask defines the size of the subnet (the number of host addresses in the subnet), VLSM allows engineers to better match the need for addresses with the size of the subnet. For example, for subnets that need fewer addresses, the engineer uses a mask with fewer host bits, so the subnet has fewer host IP addresses. This flexibility reduces the number of wasted IP addresses in each subnet. By wasting fewer addresses, more space remains to allocate more subnets.

VLSM can be helpful for both public and private IP addresses, but the benefits are more dramatic with public networks. With public networks, the address savings help engineers avoid having to obtain another registered IP network number from regional IP address assignment authorities. With private networks, as defined in RFC 1918, running out of addresses is not as big a negative, because you can always grab another private network from RFC 1918 if you run out.

Classless and Classful Routing Protocols

Before you can deploy a VLSM design created on paper, you must first use a routing protocol that supports VLSM. To support VLSM, the routing protocol must advertise the mask along with each subnet. Without mask information, the router receiving the update would be confused.

For example, if a router learned a route for 10.1.8.0, but with no mask information, what does that mean? Is that subnet 10.1.8.0/24? 10.1.8.0/23? 10.1.8.0/30? The dotted-decimal number 10.1.8.0 happens to be a valid subnet number with a variety of masks, and because multiple masks can be used with VLSM, the router has no good way to make an educated guess. To effectively support VLSM, the routing protocol needs to advertise the correct mask along with each subnet so that the receiving router knows the exact subnet that is being advertised.

By definition, *classless routing protocols* advertise the mask with each advertised route, and *classful routing protocols* do not. The classless routing protocols, as noted in Table 20-1, are the newer, more advanced routing protocols. And not only do these more advanced classless routing protocols support VLSM, but they also support manual route summarization, a feature discussed in Chapter 21, "Route Summarization."

Key Topic

Table 20-1   Classless and Classful Interior IP Routing Protocols

Routing Protocol	Is It Classless?	Sends Mask in Updates?	Supports VLSM?	Supports Manual Route Summarization?
RIP-1	No	No	No	No
IGRP	No	No	No	No
RIP-2	Yes	Yes	Yes	Yes
EIGRP	Yes	Yes	Yes	Yes
OSPF	Yes	Yes	Yes	Yes

Beyond VLSM itself, the routing protocols do not have to be configured to support VLSM or to be classless. There is no command to enable or disable the fact that classless routing protocols include the mask with each route. The only configuration choice you must make is to use a classless routing protocol, which among the routing protocols discussed for CCENT and CCNA are EIGRP and OSPF.

VLSM Configuration and Verification

Cisco routers do not configure VLSM, enable or disable it, or need any configuration to use it. From a configuration perspective, VLSM is simply a side effect of using the **ip address** interface subcommand. Routers collectively configure VLSM by virtue of having IP addresses in the same classful network but with different masks.

For example, Example 20-1 shows two of the interfaces from router Yosemite from Figure 20-1. The example shows the IP address assignments on two interfaces, one with a /24 mask and one with a /30 mask, both with IP addresses in Class A network 10.0.0.0.

Example 20-1   *Configuring Two Interfaces on Yosemite, Resulting in VLSM*

```
Yosemite# configure terminal
Yosemite(config)# interface Fa0/0
Yosemite(config-if)# ip address 10.2.1.1 255.255.255.0
Yosemite(config-if)# interface S0/1
Yosemite(config-if)# ip address 10.1.4.1 255.255.255.252
```

The use of VLSM can also be detected by a detailed look at the output of the **show ip route** command. This command lists routes in groups, by classful network, so that you see all the subnets of a single Class A, B, or C network all in a row. Just look down the list, and look to see, if any, how many different masks are listed. For example, Example 20-2 lists the routing table on Albuquerque from Figure 20-1; Albuquerque uses masks /24 and /30 inside network 10.0.0.0, as noted in the highlighted line in the example.

Example 20-2 *Albuquerque Routing Table with VLSM*

```
Albuquerque# show ip route
Codes: L - local, C - connected, S - static, R - RIP, M - mobile, B - BGP
       D - EIGRP, EX - EIGRP external, O - OSPF, IA - OSPF inter area
       N1 - OSPF NSSA external type 1, N2 - OSPF NSSA external type 2
       E1 - OSPF external type 1, E2 - OSPF external type 2
       i - IS-IS, su - IS-IS summary, L1 - IS-IS level-1, L2 - IS-IS level-2
       ia - IS-IS inter area, * - candidate default, U - per-user static route
       o - ODR, P - periodic downloaded static route, H - NHRP, l - LISP
       + - replicated route, % - next hop override

Gateway of last resort is not set

      10.0.0.0/8 is variably subnetted, 14 subnets, 3 masks
D        10.2.1.0/24 [90/2172416] via 10.1.4.1, 00:00:34, Serial0/0
D        10.2.2.0/24 [90/2172416] via 10.1.4.1, 00:00:34, Serial0/0
D        10.2.3.0/24 [90/2172416] via 10.1.4.1, 00:00:34, Serial0/0
D        10.2.4.0/24 [90/2172416] via 10.1.4.1, 00:00:34, Serial0/0
D        10.3.4.0/24 [90/2172416] via 10.1.6.2, 00:00:56, Serial0/1
D        10.3.5.0/24 [90/2172416] via 10.1.6.2, 00:00:56, Serial0/1
D        10.3.6.0/24 [90/2172416] via 10.1.6.2, 00:00:56, Serial0/1
D        10.3.7.0/24 [90/2172416] via 10.1.6.2, 00:00:56, Serial0/1
C        10.1.1.0/24 is directly connected, FastEthernet0/0
L        10.1.1.1/32 is directly connected, FastEthernet0/0
C        10.1.6.0/30 is directly connected, Serial0/1
L        10.1.6.1/32 is directly connected, Serial0/1
C        10.1.4.0/30 is directly connected, Serial0/0
L        10.1.4.1/32 is directly connected, Serial0/0
```

20

NOTE   For the purposes of understanding whether a design uses VLSM, ignore the /32 "local" routes that a router automatically creates for its own interface IP addresses.

So ends the discussion of VLSM as an end to itself. This chapter is devoted to VLSM, but it took a mere three to four pages to fully describe it. Why the entire VLSM chapter? Well, to work with VLSM, to find problems with it, to add subnets to an existing design, and to design using VLSM from scratch—in other words, to apply VLSM to real networks—takes skill and practice. To do these same tasks on the exam requires skill and practice. The rest of this chapter examines the skills to apply VLSM and provides some practice for these two key areas:

- Finding VLSM overlaps
- Adding new VLSM subnets without overlaps

Finding VLSM Overlaps

Regardless of whether a design uses VLSM, the subnets used in any IP internetwork design should not overlap their address ranges. When subnets in different locations overlap their addresses, a router's routing table entries overlap. As a result, hosts in different locations can be assigned the same IP address. Routers clearly cannot route packets correctly in these cases. In short, a design that uses overlapping subnets is considered to be an incorrect design and should not be used.

> **NOTE**   Although I've not seen the term used in other places, just to have a term to contrast with VLSM, this book refers to the non-use of VLSM—in other words, using a single mask throughout a classful network—as static-length subnet masks (SLSM).

These address overlaps are easier to see when using SLSM than when using VLSM. With SLSM, overlapped subnets have identical subnet IDs, so to find overlaps, you just have to look at the subnet IDs. With VLSM, overlapped subnets cannot have the same subnet ID. To find these overlaps, you have to look at the entire range of addresses in each subnet, from subnet ID to subnet broadcast address, and compare the range to the other subnets in the design.

An Example of Finding a VLSM Overlap

For example, imagine that a practice question for the CCENT exam shows Figure 20-2. It uses a single Class B network (172.16.0.0), with VLSM, because it uses three different masks: /23, /24, and /30.

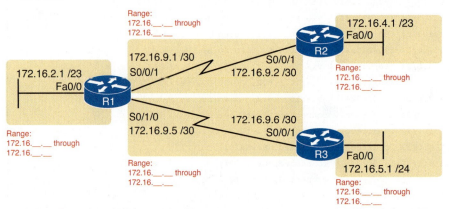

Figure 20-2   *VLSM Design with Possible Overlap*

Now imagine that the exam question shows you the figure, and either directly or indirectly asks whether overlapping subnets exist. This type of question might simply tell you that some hosts cannot ping each other, or it might not even mention that the root cause could be that some of the subnets overlap. To answer such a question, you could follow this simple but possibly laborious process:

Step 1.   Calculate the subnet ID and subnet broadcast address of each subnet, which gives you the range of addresses in that subnet.

Step 2.   List the subnet IDs in numerical order (along with their subnet broadcast addresses).

Step 3.   Scan the list from top to bottom, comparing each pair of adjacent entries, to see whether their range of addresses overlaps.

For example, Table 20-2 completes the first two steps based on Figure 20-2, listing the subnet IDs and subnet broadcast addresses, in numerical order based on the subnet IDs.

Table 20-2   Subnet IDs and Broadcast Addresses, in Numerical Order, from Figure 20-2

Subnet	Subnet Number	Broadcast Address
R1 LAN	172.16.2.0	172.16.3.255
R2 LAN	172.16.4.0	172.16.5.255
R3 LAN	172.16.5.0	172.16.5.255
R1-R2 serial	172.16.9.0	172.16.9.3
R1-R3 serial	172.16.9.4	172.16.9.7

Step 3 states the somewhat obvious step of comparing the address ranges to see whether any overlaps occur. You could just scan the list overall, but if you order the list, you can also methodically scan the list looking at each adjacent pair.

First, look closely just at the subnet number column in Table 20-2. Note that, in this case, none of the subnet numbers are identical, but two entries (highlighted) do overlap.

Next, look closely at the R2 LAN and R3 LAN subnets. All the addresses in the 172.16.5.0/24 subnet are also part of the 172.16.4.0/23 subnet. In this case, the design is invalid because of the overlap, and one of these two subnets would need to be changed.

As far as the three-step process works, note that if two adjacent entries in the list overlap, compare three entries at the next step. The two subnets already marked as overlapped can overlap with the next subnet in the list. For example, imagine a case where you had the following three subnets in a list that you were examining for VLSM overlaps:

  10.1.0.0/16 (subnet ID 10.1.0.0, broadcast 10.1.255.255)

  10.1.200.0/24 (subnet ID 10.1.200.0, broadcast 10.1.200.255)

  10.1.250.0/24 (subnet ID 10.1.250.0, broadcast 10.1.250.255)

If you compare entries 1 and 2, clearly an overlap occurs, because all the addresses in subnet 10.1.200.0/24 sit inside subnet 10.1.0.0/16. If you then compare only entries 2 and 3, those entries do not overlap. However, entries 1 and 3 do overlap. So what does this mean for the process? Anytime you find an overlap, compare all those overlapped subnets with the next line in the list of subnets until you find one that doesn't overlap.

Practice Finding VLSM Overlaps

As typical of anything to with applying IP addressing and subnetting, practice helps. To that end, Table 20-3 lists three practice problems. Just start with the five IP addresses listed in a single column, and then follow the three-step process outlined in the previous section to find any VLSM overlaps. The answers can be found near the end of this chapter, in the section "Answers to Earlier Practice Problems."

Table 20-3   VLSM Overlap Practice Problems

Problem 1	Problem 2	Problem 3
10.1.34.9/22	172.16.126.151/22	192.168.1.253/30
10.1.29.101/23	172.16.122.57/27	192.168.1.113/28
10.1.23.254/22	172.16.122.33/30	192.168.1.245/29
10.1.17.1/21	172.16.122.1/30	192.168.1.125/30
10.1.1.1/20	172.16.128.151/20	192.168.1.122/30

Adding a New Subnet to an Existing VLSM Design

The task described in this section happens frequently in real networks: choosing new subnets to add to an existing design. In real life, you can use tools that help you choose a new subnet so that you do not cause an overlap. However, for both real life and for the CCENT and CCNA exams, you need to be ready to do the mental process and math of choosing a subnet that both has the right number of host IP addresses and does not create an overlapped VLSM subnet condition. In other words, you need to pick a new subnet and not make a mistake!

For example, consider the internetwork shown earlier in Figure 20-2, with classful network 172.16.0.0. An exam question might suggest that a new subnet, with a /23 prefix length, needs to be added to the design. The question might also say, "Pick the numerically lowest subnet number that can be used for the new subnet." In other words, if both 172.16.4.0 and 172.16.6.0 would work, use 172.16.4.0.

So, you really have a couple of tasks: To find all the subnet IDs that could be used, rule out the ones that would cause an overlap, and then check to see whether the question guides you to pick either the numerically lowest (or highest) subnet ID. This list outlines the specific steps:

Step 1. Pick the subnet mask (prefix length) for the new subnet, based on the design requirements (if not already listed as part of the question).

Step 2. Calculate all possible subnet numbers of the classful network using the mask from Step 1, along with the subnet broadcast addresses.

Step 3. Make a list of existing subnet IDs and matching subnet broadcast addresses.

Step 4. Rule out overlapping new subnets by comparing the lists from the previous two steps.

Step 5. Choose the new subnet ID from the remaining subnets identified at Step 4, paying attention to whether the question asks for the numerically lowest or numerically highest subnet ID.

An Example of Adding a New VLSM Subnet

For example, Figure 20-3 shows an existing internetwork that uses VLSM. (The figure uses the same IP addresses as shown in Figure 20-2, but with R3's LAN IP address changed to fix the VLSM overlap shown in Figure 20-2.) In this case, you need to add a new subnet to support 300 hosts. Imagine that the question tells you to use the smallest subnet (least number of hosts) to meet that requirement. You use some math and logic you learned earlier in your study to choose mask /23, which gives you 9 host bits, for $2^9 - 2 = 510$ hosts in the subnet.

> **NOTE** If the logic and process in the previous paragraph were unfamiliar, it might be useful to take some time to review Chapter 19, "Subnet Design."

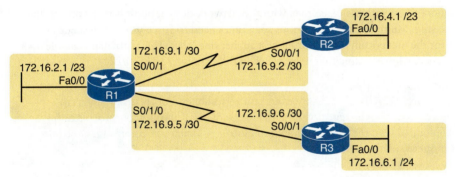

Figure 20-3 *Internetwork to Which You Need to Add a /23 Subnet, Network 172.16.0.0*

At this point, just follow the steps listed before Figure 20-3. For Step 1, you have already been given the mask (/23). For Step 2, you need to list all the subnet numbers and broadcast addresses of 172.16.0.0, assuming the /23 mask. You will not use all these subnets, but you need the list for comparison to the existing subnets. Table 20-4 shows the results, at least for the first five possible /23 subnets.

Table 20-4   First Five Possible /23 Subnets

Subnet	Subnet Number	Subnet Broadcast Address
First (zero)	172.16.0.0	172.16.1.255
Second	172.16.2.0	172.16.3.255
Third	172.16.4.0	172.16.5.255
Fourth	172.16.6.0	172.16.7.255
Fifth	172.16.8.0	172.16.9.255

Next, at Step 3, list the existing subnet numbers and broadcast addresses, as seen earlier in Figure 20-3. To do so, do the usual math to take an IP address/mask to then find the subnet ID and subnet broadcast address. Table 20-5 summarizes that information, including the locations, subnet numbers, and subnet broadcast addresses.

Table 20-5   Existing Subnet IDs and Broadcast Addresses from Figure 20-3

Subnet	Subnet Number	Subnet Broadcast Address
R1 LAN	172.16.2.0	172.16.3.255
R2 LAN	172.16.4.0	172.16.5.255
R3 LAN	172.16.6.0	172.16.6.255
R1-R2 serial	172.16.9.0	172.16.9.3
R1-R3 serial	172.16.9.4	172.16.9.7

At this point, you have all the information you need to look for the overlap at Step 4. Simply compare the range of numbers for the subnets in the previous two tables. Which of the possible new /23 subnets (Table 20-4) overlap with the existing subnets (Table 20-5)? In this case, the second through fifth subnets in Table 20-4 overlap, so rule those out as candidates to be used. (Table 20-4 denotes those subnets with gray highlights.)

20

Step 5 has more to do with the exam than with real network design, but it is still worth listing as a separate step. Multiple-choice questions sometimes need to force you into a single answer, and asking for the numerically lowest or highest subnet does that. This particular example asks for the numerically lowest subnet number, which in this case is 172.16.0.0/23.

NOTE   The answer, 172.16.0.0/23, happens to be a zero subnet. For the exam, the zero subnet should be avoided if (a) the question implies the use of classful routing protocols or (b) the routers are configured with the **no ip subnet-zero** global configuration command. Otherwise, assume that the zero subnet can be used.

Practice Adding New VLSM Subnets

Your boss wants you to add one subnet to an existing design. The existing design already has these five subnets:

10.0.0.0/24

10.0.1.0/25

10.0.2.0/26

10.0.3.0/27

10.0.6.0/28

The boss cannot decide among five competing subnet masks to use for this next new subnet to add to the internetwork. However, the boss wants you to practice VLSM and plan the subnet ID that he would use for each of those four possible masks. He tells you that the new subnet ID must be part of Class A network 10.0.0.0, that the new subnet must not overlap with the original five subnets, and that the new subnet ID must be the numerically lowest possible subnet ID (without breaking the other rules). Pick the one subnet ID that you would plan to use based on each of the following mask choices by the boss:

  1. /24

  2. /23

  3. /22

  4. /25

You can find the answers in the section "Answers to Earlier Practice Problems," later in this chapter.

Review Activities

Chapter Summary

- Variable Length Subnet Masks (VLSM) simply means that the subnet design uses more than one mask in the same classful network.

- VLSM provides many benefits for real networks, mainly related to how you allocate and use your IP address space. Because a mask defines the size of the subnet (the number of host addresses in the subnet), VLSM enables engineers to better match the need for addresses with the size of the subnets.

- VLSM can be helpful for both public and private IP addresses, but the benefits are more dramatic with public networks. With public networks, the address savings help engineers avoid having to obtain another registered IP network number from regional IP address assignment authorities.

- To support VLSM, the routing protocol must advertise the mask along with each subnet. Without mask information, the router receiving the update would be unable to determine network address from host address.

- By definition, *classless routing protocols* advertise the mask with each advertised route, and *classful routing protocols* do not.

- Cisco routers do not configure VLSM, enable or disable it, or need any configuration to use it. From a configuration perspective, VLSM is simply a side effect of the **ip address** interface subcommand. Routers collectively configure VLSM by virtue of having IP addresses in the same classful network but with different masks.

- There are basically five steps to using VLSM. You must find all the subnet IDs that could be used, rule out the ones that would cause an overlap, and then check to see whether the requirement guides you to pick either the numerically lowest (or highest) subnet ID. This list outlines the specific steps:

  Step 1. Pick the subnet mask (prefix length) for the new subnet based on the design requirements (if not already listed as part of the question).

  Step 2. Calculate all possible subnet numbers of the classful network using the mask from Step 1, along with the subnet broadcast addresses.

  Step 3. Make a list of existing subnet IDs and matching subnet broadcast addresses.

  Step 4. Rule out overlapping new subnets by comparing the lists from the previous two steps.

  Step 5. Choose the new subnet ID from the remaining subnets identified in Step 4, paying attention to whether the question asks for the numerically lowest or numerically highest subnet ID.

Review Questions

Answer these review questions. You can find the answers at the bottom of the last page of the chapter. For thorough explanations, see DVD Appendix C, "Answers to Review Questions."

1. Which of the following routing protocols support VLSM? (Choose three answers.)

    A. RIP-1

    B. RIP-2

    C. EIGRP

    D. OSPF

2.   What does the acronym VLSM stand for?

   A.   Variable-length subnet mask

   B.   Very long subnet mask

   C.   Vociferous longitudinal subnet mask

   D.   Vector-length subnet mask

   E.   Vector loop subnet mask

3.   R1 has configured interface Fa0/0 with the **ip address 10.5.48.1 255.255.240.0** command. Which of the following subnets, when configured on another interface on R1, would not be considered an overlapping VLSM subnet?

   A.   10.5.0.0 255.255.240.0

   B.   10.4.0.0 255.254.0.0

   C.   10.5.32.0 255.255.224.0

   D.   10.5.0.0 255.255.128.0

4.   R4 has a connected route for 172.16.8.0/22. Which of the following answers lists a subnet that overlaps with this subnet?

   A.   172.16.0.0/21

   B.   172.16.6.0/23

   C.   172.16.16.0/20

   D.   172.16.11.0/25

5.   A design already includes subnets 192.168.1.0/26, 192.168.1.128/30, and 192.168.1.160/29. Which of the following subnets is the numerically lowest subnet ID that could be added to the design, if you wanted to add a subnet that uses a /28 mask?

   A.   192.168.1.144/28

   B.   192.168.1.112/28

   C.   192.168.1.64/28

   D.   192.168.1.80/28

   E.   192.168.1.96/28

Review All the Key Topics

Review the most important topics from this chapter, noted with the Key Topic icon. Table 20-6 lists these key topics and where each is discussed.

Table 20-6   Key Topics for Chapter 20

Key Topic Element	Description	Page Number
Table 20-1	Classless and classful routing protocols listed and compared	496
List	Steps to analyze an existing design to discover any VLSM overlaps	498
List	Steps to follow when adding a new subnet to an existing VLSM design	500

Complete the Tables and Lists from Memory

Print a copy of DVD Appendix M, "Memory Tables," or at least the section for this chapter, and complete the tables and lists from memory. DVD Appendix N, "Memory Tables Answer Key," includes completed tables and lists to check your work.

Definitions of Key Terms

After your first reading of the chapter, try to define these key terms, but do not be concerned about getting them all correct at that time. Chapter 30 directs you in how to use these terms for late-stage preparation for the exam.

classful routing protocol, classless routing protocol, overlapping subnets, variable-length subnet masks (VLSM)

Appendix H Practice Problems

DVD Appendix H, "Practice for Chapter 20: Variable-Length Subnet Masks," lists additional practice problems and answers.

Answers to Earlier Practice Problems

Answers to Practice Finding VLSM Overlaps

This section lists the answers to the three practice problems in the section "Practice Finding VLSM Overlaps," as listed earlier in Table 20-3. Note that the tables that list details of the answer reordered the subnets as part of the process.

In Problem 1, the second and third subnet IDs listed in Table 20-7 happen to overlap. The second subnet's range completely includes the range of addresses in the third subnet.

Table 20-7 VLSM Overlap Problem 1 Answers (Overlaps Highlighted)

Reference	Original Address and Mask	Subnet ID	Broadcast Address
1	10.1.1.1/20	10.1.0.0	10.1.15.255
2	10.1.17.1/21	10.1.16.0	10.1.23.255
3	10.1.23.254/22	10.1.20.0	10.1.23.255
4	10.1.29.101/23	10.1.28.0	10.1.29.255
5	10.1.34.9/22	10.1.32.0	10.1.35.255

In Problem 2, again the second and third subnet IDs (listed in Table 20-8) happen to overlap, and again, the second subnet's range completely includes the range of addresses in the third subnet. Also, the second and third subnet IDs are the same value, so the overlap is more obvious.

Table 20-8 VLSM Overlap Problem 2 Answers (Overlaps Highlighted)

Reference	Original Address and Mask	Subnet ID	Broadcast Address
1	172.16.122.1/30	172.16.122.0	172.16.122.3
2	172.16.122.57/27	172.16.122.32	172.16.122.63
3	172.16.122.33/30	172.16.122.32	172.16.122.35
4	172.16.126.151/22	172.16.124.0	172.16.127.255
5	172.16.128.151/20	172.16.128.0	172.16.143.255

In Problem 3, three subnets overlap. Subnet 1's range completely includes the range of addresses in the second and third subnets, as shown in Table 20-9. Note that the second and third subnets do not overlap with each other, so for the process in this book to find all the overlaps, after you find that the first two subnets overlap, you should compare the next entry in the table (3) with both of the two known-to-overlap entries (1 and 2).

Table 20-9   VLSM Overlap Problem 3 Answers (Overlaps Highlighted)

Reference	Original Address and Mask	Subnet ID	Broadcast Address
1	192.168.1.113/28	192.168.1.112	192.168.1.127
2	192.168.1.122/30	192.168.1.120	192.168.1.123
3	192.168.1.125/30	192.168.1.124	192.168.1.127
4	192.168.1.245/29	192.168.1.240	192.168.1.247
5	192.168.1.253/30	192.168.1.252	192.168.1.255

Answers to Practice Adding VLSM Subnets

This section lists the answers to the four practice problems in the section "Practice Adding New VLSM Subnets," earlier in this chapter. The four problems for this section used the same set of five preexisting subnets. Table 20-10 lists those subnet IDs and subnet broadcast addresses, which define the lower and higher ends of the range of numbers in each subnet.

Table 20-10   Preexisting Subnets for the Add a VLSM Subnet Problems in This Chapter

Subnet	Subnet Number	Broadcast Address
1	10.0.0.0/24	10.0.0.255
2	10.0.1.0/25	10.0.1.127
3	10.0.2.0/26	10.0.2.63
4	10.0.3.0/27	10.0.3.31

The rest of the explanations follow the five-step process outlined earlier in the section "Adding a New Subnet to an Existing VLSM Design," except that the explanations ignore Step 3 because Step 3's results in each case are already listed in Table 20-10.

Problem 1

Step 1.   The problem statement tells us to use /24.

Step 2.   The subnets would be 10.0.0.0, 10.0.1.0, 10.0.2.0, 10.0.3.0, 10.0.4.0, 10.0.5.0, and so on, counting by 1 in the third octet.

Step 4.   The first four new possible subnets (10.0.0.0/24, 10.0.1.0/24, 10.0.2.0/24, and 10.0.3.0/24) all overlap with the existing subnets (see Table 20-11). 10.0.6.0/24 also overlaps.

Step 5.   10.0.4.0/24 is the numerically lowest new subnet number that does not overlap with the existing subnets.

Problem 2

Step 1.   The problem statement tells us to use /23.

Step 2.   The subnets would be 10.0.0.0, 10.0.2.0, 10.0.4.0, 10.0.6.0, 10.0.8.0, and so on, counting by 2 in the third octet.

Step 4. Three of the first four new possible subnets (10.0.0.0/23, 10.0.2.0/23, and 10.0.6.0/23) all overlap with existing subnets.

Step 5. 10.0.4.0/23 is the numerically lowest new subnet number that does not overlap with the existing subnets.

Problem 3

Step 1. The problem statement tells us to use /22.

Step 2. The subnets would be 10.0.0.0, 10.0.4.0, 10.0.8.0, 10.0.12.0, and so on, counting by 4 in the third octet.

Step 4. The first two new possible subnets (10.0.0.0/22 and 10.0.4.0/22) overlap with existing subnets.

Step 5. 10.0.8.0/22 is the numerically lowest new subnet number that does not overlap with the existing subnets.

Problem 4

The answer for this problem requires more detail than the others, because the /25 mask creates a larger number of subnets that might overlap with the preexisting subnets. For this problem, at Step 1, you already know to use mask /25. Table 20-11 shows the results of Step 2, listing the first 14 subnets of network 10.0.0.0 when using mask /25. For Step 4, Table 20-11 also highlights the overlapped subnets in gray. To complete the task at Step 5, search the table sequentially and find the first nongrayed subnet, 10.0.1.128/25.

Table 20-11   First 14 Subnets of Network 10.0.0.0, Using /25 Mask

Reference	Subnet Number	Broadcast Address
1	10.0.0.0	10.0.0.127
2	10.0.0.128	10.0.0.255
3	10.0.1.0	10.0.1.127
4	10.0.1.128	10.0.1.255
5	10.0.2.0	10.0.2.127
6	10.0.2.128	10.0.2.255
7	10.0.3.0	10.0.3.127
8	10.0.3.128	10.0.3.255
9	10.0.4.0	10.0.4.127
10	10.0.4.128	10.0.4.255
11	10.0.5.0	10.0.5.127
12	10.0.5.128	10.0.5.255
13	10.0.6.0	10.0.6.127
14	10.0.6.128	10.0.6.255

Answers to Review Questions:

1 B, C, and D **2** A **3** A **4** D **5** C

Chapter 21

Route Summarization

Route-summarization tools allow engineers to advertise one route that replaces several smaller routes, with the new route matching the same range of addresses. Doing so alleviates some of the waste: wasted effort, bandwidth, RAM, and CPU.

This chapter first examines manual route summarization concepts. The concepts rely on math that uses the same principles as subnetting math, and it relies on a good subnetting plan that assigns subnets in anticipation of future attempts to do route summarization. This first section of the chapter shows the math and the concepts. The second half of the chapter then shows a systematic way to find out the summary route that is the best summary route to create when configuring summary routes.

This chapter covers the following exam topics:

IP addressing (IPv4 / IPv6)

Identify the appropriate IPv4 addressing scheme using VLSM and summarization to satisfy addressing requirements in a LAN/WAN environment.

Troubleshooting

Troubleshoot and correct common problems associated with IP addressing and host configurations.

Manual Route Summarization Concepts

Small networks might have only a few dozen routes in their routers' routing tables, but the larger the internetwork, the larger the number of routes. Some enterprises might have tens of thousands of subnets, if not more. Even with the effect of decreasing the number of routes through summarization, Internet router BGP tables have come close to the 450,000 mark as of a recent check in 2012.

As a router's routing table grows, problems can occur. The tables themselves consume memory in a router. Routing (packet forwarding) requires the router to match a route in the routing table, and searching a longer table generally takes more time and more work by the CPU. Routing protocols require more work to process the routes and more bandwidth to advertise the routes. With a large routing table, it takes more time to troubleshoot problems, because the engineers working on the network need to sift through more information.

Route summarization allows network engineers to help overcome some of these scaling problems by replacing many routes for smaller subnets with one route to what looks like a larger subnet. This first major section of the chapter walks you through the basics of how route summarization works and its impact on the routers in an IPv4 network. This section also shows how the subnetting plan needs to consider the need for route summarization ahead of time and describes how to verify route summarization by using the **show ip route** command.

> **NOTE**   This chapter refers to route summarization as *manual route summarization*, in contrast to the another topic called *autosummarization*. Of the two, manual summarization is actually the tool most network engineers choose to use, while autosummarization refers to a feature of how some older routing protocols work. The term *manual* means that an engineer configures one or more commands that cause the summary route to be created. The CCNA ICND2 200-101 Official Cert Guide discusses *autosummarization*, which creates summary routes to overcome a problem with some routing protocols.

Route Summarization Basics

Imagine a small router, with limited CPU and memory, sitting in a large enterprise network. This network has over 10,000 subnets. This one small router dutifully learns all the routes with its routing protocols and adds them to its routing table. Those routes consume memory; the routing protocols take more work because of the sheer volume. Also, the long routing table means that searching the table to match a route can take longer.

Most of those 10,000 routes have the exact same forwarding instructions: to send packets out one particular interface that points toward the core of the enterprise network. Wouldn't it be great if, instead of having several thousands of those routes, this small router could have one route that matches all those same packets with instructions to forward those packets out that same interface? That's exactly what route summarization does.

Route summarization allows engineers to configure a routing protocol so that it advertises one route, replacing several smaller routes. This process creates a new summary route that matches the same range of addresses as the original routes. For example, instead of advertising routes for a lot of /24 subnets, such as 172.16.1.0/24, 172.16.2.0/24, 172.16.3.0/24, and so on, the router might simply advertise a route for 172.16.0.0/16, and not advertise all those smaller subnets.

Route summarization has many benefits. It reduces the size of routing tables, while still allowing the router to route packets to all the destinations in the network. The shorter table means that routing performance can be improved and memory can be saved inside each router. Summarization also improves convergence time for routing protocols, because the routing protocol has much less work to do.

Route Summarization and the IPv4 Subnetting Plan

For route summarization to work best, the IPv4 subnetting plan should be designed with route summarization in mind. Route summarization combines multiple routes into one route, but for that to work, the original routes must be in the same numeric range. That can happen by accident, but it works much better with planning. For example, Figure 21-1 shows a sample internetwork, with two sets of four subnets that could be summarized (some on the left, some on the right). Note that the subnetting plan placed subnets that begin with 10.2 on the left and those that begin with 10.3 on the right, which makes route summarization a little easier. To see why, focus on the right side for now, and ignore the subnets on the left. The figure shows the conditions before route summarization, for routes learned by R1, for the subnets on the right.

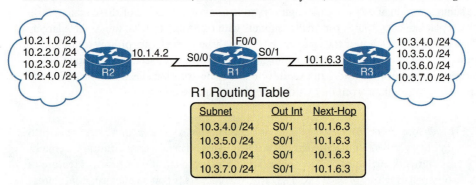

Figure 21-1   *Small Internetwork with Good Candidates for Route Summarization*

Manual route summarization causes a router to cease advertising some routes, instead advertising a route that contains a superset of all the addresses. To do so, the router that creates the summary must be configured to know the subnet number and mask to advertise in a new summary route. The routing protocol stops advertising the old smaller routes (called subordinate routes), now advertising only the summary route.

Figure 21-2 continues the example begun in Figure 21-1, showing the effect of a summary route configured on Router R3. That summary route replaces the routes for all four of the subnets on the right. Just to make the math easier, the summary route uses a subnet of 10.3.0.0/16. Note that 10.3.0.0/16 does include all the four original subnets shown in Figure 21-1 (plus other addresses).

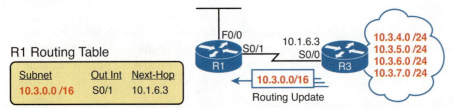

Figure 21-2   *Routes for the Four Subnets on the Right Summarized into One Route*

By creating the summary route configuration on R3, R1 (and other routers farther into the network) receive the benefit. R1's routing table decreases in size. More importantly, R1 can still forward packets to those same original four subnets, out the same S0/1 interface, to the same next-hop router (10.1.6.3, which is R3).

Verifying Manually Summarized Routes

Route summarization impacts the routing tables on the routers, with different results depending on whether a router simply learned the summary or whether the router created the summary. Example 21-1 shows R1's routing table, both before the summary route was configured on R3 (as shown in Figure 21-1) and then after R3 added the summary route configuration (as shown in Figure 21-2). (Note that the example shows only the routes learned by the routing protocol, rather than including the connected routes.)

Example 21-1   *R1 Routing Table: Before and After Summary Route Was Learned*

```
! First, the before case
R1# show ip route rip
! (Legend lines omitted for brevity)
     10.0.0.0/8 is variably subnetted, 14 subnets, 3 masks
R       10.2.1.0/24 [120/1] via 10.1.4.2, 00:00:20, Serial0/0
R       10.2.2.0/24 [120/1] via 10.1.4.2, 00:00:20, Serial0/0
R       10.2.3.0/24 [120/1] via 10.1.4.2, 00:00:20, Serial0/0
R       10.2.4.0/24 [120/1] via 10.1.4.2, 00:00:20, Serial0/0
R       10.3.4.0/24 [120/1] via 10.1.6.3, 00:00:12, Serial0/1
R       10.3.5.0/24 [120/2] via 10.1.6.3, 00:00:12, Serial0/1
R       10.3.6.0/24 [120/3] via 10.1.6.3, 00:00:12, Serial0/1
R       10.3.7.0/24 [120/4] via 10.1.6.3, 00:00:12, Serial0/1



! Now, the after case.
R1# show ip route
! (Legend lines omitted for brevity)

     10.0.0.0/8 is variably subnetted, 11 subnets, 4 masks
R       10.2.1.0/24 [120/1] via 10.1.4.2, 00:00:20, Serial0/0
R       10.2.2.0/24 [120/1] via 10.1.4.2, 00:00:20, Serial0/0
R       10.2.3.0/24 [120/1] via 10.1.4.2, 00:00:20, Serial0/0
R       10.2.4.0/24 [120/1] via 10.1.4.2, 00:00:20, Serial0/0
R       10.3.0.0/16 [120/1] via 10.1.6.3, 00:00:04, Serial0/1
```

First, look at the top half of the output, which shows the before case (based on Figure 21-1). The **show ip route rip** command lists only the RIP-learned routes, lists statistics that state R1 knows 14 subnets, and then lists eight routes learned with Routing Information Protocol (RIP). The other six routes are R1's three connected routes and three local routes for its three interfaces. In particular, note the four RIP-learned routes for subnets that begin with 10.3.

Next, look at the after case in the second part of the example. The big difference, of course, is that the before case shows the four individual subnets that begin with 10.3, and the latter case shows only the summary route for 10.3.0.0/16 instead. That summary route looks like any other route, with a subnet, mask, next-hop router (10.1.6.3), and outgoing interface (Serial 0/1). As it turns out, nothing in the line tells you that the route is a summary route as opposed to a subnet that exists somewhere in the internetwork.

Neither this book nor the ICND2 book discusses how to configure summary routes. Instead, the focus of route summarization here is to understand the big ideas, see the benefits, and be ready to work with routes that happen to be summary routes. To that end, the second half of this chapter looks at some math related to summary routes that shows how to choose the best subnet and mask to use in a summary route.

21

Choosing the Best Summary Routes

Manual route summarization works best when the subnetting plan considered summarization in the first place. For example, the earlier examples with Figures 21-1 and 21-2 used a well-thought-out plan, with the engineers only using subnets beginning with 10.2 for subnets off R2 and subnets that begin with 10.3 for subnets off R3.

When creating a summary route, some network engineer types a subnet and mask in a configuration command. Many combinations of subnet/mask can work for a given need; however, not all those options are the best option. The word *best*, when applied to choosing what summary route to configure, means that the summary should include all the subordinate subnets, but *with as few other addresses as is possible*. For the purposes of this book, the best summary route can be defined as follows:

> The summary route with the smallest range of addresses that includes all the addresses in all the subnets you want to summarize with that one summary route.

For example, in the earlier summarization example, subnets 10.3.4.0/24, 10.3.5.0/24, 10.3.6.0/24, and 10.3.7.0/24 together define a range of addresses from 10.3.4.0 to 10.3.7.255. The summary route in Example 21-1 (10.3.0.0/16) works. However, it includes a lot of IP addresses that are not in those four original subnets, because it includes the range from 10.3.0.0 to 10.3.255.255. As it turns out, a different option for this summary route—10.3.4.0/22—has a range of addresses that exactly matches the range for these four subnets (10.3.4.0–10.3.7.255). By the definition listed here, both 10.3.0.0/16 and 10.3.4.0/22 work, but 10.3.40/22 is the best summary route.

This second major section of the chapter shows how to take a set of existing routes and find the best summary route.

The Process to Find the Best Summary Route

To find the best summary route, you can use trial and error, use educated guesses, use a subnet calculator, or use any other method you like. For the purposes of CCENT and CCNA, using a simpler decimal-based process to find the best summary route probably makes the most sense. The process uses familiar skills: taking a subnet ID/mask and finding the subnet broadcast address, as discussed back in Chapter 14, "Analyzing Existing Subnets." If you can do that math with confidence, this process should be no problem. (If not, consider going back to review subnetting math from Chapter 14 before finishing this chapter.)

Here are the steps for finding the best summary route, using decimal math, with some examples to follow:

Step 1.   List all to-be-summarized (subordinate) subnet numbers in decimal, in order, from lowest to highest, along with their matching subnet broadcast addresses.

Step 2.   Note the low and high end of the range of addresses for all combined subnets by noting the numerically lowest subnet ID and numerically highest subnet broadcast address.

Step 3.   Pick a starting point prefix length /P for Step 4, as follows: Pick the shortest prefix length mask of all the subordinate subnets, and then subtract 1.

Step 4.   Calculate a new potential summary subnet/mask, with matching broadcast address, based on the lowest subordinate subnet ID from the original list and the current prefix length.

  A.   If the calculated range of addresses includes the entire range from Step 2, you have found the best summary route.

  B.   If not, subtract 1 from the prefix length used in the most recent calculation and repeat Step 4.

As usual, the steps themselves can be daunting. Here's the shorter version: Pick the lowest subnet ID from the list, keep shortening the shortest prefix-style mask, calculate a new subnet ID based on those details, and see whether the new subnet includes all the addresses in the list of original subnets. But the best way to really understand is to see a few examples and then do a few.

Sample "Best" Summary on Router R3

R3, in earlier Figures 21-1 and 21-2, connects to subnets 10.3.4.0/24, 10.3.5.0/24, 10.3.6.0/24, and 10.3.7.0/24. Figure 21-3 shows the results of the first three steps of the process, applied to the three routes off Router R3. Following the steps:

Step 1.   Relist the subnet IDs (and prefix lengths) and calculate the subnet broadcast addresses.

Step 2.   Identify 10.3.4.0 as the lowest subnet ID and 10.3.7.255 as the highest subnet broadcast address, defining the low and high end of the range that the summary must include.

Step 3.   With all four masks as /24, subtract 1 from 24, so the initial value of /P to try is /23.

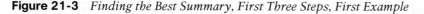

/P	① Subnet	① Broadcast
/24	② **10.3.4.0**	10.3.4.255
/24	10.3.5.0	10.3.5.255
/24	10.3.6.0	10.3.6.255
/24	10.3.7.0	② **10.3.7.255**

③ − 1
23

Figure 21-3   *Finding the Best Summary, First Three Steps, First Example*

Step 4 of the process requires some math that gets repeated until the best summary has been found. For the first time through the math at Step 4, use the /P calculated at Step 3 (in this case, /23). Then, each time Step 4's math does not result in confirming that you found the best summary route, repeat the math with a shorter prefix length mask, until the best summary is found.

This initial pass through Step 4 in this case uses subnet ID 10.3.4.0 and mask /23. At this point, you do not even know whether 10.3.4.0 would be a subnet number when using mask /23, so do the math as if you were trying to calculate both the subnet number and broadcast address. The calculation shows

   /23: subnet 10.3.4.0, broadcast 10.3.5.255

At Step 4A, you compare the newly calculated subnet address range with the range of addresses in the original subnets, as identified in Step 2. The new potential best summary route doesn't include the entire range of addresses for the original subnets. So, at Step 4B, subtract 1 from the prefix length (23 − 1 = 22) and start Step 4 again, with a /22 mask.

At the next pass through Step 4, again starting with the lowest original subnet ID (10.3.4.0), using the current prefix /22, calculating the subnet ID and broadcast, you get

   /22: subnet 10.3.4.0, broadcast 10.3.7.255

Back to Step 4A, this range exactly matches the range shown in Figure 21-3, so you have found the subnet and mask to use in the best summary route: 10.3.4.0/22.

21

Sample "Best" Summary on Router R2

Figure 21-1 shows four subnets on the right as well as four subnets on the left. So far, this chapter has mostly ignored the subnets on the left, but now you can calculate the best summary route for those subnets. Those routes are for subnets 10.2.1.0/24, 10.2.2.0/24, 10.2.3.0/24, and 10.2.4.0/24.

Figure 21-4 shows the results of the first three steps.

Step 1.   Relist the subnet IDs (and prefix lengths) and calculate the subnet broadcast addresses.

Step 2.   Identify 10.2.1.0 as the lowest subnet ID and 10.2.4.255 as the highest subnet broadcast address, defining the low and high end of the range that the summary must include.

Step 3.   As with the previous example, with all four masks as /24, you choose an initial /P to use of 1 less, or /23.

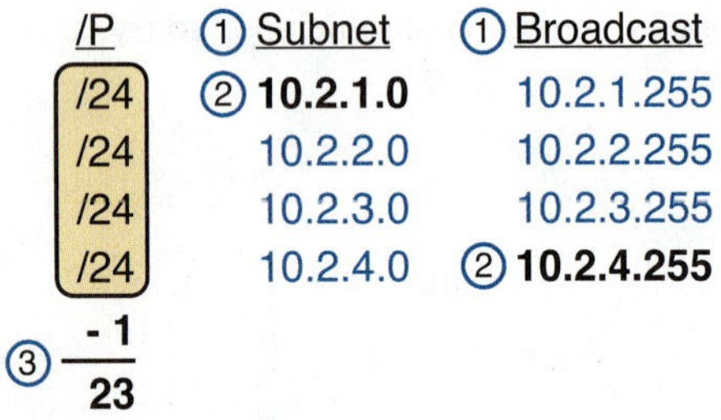

```
/P      ① Subnet     ① Broadcast
/24     ② 10.2.1.0      10.2.1.255
/24        10.2.2.0      10.2.2.255
/24        10.2.3.0      10.2.3.255
/24        10.2.4.0    ② 10.2.4.255

     -1
③  ----
     23
```

Figure 21-4   *Finding the Best Summary, First Three Steps, Second Example*

This initial pass through Step 4 uses subnet ID 10.2.1.0 and mask /23. At this point, you do not even know whether 10.2.1.0 would be a subnet number when using mask /23, so do the math as if you were trying to calculate both the subnet number and broadcast address. In this case, the calculation would show

   /23: subnet 10.2.0.0, broadcast 10.2.1.255

At Step 4A, comparing this range to the range shown in Figure 21-4, this new potential best summary route doesn't include the entire range. So, at Step 4B, subtract 1 from the prefix length (23 − 1 = 22) and start Step 4 again, with a /22 mask.

Taking the next pass through Step 4, starting with the lowest original subnet ID (10.2.1.0) and the current prefix /22, calculating the subnet ID and broadcast, you get

   /22: subnet 10.2.0.0, broadcast 10.2.3.255

This new range includes the addresses from three of the four original subordinate subnets, but not from subnet 10.2.4.0/24. So, one more pass through Step 4 is required, this time with mask /21, which gives you

   /21: subnet 10.2.0.0, broadcast 10.2.7.255

This new subnet includes the entire range, so this is the best summary route for those subnets.

Practice Choosing the Best Summary Routes

Table 21-1 lists four sets of subnets that need to be summarized as part of a summary route. Find the subnet number/mask combination that is the best summary route, at least by definition in the previous section.

Table 21-1   Practice Problems: Finding the Best Summary Route

Problem 1	Problem 2	Problem 3	Problem 4
10.1.50.0/23	172.16.112.0/24	192.168.1.160/28	172.16.125.0/24
10.1.48.0/23	172.16.114.0/25	192.168.1.152/30	172.16.126.0/24
10.1.46.0/23	172.16.116.0/23	192.168.1.192/29	172.16.127.0/24
10.1.52.0/23	172.16.111.0/24	192.168.1.128/28	172.16.128.0/24

The answers are shown in the section "Answers to Earlier Practice Problems," later in this chapter.

21

Review Activities

Chapter Summary

- Route summarization tools enable engineers to advertise one route that replaces several smaller routes, with the new route matching the same range of addresses. Doing so alleviates some of the waste: wasted effort, bandwidth, RAM, and CPU.

- Route summarization has many benefits. It reduces the size of routing tables but a router can still route packets to all the destinations in the network. The shorter table means that routing performance can be improved and memory can be saved inside each router. Summarization also improves convergence time for routing protocols because the routing protocol has much less work to do.

- Manual route summarization causes a router to cease advertising some routes, instead advertising a route that contains a superset of all the addresses. To do so, the router that creates the summary must be configured to know the subnet number and mask to advertise in a new summary route.

- The best summary route can be defined as follows:

  The summary route with the smallest range of addresses that includes all the addresses in all the subnets you want to summarize with that one summary route.

- Here are the steps for manually setting up a summary route:

  Step 1.   List all to-be-summarized (subordinate) subnet numbers in decimal, in order, lowest to highest, along with their matching subnet broadcast addresses.

  Step 2.   Note the low and high end of the range of addresses for all combined subnets by noting the numerically lowest subnet ID and numerically highest subnet broadcast address.

  Step 3.   Pick a starting point prefix length /P for Step 4, as follows: Pick the shortest prefix length mask of all the subordinate subnets, and then subtract 1.

  Step 4.   Calculate a new potential summary subnet/mask, with matching broadcast address, based on the lowest subordinate subnet ID from the original list, and the current prefix length.

  If the calculated range of addresses includes the entire range from Step 2, you have found the best summary route.

  If not, subtract 1 from the prefix length used in the most recent calculation, and repeat Step 4.

Review Questions

Answer these review questions. You can find the answers at the bottom of the last page of the chapter. For thorough explanations, see DVD Appendix C, "Answers to Review Questions."

1.   Which of the following summarized subnets is the smallest (smallest range of address-es) summary route that includes subnets 10.3.95.0, 10.3.96.0, and 10.3.97.0, mask 255.255.255.0?

   A.   10.0.0.0 255.0.0.0

   B.   10.3.0.0 255.255.0.0

   C.   10.3.64.0 255.255.192.0

   D.   10.3.64.0 255.255.224.0

2. Which of the following summarized subnets are not valid summaries that include subnets 10.1.55.0, 10.1.56.0, and 10.1.57.0, mask 255.255.255.0? (Choose two answers.)

   A. 10.0.0.0 255.0.0.0

   B. 10.1.0.0 255.255.0.0

   C. 10.1.55.0 255.255.255.0

   D. 10.1.48.0 255.255.248.0

   E. 10.1.32.0 255.255.224.0

3. Which of the following would be considered the best subnet/mask to add for a new summary route that summarizes routes for subnets 10.1.12.0/24, 10.1.14.0/24, and 10.1.15.0/24?

   A. 10.1.0.0/20

   B. 10.1.8.0/21

   C. 10.1.12.0/21

   D. 10.1.12.0/22

4. Which of the following would be considered the best subnet/mask to add for a new summary route that summarizes routes for subnets 192.168.1.64/28, 192.168.1.80/28, and 192.168.1.96/28?

   A. 192.168.1.0/25

   B. 192.168.1.64/26

   C. 192.168.1.32/26

   D. 192.168.1.64/27

Review All the Key Topics

Review the most important topics from this chapter, noted with the Key Topic icon. Table 21-2 lists these key topics and where each is discussed.

Table 21-2   Key Topics for Chapter 21

Key Topic Element	Description	Page Number
Definition	Criteria for what makes a summary route the best summary route for a given set of subnets	512
List	Process for finding the best manual summary route	512

Appendix I Practice Problems

DVD Appendix I, "Practice for Chapter 21: Route Summarization," lists additional practice problems and answers.

Definition of Key Terms

After your first reading of the chapter, try to define these key terms, but do not be concerned about getting them all correct at that time. Chapter 30 directs you in how to use these terms for late-stage preparation for the exam.

classful routing protocol, classless routing protocol, overlapping subnets, variable-length subnet masks (VLSM), contiguous network, discontiguous network, summary route

Answers to Earlier Practice Problems

This section lists the answers to the practice problems listed in the earlier section "Practice Choosing the Best Summary Routes." This section shows the answers, along with a description of how to use the process in this book to solve the problems.

For each problem, the first table lists the results of the first two steps; the gray boxes show the low and high end of the range that the new summary route must enclose. The second table for each problem shows the results of each pass through Step 4, with the final (rightmost) pass showing the correct answer.

Problem 1

Table 21-3   Practice Problem 1: First Two Steps

Subnet IDs/Masks	Subnet Broadcasts
10.1.50.0/23	10.1.51.255
10.1.48.0/23	10.1.49.255
10.1.46.0/23	10.1.47.255
10.1.52.0/23	10.1.53.255

For Problem 1, at Step 3, all masks are /23, so the initial mask will be one smaller, or /22. Finding the correct answer requires four passes through calculating a new subnet ID and mask, with the final answer shown in Table 21-4.

Table 21-4   Practice Problem 1: Multiple Passes Through Step 4 (Correct Answers Highlighted)

All Passes Use 10.1.46.0	1st Pass: /22	2nd Pass: /21	3rd Pass: /20	4th Pass: /19
Subnet ID	10.1.44.0	10.1.40.0	10.1.32.0	10.1.32.0
Broadcast Address	10.1.47.255	10.1.47.255	10.1.47.255	10.1.63.255

Problem 2

Table 21-5   Practice Problem 2: First Two Steps

Subnet IDs/Masks	Subnet Broadcasts
172.16.112.0/24	172.16.112.255
172.16.114.0/25	172.16.114.127
172.16.116.0/23	172.16.117.255
172.16.111.0/24	172.16.111.255

For Problem 2, at Step 3, the shortest mask is /23, so the initial mask will be 1 smaller, or /22. Finding the correct answer requires four passes through calculating a new subnet ID and mask, with the final answer shown in Table 21-6.

Table 21-6   Practice Problem 2: Multiple Passes Through Step 4 (Correct Answers Highlighted)

All Passes Use 172.16.111.0	1st Pass: /22	2nd Pass: /21	3rd Pass: /20	4th Pass: /19
Subnet ID	172.16.108.0	172.16.104.0	172.16.96.0	172.16.96.0
Broadcast Address	172.16.111.255	172.16.111.255	172.16.111.255	172.16.127.255

Problem 3

Table 21-7   Practice Problem 3: First Two Steps

Subnet IDs/Masks	Subnet Broadcasts
192.168.1.160/28	192.168.1.175
192.168.1.152/30	192.168.1.155
192.168.1.192/29	192.168.1.199
192.168.1.128/28	192.168.1.143

For Problem 3, at Step 3, the shortest mask is /28, so the initial mask will be 1 smaller, or /27. Finding the correct answer requires three passes through calculating a new subnet ID and mask, with the final answer shown in Table 21-8.

Table 21-8   Practice Problem 3: Multiple Passes Through Step 4 (Correct Answers Highlighted)

All Passes Use 192.168.1.128	1st Pass: /27	2nd Pass: /26	3rd Pass: /25
Subnet ID	192.168.1.128	192.168.1.128	192.168.1.128
Broadcast Address	192.168.1.159	192.168.1.191	192.168.1.255

Problem 4

Table 21-9   Practice Problem 4: First Two Steps

Subnet IDs/Masks	Subnet Broadcasts
172.16.125.0/24	172.16.125.255
172.16.126.0/24	172.16.126.255
172.16.127.0/24	172.16.127.255
172.16.128.0/24	172.16.128.255

For Problem 4, at Step 3, the shortest mask is /24, so the initial mask will be 1 smaller, or /23.

Table 21-10   Practice Problem 4: Multiple Passes Through Step 4

All Passes Use 172.16.125.0	1st Pass: /23	2nd Pass: /22	3rd Pass: /21	4th Pass: /20
Subnet ID	172.16.124.0	172.16.124.0	172.16.120.0	172.16.112.0
Broadcast Address	172.16.125.255	172.16.127.255	172.16.127.255	172.16.127.255

Table 21-10 still does not show the correct answer. If you keep going, it will take you all the way to /16 before you find the best summary: 172.16.0.0/16.

Answers to Review Questions:

1 C **2** C and D **3** D **4** B

Part V Review

Keep track of your part review progress with the checklist in Table P5-1. Details on each task follow the table.

Table P5-1   Part V Part Review Checklist

Activity	First Date Completed	Second Date Completed
Repeat all Chapter Review Questions		
Answer Part Review Questions		
Review Key Topics		
Create Process Mind Map		

Repeat All Chapter Review Questions

For this task, answer the chapter review questions again for the chapters in this part of the book, using the PCPT software. Refer to the Introduction to this book, heading "How to View Only Chapter Review Questions by Part," for help with how to make the PCPT software show you chapter review questions for this part only.

Answer Part Review Questions

For this task, answer the Part Review questions for this part of the book, using the PCPT software. Refer to the Introduction to this book, heading "How to View Only Part Review Questions by Part," for help with how to make the PCPT software show you Part Review questions for this part only.

Review Key Topics

Browse back through the chapters, and look for the Key Topic icons. If you do not remember some details, take the time to reread those topics.

Create Process Mind Map

This book part explains several types of problems that can be solved by following a process outlined in the chapter. The next mind map exercise helps to review the big ideas of what each type of problem does. This review does not focus on the details of how to find the answer to any one problem, leaving that for all the other practice suggestions included near the end of Chapters 19, 20, and 21.

Those chapters discussed the following types of problems that can be solved with some arithmetic:

- **Choosing Subnet Masks:** Based on design requirements, choose one mask to use throughout a classful IP network.

- **Finding All Subnet IDs:** Calculate all subnet IDs of a network.

- **Finding VLSM Overlaps:** Discovering mistakes in a design in which two or more subnets' address ranges overlap.

- **Adding New Subnets to an Existing VLSM Design:** Discovering an open slot in the existing subnet design into which a new VLSM subnet can be added.

- **Finding the Best Summary Route:** Based on a list of subnets/masks, find the summary route that would summarize those routes but with the least number of extra addresses within the summary.

Create a mind map with a branch for each topic in the list. For each branch, begin with the core concept and branch into three subtopics, as shown in this list and in Figure P5-1:

- **Given:** The information you have and the assumptions you make to start the problem.
- **Process:** The information or terms used during the process. Do not write the specific steps of the process; the goal here is just to make memory connections so that you know it is this process, and not some other process.
- **Result:** The facts you determine by doing the problem.

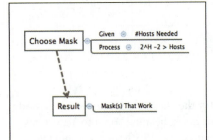

Figure P5-1 *Sample Mind Map for Part V Mind Map*

NOTE For more information on mind mapping, refer to the Introduction, in the section "About Mind Maps."

If you do choose to use mind map software, rather than paper, you might want to remember where you stored your mind map files. Table P5-2 lists the mind maps for this part review and a place to record those filenames.

Table P5-2 Configuration Mind Maps for Part V Review

Map	Description	Where You Saved It
1	Mind Map: Process Reminders	

Appendix O, "Mind Map Solutions," lists a sample mind map answer, but as usual, your mind map can and will look different.

So far, this book has shown the basics for building IPv4 networks using routers, switches, Ethernet LANs, and serial links. Part VI completes this book's topics on IPv4 networks by looking at a couple of services that help secure enterprise networks as well as create useful addressing options when connecting to the Internet.

Chapters 22 and 23 discuss the basics and more advanced features of IPv4 access control lists (ACL). ACLs are IPv4 packet filters that can be programmed to look at IPv4 packet headers, make choices, and either allow a packet through or discard the packet. Along the way, Chapter 23 also discusses some other network security topics in addition to ACLs. Chapter 24, the last chapter in this part, discusses Network Address Translation (NAT). NAT helps solve a big problem with IPv4 addressing in the Internet, and is used by almost every enterprise and home user of the Internet.

Part VI

IPv4 Services

Chapter 22

Basic IPv4 Access Control Lists

Most every other topic in the scope of CCENT focuses on achieving a core goal of any TCP/IP network: delivering IPv4 packets from the source host to the destination host. This chapter, along with the next chapter, focuses instead on preventing a subset of those packets from being allowed to reach their destinations, by using IPv4 access control lists (ACL).

IPv4 ACLs have many uses, but the CCENT exam focuses on their most commonly known use: as packet filters. You want hosts in one subnet to be able to communicate throughout your corporate network, but maybe there is a pocket of servers with sensitive data that must be protected. Maybe government privacy rules require you to further secure and protect access, not just with usernames and login, but even to protect the ability to deliver a packet to the protected host or server. IP ACLs provide a useful solution to achieve those goals.

This chapter discusses the basics of IPv4 ACLs, and in particular, one type of IP ACL: standard numbered IP ACLs. Chapter 23, "Advanced IPv4 ACLs and Device Security," completes the discussion by describing other types of IP ACLs.

> **NOTE** While IPv6 ACLs exist as well, they are not included in this book or the *Cisco CCNA Routing and Switching ICND2 200-101 Official Cert Guide*. All other references to IP ACLs in this chapter refer specifically to IPv4 ACLs.

This chapter covers the following exam topics:

IP Services

Describe the types, features, and applications of ACLs

    Standard

    Numbered

    Log option

Configure and verify ACLs in a network environment

    Numbered

    Log option

Network Device Security

Configure and verify ACLs to filter network traffic

Troubleshooting

Troubleshoot and Resolve ACL issues

    Statistics

    Permitted networks

    Direction

    Interface

Foundation Topics

IPv4 Access Control List Basics

IPv4 access control lists (IP ACL) give network engineers a way to identify different types of packets. To do so, the ACL configuration lists values that the router can see in the IP, TCP, UDP, and other headers. For example, an ACL can match packets whose source IP address is 1.1.1.1, or packets whose destination IP address is some address in subnet 10.1.1.0/24, or packets with a destination port of TCP port 23 (Telnet).

IPv4 ACLs perform many functions in Cisco routers, with the most common use as a packet filter. Engineers can enable ACLs on a router so that the ACL sits in the forwarding path of packets as they pass through the router. After it is enabled, the router considers whether each IP packet will either be discarded or allowed to continue as if the ACL did not exist.

However, ACLs can be used for many other IOS features as well. As an example, ACLs can be used to match packets for applying quality of service (QoS) features. QoS allows a router to give some packets better service, and other packets worse service. For example, packets that hold digitized voice need to have very low delay, so ACLs can match voice packets, with QoS logic in turn forwarding voice packets more quickly than data packets.

This first section introduces IP ACLs as used for packet filtering, focusing on these aspects of ACLs: the locations and direction in which to enable ACLs, matching packets by examining headers, and taking action after a packet has been matched.

ACL Location and Direction

Cisco routers can apply ACL logic to packets at the point at which the IP packets enter an interface, or the point at which they exit an interface. In other words, the ACL becomes associated with an interface and for a direction of packet flow (either in or out). That is, the ACL can be applied inbound to the router, before the router makes its forwarding (routing) decision, or outbound, after the router makes its forwarding decision and has determined the exit interface to use.

The arrows in Figure 22-1 show the locations at which you could filter packets flowing left to right in the topology. For example, imagine that you wanted to allow packets sent by host A to server S1, but to discard packets sent by host B to server S1. Each arrowed line represents a location and direction at which a router could apply an ACL, filtering the packets sent by host B.

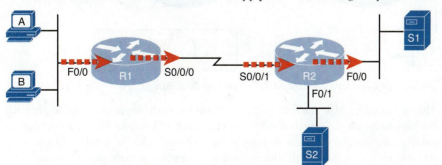

Figure 22-1 *Locations to Filter Packets from Hosts A and B Going Toward Server S1*

The four arrowed lines in the figure point out the location and direction for the router interfaces used to forward the packet from host B to server S1. In this particular example, those interfaces and direction are inbound on R1's F0/0 interface, outbound on R1's S0/0/0 interface, inbound on R2's S0/0/1 interface, and outbound on R2's F0/0 interface. If, for example, you enabled on ACL on R2's F0/1 interface, in either direction, that ACL could not possibly filter the packet sent from host B to server S1, because R2's F0/1 interface is not part of the route from B to S1.

In short, to filter a packet, you must enable an ACL on an interface that processes the packet, in the same direction the packet flows through that interface.

When enabled, the router then processes every inbound or outbound IP packet using that ACL. For example, if enabled on R1 for packets inbound on interface F0/0, R1 would compare every inbound IP packet on F0/0 to the ACL to decide that packet's fate: to continue unchanged, or to be discarded.

Matching Packets

When you think about the location and direction for an ACL, you must already be thinking about what packets you plan to filter (discard), and which ones you want to allow through. To tell the router those same ideas, you must configure the router with an IP ACL that matches packets. *Matching packets* refers to how to configure the ACL commands to look at each packet, listing how to identify which packets should be discarded, and which should be allowed through.

Each IP ACL consists of one or more configuration commands, with each command listing details about values to look for inside a packet's headers. Generally, an ACL command uses logic like "look for these values in the packet header, and if found, discard the packet." (The action could instead be to allow the packet, rather than discard.) Specifically, the ACL looks for header fields you should already know well, including the source and destination IP addresses, plus TCP and UDP port numbers.

For example, consider an example with Figure 22-2, in which you want to allow packets from host A to server S1, but to discard packets from host B going to that same server. The hosts all now have IP addresses, and the figure shows pseudocode for an ACL on R2. Figure 22-2 also shows the chosen location to enable the ACL: inbound on R2's S0/0/1 interface.

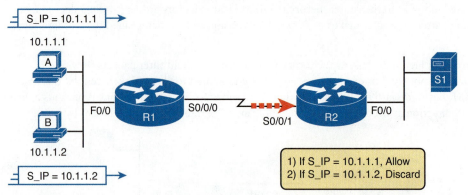

Figure 22-2 *Pseudocode to Demonstrate ACL Command-Matching Logic*

Figure 22-2 shows a two-line ACL in a rectangle at the bottom, with simple matching logic: both statements just look to match the source IP address in the packet. When enabled, R2 looks at every inbound IP packet on that interface and compares each packet to those two ACL commands. Packets sent by host A (source IP address 10.1.1.1) are allowed through, and those sourced by host B (source IP address 10.1.1.2) are discarded.

Taking Action When a Match Occurs

When using IP ACLs to filter packets, only one of two actions can be chosen. The configuration commands use keywords **deny** and **permit**, and they mean (respectively) to discard the packet or to allow it to keep going as if the ACL did not exist.

This book focuses on using ACLs to filter packets, but IOS uses ACLs for many more features. Those features typically use the same matching logic. However, in other cases, the **deny** or **permit** keywords imply some other action. For example, Chapter 24, "Network Address Translation," uses ACLs to match packets, but matching with a **permit** keyword tells the router to apply NAT functions that translate the IP addresses.

Types of IP ACLs

Cisco IOS has supported IP ACLs since the early days of Cisco routers. Beginning with the original standard numbered IP ACLs in the early days of IOS, which could enable the logic shown earlier around Figure 22-2, Cisco has added many ACL features, including:

- Standard Numbered ACLs (1–99)
- Extended Numbered ACLs (100–199)
- Additional ACL Numbers (1300–1999 standard, 2000–2699 extended)
- Named ACLs
- Improved Editing with Sequence Numbers

This chapter focuses solely on standard numbered IP ACLs, and Chapter 23 discusses the other three primary categories of IP ACLs. Briefly, IP ACLs will be either numbered or named in that the configuration identifies the ACL either using a number or a name. ACLs will also be either standard or extended, with extended ACLs having much more robust abilities in matching packets. Figure 22-3 summarizes the big ideas related to categories of IP ACLs.

Key Topic

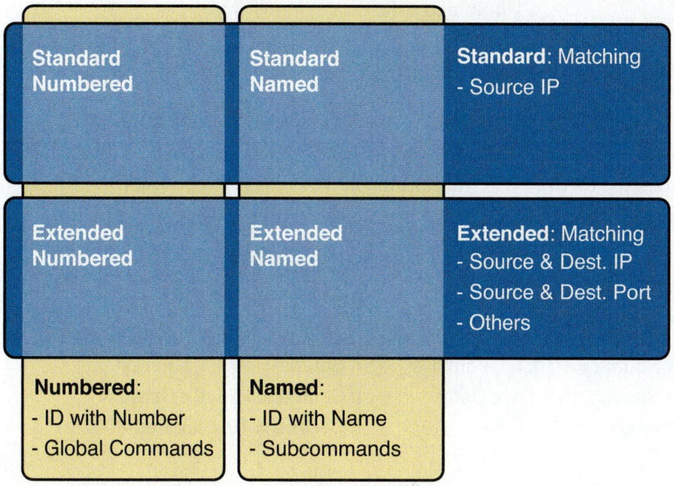

Standard Numbered	Standard Named	**Standard**: Matching - Source IP
Extended Numbered	Extended Named	**Extended**: Matching - Source & Dest. IP - Source & Dest. Port - Others
Numbered: - ID with Number - Global Commands	**Named**: - ID with Name - Subcommands	

Figure 22-3 *Comparisons of IP ACL Types*

Standard Numbered IPv4 ACLs

The title of this section serves as a great introduction, if you can decode what Cisco means by each specific word. This section is about a type of Cisco filter (ACL) that matches only the source IP address of the packet (*standard*), is configured to identify the ACL using numbers rather than names (*numbered*), and it looks at IPv4 packets.

This section examines the particulars of standard numbered IP ACLs. First, it examines the idea that one ACL is a list, and what logic that list uses. Following that, the text closely looks at how to match the source IP address field in the packet header, including the syntax of the commands. This section ends with a complete look at the configuration and verification commands to implement standard ACLs.

22

List Logic with IP ACLs

A single ACL is both a single entity and, at the same time, a list of one or more configuration commands. As a single entity, the configuration enables the entire ACL on an interface, in a specific direction, as shown earlier around Figure 22-1. As a list of commands, each command has different matching logic that the router must apply to each packet when filtering using that ACL.

When doing ACL processing, the router processes the packet, compared to the ACL, as follows:

ACLs use first-match logic. Once a packet matches one line in the ACL, the router takes the action listed in that line of the ACL, and stops looking further in the ACL.

To see exactly what that means, consider the example built around Figure 22-4. The figure shows an example ACL 1 with three lines of pseudocode. This example applies ACL 1 on R2's S0/0/1 interface, inbound (the same location as in earlier Figure 22-2).

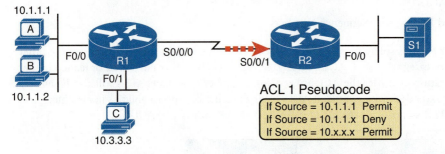

Figure 22-4   *Backdrop for Discussion of List Process with IP ACLs*

Consider the first-match ACL logic for a packet sent by host A to server S1. The source IP address will be 10.1.1.1, and it will be routed so that it enters R2's S0/0/1 interface, driving R2's ACL 1 logic. R2 compares this packet to the ACL, matching the first item in the list with a permit action. So this packet should be allowed through, as shown in Figure 22-5, on the left.

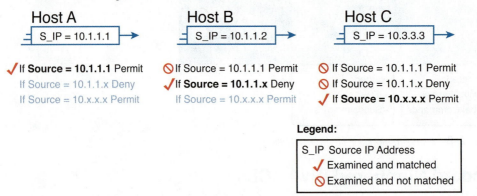

Figure 22-5   *ACL Items Compared for Packets from Hosts A, B, and C in Figure 22-4*

Next, consider a packet sent by host B, source IP address 10.1.1.2. When the packet enters R2's S0/0/1 interface, R2 compares the packet to ACL 1's first statement, and does not make a match (10.1.1.1 is not equal to 10.1.1.2). R2 then moves to the second statement, which requires some clarification. The ACL pseudocode, back in Figure 22-4, shows 10.1.1.x, which is meant to be shorthand that any value can exist in the last octet. Comparing only the first three octets, R2 decides that this latest packet does have a source IP address that begins with first three octets 10.1.1, so R2 considers that to be a match on the second statement. R2 takes the listed action (deny), discarding the packet. R2 also stops ACL processing on the packet, ignoring the third line in the ACL.

Finally, consider a packet sent by host C, again to server S1. The packet has source IP address 10.3.3.3, so when it enters R2's S0/0/1 interface, and drives ACL processing on R2, R2 looks at the first command in ACL 1. R2 does not match the first ACL command (10.1.1.1 in the command is not equal to the packet's 10.3.3.3). R2 looks at the second command, compares the first three octets (10.1.1) to the packet source IP address (10.3.3), still no match. R2 then looks at the third command. In this case, the wildcard means ignore the last three octets, and just compare the first octet (10), so the packet matches. R2 then takes the listed action (permit), allowing the packet to keep going.

This sequence of processing an ACL as a list happens for any type of IOS ACL: IP, other protocols, standard or extended, named or numbered.

Finally, if a packet does not match any of the items in the ACL, the packet is discarded. The reason is that every IP ACL has a *deny all* statement implied at the end of the ACL. It does not exist in the configuration, but if a router keeps searching the list, and no match is made by the end of the list, IOS considers the packet to have matched an entry that has a **deny** action.

Matching Logic and Command Syntax

Standard numbered IP ACLs use the following global command:

```
access-list {1-99 | 1300-1999} {permit | deny} matching-parameters
```

Each standard numbered ACL has one or more **access-list** commands with the same number, any number from the ranges shown in the preceding line of syntax. (One number is no better than the other.)

Besides the ACL number, each **access-list** command also lists the action (**permit** or **deny**), plus the matching logic. The rest of this section examines how to configure the matching parameters, which for standard ACLs, means that you can only match the source IP address, or portions of the source IP address using something called an ACL wildcard mask.

Matching the Exact IP Address

To match a specific source IP address, the entire IP address, all you have to do is type that IP address at the end of the command. For example, the previous example uses pseudocode for "permit if source = 10.1.1.1." The following command configures that logic with correct syntax using ACL number 1:

```
access-list 1 permit 10.1.1.1
```

Matching the exact full IP address is that simple.

In earlier IOS versions, the syntax included a **host** keyword. Instead of simply typing the full IP address, you first typed the **host** keyword, and then the IP address. Note that in later IOS versions, if you use the **host** keyword, IOS accepts the command, but then removes the keyword.

```
access-list 1 permit host 10.1.1.1
```

Matching a Subset of the Address with Wildcards

Often, the business goals you want to implement with an ACL does not match a single particular IP address, but rather a range of IP addresses. Maybe you want to match all IP addresses in a subnet. Maybe you want to match all IP addresses in a range of subnets, similar to a grouping you might want to collect into a route summary, like you did in Chapter 21, "Route Summarization." Regardless, you want to check for more than one IP address in a range of addresses.

IOS allows standard ACLs to match a range of addresses using a tool called a *wildcard mask*. Note that this is not a subnet mask. The wildcard mask (which this book abbreviates as *WC mask*) gives the engineer a way to tell IOS to ignore parts of the address when making comparisons, essentially treating those parts as wildcards, as if they already matched.

You can think about WC masks in decimal and in binary, and both have their uses. To begin, think about WC masks in decimal, using these rules:

Key Topic

Decimal 0: The router must compare this octet as normal.

Decimal 255: The router ignores this octet, considering it to already match.

Keeping these two rules in mind, consider Figure 22-6, which demonstrates this logic using three different but popular WC masks: one that tells the router to ignore the last octet, one that tells the router to ignore the last two octets, and one that tells the router to ignore the last three octets.

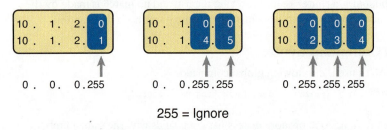

255 = Ignore

Figure 22-6 *Logic for WC Masks 0.0.0.255, 0.0.255.255, and 0.255.255.255*

All three examples in the boxes of Figure 22-6 show two numbers that are clearly different. The WC mask causes IOS to compare only some of the octets, while ignoring other octets. All three examples result in a match, because each wildcard mask tells IOS to ignore some octets. The example on the left shows WC mask 0.0.0.255, which tells the router to treat the last octet as a wildcard, essentially ignoring that octet for the comparison. Similarly, the middle example shows WC mask 0.0.255.255, which tells the router to ignore the two octets on the right. The rightmost case shows WC mask 0.255.255.255, telling the router to ignore the last three octets when comparing values.

To see the WC mask in action, think back to the earlier example related to Figure 22-4 and Figure 22-5. The pseudocode ACL in those two figures used logic that can be created using a WC mask. As a reminder, the logic in the pseudocode ACL in those two figures included the following:

- **Line 1:** Match and permit all packets with a source address of exactly 10.1.1.1.
- **Line 2:** Match and deny all packets with source addresses with first three octets 10.1.1.
- **Line 3:** Match and permit all addresses with first single octet 10.

Figure 22-7 shows the updated version of Figure 22-4, but with the completed, correct syntax, including the WC masks. In particular, note the use of WC mask 0.0.0.255 in the second command, telling R2 to ignore the last octet of the number 10.1.1.0, and the WC mask 0.255.255.255 in the third command, telling R2 to ignore the last three octets in the value 10.0.0.0.

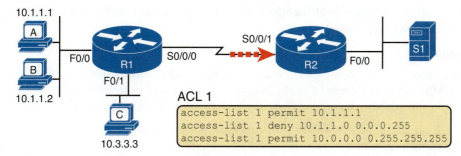

Figure 22-7 *Syntactically Correct ACL Replaces Pseudocode from Figure 22-4*

Finally, note that when using a WC mask, the **access-list** command's loosely defined *source* parameter should be a 0 in any octets where the WC mask is a 255. IOS will specify a source address to be 0 for the parts that will be ignored, even if nonzero values were configured.

Binary Wildcard Masks

Wildcard masks, as dotted-decimal number (DDN) values, actually represent a 32-bit binary number. As a 32-bit number, the WC mask actually directs the router's logic bit by bit. In short, a WC mask bit of 0 means the comparison should be done as normal, but a binary 1 means that the bit is a wildcard, and can be ignored when comparing the numbers.

Thankfully, for the purposes of CCENT and CCNA study and, frankly, for most real-world applications, you can ignore the binary WC mask. Why? Well, we generally want to match a range of addresses that can be easily identified by a subnet number and mask, whether it be a real subnet, or a summary route that groups subnets together. (See Chapter 21 for more on summary routes.) If you can describe the range of addresses with a subnet number and mask, you can find the numbers to use in your ACL with some simple math, as discussed next.

NOTE If you really want to know the binary mask logic, take the two DDN numbers the ACL will compare (one from the **access-list** command, and the other from the packet header) and convert both to binary. Then, also convert the WC mask to binary. Compare the first two binary numbers bit by bit, but also ignore any bits for which the WC mask happens to list a binary 1, because that tells you to ignore the bit. If all the bits you checked are equal, it's a match!

Finding the Right Wildcard Mask to Match a Subnet

In many cases, an ACL needs to match all hosts in a particular subnet. To match a subnet with an ACL, you can use the following shortcut:

- Use the subnet number as the source value in the **access-list** command.
- Use a wildcard mask found by subtracting the subnet mask from 255.255.255.255.

For example, for subnet 172.16.8.0 255.255.252.0, use the subnet number (172.16.8.0) as the address parameter, and then do the following math to find the wildcard mask:

```
  255.255.255.255
- 255.255.252.0
  0.  0.  3.255
```

Continuing this example, a completed command for this same subnet would be as follows:

```
access-list 1 permit 172.16.8.0 0.0.3.255
```

The upcoming section, "Practice Applying Standard IP ACLs," gives you a chance to practice matching subnets when configuring ACLs.

Matching Any/All Addresses

In some cases, you will want one ACL command to match any and all packets that reach that point in the ACL. First, you have to know the (simple) way to match all packets using the **any** keyword. More importantly, you need to think about when to match any and all packets.

First, to match any and all packets with an ACL command, just use the **any** keyword for the address. For example, to permit all packets:

```
access-list 1 permit any
```

So, when and where should you use such a command? Remember, all Cisco IP ACLs end with an implicit deny any concept at the end of each ACL. That is, if a router compares a packet to the ACL, and the packet matches none of the configured statements, the router discards the packet. Want to override that default behavior? Configure a **permit any** at the end of the ACL.

You might also want to explicitly configure a command to deny all traffic (for example, **access-list 1 deny any**) at the end of an ACL. Why, when the same logic already sits at the end of the ACL anyway? Well, the ACL **show** commands list counters for the number of packets matched by each command in the ACL, but there is no counter for that implicit *deny any* concept at the end of the ACL. So, if you want to see counters for how many packets are matched by the *deny any* logic at the end of the ACL, configure an explicit **deny any**.

Implementing Standard IP ACLs

This chapter has already introduced all the configuration steps in bits and pieces. This section summarizes those pieces as a configuration process. The process also refers to the **access-list** command, whose generic syntax is repeated here for reference:

```
access-list access-list-number {deny | permit} source [source-wildcard]
```

Key Topic

Step 1.   Plan the location (router and interface) and direction (in or out) on that interface:

   A. Standard ACLs should be placed near to the destination of the packets so that they do not unintentionally discard packets that should not be discarded.

   B. Because standard ACLs can only match a packet's source IP address, identify the source IP addresses of packets as they go in the direction that the ACL is examining.

Step 2.   Configure one or more **access-list** global configuration commands to create the ACL, keeping the following in mind:

   A. The list is searched sequentially, using first-match logic.

   B. The default action, if a packet does not match any of the **access-list** commands, is to **deny** (discard) the packet.

Step 3.   Enable the ACL on the chosen router interface, in the correct direction, using the **ip access-group** *number* {**in** | **out**} interface subcommand.

The rest of this section shows a couple of examples.

Standard Numbered ACL Example 1

The first example shows the configuration for the same requirements demonstrated with Figure 22-4 and Figure 22-5. Restated, the requirements for this ACL are as follows:

1. Enable the ACL inbound on R2's S0/0/1 interface.

2. Permit packets coming from host A.

3. Deny packets coming from other hosts in host A's subnet.

4. Permit packets coming from any other address in Class A network 10.0.0.0.

5. The original example made no comment about what to do by default, so simply deny all other traffic.

Example 22-1 shows a completed correct configuration, starting with the configuration process, followed by output from the **show running-config** command.

Example 22-1 *Standard Numbered ACL Example 1 Configuration*

```
R2# configure terminal
Enter configuration commands, one per line.  End with CNTL/Z.
R2(config)# access-list 1 permit 10.1.1.1
R2(config)# access-list 1 deny 10.1.1.0 0.0.0.255
R2(config)# access-list 1 permit 10.0.0.0 0.255.255.255
R2(config)# interface S0/0/1
R2(config-if)# ip access-group 1 in
R2(config-if)# ^Z
R2# show running-config
! Lines omitted for brevity

access-list 1 permit 10.1.1.1
access-list 1 deny 10.1.1.0 0.0.0.255
access-list 1 permit 10.0.0.0 0.255.255.255
```

First, pay close attention to the configuration process at the top of the example. Note that the **access-list** command does not change the command prompt from the global configuration mode prompt, because the **access-list** command is a global configuration command. Then, compare that to the output of the **show running-config** command: the details are identical compared to the commands that were added in configuration mode. Finally, make sure to note the **ip access-group 1 in** command, under R2's S0/0/1 interface, which enables the ACL logic (both location and direction).

Example 22-2 lists some output from Router R2 that shows information about this ACL. The **show ip access-lists** command lists details about IPv4 ACLs only, while the **show access-lists** command lists details about IPv4 ACLs plus any other types of ACLs that are currently configured, for example, IPv6 ACLs.

Example 22-2 *ACL show Commands on R2*

```
R2# show ip access-lists
Standard IP access list 1
    10 permit 10.1.1.1 (107 matches)
    20 deny   10.1.1.0, wildcard bits 0.0.0.255 (4 matches)
    30 permit 10.0.0.0, wildcard bits 0.255.255.255 (10 matches)
R2# show access-lists
Standard IP access list 1
    10 permit 10.1.1.1 (107 matches)
```

22

```
       20 deny    10.1.1.0, wildcard bits 0.0.0.255 (4 matches)
       30 permit 10.0.0.0, wildcard bits 0.255.255.255 (10 matches)
R2# show ip interface s0/0/1
Serial0/0/1 is up, line protocol is up
  Internet address is 10.1.2.2/24
  Broadcast address is 255.255.255.255
  Address determined by setup command
  MTU is 1500 bytes
  Helper address is not set
  Directed broadcast forwarding is disabled
  Multicast reserved groups joined: 224.0.0.9
  Outgoing access list is not set
  Inbound   access list is 1
! Lines omitted for brevity
```

The output of these commands shows two items of note. The first line of output in this case notes the type (standard), and the number. If more than one ACL existed, you would see multiple stanzas of output, one per ACL, each with a heading line like this one. Next, these commands list packet counts for the number of packets that the router has matched with each command. For example, 107 packets so far have matched the first line in the ACL.

Finally, the end of the example lists the **show ip interface** command output. This command lists, among many other items, the number or name of any IP ACL enabled on the interface per the **ip access-group** interface subcommand.

Standard Numbered ACL Example 2

For the second example, use Figure 22-8, and imagine your boss gave you some requirements hurriedly in the hall. At first, he tells you he wants to filter packets going from the servers on the right toward the clients on the left. Then, he says he wants you to allow access for hosts A, B, and other hosts in their same subnet to server S1, but deny access to that server to the hosts in host C's subnet. Then, he tells you that, additionally, hosts in host A's subnet should be denied access to server S2, but hosts in host C's subnet should be allowed access to server S2. All by filtering packets going right to left only, and then he tells you: put the ACL inbound on R2's F0/0 interface.

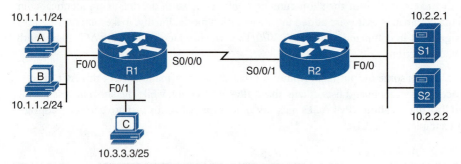

Figure 22-8 *Standard Numbered ACL Example 2*

If you cull through all the boss's comments, the requirements might reduce to the following:

1. Enable the ACL inbound on R2's F0/0 interface.

2. Permit packets from server S1 going to hosts in A's subnet.

3. Deny packets from server S1 going to hosts in C's subnet.

4. Permit packets from server S2 going to hosts in C's subnet.

5. Deny packets from server S2 going to hosts in A's subnet.

6. (There was no comment about what to do by default; use the implied **deny all** default.)

As it turns out, you cannot do everything your boss asked with a standard ACL. For example, consider the obvious command for requirement number 2: **access-list 2 permit 10.2.2.1**. That permits all traffic whose source IP is 10.2.2.1 (server S1). The very next requirement asks you to filter (deny) packets sourced from that same IP address! Even if you added another command that checked for source IP address 10.2.2.1, the router would never get to it, because routers use first-match logic when searching the ACL. You cannot check both the destination and source IP address, because standard ACLs cannot check the destination IP address.

To solve this problem, you should get a new boss! No, seriously, you have to rethink the problem and change the rules. In real life, you would probably use an extended ACL instead, as discussed in Chapter 23, which lets you check both the source and destination IP address.

For the sake of practicing another standard ACLs, imagine your boss lets you change the requirements. First, you will use two outbound ACLs, both on Router R1. Each ACL will permit traffic from a single server to be forwarded onto that connected LAN, with the following modified requirements:

1. Using an outbound ACL on R1's F0/0 interface, permit packets from server S1, and deny all other packets.

2. Using an outbound ACL on R1's F0/1 interface, permit packets from server S2, and deny all other packets.

Example 22-3 shows the configuration that completes these requirements.

Example 22-3 *Alternative Configuration in Router R1*

```
access-list 2 remark This ACL permits server S1 traffic to host A's subnet
access-list 2 permit 10.2.2.1
!
access-list 3 remark This ACL permits server S2 traffic to host C's subnet
access-list 3 permit 10.2.2.2
!
interface F0/0
 ip access-group 2 out
!
interface F0/1
 ip access-group 3 out
```

As highlighted in the example, the solution with ACL number 2 permits all traffic from server S1, with that logic enabled for packets exiting R1's F0/0 interface. All other traffic will be discarded because of the implied deny all at the end of the ACL. Additionally, ACL 3 permits traffic from server S2, which is then permitted to exit R1's F0/1 interface. Also, note that the solution shows the use of the **access-list remark** parameter, which allows you to leave text documentation that stays with the ACL.

> **NOTE** When routers apply an ACL to filter packets in the outbound direction, as shown in Example 22-3, the router checks packets that it routes against the ACL. However, a router does not filter packets that the router itself creates with an outbound ACL. Examples of those packets include OSPF routing protocol messages, and packets sent by the **ping** and **traceroute** commands on that router.

22

Troubleshooting and Verification Tips

Troubleshooting IPv4 ACLs requires some attention to detail. In particular, you have to be ready to look at the address and wildcard mask and confidently predict the addresses matched by those two combined parameters. The upcoming practice problems a little later in this chapter can help prepare you for that part of the work. But a few other tips can help you verify and troubleshoot ACL problems on the exams as well.

First, you can tell if the router is matching packets or not with a couple of tools. Example 22-2 already showed that IOS keeps statistics about the packets matched by each line of an ACL. Additionally, if you add the **log** keyword to the end of an **access-list** command, IOS then issues log messages with occasional statistics about matches of that particular line of the ACL. Both the statistics and the log messages can be helpful in deciding which line in the ACL is being matched by a packet.

For example, Example 22-4 shows an updated version of ACL 2 from Example 22-3, this time with the **log** keyword added. The bottom of the example then shows a typical log message, this one showing the resulting match based on a packet with source IP address 10.2.2.1 (as matched with the ACL), to destination address 10.1.1.1.

Example 22-4 *Creating Log Messages for ACL Statistics*

```
R1# show running-config
! lines removed for brevity
access-list 2 remark This ACL permits server S1 traffic to host A's subnet
access-list 2 permit 10.2.2.1 log
!
interface F0/0
 ip access-group 2 out
R1#

Feb  4 18:30:24.082: %SEC-6-IPACCESSLOGNP: list 2 permitted 0 10.2.2.1 -> 10.1.1.1, 1
packet
```

Anytime you troubleshoot an ACL for the first time, before getting into the details of the matching logic, take the time to think about both the interface on which the ACL is enabled, and the direction of packet flow. Sometimes, the matching logic is perfect—but the ACL has been enabled on the wrong interface, or for the wrong direction, to match the packets as configured for the ACL.

For example, Figure 22-9 repeats the same ACL shown earlier in Figure 22-7. The first line of that ACL matches the specific host address 10.1.1.1. If that ACL exists on router R2, placing that ACL as an inbound ACL on R2's S0/0/1 interface can work, because packets sent by host 10.1.1.1—on the left side of the figure—can enter R2's S0/0/1 interface. However, if R2 enables ACL 1 on it F0/0 interface, for inbound packets, the ACL will never match a packet with source IP address 10.1.1.1, because packets sent by host 10.1.1.1 will never enter that interface. Packets sent by 10.1.1.1 will exit R2's F0/0 interface, but never enter it, just because of the network topology.

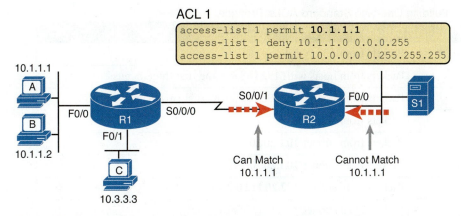

Figure 22-9 *Example of Checking the Interface and Direction for an ACL*

Practice Applying Standard IP ACLs

Some CCENT and CCNA topics, like subnetting, simply require more drills and practice than others. You can also benefit from doing practice drills with ACLs in part because ACLs require you to think of parameters to match ranges of numbers, and that of course requires some use of math, and some use of processes.

This section provides some practice problems and tips, from two perspectives. First, this section asks you to build one-line standard ACLs to match some packets. Second, this section asks you to interpret existing ACL commands to describe what packets the ACL will match. Both skills are useful for the exams.

Practice Building access-list Commands

In this section, practice getting comfortable with the syntax of the **access-list** command, particularly with choosing the correct matching logic. These skills will be helpful when reading about extended and named ACLs in the next chapter.

First, the following list summarizes some important tips to consider when choosing matching parameters to any **access-list** command:

- To match a specific address, just list the address.
- To match any and all addresses, use the **any** keyword.
- To match based only on the first one, two, or three octets of an address, use the 0.255.255.255, 0.0.255.255, and 0.0.0.255 WC masks, respectively. Also, make the source (address) parameter have 0s in the wildcard octets (those octets with 255 in the wildcard mask).
- To match a subnet, use the subnet ID as the source, and find the WC mask by subtracting the DDN subnet mask from 255.255.255.255.

Table 22-1 lists the criteria for several practice problems. Your job: Create a one-line standard ACL that matches the packets. The answers are listed in the section, "Answers to Earlier Practice Problems," later in this chapter.

Table 22-1 Building One-Line Standard ACLs: Practice

Problem	Criteria
1	Packets from 172.16.5.4
2	Packets from hosts with 192.168.6 as the first three octets
3	Packets from hosts with 192.168 as the first two octets
4	Packets from any host
5	Packets from subnet 10.1.200.0/21
6	Packets from subnet 10.1.200.0/27
7	Packets from subnet 172.20.112.0/23
8	Packets from subnet 172.20.112.0/26
9	Packets from subnet 192.168.9.64/28
10	Packets from subnet 192.168.9.64/30

Reverse Engineering from ACL to Address Range

Some exam questions might not ask that you pick the ACL statement that needs to be configured, instead asking that you interpret some existing **access-list** commands. To answer these types of questions, you need to determine the range of IP addresses matched by a particular address/wildcard mask combination in each ACL statement.

Under certain assumptions that are reasonable for CCENT and CCNA, calculating the range of addresses matched by an ACL can be relatively simple. The low end of the range is the address field, and you find the high end of the range by adding the address to the WC mask. That's it.

For example, with the command **access-list 1 permit 172.16.200.0 0.0.7.255**, the low end of the range is simply 172.16.200.0, taken directly from the command itself. Then, to find the high end of the range, just add this number to the WC mask, as follows:

$$
\begin{array}{r}
172.16.200.0 \\
+\ 0.\ 0.\quad 7.255 \\
\hline
172.16.207.255
\end{array}
$$

For this last bit of practice, look at the existing **access-list** commands in Table 22-2. In each case, make a notation about the exact IP address, or range of IP addresses, matched by the command.

Table 22-2 Finding IP Addresses/Ranges Matching by Existing ACLs

Problem	Commands for Which to Predict the Source Address Range
1	access-list 1 permit 10.7.6.5
2	access-list 2 permit 192.168.4.0 0.0.0.127
3	access-list 3 permit 192.168.6.0 0.0.0.31
4	access-list 4 permit 172.30.96.0 0.0.3.255
5	access-list 5 permit 172.30.96.0 0.0.0.63
6	access-list 6 permit 10.1.192.0 0.0.0.31
7	access-list 7 permit 10.1.192.0 0.0.1.255
8	access-list 8 permit 10.1.192.0 0.0.63.255

Interestingly, IOS lets the CLI user type an **access-list** command in configuration mode, and IOS will potentially change the address parameter before placing the command into the running config file. This process of just finding the range of addresses matched by the **access-list** command expects that the **access-list** command came from the router, so that any such changes were complete.

The change IOS can make with an **access-list** command is to convert to 0 any octet of an address for which the wildcard mask's octet is 255. For example, with a wildcard mask of 0.0.255.255, IOS ignores the last two octets. IOS expects the address field to end with two 0s. If not, IOS still accepts the **access-list** command, but IOS changes the last two octets of the address to 0s. Example 22-5 shows an example, where the configuration shows address 10.1.1.1, but wildcard mask 0.0.255.255.

Example 22-5 *IOS Changing the Address Field in an* **access-list** *Command*

```
R2# configure terminal
Enter configuration commands, one per line.  End with CNTL/Z.
R2(config)# access-list 21 permit 10.1.1.1 0.0.255.255
R2(config)# ^Z
R2#
R2# show ip access-lists
Standard IP access list 21
    10 permit 10.1.0.0, wildcard bits 0.0.255.255
```

The math to find the range of addresses relies on the fact that either the command is fully correct, or that IOS has already set these address octets to 0, as shown in the example.

NOTE The most useful WC masks, in binary, do not interleave 0s and 1s. This book assumes the use of only these types of WC masks. However, WC masks that interleave 0s and 1s are allowed, but these WC masks break the simple method of calculating the range of addresses. As you progress through to CCIE studies, be ready to dig deeper to learn how to determine what an ACL matches.

22

Review Activities

Chapter Summary

- IPv4 access control lists (IP ACL) give network engineers a way to identify different types of packets.

- IP ACLs perform many functions in Cisco routers, with the most common use as a packet filter.

- Cisco routers can apply ACL logic to packets at the point at which the IP packets enter an interface or the point at which they exit an interface. In other words, the ACL becomes associated with an interface and for a direction of packet flow (either in or out).

- Each IP ACL consists of one or more configuration commands, with each command listing details about values to look for inside a packet's headers. Generally, an ACL command uses logic like, "Look for these values in the packet header and, if found, discard the packet." (The action could instead be to allow the packet rather than discard it.) Specifically, the ACL looks for header fields you should already know well, including the source and destination IP addresses, plus TCP and UDP port numbers.

- When using IP ACLs to filter packets, only one of two actions can be chosen. The configuration commands use keywords **deny** and **permit**, and they mean (respectively) to discard the packet or to allow it to keep going as if the ACL did not exist.

- ACLs use first-match logic. When a packet matches one line in the ACL, the router takes the action listed in that line of the ACL and stops looking further in the ACL.

- Standard numbered IP ACLs use the following global command:

```
access-list {1-99 | 1300-1999} {permit | deny} source [source-wildcard]
```

Review Questions

Answer these review questions. You can find the answers at the bottom of the last page of the chapter. For thorough explanations, see DVD Appendix C, "Answers to Review Questions."

1. Barney is a host with IP address 10.1.1.1 in subnet 10.1.1.0/24. Which of the following are things that a standard IP ACL could be configured to do? (Choose two answers.)

   A. Match the exact source IP address.

   B. Match IP addresses 10.1.1.1 through 10.1.1.4 with one **access-list** command without matching other IP addresses.

   C. Match all IP addresses in Barney's subnet with one **access-list** command without matching other IP addresses.

   D. Match only the packet's destination IP address.

2. Which of the following answers list a valid number that can be used with standard numbered IP ACLs? (Choose two answers.)

   A. 1987

   B. 2187

   C. 187

   D. 87

3. Which of the following wildcard masks is most useful for matching all IP packets in subnet 10.1.128.0, mask 255.255.255.0?

    A. 0.0.0.0

    B. 0.0.0.31

    C. 0.0.0.240

    D. 0.0.0.255

    E. 0.0.15.0

    F. 0.0.248.255

4. Which of the following wildcard masks is most useful for matching all IP packets in subnet 10.1.128.0, mask 255.255.240.0?

    A. 0.0.0.0

    B. 0.0.0.31

    C. 0.0.0.240

    D. 0.0.0.255

    E. 0.0.15.255

    F. 0.0.248.255

5. ACL 1 has three statements, in the following order, with address and wildcard mask values as follows: 1.0.0.0 0.255.255.255, 1.1.0.0 0.0.255.255, and 1.1.1.0 0.0.0.255. If a router tried to match a packet sourced from IP address 1.1.1.1 using this ACL, which ACL statement does a router consider the packet to have matched?

    A. First

    B. Second

    C. Third

    D. Implied deny at the end of the ACL

6. Which of the following **access-list** commands matches all packets sent from hosts in subnet 172.16.5.0/25?

    A. access-list 1 permit 172.16.0.5 0.0.255.0

    B. access-list 1 permit 172.16.4.0 0.0.1.255

    C. access-list 1 permit 172.16.5.0

    D. access-list 1 permit 172.16.5.0 0.0.0.128

22

Review All the Key Topics

Review the most important topics from this chapter, noted with the Key Topic icon. Table 22-3 lists these key topics and where each is discussed.

Key Topic

Table 22-3   Key Topics for Chapter 22

Key Topic Element	Description	Page Number
Paragraph	Summary of the general rule of the location and direction for an ACL	530
Figure 22-3	Summary of four main categories of IPv4 ACLs in Cisco IOS	531
Paragraph	Summary of first-match logic used by all ACLs	532
List	Wildcard mask logic for decimal 0 and 255	534
List	Wildcard mask logic to match a subnet	535
List	Steps to plan and implement a standard IP ACL	536
List	Tips for creating matching logic for the source address field in the **access-list** command	541
Paragraph	How to calculate the range of numbers implied by an ACL's source and wildcard mask parameters	542

Definitions of Key Terms

After your first reading of the chapter, try to define these key terms, but do not be concerned about getting them all correct at that time. Chapter 30 directs you in how to use these terms for late-stage preparation for the exam.

standard access list, wildcard mask

Appendix J Practice Problems

DVD Appendix J, "Practice for Chapter 22: Basic IPv4 Access Control Lists," lists additional practice problems and answers.

Command Reference to Check Your Memory

Although you should not necessarily memorize the information in the tables in this section, this section includes a reference for the configuration and EXEC commands covered in this chapter. Practically speaking, you should memorize the commands as a side effect of reading this chapter and doing all the activities in this "Exam Preparation" section. To see how well you have memorized the commands as a side effect of your other studies, cover the left side of the table, read the descriptions on the right side, and see if you remember the command.

Table 22-4 Chapter 22 Configuration Command Reference

Command	Description
access-list *access-list-number* {**deny**	**permit**} *source* [*source-wildcard*] [**log**]	Global command for standard numbered access lists. Use a number between 1 and 99 or 1300 and 1999, inclusive.
access-list *access-list-number* **remark** *text*	Defines a remark that helps you remember what the ACL is supposed to do.
ip access-group *number* {**in**	**out**}	Interface subcommand to enable access lists.

Table 22-5 Chapter 22 EXEC Command Reference

Command	Description
show ip interface [*type number*]	Includes a reference to the access lists enabled on the interface.
show access-lists [*access-list-number*	*access-list-name*]	Shows details of configured access lists for all protocols.
show ip access-list [*access-list-number*	*access-list-name*]	Shows IP access lists.

Answers to Earlier Practice Problems

Table 22-6 lists the answers to the problems listed earlier in Table 22-1.

Table 22-6 Building One-Line Standard ACLs: Answers

Problem	Answers
1	**access-list 1 permit 172.16.5.4**
2	**access-list 2 permit 192.168.6.0 0.0.0.255**
3	**access-list 3 permit 192.168.0.0 0.0.255.255**
4	**access-list 4 permit any**
5	**access-list 5 permit 10.1.200.0 0.0.7.255**
6	**access-list 6 permit 10.1.200.0 0.0.0.31**
7	**access-list 7 permit 172.20.112.0 0.0.1.255**
8	**access-list 8 permit 172.20.112.0 0.0.0.63**
9	**access-list 9 permit 192.168.9.64 0.0.0.15**
10	**access-list 10 permit 192.168.9.64 0.0.0.3**

22

Table 22-7 lists the answers to the problems listed earlier in Table 22-2.

Table 22-7   Address Ranges for Problems in Table 22-2: Answers

Problem	Address Range
1	One address: 10.7.6.5
2	192.168.4.0–192.168.4.127
3	192.168.6.0–192.168.6.31
4	172.30.96.0–172.30.99.255
5	172.30.96.0–172.30.96.63
6	10.1.192.0–10.1.192.31
7	10.1.192.0–10.1.193.255
8	10.1.192.0–10.1.255.255

Answers to Review Questions:

1 A and C **2** A and D **3** D **4** E **5** A **6** B

Chapter 23

Advanced IPv4 ACLs and Device Security

Cisco routers use IPv4 access control lists (ACL) for many different applications: to match packets to make filtering decisions, to match packets for Network Address Translation (NAT), to match packets to make quality of service (QoS) decisions, and for several other reasons.

Most IP ACLs are either standard or extended ACLs, with standard ACLs matching only the source IP address, and extended matching a variety of packet header fields. At the same time, IP ACLs are either numbered or named. Figure 23-1 shows the categories, and the main features of each, as introduced in the previous chapter.

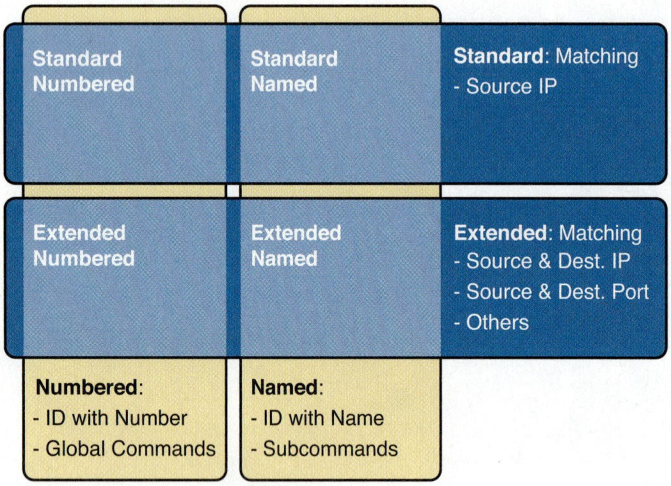

Standard Numbered	Standard Named	**Standard**: Matching - Source IP
Extended Numbered	Extended Named	**Extended**: Matching - Source & Dest. IP - Source & Dest. Port - Others
Numbered: - ID with Number - Global Commands	**Named**: - ID with Name - Subcommands	

Figure 23-1 *Comparisons of IP ACL Types*

This chapter discusses the other three categories of ACLs beyond standard numbered IP ACLs, and ends with a few miscellaneous features to secure Cisco routers and switches.

IP Services

Describe the types, features, and applications of ACLs

Sequence numbers

Editing

Extended

Named

Numbered

Configure and verify ACLs in a network environment

Named

Numbered

Configure and verify NTP as a client

Network Device Security

Configure and verify network device security features such as

Transport

Disable telnet

Physical security

Setting native VLAN to other than VLAN 1

Configure and verify ACLs to filter network traffic

Configure and verify an ACL to limit telnet and SSH access to the router

Troubleshoot and Resolve ACL issues

Statistics

Permitted networks

Direction

Interface

Foundation Topics

Extended Numbered IP Access Control Lists

Extended IP access lists have many similarities compared to the standard numbered IP ACLs discussed in the previous chapter. Just like standard IP ACLs, you enable extended access lists on interfaces for packets either entering or exiting the interface. IOS searches the list sequentially. Extended ACLs also use first-match logic, because the router stops the search through the list as soon as the first statement is matched, taking the action defined in the first-matched statement. All these features are also true of standard numbered access lists (and named ACLs).

Extended ACLs differ from standard ACLs mostly because of the larger variety of packet header fields that can be used to match a packet. One extended ACL statement can examine multiple parts of the packet headers, requiring that all the parameters be matched correctly to match that one ACL statement. That powerful matching logic makes extended access lists both more useful and more complex than standard IP ACLs.

Matching the Protocol, Source IP, and Destination IP

Like standard numbered IP ACLs, extended numbered IP ACLs also use the **access-list** global command. The syntax is identical, at least up through the **permit** or **deny** keyword. At that point, the command lists matching parameters, and those differ, of course. In particular, the extended ACL **access-list** command requires three matching parameters: the IP protocol type, the source IP address, and the destination IP address.

The IP header's Protocol field identifies the header that follows the IP header. Figure 23-2 shows the location of the IP Protocol field, the concept of it pointing to the type of header that follows, along with some details of the IP header for reference.

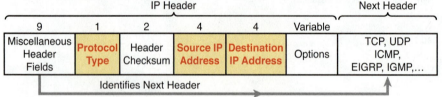

Figure 23-2   *IP Header, with Focus on Required Fields in Extended IP ACLs*

IOS requires that you configure parameters for the three highlighted parts of Figure 23-2. For the protocol type, you simply use a keyword, such as **tcp**, **udp**, or **icmp**, matching IP packets that happen to have a TCP, UDP, or ICMP header, respectively, following the IP header. Or you can use the keyword **ip**, which means "all ip packets." You also must configure some values for the source and destination IP address fields which follow; these fields use the same syntax and options for matching the IP addresses as discussed in Chapter 22, "Basic IPv4 Access Control Lists." Figure 23-3 shows the syntax.

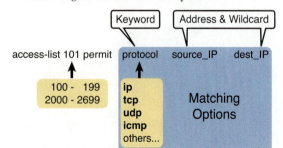

Figure 23-3   *Extended ACL Syntax, with Required Fields*

NOTE When matching IP addresses in the source and destination fields, there is one difference with standard ACLs: When matching a specific IP address, the extended ACL requires the use of the **host** keyword. You cannot simply list the IP address alone.

Table 23-1 lists several sample **access-list** commands that use only the required matching parameters. Feel free to cover the right side and use the table for an exercise, or just review the explanations to get an idea for the logic in some sample commands.

Table 23-1   Extended **access-list** Commands and Logic Explanations

access-list Statement	What It Matches
access-list 101 deny tcp any any	Any IP packet that has a TCP header
access-list 101 deny udp any any	Any IP packet that has a UDP header
access-list 101 deny icmp any any	Any IP packet that has an ICMP header
access-list 101 deny ip host 1.1.1.1 host 2.2.2.2	All IP packets from host 1.1.1.1 going to host 2.2.2.2, regardless of the header after the IP header
access-list 101 deny udp 1.1.1.0 0.0.0.255 any	All IP packets that have a UDP header following the IP header, from subnet 1.1.1.0/24, and going to any destination

The last entry in Table 23-1 helps make an important point about how IOS processes extended ACLs:

> In an extended ACL **access-list** command, all the matching parameters must match the packet for the packet to match the command.

For example, in that last example from Table 23-1, the command checks for UDP, a source IP address from subnet 1.1.1.0/24, and any destination IP address. If a packet with source IP address 1.1.1.1 were examined, it would match the source IP address check, but if it had a TCP header instead of UDP, it would not match this **access-list** command. All parameters must match.

Matching TCP and UDP Port Numbers

Extended ACLs can also examine parts of the TCP and UDP headers, particularly the source and destination port number fields. The port numbers identify the application that sends or receives the data.

The most useful ports to check are the well-known ports used by servers. For example, web servers use well-known port 80 by default. Figure 23-4 shows the location of the port numbers in the TCP header, following the IP header.

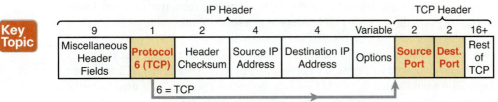

Figure 23-4 *IP Header, Followed by a TCP Header and Port Number Fields*

When an extended ACL command includes either the **tcp** or **udp** keyword, that command can optionally reference the source and/or destination port. To make these comparisons, the syntax uses keywords for equal, not equal, less than, greater than, and for a range of port numbers. Additionally, the command can use either the literal decimal port numbers, or more convenient keywords for some well-known application ports. Figure 23-5 shows the positions of the source and destination port fields in the **access-list** command and these port number keywords.

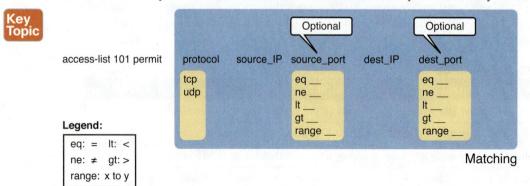

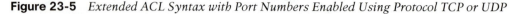

Figure 23-5 *Extended ACL Syntax with Port Numbers Enabled Using Protocol TCP or UDP*

For example, consider the simple network shown in Figure 23-6. The FTP server sits on the right, with the client on the left. The figure shows the syntax of an ACL that matches the following:

■ Packets that include a TCP header

■ Packets sent from the client subnet

■ Packets sent to the server subnet

■ Packets with TCP destination port 21 (FTP server control port)

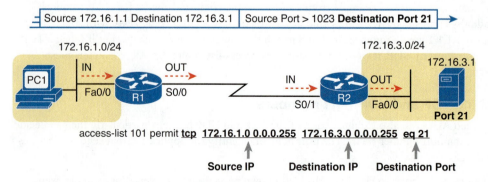

Figure 23-6 *Filtering Packets Based on Destination Port*

To fully appreciate the matching of the destination port with the **eq 21** parameters, consider packets moving from left to right, from PC1 to the server. Assuming the server uses well-known port 21 (FTP control port), the packet's TCP header has a destination port value of 21. The ACL syntax includes the **eq 21** parameters after the destination IP address. The position after the destination address parameters is important: That position identifies the fact that the **eq 21** parameters should be compared to the packet's destination port. As a result, the ACL statement shown in Figure 23-6 would match this packet, and the destination port of 21, if used in any of the four locations implied by the four dashed arrowed lines in the figure.

Conversely, Figure 23-7 shows the reverse flow, with a packet sent by the server back toward PC1. In this case, the packet's TCP header has a source port of 21, so the ACL must check the source port value of 21, and the ACL must be located on different interfaces. In this case, the **eq 21** parameters follow the source address field, but comes before the destination address field.

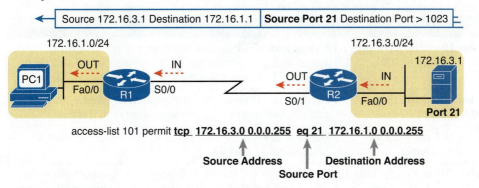

Figure 23-7 *Filtering Packets Based on Source Port*

For exam questions that require ACLs and matching of port numbers, first consider the location and direction in which the ACL will be applied. That direction determines whether the packet is being sent to the server, or from the server. At that point, you can decide whether you need to check the source or destination port in the packet, assuming you want to check the well-known port used by that service.

For reference, Table 23-2 lists many of the popular port numbers and their transport layer protocols and applications. Note that the syntax of the **access-list** commands accepts both the port numbers and a shorthand version of the application name.

Table 23-2 Popular Applications and Their Well-Known Port Numbers

Port Number(s)	Protocol	Application	access-list Command Keyword
20	TCP	FTP data	ftp-data
21	TCP	FTP control	ftp
22	TCP	SSH	—
23	TCP	Telnet	telnet
25	TCP	SMTP	smtp
53	UDP, TCP	DNS	domain
67, 68	UDP	DHCP	nameserver
69	UDP	TFTP	tftp
80	TCP	HTTP (WWW)	www
110	TCP	POP3	pop3
161	UDP	SNMP	snmp
443	TCP	SSL	—
16,384 – 32,767	UDP	RTP-based voice (VoIP) and video	—

23

Table 23-3 lists several example **access-list** commands that match based on port numbers. Cover the right side of the table, and try to characterize the packets matched by each command. Then, check the right side of the table to see if you agree with the assessment.

Table 23-3 Example Extended **access-list** Commands and Logic Explanations

access-list Statement	What It Matches
access-list 101 deny tcp any gt 1023 host 10.1.1.1 eq 23	Packets with a TCP header, any source IP address, with a source port greater than (gt) 1023, a destination IP address of exactly 10.1.1.1, and a destination port equal to (eq) 23.
access-list 101 deny tcp any host 10.1.1.1 eq 23	The same as the preceding example, but any source port matches, because that parameter is omitted in this case.
access-list 101 deny tcp any host 10.1.1.1 eq telnet	The same as the preceding example. The **telnet** keyword is used instead of port 23.
access-list 101 deny udp 1.0.0.0 0.255.255.255 lt 1023 any	A packet with a source in network 1.0.0.0/8, using UDP with a source port less than (lt) 1023, with any destination IP address.

Extended IP ACL Configuration

Because extended ACLs can match so many different fields in the various headers in an IP packet, the command syntax cannot be easily summarized in a single generic command. However, for CCNA preparation, you can rely mainly on two references for syntax, as listed in Table 23-4.

Table 23-4 Extended IP Access List Configuration Commands

Command	Configuration Mode and Description
access-list *access-list-number* {**deny**	**permit**} *protocol source source-wildcard destination destination-wildcard* [**log**	**log-input**]	Global command for extended numbered access lists. Use a number between 100 and 199 or 2000 and 2699, inclusive.
access-list *access-list-number* {**deny**	**permit**} {**tcp**	**udp**} *source source-wildcard* [*operator* [*port*]] *destination destination-wildcard* [*operator* [*port*]] [**established**] [**log**]	A version of the **access-list** command with parameters specific to TCP and/or UDP.

The configuration process for extended ACLs mostly matches the same process used for standard ACLs. You must choose the location and direction in which to enable the ACL, particularly the direction, so that you can characterize whether certain addresses and ports will be either the source or destination. Configure the ACL using **access-list** commands, and when complete, then enable the ACL using the same **ip access-group** command used with standard ACLs. All these steps mirror what you do with standard ACLs; however, when configuring, keep the following differences in mind:

- Place extended ACLs as close as possible to the source of the packets that will be filtered. Filtering close to the source of the packets saves some bandwidth.

- Remember that all fields in one **access-list** command must match a packet for the packet to be considered to match that **access-list** statement.

- Use numbers of 100–199 and 2000–2699 on the **access-list** commands; no one number is inherently better than another.

Extended IP Access Lists: Example 1

This example focuses on understanding basic syntax. In this case, the ACL denies Bob access to all FTP servers on R1's Ethernet, and it denies Larry access to Server1's web server. Figure 23-8 shows the network topology; Example 23-1 shows the configuration on R1.

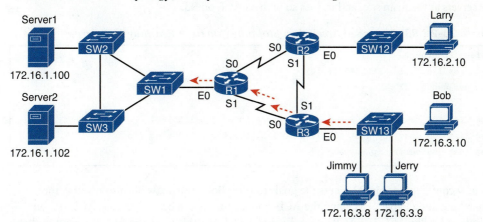

Figure 23-8 *Network Diagram for Extended Access List Example 1*

Example 23-1 *R1's Extended Access List: Example 1*

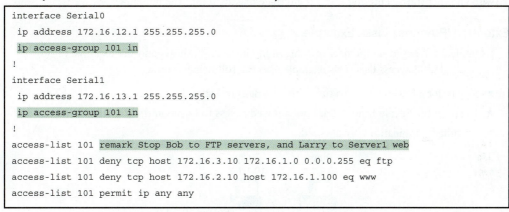

```
interface Serial0
 ip address 172.16.12.1 255.255.255.0
 ip access-group 101 in
!
interface Serial1
 ip address 172.16.13.1 255.255.255.0
 ip access-group 101 in
!
access-list 101 remark Stop Bob to FTP servers, and Larry to Server1 web
access-list 101 deny tcp host 172.16.3.10 172.16.1.0 0.0.0.255 eq ftp
access-list 101 deny tcp host 172.16.2.10 host 172.16.1.100 eq www
access-list 101 permit ip any any
```

The first ACL statement prevents Bob's access to FTP servers in subnet 172.16.1.0. The second statement prevents Larry's access to web services on Server1. The final statement permits all other traffic.

Focusing on the syntax for a moment, there are several new items to review. First, the access-list number for extended access lists falls in the range of 100–199 or 2000–2699. Following the **permit** or **deny** action, the *protocol* parameter defines whether you want to check for all IP packets or specific headers, such as TCP or UDP headers. When you check for TCP or UDP port numbers, you must specify the TCP or UDP protocol. Both FTP and web use TCP.

This example uses the **eq** parameter, meaning "equals," to check the destination port numbers for FTP control (keyword **ftp**) and HTTP traffic (keyword **www**). You can use the numeric values—or, for the more popular options, a more obvious text version is valid. (If you were to type **eq 80**, the config would show **eq www**.)

This example enables the ACL in two places on R1: inbound on each serial interface. These locations achieve the goal of the ACL. However, that initial placement was made to make the point that Cisco suggests that you locate them as close as possible to the source of the packet. Therefore, Example 23-2 achieves the same goal as Example 23-1 of stopping Bob's access to FTP servers at the main site, and it does so with an ACL on R3.

Example 23-2 *R3's Extended Access List Stopping Bob from Reaching FTP Servers Near R1*

```
interface Ethernet0
 ip address 172.16.3.1 255.255.255.0
 ip access-group 103 in

access-list 103 remark deny Bob to FTP servers in subnet 172.16.1.0/24
access-list 103 deny tcp host 172.16.3.10 172.16.1.0 0.0.0.255 eq ftp
access-list 103 permit ip any any
```

The new configuration on R3 meets the goals to filter Bob's traffic, while also meeting the overarching design goal of keeping the ACL close to the source of the packets. ACL 103 on R3 looks a lot like ACL 101 on R1 from Example 23-1, but this time, the ACL does not bother to check for the criteria to match Larry's traffic, because Larry's traffic will never enter R3's Ethernet 0 interface. ACL 103 filters Bob's FTP traffic to destinations in subnet 172.16.1.0/24, with all other traffic entering R3's E0 interface making it into the network.

Extended IP Access Lists: Example 2

Example 23-3, based on the network shown in Figure 23-9, shows another example of how to use extended IP access lists. This example uses the following criteria:

- Sam is not allowed access to the subnet of Bugs or Daffy.
- Hosts on the Seville Ethernet are not allowed access to hosts on the Yosemite Ethernet.
- All other combinations are allowed.

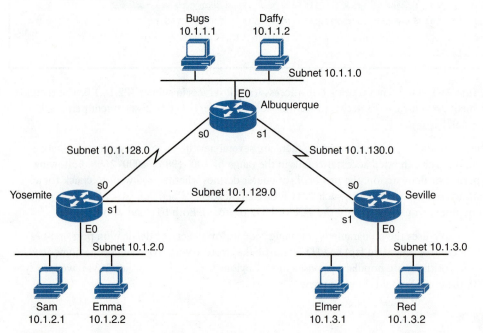

Figure 23-9 *Network Diagram for Extended Access List Example 2*

Example 23-3 *Yosemite Configuration for Extended Access List Example*

```
interface ethernet 0
 ip access-group 110 in
!
access-list 110 deny ip host 10.1.2.1 10.1.1.0 0.0.0.255
access-list 110 deny ip 10.1.2.0 0.0.0.255 10.1.3.0 0.0.0.255
access-list 110 permit ip any any
```

This configuration solves the problem with few statements while keeping to the Cisco design guideline of placing extended ACLs as close as possible to the source of the traffic. The ACL filters packets that enter Yosemite's E0 interface, which is the first router interface that packets sent by Sam enter. If the route between Yosemite and the other subnets changes over time, the ACL still applies. Also, the filtering mandated by the second requirement (to disallow Seville's LAN hosts from accessing Yosemite's) is met by the second **access-list** statement. Stopping packet flow from Yosemite's LAN subnet to Seville's LAN subnet stops effective communication between the two subnets. Alternatively, the opposite logic could have been configured at Seville.

Practice Building access-list Commands

Table 23-5 supplies a practice exercise to help you get comfortable with the syntax of the extended **access-list** command, particularly with choosing the correct matching logic. Your job: create a one-line extended ACL that matches the packets. The answers are in the section, "Answers to Earlier Practice Problems," later in this chapter. Note that if the criteria mentions a particular application protocol, for example, "web client," that means to specifically match for that application protocol.

Table 23-5 Building One-Line Extended ACLs: Practice

Problem	Criteria
1	From web client 10.1.1.1, sent to a web server in subnet 10.1.2.0/24.
2	From telnet client 172.16.4.3/25, sent to a Telnet server in subnet 172.16.3.0/25. Match all hosts in the client's subnet as well.
3	ICMP messages from the subnet in which 192.168.7.200/26 resides to all hosts in the subnet where 192.168.7.14/29 resides.
4	From web server 10.2.3.4/23's subnet to clients in the same subnet as host 10.4.5.6/22.
5	From telnet server 172.20.1.0/24's subnet to clients in the same subnet as host 172.20.44.1/23.
6	From web client 192.168.99.99/28, sent to a web server in subnet 192.168.176.0/28. Match all hosts in the client's subnet as well.
7	ICMP messages from the subnet in which 10.55.66.77/25 resides to all hosts in the subnet where 10.66.55.44/26 resides.
8	Any and every IPv4 packet.

23

Named ACLs and ACL Editing

Now that you have a good understanding of the core concepts in IOS IP ACLs, this section examines a few enhancements to IOS support for ACLs: named ACLs and ACL editing with sequence numbers. Although both features are useful and important, neither adds any function as to what a router can and cannot filter. Instead, named ACLs and ACL sequence numbers make it easier to remember ACL names and edit existing ACLs when an ACL needs to change.

Named IP Access Lists

Named IP ACLs have many similarities with numbered IP ACLs. They can be used for filtering packets, plus for many other purposes. And just like there are both standard and extended numbered ACLs that differ in regards to what packets each can match, there are also standard and extended named ACLs.

Named ACLs originally had three big differences compared to numbered ACLs:

- Using names instead of numbers to identify the ACL, making it easier to remember the reason for the ACL
- Using ACL subcommands, not global commands, to define the action and matching parameters
- ACL editing features that allow the CLI user to delete individual lines from the ACL and insert new lines

You can easily learn named ACL configuration by just converting numbered ACLs to use the equivalent named ACL configuration. Figure 23-10 shows just such a conversion, using a simple three-line standard ACL number 1. To create the three **permit** subcommands for the named ACL, you literally copy parts of the three numbered ACL commands, beginning with the **permit** keyword.

Numbered ACL

access-list 1 permit 1.1.1.1
access-list 1 permit 2.2.2.2 ⟶
access-list 1 permit 3.3.3.3

Named ACL

ip access-list standard *name*

permit 1.1.1.1
permit 2.2.2.2
permit 3.3.3.3

Figure 23-10   *Named ACL Versus Numbered ACL Configuration*

The only truly new part of the named ACL configuration is the **ip access-list** global configuration command. This command defines whether an ACL is a standard or extended ACL, and defines the name. It also moves the user to ACL configuration mode, as seen in upcoming Example 23-4. Once in ACL configuration mode, you configure **permit**, **deny**, and **remark** commands that mirror the syntax of numbered ACL **access-list** commands. If configuring a standard named ACL, these commands match the syntax of standard numbered ACLs; if configuring extended named ACLs, they match the syntax of extended numbered ACLs.

Example 23-4 shows the configuration of a named extended ACL. Pay particular attention to the configuration mode prompts, which shows ACL configuration mode.

Example 23-4   *Named Access List Configuration*

```
Router# configure terminal
Enter configuration commands, one per line.  End with Ctrl-Z.
Router(config)# ip access-list extended barney
Router(config-ext-nacl)# permit tcp host 10.1.1.2 eq www any
```

```
Router(config-ext-nacl)# deny udp host 10.1.1.1 10.1.2.0 0.0.0.255
Router(config-ext-nacl)# deny ip 10.1.3.0 0.0.0.255 10.1.2.0 0.0.0.255
Router(config-ext-nacl)# deny ip 10.1.2.0 0.0.0.255 10.2.3.0 0.0.0.255
Router(config-ext-nacl)# permit ip any any
Router(config-ext-nacl)# interface serial1
Router(config-if)# ip access-group barney out
Router(config-if)# ^Z
Router# show running-config
Building configuration...

Current configuration:

! lines omitted for brevity

interface serial 1
 ip access-group barney out
!
ip access-list extended barney
 permit tcp host 10.1.1.2 eq www any
 deny    udp host 10.1.1.1 10.1.2.0 0.0.0.255
 deny    ip 10.1.3.0 0.0.0.255 10.1.2.0 0.0.0.255
 deny    ip 10.1.2.0 0.0.0.255 10.2.3.0 0.0.0.255
 permit ip any any
```

Example 23-4 begins with the creation of an ACL named barney. The **ip access-list extended barney** command creates the ACL, naming it barney and placing the user in ACL configuration mode. This command also tells the IOS that barney is an extended ACL. Next, five different **permit** and **deny** statements define the matching logic and action to be taken upon a match. The **show running-config** command output lists the named ACL configuration before the single entry is deleted.

Named ACLs allow the user to delete and add new lines to the ACL from within ACL configuration mode. Example 23-5 shows how, with the **no deny ip . . .** command deleting a single entry from the ACL. Notice that the output of the **show access-list** command at the end of the example still lists the ACL, with four **permit** and **deny** commands instead of five.

Example 23-5   *Removing One Command from a Named ACL*

```
Router# configure terminal
Enter configuration commands, one per line.  End with Ctrl-Z.
Router(config)# ip access-list extended barney
Router(config-ext-nacl)# no deny ip 10.1.2.0 0.0.0.255 10.2.3.0 0.0.0.255
Router(config-ext-nacl)# ^Z
Router# show access-list

Extended IP access list barney
    10 permit tcp host 10.1.1.2 eq www any
    20 deny    udp host 10.1.1.1 10.1.2.0 0.0.0.255
    30 deny    ip 10.1.3.0 0.0.0.255 10.1.2.0 0.0.0.255
    50 permit ip any any
```

Editing ACLs Using Sequence Numbers

Numbered ACLs have existed in IOS since the early days of Cisco routers and IOS. However, for many years, through many IOS versions, the ability to edit a numbered IP ACL was poor. For example, to simply delete a line from the ACL, the user had to delete the entire ACL and then reconfigure it.

Today, modern IOS versions allow CLI users to easily edit both numbered and named ACLs. Cisco first introduced these enhanced ACL editing features in named ACLs only, and slowly added them to numbered ACLs as well. This section examines these great ACL editing features that have been around in IOS since Version 12.3, which as of the writing of this book, is now a relatively old IOS version.

The ACL editing feature uses an ACL sequence number that is added to each ACL **permit** or **deny** statement, with the numbers representing the sequence of statements in the ACL. ACL sequence numbers provide the following features for both numbered and named ACLs:

New Configuration Style for Numbered: Numbered ACLs use a configuration style like named ACLs, as well as the traditional style, for the same ACL; the new style is required to perform advanced ACL editing.

Deleting Single Lines: An individual ACL **permit** or **deny** statement can be deleted with a **no** *sequence-number* subcommand.

Inserting New Lines: Newly added **permit** and **deny** commands can be configured with a sequence number, dictating the location of the statement within the ACL.

Automatic Sequence Numbering: IOS adds sequence numbers to commands as you configure them, even if you do not include the sequence numbers.

To take advantage of the ability to delete and insert lines in an ACL, both numbered and named ACLs must use the same overall configuration style and commands used for named ACLs. The only difference in syntax is whether a name or number is used. Example 23-6 shows the configuration of a standard numbered IP ACL, using this alternative configuration style. The example shows the power of the ACL sequence number for editing. In this example, the following occurs:

Step 1. Numbered ACL 24 is configured using this new-style configuration, with three **permit** commands.

Step 2. The **show ip access-list** command shows the three permit commands with sequence numbers 10, 20, and 30.

Step 3. The engineer deletes only the second **permit** command using the **no 20** ACL subcommand, which simply refers to sequence number 20.

Step 4. The **show ip access-list** command confirms that the ACL now has only two lines (sequence numbers 10 and 30).

Step 5. The engineer adds a new **deny** command to the beginning of the ACL, using the **5 deny 10.1.1.1** ACL subcommand.

Step 6. The **show ip access-list** command again confirms the changes, this time listing three **permit** commands, sequence numbers 5, 10, and 30.

NOTE For this example, note that the user does not leave configuration mode, instead using the **do** command to tell IOS to issue the **show ip access-list** EXEC command from configuration mode.

Example 23-6 *Editing ACLs Using Sequence Numbers*

```
! Step 1: The 3-line Standard Numbered IP ACL is configured.
R1# configure terminal
Enter configuration commands, one per line.  End with Ctrl-Z.
R1(config)# ip access-list standard 24
R1(config-std-nacl)# permit 10.1.1.0 0.0.0.255
R1(config-std-nacl)# permit 10.1.2.0 0.0.0.255
R1(config-std-nacl)# permit 10.1.3.0 0.0.0.255


! Step 2: Displaying the ACL's contents, without leaving configuration mode.
R1(config-std-nacl)# do show ip access-list 24
Standard IP access list 24
    10 permit 10.1.1.0, wildcard bits 0.0.0.255
    20 permit 10.1.2.0, wildcard bits 0.0.0.255
    30 permit 10.1.3.0, wildcard bits 0.0.0.255


! Step 3: Still in ACL 24 configuration mode, the line with sequence number 20 is deleted.
R1(config-std-nacl)# no 20


! Step 4: Displaying the ACL's contents again, without leaving configuration mode.
! Note that line number 20 is no longer listed.
R1(config-std-nacl)#do show ip access-list 24
Standard IP access list 24
    10 permit 10.1.1.0, wildcard bits 0.0.0.255
    30 permit 10.1.3.0, wildcard bits 0.0.0.255


! Step 5: Inserting a new first line in the ACL.
R1(config-std-nacl)# 5 deny 10.1.1.1


! Step 6: Displaying the ACL's contents one last time, with the new statement
!(sequence number 5) listed first.
R1(config-std-nacl)# do show ip access-list 24
Standard IP access list 24
    5 deny    10.1.1.1
    10 permit 10.1.1.0, wildcard bits 0.0.0.255
    30 permit 10.1.3.0, wildcard bits 0.0.0.255
```

23

Note that while Example 23-6 uses a numbered ACL, named ACLs use the same process to edit (add and remove) entries.

Numbered ACL Configuration Versus Named ACL Configuration

As a brief aside about numbered ACLs, note that IOS actually allows two ways to configure numbered ACLs in the more recent versions of IOS. First, IOS supports the traditional method, using the **access-list** global commands seen earlier in Examples 23-1, 23-2, and 23-3. IOS also supports the numbered ACL configuration with commands just like named ACLs, as seen in Example 23-6.

Oddly, IOS always stores numbered ACLs with the original style of configuration, as global **access-list** commands, no matter which method is used to configure the ACL. Example 23-7 demonstrates these facts, picking up where Example 23-6 ended, with the following additional steps:

Step 7.   The engineer lists the configuration (**show running-config**), which lists the old-style configuration commands—even though the ACL was created with the new-style commands.

Step 8.   The engineer adds a new statement to the end of the ACL using the old-style **access-list 24 permit 10.1.4.0 0.0.0.255** global configuration command.

Step 9.   The **show ip access-list** command confirms that the old-style **access-list** command from the previous step followed the rule of being added only to the end of the ACL.

Step 10.   The engineer displays the configuration to confirm that the parts of ACL 24 configured with both new-style commands and old-style commands are all listed in the same old-style ACL (**show running-config**).

Example 23-7   *Adding to and Displaying a Numbered ACL Configuration*

```
! Step 7: A configuration snippet for ACL 24.
R1# show running-config
! The only lines shown are the lines from ACL 24
access-list 24 deny    10.1.1.1
access-list 24 permit 10.1.1.0 0.0.0.255
access-list 24 permit 10.1.3.0 0.0.0.255


! Step 8: Adding a new access-list 24 global command
R1# configure terminal
Enter configuration commands, one per line.   End with CNTL/Z.
R1(config)# access-list 24 permit 10.1.4.0 0.0.0.255
R1(config)# ^Z


! Step 9: Displaying the ACL's contents again, with sequence numbers. Note that even
! the new statement has been automatically assigned a sequence number.
R1# show ip access-list 24
Standard IP access list 24
    5 deny    10.1.1.1
    10 permit 10.1.1.0, wildcard bits 0.0.0.255
    30 permit 10.1.3.0, wildcard bits 0.0.0.255
    40 permit 10.1.4.0, wildcard bits 0.0.0.255


! Step 10: The numbered ACL configuration remains in old-style configuration commands.
R1# show running-config
! The only lines shown are the lines from ACL 24
access-list 24 deny    10.1.1.1
access-list 24 permit 10.1.1.0 0.0.0.255
access-list 24 permit 10.1.3.0 0.0.0.255
access-list 24 permit 10.1.4.0 0.0.0.255
```

Router and Switch Security

This final section of the chapter looks at a variety of short topics, all with some tie to how to secure routers and switches. Some features use ACLs to better secure the router or switch, while other features simply define how to use some Cisco-recommended best practices for protecting the device.

Specifically, this section reviews password security, disabling unnecessary services, disabling Telnet, securing VTY (Telnet and SSH) access with ACLs, how to choose the best locations for ACLs, and Network Time Protocol (NTP).

Review: Password Protections for the CLI

Chapter 7, "Installing and Operating Cisco LAN Switches," and Chapter 8, "Configuring Ethernet Switching," discussed how routers and switches protect CLI access using different passwords. As a reminder, Figure 23-11 reviews the locations where IOS can require a password to get into the CLI, or move to a different mode: the console, vty, and to move from user to enable mode.

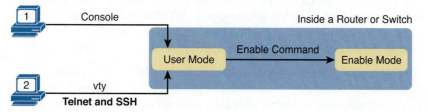

Figure 23-11   *Locations to Consider Passwords: Console, vty, and Enable*

The following list summarizes some recommendations for how to secure a router or switch CLI. Note that Chapter 8 explains the meaning of all these commands, with examples of several of these. The following list simply points out the reasons for using the various password options.

■ Use the **enable secret** command, instead of the combination of the **enable password** command plus the **service password-encryption** command. Both result in what looks like a scrambled password when displayed with the **show running-config** command. However, the **enable secret** command uses stronger password encryption, while passwords encrypted with the **service password-encryption** command can be easily broken.

■ Avoid using simple password checking for the console or VTYs with the **login** line-mode command, because this method does not identify individual users.

■ Optimally, authenticate CLI logins using an external authentication server, like a RADIUS server. However, if necessary, use locally configured **username secret** commands, which hides the passwords with a hash (as does the **enable secret** command).

■ Disable support for inbound Telnet connections, because Telnet sends the passwords as clear text, opening up the possibility of someone capturing the packets and stealing the password. Instead, configure the router and switch to allow SSH only, using the **transport input ssh** command in VTY line mode.

While all of these activities are important, all require that you also maintain solid physical security for your networking devices. The devices should be in a secured area, where only authorized personnel can physically reach the devices. Once an attacker gains physical access to a router or switch, they can remove cables, power off devices, and even reset passwords from the console, allowing them to access the devices remotely at a later time.

Disable Services

Cisco IOS, like any other OS, has to have some default settings. Those default settings include a variety of services that IOS supports for good reason. However, for most any service that a computer uses for good reason, hackers can use as a way to attack a network, or at least learn information that helps in some other attack. So, every good security plan looks at each OS used in a network, finds any default settings that can create a security exposure, and changes the default settings to minimize security risks.

23

Cisco makes several recommendations about what to disable and enable on IOS (for both routers and switches) as part of a good security plan. This section discusses a few such items, to give you an idea of the kinds of things to consider. However, this section does not attempt to list them all; the Cisco security certification track gets into more details about these features.

NOTE   For the curious: Go to Cisco.com and search for "Guide to Harden Cisco IOS Devices" for a more detailed document about recommendations for securing routers and switches.

Cisco IOS supports a graphical user interface (GUI) to do the same work as done at the CLI. To make that work, IOS acts as a web server. By default, IOS enables an HTTP web service that does not encrypt data (HTTP), with an option to configure an HTTP service that does encrypt data (HTTPS). The recommendation? Disable the HTTP service, and only enable the HTTPS service if you intend to allow users to connect to the router or switch using a web browser.

Next, Cisco Discovery Protocol (CDP), as discussed back in Chapter 10, "Troubleshooting Ethernet LANs," allows devices on the same link to learn basic information from each other. However, that basic information can help an attacker learn some useful information about the network. So, as a security recommendation, Cisco suggests disabling CDP on all interfaces connected to untrusted parts of the network. To be even more secure, CDP could be disabled globally.

NOTE   In real networks, be careful about turning off CDP on LAN switches until you understand what devices connect to the switch. Many IP phone installations require the use of CDP between the phone and the switch, and without it, the phone does not work.

As one more example, IOS has a set of services that IOS categorizes as small services. For example, the Echo service is one of these small services. It acts a lot like **ping**, with ICMP Echo Request and Echo Reply messages, but unlike these ICMP messages, the Echo application uses either TCP or UDP. So, think of it like a **ping** that also tests the transport layer, while **ping**, which uses ICMP, does not. IOS needs to run the Echo service to be ready to reply to these types of Echo messages.

Some IOS versions leave these services enabled by default, while some do not. To be thorough, disable both TCP and UDP small services.

Example 23-8 shows a configuration on Router R1 that disables the functions mentioned in this section. The notes inside the example explain the specific configuration commands.

Example 23-8   *Disabling IOS Services*

```
! Disable the HTTP service
R1(config)# no ip http server


! Disable small services, both TCP and UDP
R1(config)# no service tcp-small-servers
R1(config)# no service udp-small-servers


! Disable CDP on one interface only; no cdp run would disable
! CDP globally
R1(config)# interface gigabitEthernet 0/0
R1(config-if)# no cdp enable
R1(config-if)# ^Z
```

Controlling Telnet and SSH Access with ACLs

When an external user connects to a router or switch using Telnet or SSH, IOS uses a vty line to represent that user connection. IOS can apply an ACL to those inbound connections by applying an ACL to the vty line, filtering the addresses from which IPv4 hosts can telnet or SSH into the router or switch.

For example, imagine that all the network engineering staff uses subnet 10.1.1.0/24, and only those devices are supposed to be able to telnet into any of the Cisco routers in a network. In such a case, the configuration shown in Example 23-9 could be used on each router to deny access from IP addresses not in that subnet.

Example 23-9   *vty Access Control Using the* **access-class** *Command*

```
line vty 0 4
 login
 password cisco
 access-class 3 in
!
! Next command is a global command that matches IPv4 packets with
! a source address that begins with 10.1.1.
 access-list 3 permit 10.1.1.0 0.0.0.255
```

The **access-class** command refers to the matching logic in **access-list 3**. The keyword **in** refers to Telnet and SSH connections into this router—in other words, people telnetting into this router. As configured, ACL 3 checks the source IP address of packets for incoming Telnet connections.

IOS also supports using ACLs to filter outbound Telnet and SSH connections. For example, consider a user who first uses telnet or SSH to connect to the CLI, and now sits in user or enable mode. With an outbound vty filter, IOS will apply ACL logic if the user tries the **telnet** or **ssh** commands to connect *out of the local device* to another device.

To configure an outbound VTY ACL, use the **access-class** *acl* **out** command in VTY configuration mode. Once configured, the router filters attempts by current vty users to use the **telnet** and **ssh** commands to initiate new connections to other devices.

Of the two options—to protect inbound and outbound connections—protecting inbound connections is by far the more important and more common. However, to be complete, outbound VTY ACLs have a surprising odd feature in how they use the ACL. When using the **out** keyword, the standard IP ACL listed in the **access-class** command actually looks at the *destination IP address*, and not the source. That is, it filters based on the device to which the **telnet** or **ssh** command is trying to connect.

ACL Implementation Considerations

ACLs can be a great tool to enhance the security of a network, but engineers should think about some broader issues before simply configuring an ACL to fix a problem. To help, Cisco makes the following general recommendations in the courses on which the CCNA exams are based:

- Place extended ACLs as close as possible to the source of the packet to discard the packets quickly.
- Place standard ACLs as close as possible to the packet's destination, because standard ACLs often discard packets that you do not want discarded when they are placed close to the source.
- Place more specific statements early in the ACL.
- Disable an ACL from its interface (using the **no ip access-group** command) before making changes to the ACL.

23

The first point deals with the concept of where to locate your ACLs. If you intend to filter a packet, filtering closer to the packet's source means that the packet takes up less bandwidth in the network, which seems to be more efficient—and it is. Therefore, Cisco suggests locating extended ACLs as close to the source as possible.

However, the second point seems to contradict the first point, at least for standard ACLs, to locate them close to the destination. Why? Well, because standard ACLs look only at the source IP address, they tend to filter more than you want filtered when placed close to the source. For example, imagine that Fred and Barney are separated by four routers. If you filter Barney's traffic sent to Fred on the first router, Barney can't reach any hosts near the other three routers. So, the Cisco courses make a blanket recommendation to locate standard ACLs closer to the destination to avoid filtering traffic you don't mean to filter.

For the third item in the list, by placing more specific matching parameters early in each list, you are less likely to make mistakes in the ACL. For example, imagine that the ACL first listed a comment that permitted traffic going to 10.1.1.0/24, and denied traffic going to host 10.1.1.1. Packets sent to host 10.1.1.1 would match the first command, and never match the more specific second command. In general, placing the more specific statements first tends to ensure that you don't miss anything.

Finally, Cisco recommends that you disable the ACLs on the interfaces before you change the statements in the list. Thankfully, if you have an IP ACL enabled on an interface with the **ip access-group** command, and you delete the entire ACL, IOS does not filter any packets. (That was not always the case in earlier IOS versions!) Even so, as soon as you add a command to the ACL, the IOS starts filtering packets.

For example, suppose you have ACL 101 enabled on S0/0/0 for output packets. You delete list 101 so that all packets are allowed through. Then, you enter a single **access-list 101** command. As soon as you press Enter, the list exists, and the router filters all packets exiting S0/0/0 based on the one-line list. If you want to enter a long ACL, you might temporarily filter packets you don't want to filter! Therefore, the better way is to disable the list from the interface, make the changes to the list, and then reenable it on the interface.

Network Time Protocol

The final topic in this chapter shows how to solve an operational problem with log messages that occur on routers and switches. Solving this problem might not appear to be related to security at first, but it actually does play a key role at looking for and correlating the evidence that some kind of attack has happened.

Routers and switches issue log messages in response to different events. For example, when an interface fails, the device creates log messages. With default settings, IOS sends these messages to the console port. IOS can be configured to handle log messages in a variety of ways. The *Cisco CCNA Routing and Switching ICND2 200-101 Official Cert Guide*, Academic Edition discusses some of those ways, in Chapter 19 of that book.

One option to handle log messages uses a service called a Syslog server, where the routers and switches forward copies of all log messages to the Syslog server. The Syslog server saves copies of the messages, from all devices. With a centralized location, the network support staff can later look at the messages from all devices, and look at messages that happen at the same time, to discover if a problem has occurred. Figure 23-12 shows the idea, with a Syslog server on the right.

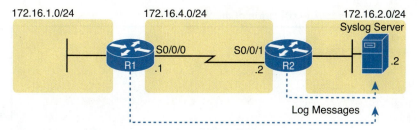

Figure 23-12 *Sample Network with a Syslog Server*

Armed with that bit of background information about syslog messages, now think about time. In particular, think about the time of day. Each device has a time-of-day clock, and most log messages list the date and time as part of the message. Why? So that when a network engineer looks back at the message, the engineer knows exactly when that message occurred.

Network Time Protocol (NTP) gives any device type, routers and switches included, a way to synchronize their time-of-day clocks. If all the network devices synchronize their clocks, then messages that list the date/time can be viewed so you know which messages happened around the same time, making troubleshooting easier.

To see why synchronizing their clocks matters, consider Example 23-10 in which Routers R1 and R2 do not synchronize their clocks. A problem keeps happening on the serial link between the two routers. A network engineer looks at all the log messages on both devices, as shown in Figure 23-12. However, when the engineer happens to see the messages on R1, at 13:38:39 (around 1:40 p.m.), and other messages from R2 at around 9:45 a.m., the engineer does not correlate the messages as being about the same problem based on the timestamps in the messages.

Example 23-10 *Log Messages from Two Routers, Compared*

```
*Oct 19 13:38:37.568: %OSPF-5-ADJCHG: Process 1, Nbr 2.2.2.2 on Serial0/0/0 from FULL to
 DOWN, Neighbor Down: Interface down or detached
*Oct 19 13:38:39.568: %LINK-5-CHANGED: Interface Serial0/0/0, changed state to
 administratively down
*Oct 19 13:38:40.568: %LINEPROTO-5-UPDOWN: Line protocol on Interface Serial0/0/0, changed
 state to down
```

```
! These messages happened on router R2
Oct 19 09:44:09.027: %LINK-3-UPDOWN: Interface Serial0/0/1, changed state to down
Oct 19 09:44:09.027: %OSPF-5-ADJCHG: Process 1, Nbr 1.1.1.1 on Serial0/0/1 from FULL to
 DOWN, Neighbor Down: Interface down or detached
Oct 19 09:44:10.027: %LINEPROTO-5-UPDOWN: Line protocol on Interface Serial0/0/1, changed
 state to down
```

As it turns out, the messages in both parts of Figure 23-12 happen within 0.5 seconds of each other, but the two routers' time-of-day clocks were not synchronized. With synchronized clocks, the two routers would have listed a timestamp of almost the exact same time when these messages occurred, making it much easier to read and correlate messages in the future. And for security issues, accurate timestamps let you correlate router and switch log messages with other events logged by other security software and hardware, creating a better defense against attacks.

To configure a router or switch to synchronize its time with an existing NTP server, only a single configuration command is required. Example 23-11 shows router R1 with the **ntp server** command. This command does not make the local device act as an NTP server; instead, it points to the IP address of an NTP server, making the local device act as an NTP client. The server is a device using IP address 172.16.2.2 in this case.

23

Example 23-11   *Configuration and Verification of an NTP Client*

```
R1# configure terminal
R1(config)# ntp server 172.16.2.2 version 4
R1(config)# ^Z
R1#


R1# show ntp status
Clock is synchronized, stratum 8, reference is 172.16.2.2
nominal freq is 250.0000 Hz, actual freq is 250.0000 Hz, precision is 2**21
ntp uptime is 4700 (1/100 of seconds), resolution is 4000
reference time is D42BD899.5FFCE014 (13:48:09.374 UTC Fri Oct 19 2012)
clock offset is -0.0033 msec, root delay is 1.28 msec
root dispersion is 3938.51 msec, peer dispersion is 187.59 msec
loopfilter state is 'CTRL' (Normal Controlled Loop), drift is 0.000000000 s/s
system poll interval is 64, last update was 42 sec ago.


R1# show ntp associations

  address         ref clock       st   when   poll reach  delay offset    disp
*172.16.2.2      127.127.1.1       7     36     64     1  1.261  -0.001 7937.5
 * sys.peer, # selected, + candidate, - outlyer, x falseticker,  configured
```

The second part of the example shows two NTP verification commands. First, the output of the **show ntp status** command gives the NTP status in the very first line. In this case, R1 has synchronized its time with the device at 172.16.2.2. This command also lists the current time and date for the timezone configured on the router. The **show ntp associations** command lists a single line of output for each other NTP device with which the router has associated.

Many variations of NTP configuration exist beyond the simple option shown in Example 23-11. For example, devices can act more like peers, influencing each other's time. Routers and switches can actually be the NTP server with just one command (**ntp master**) as well. And NTP can use authentication so that a router or switch does not get fooled into changing its timestamp, making it more difficult to discover an attack.

Review Activities

Chapter Summary

- Just like standard IP ACLs, you enable extended access lists on interfaces for packets either entering or exiting the interface. Cisco IOS searches the list sequentially. Extended ACLs also use first-match logic because the router stops the search through the list as soon as the first statement is matched, taking the action defined in the first matched statement.

- One extended ACL statement can examine multiple parts of the packet headers, requiring all the parameters to be matched correctly to match that one ACL statement. That powerful matching logic makes extended access lists both more useful and more complex than standard IP ACLs.

- Like standard numbered IP ACLs, extended numbered IP ACLs also use the **access-list** global command. The syntax is identical, at least up through the **permit** or **deny** keyword. At that point, the command lists matching parameters, and those differ, of course.

- In particular, the extended ACL **access-list** command requires three matching parameters: the IP protocol type, the source IP address, and the destination IP address.

- For the protocol type, you simply use a keyword, such as **tcp**, **udp**, or **icmp**, matching IP packets that happen to have a TCP, UDP, or ICMP header, respectively, following the IP header. Or you can use the keyword **ip**, which means "all ip packets."

- In an extended ACL **access-list** command, all the matching parameters must match the packet for the packet to match the command.

- Extended ACLs can also examine parts of the TCP and UDP headers, particularly the source and destination port number fields. The port numbers identify the application that sends or receives the data.

- When an extended ACL command includes either the **tcp** or **udp** keyword, that command can optionally reference the source and/or destination port. To make these comparisons, the syntax uses keywords for equal, not equal, less than, and greater than, and for a range of port numbers. Additionally, the command may use either the literal decimal port numbers or more convenient keywords for some well-known application ports.

- Configure the ACL using **access-list** commands and, when complete, enable the ACL using the same **ip access-group** command used with standard ACLs. All these steps mirror what you do with standard ACLs; however, when configuring, keep the following differences in mind:

  - Place extended ACLs as close as possible to the source of the packets that will be filtered. Filtering close to the source of the packets saves some bandwidth.

  - Remember that all fields in one **access-list** command must match a packet for the packet to be considered to match that **access-list** statement.

  - Use numbers between 100–199 and 2000–2699 on the **access-list** commands; no one number is inherently better than another.

- Named IP ACLs have many similarities with numbered IP ACLs. They can be used to filter packets and for many other purposes. And just as there are both standard and extended numbered ACLs that differ in regard to what packets each can match, there are also standard and extended named ACLs.

  - The only truly new part of the named ACL configuration is the **ip access-list** global configuration command. This command defines whether an ACL is a standard or extended ACL, and defines the name.

  - Named ACLs enable the user to delete and add new lines to the ACL from within ACL configuration mode.

23

- The ACL editing feature uses an ACL sequence number that is added to each ACL **permit** or **deny** statement, with the numbers representing the sequence of statements in the ACL. ACL sequence numbers provide the following features for both numbered and named ACLs:
  - **New Configuration Style for Numbered:** Numbered ACLs use a configuration style like named ACLs, as well as the traditional style, for the same ACL; the new style is required to perform advanced ACL editing.
  - **Deleting Single Lines:** An individual ACL **permit** or **deny** statement can be deleted with a **no** *sequence-number* subcommand.
  - **Inserting New Lines:** Newly added **permit** and **deny** commands can be configured with a sequence number, dictating the location of the statement within the ACL.
  - **Automatic Sequence Numbering:** IOS adds sequence numbers to commands as you configure them, even if you do not include the sequence numbers.
- When an external user connects to a router or switch using Telnet or SSH, Cisco IOS uses a vty line to represent that user connection. Cisco IOS can apply an ACL to those inbound connections by applying an ACL to the vty line, filtering the addresses from which IPv4 hosts can telnet or SSH into the router or switch.

  For example, in the command **access-class 3 in**, the keyword **in** refers to Telnet and SSH connections into this router—in other words, people telnetting into this router.
- The following statements summarize some basic ACL rules:
  - Place extended ACLs as close as possible to the source of the packet to discard the packets quickly.
  - Place standard ACLs as close as possible to the packet's destination, because standard ACLs often discard packets that you do not want discarded when they are placed close to the source.
  - Place more specific statements early in the ACL.
  - Disable an ACL from its interface (using the **no ip access-group** command) before making changes to the ACL.
- Network Time Protocol (NTP) gives any device type, routers and switches included, a way to synchronize their time-of-day clocks. If all the network devices synchronize their clocks, then messages that list the date/time can be viewed so you know which messages happened around the same time, making troubleshooting easier.

Review Questions

Answer these review questions. You can find the answers at the bottom of the last page of the chapter. For thorough explanations, see DVD Appendix C, "Answers to Review Questions."

1. Which of the following fields cannot be compared based on an extended IP ACL? (Choose two answers.)

   A. Protocol

   B. Source IP address

   C. Destination IP address

   D. TOS byte

   E. URL

   F. Filename for FTP transfers

2. Which of the following **access-list** commands permit packets going from host 10.1.1.1 to all web servers whose IP addresses begin with 172.16.5? (Choose two answers.)

   A. access-list 101 permit tcp host 10.1.1.1 172.16.5.0 0.0.0.255 eq www

   B. access-list 1951 permit ip host 10.1.1.1 172.16.5.0 0.0.0.255 eq www

   C. access-list 2523 permit ip host 10.1.1.1 eq www 172.16.5.0 0.0.0.255

   D. access-list 2523 permit tcp host 10.1.1.1 eq www 172.16.5.0 0.0.0.255

   E. access-list 2523 permit tcp host 10.1.1.1 172.16.5.0 0.0.0.255 eq www

3. Which of the following **access-list** commands permits packets going to any web client from all web servers whose IP addresses begin with 172.16.5?

   A. access-list 101 permit tcp host 10.1.1.1 172.16.5.0 0.0.0.255 eq www

   B. access-list 1951 permit ip host 10.1.1.1 172.16.5.0 0.0.0.255 eq www

   C. access-list 2523 permit tcp any eq www 172.16.5.0 0.0.0.255

   D. access-list 2523 permit tcp 172.16.5.0 0.0.0.255 eq www 172.16.5.0 0.0.0.255

   E. access-list 2523 permit tcp 172.16.5.0 0.0.0.255 eq www any

4. Which of the following fields can be compared using a named extended IP ACL but not a numbered extended IP ACL?

   A. Protocol

   B. Source IP address

   C. Destination IP address

   D. TOS byte

   E. None of the other answers are correct.

5. In a router running a recent IOS version (at least version 15.0), an engineer needs to delete the second line in ACL 101, which currently has four commands configured. Which of the following options could be used? (Choose two answers.)

   A. Delete the entire ACL and reconfigure the three ACL statements that should remain in the ACL.

   B. Delete one line from the ACL using the **no access-list...** global command.

   C. Delete one line from the ACL by entering ACL configuration mode for the ACL and then deleting only the second line based on its sequence number.

   D. Delete the last three lines from the ACL from global configuration mode, and then add the last two statements back into the ACL.

6. What general guideline should you follow when placing extended IP ACLs?

   A. Perform all filtering on output if at all possible.

   B. Put more general statements early in the ACL.

   C. Filter packets as close to the source as possible.

   D. Order the ACL commands based on the source IP addresses, from lowest to highest, to improve performance.

7. Which of the following is accurate about the NTP client function on a Cisco router?

    A. The client synchronizes its time-of-day clock based on the NTP server.

    B. It counts CPU cycles of the local router CPU to more accurately keep time.

    C. The client synchronizes its serial line clock rate based on the NTP server.

    D. The client must be connected to the same subnet as an NTP server.

Review All the Key Topics

Review the most important topics from this chapter, noted with the Key Topic icon. Table 23-6 lists these key topics and where each is discussed.

Table 23-6 Key Topics for Chapter 23

Key Topic Element	Description	Page Number
Figure 23-3	Syntax and notes about the three required matching fields in the extended ACL **access-list** command	552
Paragraph	Summary of extended ACL logic that all parameters must match in a single **access-list** statement for a match to occur	553
Figure 23-4	Drawing of the IP header followed by a TCP header	553
Figure 23-5	Syntax and notes about matching TCP and UDP ports with extended ACL **access-list** commands	554
Figure 23-7	Logic and syntax to match TCP source ports	555
List	Guidelines for using extended numbered IP ACLs	556
List	Differences between named and numbered ACLs when named ACLs introduced	560
List	Features enabled by IOS 12.3 ACL sequence numbers	562
List	ACL implementation recommendations	567

Definitions of Key Terms

After your first reading of the chapter, try to define these key terms, but do not be concerned about getting them all correct at that time. Chapter 30 directs you in how to use these terms for late-stage preparation for the exam.

extended access list, named access list, Network Time Protocol (NTP)

Command Reference to Check Your Memory

Although you should not necessarily memorize the information in the tables in this section, the following is a reference for the configuration and EXEC commands covered in this chapter.

Table 23-7 Chapter 23 ACL Configuration Command Reference

Command	Description
access-list *access-list-number* {**deny**	**permit**} *protocol source source-wildcard destination destination-wildcard* [**log**]	Global command for extended numbered access lists. Use a number between 100 and 199 or 2000 and 2699, inclusive.
access-list *access-list-number* {**deny**	**permit**} **tcp** *source source-wildcard* [*operator* [*port*]] *destination destination-wildcard* [*operator* [*port*]] [**log**]	A version of the **access-list** command with TCP-specific parameters.
access-list *access-list-number* **remark** *text*	Defines a remark that helps you remember what the ACL is supposed to do.
ip access-group {*number*	*name* [**in**	**out**]}	Interface subcommand to enable access lists.
access-class *number*	*name* [**in**	**out**]	Line subcommand to enable either standard or extended access lists on vty lines.
ip access-list {**standard**	**extended**} *name*	Global command to configure a named standard or extended ACL and enter ACL configuration mode.
{**deny**	**permit**} *source* [*source wildcard*] [**log**]	ACL mode subcommand to configure the matching details and action for a standard named ACL.
{**deny**	**permit**} *protocol source source-wildcard destination destination-wildcard* [**log**]	ACL mode subcommand to configure the matching details and action for an extended named ACL.
{**deny**	**permit**} **tcp** *source source-wildcard* [*operator* [*port*]] *destination destination-wildcard* [*operator* [*port*]] [**log**]	ACL mode subcommand to configure the matching details and action for a named ACL that matches TCP segments.
remark *text*	ACL mode subcommand to configure a description of a named ACL.

23

Table 23-8 Chapter 23 Device Security Configuration Command Reference

Command	Description
enable secret *pass-value*	Global command. Sets this switch's password that is required for any user to reach enable mode.
enable password *pass-value*	Global command. Sets this switch's password that is required for any user to reach enable mode.
login local	Console and vty configuration mode. Tells IOS to prompt for a username and password, to be checked against locally configured **username** global configuration commands on this switch or router.
username *name* **secret** *pass-value*	Global command. Defines one of possibly multiple usernames and associated passwords, used for user authentication. Used when the **login local** line configuration command has been used.
crypto key generate rsa	Global command. Creates and stores (in a hidden location in flash memory) the keys required by SSH.

Command	Description
transport input {telnet | ssh | all | none}	vty line configuration mode. Defines whether Telnet and/or SSH access is allowed into this switch. Both values can be configured on one command to allow both Telnet and SSH access (the default).
service password-encryption	Global command that (weakly) encrypts plain text passwords that might have been defined by the username, enable password, and line password commands.
[no] ip http server	Global command to disable (with the no option) or enable the HTTP service, supporting a GUI interface to the router or switch.
[no] service tcp-small-servers	Global command to disable (with the no option) or enable a group of small TCP-based services (echo, discard, daytime, and chargen)
[no] service udp-small-servers	Global command to disable (with the no option) or enable a group of small UDP-based services (echo, discard, daytime, and chargen)
[no] cdp run	Global command to disable (with the no option) or enable CDP for the entire router or switch.
[no] cdp enable	Interface subcommand to disable (with the no option) or enable CDP for that interface.
ntp server server–IP [version 1..4]	Configures the router or switch to act as a NTP client, using the listed server as the NTP server.

Table 23-9   Chapter 23 EXEC Command Reference

Command	Description
show ip interface [type number]	Includes a reference to the access lists enabled on the interface.
show access-lists [access-list-number | access-list-name]	Shows details of configured access lists for all protocols.
show ip access-lists [access-list-number | access-list-name]	Shows IP access lists.
show ntp status	Lists several lines of NTP status information, including the IP address of any NTP peers.
show ntp associations	Lists a single line identifying each other NTP peer with which this router has associated with NTP.

Answers to Earlier Practice Problems

Table 23-10 lists the answers to the practice problems listed in Table 23-5. Note that for any question that references a client, you might have chosen to match port numbers greater than 1023. The answers in this table mostly ignore that option, but just to show one sample, the answer to the first problem lists one with a reference to client ports greater than 1023 and one without. The remaining answers simply omit this part of the logic.

Table 23-10   Building One-Line Extended ACLs: Answers

	Criteria
1	access-list 101 permit tcp host 10.1.1.1 10.1.2.0 0.0.0.255 eq www or access-list 101 permit tcp host 10.1.1.1 gt 1023 10.1.2.0 0.0.0.255 eq www
2	access-list 102 permit tcp 172.16.4.0 0.0.0.127 172.16.3.0 0.0.0.127 eq telnet
3	access-list 103 permit icmp 192.168.7.192 0.0.0.63 192.168.7.8 0.0.0.7
4	access-list 104 permit tcp 10.2.2.0 0.0.1.255 eq www 10.4.4.0 0.0.3.255
5	access-list 105 permit tcp 172.20.1.0 0.0.0.255 eq 23 172.20.44.0 0.0.1.255
6	access-list 106 permit tcp 192.168.99.96 0.0.0.15 192.168.176.0 0.0.0.15 eq www
7	access-list 107 permit icmp 10.55.66.0 0.0.0.127 10.66.55.0 0.0.0.63
8	access-list 108 permit ip any any

Answers to Review Questions:

1 E and F **2** A and E **3** E **4** E **5** A and C **6** C **7** A

23

Chapter 24

Network Address Translation

This last of the chapters about IPv4 topics looks at a very popular and very important part of both enterprise and small office/home office (SOHO) networks: Network Address Translation, or NAT. NAT helped solve a big problem with IPv4: The IPv4 address space would have been completely consumed by the mid-1990s. After it was consumed, the Internet could not continue to grow, which would have significantly slowed the development of the Internet.

This chapter actually discusses two short-term solutions to the IPv4 address exhaustion issue, which also serves as a good lead-in to IP version 6 (IPv6). NAT, along with classless interdomain routing (CIDR), helped extend the life of IPv4 as the network layer protocol of the Internet from the 1990s into the 2010s. Part VII of this book discusses the long-term solution that will become the standard for the Internet: IP version 6 (IPv6).

This chapter breaks the topics into three major sections. The first section explains the challenges to the IPv4 address space caused by the Internet revolution of the 1990s. The second section explains the basic concept behind NAT, how several variations of NAT work, and how the Port Address Translation (PAT) option conserves the IPv4 address space. The final section shows how to configure NAT from the Cisco IOS Software command-line interface (CLI), and how to troubleshoot NAT.

This chapter covers the following subjects:

Operation of IP Data Networks

Predict the data flow between two hosts across a network

IP Services

Identify the basic operation of NAT

  Purpose

  Pool

  Static

  1 to 1

  Overloading

  Source addressing

  One way NAT

Configure and verify NAT for given network requirements

Foundation Topics

Perspectives on IPv4 Address Scalability

The original design for the Internet required every organization to ask for, and receive, one or more registered classful IP network numbers. The people administering the program ensured that none of the IP networks were reused. As long as every organization used only IP addresses inside its own registered network numbers, IP addresses would never be duplicated, and IP routing could work well.

Connecting to the Internet using only a registered network number, or several registered network numbers, worked well for a while. In the early to mid-1990s, it became apparent that the Internet was growing so fast that all IP network numbers would be assigned by the mid-1990s! Concern arose that the available networks would be completely assigned, and some organizations would not be able to connect to the Internet.

The main long-term solution to the IP address scalability problem was to increase the size of the IP address. This one fact was the most compelling reason for the advent of IP version 6 (IPv6). (Version 5 was defined much earlier, but was never deployed, so the next attempt was labeled as version 6.) IPv6 uses a 128-bit address, instead of the 32-bit address in IPv4. With the same or improved process of assigning unique address ranges to every organization connected to the Internet, IPv6 can easily support every organization and individual on the planet, with the number of IPv6 addresses theoretically reaching above 10^{38}.

Many short-term solutions to the addressing problem were suggested, but three standards worked together to solve the problem. Two of the standards work closely together: Network Address Translation (NAT) and private addressing. These features together allow organizations to use unregistered IP network numbers internally and still communicate well with the Internet. The third standard, classless interdomain routing (CIDR), allows ISPs to reduce the wasting of IP addresses by assigning a company a subset of a network number rather than the entire network. CIDR also can allow ISPs to summarize routes such that multiple Class A, B, or C networks match a single route, which helps reduce the size of Internet routing tables.

24

> **NOTE** These tools have worked well. Estimates in the early 1990s predicted that the world would run out of IPv4 addresses by the mid-1990s, but IANA did not exhaust the IPv4 address space until February 2011.

CIDR

CIDR is a global address assignment convention that defines how the Internet Assigned Numbers Authority (IANA), its member agencies, and ISPs should assign the globally unique IPv4 address space to individual organizations.

CIDR, defined in RFC 4632, has two main goals. First, CIDR defines a way to assign public IP addresses, worldwide, to allow route aggregation or route summarization. These route summaries greatly reduce the size of routing tables in Internet routers. Second, CIDR defines rules that allow an ISP to assign public IP addresses in blocks other than an entire Class A, B, or C network. CIDR allows ISPs to assign a public IPv4 address block of a size that better matches the needs of that customer.

Route Aggregation for Shorter Routing Tables

Imagine a router in the Internet, with a route to every Class A, B, and C network on the planet. More than 2 million Class C networks exist! If Internet routers had to list every classful network in their routing tables, the routers would require a lot of memory, and routing table searches would require a lot of processing power.

CIDR defines a route aggregation or summarization strategy for the routes to public IPv4 addresses in the Internet. This strategy relies on a worldwide IPv4 address assignment strategy, as well as some simple math to replace many routes for smaller ranges of addresses with one route for a larger range of addresses.

Figure 24-1 shows a typical case of how CIDR might be used to replace over 65,000 routes with one route. First, imagine that ISP 1 owns Class C networks 198.0.0.0 through 198.255.255.0 (these might look funny, but they are valid Class C network numbers). In other words, IANA assigned all addresses that begin with 198 to one of the five regional numbering authorities, and that organization assigned this entire range to one big ISP in that part of the world. This assignment idea is part of CIDR, because it then allows route summarization.

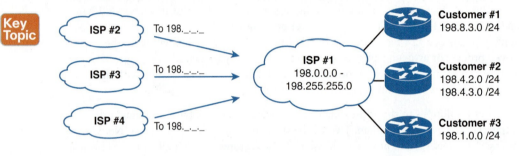

Figure 24-1 *Typical Use of CIDR*

CIDR then defines how to create one route for all of the 2^{16} Class C networks that begin with 198. Figure 24-1 shows the ISPs on the left each with one route to 198.0.0.0/8—in other words, a route to all hosts whose IP address begins with 198. 65,536 Class C IP networks begin with 198, and this one summary route represents all those IP networks.

CIDR requires the use of a classless routing protocol, which, by definition, means that the routing protocol sends the mask along with each route. Classless routing protocols treat each route more like a math problem, ignoring the Class A, B, and C rules. For example, 198.0.0.0/8 (198.0.0.0, mask 255.0.0.0) defines a set of addresses whose first 8 bits are equal to decimal 198. ISP 1 advertises this route to the other ISPs, which need a route only to 198.0.0.0/8. In its routers, ISP 1 knows which Class C networks are at which customer sites. This is how CIDR gives Internet routers a much more scalable routing table—by reducing the number of entries in the tables.

IPv4 Address Conservation

CIDR also helps reduce the chance of our running out of IPv4 addresses by allowing an ISP to allocate a subset of a Class A, B, or C network to a single customer. For example, imagine that ISP 1's customer 1 needs only ten IP addresses and that customer 3 needs 25 IP addresses. ISP 1 does something like this: It assigns IP subnet 198.8.3.16/28, with assignable addresses 198.8.3.17 to 198.8.3.30, to customer 1. For customer 3, ISP 1 suggests 198.8.3.32/27, with 30 assignable addresses (198.8.3.33 to 198.8.3.62). The ISP has met the customers' needs and still not used all of Class C network 198.8.3.0.

CIDR helps prevent the wasting of IP addresses, thereby reducing the need for registered IP network numbers. Instead of two customers consuming two entire Class C networks, each consumes a small portion of a single Class C network. At the same time, CIDR, along with the intelligent administration of consecutive network numbers to each ISP, allows the Internet routing table to support a much smaller routing table in Internet routers than would otherwise be required.

Private Addressing

Some computers might never be connected to the Internet. These computers' IP addresses could be duplicates of registered IP addresses in the Internet. When designing the IP addressing convention for such a network, an organization could pick and use any network number(s) it wanted, and all would be well. For example, you can buy a few routers, connect them in your office, and configure IP addresses in network 1.0.0.0, and it would work. The IP addresses you use might be duplicates of real IP addresses in the Internet, but if all you want to do is learn on the lab in your office, everything will be fine.

When building a private network that will have no Internet connectivity, you can use IP network numbers called *private internets*, as defined in RFC 1918, "Address Allocation for Private Internets." This RFC defines a set of networks that will never be assigned to any organization as a registered network number. Instead of using someone else's registered network numbers, you can use numbers in a range that are not used by anyone else in the public Internet. Table 24-1 shows the private address space defined by RFC 1918.

Key Topic

Table 24-1   RFC 1918 Private Address Space

Range of IP Addresses	Class of Networks	Number of Networks
10.0.0.0 to 10.255.255.255	A	1
172.16.0.0 to 172.31.255.255	B	16
192.168.0.0 to 192.168.255.255	C	256

In other words, any organization can use these network numbers. However, no organization is allowed to advertise these networks using a routing protocol on the Internet.

You might be wondering why you would bother to reserve special private network numbers when it doesn't matter whether the addresses are duplicates. Well, as it turns out, you can use private addressing in an internetwork, and connect to the Internet at the same time, as long as you use Network Address Translation (NAT). The rest of this chapter examines and explains NAT.

Network Address Translation Concepts

NAT, defined in RFC 3022, allows a host that does not have a valid, registered, globally unique IP address to communicate with other hosts through the Internet. The hosts might be using private addresses or addresses assigned to another organization. In either case, NAT allows these addresses that are not Internet ready to continue to be used and still allows communication with hosts across the Internet.

NAT achieves its goal by using a valid registered IP address to represent the private address to the rest of the Internet. The NAT function changes the private IP addresses to publicly registered IP addresses inside each IP packet, as shown in Figure 24-2.

24

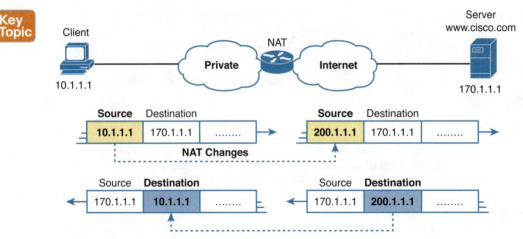

Figure 24-2 *NAT IP Address Swapping: Private Addressing*

Notice that the router, performing NAT, changes the packet's source IP address when the packet leaves the private organization. The router performing NAT also changes the destination address in each packet that is forwarded back into the private network. (Network 200.1.1.0 is a registered network in Figure 24-2.) The NAT feature, configured in the router labeled NAT, performs the translation.

Cisco IOS Software supports several variations of NAT. The next few pages cover the concepts behind several of these variations. The section after that covers the configuration related to each option.

Static NAT

Static NAT works just like the example shown in Figure 24-2, but with the IP addresses statically mapped to each other. To help you understand the implications of static NAT and to explain several key terms, Figure 24-3 shows a similar example with more information.

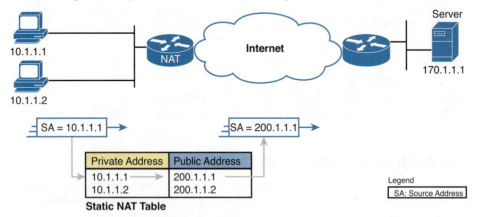

Figure 24-3 *Static NAT Showing Inside Local and Global Addresses*

First, the concepts: The company's ISP has assigned it registered network 200.1.1.0. Therefore, the NAT router must make the private IP addresses look like they are in network 200.1.1.0. To do so, the NAT router changes the source IP addresses in the packets going from left to right in the figure.

In this example, the NAT router changes the source address ("SA" in the figure) of 10.1.1.1 to 200.1.1.1. With static NAT, the NAT router simply configures a one-to-one mapping between the private address and the registered address that is used on its behalf. The NAT router has statically configured a mapping between private address 10.1.1.1 and public, registered address 200.1.1.1.

Supporting a second IP host with static NAT requires a second static one-to-one mapping using a second IP address in the public address range. For example, to support 10.1.1.2, the router statically maps 10.1.1.2 to 200.1.1.2. Because the enterprise has a single registered Class C network, it can support at most 254 private IP addresses with NAT, with the usual two reserved numbers (the network number and network broadcast address).

The terminology used with NAT, particularly with configuration, can be a little confusing. Notice in Figure 24-3 that the NAT table lists the private IP addresses as "private" and the public, registered addresses from network 200.1.1.0 as "public." Cisco uses the term *inside local* for the private IP addresses in this example and *inside global* for the public IP addresses.

Using NAT terminology, the enterprise network that uses private addresses, and therefore needs NAT, is the "inside" part of the network. The Internet side of the NAT function is the "outside" part of the network. A host that needs NAT (such as 10.1.1.1 in the example) has the IP address it uses inside the network, and it needs an IP address to represent it in the outside network. So, because the host essentially needs two different addresses to represent it, you need two terms. Cisco calls the private IP address used in the inside network the *inside local* address and the address used to represent the host to the rest of the Internet the *inside global* address. Figure 24-4 repeats the same example, with some of the terminology shown.

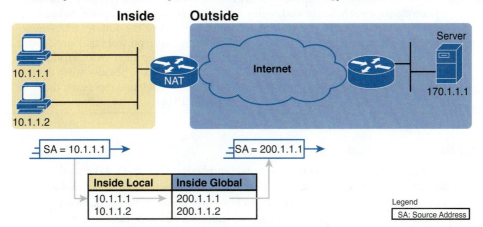

Figure 24-4 *Static NAT Terminology*

Most typical NAT configurations change only the IP address of inside hosts. Therefore, the current NAT table shown in Figure 24-4 shows the inside local and corresponding inside global registered addresses. However, the outside host IP address can also be changed with NAT. When that occurs, the terms *outside local* and *outside global* denote the IP address used to represent that host in the inside network and the outside network, respectively. Table 24-2 summarizes the terminology and meanings.

Key Topic

Table 24-2   NAT Addressing Terms

Term	Meaning
Inside local	In a typical NAT design, the term *inside* refers to an address used for a host inside an enterprise. An inside local is the actual IP address assigned to a host in the private enterprise network. A more descriptive term might be *inside private*, because oftentimes (but not always), the inside addresses are also private addresses.
Inside global	In a typical NAT design, the term *inside* refers to an address used for a host inside an enterprise. NAT uses an inside global address to represent the inside host as the packet is sent through the outside network, typically the Internet. A NAT router changes the source IP address of a packet sent by an inside host from an inside local address to an inside global address as the packet goes from the inside to the outside network.
	A more descriptive term might be *inside public*, because when using RFC 1918 addresses in an enterprise, the inside global address represents the inside host with a public IP address that can be used for routing in the public Internet.
Outside global	In a typical NAT design, the term outside refers to an address used for a host outside an enterprise—in other words, in the Internet. An outside global address is the actual IP address assigned to a host that resides in the outside network, typically the Internet. A more descriptive term might be *outside public*, because the outside global address represents the outside host with a public IP address that can be used for routing in the public Internet.
Outside local	NAT can translate the outside IP address—the IP address that represents the host outside the enterprise network—although this is not a popular option. When a NAT router forwards a packet from the inside network to the outside, when using NAT to change the outside address, the IP address that represents the outside host as the destination IP address in the packet header is called the outside local IP address. A more descriptive term might be *outside private*, because when using RFC 1918 addresses in an enterprise, the outside local address represents the outside host with a private IP address from RFC 1918.

Dynamic NAT

Dynamic NAT has some similarities and differences compared to static NAT. Like static NAT, the NAT router creates a one-to-one mapping between an inside local and inside global address, and changes the IP addresses in packets as they exit and enter the inside network. However, the mapping of an inside local address to an inside global address happens dynamically.

Dynamic NAT sets up a pool of possible inside global addresses and defines matching criteria to determine which inside local IP addresses should be translated with NAT. For example, in Figure 24-5, a pool of five inside global IP addresses has been established: 200.1.1.1 through 200.1.1.5. NAT has also been configured to translate any inside local addresses that start with 10.1.1.

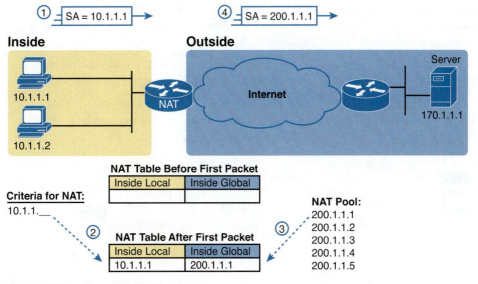

Figure 24-5 *Dynamic NAT*

The numbers 1, 2, 3, and 4 in the figure refer to the following sequence of events:

1. Host 10.1.1.1 sends its first packet to the server at 170.1.1.1.

2. As the packet enters the NAT router, the router applies some matching logic to decide whether the packet should have NAT applied. Because the logic has been configured to match source IP addresses that begin with 10.1.1, the router adds an entry in the NAT table for 10.1.1.1 as an inside local address.

3. The NAT router needs to allocate an IP address from the pool of valid inside global addresses. It picks the first one available (200.1.1.1, in this case) and adds it to the NAT table to complete the entry.

4. The NAT router translates the source IP address and forwards the packet.

The dynamic entry stays in the table as long as traffic flows occasionally. You can configure a timeout value that defines how long the router should wait, having not translated any packets with that address, before removing the dynamic entry. You can also manually clear the dynamic entries from the table using the **clear ip nat translation** * command.

NAT can be configured with more IP addresses in the inside local address list than in the inside global address pool. The router allocates addresses from the pool until all are allocated. If a new packet arrives from yet another inside host, and it needs a NAT entry, but all the pooled IP addresses are in use, the router simply discards the packet. The user must try again until a NAT entry times out, at which point the NAT function works for the next host that sends a packet. Essentially, the inside global pool of addresses needs to be as large as the maximum number of concurrent hosts that need to use the Internet at the same time—unless you use PAT, as is explained in the next section.

Overloading NAT with Port Address Translation (PAT)

Some networks need to have most, if not all, IP hosts reach the Internet. If that network uses private IP addresses, the NAT router needs a very large set of registered IP addresses. With static NAT, for each private IP host that needs Internet access, you need a publicly registered IP address, completely defeating the goal of reducing the number of public IPv4 addresses needed for that organization. Dynamic NAT lessens the problem to some degree, because every single host in an internetwork should seldom need to communicate with the Internet at the same time.

However, if a large percentage of the IP hosts in a network will need Internet access throughout that company's normal business hours, NAT still requires a large number of registered IP addresses, again failing to reduce IPv4 address consumption.

The NAT Overload feature, also called Port Address Translation (PAT), solves this problem. Overloading allows NAT to scale to support many clients with only a few public IP addresses.

The key to understanding how overloading works is to recall how hosts use TCP and User Datagram Protocol (UDP) ports. To see why, first consider the idea of three separate TCP connections to a web server, from three different hosts, as shown in Figure 24-6.

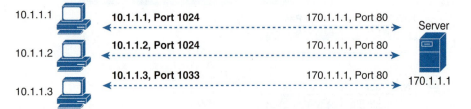

Figure 24-6   *Three TCP Connections from Three PCs*

Next, compare those three TCP connections in Figure 24-6 to three similar TCP connections, now with all three TCP connections from one client, as shown in Figure 24-7. The server does realize a difference, because the server see the IP address and TCP port number used by the clients in both figures. However, the server really does not care whether the TCP connections come from different hosts, or the same host; the server just sends and receives data over each connection.

Figure 24-7   *Three TCP Connections from One PC*

NAT takes advantage of the fact that, from a transport layer perspective, the server doesn't care whether it has one connection each to three different hosts or three connections to a single host IP address. NAT overload (PAT) translates not only the address, but the port number when necessary, making what looks like many TCP or UDP flows from different hosts look like the same number of flows from one host. Figure 24-8 outlines the logic.

Key Topic

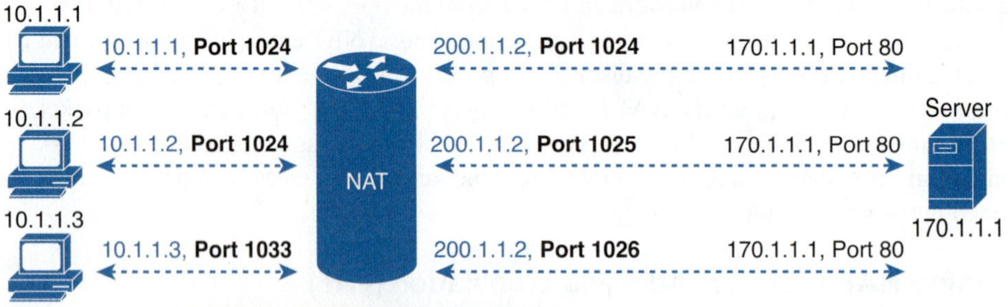

Inside Local	Inside Global
10.1.1.1: **1024**	200.1.1.2: **1024**
10.1.1.2: **1024**	200.1.1.2: **1025**
10.1.1.3: **1033**	200.1.1.2: **1026**

Dynamic NAT Table, With Overloading

Figure 24-8   *NAT Overload (PAT)*

When PAT creates the dynamic mapping, it selects not only an inside global IP address but also a unique port number to use with that address. The NAT router keeps a NAT table entry for every unique combination of inside local IP address and port, with translation to the inside global address and a unique port number associated with the inside global address. And because the port number field has 16 bits, NAT overload can use more than 65,000 port numbers, allowing it to scale well without needing many registered IP addresses—in many cases, needing only one inside global IP address.

Of the three types of NAT covered in this chapter so far, PAT is by far the most popular option. Static NAT and Dynamic NAT both require a one-to-one mapping from the inside local to the inside global address. PAT significantly reduces the number of required registered IP addresses compared to these other NAT alternatives.

NAT Overload (PAT) on Consumer Routers

The (upcoming) last major section of this chapter shows how to configure and verify NAT overload, or PAT, on an enterprise-class Cisco router. However, consumer-grade Cisco routers enable many features by default, including PAT. The strategy with consumer-grade routers allows the consumer to just physically install the router and cables, without needing to configure the router. This topic discusses how these consumer-grade routers work to enable PAT, even when using defaults.

First, as mentioned way back in Chapter 3, "Fundamentals of WANs." products sold in the store as a "router" actually have many features: a router, a LAN switch, often with a wireless LAN access point, and a security firewall. They often include the PAT function as well. As for hardware, these routers have several RJ-45 ports labeled as "LAN"; these are ports for the LAN switch function. They also have one RJ-45 port labeled "WAN," which is another Ethernet port that acts like a router interface, typically connected to a DSL or cable modem which in turn connects to the Internet, as shown in Figure 24-9.

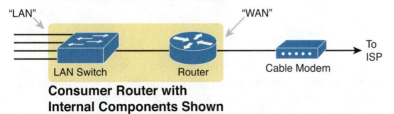

Figure 24-9 *Consumer "Router" with LAN and WAN Ports*

To understand how a consumer router does PAT by default, you first need to understand how it does DHCP. The router acts as a DHCP server on the LAN side, using a private IP network prechosen by the router vendor. (Cisco products often use private Class C network 192.168.1.0.) Then, on the WAN side, the router acts as a DHCP client, leasing an IP address from the ISP's DHCP server. But the address learned from the ISP is not a private IP address, but a public IPv4 address, as shown in Figure 24-10.

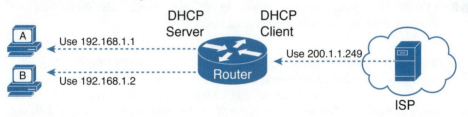

Figure 24-10 *Consumer Router as DHCP Server on LAN, DHCP Client on WAN*

NOTE   To make an enterprise-class router act like the router in Figure 24-10, on the WAN port, use the **ip address dhcp** interface subcommand. This command simply tells the router to learn its own interface IP address with DHCP. The DHCP server configuration would use the same commands detailed in Chapter 18, "Configuring and Verifying Host Connectivity."

By using DHCP on both the LAN and WAN sides, a consumer router has created a perfect match of IP addresses to use PAT. The computers on the LAN all have private IP addresses, and the one WAN port has a public IP address. All the consumer router has to do is enable PAT, with the LAN side of the router as the NAT inside, and the WAN port on the NAT outside, as shown in Figure 24-11.

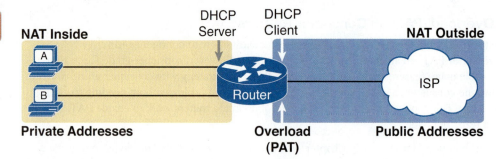

Figure 24-11   *Locations of DHCP and NAT/PAT Roles in a Consumer Router*

NAT Configuration and Troubleshooting

In the following sections, you read about how to configure the three most common variations of NAT: static NAT, dynamic NAT, and PAT, along with the **show** and **debug** commands used to troubleshoot NAT.

Static NAT Configuration

Static NAT configuration, as compared to the other variations of NAT, requires the fewest configuration steps. Each static mapping between a local (private) address and a global (public) address must be configured. Additionally, the router must be told on which interfaces it should use NAT, because NAT does not have to be enabled on every interface. In particular, the router needs to know each interface and whether the interface is an inside or outside interface. The specific steps are as follows:

Step 1.   Configure interfaces to be in the inside part of the NAT design using the **ip nat inside** interface subcommand.

Step 2.   Configure interfaces to be in the outside part of the NAT design using the **ip nat outside** interface subcommand.

Step 3.   Configure the static mappings with the **ip nat inside source static** *inside-local inside-global* global configuration command.

Figure 24-12 shows the familiar network used in the description of static NAT earlier in this chapter, which is also used for the first several configuration examples. In Figure 24-12, you can see that Certskills has obtained Class C network 200.1.1.0 as a registered network number. That entire network, with mask 255.255.255.0, is configured on the serial link between Certskills and the Internet. With a point-to-point serial link, only two of the 254 valid IP addresses in that network are consumed, leaving 252 addresses.

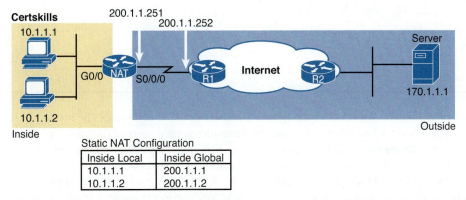

Figure 24-12   *Sample Network for NAT Examples, with Public Class C 200.1.1.0/24*

When planning a NAT configuration, you must find some IP addresses to use as inside global IP addresses. Because these addresses must be part of some registered IP address range, it is common to use the extra addresses in the subnet connecting the enterprise to the Internet—for example, the extra 252 IP addresses in network 200.1.1.0 in this case. The router can also be configured with a loopback interface and assigned an IP address that is part of a globally unique range of registered IP addresses.

Example 24-1 lists the NAT configuration, using 200.1.1.1 and 200.1.1.2 for the two static NAT mappings.

Example 24-1   *Static NAT Configuration*

```
NAT# show running-config
!
! Lines omitted for brevity
!
interface GigabitEthernet0/0
 ip address 10.1.1.3 255.255.255.0
 ip nat inside
!
interface Serial0/0/0
 ip address 200.1.1.251 255.255.255.0
 ip nat outside
!
ip nat inside source static 10.1.1.2 200.1.1.2
ip nat inside source static 10.1.1.1 200.1.1.1

NAT# show ip nat translations
Pro Inside global     Inside local     Outside local     Outside global
--- 200.1.1.1         10.1.1.1         ---               ---
--- 200.1.1.2         10.1.1.2         ---               ---

NAT# show ip nat statistics
Total active translations: 2 (2 static, 0 dynamic; 0 extended)
Outside interfaces:
  Serial0/0/0
```

```
Inside interfaces:
  GigabitEthernet0/0
Hits: 100  Misses: 0
Expired translations: 0
Dynamic mappings:
```

The static mappings are created using the **ip nat inside source static** command. The **inside** keyword means that NAT translates addresses for hosts on the inside part of the network. The **source** keyword means that NAT translates the source IP address of packets coming into its inside interfaces. The **static** keyword means that the parameters define a static entry, which should never be removed from the NAT table because of timeout. Because the design calls for two hosts, 10.1.1.1 and 10.1.1.2, to have Internet access, two **ip nat inside** commands are needed.

After creating the static NAT entries, the router needs to know which interfaces are "inside" and which are "outside." The **ip nat inside** and **ip nat outside** interface subcommands identify each interface appropriately.

A couple of **show** commands list the most important information about NAT. The **show ip nat translations** command lists the two static NAT entries created in the configuration. The **show ip nat statistics** command lists statistics, listing things such as the number of currently active translation table entries. The statistics also include the number of hits, which increments for every packet for which NAT must translate addresses.

Dynamic NAT Configuration

As you might imagine, dynamic NAT configuration differs in some ways from static NAT, but it has some similarities as well. Dynamic NAT still requires that each interface be identified as either an inside or outside interface, and of course static mapping is no longer required. Dynamic NAT uses an access control list (ACL) to identify which inside local (private) IP addresses need to have their addresses translated, and it defines a pool of registered public IP addresses to allocate. The specific steps are as follows:

Step 1.   As with static NAT, configure interfaces to be in the inside part of the NAT design using the **ip nat inside** interface subcommand.

Step 2.   As with static NAT, configure interfaces to be in the outside part of the NAT design using the **ip nat outside** interface subcommand.

Step 3.   Configure an ACL that matches the packets entering inside interfaces for which NAT should be performed.

Step 4.   Configure the pool of public registered IP addresses using the **ip nat pool** *name first-address last-address* **netmask** *subnet-mask* global configuration command.

Step 5.   Enable dynamic NAT by referencing the ACL (Step 3) and pool (Step 4) with the **ip nat inside source list** *acl-number* **pool** *pool-name* global configuration command.

The next example shows a sample dynamic NAT configuration using the same network topology as the previous example (see Figure 24-12). In this case, the same two inside local addresses, 10.1.1.1 and 10.1.1.2, need translation. However, unlike the previous static NAT example, the configuration in Example 24-2 places the public IP addresses (200.1.1.1 and 200.1.1.2) into a pool of dynamically assignable inside global addresses.

Example 24-2 *Dynamic NAT Configuration*

```
NAT# show running-config
!
! Lines omitted for brevity
!
interface GigabitEthernet0/0
 ip address 10.1.1.3 255.255.255.0
 ip nat inside
!
interface Serial0/0/0
 ip address 200.1.1.251 255.255.255.0
 ip nat outside
!
ip nat pool fred 200.1.1.1 200.1.1.2 netmask 255.255.255.252
ip nat inside source list 1 pool fred
!
access-list 1 permit 10.1.1.2
access-list 1 permit 10.1.1.1
```

Dynamic NAT configures the pool of public (global) addresses with the **ip nat pool** command listing the first and last numbers in an inclusive range of inside global addresses. For example, if the pool needed ten addresses, the command might have listed 200.1.1.1 and 200.1.1.10, which means that NAT can use 200.1.1.1 and 200.1.1.10.

Dynamic NAT also performs a verification check on the **ip nat pool** command with the required **netmask** parameter. If the address range would not be in the same subnet, assuming the configured **netmask** was used on the addresses in the configured range, then IOS will reject the **ip nat pool** command. For example, as configured with the low end of 200.1.1.1, high end of 200.1.1.2, and a mask of 255.255.255.252, IOS would use the following checks, to ensure that both calculates put 200.1.1.1 and 200.1.1.2 in the same subnet:

- 200.1.1.1 with mask 255.255.255.252 implies subnet 200.1.1.0, broadcast address 200.1.1.3.
- 200.1.1.2 with mask 255.255.255.252 implies subnet 200.1.1.0, broadcast address 200.1.1.3.

If the command had instead showed a low and high end value of 200.1.1.1 and 200.1.1.6, again with mask 255.255.255.252, IOS would reject the command. IOS would do the math spelled out in the following list, realizing that the numbers were in different subnets:

- 200.1.1.1 with mask 255.255.255.252 implies subnet 200.1.1.0, broadcast address 200.1.1.3.
- 200.1.1.6 with mask 255.255.255.252 implies subnet 200.1.1.4, broadcast address 200.1.1.7.

One other big different between the dynamic NAT and static NAT configuration in Example 24-1 has to do with two options in the **ip nat inside source** command. The dynamic NAT version of this command refers to the name of the NAT pool it wants to use for inside global addresses—in this case, fred. It also refers to an IP ACL, which defines the matching logic for inside local IP addresses. So, the logic for the **ip nat inside source list 1 pool fred** command in this example is:

> Create NAT table entries that map between hosts matched by ACL 1, for packets entering any inside interface, allocating an inside global address from the pool called fred.

24

Dynamic NAT Verification

Examples 24-3 and 24-4 show the evidence that dynamic NAT begins with no NAT table entries, but the router reacts after user traffic correctly drives the NAT function. Example 24-3 shows the output of the **show ip nat translations** and **show ip nat statistics** commands before any users generate traffic that makes NAT do some work. The **show ip nat translations** command, which lists the NAT table entries, lists a blank line; the **show ip nat statistics** command, which shows how many times NAT has created a NAT table entry, shows 0 active translations.

Example 24-3 *Dynamic NAT Verifications Before Generating Traffic*

```
! The next command lists one empty line because no entries have been dynamically
! created yet.
NAT# show ip nat translations

NAT# show ip nat statistics
Total active translations: 0 (0 static, 0 dynamic; 0 extended)
Outside interfaces:
  Serial0/0
Inside interfaces:
  Ethernet0/0
Hits: 0  Misses: 0
CEF Translated packets: 0, CEF Punted packets: 0
Expired translations: 0
Dynamic mappings:
-- Inside Source
[id 1] access-list 1 pool fred refcount 0
 pool fred: netmask 255.255.255.252
    start 200.1.1.1 end 200.1.1.2
    type generic, total addresses 2, allocated 0 (0%), misses 0

Total doors: 0
Appl doors: 0
Normal doors: 0
Queued Packets: 0
```

The **show ip nat statistics** command at the end of the example lists some particularly interesting troubleshooting information with two different counters labeled "misses," as highlighted in the example. The first occurrence of this counter counts the number of times a new packet comes along, needing a NAT entry, and not finding one. At that point, dynamic NAT reacts and builds an entry. The second misses counter toward the end of the command output lists the number of misses in the pool. This counter only increments when dynamic NAT tries to allocate a new NAT table entry and finds no available addresses, so the packet cannot be translated—probably resulting in an end user not getting to the application.

Next, Example 24-4 updates the output of both commands after the user of host at 10.1.1.1 telnets to host 170.1.1.1.

Example 24-4 *Dynamic NAT Verifications After Generating Traffic*

```
NAT# show ip nat translations
Pro Inside global      Inside local     Outside local     Outside global
--- 200.1.1.1          10.1.1.1         ---               ---


NAT# show ip nat statistics
Total active translations: 1 (0 static, 1 dynamic; 0 extended)
Outside interfaces:
  Serial0/0
Inside interfaces:
  Ethernet0/0
Hits: 69  Misses: 1
Expired translations: 0
Dynamic mappings:
-- Inside Source
access-list 1 pool fred refcount 1
 pool fred: netmask 255.255.255.252
    start 200.1.1.1 end 200.1.1.2
    type generic, total addresses 2, allocated 1 (50%), misses 0
```

The example begins with host 10.1.1.1 telnetting to 170.1.1.1 (not shown), with the NAT router creating a NAT entry. The NAT table shows a single entry, mapping 10.1.1.1 to 200.1.1.1. And, the first line in the output of the **show ip nat statistics** command lists a counter for 1 active translation, as seen in the NAT table at the top of the example.

Take an extra moment to consider the last highlighted line, where the **show ip nat statistics** command lists 1 miss and 69 hits. The first miss counter, now at 1, means that one packet arrived that needed NAT but there was no NAT table entry. NAT reacted and added a NAT table entry, so the hit counter of 69 means that the next 69 packets used the newly added NAT table entry. The second misses counter, still at 0, did not increment because the NAT pool had enough available inside global IP addresses to use to allocate the new NAT table entry. Also note that the last line lists statistics on the number of pool members allocated (1) and the percentage of the pool currently in use (50%).

The dynamic NAT table entries time out after a period of inactivity, putting those inside global addresses back in the pool for future use. Example 24-5 shows a sequence in which two different hosts make use of inside global address 200.1.1.1. Host 10.1.1.1 uses inside global address 200.1.1.1 at the beginning of the example. Then, instead of just waiting on the NAT entry to time out, the example clears the NAT table entry with the **clear ip nat translation** * command. At that point, the user at 10.1.1.2 telnets to 170.1.1.1, and the new NAT table entry appears, using the same 200.1.1.1 inside global address.

Example 24-5 *Example of Reuse of a Dynamic Inside Global IP Address*

```
! Host 10.1.1.1 current uses inside global 200.1.1.1
NAT# show ip nat translations
Pro Inside global      Inside local     Outside local     Outside global
--- 200.1.1.1          10.1.1.1         ---               ---
NAT# clear ip nat translation *

!

! telnet from 10.1.1.2 to 170.1.1.1 happened next; not shown
!
```

24

```
! Now host 10.1.1.2 uses inside global 200.1.1.1

NAT# show ip nat translations
Pro Inside global     Inside local     Outside local     Outside global
--- 200.1.1.1         10.1.1.2         ---               ---
!
! Telnet from 10.1.1.1 to 170.1.1.1 happened next; not shown
!
NAT# debug ip nat
IP NAT debugging is on

Oct 20 19:23:03.263: NAT*: s=10.1.1.1->200.1.1.2, d=170.1.1.1 [348]
Oct 20 19:23:03.267: NAT*: s=170.1.1.1, d=200.1.1.1->10.1.1.1 [348]
Oct 20 19:23:03.464: NAT*: s=10.1.1.1->200.1.1.2, d=170.1.1.1 [349]
Oct 20 19:23:03.568: NAT*: s=170.1.1.1, d=200.1.1.1->10.1.1.1 [349]
```

Finally, at the end of Example 24-5, you see that host 10.1.1.1 has telnetted to another host in the Internet, plus the output from the **debug ip nat** command. This **debug** command causes the router to issue a message every time a packet has its address translated for NAT. You generate the output results by entering a few lines from the Telnet connection from 10.1.1.1 to 170.1.1.1. The debug output tells us that host 10.1.1.1 now uses inside global address 200.1.1.2 for this new connection.

NAT Overload (PAT) Configuration

The static and dynamic NAT configuration matter, but the NAT overload (PAT) configuration in this section matters more. This is the feature that saves public IPv4 addresses and prolonged IPv4's life.

NAT overload, as mentioned earlier, allows NAT to support many inside local IP addresses with only one or a few inside global IP addresses. By essentially translating the private IP address and port number to a single inside global address, but with a unique port number, NAT can support many (over 65,000) private hosts with only a single public, global address.

Two variations of PAT configuration exist in IOS. If PAT uses a pool of inside global addresses, the configuration looks exactly like dynamic NAT, except the **ip nat inside source list** global command has an **overload** keyword added to the end. If PAT just needs to use one inside global IP address, PAT can use one of its interface IP addresses. Because NAT can support over 65,000 concurrent flows with a single inside global address, a single public IP address can support an entire organization's NAT needs.

The following statement detail the configuration different between NAT overload and 1:1 NAT when using a NAT pool:

Use the same steps for configuring dynamic NAT, as outlined in the previous section, but include the **overload** keyword at the end of the **ip nat inside source list** global command.

The following checklist details the configuration when using an interface IP address as the sole inside global IP address:

Step 1. As with dynamic and static NAT, configure inside interfaces with the **ip nat inside** interface subcommand.

Step 2. As with dynamic and static NAT, configure outside interfaces with the **ip nat outside** interface subcommand.

Step 3.   As with dynamic NAT, configure an ACL that matches the packets entering inside interfaces.

Step 4.   Configure the **ip nat inside source list** *acl-number* **interface** *type/number* **overload** global configuration command, referring to the ACL created in Step 3 and to the interface whose IP address will be used for translations.

Example 24-2 shows a dynamic NAT configuration. To convert it to a PAT configuration, the **ip nat inside source list 1 pool fred overload** command would be used instead, simply adding the **overload** keyword.

The next example shows PAT configuration using a single interface IP address. Figure 24-13 shows the same familiar network, with a few changes. In this case, the ISP has given Certskills a subset of network 200.1.1.0: CIDR subnet 200.1.1.248/30. In other words, this subnet has two usable addresses: 200.1.1.249 and 200.1.1.250. These addresses are used on either end of the serial link between Certskills and its ISP. The NAT feature on the Certskills router translates all NAT addresses to its serial IP address, 200.1.1.249.

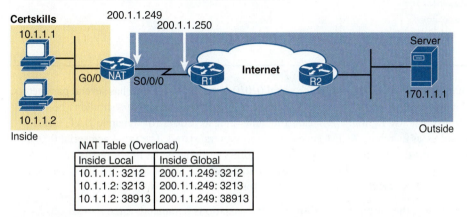

Figure 24-13   *NAT Overload and PAT*

In Example 24-6, which shows the NAT overload configuration, NAT translates using inside global address 200.1.1.249 only, so the NAT pool is not required. In the example, host 10.1.1.2 creates two Telnet connections, and host 10.1.1.1 creates one Telnet connection, causing three dynamic NAT entries, each using inside global address 200.1.1.249, but each with a unique port number.

Example 24-6   *NAT Overload Configuration*

```
NAT# show running-config
!
! Lines Omitted for Brevity
!
interface GigabitEthernet0/0
 ip address 10.1.1.3 255.255.255.0
 ip nat inside
!
interface Serial0/0/0
 ip address 200.1.1.249 255.255.255.252
 ip nat outside
!
ip nat inside source list 1 interface Serial0/0/0 overload
!
```

```
access-list 1 permit 10.1.1.2
access-list 1 permit 10.1.1.1
!

NAT# show ip nat translations
Pro Inside global        Inside local      Outside local     Outside global
tcp 200.1.1.249:3212     10.1.1.1:3212     170.1.1.1:23      170.1.1.1:23
tcp 200.1.1.249:3213     10.1.1.2:3213     170.1.1.1:23      170.1.1.1:23
tcp 200.1.1.249:38913    10.1.1.2:38913    170.1.1.1:23      170.1.1.1:23
NAT# show ip nat statistics
Total active translations: 3 (0 static, 3 dynamic; 3 extended)
Outside interfaces:
  Serial0/0/0
Inside interfaces:
  GigabitEthernet0/0
Hits: 103   Misses: 3
Expired translations: 0
Dynamic mappings:
-- Inside Source
access-list 1 interface Serial0/0/0 refcount 3
```

The **ip nat inside source list 1 interface serial 0/0/0 overload** command has several parameters, but if you understand the dynamic NAT configuration, the new parameters shouldn't be too hard to grasp. The **list 1** parameter means the same thing as it does for dynamic NAT: Inside local IP addresses matching ACL 1 have their addresses translated. The **interface serial 0/0/0** parameter means that the only inside global IP address available is the IP address of the NAT router's interface serial 0/0/0. Finally, the **overload** parameter means that overload is enabled. Without this parameter, the router does not perform overload, just dynamic NAT.

As you can see in the output of the **show ip nat translations** command, three translations have been added to the NAT table. Before this command, host 10.1.1.1 creates one Telnet connection to 170.1.1.1, and host 10.1.1.2 creates two Telnet connections. The router creates one NAT table entry for each unique combination of inside local IP address and port.

NAT Troubleshooting

The majority of NAT troubleshooting issues relate to getting the configuration correct. The following list summarizes some hints and tips about how to find the most common NAT configuration problems. Following the list, the text explains one common routing problem that can prevent NAT from working, which relates mainly to ensuring that the configuration is correct.

Key Topic

■ Ensure that the configuration includes the **ip nat inside** and **ip nat outside** interface subcommands. These commands enable NAT on the interfaces, and the inside/outside designation is important.

■ For static NAT, ensure that the **ip nat inside source static** command lists the inside local address first and the inside global IP address second.

■ For dynamic NAT, ensure that the ACL configured to match packets sent by the inside hosts match that host's packets, before any NAT translation has occurred. For example, if an inside local address of 10.1.1.1 should be translated to 200.1.1.1, ensure that the ACL matches source address 10.1.1.1, not 200.1.1.1.

- For dynamic NAT without PAT, ensure that the pool has enough IP addresses. Symptoms of not having enough addresses include a growing value in the second misses counter in the **show ip nat statistics** command output, as well as seeing all the pool addresses already in the NAT table.

- For PAT, it is easy to forget to add the **overload** option on the **ip nat inside source list** command. Without it, NAT works, but PAT does not, often resulting in users' packets not being translated and hosts not being able to get to the Internet.

- Perhaps NAT has been configured correctly, but an ACL exists on one of the interfaces, discarding the packets. Note that IOS processes ACLs before NAT for packets entering an interface, and after translating the addresses for packets exiting an interface.

- Make sure that some user traffic is entering the NAT router on an inside interface, triggering NAT to do a translation. NAT reacts to packets that come in an interface, and then matches the logic referenced in the NAT configuration. The NAT configuration can be perfect, but if no inbound traffic occurs that matches the NAT configuration, NAT does nothing.

Finally, the NAT function on one router can be impacted by a routing problem that occurs on another router. The routers in the outside part of the network, oftentimes the Internet, need to be able to route packets to the inside global IP addresses configured on the NAT router.

For example, Figure 24-4, earlier in this chapter, shows the flow of packets from inside to outside and outside to inside. Focusing on the outside-to-inside flow, the routers in the Internet needed to know how to route packets to public registered IP address 200.1.1.1. Typically, this address range would be advertised by a dynamic routing protocol. So, if a review of the NAT configuration shows that the configuration looks correct, look at the routes in both the NAT router and other routers to ensure that the routers can forward the packets, based on the addresses used on both sides of the router performing the NAT function.

24

Review Activities

Chapter Summary

- CIDR is a global address assignment convention that defines how the Internet Assigned Numbers Authority (IANA), its member agencies, and ISPs should assign the globally unique IPv4 address space to individual organizations.

- CIDR, defined in RFC 4632, has two main goals:

  - First, CIDR defines a way to assign public IP addresses, worldwide, to enable route aggregation or route summarization. These route summaries greatly reduce the size of routing tables in Internet routers.

  - Second, CIDR defines rules that enable an ISP to assign public IP addresses in blocks other than an entire Class A, B, or C network. CIDR enables ISPs to assign a public IPv4 address block of a size that better matches the needs of that customer.

- CIDR requires the use of a classless routing protocol, which, by definition, means that the routing protocol sends the mask along with each route.

- When building a private network that will have no Internet connectivity, you can use IP network numbers called *private internets*, as defined in RFC 1918, "Address Allocation for Private Internets." This RFC defines a set of networks that will never be assigned to any organization as a registered network number. Instead of using someone else's registered network numbers, you can use numbers in a range that are not used by anyone else in the public Internet.

- NAT, defined in RFC 3022, enables a host that does not have a valid, registered, globally unique IP address to communicate with other hosts through the Internet.

- NAT achieves its goal by using a valid registered IP address to represent the private address to the rest of the Internet. The NAT function changes the private IP addresses to publicly registered IP addresses inside each IP packet.

- Using NAT terminology, the enterprise network that uses private addresses, and therefore needs NAT, is the "inside" part of the network. The Internet side of the NAT function is the "outside" part of the network. A host that needs NAT has the IP address it uses inside the network, and it needs an IP address to represent it in the outside network. So, because the host essentially needs two different addresses to represent it, you need two terms. Cisco calls the private IP address used in the inside network the *inside local* address and the address used to represent the host to the rest of the Internet the *inside global* address.

- Dynamic NAT has some similarities and differences compared to static NAT. Like static NAT, the NAT router creates a one-to-one mapping between an inside local and inside global address and changes the IP addresses in packets as they exit and enter the inside network. However, the mapping of an inside local address to an inside global address happens dynamically.

- Dynamic NAT sets up a pool of possible inside global addresses and defines matching criteria to determine which inside local IP addresses should be translated with NAT.

- The NAT Overload feature, also called Port Address Translation (PAT), enables NAT to scale to support many clients with only a few public IP addresses. When PAT creates the dynamic mapping, it selects not only an inside global IP address but also a unique port number to use with that address. The NAT router keeps a NAT table entry for every unique combination of inside local IP address and port, with translation to the inside global address and a unique port number associated with the inside global address.

■ Because the port number field has 16 bits, NAT overload can use more than 65,000 port numbers, enabling it to scale well without needing many registered IP addresses—in many cases, needing only one inside global IP address.

■ Compared to the other variations of NAT, static NAT configuration requires the fewest configuration steps. Each static mapping between a local (private) address and a global (public) address must be configured. Additionally, the router must be told on which interfaces it should use NAT, because NAT does not have to be enabled on every interface. In particular, the router needs to know each interface and whether the interface is an inside or outside interface. The specific steps are as follows:

Step 1. Configure interfaces to be in the inside part of the NAT design using the **ip nat inside** interface subcommand.

Step 2. Configure interfaces to be in the outside part of the NAT design using the **ip nat outside** interface subcommand.

Step 3. Configure the static mappings with the **ip nat inside source static** *inside-local inside-global* global configuration command.

■ As you might imagine, dynamic NAT configuration differs in some ways from static NAT, but it has some similarities as well. Dynamic NAT still requires that each interface be identified as either an inside or an outside interface, and of course static mapping is no longer required. Dynamic NAT uses an access control list (ACL) to identify which inside local (private) IP addresses need to have their addresses translated, and it defines a pool of registered public IP addresses to allocate. The specific steps are as follows:

Step 1. As with static NAT, configure interfaces to be in the inside part of the NAT design using the **ip nat inside** interface subcommand.

Step 2. As with static NAT, configure interfaces to be in the outside part of the NAT design using the **ip nat outside** interface subcommand.

Step 3. Configure an ACL that matches the packets entering inside interfaces for which NAT should be performed.

Step 4. Configure the pool of public registered IP addresses using the **ip nat pool** *name first-address last-address* **netmask** *subnet-mask* global configuration command.

Step 5. Enable dynamic NAT by referencing the ACL (Step 3) and pool (Step 4) with the **ip nat inside source list** *acl-number* **pool** *pool-name* global configuration command.

■ The following statement details the configuration difference between NAT overload and 1:1 NAT when using a NAT pool:

Use the same steps for configuring dynamic NAT but include the **overload** keyword at the end of the **ip nat inside source list** global command.

24

Review Questions

Answer these review questions. You can find the answers at the bottom of the last page of the chapter. For thorough explanations, see DVD Appendix C, "Answers to Review Questions."

1. What does CIDR stand for?

   A. Classful IP default routing

   B. Classful IP D-class routing

   C. Classful interdomain routing

   D. Classless IP default routing

   E. Classless IP D-class routing

   F. Classless interdomain routing

2. Which of the following summarized subnets represent routes that could have been created for CIDR's goal to reduce the size of Internet routing tables?

   A. 10.0.0.0 255.255.255.0

   B. 10.1.0.0 255.255.0.0

   C. 200.1.1.0 255.255.255.0

   D. 200.1.0.0 255.255.0.0

3. Which of the following are not private addresses according to RFC 1918? (Choose two answers.)

   A. 172.31.1.1

   B. 172.33.1.1

   C. 10.255.1.1

   D. 10.1.255.1

   E. 191.168.1.1

4. With static NAT, performing translation for inside addresses only, what causes NAT table entries to be created?

   A. The first packet from the inside network to the outside network

   B. The first packet from the outside network to the inside network

   C. Configuration using the **ip nat inside source** command

   D. Configuration using the **ip nat outside source** command

5. With dynamic NAT, performing translation for inside addresses only, what causes NAT table entries to be created?

   A. The first packet from the inside network to the outside network

   B. The first packet from the outside network to the inside network

   C. Configuration using the **ip nat inside source** command

   D. Configuration using the **ip nat outside source** command

6. NAT has been configured to translate source addresses of packets for the inside part of the network, but only for some hosts as identified by an access control list. Which of the following commands indirectly identifies the hosts?

   A. ip nat inside source list 1 pool barney

   B. ip nat pool barney 200.1.1.1 200.1.1.254 netmask 255.255.255.0

   C. ip nat inside

   D. ip nat inside 200.1.1.1 200.1.1.2

7. Examine the following configuration commands:

```
interface Ethernet0/0
 ip address 10.1.1.1 255.255.255.0
 ip nat inside
interface Serial0/0
 ip address 200.1.1.249 255.255.255.252
ip nat inside source list 1 interface Serial0/0
access-list 1 permit 10.1.1.0 0.0.0.255
```

   If the configuration is intended to enable source NAT overload, which of the following commands could be useful to complete the configuration? (Choose two answers.)

   A. The ip nat outside command

   B. The ip nat pat command

   C. The overload keyword

   D. The ip nat pool command

8. Examine the following show command output on a router configured for dynamic NAT:

```
-- Inside Source
access-list 1 pool fred refcount 2288
 pool fred: netmask 255.255.255.240
     start 200.1.1.1 end 200.1.1.7
     type generic, total addresses 7, allocated 7 (100%), misses 965
```

   Users are complaining about not being able to reach the Internet. Which of the following is the most likely cause?

   A. The problem is not related to NAT, based on the information in the command output.

   B. The NAT pool does not have enough entries to satisfy all requests.

   C. Standard ACL 1 cannot be used; an extended ACL must be used.

   D. The command output does not supply enough information to identify the problem.

24

Review All the Key Topics

Review the most important topics from this chapter, noted with the Key Topic icon. Table 24-3 lists these key topics and where each is discussed.

Table 24-3 Key Topics for Chapter 24

Key Topic Element	Description	Page Number
Figure 24-1	CIDR global IPv4 address assignment and route aggregation concept	580
Table 24-1	List of private IP network numbers	581
Figure 24-2	Main concept of NAT translating private IP addresses into publicly unique global addresses	582
Figure 24-4	Typical NAT network diagram with key NAT terms listed	583
Table 24-2	List of four key NAT terms and their meanings	584
Figure 24-8	Concepts behind address conservation achieved by NAT Overload (PAT)	586
Figure 24-11	DHCP and NAT/PAT concepts on a consumer-grade router	588
List	Configuration checklist for static NAT	588
List	Configuration checklist for dynamic NAT	590
List	Summary of differences between dynamic NAT configuration and PAT using a pool	594
List	Configuration checklist for PAT configuration using an interface IP address ·	594
List	The most common NAT errors	596

Complete the Tables and Lists from Memory

Print a copy of DVD Appendix M, "Memory Tables," or at least the section for this chapter, and complete the tables and lists from memory. DVD Appendix N, "Memory Tables Answer Key," includes completed tables and lists for you to check your work.

Definitions of Key Terms

After your first reading of the chapter, try to define these key terms, but do not be concerned about getting them all correct at that time. Chapter 30 directs you in how to use these terms for late-stage preparation for the exam.

CIDR, inside global, inside local, NAT overload, outside global, outside local, PAT, private IP network

Command Reference to Check Your Memory

Although you should not necessarily memorize the information in the tables in this section, this section does include a reference for the configuration and EXEC commands covered in this chapter. Practically speaking, you should memorize the commands as a side effect of reading the chapter and doing all the activities in this exam preparation section. To check to see how well you have memorized the commands as a side effect of your other studies, cover the left side of the table with a piece of paper, read the descriptions on the right side, and see whether you remember the command.

Table 24-4   Chapter 24 Configuration Command Reference

Command	Description
ip nat {inside	outside}	Interface subcommand to enable NAT and identify whether the interface is in the inside or outside of the network
ip nat inside source {list {*access-list-number*	*access-list-name*}} {interface *type number*	pool *pool-name*} [overload]	Global command that enables NAT globally, referencing the ACL that defines which source addresses to NAT, and the interface or pool from which to find global addresses
ip nat pool *name start-ip end-ip* {netmask *netmask*	prefix-length *prefix-length*}	Global command to define a pool of NAT addresses
ip nat source static *inside-ip* {*outside-ip*	*interface-id*}	Global command that lists the inside and outside address (or, an outside interface whose IP address should be used) to be paired and added to the NAT translation table

Table 24-5   Chapter 24 EXEC Command Reference

Command	Description
show ip nat statistics	Lists counters for packets and NAT table entries, as well as basic configuration information
show ip nat translations [verbose]	Displays the NAT table
clear ip nat translation {*	[inside *global-ip local-ip*] [outside *local-ip global-ip*]}	Clears all or some of the dynamic entries in the NAT table, depending on which parameters are used
clear ip nat translation *protocol* inside *global-ip global-port local-ip local-port* [outside *local-ip global-ip*]	Clears some of the dynamic entries in the NAT table, depending on which parameters are used
debug ip nat	Issues a log message describing each packet whose IP address is translated with NAT

Answers to Review Questions:

1 F **2** D **3** B and E **4** C **5** A **6** A **7** A and C **8** B

Part VI Review

Keep track of your part review progress with the checklist in Table P6-1. Details on each task follow the table.

Table P6-1   Part VI Part Review Checklist

Activity	First Date Completed	Second Date Completed
Repeat All Chapter Review Questions		
Answer Part Review Questions		
Review Key Topics		
Create Command Mind Map by Category		

Repeat All Chapter Review Questions

For this task, answer the chapter review questions again for the chapters in this part of the book, using the PCPT software. Refer to the Introduction to this book, heading "How to View Only Chapter Review Questions by Part," for help with how to make the PCPT software show you chapter review questions for this part only.

Answer Part Review Questions

For this task, answer the Part Review questions for this part of the book, using the PCPT software. Refer to the Introduction to this book, heading "How to View Only Part Review Questions by Part," for help with how to make the PCPT software show you Part Review questions for this part only.

Key Topic

Review Key Topics

Browse back through the chapters, and look for the Key Topics icons. If you do not remember some details, take the time to reread those topics.

Create Command Mind Map by Category

Like Parts II and IV of this book, Part VI introduced more CLI commands. Take a few moments to let your brain sift through what you remember, and what commands your brain thinks go together, so that you can then realize which commands you need to review so that you remember them better.

The goal with this mind map exercise is to help you remember the commands. This exercise does not focus on the details, every single parameter of every command, or even their meaning. The goal is to help you organize the commands internally, so that you know which commands to consider when faced with a real-life problem or an exam question.

Create a mind map with the following categories of commands from this part of the book:

Numbered standard IPv4 ACLs, numbered extended IPv4 ACLs, named IPv4 ACLs, router and switch security, NAT, and miscellaneous

In this mind map, for each category, think of all configuration commands and all EXEC commands (mostly **show** commands). For each category, group the configuration commands separately from the EXEC commands. Figure P6-1 shows a sample of the organization.

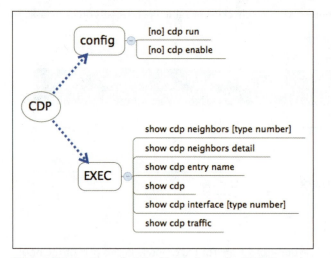

Figure P6-1 *Sample Mind Map from the CDP Branch*

Finally, keep the following important points in mind when working on this project:

- Do the activity. The learning happens when doing it, not when reading someone else's (or the sample in Appendix O, "Mind Map Solutions"). The point is to map it into your own brain.

- Do this activity without notes and without looking at the book.

- After you finish, review it versus the command summary tables at the ends of the chapters, and note which commands you had originally forgotten.

- Do not worry about every last parameter, or the exact syntax; just write down the first few words of the command.

- For later study, make a note about which commands you feel you truly understand, and which ones about which you feel less confident.

- Repeat this exercise when you have ten spare minutes, as a way to see what you remember (again without your notes).

Appendix O lists a sample mind map answer, but as usual, your mind map can and will look different.

Table P6-2   Configuration Mind Maps for Part VI Review

Map	Description	Where You Saved It
1	Commands Mind Map	

So far, this book has mostly ignored IP version 6 (IPv6). This part reverses the trend, collecting all the specific IPv6 topics into five chapters.

The chapters in this part of the book walk you through the same topics discussed throughout this book for IPv4, oftentimes using IPv4 as a point of comparison. Certainly, many details differ when comparing IPv4 and IPv6. However, many core concepts about IP addressing, subnetting, routing, and routing protocols remain the same. The chapters in this part build on those foundational concepts, adding the specific details about how IPv6 forwards IPv6 packets from one host to another.

Part VII

IP Version 6

Chapter 25

Fundamentals of IP Version 6

IPv4 has been a solid and highly useful part of the growth of TCP/IP and the Internet. For most of the long history of the Internet, and for most corporate networks that use TCP/IP, IPv4 is the core protocol that defines addressing and routing. However, even though IPv4 has many great qualities, it does have some shortcomings, creating the need for a replacement protocol: IP version 6 (IPv6).

IPv6 defines the same general functions as IPv4, but with different methods of implementing those functions. For example, both IPv4 and IPv6 define addressing, the concepts of subnetting larger groups of addresses into smaller groups, headers used to create an IPv4 or IPv6 packet, and the rules for routing those packets. At the same time, IPv6 handles the details differently, for example, using a 128-bit IPv6 address rather than the 32-bit IPv4 address.

This chapter focuses on the core network layer functions of addressing and routing. The first section of this chapter looks at the big concepts, while the second section looks at the specifics of how to write and type IPv6 addresses.

This chapter covers the following exam topics:

Operation of IP Data Networks

Predict the data flow between two hosts across a network.

IP addressing (IPv4 / IPv6)

Identify the appropriate IPv6 addressing scheme to satisfy addressing requirements in a LAN/WAN environment.

Describe IPv6 addresses

  Global unicast

IP Routing Technologies

Differentiate methods of routing and routing protocols

  next hop

  ip routing table

Troubleshooting

Troubleshoot and correct common problems associated with IP addressing and host configurations.

Foundation Topics

Introduction to IPv6

IP version 6 (IPv6) serves as the replacement protocol for IP version 4 (IPv4).

Unfortunately, that one bold statement creates more questions than it answers. Why does IPv4 need to be replaced? If IPv4 needs to be replaced, when will that happen—and will it happen quickly? What exactly happens when a company or the Internet replaces IPv4 with IPv6? And the list goes on.

While this introductory chapter cannot get into every detail of why IPv4 needs to eventually be replaced by IPv6, the clearest and most obvious reason for migrating TCP/IP networks to use IPv6 is growth. IPv4 uses a 32-bit address, which totals to a few billion addresses. Interestingly, that seemingly large number of addresses is too small. IPv6 increases the number of addresses to a 128-bit address. For perspective, IPv6 supplies over 10,000,000,000,000,000,000,000,000,000,000 times as many addresses as IPv4.

The fact that IPv6 uses a different size address field, with some different addressing rules, means that many other protocols and functions change as well. For example, IPv4 routing—in other words, the packet-forwarding process—relies on an understanding of IPv4 addresses. To support IPv6 routing, routers must understanding IPv6 addresses and routing. To dynamically learn routes for IPv6 subnets, routing protocols must support these different IPv6 addressing rules, including rules about how IPv6 creates subnets. As a result, the migration from IPv4 to IPv6 is much more than changing one protocol (IP), but it impacts many protocols.

This first section of the chapter discusses some of the reasons for the change from IPv4 to IPv6, along with the protocols that must change as a result.

The Historical Reasons for IPv6

In the last 40 years, the Internet has gone from its infancy to being a huge influence in the world. It first grew through research at universities, from the ARPANET beginnings of the Internet in the late 1960s into the 1970s. The Internet kept growing fast in the 1980s, with the Internet's fast growth still primarily driven by research and the universities that joined in that research. By the early 1990s, the Internet began to transform to allow commerce, allowing people to sell services and products over the Internet, which drove yet another steep spike upward in the growth of the Internet. Figure 25-1 shows some of these major milestones.

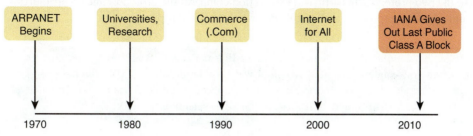

Figure 25-1 *Some Major Events in the Growth of the Internet*

Note that the figure ends the timeline with an event in which IANA/ICANN, the groups that assign public IPv4 addresses, gave out the last public IPv4 address blocks. IANA/ICANN assigned the final Class A networks to each the Regional Internet Registries (RIR) in February 2011. This event was an important event for the Internet, bringing us closer to the day when a company simply cannot get new IPv4 public address blocks.

In other words, one day, a company could want to connect to the Internet, but it cannot, just because IPv4 has no public addresses left.

Even though the press made a big deal about running out of IPv4 addresses in 2011, those who care about the Internet knew about this potential problem since the late 1980s. The problem, generally called the *IPv4 address exhaustion* problem, could literally have caused the huge growth of the Internet in the 1990s to have come to a screeching halt! Something had to be done.

The IETF came up with several short-term solutions to make IPv4 last longer, hoping to put off the day when the world ran out of public IPv4 addresses. The two primary short-term solutions were Network Address Translation / Port Address Translation (NAT/PAT) and classless inter-domain routing (CIDR). Both worked wonderfully. At the time, the Internet community hoped to extend the life of IPv4 for a few more years. In practice, these tools help extend IPv4's life another couple of decades, as seen in the timeline of Figure 25-2.

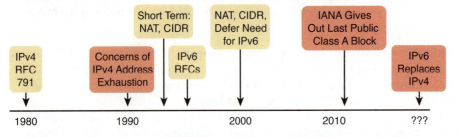

Figure 25-2   *Timeline for IPv4 Address Exhaustion and Short-/Long-Term Solutions*

NOTE   The website www.potaroo.net, by Geoff Huston, shows many interesting statistics about the growth of the Internet, including IPv4 address exhaustion.

While the short-term solutions to IPv4 address exhaustion problem gave us all a few more decades to use IPv4, IPv6 gives the world a long-term solution to the problem. IPv6 replaces IPv4 as the core Layer 3 protocol, with a new IPv6 header and new IPv6 addresses. The address size supports a huge number of addresses, solving the address shortage problem for generations (we hope).

The rest of this first section examines IPv6, comparing it to IPv4, focusing on the common features of the two protocols. In particular, this section compares the protocols (including addresses), routing, routing protocols, and miscellaneous other related topics.

NOTE   You might wonder why the next version of IP is not called IP version 5. There was an earlier effort to create a new version of IP, and it was numbered version 5. IPv5 did not progress to the standards stage. However, to prevent any issues, because version 5 had been used in some documents, the next effort to update IP was numbered as version 6.

The IPv6 Protocols

The primary purpose of the core IPv6 protocol mirrors the same purpose of the IPv4 protocol. That core IPv6 protocol, as defined in RFC 2460, defines a packet concept, addresses for those packets, and the role of hosts and routers. These rules allow the devices to forward packets sourced by hosts, through multiple routers, so that they arrive at the correct destination host. (IPv4 defines those same concepts for IPv4 back in RFC 791.)

However, because IPv6 impacts so many other functions in a TCP/IP network, many more RFCs must define details of IPv6. Some other RFCs define how to migrate from IPv4 to IPv6. Others define new versions of familiar protocols, or replace old protocols with new ones. For example:

Older OSPF Version 2 Upgraded to OSPF Version 3: The older OSPF version 2 works for IPv4, but not for IPv6, so a newer version, OSPF version 3, was created to support IPv6.

ICMP Upgraded to ICMP Version 6: Internet Control Message Protocol (ICMP) worked well with IPv4, but needed to be changed to support IPv6. The new name is ICMPv6.

ARP Replaced by Neighbor Discovery Protocol: For IPv4, Address Resolution Protocol (ARP) discovers the MAC address used by neighbors. IPv6 replaces ARP with a more general Neighbor Discovery Protocol (NDP).

NOTE But if you go to any website that lists the RFCs, like www.rfc-editor.org, you can find almost 300 RFCs that have IPv6 in the title.

While the term IPv6, when used broadly, includes many protocols, the one specific protocol called IPv6 defines the new 128-bit IPv6 address. Of course, writing these addresses in binary would be a problem—they probably would not even fit on the width of a piece of paper! IPv6 defines a shorter hexadecimal format, requiring at most 32 hexadecimal digits (one hex digit per 4 bits), with methods to abbreviate the hexadecimal addresses as well.

For example, all of the following are IPv6 addresses, each with 32 or less hex digits.

2345:1111:2222:3333:4444:5555:6666:AAAA

2000:1:2:3:4:5:6:A

FE80::1

The upcoming section "IPv6 Addressing Formats and Conventions" discusses the specifics of how to represent IPv6 addresses, including how to legally abbreviate the hex address values.

Like IPv4, IPv6 defines a header, with places to hold both the source and destination address fields. Compared to IPv4, the IPv6 header does make some other changes besides simply making the address fields larger. However, even though the IPv6 header is larger than an IPv4 header, the IPv6 header is actually simpler (on purpose), to reduce the work done each time a router must route an IPv6 packet. Figure 25-3 shows the required 40-byte part of the IPv6 header.

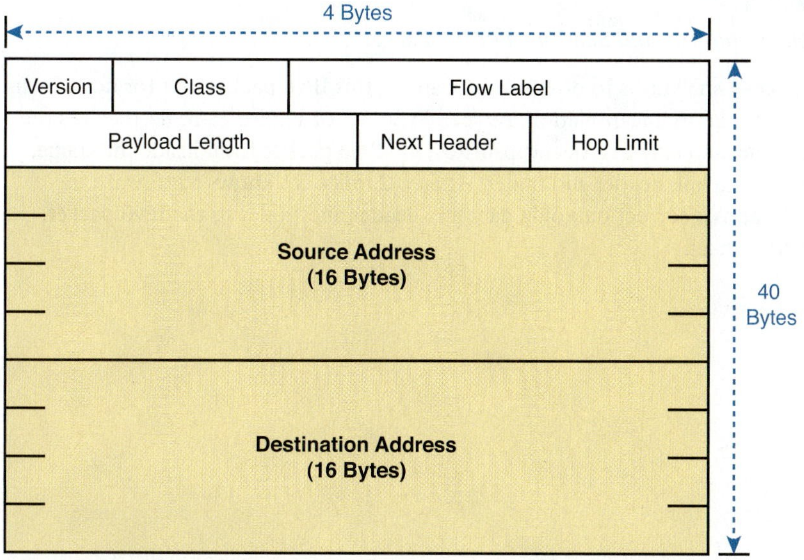

Figure 25-3 *IPv6 Header*

IPv6 Routing

As with many functions of IPv6, IPv6 routing looks just like IPv4 routing from a general perspective, with the differences being clear only once you look at the specifics. Keeping the discussion general for now, IPv6 uses these ideas the same way as IPv4:

- To be able to build and send IPv6 packets out an interface, end-user devices need an IPv6 address on that interface.

- End-user hosts need to know the IPv6 address of a default router, to which the host sends IPv6 packets if the host is in a different subnet.

- IPv6 routers deencapsulate and reencapsulate each IPv6 packet when routing the packet.

- IPv6 routers make routing decisions by comparing the IPv6 packet's destination address to the router's IPv6 routing table; the matched route list directions of where to send the IPv6 packet next.

> **NOTE**   You could take the preceding list, and replace every instance of IPv6 with IPv4, and all the statements would be true of IPv4 as well.

While the list shows some concepts that should be familiar from IPv4, the next few figures show the concepts with an example. First, Figure 25-4 shows a few settings on a host. The host (PC1) has an address of 2345::1. PC1 also knows its default gateway of 2345::2. (Both values are valid abbreviations for real IPv6 addresses.) To send an IPv6 packet to host PC2, on another IPv6 subnet, PC1 creates an IPv6 packet and sends it to R1, PC1's default gateway.

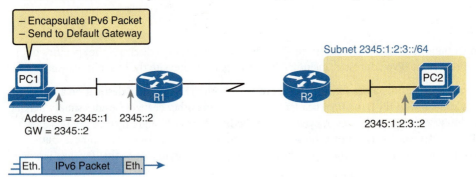

Figure 25-4   *IPv6 Host Building and Sending an IPv6 Packet*

The router (R1) has many small tasks to do when forwarding this IPv6 packet, but for now, focus on the work R1 does related to encapsulation. As seen in Step 1 of Figure 25-5, R1 receives the incoming data link frame, and extracts (deencapsulates) the IPv6 packet from inside the frame, discarding the original data link header and trailer. At Step 2, once R1 knows to forward the IPv6 packet to R2, R1 adds a correct outgoing data link header and trailer to the IPv6 packet, encapsulating the IPv6 packet.

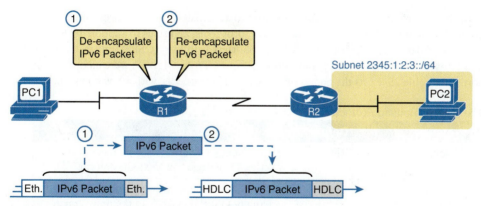

Figure 25-5 *IPv6 Router Performing Routine Encapsulation Tasks When Routing IPv6*

When a router like R1 deencapsulates the packet from the data link frame, it must also decide what type of packet sits inside the frame. To do so, the router must look at a protocol type field in the data link header, which identifies the type of packet inside the data link frame. Today, most data link frames carry either an IPv4 packet or an IPv6 packet.

To route an IPv6 packet, a router must use its IPv6 routing table instead of the IPv4 routing table. The router must look at the packet's destination IPv6 address and compare that address to the router's current IPv6 routing table. The router uses the forwarding instructions in the matched IPv6 route to forward the IPv6 packet. Figure 25-6 shows the overall process.

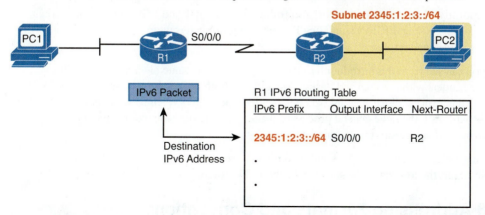

Figure 25-6 *IPv6 Router Performing Routine Encapsulation Tasks When Routing IPv6*

Note that again, the process works like IPv4, except that the IPv6 packet lists IPv6 addresses, and the IPv6 routing table lists routing information for IPv6 subnets (called prefixes).

Finally, in most enterprise networks, the routers will route both IPv4 and IPv6 packets at the same time. That is, your company will not decide to adopt IPv6, and then late one weekend night turn off all IPv4 and enable IPv6 on every device. Instead, IPv6 allows for a slow migration, during which some or all routers forward both IPv4 and IPv6 packets. (The migration strategy of running both IPv4 and IPv6 is called *dual stack*.) All you have to do is configure the router to route IPv6 packets, in addition to the existing configuration for routing IPv4 packets.

IPv6 Routing Protocols

IPv6 routers need to learn routes for all the possible IPv6 prefixes (subnets). Just like with IPv4, IPv6 routers use routing protocols, with familiar names, and generally speaking, with familiar functions.

None of the IPv4 routing protocols could be used to advertise IPv6 routes originally. They all required some kind of update to add messages, protocols, and rules to support IPv6. Over time, Routing Information Protocol (RIP), Open Shortest Path First (OSPF), Enhanced Interior Gateway Routing Protocol (EIGRP), and Border Gateway Protocol (BGP) were all updated to support IPv6. Table 25-1 lists the names of these routing protocols, with a few comments.

Table 25-1 IPv6 Routing Protocols

Routing Protocol	Defined By	Notes
RIPng (RIP Next Generation)	RFC	The "Next Generation" is a reference to a TV series, "Star Trek: the Next Generation."
OSPFv3 (OSPF version 3)	RFC	The OSPF you have worked with for IPv4 is actually OSPF version 2, so the new version for IPv6 is OSPFv3.
EIGRPv6 (EIGRP for IPv6)	Cisco	Cisco owns the rights to the EIGRP protocol, but Cisco also now publishes EIGRP as an informational RFC.
MP BGP-4 (Multiprotocol BGP version 4)	RFC	BGP version 4 was created to be highly extendable; IPv6 support was added to BGP version 4 through one such enhancement, MP BGP-4.

Additionally, these routing protocols also follow the same IGP and EGP conventions as their IPv4 cousins. RIPng, EIGRPv6, and OSPFv3 act as interior gateway protocols, advertising IPv6 routes inside an enterprise.

As you can see from this introduction, IPv6 uses many of the same big ideas as IPv4. Both define headers with a source and destination address. Both define the routing of packets, with the routing process discarding old data link headers and trailers when forwarding the packets. And routers use the same general process to make a routing decision, comparing the packet's destination IP address to the routing table.

The big differences between IPv4 and IPv6 revolve around the bigger IPv6 addresses. The next topic begins the looking at the specifics of these IPv6 addresses.

IPv6 Addressing Formats and Conventions

The CCENT and CCNA R/S exams require some fundamental skills in working with IPv4 addresses. For example, you need to be able to interpret IPv4 addresses, like 172.21.73.14. You need to be able to work with prefix-style masks, like /25, and interpret what that means when used with a particular IPv4 address. And you need to be able to take an address and mask, like 172.21.73.14/25, and find the subnet ID.

This second major section of this chapter discusses these same ideas for IPv6 addresses. In particular, this section looks at

- How to write and interpret unabbreviated 32-digit IPv6 addresses
- How to abbreviate IPv6 addresses, and how to interpret abbreviated addresses
- How to interpret the IPv6 prefix length mask
- How to find the IPv6 prefix (subnet ID), based on an address and prefix length mask

The biggest challenge with these tasks lies in the sheer size of the numbers. Thankfully, the math to find the subnet ID—often a challenge for IPv4—is easier for IPv6, at least to the depth discussed in this book.

Representing Full (Unabbreviated) IPv6 Addresses

IPv6 uses a convenient hexadecimal (hex) format for addresses. To make it more readable, IPv6 uses a format with eight sets of four hex digits, with each set of four digits separated by a colon. For example:

> 2340:1111:AAAA:0001:1234:5678:9ABC:1234

> **NOTE**   For convenience, the author uses the term *quartet* for one set of four hex digits, with eight quartets in each IPv6 address. Note that the IPv6 RFCs do not use the term *quartet*.

IPv6 addresses also have a binary format as well, but thankfully, most of the time you do not need to look at the binary version of the addresses. However, in those cases, converting from hex to binary is relatively easy. Just change each hex digit to the equivalent 4-bit value listed in Table 25-2.

Table 25-2   Hexadecimal/Binary Conversion Chart

Hex	Binary	Hex	Binary
0	0000	8	1000
1	0001	9	1001
2	0010	A	1010
3	0011	B	1011
4	0100	C	1100
5	0101	D	1101
6	0110	E	1110
7	0111	F	1111

Abbreviating and Expanding IPv6 Addresses

IPv6 also defines ways to abbreviate or shorten how you write or type an IPv6 address. Why? Although using a 32-digit hex number works much better than working with a 128-bit binary number, 32 hex digits is still a lot of digits to remember, recognize in command output, and type on a command line. The IPv6 address abbreviation rules let you shorten these numbers.

Computers and routers typically use the shortest abbreviation, even if you type all 32 hex digits of the address. So even if you would prefer to use the longer unabbreviated version of the IPv6 address, you need to be ready to interpret the meaning of an abbreviated IPv6 address as listed by a router or host. This section first looks at abbreviating addresses, and then at expanding addresses.

Abbreviating IPv6 Addresses

Two basic rules let you, or any computer, shorten or abbreviate an IPv6 address:

Key Topic

1. Inside each quartet of four hex digits, remove the leading 0s (0s on the left side of the quartet) in the three positions on the left. (Note: at this step, a quartet of 0000 will leave a single 0.)

2. Find any string of two or more consecutive quartets of all hex 0s, and replace that set of quartets with double colon (::). The :: means "two or more quartets of all 0s." However, you can only use :: once in a single address, because otherwise the exact IPv6 might not be clear.

For example, consider the following IPv6 address. The bold digits represent digits in which the address could be abbreviated.

FE00:0000:0000:0001:0000:0000:0000:0056

Applying the first rule, you would look at all eight quartets independently. In each, remove all the leading 0s. Note that five of the quartets have four 0s, so for these, only remove three 0s, leaving the following value:

FE00:0:0:1:0:0:0:56

While this abbreviation is valid, the address can be abbreviated more, using the second rule. In this case, two instances exist where more than one quartet in a row has only a 0. Pick the longest such sequence, and replace it with ::, giving you the shortest legal abbreviation:

FE00:0:0:1::56

While FE00:0:0:1::56 is indeed the shortest abbreviation, this example happens to make it easier to see the two most common mistakes when abbreviating IPv6 addresses. First, never remove trailing 0s in a quartet (0s on the right side of the quartet). In this case, the first quartet of FE00 cannot be shortened at all, because the two 0s trail. So, the following address, that begins now with only FE in the first quartet, is not a correct abbreviation of the original IPv6 address:

FE:0:0:1::56

The second common mistake is to replace all series of all 0 quartets with a double colon. For example, the following abbreviation would be incorrect for the original IPv6 address listed in this topic:

FE00::1::56

The reason this abbreviation is incorrect is because now you do not know how many quartets of all 0s to substitute into each :: to find the original unabbreviated address.

Expanding Abbreviated IPv6 Addresses

To expand an IPv6 address back into its full unabbreviated 32-digit number, use two similar rules. The rules basically reverse the logic of the previous two rules:

1. In each quartet, add leading 0s as needed until the quartet has four hex digits.

2. If a double colon (::) exists, count the quartets currently shown; the total should be less than 8. Replace the :: with multiple quartets of 0000 so that eight total quartets exist.

The best way to get comfortable with these addresses and abbreviations is to do some yourself. Table 25-3 lists some practice problems, with the full 32-digit IPv6 address on the left, and the best abbreviation on the right. The table gives you either the expanded or abbreviated address, and you need to supply the opposite value. The answers sit at the end of the chapter, in the section "Answers to Earlier Practice Problems."

Table 25-3   IPv6 Address Abbreviation and Expansion Practice

Full	Abbreviation
2340:0000:0010:0100:1000:ABCD:0101:1010	
	30A0:ABCD:EF12:3456:ABC:B0B0:9999:9009
2222:3333:4444:5555:0000:0000:6060:0707	
	3210::
210F:0000:0000:0000:CCCC:0000:0000:000D	
	34BA:B:B::20
FE80:0000:0000:0000:DEAD:BEFF:FEEF:CAFE	
	FE80::FACE:BAFF:FEBE:CAFE
FE80:000F:00E0:0D00:FACE:BAFF:FE00:0000	
	FE80:800:0:40:CAFE:FF:FE00:1

You will become more comfortable with these abbreviations as you get more experience. The "Review Activities" section at the end of this chapter lists several suggestions for getting more practice.

Representing the Prefix Length of an Address

IPv6 uses a mask concept, called the *prefix length*, similar to IPv4 subnet masks. Similar to the IPv4 prefix-style mask, the IPv6 prefix length is written as a /, followed by a decimal number. The prefix length defines how many bits of the IPv6 address defines the IPv6 prefix, which is basically the same concept as the IPv4 subnet ID.

When writing IPv6 addresses, if the prefix length matters, the prefix length follows the IPv6 address. When writing documentation, you can leave a space between the address and the /, but when typing the values into a Cisco router, you might need to configure with or without the space. For example, use either of these for an address with a 64-bit prefix length:

2222:1111:0:1:A:B:C:D/64

2222:1111:0:1:A:B:C:D /64

Finally, note that the prefix length is a number of bits, so with IPv6, the legal value range is from 0 through 128, inclusive.

Calculating the IPv6 Prefix (Subnet ID)

With IPv4, you can take an IP address and the associated subnet mask, and calculate the subnet ID. With IPv6 subnetting, you can take an IPv6 address and the associated prefix length, and calculate the IPv6 equivalent of the subnet ID: an *IPv6 prefix*.

Like with different IPv4 subnet masks, some IPv6 prefix lengths make for an easy math problem to find the IPv6 prefix, while some prefix lengths make the math more difficult. This section looks at the easier cases, mainly because the size of the IPv6 address space lets us all choose to use IPv6 prefix lengths that make the math much easier.

25

Finding the IPv6 Prefix

In IPv6, a prefix represents a group of IPv6 addresses. For now, this section focuses on the math, and only the math, for finding the number that represents that prefix. Chapter 26, "IPv6 Addressing and Subnetting," then starts putting more meaning behind the actual numbers.

Each IPv6 prefix, or subnet if you prefer, has a number that represents the group. Per the IPv6 RFCs, the number itself is also called the prefix, but many people just call it a subnet number or subnet ID, using the same terms as IPv4.

Like IPv4, you can start with an IPv6 address and prefix length, and find the prefix, with the same general rules that you use in IPv4. If the prefix length is /P, use these rules:

Key Topic

1. Copy the first P bits.
2. Change the rest of the bits to 0.

When using a prefix length that happens to be a multiple of 4, you do not have to think in terms of bits, but in terms of hex digits. A prefix length that is a multiple of 4 means that each hex digit is either copied, or changed to 0. Just for completeness, if the prefix length is indeed a multiple of 4, the process becomes

1. Identify the number of hex digits in the prefix by dividing the prefix length (which is in bits) by 4.
2. Copy the hex digits determined to be in the prefix per the first step.
3. Change the rest of the hex digits to 0.

Figure 25-7 shows an example, with a prefix length of 64. In this case, Step 1 looks at the /64 prefix length, and calculates that the prefix has 16 hex digits. Step 2 copies the first 16 digits of the IPv6 address, while Step 3 records hex 0s for the rest of the digits.

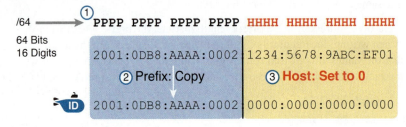

Legend:

ID Subnet ID

Figure 25-7 *Creating the IPv6 Prefix from an Address/Length*

After you find the IPv6 prefix, you should also be ready to abbreviate the IPv6 prefix using the same rules you use to abbreviate IPv6 addresses. However, you should pay extra attention to the end of the prefix, because it often has several octets of all 0 values. As a result, the abbreviation typically ends with two colons (::).

For example, consider the following IPv6 address that is assigned to a host on a LAN:

2000:1234:5678:9ABC:1234:5678:9ABC:1111/64

This example shows an IPv6 address that itself cannot be abbreviated. After you calculate the prefix for the subnet in which the address resides, by zeroing out the last 64 bits (16 digits) of the address, you find the following prefix value:

2000:1234:5678:9ABC:**0000:0000:0000:0000**/64

This value can be abbreviated, with four quartets of all 0s at the end, as follows:

2000:1234:5678:9ABC::/64

To get better at the math, take some time to work through finding the prefix for several practice problems, as listed in Table 25-4. The answers sit at the end of the chapter, in the section "Answers to Earlier Practice Problems."

Table 25-4   Finding the IPv6 Prefix from an Address/Length Value

Address/Length	Prefix
2340:0:10:100:1000:ABCD:101:1010/64	
30A0:ABCD:EF12:3456:ABC:B0B0:9999:9009/64	
2222:3333:4444:5555::6060:707/64	
3210::ABCD:101:1010/64	
210F::CCCC:B0B0:9999:9009/64	
34BA:B:B:0:5555:0:6060:707/64	
3124::DEAD:CAFE:FF:FE00:1/64	
2BCD::FACE:BEFF:FEBE:CAFE/64	
3FED:F:E0:D00:FACE:BAFF:FE00:0/64	
3BED:800:0:40:FACE:BAFF:FE00:0/64	

The "Review Activities" section at the end of this chapter lists several suggestions for getting more practice. The "Answers to Earlier Practice Problems" section at the end of the chapter also contains Table 25-8, which lists a completed version of this table so that you can check your work.

Working with More Difficult IPv6 Prefix Lengths

Some prefix lengths make the math to find the prefix very easy, some mostly easy, and some require you to work in binary. If the prefix length is a multiple of 16, the process of copying part of the address copies entire quartets. If the prefix length is not a multiple of 16, but is a multiple of 4, at least the boundary sits at the edge of a hex digit, so you can avoid working in binary.

Although the /64 prefix length is by far the most common prefix length, you should be ready to find the prefix when using a prefix length that is any multiple of 4. For example, consider the following IPv6 address and prefix length:

2000:1234:5678:9ABC:1234:5678:9ABC:1111/56

Because this example uses a /56 prefix length, the prefix includes the first 56 bits, or first 14 complete hex digits, of the address. The rest of the hex digits will be 0, resulting in the following prefix:

2000:1234:5678:9A**00:0000:0000:0000:0000**/56

This value can be abbreviated, with four quartets of all 0s at the end, as follows:

2000:1234:5678:9A**00**::/56

This example shows an easy place to make a mistake. Sometimes, people look at the /56 and think of that as the first 14 hex digits, which is correct. However, they then copy the first 14 hex digits, and add a double colon, showing the following:

2000:1234:5678:**9A**::/56

25

This abbreviation is not correct, because it removed the trailing "00" at the end of the fourth quartet. So, be careful when abbreviating when the boundary is not at the edge of a quartet.

Once again, some extra practice can help. Table 25-5 uses examples that have a prefix length that is a multiple of 4, but is not on a quartet boundary, just to get some extra practice. The answers sit at the end of the chapter, in the section "Answers to Earlier Practice Problems."

Table 25-5 Finding the IPv6 Prefix from an Address/Length Value

Address/Length	Prefix
34BA:B:B:0:5555:0:6060:707/80	
3124::DEAD:CAFE:FF:FE00:1/80	
2BCD::FACE:BEFF:FEBE:CAFE/48	
3FED:F:E0:D00:FACE:BAFF:FE00:0/48	
210F:A:B:C:CCCC:B0B0:9999:9009/40	
34BA:B:B:0:5555:0:6060:707/36	
3124::DEAD:CAFE:FF:FE00:1/60	
2BCD::FACE:1:BEFF:FEBE:CAFE/56	
3FED:F:E0:D000:FACE:BAFF:FE00:0/52	
3BED:800:0:40:FACE:BAFF:FE00:0/44	

Review Activities

Chapter Summary

- The primary purpose of the core IPv6 protocol mirrors the same purpose of the IPv4 protocol. That core IPv6 protocol, as defined in RFC 2460, defines a packet concept, addresses for those packets, and the role of hosts and routers. These rules enable the devices to forward packets sourced by hosts, through multiple routers, so that they arrive at the correct destination host.

- However, because IPv6 impacts so many other functions in a TCP/IP network, many more RFCs must define details of IPv6. Some other RFCs define how to migrate from IPv4 to IPv6. Others define new versions of familiar protocols or replace old protocols with new ones. For example:

  - **Older OSPF Version 2 Upgraded to OSPF Version 3:** The older OSPF version 2 works for IPv4 but not for IPv6, so a newer version, OSPF version 3, was created to support IPv6.

  - **ICMP Upgraded to ICMP Version 6:** ICMP worked well with IPv4 but needed to be changed to support IPv6. The new name is ICMPv6.

  - **ARP Replaced by Neighbor Discovery Protocol:** For IPv4, ARP discovers the MAC address used by neighbors. IPv6 replaces ARP with a more general Neighbor Discovery Protocol (NDP).

- Although the term IPv6, when used broadly, includes many protocols, the one specific protocol called IPv6 defines the new 128-bit IPv6 address.

- As with many functions of IPv6, IPv6 routing looks just like IPv4 routing from a general perspective, with the differences being clear only when you look at the specifics. IPv6 uses these ideas the same way as IPv4:

  - To be able to build and send IPv6 packets out an interface, end-user devices need an IPv6 address on that interface.

  - End-user hosts need to know the IPv6 address of a default router, to which the host sends IPv6 packets if the host is in a different subnet.

  - IPv6 routers deencapsulate and reencapsulate each IPv6 packet when routing the packet.

  - IPv6 routers make routing decisions by comparing the IPv6 packet's destination address to the router's IPv6 routing table; the matched route lists directions of where to send the IPv6 packet next.

- IPv6 uses a convenient hexadecimal (hex) format for addresses. To make it more readable, IPv6 uses a format with 8 sets of 4 hex digits, with each set of 4 digits separated by a colon. For example:

  2340:1111:AAAA:0001:1234:5678:9ABC:1234

- Two basic rules let you, or any computer, shorten or abbreviate an IPv6 address:

  - Inside each quartet of four hex digits, remove the leading 0s (0s on the left side of the quartet) in the three positions on the left. (Note: At this step, a quartet of 0000 will leave a single 0.)

  - Find any string of two or more consecutive quartets of all hex 0s, and replace that set of quartets with a double colon (::). The :: means "two or more quartets of all 0s." However, you can use :: only once in a single address, because otherwise the exact IPv6 might not be clear.

25

- To expand an IPv6 address back into its full unabbreviated 32-digit number, use two similar rules. The rules basically reverse the logic of the previous two rules.

  - In each quartet, add leading 0s as needed until the quartet has four hex digits.

  - If a double colon (::) exists, count the quartets currently shown; the total should be less than 8. Replace the :: with multiple quartets of 0000 so that 8 total quartets exist.

- IPv6 uses a mask concept, called the *prefix length*, similar to IPv4 subnet masks. Similar to the IPv4 prefix-style mask, the IPv6 prefix length is written as a / followed by a decimal number. The prefix length defines how many bits of the IPv6 address defines the IPv6 prefix, which is basically the same concept as the IPv4 subnet ID.

- Like IPv4, you can start with an IPv6 address and prefix length and find the prefix, with the same general rules that you use in IPv4. If the prefix length is /P, then use these rules:

  - Copy the first P bits.

  - Change the rest of the bits to 0.

- When using a prefix length that happens to be a multiple of 4, you do not have to think in terms of bits but in terms of hex digits. A prefix length that is a multiple of 4 means that each hex digit is either copied or changed to 0. Just for completeness, if the prefix length is indeed a multiple of 4, the process becomes

  - Identify the number of hex digits in the prefix by dividing the prefix length (which is in bits) by 4.

  - Copy the hex digits determined to be in the prefix per the first step.

  - Change the rest of the hex digits to 0.

Review Questions

Answer these review questions. You can find the answers at the bottom of the last page of the chapter. For thorough explanations, see DVD Appendix C, "Answers to Review Questions."

1. Which of the following was a short-term solution to the IPv4 address exhaustion problem?

   A. IP version 6

   B. IP version 5

   C. NAT/PAT

   D. ARP

2. A router receives an Ethernet frame that holds an IPv6 packet. The router then makes a decision to route the packet out a serial link. Which of the following statements is true about how a router forwards an IPv6 packet?

   A. The router discards the Ethernet data link header and trailer of the received frame.

   B. The router makes the forwarding decision based on the packet's source IPv6 address.

   C. The router keeps the Ethernet header, encapsulating the entire frame inside a new IPv6 packet before sending it over the serial link.

   D. The router uses the IPv4 routing table when choosing where to forward the packet.

3. Which of the following is the shortest valid abbreviation for FE80:0000:0000:0100:0000:0000:0000:0123?

    A. FE80::100::123

    B. FE8::1::123

    C. FE80::100:0:0:0:123:4567

    D. FE80:0:0:100::123

4. Which of the following is the shortest valid abbreviation for 2000:0300:0040:0005:6000:0700:0080:0009?

    A. 2:3:4:5:6:7:8:9

    B. 2000:300:40:5:6000:700:80:9

    C. 2000:300:4:5:6000:700:8:9

    D. 2000:3:4:5:6:7:8:9

5. Which of the following is the unabbreviated version of IPv6 address 2001:DB8::200:28?

    A. 2001:0DB8:0000:0000:0000:0000:0200:0028

    B. 2001:0DB8::0200:0028

    C. 2001:0DB8:0:0:0:0:0200:0028

    D. 2001:0DB8:0000:0000:0000:0000:200:0028

6. Which of the following is the prefix for address 2000:0000:0000:0005:6000:0700:0080:0009, assuming a mask of /64?

    A. 2000::5::/64

    B. 2000::5:0:0:0:0/64

    C. 2000:0:0:5::/64

    D. 2000:0:0:5:0:0:0:0/64

Review All the Key Topics

Review the most important topics from this chapter, noted with the Key Topic icon. Table 25-6 lists these key topics and where each is discussed.

Table 25-6   Key Topics for Chapter 25

Key Topic Element	Description	Page Number
List	Similarities between IPv4 and IPv6	614
List	Rules for abbreviating IPv6 addresses	617
List	Rules for expanding an abbreviated IPv6 address	618
List	Process steps to find an IPv6 prefix, based on the IPv6 address and prefix length	620

Complete the Tables and Lists from Memory

Print a copy of DVD Appendix M, "Memory Tables," or at least the section for this chapter, and complete the tables and lists from memory. DVD Appendix N, "Memory Tables Answer Key," includes completed tables and lists for you to check your work.

Definitions of Key Terms

After your first reading of the chapter, try to define these key terms, but do not be concerned about getting them all correct at that time. Chapter 30 directs you in how to use these terms for late-stage preparation for the exam.

IPv4 address exhaustion, IETF, NAT, CIDR, IP version 6 (IPv6), OSPF version 3 (OSPFv3), EIGRP version 6 (EIGRPv6), prefix, prefix length, quartet

Additional Practice with IPv6 Address Abbreviations

For additional practice abbreviating IPv6 addresses:

- DVD Appendix K, "Practice for Chapter 25: Fundamentals of IP Version 6," has some additional practice problems listed.
- Create your own problems using any real router or simulator. Get into the router CLI, into configuration mode, and configure a 32-digit unabbreviated IPv6 address. Then predict the shortest abbreviation. Finally, use the **show ipv6 interface** command to see if the router used the same abbreviation you used.

Answers to Earlier Practice Problems

This chapter includes practice problems spread around different locations in the chapter. The answers are located in Tables 25-7, 25-8, and 25-9.

Table 25-7   Answers to Questions in the Earlier Table 25-3

Full	Abbreviation
2340:0000:0010:0100:1000:ABCD:0101:1010	2340:0:10:100:1000:ABCD:101:1010
30A0:ABCD:EF12:3456:0ABC:B0B0:9999:9009	30A0:ABCD:EF12:3456:ABC:B0B0:9999:9009
2222:3333:4444:5555:0000:0000:6060:0707	2222:3333:4444:5555::6060:707
3210:0000:0000:0000:0000:0000:0000:0000	3210::
210F:0000:0000:0000:CCCC:0000:0000:000D	210F::CCCC:0:0:D
34BA:000B:000B:0000:0000:0000:0000:0020	34BA:B:B::20
FE80:0000:0000:0000:DEAD:BEFF:FEEF:CAFE	FE80::DEAD:BEFF:FEEF:CAFE
FE80:0000:0000:0000:FACE:BAFF:FEBE:CAFE	FE80::FACE:BAFF:FEBE:CAFE
FE80:000F:00E0:0D00:FACE:BAFF:FE00:0000	FE80:F:E0:D00:FACE:BAFF:FE00:0
FE80:0800:0000:0040:CAFE:00FF:FE00:0001	FE80:800:0:40:CAFE:FF:FE00:1

Table 25-8 Answers to Questions in the Earlier Table 25-4

Address/Length	Prefix
2340:0:10:100:1000:ABCD:101:1010/64	2340:0:10:100::/64
30A0:ABCD:EF12:3456:ABC:B0B0:9999:9009/64	30A0:ABCD:EF12:3456::/64
2222:3333:4444:5555::6060:707/64	2222:3333:4444:5555::/64
3210::ABCD:101:1010/64	3210::/64
210F::CCCC:B0B0:9999:9009/64	210F::/64
34BA:B:B:0:5555:0:6060:707/64	34BA:B:B::/64
3124::DEAD:CAFE:FF:FE00:1/64	3124:0:0:DEAD::/64
2BCD::FACE:BEFF:FEBE:CAFE/64	2BCD::/64
3FED:F:E0:D00:FACE:BAFF:FE00:0/64	3FED:F:E0:D00::/64
3BED:800:0:40:FACE:BAFF:FE00:0/64	3BED:800:0:40::/64

Table 25-9 Answers to Questions in the Earlier Table 25-5

Address/Length	Prefix
34BA:B:B:0:5555:0:6060:707/80	34BA:B:B:0:5555::/80
3124::DEAD:CAFE:FF:FE00:1/80	3124:0:0:DEAD:CAFE::/80
2BCD::FACE:BEFF:FEBE:CAFE/48	2BCD::/48
3FED:F:E0:D00:FACE:BAFF:FE00:0/48	3FED:F:E0::/48
210F:A:B:C:CCCC:B0B0:9999:9009/40	210F:A::/40
34BA:B:B:0:5555:0:6060:707/36	34BA:B::/36
3124::DEAD:CAFE:FF:FE00:1/60	3124:0:0:DEA0::/60
2BCD::FACE:1:BEFF:FEBE:CAFE/56	2BCD:0:0:FA00::/56
3FED:F:E0:D000:FACE:BAFF:FE00:0/52	3FED:F:E0:D000::/52
3BED:800:0:40:FACE:BAFF:FE00:0/44	3BED:800::/44

Answers to Review Questions::

1 C **2** A **3** D **4** B **5** A **6** C

Chapter 26

IPv6 Addressing and Subnetting

IPv4 organizes the address space in a couple of ways. First, IPv4 splits addresses by class, with Classes A, B, and C defining unicast IPv4 addresses. (The term *unicast* refers to the fact that each address is used by only one interface.) Then, within the Class A, B, and C address range, the Internet Assigned Numbers Authority (IANA) and the Internet Corporation for Assigned Names and Numbers (ICANN) reserve most of the addresses as public IPv4 addresses, with a few reserved as private IPv4 addresses.

IPv6 does not use any concept like the classful network concept used by IPv4. However, IANA does still reserve some IPv6 address ranges for specific purposes, even with some address ranges that serve as both public IPv6 addresses and private IPv6 addresses. IANA also attempts to take a practical approach to reserving ranges of the entire IPv6 address space for different purposes, using the wisdom gained from several decades of fast growth in the IPv4 Internet.

This chapter has two major sections. The first examines *global unicast addresses*, which serve as public IPv6 addresses. The second major section looks at *unique local addresses*, which serve as private IPv6 addresses.

This chapter covers the following exam topics:

IP addressing (IPv4 / IPv6)

Identify the appropriate IPv6 addressing scheme to satisfy addressing requirements in a LAN/WAN environment.

Describe IPv6 addresses

  Global unicast

  Unique local

Troubleshooting

Troubleshoot and correct common problems associated with IP addressing and host configurations.

Global Unicast Addressing Concepts

This first major section of the chapter focuses on one type of unicast IPv6 addresses: global unicast addresses. As it turns out, many of the general concepts and processes behind these global unicast IPv6 addresses follow the original intent for public IPv4 addresses. So, this section begins with a review of some IPv4 concepts, followed by the details of how a company can use global unicast addresses.

This first section also discusses IPv6 subnetting, and the entire process of taking a block of global unicast addresses and creating subnets for one company. This process takes a globally unique global routing prefix, creates IPv6 subnets, and assigns IPv6 addresses from within each subnet, much like with IPv4.

A Brief Review of Public and Private IPv4 Addresses

In the history of IPv4 addressing, the world started out with a plan that gave every single host a globally unique public IPv4 address. However, as discussed in several places already, the IPv4 address space had too few addresses. So, in the 1990s, companies started using addresses from the private IPv4 address range, as defined in RFC 1918. These companies either simply did not connect to the Internet, or to connect to the Internet, they used NAT, sharing a few public globally unique IPv4 addresses for all host connections into the Internet.

The next few pages briefly review some of the major concepts behind using public and private addresses in IPv4, as a comparison to the equivalent addresses in IPv6.

Review of Public IPv4 Addressing Concepts

In the original design for the IPv4 Internet, the Internet relied on every IPv4 host using a unicast address that was unique in the universe. To make that happen, three major steps in planning had to occur so that each unicast address was unique:

- The company or organization asked for and received the rights to the exclusive use of a public Class A, B, or C IPv4 network number.
- The engineers at that company subdivided that classful network into smaller subnets, making sure to use each subnet in only one place in the company.
- The engineers chose individual IPv4 addresses from within each subnet, making sure to use each address for only one host interface.

Figure 26-1 shows a conceptual view of the breakdown of a classful IPv4 network into subnets, with each subnet holding individual unicast IPv4 addresses. The figure represents the entire public Class A, B, or C network with the largest rectangle, and each individual unicast IPv4 address using a mailbox icon.

One Public Class A, B, or C Network

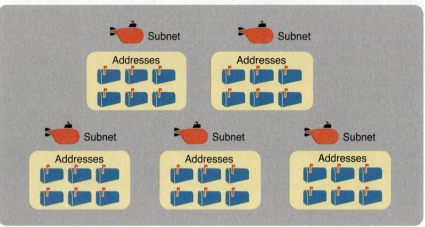

Figure 26-1 *Unique IP Network, Unique Subnets, and Unique Addresses Per Subnet*

While Figure 26-1 shows some of the general concepts behind how an enterprise could take a classful IPv4 network and subdivide it into subnets, the network engineer must also plan where to use subnets in the enterprise internetwork. By now, the ideas should be relatively familiar, but for review, for the technologies discussed for the CCENT and CCNA certifications, the following each need a separate IPv4 subnet:

Key Topic

- VLAN
- Point-to-point serial link
- Ethernet emulation WAN link (EoMPLS)
- Frame Relay PVC (not discussed in detail until the ICND2 book)

For example, in the enterprise internetwork shown in Figure 26-2, the enterprise network engineer plans for five subnets. In this example, each router LAN interface connects to a LAN that uses a single VLAN, for a total of three subnets for the three VLANs. The serial and Ethernet WAN links each need a subnet as well. (Subnets for the Internet will be assigned by the various ISPs.)

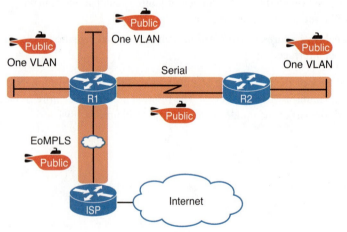

Figure 26-2 *Example Internetwork with Five IPv4 Subnets with Public Addresses*

Review of Private IPv4 Addressing Concepts

Frankly, today, most companies do not use public IPv4 addresses throughout their enterprise internetworks. The world starting running out of IPv4 addresses, and this IPv4 address exhaustion problem required some changes.

Today, most enterprise internetworks use private IPv4 addresses for most hosts. The reason being that using private IPv4 addresses (per RFC 1918), along with NAT/PAT, significantly reduces the number of public IPv4 addresses needed by that organization. Using private IPv4 addresses, with NAT/PAT, allowed one public IPv4 address to support a fairly large enterprise internetwork, putting off the day when the world would run out of public IPv4 addresses. (See Chapter 25's section "The Historical Reasons for IPv6" for a review of some of the events that drove the need for private IPv4 addresses and NAT/PAT.)

For comparison, Figure 26-3 repeats the same enterprise internetwork design shown in Figure 26-3. However, in this case, the enterprise uses private IPv4 addresses in most of the network, with Router R1 performing NAT/PAT, reducing the number of required public IPv4 addresses.

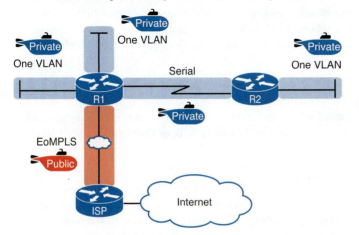

Figure 26-3   *Example Internetwork with Five IPv4 Subnets*

Public and Private IPv6 Addresses

IPv6 allows two similar options for unicast addressing, beginning with *global unicast* addressing. These addresses work like the original design for IPv4 using public addresses. Similar to public IPv4 addresses, IPv6 global unicast addresses rely on an administrative process that assigns each company a unique IPv6 address block. Each company then subnets this IPv6 address block, and only uses addresses from within that block. The result: That company uses addresses that are unique across the globe as well.

The second IPv6 option uses *unique local* IPv6 addresses, which work more like the IPv4 private addresses. Companies that do not plan to connect to the Internet, and companies that plan to use IPv6 NAT, can use these private unique local addresses. The process also works similarly to IPv4: The engineer can read the details in an RFC, pick some numbers, and start assigning IPv6 addresses, without having to register with IANA or any other authority.

The following lists summarizes these points for quicker review:

Global Unicast: Addresses that work like public IPv4 addresses. The organization that needs IPv6 addresses asks for a registered IPv6 address block, which is assigned as a global routing prefix. After that, only that organization uses the addresses inside that block of addresses, that is, the addresses that begin with the assigned prefix.

26

Unique Local: Works somewhat like private IPv4 addresses, with the possibility that multiple organizations use the exact same addresses, and with no requirement for registering with any numbering authority.

The rest of this first major section of the chapter examines global unicast addresses in more detail, while the second major section of the chapter examines unique local addresses.

> **NOTE** Just for completeness sake, note that you might also find documentation about another range of addresses called *site local*. These addresses, defined by prefix FEC0::/10 (so that they begin with FEC, FED, FEE, or FEF) were originally intended to be used like IPv4 private addresses. They have now been removed from the IPv6 standards.

The IPv6 Global Routing Prefix

IPv6 global unicast addresses allow IPv6 to work more like the original design of the IPv4 Internet. In other words, each organization asks for a block of IPv6 addresses, which no one else can use. That organization further subdivides the address block into smaller chunks, called subnets. Finally, to choose what IPv6 address to use for any host, the engineer chooses an address from the right subnet.

That reserved block of IPv6 addresses—a set of addresses that only one company can use—is called a *global routing prefix*. Each organization that wants to connect to the Internet, and use IPv6 global unicast addresses, should ask for and receive a global routing prefix. Very generally, you can think of the global routing prefix like an IPv4 Class A, B, or C network number from the range of public IPv4 addresses.

The term *global routing prefix* might not make you think of a block of IPv6 addresses at first. The term actually refers to the idea that Internet routers can have one route that refers to all the addresses inside the address block, without a need to have routes for smaller parts of that block. For example, Figure 26-4 shows three companies, with three different IPv6 global routing prefixes; the router on the right (R4) has one IPv6 route for each global routing prefix.

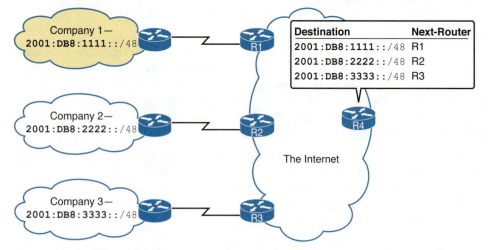

Figure 26-4   *Three Global Routing Prefixes, with One Route per Prefix*

The global routing prefix sets those IPv6 addresses apart for use by that one company, just like a public IPv4 network or CIDR address block does in IPv4. All IPv6 addresses inside that company should begin with that global routing prefix, to avoid using other companies' IPv6 addresses. No other companies should use IPv6 addresses with that same prefix. And thankfully, IPv6 has plenty of space to allow all companies to have a global routing prefix, with plenty of addresses.

Both the IPv6 and IPv4 address assignment process rely on the same organizations: IANA (along with ICANN), the Regional Internet Registries (RIR), and ISPs. For example, an imaginary company, Company1, received the assignment of a global routing prefix. The prefix means "All addresses whose first 12 hex digits are 2001:0DB8:1111," as represented by prefix 2001:0DB8:1111::/48. To receive that assignment, the process shown in Figure 26-5 happened.

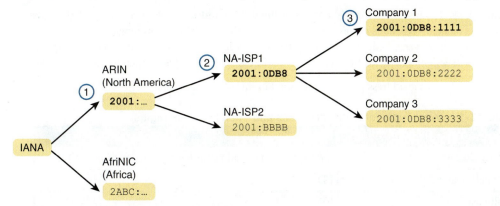

Figure 26-5 *Prefix Assignment with IANA, RIRs, and ISPs*

The event timeline in the figure uses a left-to-right flow; in other words, the event on the far left must happen first. Following the flow from left to right in the figure:

1. **IANA gives ARIN prefix 2001::/16:** ARIN (the RIR for North America) asks IANA for the assignment of a large block of addresses. In this imaginary example, IANA gives ARIN a prefix of "all addresses that begin 2001," or 2001::/16.

2. **ARIN gives NA-ISP1 prefix 2001:0DB8::/32:** NA-ISP1, an imaginary ISP based in North America, asks ARIN for a new IPv6 prefix. ARIN takes a subset of its 2001::/16 prefix, specifically all addresses that begin with the 32 bits (8 hex digits) 2001:0DB8, and gives it to the ISP.

3. **NA-ISP1 gives Company 1 2001:0DB8:1111::/48:** Company 1 decides to start supporting IPv6, so it goes to its ISP, NA-ISP1, to ask for a block of global unicast addresses. NA-ISP1 gives Company 1 a "small" piece of NA-ISP1's address block, in this case the addresses that begin with the 48 bits (12 hex digits) of 2001:0DB8:1111 (2001:0DB8:1111::/48).

> **NOTE**   If you do not plan to connect to the Internet using IPv6 for a while, and just want to experiment, you do not need to ask for an IPv6 global routing prefix to be assigned. Just make up IPv6 addresses and configure your devices.

26

Address Ranges for Global Unicast Addresses

Global unicast addresses make up the majority of the IPv6 address space. However, unlike IPv4, the rules for which IPv6 address fall into which category are purposefully more flexible than they were with IPv4 and the rules for IPv4 Classes A, B, C, D, and E.

Originally, IANA reserved all IPv6 addresses that begin with hex 2 or 3 as global unicast addresses. (This address range can be written succinctly as prefix 2000::/3.)

Later RFCs made the global unicast address range wider, basically include all IPv6 addresses not otherwise allocated for other purposes. For example, the unique local unicast addresses, discussed later in this chapter, all start with hex FD. So, while global unicast addresses would not include any addresses that begin with FD, any address ranges that are not specifically reserved, for now, are considered to be global unicast addresses.

Finally, just because an amazingly enormous number of addresses sit within the global unicast address range, IANA does not assign prefixes from all over the address range. IPv4 has survived well for over 30 years with an admittedly too-small address size. By making smart and practical choices in assigning IPv6 addresses, the IPv6 address space could last much longer than IPv4.

Table 26-1 lists the address prefixes discussed in this book, and their purpose.

Key Topic

Table 26-1   Some Types of IPv6 Addresses and Their First Hex Digit(s)

Address Type	First Hex Digits
Global Unicast	2 or 3 (originally); all not otherwise reserved (today)
Unique Local	FD
Multicast	FF
Link-Local	FE80

IPv6 Subnetting Using Global Unicast Addresses

After an enterprise has a block of reserved global unicast addresses—in other words, a global routing prefix—the company needs to subdivide that large address block into subnets.

Subnetting IPv6 addresses works generally like IPv4, but with mostly simpler math (hoorah!). Because of the absolutely large number of addresses available, most everyone uses the easiest possible IPv6 prefix length: /64. Using /64 as the prefix length for all subnets makes the IPv6 subnetting math just as easy as using a /24 mask for all IPv4 subnets. Additionally, the dynamic IPv6 address assignment process works better with a /64 prefix length as well, so in practice, and in this book, expect IPv6 designs to use a /64 prefix length.

This section does walk you through the different parts of IPv6 subnetting, while mostly using examples that use a /64 prefix length. The discussion defines the rules about which addresses should be in the same subnet, and which addresses need to be in different subnets. Plus this section looks at how to analyze the global routing prefix and associated prefix length to find all the IPv6 prefixes (subnet IDs) and the addresses in each subnet.

> **NOTE**   If the IPv4 subnetting concepts are a little vague, you might want to reread Chapter 11, "Perspectives on IPv4 Subnetting," which discusses the subnetting concepts for IPv4.

Deciding Where IPv6 Subnets Are Needed

First, IPv6 and IPv4 both use the same concepts about where a subnet is needed: one for each VLAN and one for each point-to-point WAN connection (serial and EoMPLS), with the subnetting details for Frame Relay being discussed in the ICND2 book. Figure 26-6 shows an example of the idea, using the small enterprise internetwork of Company 1. Company 1 has two LANs, with a point-to-point serial link connecting the sites. It also has an Ethernet WAN link connected to an ISP. Using the same logic you would use for IPv4, Company 1 needs four IPv6 subnets.

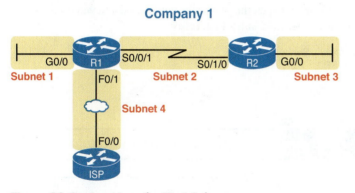

Figure 26-6 *Locations for IPv6 Subnets*

The Mechanics of Subnetting IPv6 Global Unicast Addresses

To understand how to subnet your one large block of IPv6 addresses, you need to understand some of the theory and mechanisms IPv6 uses. To learn those details, it can help to compare IPv6 with some similar concepts from IPv4.

With IPv4, without subnetting, an address has two parts: a network part and a host part. Class A, B, and C rules define the length of the network part, with the host part making up the rest of the 32-bit IPv4 address, as shown in Figure 26-7.

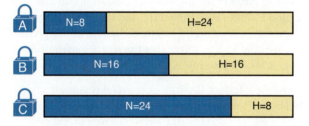

Figure 26-7 *Classful View of Unsubnetted IPv4 Networks*

To subnet an IPv4 Class A, B, or C network, the network engineer for the enterprise makes some choices. Conceptually, the engineer creates a three-part view of the addresses, adding a subnet field in the center, while shortening the host field. (Many people call this "borrowing host bits.") The size of the network part stays locked per the Class A, B, and C rules, with the line between the subnet and host part being flexible, based on the choice of subnet mask. Figure 26-8 shows the idea, for a subnetted Class B network.

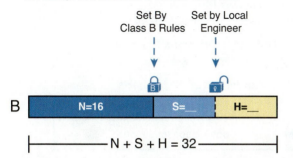

Figure 26-8 *Classful View of Subnetted IPv4 Networks*

IPv6 uses a similar concept, with the details in Figure 26-9. The structure shows three major parts, beginning with the global routing prefix, which is the initial value that must be the same in all IPv6 addresses inside the enterprise. The address ends with the interface ID, which acts like the IPv4 host field. The subnet field sits between the two other fields, used as a way to number and identify subnets, much like the subnet field in IPv4 addresses.

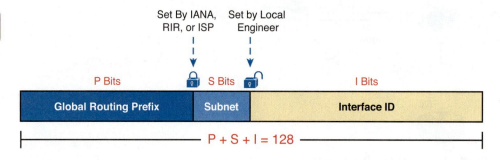

Figure 26-9   *Structure of Subnetted IPv6 Global Unicast Addresses*

First, just think about the general idea with IPv6, comparing Figure 26-9 to Figure 26-8. The IPv6 global routing prefix acts like the IPv4 network part of the address structure. The IPv6 subnet part acts like the IPv4 subnet part. And the right side of the IPv6, formally called the interface ID (short for interface identifier), acts like the IPv4 host field.

Now focus on the IPv6 global routing prefix and its prefix length. Unlike IPv4, IPv6 has no concept of address classes, so no preset rules determine the prefix length of the global routing prefix. However, when a company applies to an ISP, RIR, or any other organization that can allocate a global routing prefix, that allocation includes both the prefix, and the prefix length. After a company receives a global routing prefix and that prefix length, the length of the prefix typically does not change over time, and is basically locked. (Note that the prefix length of the global routing prefix is often between /32 and /48, or possibly as long as /56.)

Next, look to the right side of Figure 26-9 to the interface ID field. For several reasons that become more obvious the more you learn about IPv6, this field is often 64 bits long. Does it have to be 64 bits long? No. However, using a 64-bit interface ID field works well in real networks, and there are no reasons to avoid using a 64 bit interface ID field.

Finally, look to the center of Figure 26-9, and the subnet field. Similar to IPv4, this field creates a place with which to number IPv6 subnets. The length of the subnet field is based on the other two facts: the length of the global routing prefix and the length of the interface ID. And with the commonly used 64-bit interface ID field, the subnet field is typically 64 − P bits, with P being the length of the global routing prefix.

Next, consider the structure of a specific global unicast IPv6 address, 2001:0DB8:1111:0001:0000:0000:0000:0001, as seen in Figure 26-10. In this case:

- The company was assigned prefix 2001:0DB8:1111, with prefix length /48.

- The company uses the usual 64-bit interface ID.

- The company has a subnet field of 16 bits, allowing for 2^{16} IPv6 subnets.

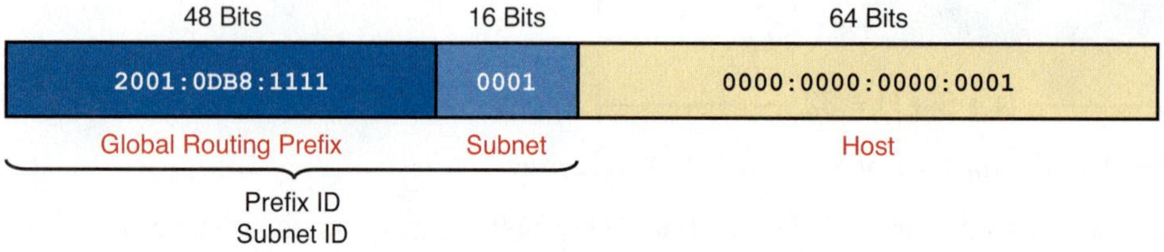

48 Bits	16 Bits	64 Bits
2001:0DB8:1111	0001	0000:0000:0000:0001
Global Routing Prefix	Subnet	Host

Prefix ID
Subnet ID

Figure 26-10   *Address Structure for Company 1 Example*

The example in Figure 26-10, along with a little math, shows one reason why so many companies use a /64 prefix length for all subnets. With this structure, Company 1 can support 2^{16} possible subnets (65,536). Few companies need that many subnets. Then, each subnet supports over 10^{18} addresses per subnet (2^{64}, minus some reserved values). So, for both subnets and hosts, the address structure supports far more than are needed. Plus, the /64 prefix length for all subnets makes the math simple, because it cuts the 128-bit IPv6 address in half.

Listing the IPv6 Subnet Identifier

Like with IPv4, IPv6 needs to identify each IPv6 subnet with some kind of a subnet identifier, or subnet ID. Figure 26-10 lists the informal names for this number (subnet ID), and the more formal name (prefix ID). Routers then list the IPv6 subnet ID in routing tables, along with the prefix length.

Chapter 25, "Fundamentals of IP Version 6," has already discussed how to find the subnet ID, given an IPv6 address and prefix length. The math works the same way when working with global unicasts, as well as the unique local addresses discussed later in the chapter. Because Chapter 25 has already discussed the math, this chapter does not repeat the math. However, for completeness, the example in Figure 26-10, the subnet ID would be

2001:DB8:1111:1::/64

List All IPv6 Subnets

With IPv4, if you choose to use a single subnet mask for all subnets, you can sit and write down all the subnets of a Class A, B, or C network using that one subnet mask. With IPv6, the same ideas apply. If you plan to use a single prefix length for all subnets, you can start with the global routing prefix and write down all the IPv6 subnet IDs as well.

To find all the subnet IDs, you simply need to find all the unique values that will fit inside the subnet part of the IPv6 address, basically following these rules:

Key Topic

■ All subnet IDs begin with the global routing prefix.

■ Use a different value in the subnet field to identify each different subnet.

■ All subnet IDs have all 0s in the interface ID.

As an example, take the IPv6 design shown in Figure 26-10, and think about all the subnet IDs. First, all subnets will use the commonly used /64 prefix length. This company uses a global routing prefix of 2001:0DB8:1111::/48, which defines the first 12 hex digits of all the subnet IDs. To find all the possible IPv6 subnet IDs, think of all the combinations of unique values in the fourth quartet, and then represent the last four quartets of all 0s with a :: symbol. Figure 26-11 shows the beginning of just such a list.

```
  2001:0DB8:1111:0000::      2001:0DB8:1111:000B::
✓ 2001:0DB8:1111:0001::      2001:0DB8:1111:000C::
✓ 2001:0DB8:1111:0002::      2001:0DB8:1111:000D::
✓ 2001:0DB8:1111:0003::      2001:0DB8:1111:000E::
✓ 2001:0DB8:1111:0004::      2001:0DB8:1111:000F::
  2001:0DB8:1111:0005::      2001:0DB8:1111:0010::
  2001:0DB8:1111:0006::      2001:0DB8:1111:0011::
  2001:0DB8:1111:0007::      2001:0DB8:1111:0012::
  2001:0DB8:1111:0008::      2001:0DB8:1111:0013::
  2001:0DB8:1111:0009::      2001:0DB8:1111:0014::
  2001:0DB8:1111:000A::      2001:0DB8:1111:0015::
```

Global Routing Prefix   Subnet   Global Routing Prefix   Subnet

Figure 26-11 *First 22 Possible Subnets with a 16-bit Subnet Field in This Example*

26

The example allows for 65,536 subnets, so clearly the example will not list all the possible subnets. However, in that fourth quartet, all combinations of hex values would be allowed.

> **NOTE**   The IPv6 subnet ID, more formally called the *subnet router anycast address*, is reserved, and should not be used as an IPv6 address for any host.

Assign Subnets to the Internetwork Topology

After an engineer lists all the possible subnet IDs (based on the subnet design), the next step is to choose which subnet ID to use for each link that needs an IPv6 subnet. Just like with IPv4, each VLAN, each serial link, each EoMPLS link, and many other data link instances need an IPv6 subnet.

Figure 26-12 shows an example using Company 1 again. The figure uses the four subnets from Figure 26-11 that have check marks beside them. The check marks are just a reminder to not use those four subnets in other locations.

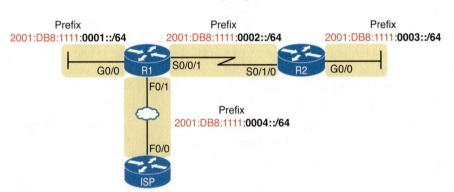

Figure 26-12   *Subnets in Company 1, with Global Routing Prefix of 2001:0DB8:1111::/48*

Assigning Addresses to Hosts in a Subnet

Now that the engineer has planned which IPv6 subnet will be used in each location, the individual IPv6 addressing can be planned and implemented. Each address must be unique, in that no other host interface uses the same IPv6 address. Also, the hosts cannot use the subnet ID itself.

The process of assigning IPv6 addresses to interfaces works similarly to IPv4. Addresses can be configured statically, along with the prefix length, default router, and DNS IPv6 addresses. Alternately, hosts can learn these same settings dynamically, using either DHCP or other a built-in IPv6 mechanism called Stateless Address Autoconfiguration, or SLAAC.

For example, Figure 26-13 shows some static IP addresses that could be chosen for the router interfaces based on the subnet choices shown in Figure 26-12. In each case, the router interfaces use an interface ID that is a relatively low number, easily remembered.

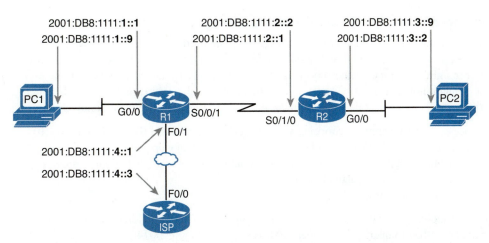

Figure 26-13 *Example Static IPv6 Addresses Based on the Subnet Design of Figure 26-12*

This chapter puts off the details of how to configure the IPv6 addresses until the next two chapters. Chapter 27, "Implementing IPv6 Addressing on Routers," looks at how to configure IPv6 addresses on routers, with both static configuration and dynamic configuration. Chapter 28, "Implementing IPv6 Addressing on Hosts," examines how to configure hosts with IPv6 addresses, with more focus on the dynamic methods and the related protocols.

Unique Local Unicast Addresses

Unique local unicast addresses act as private IPv6 addresses. These addresses have many similarities with global unicast addresses, particularly in how to subnet. The biggest difference lies in the literal number (unique local addresses begin with hex FD), and with the administrative process: The unique local prefixes are not registered with any numbering authority, and can be used by multiple organizations.

Although the network engineer creates unique local addresses without any registration or assignment process, the addresses still need to follow some rules, as follows:

- Use FD as the first two hex digits.
- Choose a unique 40-bit global ID.
- Append the global ID to "FD" to create a 48-bit prefix, used as the prefix for all your addresses.
- Use the next 16 bits as a subnet field.
- Note that the structure leaves a convenient 64-bit interface ID field.

Figure 26-14 shows the format of these unique local unicast addresses.

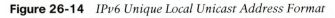

8 Bits	40 Bits	16 Bits	64 Bits
FD	**Global ID (Pseudo-Random)**	**Subnet**	**Interface ID**

Subnet ID

Figure 26-14 *IPv6 Unique Local Unicast Address Format*

> **NOTE** Just to be completely exact, IANA actually reserves prefix FC00::/7, and not FD00::/8, for these addresses. FC00::/7 includes all addresses that begin with hex FC and FD. However, an RFC (4193) requires that the eighth bit of these addresses to be set to 1, so in practice today, the unique local addresses all begin with their first two digits as FD.

26

Subnetting with Unique Local IPv6 Addresses

Subnetting using unique local addresses works just like subnetting with global unicast addresses with a 48-bit global routing prefix. The only difference is that with global unicasts, you start by asking for a global routing prefix to be assigned to your company, and that global routing prefix might or might not have a /48 prefix length. With unique local, you create that prefix locally, and the prefix begins with /48, with the first 8 bits set and the next 40 bits randomly chosen.

The process can be as simple as choosing a 40-bit value as your global ID. 40 bits requires 10 hex digits, so you can even avoid thinking in binary, and just make up a unique 10-hex-digit value. For example, imagine you chose a 40-bit global ID of 00 0001 0001. Your addresses must begin with the two hex digits FD, making the entire prefix be FD00:0001:0001::/48, or FD00:1:1::/48 when abbreviated.

To create subnets, just as you did in the earlier examples with a 48-bit global routing prefix, treat the entire fourth quartet as a subnet field, as shown in Figure 26-14.

Figure 26-15 shows an example subnetting plan using unique local addresses. The example repeats the same topology shown earlier in Figure 26-12; that figure showed subnetting with a global unicast prefix. This example uses the exact same numbers for the fourth quartet's subnet field, simply replacing the 48-bit global unicast prefix with this new local unique prefix of FD00:1:1.

Company 1 – Unique Local Prefix FD00:1:1::/48

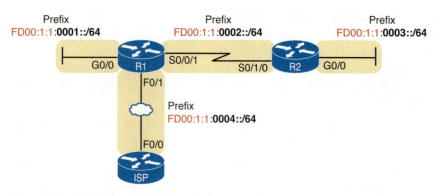

Figure 26-15 *Subnetting Using Unique Local Addresses*

The Need for Globally Unique Local Addresses

The example in Figure 26-15 shows an easy-to-remember prefix of FD00:1:1::/48. Clearly, I made up the easy-to-remember global ID in this example. What global ID would you choose for your company? Would you pick a number that you could not abbreviate, and make it shorter? If you had to pick the IPv6 prefix for you unique local addresses from the options in following list, which would you pick for your company?

- FDE9:81BE:A059::/48
- FDF0:E1D2:C3B4::/48
- FD00:1:1::/48

Given freedom to choose, most people would pick an easy-to-remember, short-to-type prefix, like FD00:1:1::/48. And in a lab or other small network used for testing, making up an easy to use number is reasonable. However, for use in real corporate networks, you should not just make up any global ID you like—you should try and follow the unique local address rules that strive to help make your addresses unique in the universe—even without registering a prefix with an ISP or RIR.

RFC 4193 defines unique local addresses. Part of that RFC stresses the importance of choosing your global ID in a way to make it statistically unlikely to be used by other companies. What is the result of unique global IDs at every company? Making all these unique local addresses unique across the globe. So if you do plan on using unique local addresses in a real network, plan on using the random number generator logic listed in RFC 4193 to create your prefix.

One of the big reasons to attempt to use a unique prefix, rather than everyone using the same easy-to-remember prefixes, is to be ready for the day that your company merges with or buys another company. Today, with IPv4, a high percentage of companies use private IPv4 network 10.0.0.0. When they merge their networks, the fact that both use network 10.0.0.0 makes the network merger more painful than if the companies had used different private IPv4 networks. With IPv6 unique local addresses, if both companies did the right thing, and randomly chose a prefix, they will most likely be using completely different prefixes, making the merger much simpler. However, companies that take the seemingly easy way out, and choose an easy-to-remember prefix like of FD00:1:1, greatly increase their risk of requiring extra effort when merging with another company that also chose to use that same prefix.

26

Review Activities

Chapter Summary

- IPv6 allows two options for unicast addressing:

    - **Global Unicast:** Addresses that work like public IPv4 addresses. The organization that needs IPv6 addresses asks for a registered IPv6 address block, which is assigned as a global routing prefix. After that, only that organization uses the addresses inside that block of addresses; that is, the addresses that begin with the assigned prefix.

    - **Unique Local:** Works somewhat like private IPv4 addresses, with the possibility that multiple organizations use the exact same addresses and with no requirement for registering with any numbering authority.

- That reserved block of IPv6 addresses—a set of addresses that only one company can use—is called a *global routing prefix*. Each organization that wants to connect to the Internet and use IPv6 global unicast addresses should ask for and receive a global routing prefix. Generally, you can think of the global routing prefix like an IPv4 Class A, B, or C network number from the range of public IPv4 addresses.

- To summarize some of the IPv6 addresses and their first hex digits:

    - Global Unicast: 2 or 3 (originally); all not otherwise reserved (today)

    - Unique Local: FD

    - Multicast: FF

    - Link Local FE80

- IPv6 and IPv4 both use the same concepts about where a subnet is needed: one for each VLAN and one for each point-to-point WAN connection (serial and EoMPLS).

- The IPV6 addressing structure shows three major parts, beginning with the global routing prefix, which is the initial value that must be the same in all IPv6 addresses inside the enterprise. The address ends with the interface ID, which acts like the IPv4 host field. The subnet field sits between the two other fields, used as a way to number and identify subnets, much like the subnet field in IPv4 addresses.

- To find all the subnet IDs, you simply need to find all the unique values that will fit inside the subnet part of the IPv6 address, basically following these rules:

    - All subnet IDs begin with the global routing prefix

    - Use a different value in the subnet field to identify each different subnet

    - All subnet IDs have all 0s in the interface ID

- Unique local unicast addresses act as private IPv6 addresses. These addresses have many similarities with global unicast addresses, particularly in how to subnet. The biggest difference lies in the literal number (unique local addresses begin with hex FD) and with the administrative process: The unique local prefixes are not registered with any numbering authority and can be used by multiple organizations.

- Although the network engineer creates unique local addresses without any registration or assignment process, the addresses still need to follow some rules, as follows:

    - Use FD as the first two hex digits.

    - Choose a unique 40-bit global ID.

    - Append the global ID to "FD" to create a 48-bit prefix, used as the prefix for all your addresses.

    - Use the next 16 bits as a subnet field.

    - Note that the structure leaves a convenient 64-bit interface ID field.

Review Questions

Answer these review questions. You can find the answers at the bottom of the last page of the chapter. For thorough explanations, see DVD Appendix C, "Answers to Review Questions."

1. Which of the following IPv6 addresses appears to be a unique local unicast address, based on its first few hex digits?

   A. 3123:1:3:5::1

   B. FE80::1234:56FF:FE78:9ABC

   C. FDAD::1

   D. FF00::5

2. Which of the following IPv6 addresses appears to be a global unicast address, based on its first few hex digits?

   A. 3123:1:3:5::1

   B. FE80::1234:56FF:FE78:9ABC

   C. FDAD::1

   D. FF00::5

3. When subnetting an IPv6 address block, an engineer shows a drawing that breaks the address structure into three pieces. Comparing this concept to a three-part IPv4 address structure, which part of the IPv6 address structure is most like the IPv4 network part of the address?

   A. Subnet

   B. Interface ID

   C. Network

   D. Global routing prefix

   E. Subnet router anycast

4. When subnetting an IPv6 address block, an engineer shows a drawing that breaks the address structure into three pieces. Assuming that all subnets use the same prefix length, which of the following answers lists the name of the field on the far right side of the address?

   A. Subnet

   B. Interface ID

   C. Network

   D. Global routing prefix

   E. Subnet router anycast

5. For the IPv6 address FD00:1234:5678:9ABC:DEF1:2345:6789:ABCD, which part of the address is considered the global ID of the unique local address?

   A. None; this address has no global ID.

   B. 00:1234:5678:9ABC

   C. DEF1:2345:6789:ABCD

   D. 00:1234:5678

   E. FD00

26

Review All the Key Topics

Review the most important topics from this chapter, noted with the Key Topic icon. Table 26-2 lists these key topics and where each is discussed.

Table 26-2   Key Topics for Chapter 26

Key Topic Element	Description	Page Number
List	Network links that need an IPv6 subnet	630
List	Two types of IPv6 unicast addresses	631
Table 26-1	Values of the initial hex digits of IPv6 addresses, and the address type implied by each	634
Figure 26-9	Subnetting concepts for IPv6 global unicast addresses	636
List	Rules for how to find all IPv6 subnet IDs, given the global routing prefix, and prefix length used for all subnets	637
List	Rules for building unique local unicast addresses	639
Figure 26-14	Subnetting concepts for IPv6 unique local addresses	639

Complete the Tables and Lists from Memory

Print a copy of DVD Appendix M, "Memory Tables," or at least the section for this chapter, and complete the tables and lists from memory. DVD Appendix N, "Memory Tables Answer Key," includes completed tables and lists for you to check your work.

Definitions of Key Terms

After your first reading of the chapter, try to define these key terms, but do not be concerned about getting them all correct at that time. Chapter 30 directs you in how to use these terms for late-stage preparation for the exam.

global unicast address, global routing prefix, unique local address, subnet ID (prefix ID), subnet router anycast address

Answers to Review Questions:

1 C **2** A **3** D **4** B **5** D

Chapter 27

Implementing IPv6 Addressing on Routers

With IPv4 addressing, some devices, like servers and routers, typically use static predefined IPv4 addresses. End-user devices do not mind if their address changes from time to time, and they typically learn an IPv4 address dynamically using DHCP. IPv6 uses the same general mode, with servers, routers, and other devices in the control of the IT group often using predefined IPv6 addresses, and with end-user devices using dynamically learned IPv6 addresses.

This chapter focuses on the addresses configured on routers, while Chapter 28, "Implementing IPv6 Addressing on Hosts," focuses on the addresses learned by IPv6 hosts.

Routers require unicast IPv6 addresses on their interfaces. At the same time, routers use a variety of other IPv6 addresses to participate in many of the protocols and roles required of a router. This chapter begins with the more obvious IPv6 addressing configuration, with features that mirror IPv4 features, showing how to configure interfaces with IPv6 addresses and view that configuration with **show** commands. The second half of the chapter introduces new IPv6 addressing concepts, showing some other addresses used by routers when doing different tasks.

This chapter covers the following exam topics:

IP addressing (IPv4 / IPv6)

Describe the technological requirements for running IPv6 in conjunction with IPv4 such as dual stack

Describe IPv6 addresses

  Multicast

  Link local

  eui 64

IP Routing Technologies

Configure and verify utilizing the CLI to set basic Router configuration

  Cisco IOS commands to perform basic router setup

Configure and verify operation status of an ethernet interface

Verify router configuration and network connectivity

  Cisco IOS commands to review basic router information and network connectivity

Troubleshooting

Troubleshoot and correct common problems associated with IP addressing and host configurations.

Implementing Unicast IPv6 Addresses on Routers

Every company bases its enterprise network on one or more protocol models, or protocol stacks. In the earlier days of networking, enterprise networks used one or more protocol stacks from different vendors, as shown on the left of Figure 27-1. Over time, companies added TCP/IP (based on IPv4) to the mix. Eventually, companies migrated fully to TCP/IP as the only protocol stack in use.

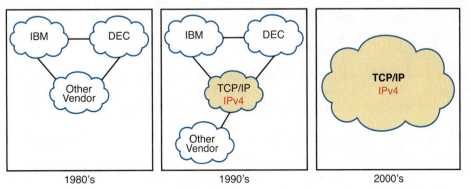

Figure 27-1 *Migration of Enterprise Networks to Use TCP/IP Stack Only, IPv4*

The emergence of IPv6 requires that IPv6 be implemented in end-user hosts, servers, routers, and other devices. However, corporations cannot just migrate all devices from IPv4 to IPv6 over one weekend. Instead, what will likely occur is some kind of long-term migration and coexistence, in which for a large number of years, most corporate networks again use multiple protocol stacks: one based on IPv4 and one based on IPv6.

Eventually, over time, we might all see the day when enterprise networks run only IPv6, without any IPv4 remaining, but that day might take a while. Figure 27-2 shows the progression, just to make the point, but who knows how long it will take?

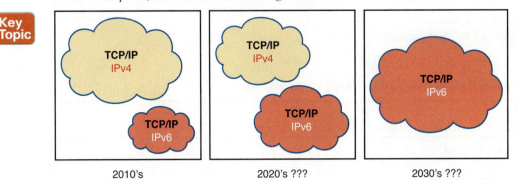

Figure 27-2 *Likely Path Through Dual-Stack (IPv4 and IPv6) over a Long Period*

One way to add IPv6 support to an established IPv4-based enterprise internetwork is to implement a dual-stack strategy. To do so, the routers can be configured to route IPv6 packets, with IPv6 addresses on their interfaces, with a similar model to how routers support IPv4. Then, hosts can implement IPv6 when ready, running both IPv4 and IPv6 (dual stacks). The first major section of this chapter shows how to configure and verify unicast IPv6 addresses on routers.

Static Unicast Address Configuration

Cisco routers give us two options for static configuration of IPv6 addresses. In one case, you configure the full 128-bit address, while in the other, you configure a 64-bit prefix, and let the router derive the second half of the address (the interface ID). The next few pages show how to configure both options, and how the router chooses the second half of the IPv6 address.

Configuring the Full 128-Bit Address

To statically configure the full 128-bit unicast address—either global unicast or unique local—the router needs an **ipv6 address** *address/prefix-length* interface subcommand on each interface. The address can be an abbreviated IPv6 address, or the full 32-digit hex address. The command includes the prefix length value, at the end, with no space between the address and prefix length.

The configuration of the router interface IPv6 address really is that simple. Figure 27-3, along with Examples 27-1 and 27-2, shows a basic example. The figure shows the global unicast IPv6 address used by two different routers, on two interfaces each. As usual, all subnets use a /64 prefix length.

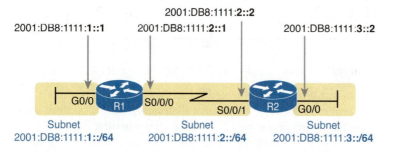

Figure 27-3   *128-bit IPv6 Addresses to Be Configured on Cisco Router Interfaces*

Example 27-1   *Configuring Static IPv6 Addresses on R1*

```
ipv6 unicast-routing
!
interface GigabitEthernet0/0
 ipv6 address 2001:DB8:1111:1::1/64
!
interface Serial0/0/0
 ipv6 address 2001:0db8:1111:0002:0000:0000:0000:0001/64
```

Example 27-2   *Configuring Static IPv6 Addresses on R2*

```
ipv6 unicast-routing
!
interface GigabitEthernet0/0
 ipv6 address 2001:DB8:1111:3::2/64
!
interface Serial0/0/1
 ipv6 address 2001:db8:1111:2::2/64
```

NOTE   Example 27-1's configuration on R1 uses both abbreviated and unabbreviated addresses, and both lowercase and uppercase hex digits, showing that all are allowed. Router **show** commands list the abbreviated value with uppercase hex digits.

Enabling IPv6 Routing

While the configuration shown in Examples 27-1 and 27-2 focus on the IPv6 address configuration, they also include an important but often overlooked step when configuring IPv6 on Cisco routers: IPv6 routing needs to be enabled.

Before routers can route (forward) IPv6 packets, IPv6 routing must be enabled. On Cisco routers, IPv4 routing is enabled by default, but IPv6 routing is not enabled by default. The solution takes only a single command—**ipv6 unicast-routing**—which enables IPv6 routing on the router.

Note that a router must enable IPv6 globally (**ipv6 unicast-routing**) and enable IPv6 on the interface (**ipv6 address**), before the router will attempt to route packets in and out an interface. (If the router happens to omit the **ipv6 unicast-routing** command, it can still be configured with interface IPv6 addresses, but the router acts like an IPv6 host, and does not route IPv6 packets.)

Verifying the IPv6 Address Configuration

IPv6 uses many **show** commands that mimic the syntax of IPv4 **show** commands. For example:

- The **show ipv6 interface brief** command gives you interface IPv6 address info, but not prefix length info, similar to the IPv4 **show ip interface brief** command.

- The **show ipv6 interface** command gives the details of IPv6 interface settings, much like the **show ip interface** command does for IPv4.

The one notable difference in the most common commands is that the **show interfaces** command still lists the IPv4 address and mask, but tells us nothing about IPv6. So, to see IPv6 interface addresses, use commands that begin with **show ipv6**. Example 27-3 lists a few samples from Router R1, with the explanations following.

Example 27-3 *Verifying Static IPv6 Addresses on Router R1*

```
! The first interface is in subnet 1
R1# show ipv6 interface GigabitEthernet 0/0
GigabitEthernet0/0 is up, line protocol is up
  IPv6 is enabled, link-local address is FE80::1FF:FE01:101
  No Virtual link-local address(es):
  Description: LAN at Site 1
  Global unicast address(es):
    2001:DB8:1111:1::1, subnet is 2001:DB8:1111:1::/64
  Joined group address(es):
    FF02::1
    FF02::2
    FF02::A
    FF02::1:FF00:1
    FF02::1:FF01:101
  MTU is 1500 bytes
  ICMP error messages limited to one every 100 milliseconds
  ICMP redirects are enabled
  ICMP unreachables are sent
  ND DAD is enabled, number of DAD attempts: 1
  ND reachable time is 30000 milliseconds (using 30000)
  ND advertised reachable time is 0 (unspecified)
  ND advertised retransmit interval is 0 (unspecified)
  ND router advertisements are sent every 200 seconds
  ND router advertisements live for 1800 seconds
```

27

```
       ND advertised default router preference is Medium
       Hosts use stateless autoconfig for addresses.


R1# show ipv6 interface S0/0/0
Serial0/0/0 is up, line protocol is up
   IPv6 is enabled, link-local address is FE80::1FF:FE01:101
   No Virtual link-local address(es):
   Description: link to R2
   Global unicast address(es):
      2001:DB8:1111:2::1, subnet is 2001:DB8:1111:2::/64
   Joined group address(es):
      FF02::1
      FF02::2
      FF02::A
      FF02::1:FF00:1
      FF02::1:FF01:101
   MTU is 1500 bytes
! Lines omitted for brevity


R1# show ipv6 interface brief
GigabitEthernet0/0      [up/up]
      FE80::1FF:FE01:101
      2001:DB8:1111:1::1
GigabitEthernet0/1      [administratively down/down]
   unassigned
Serial0/0/0             [up/up]
      FE80::1FF:FE01:101
      2001:DB8:1111:2::1
Serial0/0/1             [administratively down/down]
   unassigned
```

First, focus on the output of the two **show ipv6 interface** commands that make up most of the output in Example 27-3. The first command lists interface G0/0, showing output about that interface only. Note that the output lists the configured IPv6 address and prefix length, as well as the IPv6 subnet (2001:DB8:1111:1::/64), which the router calculated based on the IPv6 address. The second **show ipv6 interface** command shows similar details for interface S0/0/0, with some of the volume of output omitted.

The end of the example lists the output of the **show ipv6 interface brief** command. Similar to the IPv4-focused **show ip interface brief** command, this command lists IPv6 addresses, but not the prefix length or prefixes. This command also lists all interfaces on the router, whether or not IPv6 is enabled on the interfaces. For example, in this case, the only two interfaces on R1 that have an IPv6 address are G0/0 and S0/0/0, as configured earlier in Example 27-1.

Beyond the IPv6 addresses on the interfaces, the router also adds IPv6 connected routes to the IPv6 routing table off each interface. Just as with IPv4, the router keeps these connected routes in the IPv6 routing table only when the interface is in a working (up/up) state. But if the interface has an IPv6 unicast address configured, and the interface is working, the router adds the connected routes. Example 27-4 shows the connected IPv6 on Router R1 from Figure 27-3.

Example 27-4 *Displaying Connected IPv6 Routes on Router R1*

```
R1# show ipv6 route connected
IPv6 Routing Table - default - 5 entries
Codes: C - Connected, L - Local, S - Static, U - Per-user Static route
       B - BGP, R - RIP, I1 - ISIS L1, I2 - ISIS L2
       IA - ISIS interarea, IS - ISIS summary, D - EIGRP, EX - EIGRP external
       ND - ND Default, NDp - ND Prefix, DCE - Destination, NDr - Redirect
       O - OSPF Intra, OI - OSPF Inter, OE1 - OSPF ext 1, OE2 - OSPF ext 2
       ON1 - OSPF NSSA ext 1, ON2 - OSPF NSSA ext 2
C   2001:DB8:1111:1::/64 [0/0]
     via GigabitEthernet0/0, directly connected
C   2001:DB8:1111:2::/64 [0/0]
     via Serial0/0/0, directly connected
```

Generating a Unique Interface ID Using EUI-64

IPv6 follows the same general model as IPv4 regarding which types of devices typically use static, predefined addresses, and which use dynamically learned address. For example, routers inside an enterprise use a static IPv4 addresses, while end-user devices typically learn their IPv4 address using DHCP. With IPv6, routers also typically use static IPv6 addresses, while user devices use DHCP or Stateless Address Auto Configuration (SLAAC) to dynamically learn their IPv6 address.

Interestingly, routers have two options for configuring a stable and predictable IPv6 interface address that does not change. One method, discussed already in this chapter, uses the **ipv6 address** command to define the entire 128-bit address, as shown in Examples 27-1 and 27-2. The other method uses this same **ipv6 address** command to configure only the 64-bit IPv6 prefix for the interface, and lets the router automatically generate a unique interface ID.

This second method uses rules called EUI-64 (extended unique identifier). The configuration includes a keyword to tell the router to use EUI-64 rules, along with the 64-bit prefix. The router then uses EUI-64 rules to create the interface ID part of the address, as follows:

Key Topic

1. Split the 6-byte (12-hex-digit) MAC address in two halves (6 hex digits each).
2. Insert FFFE in between the two, making the interface ID now have a total of 16 hex digits (64 bits).
3. Invert the seventh bit of the interface ID.

Figure 27-4 shows the major pieces of how the address is formed.

Key Topic

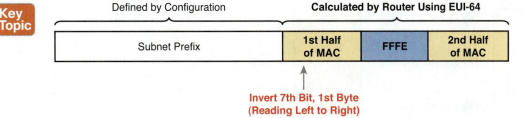

Figure 27-4 *IPv6 Address Format with Interface ID and EUI-64*

Although it might seem a bit convoluted, it works. Also, with a little practice, you can look at an IPv6 address and quickly notice the FFFE in the middle of the interface ID, and then easily find the two halves of the corresponding interface's MAC address. But you need to be ready to do the same math, in this case to predict the EUI-64 formatted IPv6 address on an interface.

27

For example, if you ignore the final step of inverting the seventh bit, the rest of the steps just require that you move the pieces around. Figure 27-5 shows two examples, just so you see the process.

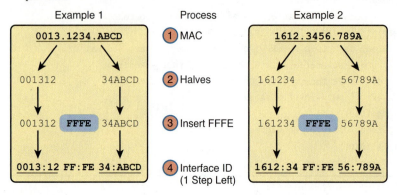

Figure 27-5 *Two Examples of Most of the EUI-64 Interface ID Process*

Both examples follow the same process. Each starts with the MAC address, breaking it into two halves (Step 2). The third step inserts FFFE in the middle, and the fourth step inserts a colon every four hex digits, keeping with IPv6 conventions.

While the examples in Figure 27-5 show most of the steps, they omit the final step. The final step requires that you convert the first byte (first two hex digits) from hex to binary, invert the seventh of the 8 bits, and convert the bits back to binary. Inverting a bit means that if the bit is a 0, make it a 1; if it is a 1, make it a 0. Most of the time, with IPv6 addresses, the original bit will be 0, and will be inverted to a 1.

> **NOTE** The bit being inverted for EUI-64 is called the universal/local bit, with a value of 0 meaning that the MAC is a universal burned-in address. All burned-in MAC addresses should have a binary 0 in this bit position. Because people seldom override their router MAC addresses, the EUI-64 calculation will typically change the seventh bit from a binary 0 to a binary 1.

For example, Figure 27-6 completes the two examples from Figure 27-5, focusing only on the first two hex digits. The examples show each pair of hex digits (Step 1) and the binary equivalent (Step 2). Step 3 shows a copy of those same 8 bits, except the seventh bit is inverted; the example on the left inverts from 0 to 1, and the example on the right inverts from 1 to 0. Finally, the bits are converted back to hex at Step 4.

Key Topic

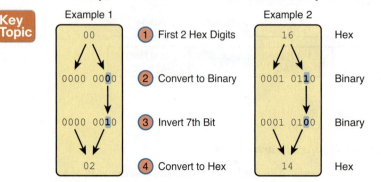

Figure 27-6 *Inverting the Seventh Bit of an EUI-64 Interface ID Field*

> **NOTE** If you do not remember how to do hex to binary conversions, take a few moments to review the process. If you memorize the 16 hex values for digits 0 through F, with the corresponding binary values, the conversion can be easy. If you do not have those handy in your memory, take a few moments to look at Table A-2 in Appendix A, "Numeric Reference Tables."

As usual, the best way to get comfortable with forming these EUI-64 interface IDs is to calculate some yourself. Table 27-1 lists some practice problems, with an IPv6 64-bit prefix in the first column and the MAC address in the second column. Your job is to calculate the full (unabbreviated) IPv6 address using EUI-64 rules. The answers sit at the end of the chapter, in the section "Answers to Earlier Practice Problems."

Table 27-1   IPv6 EUI-64 Address Creation Practice

Prefix	MAC Address	Unabbreviated IPv6 Address
2001:DB8:1:1::/64	0013.ABAB.1001	
2001:DB8:1:1::/64	AA13.ABAB.1001	
2001:DB8:1:1::/64	000C.BEEF.CAFE	
2001:DB8:1:1::/64	B80C.BEEF.CAFE	
2001:DB8:FE:FE::/64	0C0C.ABAC.CABA	
2001:DB8:FE:FE::/64	0A0C.ABAC.CABA	

Configuring a router interface to use the EUI-64 format uses the **ipv6 address** *address/prefix-length* **eui-64** interface subcommand. The **eui-64** keyword tells the router to find the interface MAC address and do the EUI-64 conversion math to find the interface ID.

Example 27-5 shows a revised configuration on Router R1, as compared to the earlier Example 27-1. In this case, R1 uses EUI-64 formatting for its IPv6 addresses.

Example 27-5   *Configuring R1's IPv6 Interfaces Using EUI-64*

```
! The next commands are on router R1
ipv6 unicast-routing
!
! The ipv6 address command now lists the a prefix
interface GigabitEthernet0/0
 ipv6 address 2001:DB8:1111:1::/64 eui-64
!
interface Serial0/0/0
 ipv6 address 2001:DB8:1111:2::/64 eui-64


R1# show ipv6 interface brief
GigabitEthernet0/0      [up/up]
    FE80::1FF:FE01:101
    2001:DB8:1111:1:0:1FF:FE01:101
GigabitEthernet0/1      [administratively down/down]
    unassigned
Serial0/0/0             [up/up]
    FE80::1FF:FE01:101
    2001:DB8:1111:2:0:1FF:FE01:101
Serial0/0/1             [administratively down/down]
    unassigned
```

27

Note that the example shows EUI-64 being used on a serial interface, which does not have an associated MAC address. For interfaces that do not have a MAC address, the router chooses the MAC of the lowest-numbered router interface that does have a MAC. In this example, R1 uses its G0/0 interface MAC to form the EUI-64 interface ID for all the serial interfaces.

> **NOTE**   When using EUI-64, the address value in the **ipv6 address** command should be the prefix, not the full 128-bit IPv6 address. However, if you mistakenly type the full address, and still use the **eui-64** keyword, IOS accepts the command, and converts the address to the matching prefix before putting the command into the running config file. For example, IOS accepts and then converts the **ipv6 address 2000:1:1:1::1/64 eui-64** command to **ipv6 address 2000:1:1:1::/64 eui-64**.

Dynamic Unicast Address Configuration

In most cases, network engineers will configure the IPv6 addresses of router interfaces so that the addresses do not change until the engineer changes the router configuration. However, routers can be configured to use dynamically learned IPv6 addresses. These can be useful for routers connecting to the Internet through some types of Internet access technologies, like DSL and cable modems.

Cisco routers support two ways for the router interface to dynamically learn an IPv6 address to use:

- Stateful DHCP
- Stateless Address Autoconfiguration (SLAAC)

Both methods use the familiar **ipv6 address** command. Of course, neither option configures the actual IPv6 address; instead, the commands configure a keyword that tells the router which method to use to learn its IPv6 address. Example 27-6 shows the configuration, with one interface using stateful DHCP, and one using SLAAC.

Example 27-6   *Router Configuration to Learn IPv6 Addresses with DHCP and SLAAC*

```
! This interface uses DHCP to learn its IPv6 address
interface FastEthernet0/0
 ipv6 address dhcp
!
! This interface uses SLAAC to learn its IPv6 address
interface FastEthernet0/1
 ipv6 address autoconfig
```

Cisco routers also have to be ready to play a role with DHCP and SLAAC on behalf of other IPv6 devices in the network. Chapter 28, which focuses on implementing IPv6 on hosts, discusses the protocols and the responsibilities of the routers.

Special Addresses Used by Routers

IPv6 configuration on a router begins with the simple steps discussed in the first part of this chapter. After configuring the **ipv6 unicast-routing** global configuration command, to enable the function of IPv6 routing, the addition of a unicast IPv6 address on an interface causes the router to do the following:

- Gives the interface a unicast IPv6 address
- Enables the routing of IPv6 packets in/out that interface

- Defines the IPv6 prefix (subnet) that exists off that interface
- Tells the router to add a connected IPv6 route for that prefix, to the IPv6 routing table, when that interface is up/up

> **NOTE**   In fact, if you pause and look at the list again, the same ideas happen for IPv4 when you configure an IPv4 address on a router interface.

While all the IPv6 features in this list work much like similar features in IPv4, IPv6 also has a number of additional functions not seen in IPv4. Often, these additional functions use other IPv6 addresses, many of which are multicast addresses. This second major section of this chapter examines the additional IPv6 addresses seen on routers, with a brief description of how they are used.

Link-Local Addresses

IPv6 uses link-local addresses as a special kind of unicast IPv6 address. These addresses are not used for normal IPv6 packet flows that contain data for applications. Instead, these addresses are used by some overhead protocols and for routing. This next topic first looks at how IPv6 uses link-local addresses and then how routers create link-local addresses.

Link-Local Address Concepts

Each IPv6 host (routers included) use an additional unicast address called a link-local address. Packets sent to a link-local address do not leave the IPv6 subnet, because routers do not forward packets sent to a link-local address.

IPv6 uses link-local addresses for a variety of protocols. Many IPv6 protocols that need to send messages inside a single subnet typically use link-local addresses, rather than the host's global unicast or unique local address. For example, Neighbor Discovery Protocol (NDP), which replaces the functions of IPv4's ARP, uses link-local addresses.

Routers also use link-local addresses as the next-hop IP addresses in IPv6 routes, as shown in Figure 27-7. IPv6 hosts also use a default router (default gateway) concept, like IPv4, but instead of the router address being in the same subnet, hosts refer to the router's link-local address. The **show ipv6 route** command lists the link-local address of the neighboring router, and not the global unicast or unique local unicast address.

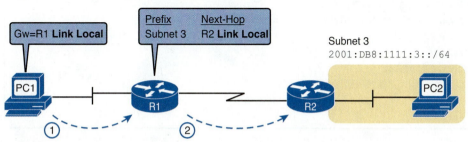

Figure 27-7   *IPv6 Using Link-Local Addresses as the Next-Hop Address*

The following list summarizes the key facts about link-local addresses:

Unicast (not multicast): Link-local addresses represent a single host, and packets sent to a link-local address should be processed by only that one IPv6 host.

Forwarding scope is the local link only: Packets sent to a link-local address do not leave the local data link, because routers do not forward packets with link-local destination addresses.

27

Automatically generated: Every IPv6 host interface (and router interface) can create their own link-local address automatically, solving some initialization problems for hosts before they learn a dynamically learned global unicast address.

Common uses: Used for some overhead protocols that stay local to one subnet, and as the next-hop address for IPv6 routes.

Creating Link-Local Addresses on Routers

IPv6 hosts and routers can calculate their own link-local address, for each interface, using some basic rules. First, all link-local addresses start with the same prefix, as shown on the left side of Figure 27-8. By definition, the first 10 bits must match prefix FE80::/10, meaning that the first three hex digits will be either FE8, FE9, FEA, or FEB. However, when following the RFC, the next 54 bits should be binary 0, so the link-local address should always start with FE80:0000:0000:0000 as the first four unabbreviated quartets.

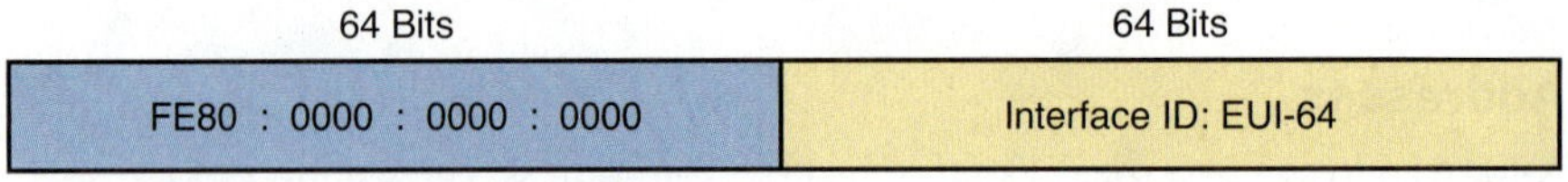

64 Bits	64 Bits
FE80 : 0000 : 0000 : 0000	Interface ID: EUI-64

Figure 27-8 *Link-Local Address Format*

The second half of the link-local address, in practice, can be formed with different rules. Cisco routers use the EUI-64 format to create the interface ID (see the earlier section "Generating a Unique Interface ID Using EUI-64"). As a result, a router's complete link-local address should be unique, because the MAC address that feeds into the EUI-64 process should be unique. Other OSs randomly generate the interface ID. For example, Microsoft OSs use a somewhat random process to choose the interface ID, and change it over time, in an attempt to prevent some forms of attacks. Finally, link-local addresses can simply be configured.

IOS creates a link-local address for any interface that has configured at least one other unicast address using the **ipv6 address** command (global unicast or unique local). To see the link-local address, just use the usual commands that also list the unicast IPv6 address: **show ipv6 interface** and **show ipv6 interface brief**. Example 27-7 shows an example from Router R1.

Example 27-7 *Comparing Link-Local Addresses with EUI-Generated Unicast Addresses*

```
R1# show ipv6 interface brief
GigabitEthernet0/0      [up/up]
    FE80::1FF:FE01:101
    2001:DB8:1111:1:0:1FF:FE01:101
GigabitEthernet0/1      [administratively down/down]
    unassigned
Serial0/0/0             [up/up]
    FE80::1FF:FE01:101
    2001:DB8:1111:2:0:1FF:FE01:101
Serial0/0/1             [administratively down/down]
    unassigned
```

First, examine the two pair of highlighted entries in the example. For each of the two interfaces that have a global unicast address (G0/0 and S0/0/0), the output lists the global unicast, which happens to begin with 2001 in this case. At the same time, the output also lists the link-local address for each interface, beginning with FE80.

Next, focus on the two addresses listed under interface G0/0. If you look closely at the second half of the two addresses listed for interface G0/0, you will see that both addresses have the same interface ID value. The global unicast address was configured in this case with the **ipv6 address 2001:DB8:1111:1::/64 eui-64** command, so the router used EUI-64 logic to form both the global unicast address and the link-local address. The interface MAC address in this case is 0200.0101.0101, so the router calculates an interface ID portion of both addresses as 0000:01FF:FE01:0101 (unabbreviated). After abbreviation, router R1's link-local address on interface G0/0 becomes FE80::1FF:FE01:101.

IOS can either automatically create the link-local address, or it can be configured. IOS chooses the link-local address for the interface based on the following rules:

- If configured, the router uses the value in the **ipv6 address** *address* **link-local** interface subcommand. Note that the configured link-local address must be from the correct address range for link-local addresses, that is, an address from prefix FE80::/10. In other words, the address must begin with FE8, FE9, FEA, or FEB.

- If not configured, the IOS calculates the link-local address using EUI-64 rules, as discussed and demonstrated in and around Example 27-7. The calculation uses EUI-64 rules even if the interface unicast address does not use EUI-64.

IPv6 Multicast Addresses

IPv6 uses multicast IPv6 addresses for several purposes. In some cases, overhead protocols use these addresses to send packets to multiple IPv6 hosts at once. In other cases, applications use multicast addresses to send IPv6 packets to many hosts, rather than sending a different packet to each individual host.

This next topic first compares the use of broadcast address with the use of multicast addresses. It then looks at some common multicast addresses used with IPv6.

Broadcasts Versus Multicasts

The terms *broadcast* and *multicast* have subtle and slightly different meanings. After you learn more about both, particularly multicasts, the differences become obvious. However, CCENT and CCNA R/S do not get into much depth on either topic, so briefly, take a moment to consider a basic comparison.

First, think about IPv4, and an IPv4 subnet. IPv4 uses broadcasts, meaning that IPv4 allows a host to send a packet to a broadcast address, such that all IPv4 hosts in that subnet must listen for the packet, read the packet, and at least spend some CPU cycles deciding whether they need to respond. In short, a broadcast goes to all devices, and all must consider the message.

Broadcasts can be wasteful of the CPU cycles on the hosts in a subnet, because oftentimes, a broadcast is used to get a response for only one host, or just a few hosts, in that subnet. Multicasts help solve that problem, by causing a packet to be processed only by the correct subset of hosts. Because using multicasts is more efficient for the devices in the network, IPv6 does not use broadcasts, instead using multicast addresses.

To complete the comparison, now think about IPv6, and an IPv6 subnet with 100 hosts and 3 routers. Sometimes, a host wants to send a packet to "all hosts running IPv6"—well, IPv6 defines a multicast address for that (FF02::1). Packets sent to FF02::1 arrive at all devices that have IPv6 enabled (including routers) and should be processed by all. However, if a protocol message needs to go to all IPv6 routers, but not to hosts, the packet can be sent to address FF02::2—a multicast address used only by IPv6 routers. Packets sent to FF02::2 do not require any processing by the nonrouters, saving their CPU cycles.

Continuing the comparison one step further, a packet could be sent to a subset of the routers. Enhanced Interior Gateway Routing Protocol (EIGRP) uses a reserved multicast address (FF02::A), while Open Shortest Path First (OSPF) uses two (FF02::5 and FF02::6). These routing protocols send their Update messages to these reserved multicast addresses, so a router running EIGRP does not bother a router running OSPF, or vice versa.

27

Common Local Scope Multicast Addresses

In some cases, multicast messages need to stay within one subnet, but in other cases, they need to be able to flow to many subnets. Some multicast addresses imply that a packet sent to that address should stay on the link; these addresses have a link-local scope. Multicast addresses that allow the packets to be routed to other subnets inside the enterprise have an organization-local scope.

For the purposes of this book, you will see a few link-local scope addresses on a regular basis. The Internet Assigned Numbers Authority (IANA) reserves all IPv6 addresses that begin with FF, or more formally, prefix FF00::/8, for IPv6 multicasts. Within that range, IANA reserves all that begin with FF02 (formally, FF02::/16) for link-local scope multicast addresses.

Table 27-2 lists the most common local-scope IPv6 multicast addresses.

Table 27-2   Key IPv6 Local-Scope Multicast Addresses

Short Name	Multicast Address	Meaning	IPv4 Equivalent
All-nodes	FF02::1	All-nodes (all interfaces that use IPv6 that are on the link)	A subnet broadcast address
All-routers	FF02::2	All-routers (all IPv6 router interfaces on the link)	None
All-OSPF, All-OSPF-DR	FF02::5, FF02::6	All OSPF routers and all OSPF designated routers, respectively	224.0.0.5, 224.0.0.6
EIGRPv6 Routers	FF02::A	All routers using EIGRP for IPv6 (EIGRPv6)	224.0.0.10

Example 27-8 repeats the output of the **show ipv6 interface** command to show the multicast addresses used by Router R1 on its G0/0 interface. In this case, the highlighted lines show the all-nodes address (FF02::1), all-routers (FF02::2), and EIGRPv6 (FF02::A).

Example 27-8   *Verifying Static IPv6 Addresses on Router R1*

```
R1# show ipv6 interface GigabitEthernet 0/0
GigabitEthernet0/0 is up, line protocol is up
  IPv6 is enabled, link-local address is FE80::1FF:FE01:101
  No Virtual link-local address(es):
  Description: LAN at Site 1
  Global unicast address(es):
    2001:DB8:1111:1::1, subnet is 2001:DB8:1111:1::/64
  Joined group address(es):
    FF02::1
    FF02::2
    FF02::A
    FF02::1:FF00:1
    FF02::1:FF01:101
  ! Lines omitted for brevity
```

Solicited-Node Multicast Addresses

Many of the multicast addresses used by protocols in the scope of the CCENT and CCNA exams are simply numbers reserved by an RFC. We just need to remember the numbers and notice them in **show** commands. However, one particular type of multicast address, called the solicited-node multicast address, varies from host to host, so its value is not preset. This last topic of the chapter briefly describes this type of multicast address.

Some IPv6 multicast addresses have clear and meaningful short names. Terms like "all-nodes" (for multicast address FF02::1) or "all-routers" (for multicast address FF02::2) pretty much define the meaning. Frankly, the term "solicited-node" does not make the idea behind this multicast address jump off the page.

Generally speaking, the solicited-node multicast address provides a destination address so that one packet can be sent inside one IPv6 subnet (link-local), to all hosts whose unicast addresses happen to have the same value in the last six hex digits. While true, that first sentence is relatively long. The following list breaks down the concepts that effectively define what the solicited-node multicast address is, for a particular host:

- A multicast address (not a unicast address)
- Link-local scope
- Based on the unicast IPv6 address of the host
- Specifically based on the only last six hex digits of the unicast address
- Each host must listen for packets sent to its solicited-node multicast address
- All hosts whose unicast IPv6 addresses have the same value in the last six hex digits use this same solicited node multicast address, and process the same packets

This last bullet item gets to the key function of these solicited node multicast addresses. Packets sent to a particular solicited-node multicast address might go to just one host. However, if more than one host in a subnet happens to have equal values in the last six hex digits of its unicast addresses, that same multicast packet is processed by both/all hosts. And some protocols want this kind of logic, of sending one multicast packet to all hosts who happen to have these similar unicast IPv6 addresses. As a result, the solicited-node multicast address was born.

> **NOTE** An alternate name, like "The link-local multicast address in common to all hosts with the same last six hex digits of their respective unicast addresses," would be a much more meaningful name instead of "solicited-node" multicast. However, as long as you know the meaning, just memorize the true name.

All IPv6 hosts must listen for messages sent to their solicited-node multicast address(es). So, for each interface, and for each unicast address on each interface, the device must determine its solicited node multicast address(es), and listen for packets sent to those addresses.

The logic to find a solicited-node multicast address, after you know the unicast address, is simple. Start with the predefined /104 prefix shown in Figure 27-9. In other words, all the solicited-node multicast addresses begin with the abbreviated FF02::1:FF. In the last 24 bits (6 hex digits), copy the unicast address into the solicited-node address.

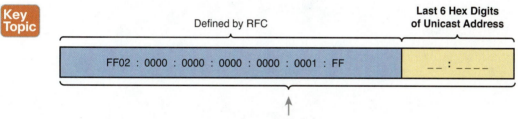

Figure 27-9 *Solicited-Node Multicast Address Format*

To see samples of these addresses on a router, look back to the previous Example 27-8. The last two lines of command output show the solicited-node multicast addresses for Router R1's G0/0 interface: FF02::1:FF00:1 and FF02::1:FF01:101. Note that in this case, the reason R1's G0/0 has two such addresses is that one matches the router's global unicast address on that interface, while the other matches the link-local (unicast) address.

Miscellaneous IPv6 Addresses

Together, this chapter and the previous chapter have introduced most of the IPv6 addressing concepts included in this book. This short topic mentions a few remaining IPv6 addressing ideas and summarizes the topics for easy study.

First, all IPv6 hosts can use two additional special addresses:

- The unknown (unspecified) IPv6 address, ::, or all 0s
- The loopback IPv6 address, ::1, or 127 binary 0s with a single 1

The unknown address (::) can be used by a host when it's own IPv6 address is not yet known, or when the host wonders if its own IPv6 address might have problems. For example, hosts use the unknown address during the early stages of dynamically discovering their IPv6 address. When a host does not yet know what IPv6 address to use, it can use the :: address as its source IPv6 address.

The IPv6 loopback address gives each IPv6 host a way to test its own protocol stack. Just like the IPv4 127.0.0.1 loopback address, packets sent to ::1 do not leave the host, but are instead simply delivered down the stack to IPv6, and back up the stack to the application on the local host.

Review Activities

Chapter Summary

- Cisco routers give us two options for static configuration of IPv6 addresses. In one case, you configure the full 128-bit address, while in the other, you configure a 64-bit prefix and let the router derive the second half of the address (the interface ID).

- To statically configure the full 128-bit unicast address—either global unicast or unique local—the router needs an **ipv6 address** *address/prefix-length* interface subcommand on each interface.

- Note that a router must enable IPv6 globally (**ipv6 unicast-routing**), and enable IPv6 on the interface (**ipv6 address**), before the router will attempt to route packets into and out of an interface. (If the router happens to omit the **ipv6 unicast-routing** command, it can still be configured with interface IPv6 addresses, but the router acts like an IPv6 host and does not route IPv6 packets.)

- IPv6 uses many **show** commands that mimic the syntax of IPv4 **show** commands. For example:

  - The **show ipv6 interface brief** command gives you interface IPv6 address info but not prefix length info, similar to the IPv4 **show ip interface brief** command.

  - The **show ipv6 interface** command gives the details of IPv6 interface settings, much like the **show ip interface** command does for IPv4.

- To generate a unique interface ID using EUI-64:

  - Configure a router interface to use the EUI-64 format using the **ipv6 address** *address/prefix-length* **eui-64** interface subcommand. The **eui-64** keyword tells the router to find the interface MAC address and do the EUI-64 conversion math to find the interface ID.

  - The router then uses EUI-64 rules to create the interface ID part of the address, as follows:

    - Split the 6-byte (12 hex digit) MAC address in two halves (6 hex digits each).

    - Insert FFFE in between the two, making the interface ID now have a total of 16 hex digits (64 bits).

    - Invert the seventh bit of the interface ID.

- Cisco routers support two ways for the router interface to dynamically learn an IPv6 address to use

  - Stateful DHCP

  - Stateless Address Autoconfiguration (SLAAC)

- After configuring the **ipv6 unicast-routing** global configuration command, to enable the function of IPv6 routing, the addition of a unicast IPv6 address on an interface causes the router to do the following:

  - Gives the interface a unicast IPv6 address

  - Enables the routing of IPv6 packets in/out that interface

  - Defines the IPv6 prefix (subnet) that exists off that interface

  - Tells the router to add a connected IPv6 route for that prefix to the IPv6 routing table when that interface is up/up

- Each IPv6 host (routers included) uses an additional unicast address called a link-local address. Packets sent to a link-local address do not leave the IPv6 subnet because routers do not forward packets sent to a link-local address.

27

- The following list summarizes the key facts about link-local addresses:

  - **Unicast (not multicast):** Link-local addresses represent a single host, and packets sent to a link-local address should be processed only by that one IPv6 host.

  - **Forwarding scope is the local link only:** Packets sent to a link-local address do not leave the local data link because routers do not forward packets with link-local destination addresses.

  - **Automatically generated:** Each IPv6 host interface (and router interface) can create its own link-local address automatically, solving some initialization problems for hosts before they learn a dynamically learned global unicast address.

  - **Common Uses:** Used for some overhead protocols that stay local to one subnet, and as the next-hop address for IPv6 routes.

- All IPv6 hosts can use two additional special addresses:

  - The unknown (unspecified) IPv6 address, ::, or all 0s
  - The loopback IPv6 address, ::1, or 127 binary 0s with a single 1

Review Questions

Answer these review questions. You can find the answers at the bottom of the last page of the chapter. For thorough explanations, see DVD Appendix C, "Answers to Review Questions."

1. Router R1 has an interface named Gigabit Ethernet 0/1, whose MAC address has been set to 0200.0001.000A. Which of the following commands, added in R1's Gigabit Ethernet 0/1 configuration mode, gives this router's G0/1 interface a unicast IPv6 address of 2001:1:1:1:1:200:1:A, with a /64 prefix length?

   A. **ipv6 address 2001:1:1:1:1:200:1:A/64**

   B. **ipv6 address 2001:1:1:1:1:200:1:A/64 eui-64**

   C. **ipv6 address 2001:1:1:1:1:200:1:A /64 eui-64**

   D. **ipv6 address 2001:1:1:1:1:200:1:A /64**

   E. None of the other answers are correct.

2. Router R1 has an interface named Gigabit Ethernet 0/1, whose MAC address has been set to 5055.4444.3333. This interface has been configured with the **ipv6 address 2000:1:1:1::/64 eui-64** subcommand. What unicast address will this interface use?

   A. 2000:1:1:1:52FF:FE55:4444:3333

   B. 2000:1:1:1:5255:44FF:FE44:3333

   C. 2000:1:1:1:5255:4444:33FF:FE33

   D. 2000:1:1:1:200:FF:FE00:0

3. Router R1 currently supports IPv4, routing packets in and out all its interfaces. R1's configuration needs to be migrated to support dual-stack operation, routing both IPv4 and IPv6. Which of the following tasks must be performed before the router can also support routing IPv6 packets? (Choose two answers.)

   A. Enable IPv6 on each interface using an **ipv6 address** interface subcommand.

   B. Enable support for both versions with the **ip versions 4 6** global command.

   C. Additionally enable IPv6 routing using the **ipv6 unicast-routing** global command.

   D. Migrate to dual-stack routing using the **ip routing dual-stack** global command.

4. Router R1 has an interface named Gigabit Ethernet 0/1, whose MAC address has been set to 0200.0001.000A. The interface is then configured with the **ipv6 address 2001:1:1:1:200:FF:FE01:B/64** interface subcommand; no other **ipv6 address** commands are configured on the interface. Which of the following answers lists the link-local address used on the interface?

   A. FE80::FF:FE01:A

   B. FE80::FF:FE01:B

   C. FE80::200:FF:FE01:A

   D. FE80::200:FF:FE01:B

5. Which of the following multicast addresses is defined as the address for sending packets to only the IPv6 routers on the local link?

   A. FF02::1

   B. FF02::2

   C. FF02::5

   D. FF02::A

6. Router R1 has an interface named Gigabit Ethernet 0/1, whose MAC address has been set to 0200.0001.000A. Which of the following commands, added in R1's Gigabit Ethernet 0/1 configuration mode, results in R1 using a solicited node multicast address of FF02::1:FF00:A?

   A. ipv6 address 2001:1:1:1:1:200:1:A/64

   B. ipv6 address 2001:1:1:1::/64 eui-64

   C. ipv6 address 2001:1:1:1::A/64

   D. None of the other answers results in R1 using that multicast address.

Review All the Key Topics

Review the most important topics from this chapter, noted with the Key Topic icon. Table 27-3 lists these key topics and where each is discussed.

Key Topic

Table 27-3   Key Topics for Chapter 27

Key Topic Element	Description	Page Number
Figure 27-2	Concept drawing about the need for dual stacks for the foreseeable future	647
List	Rules for creating an IPv6 address using EUI-64 rules	651
Figure 27-4	Conceptual drawing of how to create an IPv6 address using EUI-64 rules	651
Figure 27-6	Example of performing the bit inversion when using EUI-64	652
List	Functions IOS enables when an IPv6 is configured on a working interface	654
List	Key facts about IPv6 link-local addresses	655
Figure 27-9	Conceptual drawing of how to make a solicited-node multicast address	659
List	Other special IPv6 addresses	660

27

Complete the Tables and Lists from Memory

Print a copy of DVD Appendix M, "Memory Tables," or at least the section for this chapter, and complete the tables and lists from memory. DVD Appendix N, "Memory Tables Answer Key," includes completed tables and lists for you to check your work.

Definitions of Key Terms

After your first reading of the chapter, try to define these key terms, but do not be concerned about getting them all correct at that time. Chapter 30 directs you in how to use these terms for late-stage preparation for the exam.

dual stacks, EUI-64, link-local address, link-local scope, solicited-node multicast address, all-nodes multicast address, all-routers multicast address

Additional Practice with IPv6 Address Abbreviations

For additional practice with finding EUI-64 addresses and with solicited-node multicast addresses:

■ DVD Appendix L, "Practice for Chapter 27: Implementing IPv6 Addressing on Routers," has some additional practice problems listed for both EUI-64 and solicited-node multicast addresses.

■ Create your own problems using any real router or simulator. Get into the router CLI, into configuration mode, and configure the **mac-address** *address* and **ipv6 address** *prefix***/64 eui-64** command. These commands (respectively) change the MAC address used on the interface and tell the router to create an IPv6 using EUI-64 rules. Then, before looking at the IPv6 address chosen by the router, do the calculations yourself. Finally, use the **show ipv6 interface** command to see the unicast address as well as the solicited-node multicast address.

Command Reference to Check Your Memory

Although you should not necessarily memorize the information in the tables in this section, this section does include a reference for the configuration and EXEC commands covered in this chapter. Practically speaking, you should memorize the commands as a side effect of reading the chapter and doing all the activities in this exam preparation section. To check to see how well you have memorized the commands as a side effect of your other studies, cover the left side of the table with a piece of paper, read the descriptions on the right side, and see whether you remember the command.

Table 27-4   Chapter 27 Configuration Command Reference

Command	Description
ipv6 unicast-routing	Global command that enables IPv6 routing on the router
ipv6 address *ipv6-address/ prefix-length* [eui-64]	Interface subcommand that manually configures either the entire interface IP address, or a /64 prefix with the router building the EUI-64 format interface ID automatically

Table 27-5   Chapter 27 EXEC Command Reference

Command	Description
show ipv6 route [connected]	Lists IPv6 routes, or just the connected routes
show ipv6 interface [*type number*]	Lists IPv6 settings on an interface, including link-local and other unicast IP addresses
show ipv6 interface brief	Lists interface status and IPv6 addresses for each interface

Answers to Earlier Practice Problems

Table 27-1, earlier in this chapter, listed several practice problems in which you needed to calculate the IPv6 address based on EUI-64 rules. Table 27-6 lists the answers to those problems.

Table 27-6   Answers to IPv6 EUI-64 Address Creation Practice

Prefix	MAC Address	Unabbreviated IPv6 Address
2001:DB8:1:1::/64	0013.ABAB.1001	2001:DB8:1:1:0213:ABFF:FEAB:1001
2001:DB8:1:1::/64	AA13.ABAB.1001	2001:DB8:1:1:A813:ABFF:FEAB:1001
2001:DB8:1:1::/64	000C.BEEF.CAFE	2001:DB8:1:1:020C:BEFF:FEEF:CAFE
2001:DB8:1:1::/64	B80C.BEEF.CAFE	2001:DB8:1:1:BA0C:BEFF:FEEF:CAFE
2001:DB8:FE:FE::/64	0C0C.ABAC.CABA	2001:DB8:FE:FE:0E0C:ABFF:FEAC:CABA
2001:DB8:FE:FE::/64	0A0C.ABAC.CABA	2001:DB8:FE:FE:080C:ABFF:FEAC:CABA

Answers to Review Questions:

1 A **2** B **3** A and C **4** A **5** B **6** C

Chapter 28

Implementing IPv6 Addressing on Hosts

IPv6 hosts act like IPv4 hosts in many ways, using similar ideas, similar protocols, and even similar or identical commands for the same purpose. At the same time, IPv6 sometimes takes a much different approach than does IPv4, using a much different solution with a new protocol or command. For example:

- Similar to IPv4, IPv6 hosts use a unicast address, prefix length (mask), default router, and DNS server.

- Similar to IPv4, IPv6 uses a protocol to dynamically learn the MAC address of other hosts in the same LAN-based subnet.

- Unlike IPv4, IPv6 hosts use the Neighbor Discovery Protocol (NDP) for many functions, including the functions done by IPv4's ARP.

- Similar to IPv4, IPv6 hosts can use DHCP to learn their four primary IPv6 settings.

- Unlike IPv4, IPv6 supports another dynamic address assignment process other than DHCP, called Stateless Address Autoconfiguration (SLAAC).

This chapter focuses on the four primary IPv6 settings on hosts: the address, prefix length, default router address, and DNS server address. However, to understand how hosts dynamically learn those addresses, this chapter begins its first major section devoted to NDP, which plays a key role in several IPv6 processes. The middle section of the chapter then focuses on how hosts dynamically learn their IPv6 settings, with both DHCP and SLAAC. The final major section of this chapter looks at the tools to verify a host's IPv6 settings—many of which use the same commands used for IPv4.

LAN Switching Technologies

Verify network status and switch operation using basic utilities such as ping, telnet and ssh.

IP addressing (IPv4 / IPv6)

Describe the technological requirements for running IPv6 in conjunction with IPv4 such as dual stack

Describe IPv6 addresses

autoconfiguration

IP Routing Technologies

Verify router configuration and network connectivity

IP Services

Configure and verify DHCP (IOS Router)

configuring router interfaces to use DHCP

Troubleshooting

Troubleshoot and correct common problems associated with IP addressing and host configurations.

Foundation Topics

The Neighbor Discovery Protocol

IPv6 hosts need to know several important IPv6 settings that mirror the settings needed on IPv4 hosts: an address, the associated prefix length (mask equivalent), the default router address, and the DNS server address(es). Figure 28-1 shows those four concepts for PC1 on the left.

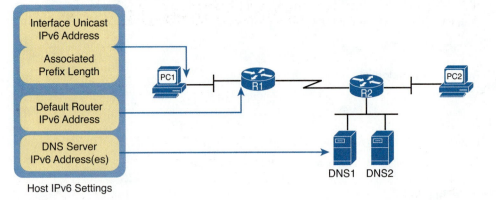

Figure 28-1 *IPv6 Settings Needed on Hosts*

Note that of the four settings, three are unicast IPv6 addresses. The PC's own IPv6 address is typically a global unicast or unique local unicast, as are the PC's references to the DNS servers. However, because the default router must be locally reachable, the default router setting typically refers to the router's link-local address.

Neighbor Discovery Protocol (NDP) defines several different functions related to IPv6 addressing, as follows:

- **SLAAC:** When using Stateless Address Autoconfiguration (SLAAC), the host uses NDP messages to learn the first part of its address, plus the prefix length.

- **Router Discovery:** Hosts learn the IPv6 addresses of the available IPv6 routers in the same subnet using NDP messages.

- **Duplicate Address Detection:** No matter how a host sets or learns its IPv6 address, the host waits to use the address until the host knows that no other host uses the same address. How does a host detect this problem? Using NDP messages, of course, through a process called Duplicate Address Detection (DAD).

- **Neighbor MAC Discovery:** After a host has passed the DAD process, and uses its IPv6 address, a LAN-based host will need to learn the MAC address of other hosts in the same subnet. NDP replaces IPv4's ARP, providing messages that replace the ARP Request and Reply messages.

The rest of this section steps through each of these four functions to varying degrees. Note that this section defers most of the discussion of the SLAAC process until later in the chapter, focusing more on the core NDP functions in this section.

Discovering Routers with NDP RS and RA

NDP defines a matched pair of messages that let a host dynamically discover all potential default routers that sit on the same data link. Basically, the process works with the host multicasting a message asking "routers, tell me about yourselves," and the routers reply. The messages are:

Router Solicitation (RS): Sent to the "all-IPv6-routers" local-scope multicast address of FF02::2, so that the message asks all routers, on the local link only, to identify themselves.

Router Advertisement (RA): This message, sent by the router, lists many facts, including the link-local IPv6 address of the router. When unsolicited, it is sent to the all-IPv6-hosts local-scope multicast address of FF02::1. When sent in response to an RS message, it flows back to either the unicast address of the host that sent the NS, or to the all-IPv6-hosts address FF02::1.

For example, Figure 28-2 shows how host PC1 can learn R1's link-local address. The process is indeed simple, with PC1 first asking and R1 replying.

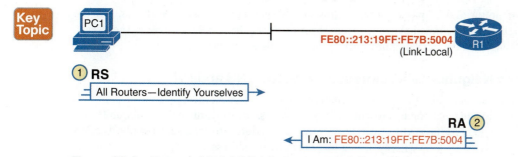

Figure 28-2 *Example NDP RS/RA Process to Find the Default Routers*

> **NOTE** IPv6 allows multiple prefixes and multiple default routers to be listed in the RA message; the figure just shows one of each for simplicity's sake.

IPv6 does not use broadcasts, but it does use multicasts. In this case, the RS message flows to the all-routers multicast address (FF02::2) so that all routers will receive the message. It has the same good effect as a broadcast with IPv4, without the negatives of a broadcast. In this case, only IPv6 routers will spend any CPU cycles processing the RS message. The RA message can flow either to the unicast IPv6 address of PC1 or to the all nodes FF02::1 address.

Note that while Figure 28-2 shows how a host can ask to learn about any routers, routers also periodically send unsolicited RA messages, even without an incoming RS. When routers send these periodic RA messages, they basically advertise details about IPv6 on the link. In this case, the RA messages flow to the FF02::1 all-nodes IPv6 multicast address.

Discovering Addressing Info for SLAAC with NDP RS and RA

While the NDP RS and RA messages identify IPv6 routers, these messages also supply other pieces of information as well. If you think about the messages more generally, RS gives a host a means to request information more general, like this: "IPv6 routers, tell me information that you know!" The RA message gives IPv6 routers a means to distribute the information: "Here is the information that I know!" Figure 28-2 just happens to show one fact learned through the RS and RA messages, namely the IPv6 address of the IPv6 router.

28

Another fact that routers know is the prefix and prefix length used on the local link. Routers typically have an **ipv6 address** command on each interface; that command lists the prefix length and enough information for the router to calculate the associated IPv6 prefix. A host can learn these details using the RS and RA message exchange, as shown in Figure 28-3.

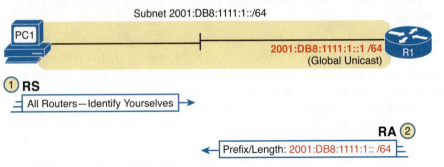

Subnet 2001:DB8:1111:1::/64

PC1

2001:DB8:1111:1::1 /64
(Global Unicast)   R1

① **RS**

All Routers—Identify Yourselves

RA ②

Prefix/Length: 2001:DB8:1111:1:: /64

Figure 28-3   *Using NDP RS/RA to Discover the Prefix/Length on the LAN*

As it turns out, the SLAAC process, used by hosts to dynamically learn an IPv6 address, uses the prefix/prefix length information learned from the router using RS and RA messages. The later section "Using Stateless Address Autoconfiguration" discusses the entire process.

Discovering Neighbor Link Addresses with NDP NS and NA

NDP defines a second pair of matched solicitation and advertisement messages: the neighbor solicitation (NS) and neighbor advertisement (NA) messages. Basically, the NS acts like an IPv4 ARP request, asking the host with a particular unicast IPv6 address to send back a reply. The NA message acts like an IPv4 ARP Reply, listing that host's MAC address.

The process of sending the NS and NA messages follows the same general process as RS and RA: The NS message asks for information and the NA supplies the information. The most obvious difference is that while RS/RA focuses on information held by routers, NS/NA focuses on information that could be held by any IPv6 host. Also, note that the NS messages goes to the solicited-node multicast address associated with the target; see Chapter 27's topic "Solicited-Node Multicast Addresses" for a reminder of this type of address.

Neighbor Solicitation (NS): Asks a host with a particular IPv6 address (the target address) to send back an NA with its MAC address listed. The NS message is sent to the solicited-node multicast address associated with the target address, so that the message is processed only by hosts whose last six hex digits match the address which is being queried.

Neighbor Advertisement (NA): This message lists the sender's address as the target address, along with the matching MAC address. It is sent back to the unicast address of the host that sent the original NS message. In some cases, a host sends an unsolicited NA, in which case the message is sent to the all-IPv6-hosts local-scope multicast address FF02::1.

NOTE   With NDP, the word "neighbor" refers to the fact that the devices will be on the same data link, for example, the same VLAN.

Figure 28-4 shows an example of how a host (PC1) uses an NS message to learn the MAC address used by another host. The NDP NS and NA messages replace the IPv4 ARP protocol in that it lets hosts discover the link-layer address of other IPv6 hosts on the same data link. (IPv6 refers to hosts on the same data link as simply *on-link*.) The NS message lists a target IPv6 unicast address, with the implied question: "What is your link address?" The NA message, in this example sent back to the original host that asked the question, lists that link address. Figure 28-4 shows an example.

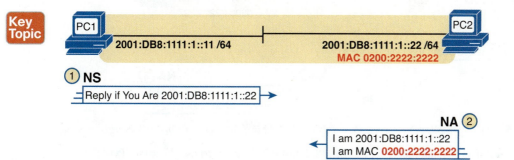

Figure 28-4   *Example NDP NS/NA Process to Find the Link Address of On-Link Neighbors*

At Step 1 of this particular example, PC1 sends the solicitation to find PC2's MAC address. PC1 first looks in its NDP neighbor table, the equivalent of the IPv4 ARP cache, and does not find the MAC address for IPv6 address 2001:DB8:1111:1::22. So, at Step 1, PC1 sends the NDP NS message to the matching solicited-node multicast address for 2001:DB8:1111:1::22, or FF02::1:FF00:22. Only IPv6 hosts whose address ends with 00:0022 will listen for this solicited-node multicast address. As a result, only a small subset of hosts on this link will process the received NDP NS message.

At Step 2, PC2 reacts to the received NS message. PC2 sends back an NA message in reply, listing PC2's MAC address. PC1 records PC2's MAC address in PC1's NDP neighbor table.

> **NOTE**   To view a host's NDP neighbor table, use these commands: (Windows) **netsh interface ipv6 show neighbors**; (Linux) **ip -6 neighbor show**; (Mac OS) **ndp -an**.

Discovering Duplicate Addresses Using NDP NS and NA

The NDP NS/NA messages also require hosts to do an important check to avoid using duplicate IPv6 addresses. IPv6 uses the Duplicate Address Detection (DAD) process before using a unicast address to make sure that no other node on that link is already using the address. If another host already uses that address, the first host simply does not use the address until the problem is resolved.

The term DAD refers to the function, but the function uses NDP NS and NA messages. Basically, a host sends an NS message, but it lists the address the host wants to use as the target address. If no duplicate exists, no other host should reply with an NA. However, if another host already uses that address, that host will reply with an NA, identifying a duplicate use of the address. Figure 28-5 shows an example in which a duplicate is detected.

28

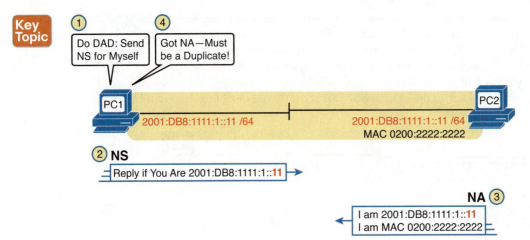

Figure 28-5 *Example NDP NS/NA Process to Find the Link Address of On-Link Neighbors*

Figure 28-5 shows an example in which both PC1 and PC2 attempt to use the same IPv6 address. PC2 is already using the address, and PC1 uses DAD before using the address. The figure shows the following steps:

1. PC1, before using address 2001:DB8:1111:1::11, must use DAD.

2. PC1 sends an NS message, listing the address PC1 now wants to use (2001:DB8:1111:1::11) as the target.

3. PC2 receives the NS, sees what PC2 already uses as its own address, and sends back an NA.

4. PC1, on receiving the NA message for its own IPv6 address, realizes a duplicate address exists.

Hosts do the DAD check for each of their unicast addresses, link-local addresses included, both when the address is first used and each time the host's interface comes up.

NDP Summary

This chapter explains some of the more important functions performed by NDP. NDP does more than what is listed in this chapter, and the protocol allows for addition of other functions, so NDP might continue to grow. For now, use Table 28-1 as a study reference for the four NDP features discussed here.

Table 28-1 NDP Function Summary

Function	Protocol Messages	Who Discovers Info	Who Supplies Info	Info Supplied
Router discovery	RS and RA	Any IPv6 host	Any IPv6 router	Link-local IPv6 address of router
Prefix/length discovery	RS and RA	Any IPv6 host	Any IPv6 router	Prefix(es) and associated prefix lengths used on local link
Neighbor discovery	NS and NA	Any IPv6 host	Any IPv6 host	Link-layer address (for example, MAC address) used by a neighbor
Duplicate Address Detection	NS and NA	Any IPv6 host	Any IPv6 host	Simple confirmation whether a unicast address is already in use

Dynamic Configuration of Host IPv6 Settings

By the time IPv6 was created back in the early to mid 1990s, the world had a decade or two of experience with IPv4. That experience with IPv4 had already shown the need for hosts to dynamically learn their IPv4 settings, including the host's IPv4 address. By the time IPv6 was being created, DHCP for IPv4 had already become the preferred IPv4 solution to allow hosts to dynamically learn their IPv4 address and other settings.

DHCP worked well for IPv4, so creating a version of DHCP for IPv6 (DHCPv6) made perfect sense. However, while DHCP has many advantages, one possible disadvantage is that DHCP requires a server which keeps information about each host (client) and their address. The designers of IPv6 wanted an alternative dynamic address assignment tool, one that did not require a server. The answer? SLAAC.

This second major section of the chapter first looks at DHCPv6, followed by SLAAC.

Dynamic Configuration Using Stateful DHCP and NDP

DHCP for IPv6 (DHCPv6) gives an IPv6 host a way to learn host IPv6 configuration settings, using the same general concepts as DHCP for IPv4. The host exchanges messages with a DHCP server, and the server supplies the host with configuration information, including a lease of an IPv6 address, along with prefix length and DNS server address information.

> **NOTE** The DHCP version is not actually version 6; the name just ends in "v6" in reference to the support for IPv6.

More specifically, stateful DHCPv6 works like the more familiar DHCP for IPv4 in many other general ways, as follows:

- DHCP clients on a LAN send messages that flow only on the local LAN, hoping to find a DHCP server.

- If the DHCP server sits on the same LAN as the client, the client and server can exchange DHCP messages directly, without needing help from a router.

- If the DHCP server sits on another link as compared to the client, the client and server rely on a router to forward the DHCP messages.

- The router that forwards messages from one link, to a server in a remote subnet, must be configured as a DHCP Relay Agent, with knowledge of the DHCP server's IPv6 address.

- Servers have configuration that lists pools of addresses for each subnet from which the server allocates addresses.

- Servers offer a lease of an IP address to a client, from the pool of addresses for the client's subnet; the lease lasts a set time period (usually days or weeks).

- The server tracks state information, specifically a client identifier (often based on the MAC address), along with the address that is currently leased to that client.

DHCPv6 has two major branches of how it can be used: stateful DHCPv6 and stateless DHCPv6. Stateful DHCPv6 works more like the DHCPv4 model, especially related to that last item in the list. A stateful DHCPv6 server tracks information about which client has a lease for what IPv6 address; the fact that the server knows information about a specific client is called state information, making the DHCP server a stateful DHCP server.

Stateless DHCP servers do not track any per-client information. The upcoming section "Using Stateless Address Autoconfiguration" discusses how stateless DHCPv6 servers have an important role when a company decides to use SLAAC.

28

Differences Between DHCPv6 and DHCPv4

While stateful DHCPv6 has many similarities to DHCPv4, many particulars differ as well. Figure 28-6 shows one key difference: Stateful DHCPv6 does not supply default router information to the client. Instead, the client host uses the built-in NDP protocol to learn the routers' IPv6 addresses directly from the local routers.

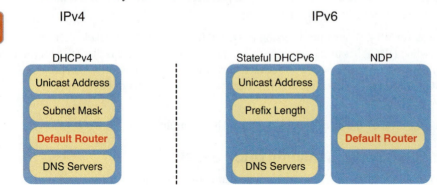

Figure 28-6 *Sources of Specific IPv6 Settings When Using Stateful DHCP*

DHCPv6 also updates the protocol messages to use IPv6 packets instead of IPv4 packets, with new messages and fields as well. For example, Figure 28-7 shows the names of the DHCPv6 messages, which replace the DHCPv4 Discover, Offer, Request, and Acknowledgment (DORA) messages. Instead, DHCPv6 uses the Solicit, Advertise, Request, and Reply messages.

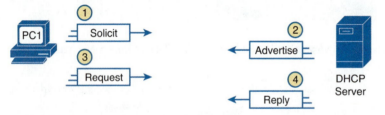

Figure 28-7 *Four Stateful DHCPv6 Messages Between Client and Server*

The four DHCPv6 messages work in two matched pairs with the same general flow as the similar DHCPv4 messages. The Solicit and Advertise messages complete the process of the client searching for the IPv6 address of a DHCPv6 server (the Solicit message), and the server advertising an address (and other configuration settings) for the client to possibly use (the Advertise message). The Request and Reply messages let the client ask to lease the address, with the server confirming the lease in the Reply message.

DHCPv6 Relay Agents

For enterprises that choose to use stateful DHCPv6, oftentimes the DHCP server sits at a central site, far away from many of the clients that use the DHCPv6 server. In those cases, the local router at each site must act as a DHCP relay agent.

The concepts of DHCPv6 relay work like DHCPv4 relay, as discussed in Chapter 18's section "Supporting DHCP for Remote Subnets with DHCP Relay." The client sends a message that only flows inside the local LAN. The router then changes the source and destination IP address, forwarding the packet to the DHCP server. When the server sends a reply, it actually flows to an address on the router (the relay agent), which changes the addresses in that packet as well.

The differences for IPv6 become more obvious when you look at some of the IPv6 addresses used in DHCPv6 messages, like the Solicit message used to lead off a DHCPv6 flow. As shown in Figure 28-8, the client uses the following addresses in the solicit message:

Source of link-local: The client uses its own link-local address as the source address of the packet.

Destination address of "all-DHCP-agents" FF02::1:2: This link-local scope multicast address is used to send packets to two types of devices: DHCP servers and routers acting as DHCP relay agents.

With a link-local scope multicast destination address, the Solicit message sent by a host would only flow on the local LAN. Figure 28-8 shows some of the particulars of how R1, acting as a DHCPv6 relay agent, assists DHCPv6 clients like host A to deliver DHCPv6 packets to the DHCPv6 server.

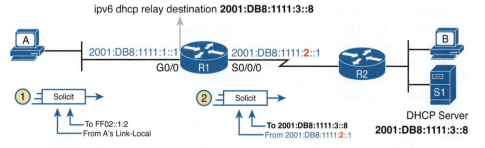

Figure 28-8 *DHCPv6 Relay Agent and DHCP IPv6 Addresses*

Focus first on Step 1, in which host A, the DHCPv6 client, builds and sends its DHCPv6 Solicit message. The message flows from host A's link-local address, and to the all-DHCP-agents multicast address FF02::1:2. With a link-local scope multicast destination address, the Solicit message sent by a host would only flow on the local LAN.

Step 2 shows the results of R1's work as the DHCPv6 relay agent. R1 listens for incoming DHCPv6 messages sent to FF02::1:2, and processes the message sent by host A. R1 changes the destination IPv6 address of the packet to match the DHCPv6 server on the right. R1 also changes the source IPv6 address to be one of R1's IPv6 addresses. With DHCPv6, by default R1 uses the address of its outgoing interface (S0/0/0) as the source IPv6 address, which is slightly different from the DHCPv4 relay agent. R1 then forwards the Solicit message to the server.

The return DHCPv6 messages from the server to the client (not shown in the figure) flow first to the relay agent router's IPv6 address—in other words, to 2001:DB8:1111:2::1 in this case. The relay agent then converts the destination address of those messages as well, and forwards the DHCPv6 messages to the client's link-local address.

Example 28-1 shows the DHCPv6 relay agent configuration for R1 in Figure 28-8. The top of the example shows the **ipv6 dhcp relay** interface subcommand, with reference to the IPv6 address of the DHCPv6 server. The bottom of the figure shows the output of the **show ipv6 interface** command, which confirms that R1 is now listening for multicasts sent to the all-DHCP-agents multicast address FF02::1:2.

Example 28-1 *Configuring Router R1 to Support Remote DHCPv6 Server*

```
interface GigabitEthernet0/0
 ipv6 dhcp relay destination 2001:DB8:1111:3::8


R1# show ipv6 interface g0/0
GigabitEthernet0/0 is up, line protocol is up
  IPv6 is enabled, link-local address is FE80::FF:FE00:1
  No Virtual link-local address(es):
  Description: to SW1 port F0/1
  Global unicast address(es):
```

28

```
        2001:DB8:1111:1::1, subnet is 2001:DB8:1111:1::/64 [EUI]
   Joined group address(es):
    FF02::1
    FF02::2
    FF02::A
    FF02::1:2
    FF02::1:FF00:1
 ! Lines omitted for brevity
```

Using Stateless Address Autoconfiguration

The stateful nature of DHCPv4, as well as its newer cousin stateful DHCPv6, causes some challenges. Someone has to configure, administer, and manage the DHCP server(s). The configuration includes ranges of IP addresses for every subnet. Then, when a host (client) leases the address, the server notes which client is using which address. All these functions work, and work well, but the reliance on a stateful DHCP server requires some thought and attention from the IT staff.

IPv6's Stateless Address Autoconfiguration (SLAAC) provides an alternative method for dynamic IPv6 address assignment—without needing a stateful server. In other words, SLAAC does not require a server to assign or lease the IPv6 address, does not require the IT staff to preconfigure data per subnet, and does not require the server to track which device uses which IPv6 address.

The term SLAAC refers to both a specific part of how a host learns one IPv6 setting—its IPv6 address—plus the overall process of learning all four key host IPv6 settings (address, prefix length, default router, and DNS server addresses). This next topic begins by looking at the tasks done by SLAAC related to the IPv6 address. Then, the text looks at the overall process that uses SLAAC to find all four host settings—a process that uses NDP as well as stateless DHCP.

Building an IPv6 Address Using SLAAC

When using SLAAC, a host does not lease its IPv6 address, or even learn its IPv6 address. Instead, the host learns part of the address—the prefix—and then makes up the rest of its own IPv6 address. Specifically, a host using SLAAC to choose its own IPv6 address uses the following steps:

Key Topic

1. Learn the IPv6 prefix used on the link, from any router, using NDP RS/RA messages
2. Choose its own IPv6 address by making up the interface ID value to follow the just-learned IPv6 prefix
3. Before using the address, first use DAD to make sure that no other host is already using the same address

Figure 28-9 summarizes the first two steps, while noting the two most common ways a host completes the address. Hosts can use EUI-64 rules, as discussed back in Chapter 27's section "Generating a Unique Interface ID Using EUI-64." Alternately, the host can use a process to choose a random number.

Key Topic

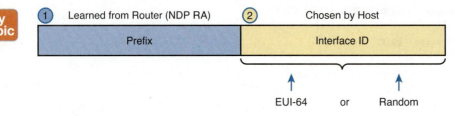

Figure 28-9 *Host IPv6 Address Formation Using SLAAC*

NOTE Microsoft OSs generally use the option to randomly pick the interface ID, with clients picking different values over time, as a security measure.

Combining SLAAC with NDP and Stateless DHCP

When using SLAAC, a host actually makes use of three different tools to find its four IPv6 settings, as noted in Figure 28-10. SLAAC itself focuses on the IPv6 address only. The host then uses NDP messages to learn both the prefix length, as well as the IPv6 addresses of the available routers on the link. Finally, the host makes use of stateless DHCP to learn the IPv6 addresses of any DNS servers.

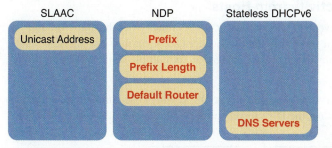

Figure 28-10 *Sources of Specific IPv6 Settings When Using SLAAC*

Stateless DHCP solves the last piece of this puzzle when also using SLAAC. The host needs to know the DNS servers' IPv6 addresses. The solution? Use DHCPv6. However, the host, acting as the DHCPv6 client, asks the server for only the DNS server addresses, and not for a lease of an IPv6 address.

So, why does the world need to call this service *stateless DHCPv6*? The DHCP server with stateless DHCPv6 has far less work to do, and the network engineer has far less administrative work to do. With stateless DHCPv6, the DHCPv6 server:

- Needs simple configuration only, specifically a small number of addresses for the DNS servers, but nothing else

- Needs no per-subnet configuration: no subnet list, no per-subnet address pools, no list of excluded addresses per subnet, and no per-subnet prefix lengths

- Has no need to track state information about DHCP leases—that is, which devices lease which IPv6 address—because the server does not lease addresses to any clients

Table 28-2 summarizes the key comparison points between stateless DHCP and stateful DHCP.

Table 28-2 Comparison of Stateless and Stateful DHCPv6 Services

Feature	Stateful DHCP	Stateless DHCP
Remembers IPv6 address (state information) of clients that make requests	Yes	No
Leases IPv6 address to client	Yes	No
Supplies list of DNS server addresses	Yes	Yes
Commonly used with SLAAC	No	Yes

28

Verification of Host IPv6 Connectivity

This third and final major section of the chapter examines a few commands to verify the settings on hosts. Specifically, this section examines the host's IPv6 settings, and then looks at the usual commands to test whether a host can send packets: **ping** and **traceroute**.

Note that this section lists some commands on different host OSs. As usual, the goal of listing host commands is to give a general idea of the information that can be viewed on a host. However, keep in mind that this and other chapters do not attempt to show each variation of every networking command on every OS; instead, the goal is to reinforce the ideas seen earlier in the chapter.

Verifying Host IPv6 Connectivity from Hosts

Most end-user OSs support a convenient way to look at IPv6 settings from the graphical user interface. In some cases, all four of the key IPv6 host settings can be on the same window, while in other cases, seeing all the settings might require navigation to multiple windows or tabs in the same window.

As an example, Figure 28-11 shows a window from Mac OS X, which lists three of the four IPv6 host settings. The one missing setting, the DNS server setting, is in another tab (as seen near the top of the image).

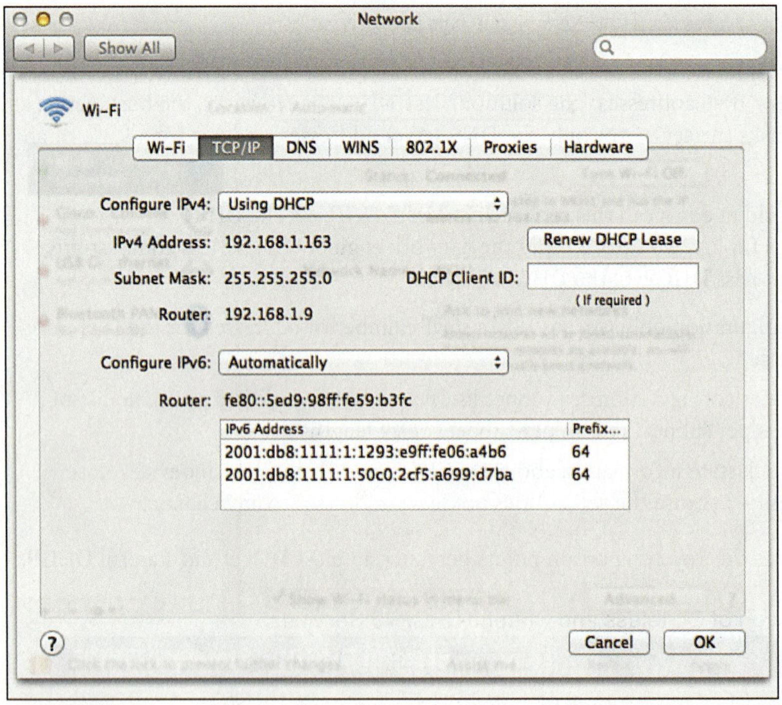

Figure 28-11 *Three IPv6 Settings for Dynamic Address Assignment on Mac OS*

Take a moment to look at the details in Figure 28-11's image. The image shows the IPv4 settings at the top, as being learned with DHCP. The lower half of the window shows the IPv6 settings as having been learned "Automatically," which means that the host will use either stateful DHCP or SLAAC. In this case, the host used SLAAC to give itself two IPv6 addresses inside the same 2001:DB8:1111:1::/64 subnet—one using EUI-64 rules and one with a random interface ID. (Note that IPv6 host logic includes many details not discussed in this chapter, including the reasons why a host might use two rather than one address.)

Hosts also support a range of commands to check the same information. For IPv6 settings, many OSs use familiar commands: **ipconfig** on Windows OSs and **ifconfig** on Linux and Mac OS. Example 28-2 shows an **ifconfig** command from the same Mac used to create Figure 28-11, for comparison. In particular, if you look at the two highlighted fields, you can see the EUI-64 interface ID that resulted from using this host's MAC address.

Example 28-2 *Sample ifconfig Command from a Mac*

```
WOair$ ifconfig en0
en0: flags=8863<UP,BROADCAST,SMART,RUNNING,SIMPLEX,MULTICAST> mtu 1500
        ether 10:93:e9:06:a4:b6
        inet6 fe80::1293:e9ff:fe06:a4b6%en0 prefixlen 64 scopeid 0x4
        inet 192.168.1.163 netmask 0xffffff00 broadcast 192.168.1.255
        inet6 2001:db8:1111:1:1293:e9ff:fe06:a4b6 prefixlen 64 autoconf
        inet6 2001:db8:1111:1:50c0:2cf5:a699:d7ba prefixlen 64 autoconf temporary
        media: autoselect
        status: active
```

Beyond simply checking the four key IPv6 settings on the host, testing the installation of a new host also requires testing whether the host has connectivity to the rest of the internetwork, using the usual tools: the **ping** and **traceroute** commands.

As for the commands themselves, some OSs (notably Microsoft Windows variants and Cisco routers and switches) let you use the same **ping** and **traceroute** commands used with IPv4. Some other OSs require a different command, like the **ping6** and **traceroute6** commands used with Mac OS and Linux. (The upcoming examples show both variations.)

As for the output of the **ping** and **traceroute** commands, most people who understand the IPv4 version of these commands need no coaching whatsoever to understand the IPv6 version. The output is mostly unchanged compared to the IPv4 equivalents, other than the obvious differences with listing IPv6 addresses. For comparison, upcoming Examples 28-3 and 28-4 show sample output, using the internetwork displayed in Figure 28-12.

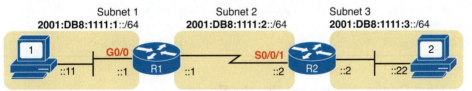

Figure 28-12 *Sample IPv6 Internetwork for ping and traceroute Examples*

Example 28-3 shows three **ping** commands, taken from PC1, a Linux host. (Linux happens to replace the older commands with the **ping6** and **traceroute6** commands.) The first two commands show IPv6 pings, the first to R1's LAN IPv6 address, followed by PC1 pinging PC2's IPv6 address. The final command shows an IPv4 ping for comparison.

Example 28-3 *The ping6 Command from PC1, for R1 and PC2*

```
Master@PC1:$ ping6 2001:db8:1111:1::1
PING 2001:db8:1111:1::1 (2001:db8:1111:1::1) 56 data bytes
64 bytes from 2001:db8:1111:1::11: icmp_seq=1 ttl=64 time=1.26 ms
64 bytes from 2001:db8:1111:1::11: icmp_seq=2 ttl=64 time=1.15 ms
^C
--- 2001:db8:1111:1::1 ping statistics ---
2 packets transmitted, 2 received, 0% packet loss, time 1001 ms
rtt min/avg/max/mdev = 1.156/1.210/1.263/0.062 ms
```

Key Topic

28

```
Master@PC1:$ ping6 2001:db8:1111:3::22
PING 2001:db8:1111:3::22 ( 2001:db8:1111:3::22) 56 data bytes
64 bytes from 2001:db8:1111:3::22: icmp_seq=1 ttl=64 time=2.33 ms
64 bytes from 2001:db8:1111:3::22: icmp_seq=2 ttl=64 time=2.59 ms
64 bytes from 2001:db8:1111:3::22: icmp_seq=3 ttl=64 time=2.03 ms
^C
--- 2001:db8:1111:3::22 ping statistics ---
3 packets transmitted, 3 received, 0% packet loss, time 2003 ms
rtt min/avg/max/mdev = 2.039/2.321/2.591/0.225 ms


! An IPv4 ping next, for comparison - ping of PC2 from PC1
Master@PC1:$ ping 10.1.3.22
PING 10.1.3.22 (10.1.3.22) 56 data bytes
64 bytes from 10.1.3.22: icmp_seq=1 ttl=64 time=2.45 ms
64 bytes from 10.1.3.22: icmp_seq=2 ttl=64 time=2.55 ms
64 bytes from 10.1.3.22: icmp_seq=3 ttl=64 time=2.14 ms
^C
--- 10.1.3.22 ping statistics ---
3 packets transmitted, 3 received, 0% packet loss, time 2014 ms
rtt min/avg/max/mdev = 2.04/2.318/2.604/0.224 ms
```

Example 28-4 shows a **traceroute6** command on PC1, finding the route to PC2. The output mirrors the style of output for most IPv4 **traceroute** commands, other than the obvious difference of listing IPv6 addresses. Note that the output lists R1's G0/0 IPv6 address, then R2's S0/0/1 IPv6 address, and then finally PC2's address to end the output.

Example 28-4   *The* traceroute6 *Command from PC1, for PC2*

```
Master@PC1:$ traceroute6 2001:db8:1111:3::22
traceroute to 2001:db8:1111:3::22 (2001:db8:1111:3::22) from 2001:db8:1111:1::11,
  30 hops max, 24 byte packets
1   2001:db8:1111:1::1 (2001:db8:1111:1::1)   0.794 ms   0.648 ms   0.604 ms
2   2001:db8:1111:2::2 (2001:db8:1111:2::2)   1.606 ms   1.49 ms   1.497 ms
3   2001:db8:1111:3::22 (2001:db8:1111:3::22)   2.038 ms   1.911 ms   1.899 ms
```

Verifying Host Connectivity from Nearby Routers

For router verification commands for IPv6, some IPv6 features use the exact same command as with IPv4, but some substitute "ipv6" for "ip." And in some cases, particularly with functions that do not exist in IPv4 or have changed quite a bit, routers support brand new commands. This section looks at a couple of router commands useful to verify IPv6 host connectivity, some old and some new for IPv6.

First, for the more familiar commands. Cisco routers and switches support the **ping** and **traceroute** commands with the same basic features for IPv6 as with IPv4. For the standard version of the commands, the commands accept either an IPv4 or an IPv6 address as input. For the extended versions of these commands, the first prompt question asks for the protocol—just type **ipv6**, instead of using the default of **ip**, and answer the rest of the questions.

Of course, an example helps, particularly for the extended commands. Example 28-5 begins with an extended IPv6 **ping**, from R1 to PC2, using R1's G0/0 interface as the source of the packets. The second command shows a standard IPv6 **traceroute** from R1 to PC2.

Example 28-5 *Extended* **ping** *and Standard* **traceroute** *for IPv6 from Router R1*

```
R1# ping
Protocol [ip]: ipv6
Target IPv6 address: 2001:db8:1111:3::22
Repeat count [5]:
Datagram size [100]:
Timeout in seconds [2]:
Extended commands? [no]: yes
Source address or interface: GigabitEthernet0/0
UDP protocol? [no]:
Verbose? [no]:
Precedence [0]:
DSCP [0]:
Include hop by hop option? [no]:
Include destination option? [no]:
Sweep range of sizes? [no]:
Type escape sequence to abort.
Sending 5, 100-byte ICMP Echos to 2001:DB8:1111:3::22, timeout is 2 seconds:
Packet sent with a source address of 2001:DB8:1111:1::1
!!!!!
Success rate is 100 percent (5/5), round-trip min/avg/max = 0/1/4 ms

R1# traceroute 2001:db8:1111:3::22
Type escape sequence to abort.
Tracing the route to 2001:DB8:1111:3::22

  1 2001:DB8:1111:2::2 4 msec 0 msec 0 msec
  2 2001:DB8:1111:3::22 0 msec 4 msec 0 msec
```

Another way to verify host settings from a router is to look at the router's neighbor table. All IPv6 hosts, routers included, keep an IPv6 neighbor table: a list of all neighboring IPv6 addresses and matching MAC addresses. Basically, this table replaces the IPv4 ARP table, and it contains the content learned with NDP NS and NA messages.

One way to verify whether a neighboring host is responsive is to find out whether it will send back an NDP NA when the router sends it an NDP NS (to discover the host's MAC address). To do so, the router could clear its neighbor table (**clear ipv6 neighbor**) and then ping a host on some connected interface. The router will first need to send an NDP NS, and the host must send an NDP NA back. If the router shows that host's MAC address in the neighbor table, then the host must have just replied with an NDP NA. Example 28-6 shows a sample of an IPv6 neighbor table, from Router R2 in upcoming Figure 28-13, using the **show ipv6 neighbors** command.

Example 28-6 *The* **show ipv6 neighbors** *Command on Router R2*

```
R2# show ipv6 neighbors
IPv6 Address                     Age Link-layer Addr State Interface
FE80::11FF:FE11:1111               0 0200.1111.1111  STALE Gi0/0
FE80::22FF:FE22:2222               1 0200.2222.2222  STALE Gi0/0
2001:DB8:1111:3::22                0 0200.2222.2222  REACH Gi0/0
FE80::FF:FE00:3333                 1 0200.0000.3333  DELAY Gi0/0
2001:DB8:1111:3::33                0 0200.1111.1111  REACH Gi0/0
2001:DB8:1111:3::3                 0 0200.0000.3333  REACH Gi0/0
```

28

Finally, routers can also list information about the available routers on a LAN subnet, which impacts the connectivity available to hosts. As a reminder, routers send NDP RA messages to announce their willingness to act as an IPv6 router on a particular LAN subnet. Cisco routers watch for RA messages received from other routers (routers send periodic unsolicited RA messages, by the way). The **show ipv6 routers** command lists any other routers, but not the local router.

As an example, consider the topology shown in Figure 28-13. R1 is the only IPv6 router on the LAN on the left, so R1 does not hear an RA messages from other routers on that LAN subnet. However, R2 and R3, connected to the same subnet, hear NDP RA's from each other. Example 28-7 lists the output of the **show ipv6 routers** command on R1 (with no routers listed) and R2 (with one router listed) for comparison's sake.

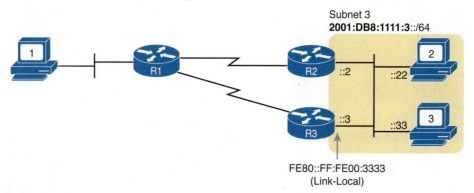

Figure 28-13   *Sample IPv6 Internetwork with Two Routers on the Same Link (VLAN)*

Example 28-7   *Listing All Routers with the* **show ipv6 routers** *Command*

```
! No routers listed by this command on R1
R1# show ipv6 routers
R1#
! The next command happens on R2 - one router (R3) listed
R2# show ipv6 routers
Router FE80::FF:FE00:3333 on GigabitEthernet0/0, last update 0 min
  Hops 64, Lifetime 1800 sec, AddrFlag=0, OtherFlag=0, MTU=1500
  HomeAgentFlag=0, Preference=Medium
  Reachable time 0 (unspecified), Retransmit time 0 (unspecified)
  Prefix 2001:DB8:1111:3::/64 onlink autoconfig
    Valid lifetime 2592000, preferred lifetime 604800
```

Finally, one last thought related to commands on hosts themselves: The host can of course list its own NDP information. Interestingly, most hosts list the neighbor table, and then just flag which entries also happen to be routers (the ones that also sent an NDP RA at some point).

Example 28-8 shows an example, this time from a host using Mac OS. Of the two highlighted entries, the first, with the flags field ("Flgs") listing an "R," is a router that formerly sent an RA to announce itself. The second highlighted entry is for a host, so the letter "R" is not listed under the "Flgs" (flags) heading.

Example 28-8   *Example NDP Neighbor Table, Mac OS*

```
WOAir$ ndp -an
Neighbor                        Linklayer Address   Netif Expire     St Flgs Prbs
::1                             (incomplete)        lo0   permanent  R
2001:db8:1111:1::1              5c:d9:98:59:b3:fc    en0   1s         D  R
2001:db8:1111:1:1293:e9ff:fe06:a4b6 10:93:e9:6:a4:b6 en0   5s                R
```

Review Activities

Chapter Summary

- Neighbor Discovery Protocol (NDP) defines several different functions related to IPv6 addressing, as follows:

  - **SLAAC:** When using Stateless Address Autoconfiguration (SLAAC), the host uses NDP messages to learn the first part of its address, plus the prefix length.

  - **Router Discovery:** Hosts learn the IPv6 addresses of the available IPv6 routers in the same subnet using NDP messages.

  - **Duplicate Address Detection:** No matter how a host sets or learns its IPv6 address, the host waits to use the address until the host knows that no other host uses the same address. How does a host detect this problem? Using NDP messages through a process called duplicate address detection (DAD).

  - **Neighbor MAC Discovery:** After a host has passed the DAD process and uses its IPv6 address, a LAN-based host will need to learn the MAC address of other hosts in the same subnet. NDP replaces IPv4's ARP, providing messages that replace the ARP Request and Reply messages.

- The PC's own IPv6 address is typically a global unicast or unique local unicast, as are the PC's references to the DNS servers. However, because the default router must be locally reachable, the default router setting typically refers to the router's link-local address.

- NDP defines a matched pair of messages that let a host dynamically discover all potential default routers that sit on the same data link. Basically, the process works with the host multicasting a message saying, "Routers, tell me about yourselves," and the routers reply. The messages are

  - **Router Solicitation (RS):** Sent to the "all-IPv6-routers" local-scope multicast address of FF02::2, so that the message asks all routers, on the local link only, to identify themselves.

  - **Router Advertisement (RA):** This message, sent by the router, lists many facts, including the link-local IPv6 address of the router. When unsolicited, it is sent to the all-IPv6-hosts local-scope multicast address of FF02::1. When sent in response to an RS message, it flows back to either the unicast address of the host that sent the NS or to the all-IPv6-hosts address FF02::1.

- NDP defines a second pair of matched solicitation and advertisement messages: the neighbor solicitation (NS) and neighbor advertisement (NA) messages. Basically, the NS acts like an IPv4 ARP request, asking the host with a particular unicast IPv6 address to send back a reply. The NA message acts like an IPv4 ARP reply listing that host's MAC address.

- DHCP for IPv6 (DHCPv6) gives an IPv6 host a way to learn host IPv6 configuration settings using the same general concepts as DHCP for IPv4. The host exchanges messages with a DHCP server, and the server supplies the host with configuration information, including a lease of an IPv6 address, along with prefix length and DNS server address information.

- Stateful DHCPv6 works like the more familiar DHCP for IPv4 in many other general ways, as follows:

  - DHCP clients on a LAN send messages that flow only on the local LAN, hoping to find a DHCP server.

  - If the DHCP server sits on the same LAN as the client, the client and server can exchange DHCP messages directly, without needing help from a router.

  - If the DHCP server sits on another link compared to the client, the client and server rely on a router to forward the DHCP messages.

28

- The router that forwards messages from one link to a server in a remote subnet must be configured as a DHCP relay agent, with knowledge of the DHCP server's IPv6 address.

- Servers have configuration that lists pools of addresses for each subnet from which the server allocates addresses.

- Servers offer a lease of an IP address to a client from the pool of addresses for the client's subnet; the lease lasts a set time period (usually days or weeks).

- The server tracks state information; specifically, a client identifier (often based on the MAC address), along with the address that is currently leased to that client.

- When using SLAAC, a host does not lease its IPv6 address or even learn it. Instead, the host learns part of the address—the prefix—and then makes up the rest of its own IPv6 address. Specifically, a host using SLAAC to choose its own IPv6 address uses the following steps:

Step 1.   Learns the IPv6 prefix used on the link, from any router, using NDP RS/RA messages

Step 2.   Chooses its own IPv6 address by making up the interface ID value to follow the just-learned IPv6 prefix

Step 3.   Before using the address, first uses DAD to make sure no other host is already using the same address

Review Questions

Answer these review questions. You can find the answers at the bottom of the last page of the chapter. For thorough explanations, see DVD Appendix C, "Answers to Review Questions."

1. PC1, PC2, and Router R1 all connect to the same VLAN and IPv6 subnet. PC1 wants to send its first IPv6 packet to PC2. What protocol or message will PC1 use to discover the MAC address to which PC1 should send the Ethernet frame that encapsulates this IPv6 packet?

    A. ARP

    B. NDP NS

    C. NDP RS

    D. SLAAC

2. PC1 and Router R1 connect to the same VLAN and IPv6 subnet. The user of PC1 pings the IPv6 address of a host that sits at a remote site, so that the packets flow through R1, PC1's default router. PC1 did not statically configure its default router setting. Which of the following answers lists a protocol or message that PC1 could have used when trying to learn what IPv6 address to use as its default router?

    A. EUI-64

    B. NDP NS

    C. DAD

    D. NDP RS

3. Which of the following pieces of information does a router supply in an NDP Router Advertisement (RA) message? (Choose two answers.)

   A. Router IPv6 address

   B. Host name of the router

   C. IPv6 prefix(es) on the link

   D. IPv6 address of DHCP server

4. Host PC1 dynamically learns its IPv6 settings using stateful DHCPv6. Which one of PC1's settings is least likely to be learned from the stateful DHCPv6 server?

   A. Host address

   B. Prefix length

   C. Default router address

   D. DNS server address(es)

5. Host PC1 dynamically learns its IPv6 settings using Stateless Address Autoconfiguration (SLAAC). Which one of PC1's settings is most likely to be learned from the stateless DHCPv6 server?

   A. Host address

   B. Prefix length

   C. Default router address

   D. DNS server address(es)

6. Host PC1 dynamically learns its IPv6 settings using Stateless Address Autoconfiguration (SLAAC). Think about the host's unicast address as two parts: the prefix and the interface ID. Which of the answers list a way that SLAAC learns or builds the value of the interface ID portion of the host's address? (Choose two answers.)

   A. Learned from a DHCPv6 server

   B. Built by the host using EUI-64 rules

   C. Learned from a router using NDP RS/RA messages

   D. Built by the host using a random value

7. Three routers connect to the same VLAN and IPv6 subnet. All three routers have sent NDP RA messages, in reply to various IPv6 hosts' NDP RS messages, asking to learn about the available IPv6 routers in the subnet. A network engineer issues the **show ipv6 neighbors** command on R1. Which of the answers best describes the kind of NDP information held in this output?

   A. IPv6 neighbors (both routers and hosts) plus their MAC addresses, without noting which are routers

   B. IPv6 neighbors (both routers and hosts) plus their MAC addresses, and also noting which are routers

   C. IPv6 routers, with no information about nonrouters, with no MAC address info

   D. IPv6 routers, with no information about nonrouters, with MAC address info

28

Review All the Key Topics

Review the most important topics from this chapter, noted with the Key Topic icon. Table 28-3 lists these key topics and where each is discussed.

Table 28-3   Key Topics for Chapter 28

Key Topic Element	Description	Page Number
List	Four functions for which NDP plays a major role	668
List	Descriptions of the NDP Router Solicitation (RS) and Router Advertisement (RA) messages	669
Figure 28-2	Example use of NDP RS and RA	669
List	Descriptions of the NDP Neighbor Solicitation (NS) and Neighbor Advertisement (NA) messages	670
Figure 28-4	Example use of NDP NS and NA	671
Figure 28-5	Example use of NDP for Duplicate Address Detection (DAD)	672
Table 28-1	Summary of NDP functions discussed in this chapter	672
List	Similarities between DHCP for IPv4 and stateful DHCP for IPv6	673
Figure 28-6	Key difference between DHCPv4 and stateful DHCPv6	674
List	Steps a host takes to build its IPv6 address when using SLAAC	676
Figure 28-9	SLAAC address creation concepts	676
Example 28-3	Examples of the **ping6** command	679

Complete the Tables and Lists from Memory

Print a copy of DVD Appendix M, "Memory Tables," or at least the section for this chapter, and complete the tables and lists from memory. DVD Appendix N, "Memory Tables Answer Key," includes completed tables and lists to check your work.

Definitions of Key Terms

After your first reading of the chapter, try to define these key terms, but do not be concerned about getting them all correct at that time. Chapter 30 directs you in how to use these terms for late-stage preparation for the exam.

Neighbor Discovery Protocol (NDP), Router Solicitation (RS), Router Advertisement (RA), Neighbor Solicitation (NS), Neighbor Advertisement (NA), Stateless Address Autoconfiguration (SLAAC), Duplicate Address Detection (DAD), stateful DHCPv6, stateless DHCPv6, IPv6 neighbor table

Command Reference to Check Your Memory

Although you should not necessarily memorize the information in the tables in this section, this section does include a reference for the configuration and EXEC commands covered in this chapter. Practically speaking, you should memorize the commands as a side effect of reading the chapter and doing all the activities in this exam preparation section. To check to see how well you have memorized the commands as a side effect of your other studies, cover the left side of the table with a piece of paper, read the descriptions on the right side, and see whether you remember the command.

Table 28-4 Chapter 28 Configuration Command Reference

Command	Description
ipv6 dhcp relay destination *server-address*	Interface subcommand that enables the IPv6 DHCP relay agent

Table 28-5 Chapter 28 EXEC Command Reference

Command	Description
ping {*host-name* | *ipv6-address*}	Tests IPv6 routes by sending an ICMP packet to the destination host
traceroute {*host-name* | *ipv6-address*}	Tests IPv6 routes by discovering the IP addresses of the routes between a router and the listed destination
show ipv6 neighbors	Lists the router's IPv6 neighbor table
show ipv6 routers	Lists any neighboring routers that advertised themselves through an NDP RA message

Table 28-6 Chapter 28 Host Command Reference

Command (Microsoft, Apple, Linux)	Description
ipconfig / ifconfig / ifconfig	Lists interface settings, including IPv4 and IPv6 addresses
ping / ping6 / ping6	Tests IP routes by sending an ICMPv6 packet to the destination host
tracert / traceroute6 / traceroute6	Tests IP routes by discovering the IPv6 addresses of the routes between a router and the listed destination
netsh interface ipv6 show neighbors / ndp -an / ip -6 neighbor show	Lists a host's IPv6 neighbor table

---

Answers to Review Questions:

1 B **2** D **3** A and C **4** C **5** D **6** B and D **7** A

28

Chapter 29

Implementing IPv6 Routing

The one remaining piece of the IPv6 story for this book is how routers learn IPv6 routes. The easiest and most common way to make all routers learn all the correct routes is to use a dynamic IPv6 routing protocol, like Open Shortest Path First (OSPF) version 3 (OSPFv3). So, this chapter discusses the basics of OSPFv3 implementation, in the third major section of this chapter.

However, so far this book has not yet discussed other simpler ways that routers can add IPv6 routes to their routing tables: connected, local, and static routes. The first section of this chapter walks you through the details of how IPv6, similar to IPv4, adds both connected and local routes based on each interface IPv6 address. The second major section of this chapter then looks at how to configure static IPv6 routes by typing in commands, in this case using the **ipv6 route** command instead of IPv4's **ip route** command.

This chapter covers the following exam topics:

IP addressing (IPv4 / IPv6)

Describe the technological requirements for running IPv6 in conjunction with IPv4 such as dual stack

IP Routing Technologies

Verify router configuration and network connectivity

  Cisco IOS commands to review basic router information and network connectivity

Configure and verify routing configuration for a static or default route given specific routing requirements

Differentiate methods of routing and routing protocols

  Static vs. Dynamic

  Passive interfaces

Configure and verify OSPF (single area)

  Benefit of single area

  Configure OSPF v3

  Router ID

  Passive interface

Connected and Local IPv6 Routes

A Cisco router adds IPv6 routes to its IPv6 routing table for several reasons. Many of you could predict those reasons at this point in your reading, in part because the logic mirrors the logic routers use for IPv4. Specifically, a router adds IPv6 routes based on the following:

- The configuration of IPv6 addresses on working interfaces (connected and local routes)
- The direct configuration of a static route (static routes)
- The configuration of a routing protocol, like OSPFv3, on routers that share the same data link (dynamic routes, in this case, OSPF routes)

The three sections of this chapter follow this same outline, and in the same order.

Rules for Connected and Local Routes

Routers add and remove connected routes, and local routes, based on the interface configuration and the interface state. First, the router looks for any configured unicast addresses on any interfaces by looking for the **ipv6 address** command. Then, if the interface is working—if the interface has a "line status is up, protocol status is up" notice in the output of the **show interfaces** command—the router adds both a connected and local route.

> **NOTE** Routers do not create IPv6 routes for link-local addresses.

The connected and local routes themselves follow the same general logic as with IPv4. The connected route represents the subnet connected to the interface, while the local route is a host route for only the specific IPv6 address configured on the interface.

As an example, consider a router, with a working interface, configured with the **ipv6 address 2000:1:1:1::1/64** command. The router will calculate the subnet ID based on this address and prefix list, and place a connected route for that subnet (2000:1:1:1::/64) into the routing table. The router also takes the listed IPv6 address and creates a host route for that address, with a /128 prefix length. (With IPv4, host routes have a /32 prefix length, while IPv6 uses a /128 prefix length, meaning "exactly this one address.")

The following list summarizes these rules for easier review and study:

1. Routers create IPv6 routes based each unicast IPv6 address on an interface, as configured with the **ipv6 address** command, as follows:

   A. The router creates a route for the subnet (a connected route).

   B. The router creates a host route (/128 prefix length) for the router IPv6 address (a local route).

2. Routers do not create routes based on the link-local addresses associated with the interface.

3. Routers remove the connected and local routes for an interface if the interface fails, and re-adds these routes when the interface is again in a working (up/up) state.

29

Example of Connected IPv6 Routes

While the concept of connected and local IPv6 routes works much like IPv4 routes, seeing a few examples can certainly help. To show some example routes, Figure 29-1 gives the details of one sample internetwork used in this chapter. The figure shows the IPv6 subnet IDs. The upcoming examples focus on the connected and local routes on Router R1.

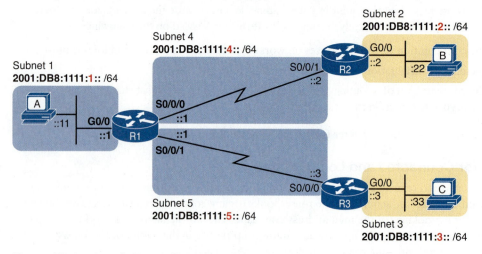

Figure 29-1 *Sample Network Used to Show Connected and Local Routes*

To clarify the notes in the figure, note that the figure shows IPv6 prefixes (subnets), with a shorthand notation for the interface IPv6 addresses. The figure shows only the abbreviated interface ID portion of each interface address near each interface. For example, R1's G0/0 interface address would begin with subnet ID value 2001:DB8:1111:1, added to ::1, for 2001:DB8:1111:1::1.

Now on to the example of connected routes. To begin, consider the configuration of Router R1 from Figure 29-1, as shown in Example 29-1. The excerpt from the **show running-config** command on R1 shows three interfaces, all of which are working. Also note that no static route or OSPFv3 configuration exists.

Example 29-1 *IPv6 Addressing Configuration on Router R1*

```
ipv6 unicast-routing
!
interface serial0/0/0
  ipv6 address 2001:db8:1111:4::1/64
!
interface serial0/0/1
  ipv6 address 2001:db8:1111:5::1/64
!
interface gigabitethernet0/0
  ipv6 address 2001:db8:1111:1::1/64
```

Based on Figure 29-1 and Example 29-1, R1 should have three connected IPv6 routes, as highlighted in Example 29-2.

Example 29-2 *Routes on Router R1 Before Adding Static or OSPF Routes*

```
R1# show ipv6 route
IPv6 Routing Table - default - 7 entries
Codes: C - Connected, L - Local, S - Static, U - Per-user Static route
       B - BGP, R - RIP, I1 - ISIS L1, I2 - ISIS L2
       IA - ISIS interarea, IS - ISIS summary, D - EIGRP, EX - EIGRP external
       ND - Neighbor Discovery, l - LISP
       O - OSPF Intra, OI - OSPF Inter, OE1 - OSPF ext 1, OE2 - OSPF ext 2
       ON1 - OSPF NSSA ext 1, ON2 - OSPF NSSA ext 2
C    2001:DB8:1111:1::/64 [0/0]
     via GigabitEthernet0/0, directly connected
L    2001:DB8:1111:1::1/128 [0/0]
     via GigabitEthernet0/0, receive
C    2001:DB8:1111:4::/64 [0/0]
     via Serial0/0/0, directly connected
L    2001:DB8:1111:4::1/128 [0/0]
     via Serial0/0/0, receive
C    2001:DB8:1111:5::/64 [0/0]
     via Serial0/0/1, directly connected
L    2001:DB8:1111:5::1/128 [0/0]
     via Serial0/0/1, receive
L    FF00::/8 [0/0]
     via Null0, receive
```

All three highlighted routes show the same basic kinds of information, so for discussion, focus on the first pair of highlighted lines, which detail the connected route for subnet 2001:DB8:1111:1::/64. Much of the information is self-explanatory: the phrase "directly connected" referring to the fact that the route is a connected route, the interface identifier, and the prefix/length of 2001:DB8:1111:1::/64. At the far left, the code letter "C" identifies the route as a connected route (per the legend above). Also note that the numbers in brackets mirror the same ideas as IPv4's **show ip route** command: The first number represents the administrative distance and the second is the metric.

Examples of Local IPv6 Routes

Continuing this same example, three local routes should exist on R1 for the same three interfaces as the connected routes. Indeed that is the case, with one extra local route for other purposes. Example 29-3 shows only the local routes, as listed by the **show ipv6 route local** command, with highlights of one particular local route for discussion.

Example 29-3 *Local IPv6 Routes on Router R1*

```
R1# show ipv6 route local
! Legend omitted for brevity

L    2001:DB8:1111:1::1/128 [0/0]
     via GigabitEthernet0/0, receive
L    2001:DB8:1111:4::1/128 [0/0]
     via Serial0/0/0, receive
L    2001:DB8:1111:5::1/128 [0/0]
     via Serial0/0/1, receive
L    FF00::/8 [0/0]
     via Null0, receive
```

29

For the highlighted local route, look for a couple of quick facts. First, look back to R1's configuration in Example 29-1, and note R1's IPv6 address on its G0/0 interface. This local route lists the exact same address. Also note the /128 prefix length, meaning this route matches packet sent to that address (2001:DB8:1111:1::1), and only that address.

Static IPv6 Routes

While routers automatically add connected and local routes based on the interface configuration, static routes require direct configuration with the **ipv6 route** command. Simply put, someone configures the command, and the router places the details from the command into a route in the IPv6 routing table.

The **ipv6 route** command follows the same general logic as does IPv4's **ip route** command, as discussed back in Chapter 16, "Configuring IPv4 Addresses and Routes." For IPv4, the **ip route** command starts by listing the subnet ID and mask, so for IPv6, the **ipv6 route** command begins with the prefix and prefix length. Then, the respective commands list the directions of how this router should forward packets towards that destination subnet or prefix, by listing the outgoing interface, or the address of the next-hop router.

Figure 29-2 shows the concepts behind a single **ipv6 route** command, demonstrating the concepts behind a static route on Router R1 for the subnet on the right (subnet 2, or 2001:DB8:1111:2::/64). A static route on R1, for this subnet, will begin with **ipv6 route 2001:DB8:1111:2::/64**, followed by either the outgoing interface (S0/0/0) or the next-hop IPv6 address, or both.

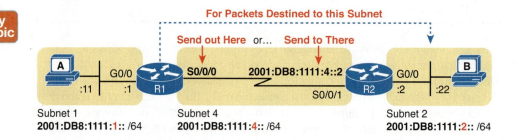

Figure 29-2 *Logic Behind IPv6 Static Route Commands (IPv6 route)*

Now that you understand the big ideas with IPv6 static routes, the next few pages walk you through a series of examples. In particular, the examples look at configuring static routes with an outgoing interface, then with a next-hop global unicast address, and then with a next-hop link-local address. This section ends with a discussion of static IPv6 default routes.

Static Routes Using the Outgoing Interface

This first IPv6 static route example uses the outgoing interface option. As a reminder, for both IPv4 and IPv6 static routes, when the command references an interface, the interface is a local interface. That is, it is an interface on the router where the command is added. In this case, as shown in Figure 29-2, R1's **ipv6 route** command would use interface S0/0/0, as shown in the top of Example 29-4.

Example 29-4 *Static IPv6 Routes on Router R1*

```
! Static route on router R1
R1(config)# ipv6 route 2001:db8:1111:2::/64 s0/0/0
```

While Example 29-4 shows the correct syntax of the route, if using static routes throughout this internetwork, more static routes are needed. For example, to support traffic between hosts A and B, R1 is now prepared. Host A will forward all its IPv6 packets to its default router (R1), and R1 can now routes those packets out S0/0/0 to R2 next. However, Router R2 does not yet have a route back to host A's subnet, subnet 1 (2001:DB8:1111:1::/64), so a complete solution requires more routes.

Example 29-5 solves this problem by giving Router R2 a static route for subnet 1 (2001:DB8:1111:1:/64). After adding this route, hosts A and B should be able to ping each other.

Example 29-5 *Static IPv6 Routes on Router R2*

```
! Static route on router R2
R2(config)# ipv6 route 2001:db8:1111:1::/64 s0/0/1
```

Many options exist for verifying the existence of the static route and testing whether hosts can use the route. **ping** and **traceroute**, as discussed in Chapter 28, "Implementing IPv6 Addressing on Hosts" can test connectivity. From the router command line, the **show ipv6 route** command will list all the IPv6 routes. The shorter output of the **show ipv6 route static** command, which lists only static routes, could also be used; Example 29-6 shows that output, with the legend omitted.

Example 29-6 *Verification of Static Routes Only on R1*

```
R1# show ipv6 route static
! Legend omitted for brevity
S    2001:DB8:1111:2::/64 [1/0]
     via Serial0/0/0, directly connected
```

This command lists many facts about the one static route on R1. First, the code "S" in the left column does identify the route as a static route. (However, the later phrase "directly connected" might mislead you to think this is a connected route; trust the "S" code.) Note that the prefix (2001:DB8:1111:2::/64) matches the configuration (in Example 29-4), as does the outgoing interface (S0/0/0).

While this command lists basic information about each static route, it does not state whether this route would be used when forwarding packets to a particular destination. For example, if host A sent an IPv6 packet to host B (2001:DB8:1111:2::22), would R1 use this static route? As it turns out, the **show ipv6 route 2001:DB8:1111:2::22** command answers this question. This command asks the router to list the route the router would use when forwarding packets to that particular address. Example 29-7 shows an example.

Example 29-7 *Displaying the Router R1 Uses to Forward to Host B*

```
R1# show ipv6 route 2001:db8:1111:2::22
Routing entry for 2001:DB8:1111:2::/64
  Known via "static", distance 1, metric 0
  Route count is 1/1, share count 0
  Routing paths:
    directly connected via Serial0/0/0
      Last updated 00:01:29 ago
```

Static Routes Using Next-Hop IPv6 Address

Static IPv6 routes that refer to a next-hop address have two options: the unicast address on the neighboring router (global unicast or unique local), or the link-local address of that same neighboring router. Figure 29-3 spells out those two options with an updated version of Figure 29-2, this time showing Router R2's global unicast as well as R2's link-local address.

29

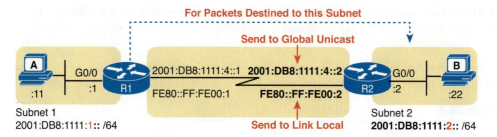

Figure 29-3   *Using Unicast or Link-Local as Next-Hop Address for Static Routes*

The next few pages walk you through examples, first with a global unicast as next-hop and then with a link-local as next-hop.

Example Static Route with a Global Unicast Next-Hop Address

This example uses the internetwork in Figure 29-3, but with the earlier static routes removed. That is, both routers have only connected and local routes to begin the example.

For this example, as shown in Example 29-8, both R1 and R2 add static routes that refer to the neighbor's global unicast address. R1 adds a route for subnet 2 (on the right), while R2 adds a route for subnet 1 (on the left). Note that the example shows routes in both directions so that the two hosts can send packets to each other.

Example 29-8   *Static IPv6 Routes Using Global Unicast Addresses*

```
! The first command is on router R1, listing R2's global unicast address
R1(config)# ipv6 route 2001:db8:1111:2::/64 2001:DB8:1111:4::2
```
```
! The next command is on router R2, listing R1's global unicast address
R2(config)# ipv6 route 2001:db8:1111:1::/64 2001:db8:1111:4::1
```

The **ipv6 route** command itself is relatively straightforward. Focus on R1's route, which matches the logic shown in Figure 29-3. The command lists subnet 2 (2001:DB8:1111:2::/64). It then lists R2's global unicast address (ending in 4::2).

The verification commands on R1, as shown in Example 29-9, list the usual information. Example 29-9 shows two commands, first listing R1's only static route (the one configured in Example 29-8). The end of the example lists the **show ipv6 route 2001:DB8:1111:2::22** command, which lists the route R1 uses when forwarding packets to Host B, proving that R1 uses this new static route when forwarding packets to that host.

Example 29-9   *Verification of Static Routes to a Next-Hop Global Unicast Address*

```
R1# show ipv6 route static
! Legend omitted for brevity
S   2001:DB8:1111:2::/64 [1/0]
     via 2001:DB8:1111:4::2


R1# show ipv6 route 2001:db8:1111:2::22/64
Routing entry for 2001:DB8:1111:2::/64
 Known via "static", distance 1, metric 0
 Backup from "ospf 1 [110]"
 Route count is 1/1, share count 0
 Routing paths:
   2001:DB8:1111:4::2
     Last updated 00:07:43 ago
```

Example Static Route with a Link-Local Next-Hop Address

Static routes that refer to a neighbor's link-local address work a little like both of the previous two styles of static routes. First, the **ipv6 route** command refers to a next-hop address, namely a link-local address. However, the command must also refer to the router's local outgoing interface. Why both? The **ipv6 route** command cannot simply refer to a link-local next-hop address by itself, because the link-local address does not, by itself, tell the local router which outgoing interface to use.

Interestingly, when the **ipv6 route** command refers to a global unicast next-hop address, the router can deduce the outgoing interface. For example, the earlier example on R1, as shown in Example 29-8, shows R1 with a static IPv6 route with a next-hop IPv6 address of 2001:DB8:1111:4::2. R1 can look at its IPv6 routing table, see its connected route that includes this 2001:DB8:1111:4::2 address, and see a connected route off R1's S0/0/0. As a result, with a next-hop global unicast address, R1 can deduce the correct outgoing interface (R1's S0/0/0).

With a link-local next-hop address, a router cannot work through this same logic, so the outgoing interface must also be configured. Example 29-10 shows the configuration of static routes on R1 and R2, replacements for the two routes previously configured in Example 29-8.

Example 29-10   *Static IPv6 Routes Using Link-Local Neighbor Addresses*

```
! The first command is on router R1, listing R2's link-local address
R1(config)# ipv6 route 2001:db8:1111:2::/64 S0/0/0 FE80::FF:FE00:2
! The next command is on router R2, listing R1's link-local address
R2(config)# ipv6 route 2001:db8:1111:1::/64 S0/0/1 FE80::FF:FE00:1
```

Example 29-11 verifies the configuration in Example 29-10 by repeating the **show ipv6 route static** and **show ipv6 route 2001:DB8:1111:2::22** commands used in Example 29-9. Note that the output from both commands differs slightly in regards to the forwarding details. Because the new commands list both the next-hop address and outgoing interface, the **show** commands also list both the next-hop (link-local) address and the outgoing interface. If you refer back to Example 29-9, you will see only a next-hop address listed.

Example 29-11   *Verification of Static Routes to a Next-Hop Link-Local Address*

```
R1# show ipv6 route static
! Legend omitted for brevity

S    2001:DB8:1111:2::/64 [1/0]
       via FE80::FF:FE00:2, Serial0/0/0


R1# show ipv6 route 2001:db8:1111:2::22
Routing entry for 2001:DB8:1111:2::/64
  Known via "static", distance 1, metric 0
  Backup from "ospf 1 [110]"
  Route count is 1/1, share count 0
  Routing paths:
    FE80::FF:FE00:2, Serial0/0/0
      Last updated 00:08:10 ago
```

29

Static Default Routes

IPv6 supports a default route concept, similar to IPv4. The default route tells the router what to do with an IPv6 packet when the packet matches no other IPv6 route. The logic is pretty basic:

- With no default route, the router discards the IPv6 packet.

- With a default route, the router forwards the IPv6 packet based on the default route.

Default routes can be particularly useful in a couple of network design cases. For example, with an enterprise network design that uses a single router at each branch office, with one WAN link to each branch, the branch routers have only one possible path over which to forward packets. In a large network, when using a routing protocol, the branch router could learn thousands of routes—all of which point back toward the core of the network over that one WAN link.

Branch routers could use default routes instead of a routing protocol. The branch router would forward all traffic to the core of the network. Figure 29-4 shows just such an example, with two sample branch routers on the right and a core site router on the left.

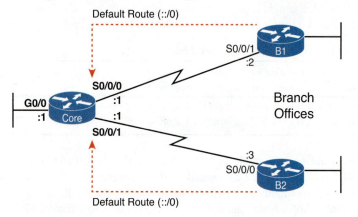

Figure 29-4 *Using Static Default Routes at Branches to Forward Back to the Core*

To configure a static default route, use the same rules already discussed in this section of the chapter, but use a specific value to note the route as a default route: ::/0. Taken literally, the double colon (::) is the IPv6 abbreviation for all 0s, and the /0 means the prefix length is 0. This idea mirrors the IPv4 convention to refer to the default route as 0.0.0.0/0. Otherwise, just configure the **ipv6 route** command as normal.

Example 29-12 shows one such example static default route on Router B1 from Figure 29-4. This example uses the outgoing interface option.

Example 29-12 *Static Default Route for Branch Router B1*

```
!Forward out B1's S0/0/1 local interface…
B1(config)# ipv6 route ::/0 S0/0/1
```

With IPv6, the router displays the default a little more cleanly than with IPv4. The **show ipv6 route** command simply includes the route in the output of the command, along with the other routes. Example 29-13 shows an example, with "::/0" listed to denote this route as the default route.

Example 29-13   *Router B1's Static Default Route (Using Global Unicast Next-Hop)*

```
B1# show ipv6 route static
IPv6 Routing Table - default - 10 entries
Codes: C - Connected, L - Local, S - Static, U - Per-user Static route
       B - BGP, R - RIP, I1 - ISIS L1, I2 - ISIS L2
       IA - ISIS interarea, IS - ISIS summary, D - EIGRP, EX - EIGRP external
       ND - ND Default, NDp - ND Prefix, DCE - Destination, NDr - Redirect
       O - OSPF Intra, OI - OSPF Inter, OE1 - OSPF ext 1, OE2 - OSPF ext 2
       ON1 - OSPF NSSA ext 1, ON2 - OSPF NSSA ext 2
S    ::/0 [1/0]
     via Serial0/0/1, directly connected
```

Dynamic Routes with OSPFv3

While static routes work, most internetworks use a dynamic routing protocol to learn the IPv6 routes for all subnets not connected to a local router. This last major section of the chapter looks at one IPv6 routing protocol—OSPF version 3—focusing on the similarities with OSPF version 2 and the configuration.

This section begins by working through some conceptual and theoretical details about OSPF version 3 (OSPFv3). After going through a short discussion of theory, this section walks you through the configuration, which is both different and simpler than the equivalent OSPFv2 configuration for IPv4. This section ends with many examples of **show** commands to find out if OSPFv3 is working correctly, learning IPv6 routes.

Comparing OSPF for IPv4 and IPv6

As you might expect, OSPFv3—the version of OSPF that supports IPv6—works a lot like OSPFv2, which supports IPv4. The next few pages work through some of the terminology, concepts, similarities, and differences in how OSPF works for IPv6 versus IPv4.

OSPF Routing Protocol Versions and Protocols

First, when most engineers refer to "OSPF," they most likely refer to OSPF as used with IPv4, and specifically, OSPF version 2 (OSPFv2). Once, there was an OSPF version 1, but OSPF version 2 (OSPFv2) followed soon afterward. When OSPF became widely used as an IPv4 routing protocol, back in the early to mid 1990s, everyone used OSPFv2 and not OSPFv1. So, even in the early days of OSPF, there was no need for people to talk about whether they used OSPFv1 or OSPFv2; everyone used OSPFv2 and just called it OSPF.

Next, consider the development of the original IPv6 protocols, back in early to mid 1990s. Beyond IPv6 itself, many other protocols needed to be updated to make IPv6 work: ICMP, TCP, UDP, and so on, including OSPF. When a working group updated OSPF to support IPv6, what did they call it? OSPF version 3, of course.

Interestingly, OSPFv3 supports advertising IPv6 routes, but not IPv4 routes. So, OSPFv3 does not attempt to add IPv6 support to the preexisting OSPFv2. While the protocols share many similarities, think of OSPFv2 and OSPFv3 as different routing protocols: one for IPv4 routes (OSPFv2) and one for IPv6 routes (OSPFv3).

Because OSPFv3 advertises IPv6 routes, and only IPv6 routes, an enterprise network that uses a dual-stack strategy actually needs to run both OSPFv2 and OSPFv3 (assuming they use OSPF at all). Are their underlying concepts very similar? Yes. However, each router would run both an

29

OSPFv2 and OSPFv3 routing protocol process, with both processes forming neighbor relationships, both sending database updates, and both calculating routes. So, a typical migration from an OSPFv2, IPv4-only enterprise network, to instead support a dual-stack IPv4/IPv6 approach (running both IPv4 and IPv6 on each host/router), would use these basic steps:

Step 1. Before IPv6, the company supports IPv4 using OSPFv2.

Step 2. When planning to add IPv6 support, the company plans to use a dual-stack approach, supporting both IPv4 and IPv6 routing on the routers in the enterprise network.

Step 3. To support IPv6 routing, companies add OSPFv3 configuration to all the routers, but they must keep the OSPFv2 configuration to continue to route IPv4 packets.

Other routing protocols followed a similar progression for updates to support IPv6, although with more unusual names. In the case of Routing Information Protocol (RIP), RIP has two versions that support IPv4, with the expected names of RIP version 1 (RIPv1) and RIP version 2 (RIPv2). To support IPv6, a working group created a new version of RIP, called *RIP Next Generation (RIPng)*, with the name chosen in reference to the "Star Trek" TV series. (Yep.) Enhanced Interior Gateway Routing Protocol (EIGRP), as a Cisco-proprietary routing protocol, has always been known simply as "EIGRP." However, to make discussions easier, some documents refer to EIGRP IPv4 support as "EIGRP," and EIGRP for IPv6 as "EIGRPv6."

Table 29-1 summarizes the terminology for these main three interior IP routing protocols.

Table 29-1 Summary of Version Terminology for Interior Routing Protocols

	RIP	OSPF	EIGRP
Latest version that supports IPv4 routes	RIP version 2 (RIPv2)	OSPF version 2 (OSPFv2)	EIGRP
Version that supports IPv6 routes	RIP Next Generation (RIPng)	OSPF version 3 (OSPFv3)	EIGRP for IPv6 (EIGRPv6)

Comparing OSPFv2 and OSPFv3

To the depth that this book discusses OSPF theory and concepts, OSPFv3 acts very much like OSPFv2. For example, both use link-state logic. Both use the same metric. And the list keeps getting longer, because the protocols do have many similarities. The following list notes many of the similarities for the features discussed both in this chapter in Chapter 17, "Learning IPv4 Routes with OSPFv2":

Key Topic

■ Both are link-state protocols.

■ Both use the same area design concepts and design terms.

■ Both require that the routing protocol be enabled on an interface.

■ Once enabled on an interface, both then attempt to discover neighbors connected to the data link connected to an interface.

■ Both perform a check of certain settings before a router will become neighbors with another router (the list of checks is slightly different between OSPFv2 and OSPFv3).

■ After two routers become neighbors, both OSPFv2 and OSPFv3 proceed by exchanging the contents of their link-state databases (LSDB)—the link-state advertisements (LSA) that describe the network topology—between the two neighbors.

- After all the LSAs have been exchanged, both OSPFv2 and OSPFv3 use the shortest path first (SPF) algorithm to calculate the best route to each subnet.

- Both use the same metric concept, based on the interface cost of each interface, with the same default cost values.

- Both use LSAs to describe the topology, with some differences in how LSAs work.

The biggest differences between OSPFv3 and the older OSPFv2 lay with internals and with configuration. OSPFv3 changes the structure of some OSPF LSAs; however, these differences do not sit within the scope of this book. OSPFv3 uses a more direct approach to configuration, enabling OSPFv3 on each interface using an interface subcommand.

For later comparison to OSPFv3 configuration, Figure 29-5 shows the structure of the configuration for OSPFv2. It shows the fact that the OSPFv2 **network** subcommand—a subcommand in router configuration mode—refers to the IPv4 address on an interface, which then identifies the interface on which OSPFv2 should be enabled. In other words, the OSPFv2 configuration does not mention the interface directly.

Configuration

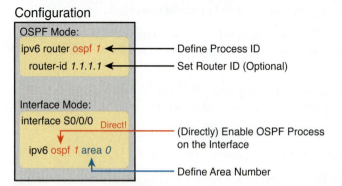

Figure 29-5   *OSPFv2 Indirectly Enables OSPF on the Interface*

OSPFv3 configuration directly enables OSPF on the interface by adding a subcommand in interface configuration mode to enable OSPFv3 on that interface. In fact, OSPFv3 does not use a **network** subcommand in router configuration mode. Instead, OSPFv3 uses the **ipv6 ospf** *process-id* **area** *area-id* interface subcommand, as shown in Figure 29-6. This command enables the listed OSPFv3 process on that interface, and sets the OSPFv3 area.

Configuration

```
OSPF Mode:
ipv6 router ospf 1        ──── Define Process ID
    router-id 1.1.1.1     ──── Set Router ID (Optional)


Interface Mode:
interface S0/0/0  Direct!

                          ──── (Directly) Enable OSPF Process
ipv6 ospf 1 area 0             on the Interface

                          ──── Define Area Number
```

Figure 29-6   *OSPFv3 Configuration Directly Enables OSPF on the Interface*

29

> **NOTE**   Cisco IOS actually supports configuration of OSPFv2 using the same style of commands shown for OSPFv3 in Figure 29-6 as well. IOS supports only the new, more direct configuration style for OSPFv3, as shown in the figure.

Now that you have a general idea about the similarities and differences between OSPFv3 and OSPFv2, the rest of this section shows examples of how to configure and verify OSPFv3.

Configuring Single-Area OSPFv3

OSPFv3 configuration requires some basic steps: pick and configure a process ID, and enable the process on each interface, while assigning the correct OSPF area to each interface. These details should be listed in any planning information. Also, this book uses single-area designs only, so all the interfaces should be assigned to the same area.

The one potential configuration issue is the OSPFv3 router ID (RID).

For review, OSPFv2 uses a 32-bit RID, chosen when the OSPF process initializes. That is, when OSPF is first configured, or later, when the router is reloaded, the OSPFv2 process chooses a number to use as its RID. When choosing the OSPFv2 process chooses its RID based using this list until it finds a RID:

1.   If the **router-id** *rid* OSPF subcommand is configured, use this value, and ignore interface IPv4 addresses.

2.   If the router ID is not set with the **router-id** command, check any loopback interfaces that have an IPv4 address configured and an interface status of up. Among these, pick the highest numeric IP address.

3.   If neither of the first two items supply a router ID, the router picks the highest numeric IPv4 address from all other interfaces whose interface status code (first status code) is up. (In other words, an interface is up/down state will be included by OSPF when choosing its router ID.)

Interestingly, OSPFv3 also uses a 32-bit RID, using the exact same rules as OSPFv2. The number is typically listed in dotted-decimal notation (DDN). That is, OSPFv3, which supports IPv6, has a router ID that looks like an IPv4 address.

Using the same RID selection rules for OSPFv3 as for OSPFv2 leaves open one unfortunate potential misconfiguration: a router that does not use the OSPFv3 **router-id** command, and does not have any IPv4 addresses configured, cannot choose a RID. If the OSPFv3 process does not have an RID, the process cannot work correctly, form neighbor relationships, or exchange routes.

This problem can be easily solved. When configuring OSPFv3, if the router does not have any IPv4 addresses, make sure to configure the RID using the **router-id** router subcommand.

Beyond that one small issue, the OSPFv3 configuration is relatively simple. The following list summarizes the configuration steps and commands for later reference and study, with examples to follow:

Step 1.   Create an OSPFv3 process number, and enter OSPF configuration mode for that process, using the **ipv6 router ospf** *process-id* global command.

Step 2.   Ensure the router has an OSPF router ID, through either:

   A. Configuring the **router-id** *id-value* router subcommand

   B. Preconfiguring an IPv4 address on any loopback interface whose line status is up

   C. Preconfiguring an IPv4 address on any working interface whose line status is up

Step 3.   Configure the **ipv6 ospf** *process-id* **area** *area-number* command on each interface on which OSPFv3 should be enabled, to both enable OSPFv3 on the interface and set the area number for the interface.

OSPFv3 Single-Area Configuration Example

Figure 29-7 shows the details of an internetwork used for an OSPFv3 configuration example. The figure shows a single area (area 0). Also, note that Routers R2 and R3 connect to the same VLAN and IPv6 prefix on the right.

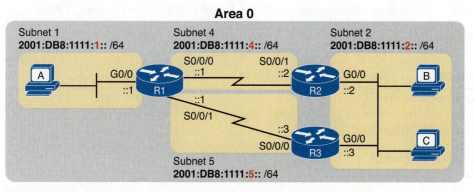

Figure 29-7   *Single-Area Design in OSPFv3 Configuration Example*

The upcoming OSPFv3 configuration example uses the following requirements:

■ All interfaces will be in area 0, so all the **ipv6 ospf** *process-id* **area** *area-number* commands will refer to area 0.

■ Each router uses a different OSPF process ID number, just to emphasize the point that the process IDs do not have to match on neighboring OSPFv3 routers.

■ Each router sets its router ID directly with the **router-id** command to an obvious number (1.1.1.1, 2.2.2.2, and 3.3.3.3, for R1, R2, and R3, respectively).

■ The routers do not use IPv4.

To begin, Example 29-14 shows an excerpt from R1's **show running-config** command before adding the OSPFv3 configuration with the **ipv6 unicast-routing** command, plus an **ipv6 address** command on each interface.

Example 29-14   *R1 IPv6 Configuration Reference (Before Adding OSPFv3 Configuration)*

```
ipv6 unicast-routing
!
interface serial0/0/0
 no ip address
 ipv6 address 2001:db8:1111:4::1/64
!
interface serial0/0/1
 no ip address
 ipv6 address 2001:db8:1111:5::1/64
!
interface GigabitEthernet0/0
 no ip address
 ipv6 address 2001:db8:1111:1::1/64
```

29

Example 29-15 begins to show the OSPFv3 configuration, starting on Router R1. Note that at this point, Router R1 has no IPv4 addresses configured, so R1 cannot possibly choose an OSPFv3 RID; it must rely on the configuration of the **router-id** command. Following the example in sequence, the following occurs:

Step 1.   The engineer adds the **ipv6 router ospf 1** global command, creating the OSPFv3 process.

Step 2.   The router tries to allocate an OSPFv3 RID and fails, so it issues an error message.

Step 3.   The engineer adds the **router-id 1.1.1.1** to give R1's OSPFv3 process an RID.

Step 4.   The engineer adds **ipv6 ospf 1 area 0** commands to all three interfaces.

Example 29-15 *Additional Configuration on R1 to Enable OSPFv3 on Three Interfaces*

```
R1# configure terminal
Enter configuration commands, one per line.  End with CNTL/Z.
R1(config)# ipv6 router ospf 1
Jan  4 21:03:50.622: %OSPFv3-4-NORTRID: OSPFv3 process 1 could not pick a router-id,
please configure manually
R1(config-rtr)# router-id 1.1.1.1
R1(config-rtr)#
R1(config-rtr)# interface serial0/0/0
R1(config-if)# ipv6 ospf 1 area 0
R1(config-if)# interface serial0/0/1
R1(config-if)# ipv6 ospf 1 area 0
R1(config-if)# interface GigabitEthernet0/0
R1(config-if)# ipv6 ospf 1 area 0
R1(config-if)# end
R1#
```

When looking at the configuration on a single OSPFv3 router, only two other types of parameters can be an issue: the OSPF process ID and the area number. When checking an OSPFv3 configuration for errors, first check the process ID numbers, and make sure that all the values match on that router. For example, the **ipv6 router ospf** *process-id* command's process ID should match all the **ipv6 ospf** *process-id* . . . interface subcommands. The other value, the area number, simply needs to match the planning diagram that shows which interfaces should be in which area.

When comparing two neighboring routers, some parameters must match, or the routers will not become neighbors. Troubleshooting these kinds of problems sits within the scope of the 200-101 ICND2 exam, not the 100-101 ICND1 exam. However, the one big difference between OSPFv2 and OSPFv3 in this neighbor checklist is that OSPFv3 neighbors do not have to have IPv6 prefixes (subnets) or prefix lengths that match. Otherwise, OSPFv3 neighbors must match with items such as both routers being in the same area, having the same Hello interval and the same dead interval.

Example 29-16 shows a completed configuration for Router R2. In this case, Router R2 uses a different OSPF process ID than R1; the process IDs on neighbors do not have to match with OSPFv2 or OSPFv3. R2 creates its OSPFv3 process (2), sets its RID (2.2.2.2), and enables OSPFv3 on all three of its interfaces with the **ipv6 ospf 2 area 0** interface subcommand.

Example 29-16   *Complete IPv6 Configuration, Using OSPFv3, on Router R2*

```
ipv6 unicast-routing
!
ipv6 router ospf 2
 router-id 2.2.2.2
!
interface serial0/0/1
 ipv6 address 2001:db8:1111:4::2
 ipv6 ospf 2 area 0
!
interface GigabitEthernet0/0
 ipv6 address 2001:db8:1111:2::2
 ipv6 ospf 2 area 0
```

OSPFv3 Passive Interfaces

Like OSPFv2, OSPFv3 can be configured to make interfaces passive. Some IPv6 subnets have only one router connected to the subnet. In those cases, the router needs to enable OSPFv3 on the interface, so that the router advertises about the connected subnet, but the router does not need to attempt to discover OSPFv3 neighbors on the interface. In those cases, the engineer can configure the interface as on OSPFv3 passive interface, telling the router to do the following:

- Quit sending OSPF Hellos on the interface
- Ignore received Hellos on the interface
- Do not form neighbor relationships over the interface
- Continue to advertise about any subnets connected to the interface

Interestingly, passive interface configuration works the same for both OSPFv2 and OSPFv3. For example, in the configuration example based on Figure 29-7, only R1 connects to the LAN subnet on the left side of the figure, so R1's G0/0 interface could be made passive to OSPFv3. To do so, the engineer could add the **passive-interface gigabitethernet0/0** subcommand in OSPFv3 configuration mode on Router R1.

For a more complete discussion of how to configure passive interfaces for OSPF, refer to Chapter 17's section "OSPF Passive Interfaces."

Verifying OSPFv3 Status and Routes

To verify whether OSPFv3 works, you can take two different approaches. You can start at the end, looking at the IPv6 routes added by OSPFv3. If the correct routes show up in the correct routers' routing tables, OSPFv3 must be working correctly. Alternately, you can proceed in the same order that OSPF uses to build the routes: First confirm the configuration settings, then look at the OSPF neighbors, then the OSPF database, and finally look at the routes OSPF added to the routing tables.

When speed matters, look at the routing table first. However, for the sake of learning, it helps to walk through the steps from start to finish, working through a variety of OSPFv3 **show** commands. The rest of this section works through several OSPFv3 **show** commands, in this order:

- Verifying the configuration settings (OSPFv3 process and interfaces)
- Verifying OSPFv3 neighbors
- Verifying the OSPFv3 link-state database (LSDB) and LSAs
- Verifying OSPFv3 routes

This section happens to mention a wide variety of OSPFv3 **show** commands that have a matching and similar OSPFv2 **show** command. Table 29-2 lists these **show** commands for easier reference and study.

Key Topic

Table 29-2   OSPFv2 and Matching OSPFv3 **show** Commands

To Display Details About...	OSPFv2	OSPFv3
OSPF process	show ip ospf	show ipv6 ospf
All sources of routing information	show ip protocols	show ipv6 protocols
Details about OSPF-enabled interfaces	show ip ospf interface	show ipv6 ospf interface
Concise info about OSPF-enabled interfaces	show ip ospf interface brief	show ipv6 ospf interface brief
List of neighbors	show ip ospf neighbor	show ipv6 ospf neighbor
Summary of LSDB	show ip ospf database	show ipv6 ospf database
OSPF-learned routes	show ip route ospf	show ipv6 route ospf

NOTE   Note that all the OSPFv3 commands use the exact same commands as those for IPv4, except they use **ipv6** instead of the **ip** parameter.

Verifying OSPFv3 Configuration Settings

To verify the OSPFv3 configuration on a router, a simple **show running-config** command works well. However, in some cases in real life, and on the exams with many Simlet questions, you might not be allowed to enter enable mode to use commands like **show running-config**. In those cases, you can re-create the OSPFv3 configuration using several show commands.

To start re-creating the OSPFv3 configuration, look at the output of the **show ipv6 ospf** command. This command lists information about the OSPFv3 process itself. In fact, the first line of output, highlighted in Example 29-17, tells you the following facts about the configuration:

■ The router has been configured with OSPFv3 process ID 1, meaning the **ipv6 router ospf 1** command is configured.

■ The router uses router ID 1.1.1.1, which means either the **router-id 1.1.1.1** command is configured or the **ip address 1.1.1.1** *mask* command is configured on some interface on the router.

Example 29-17   *Verifying OSPFv3 Process Configuration*

```
R1# show ipv6 ospf
Routing Process "ospfv3 1" with ID 1.1.1.1
Event-log enabled, Maximum number of events: 1000, Mode: cyclic
Initial SPF schedule delay 5000 msecs
Minimum hold time between two consecutive SPFs 10000 msecs
Maximum wait time between two consecutive SPFs 10000 msecs
Minimum LSA interval 5 secs
Minimum LSA arrival 1000 msecs
LSA group pacing timer 240 secs
```

```
Interface flood pacing timer 33 msecs
Retransmission pacing timer 66 msecs
Number of external LSA 0. Checksum Sum 0x000000
Number of areas in this router is 1. 1 normal 0 stub 0 nssa
Graceful restart helper support enabled
Reference bandwidth unit is 100 mbps
    Area BACKBONE(0)
        Number of interfaces in this area is 3
        SPF algorithm executed 4 times
        Number of LSA 13. Checksum Sum 0x074B38
        Number of DCbitless LSA 0
        Number of indication LSA 0
        Number of DoNotAge LSA 0
        Flood list length 0
```

The highlights toward the end of Example 29-17 give some hints about the rest of the configuration, but not enough detail to list every part of the remaining OSPFv3 configuration. The highlighted lines mention three interfaces are in "this area" and that the area is backbone area 0. All these message sit under the heading line at the top of the example, for OSPFv3 process "1." These facts together tell us that this router (R1) uses the following configuration:

- Interface subcommand **ipv6 ospf 1 area 0**.

- The router uses this interface subcommand on three interfaces.

However, the **show ipv6 ospf** command does not identify the interfaces on which OSPFv3 is working. To find those interfaces, use either of the two commands in Example 29-18. Focusing first on the **show ipv6 ospf interface brief** command, this command lists one line for each interface on which OSPFv3 is enabled. Each line lists the interface, the OSPFv3 process ID (under the heading "PID"), the area assigned to the interface, and the number of OSPFv3 neighbors ("Nbrs" heading) known out that interface.

Example 29-18 *Verifying OSPFv3 Interfaces*

```
R1# show ipv6 ospf interface brief
Interface    PID    Area          Intf ID    Cost   State Nbrs F/C
Gi0/0        1      0             3          1      DR    0/0
Se0/0/1      1      0             7          64     P2P   1/1
Se0/0/0      1      0             6          64     P2P   1/1

R1# show ipv6 protocols
IPv6 Routing Protocol is "connected"
IPv6 Routing Protocol is "ND"
IPv6 Routing Protocol is "ospf 1"
  Interfaces (Area 0):
    GigabitEthernet0/0
    Serial0/0/1
    Serial0/0/0
  Redistribution:
    None
```

NOTE Just as with the **show ip ospf interface brief** command, the **show ipv6 ospf interface brief** command lists both nonpassive and passive OSPFv3 interfaces.

29

The second half of the output in Example 29-18, listing the **show ipv6 protocols** command, lists information about every source of IPv6 routes on the router. This command lists noticeably less detail about OSPFv3 than the **show ip protocol** command lists about OSPFv2. However, both commands list the interfaces on which OSPFv3 is enabled.

Both of the commands in Example 29-18 give enough information to predict that this router (R1) has an **ipv6 ospf 1 area 0** subcommand under three interfaces: G0/0, S0/0/0, and S0/0/1.

Verifying OSPFv3 Neighbors

Verifying OSPFv3 neighbors requires a brief look at a single command: **show ipv6 ospf neighbor**. This command lists one line per neighbor, listing key facts about that neighbor. In particular, it lists the neighbor's RID, the local router's interface through which that neighbor is reached, and the status of the neighbor relationship.

In the OSPFv3 example used in this chapter, each router should have two neighbor relationships. R1 has two serial links, one each to Routers R2 and R3, so R1 will form a neighbor relationship with each of these routers. R2 and R3 both connect to the same IPv6 subnet over a LAN, and will form a neighbor relationship over that LAN. Figure 29-8 shows the expected OSPFv3 neighbor relationships.

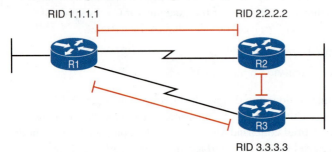

Figure 29-8   *Expected OSPFv3 Neighbor Relationships Compared to Figure 29-7*

Example 29-19 shows the OSPFv3 neighbor relationships on Routers R1 and R2. The highlighted portions point out the basics, with the neighboring routers' RIDs, local interface, and state. The "FULL" state means that the neighbor relationship is working, and that the neighbors have "fully" completed the exchange of LSAs.

Example 29-19   *Verifying OSPFv3 Neighbors on Routers R1 and R2*

```
! The first command is from router R1, listing R2 and R3

R1# show ipv6 ospf neighbor

Neighbor ID     Pri   State        Dead Time   Interface ID   Interface
3.3.3.3           0   FULL/  -     00:00:39    6              Serial0/0/1
2.2.2.2           0   FULL/  -     00:00:31    7              Serial0/0/0


! The next command is from router R2, listing R1 and R3

R2# show ipv6 ospf neighbor

Neighbor ID     Pri   State        Dead Time   Interface ID   Interface
1.1.1.1           0   FULL/  -     00:00:39    6              Serial0/0/1
3.3.3.3           1   FULL/DR      00:00:33    3              GigabitEthernet0/0
```

Before speeding along to the next topic, take a moment to look again at the output in Example 29-19. Do you see anything in the output that makes you think of IPv6 instead of IPv4? OSPFv3 uses 32-bit RIDs, listed in dotted-decimal notation, so the output looks literally just like the output from the **show ip ospf neighbor** command. The only difference is the command itself, with the **ipv6** keyword.

Examining the OSPFv3 Database

OSPFv3 does differ from OSPFv2 with the theory and details of OSPF LSAs. However, this book mostly ignores LSA details, with the ICND2 book discussing LSAs in a small amount of detail. To understand the differences between OSPFv2 and OSPFv3, the discussion would need to be much deeper.

However, an easy way to do a basic check of the LSDB is to check for Type 1 router LSAs. Both OSPFv2 and OSPFv3 use a Type 1 LSA for every router, with the LSA describing the router itself. The LSA has an identifier equal to the RID of that router. Inside an area, the LSDB should contain one Type 1 LSA for every router in the area. Example 29-20 shows the first section of output from the **show ipv6 ospf database** command and tells you whether a router has learned the Type 1 Router LSA from all the routers.

Example 29-20 *Verifying OSPFv3 LSDB on R1*

```
R2# show ipv6 ospf database

            OSPFv3 Router with ID (2.2.2.2) (Process ID 2)

               Router Link States (Area 0)

ADV Router       Age         Seq#        Fragment ID Link count  Bits
1.1.1.1          452         0x80000002  0           2           None
2.2.2.2          456         0x80000004  0           2           None
3.3.3.3          457         0x80000005  0           2           None

! Lines omitted for brevity
```

The example shows three lines of data under the heading lines in the section titled "Router Link States." This section shows data about the Type 1 Router LSAs. In that section, the heading "ADV Router" referring to the router that advertised the LSA. In this case, R1 (RID 1.1.1.1) knows its own Type 1 LSA, plus R2's (RID 2.2.2.2) and R3's (RID 3.3.3.3).

Examining IPv6 Routes Learned by OSPFv3

Finally, the real proof of whether OSPFv3 works is whether the routers learn and add any IPv6 routes to the IPv6 routing table. This section completes the verification process with a look at the IPv6 routes added by OSPFv3.

When working correctly, OSPFv3 routers learn enough information to create routes for all IPv6 prefixes (subnets) in the internetwork. The one big difference as compared with OSPFv2 is that OSPFv3-learned routes use a link-local next-hop address. For example, in the internetwork shown in Figure 29-9, which is the same design used for the OSPFv3 configuration example, R2 adds a route to subnet 1 on the left (subnet 2001:DB8:1111:1::/64). R2 uses R1's link-local address as the next-hop address, as shown in the figure.

29

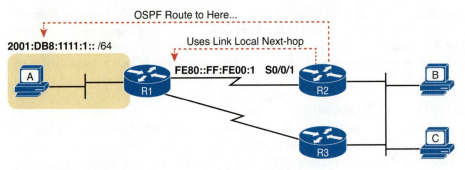

Figure 29-9 *OSPFv3 and Its Use of Link-Local Addresses*

Example 29-21 lists the output from the **show ipv6 route ospf** command on Router R2, for the route highlighted in Figure 29-9. Of particular importance, note

- Code letter "O" meaning "OSPF"
- In brackets, 110, the administrative distance of OSPF, and 65, the metric for this route
- The fact that the route lists both the link-local address and the outgoing interface

Example 29-21 *OSPFv3 Routes on Router R2*

```
R2# show ipv6 route ospf
IPv6 Routing Table - default - 9 entries
! Legend omitted for brevity

O   2001:DB8:1111:1::/64 [110/65]
     via FE80::FF:FE00:1, Serial0/0/1
O   2001:DB8:1111:5::/64 [110/65]
     via FE80::FF:FE00:3, GigabitEthernet0/0
```

Review Activities

Chapter Summary

- A router adds IPv6 routes based on the following:
  - The configuration of IPv6 addresses on working interfaces (connected and local routes)
  - The direct configuration of a static route (static routes)
  - The configuration of a routing protocol, like OSPFv3, on routers that share the same data link (dynamic routes; in this case, OSPF routes)

- Routers add and remove connected routes, and local routes, based on the interface configuration and the interface state. First, the router looks for any configured unicast addresses on any interfaces by looking for the **ipv6 address** command. Then, if the interface is working—if the interface has a "line status is up, protocol status is up" notice in the output of the **show interfaces** command—the router adds both a connected and local route.

- The following list summarizes IPv6 routing for easier review and study:
  - Routers create IPv6 routes based on each unicast IPv6 address on an interface, as configured with the **ipv6 address** command, as follows:
    - The router creates a route for the subnet (a connected route).
    - The router creates a host route (/128 prefix length) for the router IPv6 address (a local route).
  - Routers do not create routes based on the link-local addresses associated with the interface.
  - Routers remove the connected and local routes for an interface if the interface fails, and re-add these routes when the interface is again in a working (up/up) state.

- Whereas routers automatically add connected and local routes based on the interface configuration, static routes require direct configuration with the **ipv6 route** command. Simply put, someone configures the command, and the router places the details from the command into a route in the IPv6 routing table.

- IPv6 supports a default route concept, similar to IPv4. The default route tells the router what to do with an IPv6 packet when the packet matches no other IPv6 route. The logic is pretty basic:
  - With no default route, the router discards the IPv6 packet.
  - With a default route, the router forwards the IPv6 packet based on the default route.

- OSPFv3 configuration requires some basic steps: Pick and configure a process ID, enable the process on each interface while assigning the correct OSPF area to each interface. These details should be listed in any planning information. Also, this book uses single-area designs only, so all the interfaces should be assigned to the same area.

- The OSPFv3 configuration is relatively simple. The following list summarizes the configuration steps and commands for later reference and study:

  Step 1.   Create an OSPFv3 process number, and enter OSPF configuration mode for that process using the **ipv6 router ospf** *process-id* global command.

  Step 2.   Ensure that the router has an OSPF router ID, through either
  - Configuring the **router-id** *id-value* router subcommand
  - Preconfiguring an IPv4 address on any loopback interface whose line status is up
  - Preconfiguring an IPv4 address on any working interface whose line status is up

29

Step 3.   Configure the **ipv6 ospf** *process_id* **area** *area_number* command on each interface on which OSPFv3 should be enabled, to both enable OSPFv3 on the interface and set the area number for the interface.

■ To verify the OSPFv3 configuration on a router, a simple **show running-config** command works well. However, in some cases in real life, and on the exams with many Simlet questions, you might not be allowed to enter enable mode to use commands like **show running-config**. In those cases, you can re-create the OSPFv3 configuration using several **show** commands.

■ Verifying OSPFv3 neighbors requires a brief look at a single command: **show ipv6 ospf neighbor**. This command lists one line per neighbor, listing key facts about that neighbor. In particular, it lists the neighbor's RID, the local router's interface through which that neighbor is reached, and the status of the neighbor relationship.

Review Questions

Answer these review questions. You can find the answers at the bottom of the last page of the chapter. For thorough explanations, see DVD Appendix C, "Answers to Review Questions."

1. A router has been configured with the **ipv6 address 2000:1:2:3::1/64** command on its G0/1 interface. The router creates a link-local address of FE80::FF:FE00:1 as well. The interface is working. Which of the following routes will the router add to its IPv6 routing table? (Choose two answers.)

A.   A route for 2000:1:2:3::/64

B.   A route for FE80::FF:FE00:1/64

C.   A route for 2000:1:2:3::1/128

D.   A route for FE80::FF:FE00:1/128

2. An engineer needs to add a static IPv6 route for prefix 2000:1:2:3::/64 to Router R5, in the figure shown with the previous question. Which of the following answers shows a valid static IPv6 route for that subnet, on Router R5?

A.   ipv6 route 2000:1:2:3::/64 S0/1/1

B.   ipv6 route 2000:1:2:3::/64 S0/1/0

C.   ip route 2000:1:2:3::/64 S0/1/1

D.   ip route 2000:1:2:3::/64 S0/1/0

3. An engineer needs to add a static IPv6 route for prefix 2000:1:2:3::/64 to Router R5 in the figure shown with Question 1. Which of the following answers shows a valid static IPv6 route for that subnet, on Router R5?

A.   ipv6 route 2000:1:2:3::/64 2000:1:2:56::5

B.   ipv6 route 2000:1:2:3::/64 2000:1:2:56::6

C.   ipv6 route 2000:1:2:3::/64 FE80::FF:FE00:5

D.   ipv6 route 2000:1:2:3::/64 FE80::FF:FE00:6

4. An engineer needs to add IPv6 support to an existing router, R1. R1 already has IPv4 and OSPFv2 implemented on all interfaces. The new project requires the addition of IPv6 addresses and OSPFv3 on all interfaces. Which of the following answers list a command that must be part of the completed configuration to support IPv6 and OSPFv3? (Choose two answers.)

   A. The **ipv6 router ospf** *process-id* global command

   B. The **router-id** command in OSPFv3 configuration mode

   C. The **network** *prefix/length* command in OSPFv3 configuration mode

   D. The **ipv6 ospf** *process-id* **area** *area-id* command on each IPv6-enabled interface

5. Which of the following commands list the interfaces on which OSPFv3 has been enabled? (Choose two answers.)

   A. show ipv6 ospf database

   B. show ipv6 ospf interface brief

   C. show ipv6 ospf

   D. show ipv6 protocols

6. Which of the following answers list a routing protocol that advertises IPv6 routes? (Chooses two answers.)

   A. OSPFv6

   B. OSPFv3

   C. EIGRPv6

   D. EIGRPv3

Review All the Key Topics

Review the most important topics from this chapter, noted with the Key Topic icon. Table 29-3 lists these key topics and where each is discussed.

Table 29-3   Key Topics for Chapter 29

Key Topic Element	Description	Page Number
List	Methods by which a router can build IPv6 routes	689
List	Rules for IPv6 connected and local routes	689
Figure 29-2	IPv6 static route concepts	692
List	List of similarities between OSPFv2 and OSPFv3	698
List	Rules for setting the OSPFv3 router ID (RID)	700
List	OSPFv3 configuration checklist	700
List	Actions taken and not taken for OSPFv3 passive interfaces	703
Table 29-2	OSPFv2 and OSPFv3 verification commands compared	704

29

Complete the Tables and Lists from Memory

Print a copy of DVD Appendix M, "Memory Tables," or at least the section for this chapter, and complete the tables and lists from memory. DVD Appendix N, "Memory Tables Answer Key," includes completed tables and lists to check your work.

Definitions of Key Terms

Because this chapter has so many concepts in common with the IPv4-equivalent tools, the only new term is OSPF version 3. Feel free to check your mental definition of OSPFv3 versus the definition in the glossary.

Command Reference to Check Your Memory

Table 29-4   Chapter 29 Configuration Command Reference

Command	Description
ipv6 route *prefix/length* *next-hop-address*	Global command to define an IPv6 static route to a next-hop router IPv6 address.
ipv6 route *prefix/length* *outgoing-interface*	Global command to define an IPv6 static route, with packets forwarded out the local router interface listed in the command.
ipv6 route *prefix/length* *next-hop-address* *outgoing-interface*	Global command to define an IPv6 static route, with both the next-hop address and local router outgoing interface listed in the command.
ipv6 route ::/0 *{[next-hop-address] [outgoing-interface]}*	Global command to define a default IPv6 static route, with the forwarding details (outgoing interface, next-hop address) working the same way as the nondefault versions of the **ipv6 route** command.
ipv6 router ospf *process-id*	Enters OSPFv3 configuration mode for the listed process.
router-id *id*	OSPF subcommand that statically sets the router ID.
ipv6 ospf *process-id* **area** *area-number*	Interface subcommand that enables OSPFv3 on the interface, for a particular process, and defines the OSPFv3 area.
passive-interface *type number*	OSPF subcommand that tells OSPF to be passive on that interface or subinterface.
passive-interface default	OSPF subcommand that changes the OSPF default for interfaces to be passive instead of active (not passive).
no passive-interface *type number*	OSPF subcommand that tells OSPF to be active (not passive) on that interface or subinterface.

Table 29-5   Chapter 29 EXEC Command Reference

Command	Description
show ipv6 route [ospf]	Lists routes in the routing table learned by OSPFv3.
show ipv6 ospf	Shows routing protocol parameters and current timer values for OSPFv3, and the OSPFv3 router ID.
show ipv6 ospf interface brief	Lists one line of output per OSPFv3-enabled interface, with basic settings listed, like OSPFv3 process, area number, and interface cost.
show ipv6 ospf neighbor [*neighbor-RID*]	Lists neighbors and current status with neighbors, per interface, and optionally lists details for the router ID listed in the command.
show ipv6 ospf database	Lists a summary of the LSAs in the local router's LSDB, listing one line for each LSA.
show ipv6 protocols	Lists briefer information than the IPv4 **show ip protocols** command, primarily listing all means through which a router can learn or build IPv6 routes, and interfaces on which a routing protocol is enabled.

Answers to Review Questions:

1 A and C **2** A **3** B **4** A and D **5** B and D **6** B and C

Part VII Review

Keep track of your part review progress with the checklist in Table P7-1. Details on each task follow the table.

Table P7-1 Part VII Part Review Checklist

Activity	First Date Completed	Second Date Completed
Repeat All Chapter Review Questions		
Answer Part Review Questions		
Review Key Topics		
Create IPv6 Addressing Mind Map		
Create IPv6 Configuration and Verification Command Mind Map		

Repeat All Chapter Review Questions

For this task, answer the chapter review questions again for the chapters in this part of the book, using the PCPT software. Refer to the Introduction to this book, heading "How to View Only Chapter Review Questions by Part," for help with how to make the PCPT software show you chapter review questions for this part only.

Answer Part Review Questions

For this task, answer the Part Review questions for this part of the book, using the PCPT software. Refer to the Introduction to this book, heading "How to View Only Part Review Questions by Part," for help with how to make the PCPT software show you Part Review questions for this part only.

Review Key Topics

Browse back through the chapters, and look for the Key Topics icons. If you do not remember some details, take the time to reread those topics.

Create IPv6 Addressing Mind Map

Addressing is the biggest difference between IPv4 and IPv6. Think about IPv6 addresses for a few moments—the terms, the structure, the types, and anything related to addressing. Then make a mind map that collects all the addressing concepts and terms into one mind map.

When thinking about addressing, try to organize the information to your liking. There is no one right answer. However, if you want some guidance on how to organize the information, some of the concepts and terms can be organized by type of address. For instance, link-local addresses would be one type. In that part of the mind map, you could list all terms and facts about link-local addresses, as shown in Figure P7-1.

Figure P7-1   *Sample Mind Map for the Link-Local Branch*

Chapter 25, "Fundamentals of IP Version 6," through Chapter 27, "Implementing IPv6 Addressing on Routers," contain most of the IPv6 addressing concepts in this book. Try to fit all the addressing terms from the Key Terms sections of those chapters into the map, along with all IPv6 addressing concepts and the values that identify an address as being a particular type of IPv6 address.

Create IPv6 Configuration and Verification Command Mind Map

Without referring to your notes or the book, create a mind map of all the IPv6 router commands you can recall. The goal with this mind map exercise is to help you remember the commands, but not necessarily every last parameter. The goal is to help you organize the commands internally so that you know which commands to consider when faced with a real-life problem or an exam question.

Organize your commands first by a major topic. Then, for a given topic, separate the commands based on configuration versus verification command. Some suggested major topics:

addresses, static routes, OSPFv3

Appendix O, "Mind Map Solutions," lists sample mind map answers, but as usual, your mind map can and will look different.

Table P7-2   Configuration Mind Maps for Part VII Review

Map	Description	Where You Saved It
1	IPv6 Addressing Mind Map	
2	IPv6 Commands Mind Map	

Part VIII

Final Review

Chapter 30: Final Review

Chapter 30

Final Review

Congratulations! You made it through the book, and now it's time to finish getting ready for the exam. This chapter helps you get ready to take and pass the exam in two ways.

This chapter begins by talking about the exam itself. You know the content and topics. Now you need to think about what happens during the exam, and what you need to do in these last few weeks before taking the exam. At this point, everything you do should be focused on getting you ready to pass so that you can finish up this hefty task.

The second section of this chapter gives you some exam review tasks as your final preparation for your ICND1, ICND2, or CCNA exam.

Advice About the Exam Event

Now that you have finished the bulk of this book, you could just register for your Cisco ICND1, ICND2, or CCNA exam; show up; and take the exam. However, if you spend a little time thinking about the exam event itself, learning more about the user interface of the real Cisco exams, and the environment at the Vue testing centers, you will be better prepared, particularly if this is your first Cisco exam. This first of three major sections in this chapter gives some advice about the Cisco exams and the exam event itself.

Learn the Question Types Using the Cisco Certification Exam Tutorial

In the weeks leading up to your exam, you should think more about the different types of exam questions and have a plan for how to approach those questions. One of the best ways to learn about the exam questions is to use the Cisco Exam Tutorial.

To find the Cisco Certification Exam Tutorial, go to www.cisco.com and search for "exam tutorial." The tutorial sits inside a web page with a Flash presentation of the exam user interface. The tutorial even lets you take control as if you were taking the exam. When using the tutorial, make sure that you take control and try the following:

- Try to click next on the multichoice, single-answer question without clicking an answer, and see that the testing software tells you that you have too few answers.

- On the multichoice, multianswer question, select too few answers and click Next to again see how the user interface responds.

- In the drag-and-drop question, drag the answers to the obvious answer locations, but them drag them back to the original location. (You might do this on the real exam, if you change your mind when answering the question.)

- On the Simulation question, first just make sure that you can get to the command-line interface (CLI) on one of the routers. To do so, you have to click the PC icon for a PC connected to the router console; the console cable appears as a dashed line, while network cables are solid lines.

- Still on the Sim question, make sure that you look at the scroll areas at the top, at the side, and in the terminal emulator window.

- Still on the Sim question, make sure that you can toggle between the topology window and the terminal emulator window by clicking "Show topology" and "Hide topology."

- On the Testlet question, answer one multichoice question, move to the second and answer it, and then move back to the first question, confirming that inside a Testlet, you can move around between questions.

- Again on the Testlet question, click the Next button to see the pop-up window that Cisco uses as a prompt to ask whether you want to move on. Testlets might actually allow you to give too few answers and still move on. After you click to move past the Testlet, you cannot go back to change your answer for any of these questions.

Think About Your Time Budget Versus Numbers of Questions

On exam day, you need to keep an eye on your speed. Going too slowly hurts you because you might not have time to answer all the questions. Going too fast can be hurtful, if your fast speed is because you are rushing and not taking the time to fully understand the questions. So, you need to be able to somehow know whether you are moving quickly enough to answer all the questions, while not rushing.

The exam user interface shows some useful information, namely a countdown timer as well as question counter. The question counter shows a question number for the question you are answering, and it shows the total number of questions on your exam.

Unfortunately, treating each question as equal does not give you an accurate time estimate. For example, if your exam allows 90 minutes, and your exam has 45 questions, you would have two minutes per question. After answering 20 questions, if you had taken 40 minutes, you would be right on time. However, several factors make that kind of estimate difficult.

First, Cisco does not tell us beforehand the exact number of questions for each exam. For example, the Cisco website might list the CCNA exam as having from 45 to 55 questions. (The ICND1 and ICND2 exams have similar ranges.) But you do not know how many questions are on your exam until it begins, when you go through the screens that lead up to the point where you click "Start exam."

Next, some questions (call them *time burners*) clearly take a lot more time to answer:

Normal-time questions: Multichoice and drag-and-drop, approximately 1 minute each

Time burners: Sims, Simlets, and Testlets, approximately 6–8 minutes each

Finally, in the count of 45–55 questions on a single exam, even though Testlet and Simlet questions contain several multichoice questions, the exam software counts each Testlet and Simlet question as one question in the question counter. For example, if a Testlet question has four embedded multiple-choice questions, in the exam software's question counter, that counts as one question.

> **NOTE** While Cisco does not tell us why you might get 45 questions, while someone else taking the same exam might get 55 questions, it seems reasonable to think that the person with 45 questions might have a few more of the time burners, making the two exams equivalent.

You need a plan for how you will check your time, a plan that does not distract you from the exam. It might be worth taking a bit of a guess, to keep things simple, like this:

50 questions, 90 minutes, is a little less than two minutes per question, and just guess a little based on how many time-burner questions you have seen so far.

No matter how you plan to check your time, think about it before exam day. You can even use the method listed under the next heading.

A Suggested Time-Check Method

The following math can be used to do your time check in a way that weights the time based on those time-burner questions. You do not have to use this method. But this math uses only addition of whole numbers, to keep it simple. It gives you a pretty close time estimate, in my opinion.

The concept is simple. Just do a simple calculation that estimates the time you should have used so far. Here's the math:

Number of Questions Answered So Far + 7 Per Time Burner

Then, you check the timer to figure out how much time you have spent:

- You have used exactly that much time, or a little more: Your timing is perfect.
- You have used less time: You are ahead of schedule.
- You have used noticeably more time: You are behind schedule.

For example, if you have already finished 17 questions, 2 of which were time burners, your time estimate is 17 + 7 + 7 = 31 minutes. If your actual time is also 31 minutes, or maybe 32 or 33 minutes, you are right on schedule. If you have spent less than 31 minutes, you are ahead of schedule.

So, the math is pretty easy: Questions answered, plus 7 per time burner, is the guesstimate of how long you should take if you are right on time.

NOTE   This math is an estimate; I make no guarantees that the math will be an accurate predictor on every exam.

Miscellaneous Pre-Exam Suggestions

Here are just a few more suggestions for things to think about before exam day arrives:

- Get some earplugs. Testing centers often have some, but if you do not want to chance it, come prepared. The testing center is typically a room inside the space of a company that does something else as well, oftentimes a training center. So, there are people talking in nearby rooms and others office noises. Earplugs can help. (Headphones, as electronic devices, would not be allowed.)
- Some people like to spend the first minute of the exam writing down some notes for reference. For example, maybe you want to write down the table of magic numbers for finding IPv4 subnet IDs. If you plan to do that, practice making those notes. Before each practice exam, transcribe those lists, just like you expect to do at the real exam.
- Plan your travel to the testing center with enough time so that you will not be rushing to make it just in time.
- If you tend to be nervous before exams, practice your favorite relaxation techniques for a few minutes before each practice exam, just to be ready to use them.

Exam-Day Advice

I hope the exam goes well for you. Certainly, the better prepared you are, the better chances you have on the exam. But these small tips can help you do your best on exam day:

- Rest the night before the exam, rather than staying up late to study. Clarity of thought is more important than one extra fact, especially because the exam requires so much analysis and thinking rather than just remembering facts.

- If you did not bring earplugs, ask the testing center for some, even if you cannot imagine you would use them. You never know whether it might help.

- You can bring personal effects into the building and testing company's space, but not into the actual room in which you take the exam. So, take as little extra stuff with you as possible. If you have a safe place to leave briefcases, purses, electronics, and so on, leave them there. However, the testing center should have a place to store your things as well. Simply put, the less you bring, the less you have to worry about storing. (For example, I have even been asked to remove even my analog wristwatch on more than one occasion.)

- The exam center will give you a laminated sheet and pen, as a place to take notes. (Test center personnel typically do not let you bring paper and pen into the room, even if supplied by the testing center.)

- Leave for the testing center with extra time, so you do not have to rush.

- Plan on finding a restroom before going into the testing center. If you cannot find one, of course you can use one in the testing center, and test personnel will direct you and give you time before your exam starts.

- Do not drink a 64-ounce drink on the trip to the testing center. After the exam starts, the exam timer will not stop while you go to the restroom.

- On exam day, use any relaxation techniques that you have practiced to help get your mind focused while you wait for the exam.

Exam Review

This exam review completes the Study Plan materials as suggested by this book. At this point, you have read the other chapters of the book, and you have done the Review Activities and Part Review tasks. Now you need to do the final study and review activities before taking the exam, as detailed in this section.

The Exam Review section suggests some new activities, as well as repeating some old. However, whether new or old, the activities all focus on filling in your knowledge gaps, finishing off your skills, and completing the study process. While repeating some tasks you did at chapter review and part review can help, you need to be ready to take an exam, so the exam review asks you to spend a lot of time answering exam questions.

The exam review walks you through suggestions for several types of tasks, and gives you some tracking tables for each activity. The main categories are

- Practicing for speed
- Taking practice exams
- Finding what you do not know well yet (knowledge gaps)
- Configuring and verifying functions from the CLI
- Repeating the chapter and Part Review tasks

Practice Subnetting and Other Math-Related Skills

Like it or not, some of the questions on the Cisco ICND1, ICND2, and CCNA exams require you to do some math. To pass, you have to be good at the math. You also need to know when to use each process.

The Cisco exams also have a timer. Some of the math crops up often enough so that, if you go slow with the math, or if you have to write down all the details of how you compute the answers, you might well run out of time to answer all the questions. (The two biggest reasons I hear about why people do not finish on time are these: slow speed with the math-related work and slow speed when doing simulator questions using the CLI.)

However, look at these math processes and the time crunch as a positive instead of a negative. Right now, before the exam, you know about the challenge. You know that if you keep practicing subnetting and other math, you will keep getting faster and better. As exam day approaches, if you have spare minutes, try more practice with anything to do with subnetting in particular. Look at it as a way to prepare now so that you do not have to worry about time pressure so much on the day of the exam.

Table 30-1 lists the topics in this chapter that both require math and require speed. Table 30-2 lists items for which the math or process is important, but speed is probably less important. By this point in your study, you should already be confident at finding the right answer to these kinds of problems. Now is the time to finish off your skills at getting the right answers, plus getting faster so that you reduce your time pressure on the exams.

> **NOTE** The time goals in the table are goals chosen by the author to give you an idea of a good time. If you happen to be a little slower on a few tasks, that does not mean you cannot do well on the test. But if you take several times as much time for almost every task, know that the math-related work can cause you some time problems.

Table 30-1 ICND1 Math-Related Activities That Benefit from Speed Practice

Chapter	Activity	Book's Excellent Speed Goal (Seconds)	Self Check: Date/Time	Self Check: Date/Time
12	From a unicast IPv4 address, find key facts about its classful network.	10		
13	From one mask in any format, convert to the other two mask formats.	10		
13	Given an IPv4 address and mask, find the number of network, subnet, and host bits, plus the number of hosts/subnet and number of subnets.	15		
14	Given an IPv4 address and mask, find the resident subnet, subnet broadcast address, and range of usable addresses.	20–30		
19	Given a set of mask requirements, choose the best subnet mask.	15		
19	Given a classful network and one mask, find all subnet IDs.	45		

Table 30-2   ICND1 Math-Related Activities That Can Be Less Time Sensitive

Chapter	Activity	Self Check: Date/Time	Self Check: Date/Time
20	Find VLSM overlaps, with problems that contain 5–6 subnets.		
20	Add VLSM subnets, with problems that contain 5–6 subnets.		
21	Find the best summary route, with problems that list four routes.		
22	Building an ACL command to match a subnet's addresses.		
22	Listing the addresses matched by one existing ACL command.		
25	Find the best abbreviation for one IPv6 address.		
27	Find the IPv6 address of one router interface when using EUI-64.		

To practice the math listed in both Tables 30-1 and 30-2, look at the end of the respective chapters for some suggestions. For example, for many subnetting problems, you can make up your own problems and check your work with any subnet calculator. Additionally, all these chapters have matching DVD appendices with additional practice. Finally, the author's blogs include extra practice problems, created just to give you another source from which to practice.

Take Practice Exams

One day soon, you need to pass a real Cisco exam at a Vue testing center. So, it's time to practice the real event as much as possible.

A practice exam using the Pearson IT Certification Practice Test (PCPT) exam software lets you experience many of the same issues as when taking a real Cisco exam. The software gives you a number of questions, with a countdown timer shown in the window. After you answer a question, you cannot go back to it (yes, that's true on Cisco exams). If you run out of time, the questions you did not answer count as incorrect.

The process of taking the timed practice exams helps you prepare in three key ways:

- To practice the exam event itself, including time pressure, the need to read carefully, with a need to concentrate for long periods
- To build your analysis and critical thinking skills when examining the network scenario built into many questions
- To discover the gaps in your networking knowledge so that you can study those topics before the real exam

As much as possible, treat the practice exam events as if you were taking the real Cisco exam at a Vue testing center. The following list gives some advice on how to make your practice exam more meaningful, rather than as just one more thing to do before exam day rolls around:

- Set aside two hours for taking the 90-minute timed practice exam.
- Make a list of what you expect to do for the ten minutes before the real exam event. Then visualize yourself doing those things. Before taking each practice exam, practice those final ten minutes before your exam timer starts. (The earlier section "Exam-Day Advice" lists some suggestions about what to do in those last ten minutes.)

30

- You cannot bring anything with you into the Vue exam room, so remove all notes and help materials from your work area before taking a practice exam. You can use blank paper, a pen, and your brain only. Do not use calculators, notes, web browsers, or any other app on your computer.

- Real life can get in the way, but if at all possible, ask anyone around you to leave you alone for the time you will practice. If you must do your practice exam in a distracting environment, wear headphones or earplugs to reduce distractions.

- Do not guess, hoping to improve your score. Answer only when you have confidence in the answer. Then, if you get the question wrong, you can go back and think more about the question in a later study session.

Practicing Taking the ICND1 Exam

Because you are reading this chapter in the *Cisco CCENT/CCNA ICND1 100-101 Official Cert Guide*, Academic Edition, you should be preparing for either the ICND1 exam or the CCNA exam. The PCPT exam software, and the exams you get with this ICND1 book, let you take practice exams for both the ICND1 and CCNA exams.

To take an ICND1 practice exam, you need to select one or more of the ICND1 exams from PCPT. If you followed the study plan in this book, you will not have seen any of the questions in these exam databases before now. After you select one of these exams, you simply need to choose the Practice Exam option in the upper right and start the exam.

You have several options for using these practice exams. First, if you select a single practice exam each time, you can take four such practice exam events without seeing a question repeated. At that point, you could select all four exams, and the PCPT software will randomly choose a mix of questions from all four exams. By using this strategy, you should be able to have many practice exam attempts before you start to memorize the specific questions.

Table 30-3 gives you a checklist to record your different practice exam events. Note that recording both the date and the score is helpful for some other work you will do, so note both. Also, in the Time Notes section, if you finish on time, note how much extra time you had; if you run out of time, note how many questions you did not have time to answer.

Table 30-3   ICND1 Practice Exam Checklist

Exam	Date	Score	Time Notes
ICND1			
ICND1			
ICND1			
ICND1			

Practicing Taking the CCNA Exam

If you plan on using the one-exam path to CCNA, and taking the CCNA exam, you should plan on taking CCNA practice exams and avoid the ICND1 and ICND2 practice exams. The CCNA practice exams use the same mix of questions as do the ICND1 and ICND2 practice exams, and it is best to save those questions for your CCNA practice exams.

Both the ICND1 book and the ICND2 book give you the rights to four CCNA exam question banks each. If you own only one of those two books, simply use the four exams with "CCNA Full Exam" in the title. If you own both books, you have two sets of four CCNA exam banks, for a total of eight unique CCNA exams. Figure 30-1 shows the ideas and the names of the exam in the PCPT software.

ICND1 Book

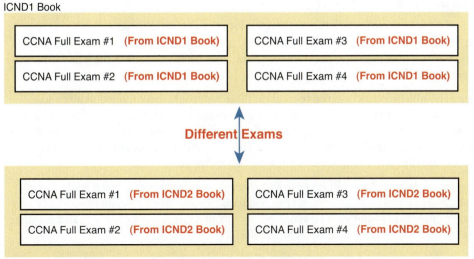

Figure 30-1   *CCNA Exam Banks in the ICND1 and ICND2 Books*

To take a CCNA exam, select one of the CCNA exam databases from the PCPT window. Then choose the Mode option of "Practice Exam" and start the exam.

Table 30-4 gives you a checklist to record your different practice exam events. Note that recording both the date and the score is helpful for some other work you will do, so note both. Also, in the Time Notes section, if you finish on time, note how much extra time you had; if you run out of time, note how many questions you did not have time to answer.

Table 30-4   CCNA Practice Exam Checklist

Exam Database Name	Date	Score	Time Notes
CCNA Exam 1 (From ICND1 Book)			
CCNA Exam 2 (From ICND1 Book)			
CCNA Exam 3 (From ICND1 Book)			
CCNA Exam 4 (From ICND1 Book)			
CCNA Exam 1 (From ICND2 Book)			
CCNA Exam 2 (From ICND2 Book)			
CCNA Exam 3 (From ICND2 Book)			
CCNA Exam 4 (From ICND2 Book)			

NOTE   The PCPT software lists, for the ICND1 book, four exam databases with the name ICND1 and four with the name CCNA. The questions in these exam databases overlap with the CCNA exams, so it makes sense to either take ICND1 practice exams or CCNA practice exams, depending on what test you are preparing for, but not both.

Advice on How to Answer Exam Questions

Open a web browser. Yes, take a break and open a web browser on any device. Do a quick search on a fun topic. Then, before you click a link, get ready to think where your eyes go for the first 5–10 seconds after you click the link. Now, click a link and look at the page. Where did your eyes go?

Interestingly, web browsers, and the content on those web pages, have trained us all to scan. Web page designers actually design content with the expectation that people will scan with different patterns. Regardless of the pattern, when reading a web page, almost no one reads sequentially, and no one reads entire sentences. They scan for the interesting graphics and the big words, and then scan the space around those noticeable items.

Other parts of our electronic culture have also changed how the average person reads. For example, many of you grew up using texting and social media, sifting through hundreds or thousands of messages—but each messages barely fills an entire sentence. (In fact, that previous sentence would not fit in a tweet, being longer than 140 characters.)

Those everyday habits have changed how we all read and think in front of a screen. Unfortunately, those same habits often hurt our scores when taking computer-based exams.

If you scan exam questions like you read web pages, texts, and tweets, you will probably make some mistakes because you missed a key fact in the question, answer, or exhibits. It helps to start at the beginning, and read all the words—a process that is amazingly unnatural for many people today.

> **NOTE** I have talked to many college professors, in multiple disciplines, and Cisco Networking Academy instructors, and they consistently tell me that the number-one test-taking issue today is that people do not read the question well enough to understand the details.

When taking the practice exams, and answering individual questions, let me make two suggestions. First, before the practice exam, think about your own personal strategy for how you will read a question. Make your approach to multiple-choice questions in particular be a conscious decision on your part. Second, if you want some suggestions on how to read an exam question, use the following strategy:

Step 1. Read the question itself, thoroughly, from start to finish.

Step 2. Scan any exhibit (usually command output) or figure.

Step 3. Scan the answers to look for the types of information. (Numeric? Terms? Single words? Phrases?)

Step 4. Reread the question thoroughly, from start to finish, to make sure that you understand it.

Step 5. Read each answer thoroughly, while referring to the figure/exhibit as needed. After reading each answer, before reading the next answer:

   A. If correct, select as correct.

   B. If for sure it is incorrect, mentally rule it out.

   C. If unsure, mentally note it as a possible correct answer.

NOTE   Cisco exams will tell you the number of correct answers. The exam software also helps you finish the question with the right number of answers noted. For example, the software prevents you from selecting too many answers. Also, if you try to move on to the next question, but have too few answers noted, the exam software asks if you truly want to move on.

Use the practice exams as a place to practice your approach to reading. Every time you click to the next question, try to read the question following your approach. If you are feeling time pressure, that is the perfect time to keep practicing your approach, to reduce and eliminate questions you miss because of scanning the question instead of reading thoroughly.

Find Knowledge Gaps Through Question Review

You just took a number of practice exams. You probably learned a lot, gained some exam-taking skills, and improved your networking knowledge and skills. But if you go back and look at all the questions you missed, you might be able to find a few small gaps in your knowledge.

One of the hardest things to find when doing your final exam preparation is to discover gaps in your knowledge and skills. In other words, what topics and skills do you need to know that you do not know? Or what topics do you think you know, but you misunderstand about some important fact? Finding gaps in your knowledge at this late stage requires more than just your gut feel about your strengths and weaknesses.

This next task uses a feature of PCPT to help you find those gaps. The PCPT software tracks each practice exam you take, remembering your answer for every question, and whether you got it wrong. You can view the results and move back and forth between seeing the question and seeing the results page. To find gaps in your knowledge, follow these steps:

Step 1.   Pick and review one of your practice exams.

Step 2.   Review each incorrect question until you are happy that you understand the question.

Step 3.   When finished with your review for a question, mark the question.

Step 4.   Review all incorrect questions from your exam until all are marked.

Step 5.   Move on to the next practice exam.

Figure 30-2 shows a sample "Question Review" page, in which all the questions were answered incorrectly. The results list a "Correct" column, with no check mark meaning that the answer was incorrect.

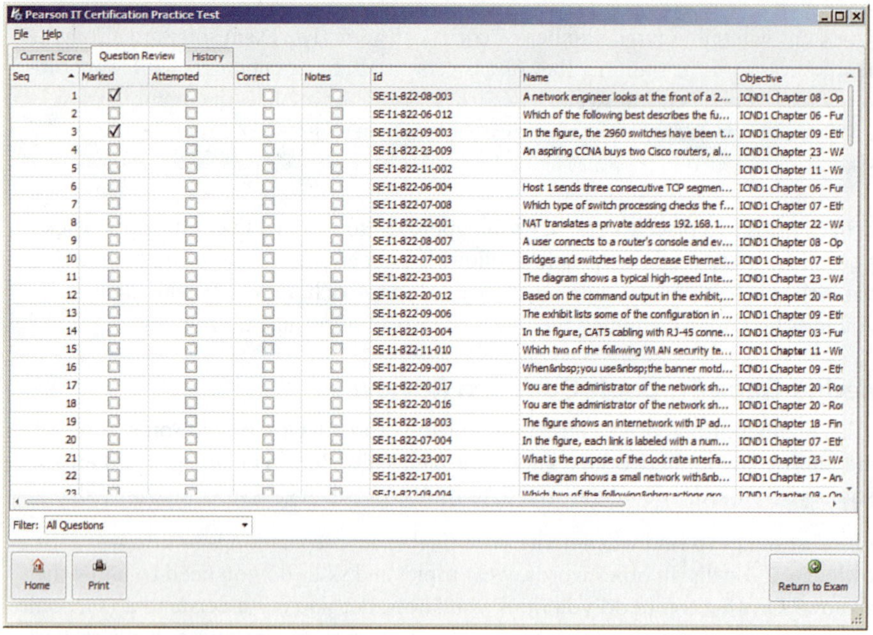

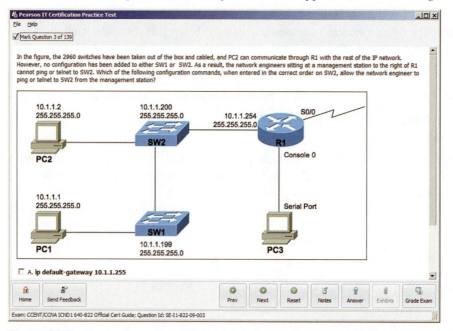

Figure 30-2 *PCPT Grading Results Page*

To perform the process of reviewing questions and marking them as complete, you can move between this Question Review page and the individual questions. Just double-click a question to move back to that question. From the question, you can click "Grade Exam" to move back to the grading results and to the Question Review page shown in Figure 30-2. The question window also shows the place to mark the question, in the upper left, as shown in Figure 30-3.

Figure 30-3 *Reviewing a Question, with Mark Feature in Upper Left*

If you want to come back later to look through the questions you missed from an earlier exam, start at the PCPT home screen. From there, instead of clicking the Start button to start a new exam, click the "View Grade History" button to see your earlier exam attempts and work through any missed questions.

Track your progress through your gap review in Table 30-5. PCPT lists your previous practice exams by date and score, so it helps to note those values in the table for comparison to the PCPT menu.

Table 30-5   Tracking Checklist for Gap Review of Practice Exams

Exam (ICND1, ICND2, or CCNA)	Original Practice Exam Date	Original Exam Score	Date Gap Review Was Completed

Practice Hands-On CLI Skills

To do well on Sim and Simlet questions, you need to be comfortable with many Cisco router and switch commands, as well as how to use them from a Cisco CLI. As described in the introduction to this book, Sim questions require you to decide what configuration command(s) need to be configured to fix a problem or to complete a working configuration. Simlet questions require you to answer multichoice questions by first using the CLI to issue **show** commands to look at the status of routers and switches in a small network.

To be ready for the exam, you need to know the following kinds of information:

CLI navigation: Basic CLI mechanics of moving into and out of user, enable, and configuration modes

Individual configuration: The meaning of the parameters of each configuration command

Feature configuration: The set of configuration commands, both required and optional, for each feature

Verification of configuration: The **show** commands that directly identify the configuration settings

Verification of status: The **show** commands that list current status values, and the ability to decide incorrect configuration or other problem causes of less-than-optimal status values

To help remember and review all this knowledge and skill, you can do the tasks listed in the next several pages.

Review Mind Maps from Part Review

During Part Review, you created different mind maps with both configuration and verification commands. To remember the specific mind maps, flip back to each part's Part Review section.

Do Labs

Whatever method you chose for building hands-on CLI skills, take some time to review and do some labs to practice the commands. At this point, you should have thought about configuration quite a bit, whether in a Simulator, on real gear, or even just as paper exercises. While it might be impractical to repeat every lab, make it a point to practice any commands and features for which you feel a little unsure about the topics from your review of the mind maps. Make sure to review lab exercises on the major topics in Table 30-6.

30

Table 30-6 Lab Checklist

Topic	Chapter	Date You Finished Lab Review
CLI basics: passwords, host name, banners, and so on	7	
Switch IPv4	8	
Switch port security	8	
VLANs	9	
VLAN trunking	9	
Router IPv4 addresses and static routes	16	
OSPFv2	17	
Standard ACLs	22	
Extended and named ACLs	23	
NAT	24	
IPv6 addressing on routers	27	
IPv6 static routes	29	
OSPFv3 (for IPv6)	29	

One great way to practice is to use the Pearson Network Simulator (the Sim) at pearsonitcertification.com/networksimulator.

As a free alternative, you can do some short 5–10-minute paper configuration labs listed on the author's blogs. Just browse the Config Museum labs in those blogs (one blog for ICND1 and one for ICND2), and choose the labs you want to use. You can try these on paper or on your own lab gear. To find the blogs, start at www.certskills.com/blogs.

Other Study Tasks

If you get to this point, and still feel the need to prepare some more, this last topic gives you two suggestions.

First, the chapter Review Activities and Part Review sections give you some useful study tasks.

Second, join in the discussions on the Cisco Learning Network. Try to answer questions asked by other learners; the process of answering makes you think much harder about the topic. When someone posts an answer with which you disagree, think about why and talk about it online. This is a great way to both learn more and build confidence.

Final Thoughts

You have studied quite a bit, worked hard, and sacrificed time and money to be ready for the exam. I hope your exam goes well, that you pass, and that you pass because you really know your stuff and will do well in your IT and networking career.

I would encourage you to celebrate when you pass, and ask advice when you do not. The Cisco Learning Network is a great place to make posts to celebrate and to ask advice for the next time around. I personally would love to hear about your progress through Twitter (@wendellodom) or my Facebook fan page (facebook.com/wendellodom). I wish you well, and congratulations for working through the entire book!

Part IX

Appendixes

Appendix A: Numeric Reference Tables

Appendix B: ICND1 Exam Updates

Glossary

Appendix A

Numeric Reference Tables

This appendix provides several useful reference tables that list numbers used throughout this book. Specifically:

Table A-1: A decimal-binary cross reference, useful when converting from decimal to binary and vice versa.

Table A-1   Decimal-Binary Cross Reference, Decimal Values 0–255

Decimal Value	Binary Value	Decimal Value	Binary Value	Decimal Value	Binary Value	Decimal Value	Binary Value
0	00000000	32	00100000	64	01000000	96	01100000
1	00000001	33	00100001	65	01000001	97	01100001
2	00000010	34	00100010	66	01000010	98	01100010
3	00000011	35	00100011	67	01000011	99	01100011
4	00000100	36	00100100	68	01000100	100	01100100
5	00000101	37	00100101	69	01000101	101	01100101
6	00000110	38	00100110	70	01000110	102	01100110
7	00000111	39	00100111	71	01000111	103	01100111
8	00001000	40	00101000	72	01001000	104	01101000
9	00001001	41	00101001	73	01001001	105	01101001
10	00001010	42	00101010	74	01001010	106	01101010
11	00001011	43	00101011	75	01001011	107	01101011
12	00001100	44	00101100	76	01001100	108	01101100
13	00001101	45	00101101	77	01001101	109	01101101
14	00001110	46	00101110	78	01001110	110	01101110
15	00001111	47	00101111	79	01001111	111	01101111
16	00010000	48	00110000	80	01010000	112	01110000
17	00010001	49	00110001	81	01010001	113	01110001
18	00010010	50	00110010	82	01010010	114	01110010
19	00010011	51	00110011	83	01010011	115	01110011
20	00010100	52	00110100	84	01010100	116	01110100
21	00010101	53	00110101	85	01010101	117	01110101
22	00010110	54	00110110	86	01010110	118	01110110
23	00010111	55	00110111	87	01010111	119	01110111
24	00011000	56	00111000	88	01011000	120	01111000
25	00011001	57	00111001	89	01011001	121	01111001
26	00011010	58	00111010	90	01011010	122	01111010
27	00011011	59	00111011	91	01011011	123	01111011
28	00011100	60	00111100	92	01011100	124	01111100
29	00011101	61	00111101	93	01011101	125	01111101
30	00011110	62	00111110	94	01011110	126	01111110
31	00011111	63	00111111	95	01011111	127	01111111

Decimal Value	Binary Value	Decimal Value	Binary Value	Decimal Value	Binary Value	Decimal Value	Binary Value
128	10000000	160	10100000	192	11000000	224	11100000
129	10000001	161	10100001	193	11000001	225	11100001
130	10000010	162	10100010	194	11000010	226	11100010
131	10000011	163	10100011	195	11000011	227	11100011
132	10000100	164	10100100	196	11000100	228	11100100
133	10000101	165	10100101	197	11000101	229	11100101
134	10000110	166	10100110	198	11000110	230	11100110
135	10000111	167	10100111	199	11000111	231	11100111
136	10001000	168	10101000	200	11001000	232	11101000
137	10001001	169	10101001	201	11001001	233	11101001
138	10001010	170	10101010	202	11001010	234	11101010
139	10001011	171	10101011	203	11001011	235	11101011
140	10001100	172	10101100	204	11001100	236	11101100
141	10001101	173	10101101	205	11001101	237	11101101
142	10001110	174	10101110	206	11001110	238	11101110
143	10001111	175	10101111	207	11001111	239	11101111
144	10010000	176	10110000	208	11010000	240	11110000
145	10010001	177	10110001	209	11010001	241	11110001
146	10010010	178	10110010	210	11010010	242	11110010
147	10010011	179	10110011	211	11010011	243	11110011
148	10010100	180	10110100	212	11010100	244	11110100
149	10010101	181	10110101	213	11010101	245	11110101
150	10010110	182	10110110	214	11010110	246	11110110
151	10010111	183	10110111	215	11010111	247	11110111
152	10011000	184	10111000	216	11011000	248	11111000
153	10011001	185	10111001	217	11011001	249	11111001
154	10011010	186	10111010	218	11011010	250	11111010
155	10011011	187	10111011	219	11011011	251	11111011
156	10011100	188	10111100	220	11011100	252	11111100
157	10011101	189	10111101	221	11011101	253	11111101
158	10011110	190	10111110	222	11011110	254	11111110
159	10011111	191	10111111	223	11011111	255	11111111

A

Table A-2: A hexadecimal-binary cross reference, useful when converting from hex to binary and vice versa.

Table A-2   Hex-Binary Cross Reference

Hex	4-Bit Binary
0	0000
1	0001
2	0010
3	0011
4	0100
5	0101
6	0110
7	0111
8	1000
9	1001
A	1010
B	1011
C	1100
D	1101
E	1110
F	1111

Table A-3: Powers of 2, from 2^1 through 2^{32}.

Table A-3   Powers of 2

X	2^x	X	2^x
1	2	17	131,072
2	4	18	262,144
3	8	19	524,288
4	16	20	1,048,576
5	32	21	2,097,152
6	64	22	4,194,304
7	128	23	8,388,608
8	256	24	16,777,216
9	512	25	33,554,432
10	1024	26	67,108,864
11	2048	27	134,217,728
12	4096	28	268,435,456
13	8192	29	536,870,912
14	16,384	30	1,073,741,824
15	32,768	31	2,147,483,648
16	65,536	32	4,294,967,296

A

Table A-4: Table of all 33 possible subnet masks, in all three formats.

Table A-4   All Subnet Masks

Decimal	Prefix	Binary
0.0.0.0	/0	00000000 00000000 00000000 00000000
128.0.0.0	/1	10000000 00000000 00000000 00000000
192.0.0.0	/2	11000000 00000000 00000000 00000000
224.0.0.0	/3	11100000 00000000 00000000 00000000
240.0.0.0	/4	11110000 00000000 00000000 00000000
248.0.0.0	/5	11111000 00000000 00000000 00000000
252.0.0.0	/6	11111100 00000000 00000000 00000000
254.0.0.0	/7	11111110 00000000 00000000 00000000
255.0.0.0	/8	11111111 00000000 00000000 00000000
255.128.0.0	/9	11111111 10000000 00000000 00000000
255.192.0.0	/10	11111111 11000000 00000000 00000000
255.224.0.0	/11	11111111 11100000 00000000 00000000
255.240.0.0	/12	11111111 11110000 00000000 00000000
255.248.0.0	/13	11111111 11111000 00000000 00000000
255.252.0.0	/14	11111111 11111100 00000000 00000000
255.254.0.0	/15	11111111 11111110 00000000 00000000
255.255.0.0	/16	11111111 11111111 00000000 00000000
255.255.128.0	/17	11111111 11111111 10000000 00000000
255.255.192.0	/18	11111111 11111111 11000000 00000000
255.255.224.0	/19	11111111 11111111 11100000 00000000
255.255.240.0	/20	11111111 11111111 11110000 00000000
255.255.248.0	/21	11111111 11111111 11111000 00000000
255.255.252.0	/22	11111111 11111111 11111100 00000000
255.255.254.0	/23	11111111 11111111 11111110 00000000
255.255.255.0	/24	11111111 11111111 11111111 00000000
255.255.255.128	/25	11111111 11111111 11111111 10000000
255.255.255.192	/26	11111111 11111111 11111111 11000000
255.255.255.224	/27	11111111 11111111 11111111 11100000
255.255.255.240	/28	11111111 11111111 11111111 11110000
255.255.255.248	/29	11111111 11111111 11111111 11111000
255.255.255.252	/30	11111111 11111111 11111111 11111100
255.255.255.254	/31	11111111 11111111 11111111 11111110
255.255.255.255	/32	11111111 11111111 11111111 11111111

Appendix B

ICND1 Exam Updates

Over time, reader feedback allows Cisco Press to gauge which topics give our readers the most problems when taking the exams. Additionally, Cisco might make small changes in the breadth of exam topics or in the emphasis of certain topics. To assist readers with those topics, the author creates new materials clarifying and expanding upon those troublesome exam topics.

The document you are viewing is Version 1.0 of this appendix and there are no updates. You can check for an updated version at www.ciscopress.com/title/9781587144851.

Glossary

10BASE-T The 10-Mbps baseband Ethernet specification using two pairs of twisted-pair cabling (Categories 3, 4, or 5): One pair transmits data and the other receives data. 10BASE-T, which is part of the IEEE 802.3 specification, has a distance limit of approximately 100 m (328 feet) per segment.

100BASE-T A name for the IEEE Fast Ethernet standard that uses two-pair copper cabling, a speed of 100 Mbps, and a maximum cable length of 100 meters.

1000BASE-T A name for the IEEE Gigabit Ethernet standard that uses four-pair copper cabling, a speed of 1000 Mbps (1 Gbps), and a maximum cable length of 100 meters.

802.1Q The IEEE standardized protocol for VLAN trunking.

802.11a The IEEE standard for wireless LANs using the U-NII spectrum, OFDM encoding, at speeds of up to 54 Mbps.

802.11b The IEEE standard for wireless LANs using the ISM spectrum, DSSS encoding, and speeds of up to 11 Mbps.

802.11g The IEEE standard for wireless LANs using the ISM spectrum, OFDM or DSSS encoding, and speeds of up to 54 Mbps.

802.11n The IEEE standard for wireless LANs using the ISM spectrum, OFDM encoding, and multiple antennas for single-stream speeds up to 150 Mbps.

A

AAA Authentication, authorization, and accounting. Authentication confirms the identity of the user or device. Authorization determines what the user or device is allowed to do. Accounting records information about access attempts, including inappropriate requests.

access interface A LAN network design term that refers to a switch interface connected to end-user devices, configured so that it does not use VLAN trunking.

access link In Frame Relay, the physical serial link that connects a Frame Relay DTE device, usually a router, to a Frame Relay switch. The access link uses the same physical layer standards as do point-to-point leased lines.

access point A wireless LAN device that provides a means for wireless clients to send data to each other and to the rest of a wired network, with the AP connecting to both the wireless LAN and the wired Ethernet LAN.

accounting In security, the recording of access attempts. *See* AAA.

address block In both IPv4 and IPv6, a set of consecutive addresses. This term is typically used for public addresses, assigned by some numbering authority (IANA/ICANN, an RIR, or an ISP).

adjacent-layer interaction The general topic of how on one computer, two adjacent layers in a networking architectural model work together, with the lower layer providing services to the higher layer.

administrative distance   In Cisco routers, a means for one router to choose between multiple routes to reach the same subnet when those routes were learned by different routing protocols. The lower the administrative distance, the better the source of the routing information.

ADSL   Asymmetric digital subscriber line. One of many DSL technologies, ADSL is designed to deliver more bandwidth downstream (from the central office to the customer site) than upstream.

All-nodes multicast address   A specific IPv6 multicast address, FF02::1, with link-local scope, used to send packets to all devices on the link that support IPv6.

All-routers multicast address   A specific IPv6 multicast address, FF02::2, with link-local scope, used to send packets to all devices that act as IPv6 routers on the local link.

Anti-X   The term used by Cisco to refer to a variety of security tools that help prevent various attacks, including antivirus, antiphishing, and antispam.

Area Border Router (ABR)   A router using OSPF in which the router has interfaces in multiple OSPF areas.

ARP   Address Resolution Protocol. An Internet protocol used to map an IP address to a MAC address. Defined in RFC 826.

ARP table   A list of IP addresses of neighbors on the same VLAN, along with their MAC addresses, as kept in memory by hosts and routers.

ARPANET   The first packet-switched network, first created around 1970, which served as the predecessor to the Internet.

asymmetric   A feature of many Internet access technologies, including DSL, cable, and modems, in which the downstream transmission rate is higher than the upstream transmission rate.

asynchronous   The lack of an imposed time ordering on a bit stream. Practically, both sides agree to the same speed, but there is no check or adjustment of the rates if they are slightly different. However, because only 1 byte per transfer is sent, slight differences in clock speed are not an issue.

ATM   Asynchronous Transfer Mode. The international standard for cell relay in which multiple service types (such as voice, video, and data) are conveyed in fixed-length (53-byte) cells. Fixed-length cells allow cell processing to occur in hardware, thereby reducing transit delays.

authentication   In security, the verification of the identity of a person or a process. *See* AAA.

authorization   In security, the determination of the rights allowed for a particular user or device. *See* AAA.

autonegotiation   An IEEE standard mechanism (802.3u) with which two nodes can exchange messages for the purpose of choosing to use the same Ethernet standards on both ends of the link, ensuring that the link functions and functions well.

autonomous system   An internetwork in the administrative control of one organization, company, or governmental agency, inside which that organization typically runs an interior gateway protocol (IGP).

auxiliary port   A physical connector on a router that is designed to be used to allow a remote terminal, or PC with a terminal emulator, to access a router using an analog modem.

B

back-to-back link   A serial link between two routers, created without CSU/DSUs, by connecting a DTE cable to one router and a DCE cable to the other. Typically used in labs to build serial links without the expense of an actual leased line from the telco.

balanced hybrid   A term that, over the years, has been used to refer to the logic behind the EIGRP routing protocol. More commonly today, this logic is referred to as advanced distance vector logic.

bandwidth   A reference to the speed of a networking link. Its origins come from earlier communications technology in which the range, or width, of the frequency band dictated how fast communications could occur.

basic service set (BSS)   In wireless LANs, a WLAN with a single access point.

bitwise Boolean AND   A Boolean AND between two numbers of the same length in which the first bit in each number is ANDed, and then the second bit in each number, and then the third, and so on.

Boolean AND   A math operation performed on a pair of one-digit binary numbers. The result is another one-digit binary number. 1 AND 1 yields 1; all other combinations yield a 0.

boot field   The low-order 4 bits of the configuration register in a Cisco router. The value in the boot field in part tells the router where to look for a Cisco IOS image to load.

broadcast address   Generally, any address that represents all devices, and can be used to send one message to all devices. In Ethernet, the MAC address of all binary 1s, or FFFF.FFFF.FFFF in hex. For IPv4, *see* subnet broadcast address.

broadcast domain   A set of all devices that receive broadcast frames originating from any device within the set. Devices in the same VLAN are in the same broadcast domain.

broadcast frame   An Ethernet frame sent to destination address FFFF.FFFF.FFFF, meaning that the frame should be delivered to all hosts on that LAN.

broadcast subnet   When subnetting a Class A, B, or C network, the one subnet in each classful network for which all subnet bits have a value of binary 1. The subnet broadcast address in this subnet has the same numeric value as the classful network's network-wide broadcast address.

bus   A common physical signal path composed of wires or other media across which signals can be sent from one part of a computer to another.

C

cable internet   An Internet access technology that uses a cable TV (CATV) cable, normally used for video, to send and receive data.

CDP   Cisco Discovery Protocol. A media- and protocol-independent device-discovery protocol that runs on most Cisco-manufactured equipment, including routers, access servers, and switches. Using CDP, a device can advertise its existence to other devices and receive information about other devices on the same LAN or on the remote side of a WAN.

CDP neighbor   A device on the other end of some communications cable that is advertising CDP updates.

CIDR   Classless interdomain routing. An RFC-standard tool for global IP address range assignment. CIDR reduces the size of Internet routers' IP routing tables, helping deal with the rapid growth of the Internet. The term *classless* refers to the fact that the summarized groups of networks represent a group of addresses that do not conform to IPv4 classful (Class A, B, and C) grouping rules.

CIDR notation   *See* prefix notation.

circuit switching   A generic reference to network services, typically WAN services, in which the provider sets up a (Layer 1) circuit between two devices, and the provider makes no attempt to interpret the meaning of the bits. *See also* packet switching.

Cisco Express Forwarding (CEF)   A method of internal processing on Cisco routers, meant to make the routing process very efficient, doing so by caching IP routes in a table that can be searched very quickly, and by remembering data link headers rather than building them for every packet that is forwarded.

classful IP network   An IPv4 Class A, B, or C network; called a classful network because these networks are defined by the class rules for IPv4 addressing.

classful routing protocol   Does not transmit the mask information along with the subnet number, and therefore must consider Class A, B, and C network boundaries and perform autosummarization at those boundaries. Does not support VLSM.

classless routing protocol   An inherent characteristic of a routing protocol, specifically that the routing protocol does send subnet masks in its routing updates, thereby removing any need to make assumptions about the addresses in a particular subnet or network, making it able to support VLSM and manual route summarization.

CLI   Command-line interface. An interface that enables the user to interact with the operating system by entering commands and optional arguments.

clock rate   The speed at which a serial link encodes bits on the transmission medium.

clock source   The device to which the other devices on the link adjust their speed when using synchronous links.

clocking   The process of supplying a signal over a cable, either on a separate pin on a serial cable or as part of the signal transitions in the transmitted signal, so that the receiving device can keep synchronization with the sending device.

codec   Coder-decoder. An integrated circuit device that transforms analog voice signals into a digital bit stream and then transforms digital signals back into analog voice signals.

collision domain   A set of network interface cards (NIC) for which a frame sent by one NIC could result in a collision with a frame sent by any other NIC in the same collision domain.

command-line interface   *See* CLI.

configuration mode   A part of the Cisco IOS Software CLI in which the user can type configuration commands that are then added to the device's currently used configuration file (running config).

configuration register   In Cisco routers, a 16-bit, user-configurable value that determines how the router functions during initialization. In software, the bit position is set by specifying a hexadecimal value using configuration commands.

connected   The single-item status code listed by a switch **show interfaces status** command, with this status referring to a working interface.

connected route   On a router, an IP route added to the routing table when the router interface is both up and has an IP address configured. The route is for the subnet that can be calculated based on the configured IP address and mask.

connection establishment   The process by which a connection-oriented protocol creates a connection. With TCP, a connection is established by a three-way transmission of TCP segments.

console port   A physical socket on a router or switch to which a cable can be connected between a computer and the router/switch, for the purpose of allowing the computer to use a terminal emulator and use the CLI to configure, verify, and troubleshoot the router/switch.

convergence   The time required for routing protocols to react to changes in the network, removing bad routes and adding new, better routes so that the current best routes are in all the routers' routing tables.

CPE   Customer premises equipment. Any equipment related to communications that is located at the customer site, as opposed to inside the telephone company's network.

crossover cable   An Ethernet cable that swaps the pair used for transmission on one device to a pair used for receiving on the device on the opposite end of the cable. In 10BASE-T and 100BASE-TX networks, this cable swaps the pair at pins 1,2 to pins 3,6 on the other end of the cable, and the pair at pins 3,6 to pins 1,2 as well.

CSMA/CD   Carrier sense multiple access with collision detection. A media-access mechanism in which devices ready to transmit data first check the channel for a carrier. If no carrier is sensed for a specific period of time, a device can transmit. If two devices transmit at once, a collision occurs and is detected by all colliding devices. This collision subsequently delays retransmissions from those devices for some random length of time.

CSU/DSU   Channel service unit/data service unit. A device that understands the Layer 1 details of serial links installed by a telco and how to use a serial cable to communicate with networking equipment such as routers.

cut-through switching   One of three options for internal processing on some models of Cisco LAN switches in which the frame is forwarded as soon as enough of the Ethernet header has been received for the switch to make a forwarding decision, including forwarding the first bits of the frame before the whole frame is received.

D

DCE   Data communications equipment. From a physical layer perspective, the device providing the clocking on a WAN link, typically a CSU/DSU, is the DCE. From a packet-switching perspective, the service provider's switch, to which a router might connect, is considered the DCE.

deencapsulation   On a computer that receives data over a network, the process in which the device interprets the lower-layer headers and, when finished with each header, removes the header, revealing the next-higher-layer PDU.

default gateway/default router   On an IP host, the IP address of some router to which the host sends packets when the packet's destination address is on a subnet other than the local subnet.

default mask   The mask used in a Class A, B, or C network that does not create any subnets; specifically, mask 255.0.0.0 for Class A networks, 255.255.0.0 for Class B networks, and 255.255.255.0 for Class C networks.

default route   On a router, the route that is considered to match all packets that are not otherwise matched by some more specific route.

demarc   The legal term for the demarcation or separation point between the telco's equipment and the customer's equipment.

denial of service (DoS)   A type of attack whose goal is to cause problems by preventing legitimate users from being able to access services, thereby preventing the normal operation of computers and networks.

DHCP   Dynamic Host Configuration Protocol. A protocol used by hosts to dynamically discover and lease an IP address, and learn the correct subnet mask, default gateway, and DNS server IP addresses.

DHCP Client   Any device that uses DHCP protocols to ask to lease an IP address from a DHCP server, or to learn any IP settings from that server.

DHCP Relay   The name of the router IOS feature that forwards DHCP messages from client to servers by changing the destination IP address from 255.255.255.255 to the IP address of the DHCP server.

DHCP Server   Software that waits for DHCP clients to request to lease IP addresses, with the server assigning a lease of an IP address as well as listing other important IP settings for the client.

directed broadcast address   *See* subnet broadcast address.

distance vector   The logic behind the behavior of some interior routing protocols, such as RIP. Distance vector routing algorithms call for each router to send its entire routing table in each update, but only to its neighbors. Distance vector routing algorithms can be prone to routing loops but are computationally simpler than link-state routing algorithms.

DNS   Domain Name System. An application layer protocol used throughout the Internet for translating host names into their associated IP addresses.

dotted-decimal notation (DDN)   The format used for IP version 4 addresses, in which four decimal values are used, separated by periods (dots).

DS0   Digital signal level 0. A 64-kbps line, or channel of a faster line inside a telco, whose origins are to support a single voice call using the original voice (PCM) codecs.

DS1   Digital signal level 1. A 1.544-Mbps line from the telco, with 24 DS0 channels of 64 kbps each, plus an 8-kbps management and framing channel. Also called a T1.

DS3   Digital signal level 3. A 44.736-Mbps line from the telco, with 28 DS1 channels plus overhead. Also called a T3.

DSL   Digital subscriber line. Public network technology that delivers high bandwidth over conventional telco local-loop copper wiring at limited distances. Typically used as an Internet access technology, connecting a user to an ISP.

DSL modem   A device that connects to a telephone line, using DSL standards, to transmit and receive data to/from a telco using DSL.

DTE   Data terminal equipment. From a Layer 1 perspective, the DTE synchronizes its clock based on the clock sent by the DCE. From a packet-switching perspective, the DTE is the device outside the service provider's network, typically a router.

dual stack   A mode of operation in which a host or router runs both IPv4 and IPv6.

duplex mismatch   On opposite ends of any Ethernet link, the condition in which one of the two devices uses full-duplex logic and the other uses half-duplex logic, resulting in unnecessary frame discards and retransmissions on the link.

Duplicate Address Detection (DAD)   A term used in IPv6 to refer to how hosts first check whether another host is using a unicast address before the first host uses that address.

E

E1   Similar to a T1, but used in Europe. It uses a rate of 2.048 Mbps and 32 64-kbps channels, with one channel reserved for framing and other overhead.

EIGRP   Enhanced Interior Gateway Routing Protocol. An advanced version of IGRP developed by Cisco. Provides superior convergence properties and operating efficiency and combines the advantages of link-state protocols with those of distance vector protocols.

EIGRP version 6   The version of the EIGRP routing protocol that supports IPv6, and not IPv4.

enable mode   A part of the Cisco IOS CLI in which the user can use the most powerful and potentially disruptive commands on a router or switch, including the ability to then reach configuration mode and reconfigure the router.

encapsulation   The placement of data from a higher-layer protocol behind the header (and in some cases, between a header and trailer) of the next-lower-layer protocol. For example, an IP packet could be encapsulated in an Ethernet header and trailer before being sent over an Ethernet.

encryption   Applying a specific algorithm to data to alter the appearance of the data, making it incomprehensible to those who are not authorized to see the information.

error detection   The process of discovering whether a data link level frame was changed during transmission. This process typically uses a Frame Check Sequence (FCS) field in the data link trailer.

error disabled   An interface state on LAN switches that can be the result of one of many security violations.

error recovery   The process of noticing when some transmitted data was not successfully received and resending the data until it is successfully received.

Ethernet   A series of LAN standards defined by the IEEE, originally invented by Xerox Corporation and developed jointly by Xerox, Intel, and Digital Equipment Corporation.

Ethernet address   A 48-bit (6-byte) binary number, usually written as a 12-digit hexadecimal number, used to identify Ethernet nodes in an Ethernet network. Ethernet frame headers list a destination and source address field, used by the Ethernet devices to deliver Ethernet frames to the correct destination.

Ethernet frame   A term referring to an Ethernet data link header and trailer, plus the data encapsulated between the header and trailer.

Ethernet link   A generic term for any physical link between two Ethernet nodes, no matter what type of cabling is used.

Ethernet port   A generic term for the opening on the side of any Ethernet node, typically in an Ethernet NIC or LAN switch, into which an Ethernet cable can be connected.

EtherType   Jargon that shortens the term "Ethernet Type," which refers to the Type field in the Ethernet header. The Type field identifies the type of packet encapsulated inside an Ethernet frame.

EUI-64   Literally, a standard for an extended unique identifier that is 64 bits long. Specifically for IPv6, a set of rules for forming the a 64-bit identifier, used as the interface ID in IPv6 addresses, by starting with a 48-bit MAC address, inserting FFFE (hex) in the middle, and inverting the seventh bit.

extended access list   A list of IOS **access-list** global configuration commands that can match multiple parts of an IP packet, including the source and destination IP address and TCP/UDP ports, for the purpose of deciding which packets to discard and which to allow through the router.

exterior gateway protocol (EGP)   A routing protocol that was designed to exchange routing information between different autonomous systems.

F

Fast Ethernet   The common name for all the IEEE standards that send data at 100 megabits per second.

filter   Generally, a process or a device that screens network traffic for certain characteristics, such as source address, destination address, or protocol, and determines whether to forward or discard that traffic based on the established criteria.

firewall   A device that forwards packets between the less secure and more secure parts of the network, applying rules that determine which packets are allowed to pass, and which are not.

flash   A type of read/write permanent memory that retains its contents even with no power applied to the memory, and uses no moving parts, making the memory less likely to fail over time.

flooding   The result of the LAN switch forwarding process for broadcasts and unknown unicast frames. Switches forward these frames out all interfaces, except the interface in which the frame arrived. Switches also flood multicasts by default, although this behavior can be changed.

flow control   The process of regulating the amount of data sent by a sending computer toward a receiving computer. Several flow control mechanisms exist, including TCP flow control, which uses windowing.

forward   To send a frame received in one interface out another interface, toward its ultimate destination.

forward acknowledgment   A process used by protocols that do error recovery, in which the number that acknowledges data lists the next data that should be sent, not the last data that was successfully received.

four-wire circuit   A line from the telco with four wires, composed of two twisted-pair wires. Each pair is used to send in one direction, so a four-wire circuit allows full-duplex communication.

fragment-free switching   One of three internal processing options on some Cisco LAN switches in which the first bits of the frame can be forwarded before the entire frame is received, but not until the first 64 bytes of the frame are received, in which case, in a well-designed LAN, collision fragments should not occur as a result of this forwarding logic.

frame   A term referring to a data link header and trailer, plus the data encapsulated between the header and trailer.

Frame Check Sequence   A field in many data link trailers used as part of the error-detection process.

Frame Relay   An international standard data link protocol that defines the capabilities to create a frame-switched (packet-switched) service, allowing DTE devices (typically routers) to send data to many other devices using a single physical connection to the Frame Relay service.

Frequency Hopping Spread Spectrum   A method of encoding data on a wireless LAN in which consecutive transmissions occur on different nearby frequency bands as compared with the prior transmission. Not used in modern WLAN standards.

full-duplex   Generically, any communication in which two communicating devices can concurrently send and receive data. In Ethernet LANs, the allowance for both devices to send and receive at the same time, allowed when both devices disable their CSMA/CD logic.

full mesh   A network topology in which more than two devices can physically communicate and, by choice, all pairs of devices are allowed to communicate directly.

G

Gigabit Ethernet   The common name for all the IEEE standards that send data at 1 gigabit per second.

global routing prefix   An IPv6 prefix that defines an IPv6 address block made up of global unicast addresses, assigned to one organization, so that the organization has a block of globally unique IPv6 addresses to use in its network.

global unicast address   A type of unicast IPv6 address that has been allocated from a range of public globally unique IP addresses, as registered through IANA/ICANN, its member agencies, and other registries or ISPs.

H

half-duplex   Generically, any communication in which only one device at a time can send data. In Ethernet LANs, the normal result of the CSMA/CD algorithm that enforces the rule that only one device should send at any point in time.

HDLC   High-Level Data Link Control. A bit-oriented synchronous data link layer protocol developed by the International Organization for Standardization (ISO).

head end   The upstream, transmit end of a cable TV (CATV) installation.

header   In computer networking, a set of bytes placed in front of some other data, encapsulating that data, as defined by a particular protocol.

host   Any device that uses an IP address.

host address   The IP address assigned to a network card on a computer.

host name   The alphameric name of an IP host.

host part   A term used to describe a part of an IPv4 address that is used to uniquely identify a host inside a subnet. The host part is identified by the bits of value 0 in the subnet mask.

host route   A route with a /32 mask, which by virtue of this mask represents a route to a single host IP address.

HTML   Hypertext Markup Language. A simple document-formatting language that uses tags to indicate how a given part of a document should be interpreted by a viewing application, such as a web browser.

HTTP   Hypertext Transfer Protocol. The protocol used by web browsers and web servers to transfer files, such as text and graphic files.

hub   A LAN device that provides a centralized connection point for LAN cabling, repeating any received electrical signal out all other ports, thereby creating a logical bus. Hubs do not interpret the electrical signals as a frame of bits, so hubs are considered to be Layer 1 devices.

I

IANA   The Internet Assigned Numbers Authority (IANA). An organization that owns the rights to assign many operating numbers and facts about how the global Internet works, including public IPv4 and IPv6 addresses. *See also* ICANN.

ICANN   The Internet Corporation for Assigned Names and Numbers. An organization appointed by IANA to oversee the distributed process of assigning public IPv4 and IPv6 addresses across the globe.

ICMP   Internet Control Message Protocol. A TCP/IP network layer protocol that reports errors and provides other information relevant to IP packet processing.

IEEE   Institute of Electrical and Electronics Engineers. A professional organization that develops communications and network standards, among other activities.

IEEE 802.2   An IEEE LAN protocol that specifies an implementation of the LLC sublayer of the data link layer.

IEEE 802.3   A set of IEEE LAN protocols that specifies the many variations of what is known today as an Ethernet LAN.

IETF   The Internet Engineering Task Force. The IETF serves as the primary organization that works directly to create new TCP/IP standards.

inactivity timer   For switch MAC address tables, a timer associated with each entry that counts time upward from 0 and is reset to 0 each time a switch receives a frame with the same MAC address. The entries with the largest timers can be removed to make space for additional MAC address table entries.

inside global   For packets sent to and from a host that resides inside the trusted part of a network that uses NAT, a term referring to the IP address used in the headers of those packets when those packets traverse the global (public) Internet.

inside local   For packets sent to and from a host that resides inside the trusted part of a network that uses NAT, a term referring to the IP address used in the headers of those packets when those packets traverse the enterprise (private) part of the network.

interior gateway protocol (IGP)   *See* interior routing protocol.

interior routing protocol   A routing protocol designed for use within a single organization.

intrusion detection system (IDS)   A security function that examines more complex traffic patterns against a list of both known attack signatures and general characteristics of how attacks can be carried out, rating each perceived threat and reporting the threats.

intrusion prevention system (IPS)   A security function that examines more complex traffic patterns against a list of both known attack signatures and general characteristics of how attacks can be carried out, rating each perceived threat, and reacting to prevent the more significant threats.

IOS   Cisco Internetwork Operating System Software that provides the majority of a router's or switch's features, with the hardware providing the remaining features.

IOS image   A file that contains the IOS.

IP   Internet Protocol. The network layer protocol in the TCP/IP stack, providing routing and logical addressing standards and services.

IP address (IP version 4)   In IP version 4 (IPv4), a 32-bit address assigned to hosts using TCP/IP. Each address consists of a network number, an optional subnetwork number, and a host number. The network and subnetwork numbers together are used for routing, and the host number is used to address an individual host within the network or subnetwork.

IP address (IP version 6)   In IP version 6 (IPv6), a 128-bit address assigned to hosts using TCP/IP. Addresses use different formats, commonly using a routing prefix, subnet, and interface ID, corresponding to the IPv4 network, subnet, and host parts of an address.

IP network   *See* classful IP network.

IP packet   An IP header, followed by the data encapsulated after the IP header, but specifically not including any headers and trailers for layers below the network layer.

IP subnet   Subdivisions of a Class A, B, or C network, as configured by a network administrator. Subnets allow a single Class A, B, or C network to be used instead of multiple networks, and still allow for a large number of groups of IP addresses, as is required for efficient IP routing.

IP version 4   Literally, the version of the Internet Protocol defined in an old RFC 791, standardized in 1980, and used as the basis of TCP/IP networks and the Internet for over 30 years.

IP version 6   A newer version of the Internet Protocol defined in RFC 2460, as well as many other RFCs, whose creation was motivated by the need to avoid the IPv4 address exhaustion problem.

IPv4 address exhaustion   The process by which the public IPv4 addresses, available to create the Internet, were consumed through the 1980s until today, with the expectation that eventually the world would run out of available IPv4 addresses.

IPv6 neighbor table   The IPv6 equivalent of the ARP table. A table that lists IPv6 addresses of other hosts on the same link, along with their matching MAC addresses, as typically learned using Neighbor Discovery Protocol (NDP).

ISDN   Integrated Services Digital Network. A service offered by telephone companies that permits telephone networks to carry data, voice, and other traffic. Often used as an Internet access technology, as well as dial backup when routers lose their normal WAN communications links.

ISL   Inter-Switch Link. A Cisco-proprietary protocol that maintains VLAN information as traffic flows between switches and routers.

ISO   International Organization for Standardization. An international organization that is responsible for a wide range of standards, including many standards relevant to networking. The ISO developed the OSI reference model, a popular networking reference model.

K

keepalive   A proprietary feature of Cisco routers in which the router sends messages on a periodic basis as a means of letting the neighboring router know that the first router is still alive and well.

L

L4PDU   Layer 4 protocol data unit. The data compiled by a Layer 4 protocol, including Layer 4 headers and encapsulated high-layer data, but not including lower-layer headers and trailers.

Layer 3 protocol   A protocol that has characteristics like OSI Layer 3, which defines logical addressing and routing. IPv4 and IPv6 are Layer 3 protocols.

Layer 3 switch   *See* multilayer switch.

learning   The process used by switches for discovering MAC addresses, and their relative location, by looking at the source MAC address of all frames received by a bridge or switch.

leased line   A serial communications circuit between two points, provided by some service provider, typically a telephone company (telco). Because the telco does not sell a physical cable between the two endpoints, instead charging a monthly fee for the ability to send bits between the two sites, the service is considered to be a leased service.

link-local address   A type of unicast IPv6 address that represents an interface on a single data link. Packets sent to a link-local address cross only that particular link and are never forwarded to other subnets by a router. Used for communications that do not need to leave the local link.

link-local scope   With IPv6 multicasts, a term that refers to the parts (scope) of the network to which a multicast packet can flow, with link-local referring to the fact that the packet stays on the subnet in which it originated.

link-state   A classification of the underlying algorithm used in some routing protocols. Link-state protocols build a detailed database that lists links (subnets) and their state (up, down), from which the best routes can then be calculated.

link-state advertisement (LSA)   In OSPF, the name of the data structure that resides inside the LSDB and describes in detail the various components in a network, including routers and links (subnets).

link-state database (LSDB)   In OSPF, the data structure in RAM of a router that holds the various LSAs, with the collective LSAs representing the entire topology of the network.

LLC   Logical Link Control. The higher of the two data link layer sublayers defined by the IEEE. Synonymous with IEEE 802.2.

local loop   A line from the premises of a telephone subscriber to the telephone company CO.

local subnet broadcast address   IPv4 address 255.255.255.255. A packet sent to this address is sent as a data link broadcast, but only flows to hosts in the subnet into which it was originally sent. Routers do not forward these packets.

local username   A username (with matching password), configured on a router or switch. It is considered local because it exists on the router or switch, and not on a remote server.

logical address   A generic reference to addresses as defined by Layer 3 protocols that do not have to be concerned with the physical details of the underlying physical media. Used mainly to contrast these addresses with data link addresses, which are generically considered to be physical addresses because they differ based on the type of physical medium.

M

MAC   Media Access Control. The lower of the two sublayers of the data link layer defined by the IEEE. Synonymous with IEEE 802.3 for Ethernet LANs.

MAC address   A standardized data link layer address that is required for every device that connects to a LAN. Ethernet MAC addresses are 6 bytes long and are controlled by the IEEE. Also known as a *hardware address*, a *MAC layer address*, and a *physical address*.

metric   A unit of measure used by routing protocol algorithms to determine the best route for traffic to use to reach a particular destination.

microsegmentation   The process in LAN design by which every switch port connects to a single device, with no hubs connected to the switch ports, creating a separate collision domain per interface. The term's origin relates to the fact that one definition for the word "segment" is "collision domain," with a switch separating each switch port into a separate collision domain or segment.

modem   Modulator-demodulator. A device that converts between digital and analog signals so that a computer can send data to another computer using analog telephone lines. At the source, a modem converts digital signals to a form suitable for transmission over analog communication facilities. At the destination, the analog signals are returned to their digital form.

multilayer switch   A LAN switch that can also perform Layer 3 routing functions. The name comes from the fact that this device makes forwarding decisions based on logic from multiple OSI layers (Layers 2 and 3).

multimode   A type of fiber-optic cabling with a larger core than single-mode cabling, allowing light to enter at multiple angles. Such cabling has lower bandwidth than single-mode fiber but requires a typically cheaper light source, such as an LED rather than a laser.

N

name server   A server connected to a network that resolves network names into network addresses.

named access list   An ACL that identifies the various statements in the ACL based on a name, rather than a number.

NAT   Network Address Translation. A mechanism for reducing the need for globally unique IP addresses. NAT allows an organization with addresses that are not globally unique to connect to the Internet, by translating those addresses into public addresses in the globally routable address space.

neighbor   In routing protocols, another router with which a router decides to exchange routing information.

Neighbor Advertisement (NA)   A message defined by the IPv6 Neighbor Discovery Protocol (NDP), used to declare to other neighbors a host's MAC address. Sometimes sent in response to a previously received NDP Neighbor Solicitation (NS) message.

Neighbor Discovery Protocol (NDP)   A protocol that is part of the IPv6 protocol suite, used to discover and exchange information about devices on the same subnet (neighbors). In particular, it replaces the IPv4 ARP protocol.

Neighbor Solicitation (NS)   A message defined by the IPv6 Neighbor Discovery Protocol (NDP), used to ask a neighbor to reply with a Neighbor Advertisement, which lists the neighbor's MAC address.

network   A collection of computers, printers, routers, switches, and other devices that can communicate with each other over some transmission medium.

network address   *See* network number.

network broadcast address   In IPv4, a special address in each classful network that can be used to broadcast a packet to all hosts in that same classful network. Numerically, the address has the same value as the network number in the network part of the address and all 255s in the host octets—for example, 10.255.255.255 is the network broadcast address for classful network 10.0.0.0.

network interface card (NIC)   A computer card, sometimes an expansion card and sometimes integrated into the motherboard of the computer, that provides the electronics and other functions to connect to a computer network. Today, most NICs are specifically Ethernet NICs, and most have an RJ-45 port, the most common type of Ethernet port.

network number   A number that uses dotted-decimal notation like IP addresses, but the number itself represents all hosts in a single Class A, B, or C IP network.

network part   The portion of an IPv4 address that is either 1, 2, or 3 octets/bytes long, based on whether the address is in a Class A, B, or C network.

Network Time Protocol (NTP)   A protocol used to synchronize time-of-day clocks so that multiple devices use the same time of day, which allows log messages to be more easily matched based on their timestamps.

networking model   A generic term referring to any set of protocols and standards collected into a comprehensive grouping that, when followed by the devices in a network, allows all the devices to communicate. Examples include TCP/IP and OSI.

next-hop router   In an IP route in a routing table, part of a routing table entry that refers to the next IP router (by IP address) that should receive packets that match the route.

NIC   *See* network interface card.

NVRAM   Nonvolatile RAM. A type of random-access memory (RAM) that retains its contents when a unit is powered off.

O

ordered data transfer   A networking function, included in TCP, in which the protocol defines how the sending host should number the data transmitted, defines how the receiving device should attempt to reorder the data if it arrives out of order, and specifies to discard the data if it cannot be delivered in order.

OSI   Open System Interconnection reference model. A network architectural model developed by the ISO. The model consists of seven layers, each of which specifies particular network functions, such as addressing, flow control, error control, encapsulation, and reliable message transfer.

OSPF   Open Shortest Path First. A popular link-state IGP that uses a link-state database and the Shortest Path First (SPF) algorithm to calculate the best routes to reach each known subnet.

OSPF version 2   The version of the OSPF routing protocol that supports IPv4, and not IPv6, and has been commonly used for over 20 years.

OSPF version 3   The version of the OSPF routing protocol that supports IPv6, and not IPv4.

outgoing interface   In an IP route in a routing table, part of a routing table entry that refers to the local interface out which the local router should forward packets that match the route.

overlapping subnets   An (incorrect) IP subnet design condition in which one subnet's range of addresses includes addresses in the range of another subnet.

P

packet   A logical grouping of bytes that includes the network layer header and encapsulated data, but specifically does not include any headers and trailers below the network layer.

packet switching   A generic reference to network services, typically WAN services, in which the service examines the contents of the transmitted data to make some type of forwarding decision. This term is mainly used to contrast with the WAN term *circuit switching*, in which the provider sets up a (Layer 1) circuit between two devices and the provider makes no attempt to interpret the meaning of the bits.

partial mesh   A network topology in which more than two devices could physically communicate but, by choice, only a subset of the pairs of devices connected to the network is allowed to communicate directly.

patch cable   An Ethernet cable, usually short, that connects from a device's Ethernet port to a wall plate or switch. With wiring inside a building, electricians prewire from the wiring closet to each cubicle or other location, with a patch cable connecting the short distance from the wall plate to the user device.

PDU   Protocol data unit. An OSI term to refer generically to a grouping of information by a particular layer of the OSI model. More specifically, an L*x*PDU would imply the data and headers as defined by Layer *x*.

ping   An Internet Control Message Protocol (ICMP) echo message and its reply; ping often is used in IP networks to test the reachability of a network device.

pinout   The documentation and implementation of which wires inside a cable connect to each pin position in any connector.

port   In TCP and UDP, a number that is used to uniquely identify the application process that either sent (source port) or should receive (destination port) data. In LAN switching, another term for switch interface.

Port Address Translation (PAT)   A NAT feature in which one inside global IP address supports over 65,000 concurrent TCP and UDP connections.

port number   A field in a TCP or UDP header that identifies the application that either sent (source port) or should receive (destination port) the data inside the data segment.

port security   A Cisco switch feature in which the switch watches Ethernet frames that come in an interface (a port), tracks the source MAC addresses of all such frames, and takes a security action if the number of different such MAC addresses is exceeded.

PPP   Point-to-Point Protocol. A protocol that provides router-to-router and host-to-network connections over synchronous point-to-point and asynchronous point-to-point circuits.

prefix   In IPv6, this term refers to the number that identifies a group of IPv6 addresses. An IPv6 subnet identifier.

prefix length   In IPv6, the number of bits in an IPv6 prefix.

prefix notation (IP version 4)   A shorter way to write a subnet mask in which the number of binary 1s in the mask is simply written in decimal. For example, /24 denotes the subnet mask with 24 binary 1 bits in the subnet mask. The number of bits of value binary 1 in the mask is considered to be the prefix length.

private addresses   IP addresses in several Class A, B, and C networks that are set aside for use inside private organizations. These addresses, as defined in RFC 1918, are not routable through the Internet.

problem isolation   The part of the troubleshooting process in which the engineer attempts to rule out possible causes of the problem until the root cause of the problem can be identified.

protocol data unit (PDU)   A generic term referring to the header defined by some layer of a networking model, and the data encapsulated by the header (and possibly trailer) of that layer, but specifically not including any lower-layer headers and trailers.

Protocol Type field   A field in a LAN header that identifies the type of header that follows the LAN header. Includes the DIX Ethernet Type field, the IEEE 802.2 DSAP field, and the SNAP protocol Type field.

PSTN   Public switched telephone network. A general term referring to the variety of telephone networks and services in place worldwide. Sometimes called *POTS*, or *plain old telephone service*.

PTT   Post, telephone, and telegraph. A government agency that provides telephone services. PTTs exist in some areas outside of North America and provide both local and long-distance telephone services.

public IP address   An IP address that is part of a registered network number, as assigned by an Internet Assigned Numbers Authority (IANA) member agency, so that only the organization to which the address is registered is allowed to use the address. Routers in the Internet should have routes allowing them to forward packets to all the publicly registered IP addresses.

Q

quartet   A term used in this book, but not in other references, to refer to a set of four hex digits in an IPv6 address.

R

RAM   Random-access memory. A type of volatile memory that can be read and written by a microprocessor.

RFC   Request For Comments. A document used as the primary means for communicating information about the TCP/IP protocols. Some RFCs are designated by the Internet Architecture Board (IAB) as Internet standards, and others are informational. RFCs are available online from numerous sources, including www.rfc-editor.org.

RIP   Routing Information Protocol. An interior gateway protocol (IGP) that uses distance vector logic and router hop count as the metric. RIP version 2 (RIP-2) replaced the older RIP version 1 (RIP-1), with RIP-2 providing more features, including support for VLSM.

RJ-45   A popular type of cabling connector used for Ethernet cabling. It is similar to the RJ-11 connector used for telephone wiring in homes in the United States. RJ-45 allows the connection of eight wires.

ROM   Read-only memory. A type of nonvolatile memory that can be read but not written to by the microprocessor.

root cause   A troubleshooting term that refers to the reason why a problem exists, specifically a reason for which, if changed, the problem would either be solved or changed to a different problem.

routed protocol   A protocol that defines packets that can be routed by a router. Examples of routed protocols include IPv4 and IPv6.

Router Advertisement (RA)   A message defined by the IPv6 Neighbor Discovery Protocol (NDP), used by routers to announce their willingness to act as an IPv6 router on a link. These can be sent in response to a previously received NDP Router Solicitation (RS) message.

router ID (RID)   In OSPF, a 32-bit number, written in dotted-decimal notation, that uniquely identifies each router.

Router Solicitation (RS)   A message defined by the IPv6 Neighbor Discovery Protocol (NDP), used to ask any routers on the link to reply, identifying the router, plus other configuration settings (prefixes and prefix lengths).

routing protocol   A set of messages and processes with which routers can exchange information about routes to reach subnets in a particular network. Examples of routing protocols include the Enhanced Interior Gateway Routing Protocol (EIGRP), the Open Shortest Path First (OSPF) protocol, and the Routing Information Protocol (RIP).

routing table   A list of routes in a router, with each route listing the destination subnet and mask, the router interface out which to forward packets destined to that subnet, and as needed, the next-hop router's IP address.

routing update   A generic reference to any routing protocol's messages in which it sends routing information to a neighbor.

running-config file   In Cisco IOS switches and routers, the name of the file that resides in RAM memory, holding the device's currently used configuration.

S

same-layer interaction   The communication between two networking devices for the purposes of the functions defined at a particular layer of a networking model, with that communication happening by using a header defined by that layer of the model. The two devices set values in the header, send the header and encapsulated data, with the receiving device(s) interpreting the header to decide what action to take.

Secure Shell (SSH)   A TCP/IP application layer protocol that supports terminal emulation between a client and server, using dynamic key exchange and encryption to keep the communications private.

segment   In TCP, a term used to describe a TCP header and its encapsulated data (also called an *L4PDU*). Also in TCP, the process of accepting a large chunk of data from the application layer and breaking it into smaller pieces that fit into TCP segments. In Ethernet, a segment is either a single Ethernet cable or a single collision domain (no matter how many cables are used).

segmentation   The process of breaking a large piece of data from an application into pieces appropriate in size to be sent through the network.

serial cable   A type of cable with many different styles of connectors used to connect a router to an external CSU/DSU on a leased-line installation.

serial interface   A type of interface on a router, used to connect to some types of WAN links, particularly leased lines and Frame Relay access links.

setup mode   An option on Cisco IOS switches and routers that prompts the user for basic configuration information, resulting in new running-config and startup-config files.

shared Ethernet   An Ethernet that uses a hub, or even the original coaxial cabling, that results in the devices having to take turns sending data, sharing the available bandwidth.

Shortest Path First (SPF) algorithm   The name of the algorithm used by link-state routing protocols to analyze the LSDB and find the least-cost routes from that router to each subnet.

single-mode   A type of fiber-optic cabling with a narrow core that allows light to enter only at a single angle. Such cabling has a higher bandwidth than multimode fiber but requires a light source with a narrow spectral width (such as a laser).

sliding windows   For protocols such as TCP that allow the receiving device to dictate the amount of data the sender can send before receiving an acknowledgment—a concept called a *window*—a reference to the fact that the mechanism to grant future windows is typically just a number that grows upward slowly after each acknowledgment, sliding upward.

solicited-node multicast address   A type of IPv6 multicast address, with link-local scope, used to send packets to all hosts in the subnet that share the same value in the last six hex digits of their unicast IPv6 addresses. Begins with FF02::1:FF00:0/104.

SONET   Synchronous Optical Network. A standard format for transporting a wide range of digital telecommunications services over optical fiber.

Spanning Tree Protocol (STP)   A protocol that uses the Spanning Tree algorithm, allowing a switch to dynamically work around loops in a network topology by creating a spanning tree. Switches exchange bridge protocol data unit (BPDU) messages with other switches to detect loops and then remove the loops by blocking selected switch interfaces.

standard access list   A list of IOS global configuration commands that can match only a packet's source IP address, for the purpose of deciding which packets to discard and which to allow through the router.

star   A network topology in which endpoints on a network are connected to a common central device by point-to-point links.

startup-config file   In Cisco IOS switches and routers, the name of the file that resides in NVRAM memory, holding the device's configuration that will be loaded into RAM as the running-config file when the device is next reloaded or powered on.

stateful DHCP   A term used in IPv6 to contrast with stateless DHCP. Stateful DHCP keeps track of which clients have been assigned which IPv6 addresses (state information).

Stateless Address Autoconfiguration (SLAAC)   A feature of IPv6 in which a host or router can be assigned an IPv6 unicast address without the need for a stateful DHCP server.

stateless DHCP   A term used in IPv6 to contrast with stateful DHCP. Stateless DHCP servers don't lease IPv6 addresses to clients. Instead, they supply other useful information, such as DNS server IP addresses, but with no need to track information about the clients (state information).

static route   An IP route on a router created by the user configuring the details of the route on the local router.

store-and-forward switching   One of three internal processing options on some Cisco LAN switches in which the Ethernet frame must be completely received before the switch can begin forwarding the first bit of the frame.

STP   Shielded twisted-pair. This type of cabling has a layer of shielded insulation to reduce electromagnetic interference (EMI).

straight-through cable   In Ethernet, a cable that connects the wire on pin 1 on one end of the cable to pin 1 on the other end of the cable, pin 2 on one end to pin 2 on the other end, and so on.

subnet   Subdivisions of a Class A, B, or C network, as configured by a network administrator. Subnets allow a single Class A, B, or C network to be used instead of multiple networks, and still allow for a large number of groups of IP addresses, as is required for efficient IP routing.

subnet address   *See* subnet number.

subnet broadcast address   A special address in each subnet, specifically the largest numeric address in the subnet, designed so that packets sent to this address should be delivered to all hosts in that subnet.

subnet ID (IPv4)   *See* subnet number.

subnet ID (IPv6)   The number that represents the IPv6 subnet. Also known as the IPv6 prefix, or more formally as the subnet router anycast address.

subnet mask   A 32-bit number that numerically describes the format of an IP address, by representing the combined network and subnet bits in the address with mask bit values of 1, and representing the host bits in the address with mask bit values of 0.

subnet number   In IPv4, a dotted-decimal number that represents all addresses in a single subnet. Numerically, the smallest value in the range of numbers in a subnet, reserved so that it cannot be used as a unicast IP address by a host.

subnet part   In a subnetted IPv4 address, interpreted with classful addressing rules, one of three parts of the structure of an IP address, with the subnet part uniquely identifying different subnets of a classful IP network.

subnetting   The process of subdividing a Class A, B, or C network into smaller groups called subnets.

switch   A network device that filters, forwards, and floods Ethernet frames based on the destination address of each frame.

switched Ethernet   An Ethernet that uses a switch, and particularly not a hub, so that the devices connected to one switch port do not have to contend to use the bandwidth available on another port. This term contrasts with *shared Ethernet*, in which the devices must share bandwidth, whereas switched Ethernet provides much more capacity, as the devices do not have to share the available bandwidth.

symmetric   A feature of many Internet access technologies in which the downstream transmission rate is the same as the upstream transmission rate.

synchronous   The imposition of time ordering on a bit stream. Practically, a device will try to use the same speed as another device on the other end of a serial link. However, by examining transitions between voltage states on the link, the device can notice slight variations in the speed on each end and can adjust its speed accordingly.

T

T1   A line from the telco that allows transmission of data at 1.544 Mbps, with the ability to treat the line as 24 different 64-kbps DS0 channels (plus 8 kbps of overhead).

TCP   Transmission Control Protocol. A connection-oriented transport layer TCP/IP protocol that provides reliable data transmission.

TCP/IP   Transmission Control Protocol/Internet Protocol. A common name for the suite of protocols developed by the U.S. Department of Defense in the 1970s to support the construction of worldwide internetworks. TCP and IP are the two best-known protocols in the suite.

telco   A common abbreviation for telephone company.

Telnet   The standard terminal-emulation application layer protocol in the TCP/IP protocol stack. Telnet is used for remote terminal connection, enabling users to log in to remote systems and use resources as if they were connected to a local system. Telnet is defined in RFC 854.

trace   Short for traceroute. A program available on many systems that traces the path that a packet takes to a destination. It is used mostly to troubleshoot routing problems between hosts.

trailer   In computer networking, a set of bytes placed behind some other data, encapsulating that data, as defined by a particular protocol. Typically, only data link layer protocols define trailers.

transparent bridge   The name of a networking device that was a precursor to modern LAN switches. Bridges forward frames between LAN segments based on the destination MAC address. Transparent bridging is so named because the presence of bridges is transparent to network end nodes.

trunk   In campus LANs, an Ethernet segment over which the devices add a VLAN header that identifies the VLAN in which the frame exists.

trunk interface   A switch interface configured so that it operates using VLAN trunking (either 802.1Q or ISL).

trunking   Also called VLAN trunking. A method (using either the Cisco ISL protocol or the IEEE 802.1Q protocol) to support multiple VLANs, allowing traffic from those VLANs to cross a single link.

trunking administrative mode   The configured trunking setting on a Cisco switch interface, as configured with the **switchport mode** command.

trunking operational mode   The current behavior of a Cisco switch interface for VLAN trunking.

twisted-pair   Transmission medium consisting of two insulated wires, with the wires twisted around each other in a spiral. An electrical circuit flows over the wire pair, with the current in opposite directions on each wire, which significantly reduces the interference between the two wires.

U

UDP   User Datagram Protocol. Connectionless transport layer protocol in the TCP/IP protocol stack. UDP is a simple protocol that exchanges datagrams without acknowledgments or guaranteed delivery.

unicast address   Generally, any address in networking that represents a single device or interface, instead of a group of addresses (as would be represented by a multicast or broadcast address).

unicast IP address   An IP address that represents a single interface. In IPv4, these addresses come from the Class A, B, and C ranges.

unique local address   A type of IPv6 unicast address meant as a replacement for IPv4 private addresses.

unknown unicast frame   An Ethernet frame whose destination MAC address is not listed in a switch's MAC address table, so the switch must flood the frame.

up and up   Jargon referring to the two interface states on a Cisco IOS router or switch (line status and protocol status), with the first "up" referring to the line status and the second "up" referring to the protocol status. An interface in this state should be able to pass data link frames.

update timer   A timer used by a router to indicate when to send the next routing update.

URL   Uniform Resource Locator. A standard for how to refer to any piece of information retrievable via a TCP/IP network, most notably used to identify web pages. For example, http://www.certskills.com/blog is a URL that identifies the protocol (HTTP), host name (www.certskills.com), and web page (blog).

user mode   A mode of the user interface to a router or switch in which the user can type only nondisruptive EXEC commands, generally just to look at the current status, but not to change any operational settings.

UTP   Unshielded twisted-pair. A type of cabling, standardized by the Telecommunications Industry Association (TIA), that holds twisted pairs of copper wires (typically four pair) and does not contain any shielding from outside interference.

V

variable-length subnet mask (VLSM)   The capability to specify a different subnet mask for the same Class A, B, or C network number on different subnets. VLSM can help optimize available address space.

virtual circuit (VC)   In packet-switched services like Frame Relay, VC refers to the ability of two DTE devices (typically routers) to send and receive data directly to each other, which supplies the same function as a physical leased line (leased circuit), but doing so without a physical circuit. This term is meant as a contrast with a leased line or leased circuit.

virtual LAN (VLAN)   A group of devices, connected to one or more switches, with the devices grouped into a single broadcast domain through switch configuration. VLANs allow switch administrators to separate the devices connected to the switches into separate VLANs without requiring separate physical switches, gaining design advantages of separating the traffic without the expense of buying additional hardware.

Virtual Private Network (VPN)   The process of securing communication between two devices whose packets pass over some public and unsecured network, typically the Internet. VPNs encrypt packets so that the communication is private, and authenticate the identity of the endpoints.

VLAN   *See* virtual LAN.

VLAN configuration database   The name of the collective configuration of VLAN IDs and names on a Cisco switch.

VLAN interface   A configuration concept inside Cisco switches, used as an interface between IOS running on the switch and a VLAN supported inside the switch, so that the switch can assign an IP address and send IP packets into that VLAN.

VLAN Trunking Protocol (VTP)   A Cisco-proprietary messaging protocol used between Cisco switches to communicate configuration information about the existence of VLANs, including the VLAN ID and VLAN name.

vlan.dat   The default file used to store a Cisco switch's VLAN configuration database.

VoIP   Voice over IP. The transport of voice traffic inside IP packets over an IP network.

VTP   *See* VLAN Trunking Protocol.

VTP client mode   One of three VTP operational modes for a switch with which switches learn about VLAN numbers and names from other switches, but which does not allow the switch to be directly configured with VLAN information.

VTP server mode   One of three VTP operational modes. Switches in server mode can configure VLANs, tell other switches about the changes, and learn about VLAN changes from other switches.

VTP transparent mode   One of three VTP operational modes. Switches in transparent mode can configure VLANs, but they do not tell other switches about the changes, and they do not learn about VLAN changes from other switches.

W

web server   Software, running on a computer, that stores web pages and sends those web pages to web clients (web browsers) that request the web pages.

well-known port   A TCP or UDP port number reserved for use by a particular application. The use of well-known ports allows a client to send a TCP or UDP segment to a server, to the correct destination port for that application.

Wi-Fi Alliance   An organization formed by many companies in the wireless industry (an industry association) for the purpose of getting multivendor certified-compatible wireless products to market in a more timely fashion than would be possible by simply relying on standardization processes.

wide-area network (WAN)   A part of a larger network that implements mostly OSI Layer 1 and 2 technology, connects sites that typically sit far apart, and uses a business model in which a consumer (individual or business) must lease the WAN from a service provider (often a telco).

wildcard mask   The mask used in Cisco IOS ACL commands and OSPF and EIGRP **network** commands.

window   Represents the number of bytes that can be sent without receiving an acknowledgment.

wireless LAN   A local-area network (LAN) that physically transmits bits using radio waves. The name "wireless" compares these LANs to more traditional "wired" LANs, which are LANs that use cables (which often have copper wires inside).

WLAN client   A wireless device that wants to gain access to a wireless access point for the purpose of communicating with other wireless devices or other devices connected to the wired internetwork.

Z

zero subnet   For every classful IPv4 network that is subnetted, the one subnet whose subnet number has all binary 0s in the subnet part of the number. In decimal, the zero subnet can be easily identified because it is the same number as the classful network number.

Index

Symbols & Numerics

J-K

L

M

N

V

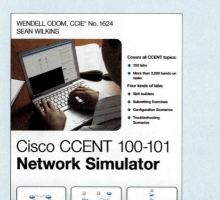
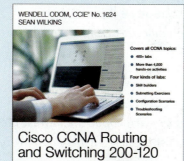